THE EUROPEAN CONVENTION ON HUMAN RIGHTS

JACOBS AND WHITE,
THE EUROPEAN CONVENTION ON HUMAN RIGHTS

CLARE OVEY AND ROBIN WHITE

Third Edition

OXFORD

UNIVERSITY PRESS

OXFORD

UNIVERSITY PRESS

Great Clarendon Street, Oxford OX2 6DP

Oxford University Press is a department of the University of Oxford.
It furthers the University's objective of excellence in research, scholarship,
and education by publishing worldwide in

Oxford New York

Auckland Bangkok Buenos Aires Cape Town Chennai
Dar es Salaam Delhi Hong Kong Istanbul Karachi Kolkata
Kuala Lumpur Madrid Melbourne Mexico City Mumbai Nairobi
São Paulo Shanghai Singapore Taipei Tokyo Toronto

with an associated company in Berlin

Oxford is a registered trade mark of Oxford University Press
in the UK and in certain other countries

Published in the United States
by Oxford University Press Inc., New York

British Library Cataloguing in Publication Data

Data available

Library of Congress Cataloging in Publication Data

Data available

ISBN 0–19–876 5800

1 3 5 7 9 10 8 6 4 2

Typeset in Adobe Minion
by RefineCatch Limited, Bungay, Suffolk
Printed in Great Britain by
Biddles Ltd., Guildford and King's Lynn

For Margaret and Neil

For Bessie

CONTENTS

PREFACE TO THE THIRD EDITION

The first edition of this work in 1975 was published when there were few systematic treatments of the Convention and its case law. The second edition was published in 1996 when there was increasing interest in the contribution of the Convention and the work of the Strasbourg organs in the protection of human rights in a widening European forum. By 1996 the case law had developed significantly into a substantial body of principles. This third edition is published against the background of the successful revision of the Convention machinery and the increasing participation of the countries of central and Eastern Europe, and the introduction of a pan-European system governed by a wholly judicial process for handling both individual and inter-State complaints. In the United Kingdom, the incorporation of the Convention in the Human Rights Act 1998 (and its entry into force on 2 October 2000) has resulted in a major focus on Convention rights and their enforcement in the national legal order.

However, this book is about the European Convention rather than about its implementation in a particular State and uses as its reference point the case law of the Strasbourg organs. This edition has been written by Clare Ovey and Robin White, though Francis Jacobs has seen and commented on much of the revised text. We have retained the article by article analysis of the European Convention, since this is helpful to those coming to the Convention for the first time, whether as students or as practitioners. We have also tried to retain, in the context of an ever-increasing volume of case law, the statement of principles which characterized the first and second editions. This has involved seeking to order the now voluminous case law of the Court in a way which helps the reader both to see the historical development of the principles established by the Strasbourg organs, and the current state of the case law. However, now that the new Court is established and is handing down many interesting judgments, we have taken the opportunity to remove some of the lengthy discussions of early Commission case law which appeared in the earlier editions, since this has been overtaken by the establishment of principles discernable from the case law of the 'old' Court and, more particularly, the 'new' Court. There is also consideration of the procedural aspects of bringing a claim before the Court.

We have both been struck by the significant advances which have been made in the state of the case law since the publication of the second edition. This has necessitated the wholesale re-drafting of virtually every chapter of the book. So we offer much more than an updating of the 1996 text; this book represents an attempt to show the real advances made in the case law in the past five years, and to offer some sense of the direction the new Court is taking in some key areas. There has been some re-ordering of material. The material on Article 6 is

now split across two chapters, with the second chapter focusing on some specific issues relating to the fairness of criminal trials in addition to dealing with
issues under Article 7. The chapter on limitations common to Articles 8 to 11
appears before rather than after the treatment of the individual articles. The
procedural material has been completely re-written to reflect not only the role
of the new Court in dealing with questions of admissibility as well as the merits
of applications alleging violations of the Convention but also the changing role
of the Committee of Ministers.

Both of us have benefited from discussions with our colleagues either at the
Court or at the University of Leicester, and beyond, in preparing this new
edition, and we are grateful to our colleagues for the fruits of those discussions.
However, we must stress that the views expressed in the book are our own. Clare
Ovey is a legal officer at the Court and the views expressed in this book are her
own and not those of the Court. Robin White sits as a Deputy Social Security
Commissioner and, in so far as there are any matters of overlap with his judicial
function, any views expressed are again purely personal and are not those of the
Office of the Social Security Commissioners.

The text is intended to be up to date to 1 January 2002.

Clare Ovey
Robin White

Leicester and Strasbourg
March 2002

A NOTE ON CITATION CONVENTIONS

COMMISSION DECISIONS AND REPORTS

These are cited by application number in roman, followed by the names of the parties in italics and the date of the decision or report, and, where the decision or report is reported, the relevant report reference.

COURT DECISIONS AND JUDGMENTS

JUDGMENTS

Older judgments of the Court were give a Series number, but for more modern judgments this practice has been abandoned.

In every case the date of the judgment is given. Where there is a Series number this is used, but for cases where there is no Series number, the application number is given in parentheses and in roman after the names of the parties to the case. Where the case is reported in the *European Human Rights Reports*, a reference to those reports is also given.

DECISIONS

The Court is now responsible for admissibility decisions as well as judgments. Admissibility decisions are listed separately from judgments, but the structure of the reference follows the same principles: names of the parties followed by the application number and the date of the decision. If there is a report available that is given.

Note that nearly all Court decisions and judgments are available on the Court's website echr.coe.int/Hudoc.htm

TABLE OF JUDGMENTS AND DECISIONS OF THE COURT OF HUMAN RIGHTS

JUDGMENTS

DECISIONS ON ADMISSIBILITY

TABLE OF DECISIONS AND REPORTS OF THE COMMISSION OF HUMAN RIGHTS

TABLE OF TREATIES AND RELATED DOCUMENTS

TABLE OF CASES

INTER-AMERICAN COURT OF HUMAN RIGHTS

INTERNATIONAL COURT OF JUSTICE

ABBREVIATIONS

AC	Appeal Court
AJCL	*American Journal of Comparative Law*
AJIL	*American Journal of International Law*
BYIL	*British Yearbook of International Law*
CD	Collection of Decisions of the Commission of Human Rights
CLP	*Current Legal Problems*
CML Rev	*Common Market Law Review*
Crim L R	*Criminal Law Review*
CSCE	Conference on Security and Co-operation in Europe
DH	*Droits de l'Homme*
DR	Decisions and Reports of the Commission of Human Rights
E L Rev	*European Law Review*
EC	European Community
ECR	European Court Reports
EEC	European Economic Community
EHRLR	*European Human Rights Law Review*
EHRR	European Human Rights Reports
ETS	European Treaty Series
European J of Int'l L	*European Journal of International Law*
EWHC	England and Wales: High Court
HRLJ	*Human Rights Law Journal*
ICCPR	International Covenant on Civil and Political Rights
ICLQ	*International and Comparative Law Quarterly*
ILO	International Labour Organisation
KCLJ	*King's College Law Journal*
LIEI	*Legal Issues of European Integration*
LQR	*Law Quarterly Review*
MLR	*Modern Law Review*
NATO	North Atlantic Treaty Organisation
NQHR	*Netherlands Quarterly of Human Rights*
PL	*Public Law*
UN GAOR	*United Nations General Assembly Official Records*
UNESCO	United Nations Educational, Scientific, and Cultural Organisation
WLR	Weekly Law Reports
Yearbook	*Yearbook of the European Convention on Human Rights*
YEL	*Yearbook of European Law*

1

HISTORICAL BACKGROUND
AND INSTITUTIONS

INTRODUCTION

The subject of this book brings together a number of threads which, however precariously, have brought developments in the ordering of international society that can only be described as spectacular if compared with the situation in 1945. One of these threads is European integration on a level to serve not only technical needs and economic interests, but also to embody a system of liberal values which crystallize centuries of political development.

The second is a concern, despite grim reality, in relations between States both within and beyond Europe, for the protection of human rights. The international protection of human rights has of course many other dimensions, but it has, arguably, been most fully and systematically developed under the law of the European Convention on Human Rights. European integration, also, has many other facets, but both the construction of the European Union, and cooperation in various fields among the States of Western Europe, have been progressively based on a set of ideas and values of which the system described here is the most complete expression.[1]

The third is the spread of democracy to the countries of central and eastern Europe and their embracing of the system of protection of human rights embodied in the European Convention on Human Rights, which has become a truly pan-European system offering a judicial approach to the protection of the fundamental rights and freedoms listed in the Convention and its Protocols.

After the Second World War, European movements arose, simultaneously and spontaneously, throughout the European democracies. They arose in response to the threat to fundamental human rights and to political freedom which had all but overwhelmed the European continent in the War, and which

---

[1] See A. Clapham, *Human Rights and the European Community: A Critical Overview* (Nomos, 1991); A. Casese, A. Clapham, and J. Weiler (eds), *Human Rights and the European Community: Methods of Protection* (Nomos, 1991); and A. Casese, A. Clapham, and J. Weiler (eds), *Human Rights and the European Community: The Substantive Law* (Nomos, 1991); and P. Alston, *The EU and Human Rights* (Oxford, 1999).

reappeared after the War in new forms of totalitarianism. The most significant immediate results of the International Committee of Movements for European Unity, and of its Congress at The Hague in May 1948, were the foundation of the Council of Europe on 5 May 1949 and the drafting by its Member States of the Convention for the Protection of Human Rights and Fundamental Freedoms of 4 November 1950,[2] generally known as the European Convention on Human Rights.

The Convention reflected the concerns and objects of this novel international organization,[3] as set out in its Constitution, the Statute of the Council of Europe. In the Preamble to the Statute, the Contracting States reaffirmed,

their devotion to the spiritual and moral values which are the common heritage of their peoples and the true source of individual freedom, political liberty and the rule of law, principles which form the basis of all genuine democracy.

The aim of the Council of Europe was, and remains, 'to achieve a greater unity between its Members for the purpose of safeguarding and realising the ideals and principles which are their common heritage and facilitating their economic and social progress',[4] and this aim was to be pursued 'through the organs of the Council by discussion of questions of common concern and by agreements and common action in economic, social, cultural, scientific, legal and administrative matters and in the maintenance and further realisation of human rights and fundamental freedoms.'[5]

Given the concern of the Council of Europe with parliamentary democracy it was appropriate that the organs of the Council of Europe should include not only a Committee of Ministers as its executive organ, consisting of the Minister for Foreign Affairs of each Member State, or their deputy,[6] but also the first European parliamentary organ, the Consultative Assembly, comprising members of the Parliaments of the Member States.[7] The Consultative Assembly has, since September 1974, styled itself the Parliamentary Assembly.[8]

Another feature unique in the history of international organizations was the requirement in Article 3 of the Statute that every Member State 'must accept the principles of the rule of law and of the enjoyment by all persons within its jurisdiction of human rights and fundamental freedoms.'

Under Article 8, a Member State which has seriously violated Article 3 of the

---

[2] The Convention entered into force on 3 September 1953. See G. Marston, 'The United Kingdom's Part in the Preparation of the European Convention on Human Rights' (1993) 42 ICLQ 796 for an account of some aspects of the drafting of the Convention.

[3] See generally, Council of Europe, *Manual of the Council of Europe. Its Structure, Functions and Achievements* (London, 1970).

[4] Art. 1(a) of the Statute.

[5] Art. 1(b).

[6] Arts. 13 and 14.

[7] Arts. 22 and 25.

[8] And is referred to by this title throughout this book.

Statute may be suspended from its rights of representation and requested by the Committee of Ministers to withdraw from the Council of Europe under Article 7 and, if it does not comply, may be expelled.[9]

The uniqueness of these provisions lay in the fact that questions of human rights fell traditionally within the domestic jurisdiction of States, and were of concern to international law only if the interests of another State were affected, as for example by the treatment of its nationals. History had all too convincingly demonstrated the inadequacy of those traditional concepts of international law and State sovereignty which made the protection of individuals the exclusive prerogative of the State of which they were nationals. Their rights may require protection, above all, against their own State—and the values of democratic government require a collective guarantee—for there are no boundaries to the denial of liberty. The creation of the Council of Europe and the adoption of the Convention on Human Rights[10] are an acknowledgement that the protection of human rights is viewed as an indispensable element of European democracy.

The principle of respect for human rights had been established in international law by the Charter of the United Nations.[11] The Universal Declaration of Human Rights, adopted by the General Assembly of the United Nations on 10 December 1948, proclaims as a 'common standard of achievement' an extensive list of human rights, which, although the Declaration is not legally binding as such, is an authoritative guide to the interpretation of the Charter.[12]

Further work in the United Nations, which led to the adoption in 1966 of two Covenants, the Covenant on Economic, Social and Cultural Rights and the Covenant on Civil and Political Rights, drew a distinction between two different classes of fundamental rights. Social and economic rights, although they appear in the Universal Declaration, are less universal in the sense that they constitute standards to be attained, depending on the level of economic development. They require action by governments, whereas civil and political rights often

---

[9] It was in consequence of proceedings started under this provision, following an initiative in the Parliamentary Assembly, that Greece announced in 1969 its withdrawal from the Council of Europe and denounced the Convention. Greece was readmitted in 1974. See also ch. 25.

[10] For a detailed consideration of the background to particular provisions of the Convention, see Council of Europe, *Collected Edition of the travaux préparatoires of the European Convention on Human Rights* (The Hague, 1977). See also G. Marston, 'The United Kingdom's Part in the Preparation of the European Convention on Human Rights' (1993) 42 ICLQ 796.

[11] See, in particular, Arts. 55 and 56 of the United Nations Charter.

[12] While the Universal Declaration itself is not a binding instrument of international law, the principles it enshrines may acquire legal force as the 'general principles of law recognized by civilized nations' under Art. 38(1)(c) of the Statute of the International Court of Justice, or as customary law reflecting the general practice of States (cf. Art. 38(1)(b) of the Statute), or even as 'a peremptory norm of general international law' (*jus cogens*), that is, a norm accepted and recognized by the international community of States as a whole as a norm from which no derogation is permitted (cf. Art. 53 of the Vienna Convention on the Law of Treaties).

require protection against executive action. Within the Council of Europe, social and economic rights are the concern of the European Social Charter,[13] which provides for progressive implementation and for supervision by the examination of periodic reports on progress achieved.

The European Convention on Human Rights guarantees, for the most part, civil and political rights: the right to life, liberty, and security; freedom from inhuman or degrading treatment, slavery, servitude, and forced labour; the right to a fair trial; freedom of conscience, of speech, and of assembly. However, Article 1 of the First Protocol, which protects property rights, and Article 2 which guarantees the right to education, are limited exceptions to this principle.

Section I of the European Convention spells out, generally in more detailed form, most of the basic civil and political rights contained in the Universal Declaration, while the First, Fourth, Sixth, and Seventh Protocols guarantee certain further rights and freedoms. The remaining Protocols amended procedural provisions of the Convention, while Protocol 12 will add a new dimension to the Convention approach to discrimination.[14]

The rights set out in the Convention and Protocols are thus derived essentially from the Universal Declaration. For the purpose of an instrument which was to be binding in law, the content of these rights was often made more specific, and the circumstances in which limitations might legitimately be imposed on them are also more specific.

The membership of the Council of Europe is broad and now encompasses the new democracies of Central and Eastern Europe. New members of the Council of Europe are expected to accede to the European Convention, which in its form as amended by Protocol 11 carries with it recognition both of an individual right of application to the Court of Human Rights and of a wholly judicial system for the protection of human rights.

IS THERE A HIERARCHY OF RIGHTS?

There is no formal hierarchy of rights set out in the Convention; this means that the Convention does not have a system in which priority is given to one right over another if they are in conflict. But it has been accepted that there will be occasions when a balance has to be achieved between conflicting

[13] The Charter entered into force on 26 February 1965. See generally D. Harris, *The European Social Charter* (Charlottesville, 1984); D. Gomien, D. Harris, and L. Zwaak, *Law and Practice of the European Convention on Human Rights and the European Social Charter* (Council of Europe, 1996); and *Fundamental Social Rights: Case Law of the European Social Charter* (Council of Europe, 2000).

[14] See ch. 19.

interests. This is reflected in the internal structure of many of the Convention rights.

Although there is no hierarchy of rights, the rights set out in the Convention can be split into two categories: unqualified rights, some of which are non-derogable, and qualified rights.

Unqualified rights are the right to life, subject to the exceptions listed in the article, in Article 2; the prohibition of torture, inhuman or degrading treatment in Article 3; the prohibition of slavery and forced labour as defined in Article 4; the right to liberty and security in Article 5; the right to a fair trial in Article 6; the prohibition on punishment without law in Article 7; the right to marry in Article 12; the right to an effective remedy in Article 13; the prohibition of discrimination in Article 14; the right to education and the right to free elections in Protocol 1; and the prohibition of the death penalty (except in time of war or of imminent threat of war) in Protocol 6.

Some of these rights are said to be absolute in the sense that no derogations under Article 15 are permitted; these are to be found in Articles 2, 3, 4, and 7, and Article 4 of Protocol 7.

Qualified rights arise where the Convention specifies a right, but goes on to indicate that the State may interfere with it in order to secure certain interests. Such rights are the right to respect for private and family life in Article 8; freedom of thought, conscience, and religion in Article 9; freedom of expression in Article 10; freedom of assembly and association in Article 11; and the protection of property in Protocol 1.

Generally, the person alleging a violation of a right protected by the Convention has the burden of establishing the violation on the balance of probabilities, but where an interference can be shown with one of the qualified rights, it will be for the State to establish on the balance of probabilities that its interference is justified. This will involve showing that the interference was in accordance with the law, that the aim of the interference was to protect a recognized interest, and that the interference was necessary in a democratic society. This final criterion will require the State to show that the interference with the qualified right was the minimum needed to secure the legitimate aim. This is the application of the doctrine of proportionality.[15]

---

[15] See below ch. 10.

THE SYSTEM OF PROTECTION

Protocol 11 to the Convention[16] entered into force on 1 November 1998 and restructured the institutional framework of the Convention. But an under-standing of the system of protection prior to 1 November 1998 remains necessary because decisions made by the Convention organs prior to the change continue to have an influence on the development of Convention rights.

THE 'OLD' SYSTEM OF PROTECTION

The Convention created two organs 'to ensure the observance of the engagements undertaken by the High Contracting Parties':[17] the European Commission of Human Rights[18] and the European Court of Human Rights.[19] The main function of these two organs, sometimes collectively referred to as the Strasbourg organs,[20] was to deal with applications made by States and by individuals alleging violations of the Convention. Under former Article 24, any State party to the Convention may refer to the Commission any alleged breach of the provisions of the Convention by another State party. Under former Article 25, the Commission could receive applications from any person, non-governmental organization, or group of individuals claiming to be the victim of a violation by one of the Member States of the rights set forth in the Conven-tion and any relevant Protocols. Initially, acceptance of the jurisdiction of the Commission to receive individual petitions was optional, but in the 1990s came to be an expected requirement of participation in the Convention system. The procedure differs depending on whether the application is made under Article 24 or 25; what follows describes the process in relation to individual applications under Article 25.

Once an application was registered, the Commission first considered, and issued a *decision* on whether the application met the admissibility

---

[16] See N. Rowe and V. Schlette, 'The Protection of Human Rights in Europe after the Eleventh Protocol to the ECHR' (1998) 23 E.L. Rev HR/1; A. Drzemczewski, 'The European Human Rights Convention: Protocol No 11—Entry into force and first year of application (2000) 21 HRLJ 1; Drzemc-zewski, 'A major overhaul of the European Human Rights Convention control mechanism: Protocol No. 11' in *Collected Courses of the Academy of European Law, Volume VI* (Florence, 1997) at 121; H.G. Schermers, 'The Eleventh Protocol to the European Convention on Human Rights' (1994) 19 E L Rev 367; Schermers, 'Adaptation of the 11th Protocol to the European Convention on Human Rights' (1995) 20 E L Rev 559; and Schermers, 'Election of Judges to the European Court of Human Rights' (1998) 23 E L Rev 568

[17] Former Art. 19 ECHR

[18] Referred to as 'the Commission'.

[19] Referred to as 'the Court of Human Rights'.

[20] Together with the Committee of Ministers: see below.

requirements.[21] If it did not, that was an end of the matter. If the application was declared admissible, the Commission went on to conduct an investigation into the merits of the complaint and to consider whether there had been a violation of the Convention. The result was a *report* from the Commission expressing an *opinion*[22] as to whether or not there had been a violation. The report was communicated on a confidential basis to the applicant and to the State concerned and was delivered to the Committee of Ministers, the political organ of the Council of Europe. Throughout this time, attempts would have been made to secure a friendly settlement 'on the basis of respect for human rights'.[23]

Final decisions on cases on which the Commission had reported and which had not resulted in a friendly settlement were made by the Committee of Ministers, or the Court of Human Rights. Recognition of the jurisdiction of the Court was technically voluntary under former Article 46 of the Convention, but a clear expectation had arisen that Contracting Parties would recognize the competence of the Court.[24] Within three months of the transmission of the Commission report to the Committee of Ministers, the application could be referred to the Court by the Commission, the defendant State, or the State whose national was alleged to be the victim.[25] The applicant had no standing to refer the application to the Court, unless the defendant State was a party to Protocol 9.[26] Where that was so, the applicant could refer the matter to the Court, but (unless it was also referred to the Court by the Commission or a State) it had first to be submitted to a panel of three judges, who could decide unanimously that the application should not be considered by the Court because it did not raise a serious question affecting the interpretation or application of the Convention.

If the case was referred to the Court and heard by it, there was a full judicial procedure, and even where Protocol 9 had not been ratified, some accommodations were made which allowed limited participation by the applicant. The Court sat in plenary session or in Chambers of nine.[27] Decisions were made by a majority of the judges present and voting, with the President enjoying a casting vote if necessary. Separate opinions could be attached to the judgment of the majority.

Those cases which were not referred to the Court within three months of transmission of the Commission's report to the Committee of Ministers were automatically decided by the Committee of Ministers. Latterly, the practice of

---

[21] See below.
[22] This is not legally binding.
[23] Former Art. 28 ECHR.
[24] And this happened.
[25] Former Art. 48 ECHR.
[26] 24 Contracting Parties (not including the UK) ratified Protocol 9.
[27] Former Art. 43 ECHR.

the Committee of Ministers was to endorse the Commission report without any further investigation of the merits of the case.

The use of a political organ was a compromise to ensure that all applications resulted in a final determination. In the early years, there were States which had not recognized the competence of the Court, and there have always been cases which no one has referred to the Court.

THE 'NEW' SYSTEM OF PROTECTION

Protocol 11 amended the Convention to make provision for a new wholly judicial system of determination of applications. The Commission and the Court have been replaced from 1 November 1998 by a new permanent Court, which handles both the admissibility and merits phases of application. The Court is also charged with seeking to secure friendly settlement of matters before it.[28]

Individual applications are made to the Court under Article 34 and individuals have full standing before the Court. There will, undoubtedly continue to be a filtering process by Court staff before applications are registered. In the calendar year 2000 the Court registered 10,486 applications,[29] but will have opened many more provisional files.[30] The difference in the figures is explained by the practice of the Court Secretariat of explaining in correspondence why certain applications are destined to fail—for example, because the complaint is made about a State which is not a party to the Convention or the violation alleged is not of a right protected by the Convention.[31] Complaints are initially considered by a three-judge committee which will consider whether the application meets the Convention's admissibility criteria,[32] but it can only rule an application to be inadmissible if it is unanimous.[33] These criteria have not changed with the amendments made by Protocol 11 and flow from the terms of Articles 34 and 35[34] and involve the consideration of nine questions:

1   Can the applicant claim to be a victim?
2   Is the defendant State a party to the Convention?
3   Have domestic remedies been exhausted?
4   Is the application filed within the six-month time-limit?
5   Is the application signed?

---

[28] Art. 38(1)(b).

[29] *Information Note on the Court's Statistics 2000.*

[30] The total number of provisional files between 1955 and the end of 1999 was 153,921 producing 53,424 registered applications. In 1999, there were 20,888 provisional files; in 2000, 26,775; and in 2001, 31,843 files.

[31] See E. Fribergh, 'The Commission Secretariat's Handling of Provisional Files' in F. Matscher and H. Petzold (eds.) *Protecting Human Rights: The European Dimension. Essays in Honour of Gérard Wiarda* (Köln: Carl Heymans Verlag KG, 1990), 181.

[32] Arts. 27–8 ECHR. For a discussion of the conditions of admissibility, see ch. 24.

[33] Art. 28 ECHR.   [34] Formerly Arts. 25 and 26.

6   Has the application been brought before?
7   Is the application compatible with the Convention?
8   Is the application manifestly ill-founded?
9   Is there an abuse of the right of petition?

In recent years somewhere around one in four to one in seven applications has been declared admissible, though over the life of the Convention fewer than one in ten applications has progressed beyond the admissibility phase.

Those cases which are not ruled inadmissible by the three-judge committee are put before a seven-judge chamber of the Court, which will include the judge sitting in respect of the defendant State. The chamber will consider the written arguments of the parties, investigate the material facts if these are in contention, and hear oral argument. This stage of the proceedings concludes with a decision whether the complaint is admissible and whether a friendly settlement is possible.[35] There follows a consideration of the merits. In some cases the admissibility and merits phases are joined.

Certain cases of special difficulty can be referred by a chamber to a Grand Chamber of seventeen judges.[36]

The Contracting Parties undertake to abide by the final judgment of the Court in any case to which they are parties.[37] The final judgment is transmitted to the Committee of Ministers whose sole role in the process is now to supervise the execution of judgments.[38]

ADVISORY OPINIONS OF THE EUROPEAN COURT OF HUMAN RIGHTS

Under Article 47 ECHR[39] the Court has jurisdiction to give advisory opinions at the request of the Committee of Ministers[40] on legal questions concerning the interpretation of the Convention and its accompanying Protocols. The Court is

---

[35] Arts. 29 and 38, ECHR.   [36] Arts. 30–31 and 43 ECHR.   [37] Art. 46(1).
[38] Art.46(2). There has in recent times been concern over the failure of Contracting States to abide by final judgments. See e.g. Interim Resolution DH (2000) 105 adopted on 24 July 2000 on the non-execution of the judgment in the case of *Loizidou* v. *Turkey*, reproduced at (2000) 21 HRLJ 272, Resolution 1226 (2000) of the Parliamentary Assembly adopted on 28 September 2000 on execution of judgments of the European Court of Human Rights; Recommendation 1477 (2000) of the Parliamentary Assembly adopted on 28 September 2000 on the execution of judgments of the European Court of Human Rights, E. Jurgens *Report on the execution of judgments of the European Court of Human Rights* adopted by the Parliamentary Assembly on 28 September 2000, reproduced at (2000) 21 HRLJ 275; and J. Harman, 'Complementary Mechanisms within the Council of Europe. Perspectives of the Committee of Ministers' (2000) 21 HRLJ 296.
[39] Formerly the Second Protocol which has been in force since 21 September 1970.
[40] Decisions to request an advisory opinion require a majority vote: Article 47(3) ECHR.

required to sit as a Grand Chamber in considering such requests and must deliver a reasoned opinion on the questions referred; separate opinions are permitted.[41] To date, the procedure has not been used. This is hardly surprising since Article 47(2) provides:

Such opinions shall not deal with any question relating to the content or scope of the rights or freedoms defined in Section I of the Convention and in the protocols thereto, or with any other questions which the Commission, the Court or the Committee of Ministers might have to consider in consequence of any such proceedings as could be instituted in accordance with the Convention.

The restrictive framing of the conditions for advisory opinions of the European Court of Human Rights is unfortunate. The advisory opinion procedure under the Inter-American Convention on Human Rights, which is open to Member States of the Organization of American States, has proved to be a particularly fruitful source of case law under that Convention.[42] Advisory opinions of the International Court of Justice have also had a significant influence on the development of international law,[43] and the preliminary ruling procedure[44] under Article 234 of the EC Treaty[45] has been an outstanding success in securing both the development of European Community law and its uniform application throughout the Member States.[46]

THE ROLE OF THE SECRETARY-GENERAL OF THE COUNCIL OF EUROPE

The Secretary-General is the senior official of the Council of Europe, elected for a period of five years by the Parliamentary Assembly from a list of candidates drawn up by the Committee of Ministers.[47] The Secretary-General is the depository for ratifications of the Convention[48] with all the duties that entails.

---

[41] Art. 31b ECHR. See the Rules of Court for the procedural rules surrounding advisory opinions.

[42] See Art. 64 of the American Convention on Human Rights of 22 November 1969, OAS Treaty Series No 36.

[43] See I. Brownlie, *Principles of Public International Law* (Oxford, 1991), at 730–5.

[44] The jurisdiction of the Court of Justice is not advisory in the sense used above, though it does operate as an effective partnership between national courts and the Community court by providing national courts with authoritative interpretations of Community law which they must apply to the cases before them.

[45] Formerly Art. 177 of the EC Treaty.

[46] See generally L. Neville Brown and T. Kennedy, *The Court of Justice of the European Communities* (London, 2000), at ch. 10.

[47] Art. 36 of the Statute of the Council of Europe.

[48] Art. 59 of the Convention.

Denunciations of the Convention and derogations permitted by the Convention, as well as any declarations required under Convention provisions, are filed with the Secretary-General.

The Secretary-General also has an important monitoring function under Article 52,[49] which provides:

On receipt of a request from the Secretary-General of the Council of Europe any High Contracting Party shall furnish an explanation of the manner in which its internal law ensures the effective implementation of any of the provisions of this Convention.

Reporting systems are, of course, common measures for securing implementation of human rights obligations.[50] Such procedures are proactive, requiring States to examine the state of their own law rather than reactive, requiring responses to alleged violations of international obligations. This kind of self-assessment or compliance audit can be very valuable if undertaken in the spirit required by the Convention.

Article 52 of the Convention is, however, silent on the circumstances in which the Secretary-General will exercise the powers given under the Article. The Secretary-General has stated that it is a matter entirely within 'his own responsibility and at his own discretion'.[51] States Parties to the Convention have acquiesced in this interpretation.

General practice to date has been to address requests to all States Parties, but recently the Secretary-General has put individual questions to Moldova concerning Transnistria, and to Russia concerning the situation in Chechnya. In October 1964 States were asked to report generally on how their legal systems guaranteed the rights protected in the Convention and First Protocol; in July 1970 on the implementation of the rights protected by Article 5(5); in April 1975 on the application of Articles 8, 9, 10, and 11; in March 1983 on the implementation of the Convention in respect of children and young persons placed in the care of institutions following a decision of the administrative or judicial authorities; and in July 1988 on the rights protected by Article 6(1) and (3).

---

[49] Formerly Art. 57. See generally, P. Mahoney, 'Does Article 57 of the European Convention on Human Rights serve any useful purpose?' in F. Matscher and H. Petzold (ed.), *Protecting Human Rights: The European Dimension. Studies in Honour of Gérard J. Wiarda* (Köln, 1988), at 373–93. See also J. Melander, 'Report on "Responses from the Organs of the European Convention including the Committee of Ministers"' and Zanghi, 'Written Communication on "Responsibilities Resulting for the Committee of Ministers and the Secretary General of the Council of Europe for the Implementation of the European Convention on Human Rights"' in Council of Europe, *Proceedings of the Sixth Colloquy about the European Convention on Human Rights, 13–16 November 1985* (Dordrecht, 1988), at 842–904 (esp. 892–904) and 920–64 (esp. 957–64) respectively.

[50] See e.g. Arts. 40 of the International Covenant on Civil and Political Rights; Arts. 16–22 of the International Covenant on Economic, Social and Cultural Rights; Articles 22–3 of the Constitution of the International Labour Organisation; Arts. 42–3 of the American Convention on Human Rights; and Art. 62 of the African Charter on Human and Peoples' Rights.

[51] Statement of Secretary-General to the Legal Committee of the Consultative Assembly in Oslo on 29 August 1964, Council of Europe, *Collected Texts* (Strasbourg, 1987), at 235–6.

The Secretary-General has compiled the responses received from the States and brought these to the notice of the Parliamentary Assembly, and latterly also to the Commission and the Court.[52] The responses are not subject to any critical scrutiny.[53] The responses of the States are published,[54] though each State is consulted to seek its views on whether it would wish the information supplied by it not to be published. The Secretary-General has no standing to bring violations which might be evidenced in the responses from the States to the attention of the Court, though it would be open to any State Party to the Convention to make a complaint under Article 33[55] provided that the usual admissibility conditions were met. In cases of the most serious violations, the matter could be referred to the Committee of Ministers with a view to its exercising its powers of suspension and expulsion under Articles 7 and 8 of the Statute of the Council of Europe.

THE COMMISSIONER FOR HUMAN RIGHTS

The Commissioner for Human Rights is an office established by resolution of the Committee of Ministers.[56] The Commissioner[57] is elected by the Parliamentary Assembly and is charged with promoting education in, and awareness of, human rights in the territories of the Contracting Parties. Additionally the Commissioner helps to promote the effective observance and full enjoyment of human rights as embodied in a variety of Council of Europe instruments. But the Commissioner may not take up any individual complaints. Particular activities to date have included studies of the human rights situation in Georgia and in Chechnya. An annual report is submitted to the Committee of Ministers and to the Parliamentary Assembly. The Commissioner may also issue recommendations, opinions, and reports on any matters within his competence.

---

[52] Council of Europe, *Human Rights Information Sheet No. 21*, H/INF(87)1, at 95 and *Human Rights Information Sheet No. 23*, H/INF(88)2, at 59.

[53] Cf. the procedure under Article 40 of the International Covenant on Civil and Political Rights where the Human Rights Committee questions States on their responses. See generally, D. McGoldrick, *The Human Rights Committee* (Oxford, 1991), ch.3.

[54] See above, n. 49 and see Council of Europe Documents H(67)2, H(72)2, H(76)15, and H(86)1.

[55] Formerly Art. 24

[56] Resolution (99) 50 of 7 May 1999, adopted by the Committee of Ministers at its 104th session.

[57] Currently Alvaro Gil-Robles.

OTHER HUMAN RIGHTS INSTRUMENTS OF THE
COUNCIL OF EUROPE

Mention has already been made of the European Social Charter as the Council of Europe instrument which addresses economic, social, and cultural rights. But there are now 185 Council of Europe treaties, many of which address human rights issues.[58] The following are of particular significance:

- the European Agreement relating to persons participating in proceedings of the European Commission and Court of Human Rights of 6 May 1969;[59]
- the European Agreement relating to persons participating in proceedings of the European Court of Human Rights of 5 March 1996;[60]
- the European Convention for the Prevention of Torture and Inhuman and Degrading Treatment of 26 November 1987 and its two Protocols;[61]
- the European Charter for Regional or Minority Languages of 5 November 1992;[62] and
- the Framework Convention for the Protection of National Minorities of 1 February 1995.[63]

Though this work is concerned with the European Convention on Human Rights, the contribution of the Council of Europe to the protection of human rights goes far beyond this Convention. Conventions such as the European Convention for the Prevention of Torture are having a significant impact on the work of the Court in dealing with cases involving allegations of violations of Article 3 prohibiting torture, inhuman, and degrading treatment.[64]

---

[58] For a full list, see conventions.coe.int.
[59] ETS No. 67.
[60] ETS No. 161
[61] ETS No. 126, ETS No 151, and ETS No. 152
[62] ETS No. 148
[63] ETS No. 157.
[64] See ch. 5 below.

2

THE SCOPE OF THE CONVENTION

GENERAL SCOPE OF THE CONVENTION

Article 1 provides that 'The High Contracting Parties shall secure to everyone within their jurisdiction the rights and freedoms defined in Section I of this Convention.'

Section I of the Convention contains, in Articles 2 to 18, a list of the rights and freedoms guaranteed, similar to and indeed partly modelled on the Universal Declaration of Human Rights. The whole of Section I, however, does not in terms impose any obligations on States; it takes the form of a declaration of rights. It is Article 1 which transforms this declaration of rights into a set of obligations for the States which ratify the Convention.

The overall approach of the Convention is based on the principles of solidarity and subsidiarity. Solidarity refers to the undertaking by Contracting Parties to secure the rights protected under the Convention in their national legal orders, while subsidiarity[1] refers to the role of the Court of Human Rights being subsidiary to the institutions of national legal systems in adjudicating on claims that the rights have been violated. It is for this reason that a complaint cannot be made to the Court of Human Rights until all efforts to resolve the dispute have been undertaken within the national legal order. This principle also explains why the Court of Human Rights does not regard itself as a court of appeal from decisions of institutions within national legal orders.

Writers have differed on the nature of the guarantee in Article 1. Some have argued that there is an obligation to incorporate the actual text of the Convention, or of Section I at least, into domestic law.[2] A former President of the Court has spoken of the merits of incorporation in the following terms:

---

[1] See H. Petzold, 'The Convention and the Principle of Subsidiarity', in R. Macdonald, F. Matscher, and H. Petzold, *The European System for the Protection of Human Rights* (Dordrecht, 1993), at 41.

[2] See H. Golsong, 'Die europäishe Konvention zum Schutze der Menschenrechte und Grundfreiheiten', *Jaarbuch des öffentlichen Rechts*, Book 10, 1961, 123–57, and T. Buergenthal, 'The effect of the European Convention on Human Rights on the Internal Law of Member States', in *The European*

Incorporation of the Convention into domestic law, as known in many States, is one of the most effective means of reducing the need for recourse to Strasbourg.[3]

The advantages of incorporation are spelled out in other speeches:

It has in fact two advantages: it provides the national court with the possibility of taking account of the Convention and the Strasbourg case-law to resolve the dispute before it, and at the same time it gives the European organs an opportunity to discover the views of the national courts regarding the interpretation of the Convention and its application to a specific set of circumstances. The dialogue which thus develops between those who are called upon to apply the Convention on the domestic level and those who must do so on the European level is crucial for an effective protection of the rights guaranteed under the Convention.[4]

One final quotation will serve to emphasize the importance of incorporation:

It was [the] clear intention [of those who drafted the Convention] to secure directly for the individual the rights and freedoms set out in the Convention and, as the Strasbourg Court has said in one of its judgments, that intention finds a particularly faithful reflection in those instances where the Convention has been incorporated into domestic law.[5]

There is no dispute, however, that domestic law must give full effect to the rights guaranteed by the Convention; and the States Parties have in fact chosen to implement its guarantees by different methods, according to their own constitutional practices.[6] Thus the Convention has the status of domestic law in Germany and of constitutional law in Austria. In France the Convention has an intermediate status, higher than ordinary legislation but lower than the Constitution. Prior to 2 October 2000, the Convention had not been enacted as part of the law of the United Kingdom and therefore did not have the force of

Convention on Human Rights, British Institute of International and Comparative Law, Supplementary Publication No. 11, 1965, 57 *et seq.*, and for the opposite view K. Partsch, *Die Rechte und Freiheiten der europäischen Menschrechtskonvention* (Berlin, 1966), 272 ff., and T. Sørensen, 'Obligations of a State Party to a Treaty as Regards its Municipal Law' in A. H. Robertson (ed.), *Human Rights in National and International Law* (Manchester, 1968), at 11–31. See also A. Drzemczewski, *European Human Rights Convention in Domestic Law. A Comparative Study* (Oxford, 1983).

[3] R. Ryssdal, Speech to the Informal Ministerial Conference on Human Rights and Celebration of the 40th Anniversary of the European Convention on Human Rights, Rome, 5 November 1990, p.2, Council of Europe document Cour (90) 289.

[4] R. Ryssdal, Speech at the ceremony for the 40th anniversary of the European Convention on Human Rights at Trieste, 18 December 1990, Council of Europe document Cour (90) 318, p.2.

[5] R. Ryssdal, Address to Conference of Presidents and Attorney Generals of the Supreme Courts of the European Communities, 19–22 May 1992, Council of Europe document Cour (92) 135. See dictum in *Ireland* v. *United Kingdom*, Judgment of 18 January 1978, Series A No. 25; (1979–80) 2 EHRR 25, para. 239 of the judgment. See also J. Frowein, 'Incorporation of the Convention into Domestic Law' in J. P. Gardner (ed.), *Aspects of Incorporation of the European Convention of Human Rights into Domestic Law* (London, 1993).

[6] Buergenthal, n.1 above, at 79–106.

law.[7] It was argued that the general law of the land guaranteed all the rights contained in the Convention. That has now changed with the entry into force of the Human Rights Act 1998 which gives 'further effect' to the Convention in United Kingdom law.[8]

The question by what means the rights are implemented may in the end be a matter of legal technique, though certainly some techniques may be more effective than others. The protection of the individual is plainly more effective if the substantive rights guaranteed by the Convention can be enforced by the national courts. Where the rights are not expressly enacted in domestic law, or cannot be invoked before the domestic courts, there is no alternative to the European procedure. The experience of incorporation into the law of the United Kingdom is that the rights guaranteed gain a much higher profile within the national legal order, as the authorities in Contracting Parties determine the extent to which action is compatible with the rights guaranteed in the Convention.

Whether or not they incorporate the actual text of the Convention into domestic law, States are obliged, by appropriate means, 'to ensure that their domestic legislation is compatible with the Convention and, if need be, to make any necessary adjustments to this end'.[9] Further, the terms of Article 52[10] show that domestic law must be such as to 'ensure the effective implementation' of all the provisions of the Convention.

This does not, however, exhaust the effect of Article 1. States are liable for violations of the Convention which may result not only from legislation incompatible with it, but also from acts of all public authorities, at every level, including the executive and the courts. But decisions taken by international organizations, of which the State is a member, such as the European Patent Organization, do not involve the exercise of national jurisdiction within the meaning of Article 1.[11]

The double aspect of Article 1, requiring States to implement the Convention, on the one hand, and not to infringe it, on the other, explains their obligation to 'secure' the rights guaranteed to everyone 'within their jurisdiction'. Clearly these words do not mean that States are not liable for violations committed by them outside their territory; such an interpretation would be manifestly unreasonable, and would misconstrue the function of Article 1. A State must be

---

[7] *R* v. *Chief Immigration officer, Heathrow Airport, ex parte Salamat Bibi*, [1976] 1 WLR 979; [1976] 3 All ER 843, CA; *R* v. *Secretary of State for the Home Department, ex parte Brind*, [1991] 1 AC 696; [1991] 2 WLR 588, HL.

[8] See below in this chapter.

[9] App. 214/56, *De Becker* v. *Belgium*, 9 June 1958; (1959–60) 2 *Yearbook* 214, at 234.

[10] Formerly Art. 57.

[11] App. 12090/92, *Heinz* v. *Contracting Parties who are also Parties to the European Patent Convention*, 10 January 1994, (1994) 76-A DR 125. See now *Matthews* v. *United Kingdom* (App. 24833/94), Judgment of 18 February 1999; (1999) 28 EHRR 361; and *Waite and Kennedy* v. *Germany* (App. 26083/94), Judgment of 18 February 1999; (1999) 30 EHRR 261. For a discussion of the *Matthews* case, see below in this chapter, and see ch. 17.

responsible for its own violations of the Convention, wherever they are committed, but it can be responsible for securing human rights, in the sense of implementing them by the necessary legislation, only within its jurisdiction.[12]

In both the *Swedish Engine Drivers' Union* case[13] and the *Schmidt and Dahlström* case[14] the applicants' complaints under Articles 11 and 14 were arguably directed partly against the State as employer and partly against the State's exercise of public authority. The Swedish Government contended that the applicants were attacking not the Swedish legislative, executive, and judicial authorities, but rather the National Collective Bargaining Office and thus the 'State as employer'; and that, in the sphere of work and employment conditions, the Convention could not impose upon the State obligations that were not incumbent on private employers.

According to the Commission, on the other hand, the disputed decision adopted by the Office could in principle be challenged under Article 11, even if the Office fulfilled typical employer functions. The Court had no difficulty in concluding that the Convention was applicable in this situation.

Questions have arisen as to whether a State can violate the Convention by becoming party to another treaty. In one case, the Commission said:

If a State contracts treaty obligations and subsequently concludes another international agreement which disables it from performing its obligations under the first treaty, it will be answerable for any resulting breach of its obligations under the treaty.[15]

In another case, the Commission held that the transfer of powers by the Contracting States to an international organization is compatible with the Convention, provided that within the organization fundamental rights receive an equivalent protection. In the context of Article 1 of Protocol 1, the European Patents Convention contains detailed safeguards for the protection of intellectual property rights. The transfer of power which it entails is therefore compatible with the Convention. The application was outside the scope of the Convention *ratione personae*.[16]

In the *Matthews* case,[17] the Court of Human Rights was called upon to

[12] See further below in this chapter.

[13] *Swedish Engine Drivers' Union* v. *Sweden*, Judgment of 6 February 1976, Series A No. 20; (1979–80) 1 EHRR 617.

[14] *Schmidt and Dahlström* v. *Sweden*, Judgment of 6 February 1976, Series A No. 21; (1979–80) 1 EHRR 632.

[15] App. 235/56, X v. *Federal Republic of Germany*, 10 June 1958, (1958–9) 2 *Yearbook* 256, at 300.

[16] App. 12090/92, *Heinz* v. *Contracting Parties who are also Parties to the European Patent Convention*, 10 January 1994 (1994) 76-A DR 125. See also App. 13258/77, M & Co. v. *Federal Republic of Germany*, 9 February 1990, (1990) 64 DR 138, at 144, making the same point in connection with the EEC Treaty.

[17] *Matthews* v. *United Kingdom*, Judgment of 18 February 1999; (1999) 28 EHRR 361; see also Canor, '*Primus inter pares*. Who is the ultimate guardian of fundamental rights in Europe?' (2000) 25 E L Rev 3; T. King, 'Ensuring human rights review of intergovernmental acts in Europe' (2000) 25 E L Rev 79; and H. Schermers, 'European Remedies in the Field of Human Rights' in C. Kilpatrick, N. Novitz, and P. Skidmore, *The Future of Remedies in Europe* (Oxford, 2000), at 205.

consider a complaint against the United Kingdom about participation in elections to the European Parliament which were set out in an act of the Community's institutions. The Community Act establishing the rules for direct elections provided in Annex II that the United Kingdom would apply the provisions only in respect of the United Kingdom. Denise Matthews was a United Kingdom national living in Gibraltar, a dependent territory of the United Kingdom. She sought to register as a voter in respect of the elections to the European Parliament, but was refused on the grounds that the Community Act did not include Gibraltar within the franchise for these elections. She complained that this refusal violated her rights under Article 3 of Protocol 1 on free elections.[18]

The Court of Human Rights decided that the United Kingdom remained responsible for securing the rights in Article 3 of Protocol 1 in respect of Community legislation in the same way as if the restriction on the franchise had been included in national law. The Court went on to find that Article 3 applied, since it was possible to interpret the European Parliament as being a legislature within the article, and concluded that there had been a violation of the article. The significance of the case is that the Court of Human Rights has stated in the clearest terms that the Contracting Parties remain responsible for guaranteeing the rights contained in the Convention even where they create an international organization and transfer competence to it in particular areas, and that, where no other judicial body is competent to review acts of the international organization, the Court of Human Rights will consider complaints of violations of the Convention's guaranteed rights.

A difficult question is how far a State is responsible for violations of the rights guaranteed by the Convention, committed within its territory by private persons. Where Section I of the Convention is enacted as part of domestic law, or can be invoked before the domestic courts, a limited effect on third parties[19] may be allowed, since Section I does not itself confine liability to the State.[20] On

---

[18] See ch. 17 below.

[19] See for this effect on third parties *(Drittwirkung)* in national law, as well as on the European level, M. Eissen, 'La Convention et les devoirs de l'individu' in *La protection internationale des Droits de l'homme dans le cadre européen* (Paris, 1961), 167; Eissen, 'The European Convention on Human Rights and the Duties of the Individual' in (1962) 32 *Acta Scandinavica Juris Gentium* 230; Eissen, 'La Convention européenne des Droits de l'Homme et les obligations de l'individu: une mise à jour', in R. Cassin, *Amicorum Discipulorumque Liber* III (Paris, 1971), 151; A. Drzemczewski, 'The domestic status of the European Convention on Human Rights. New Dimensions' [1977/1] LIEI 1–85; and E. A. Alkema, 'The third party applicability or "Drittwirkung" of the European Convention on Human Rights' in F. Matscher and H. Petzold, *Protecting Human Rights: The European Dimension. Studies in Honour of Gérard J. Wiarda* (Köln, 1988), at 33–45. See also A. Clapham, *Human Rights in the Private Sphere* (Oxford, 1993).

[20] On the effect of incorporation and the notion of the horizontal effect of the Convention within a national legal order, see M. Hunt, 'The "horizontal effect" of the Human Rights Act' [1998] PL 423, and G. Phillipson, 'The Human Rights Act, "Horizontal Effect" and the Common Law: a Bang or a Whimper' (1999) 62 MLR 824, on this issue in the UK following the passing of the Human Rights Act 1998.

the European level, however, the Commission can only deal, under Article 34,[21] with an application by an individual claiming to be a victim of a violation by one of the Contracting Parties. If the violation is by a private individual, therefore, a State may have fulfilled its obligations if its law adequately protects the rights guaranteed and provides for an effective remedy in the event of such violation.

The precise extent to which a State may be liable for the conduct of a private individual must ultimately depend on the terms of the individual articles of the Convention, and must be examined separately in relation to each of the rights guaranteed. For example, issues have arisen as to how far the conduct of a lawyer may involve the responsibility of the State in relation to its duty to provide a fair trial;[22] how far the State is liable, in relation to trade union freedoms, for the acts of private employers;[23] and how far the rights relating to education are guaranteed where children are educated at private schools.[24]

TEMPORAL SCOPE

In the *Nielsen* case, the Commission said:

Under a generally recognised rule of international law, the Convention only governs for each Contracting Party those facts which are subsequent to the date of its entry into force with regard to the Party in question.[25]

The Convention, therefore, can have no retroactive effect. The Convention entered into force, in accordance with Article 66(2), after ratification by ten States; this figure was achieved on 3 September 1953.[26] For any State ratifying the Convention and Protocols after these dates, they enter into force on the date of ratification.[27] An application cannot relate back to an event earlier than the entry into force of the instrument in question in respect of the State against which the application is brought, unless that event has consequences which may raise the question of a continuing violation.[28]

---

[21] Formerly Art. 25.

[22] App. 2656/65, *X* v. *Austria*, 3 April 1967, (1967) 23 CD 31.

[23] App. 4125/69, *X* v. *Ireland*, 1 February 1971, (1971) 14 *Yearbook* 198.

[24] App. 14229/88, *X and Y* v. *United Kingdom*, 13 December 1990, (1991) 12 HRLJ 61.

[25] App. 343/57, *Nielsen* v. *Denmark*, 2 September 1959, (1959–60) 2 *Yearbook* 412, at 454.

[26] The various Protocols entered into force on the following dates: Protocol 1: 18 May 1954; Protocol 2: 21 September 1970; Protocol 3: 21 September 1970; Protocol 4: 2 May 1968; Protocol 5: 21 December 1971; Protocol 6: 1 March 1985; Protocol 7: 1 November 1988; Protocol 8: 1 January 1990; Protocol 9: 1 October 1994; Protocol 10: not in force; Protocol 11: 1 November 1998; and Protocol 12: not yet in force.

[27] See Art. 66(3) of the Convention; the Protocols adopt a similar rule.

[28] As in App. 214/56, *De Becker* v. *Belgium*, 9 January 1958, (1958–8) 2 *Yearbook* 214.

On the other hand, accepting the competence of the Commission, under former Article 25, to deal with individual applications, had in principle a retro-active effect.[29] So if an alleged violation was subsequent to the entry into force of the Convention in respect of the State concerned, but prior to its declaration under Article 25, the Commission was competent *ratione temporis*. Similar considerations applied to declarations accepting the compulsory jurisdiction of the Court. Despite this general rule, it became clear that it was possible to frame a declaration in such terms that acceptance of the competence of the Commission and the Court had no retrospective effect. The United Kingdom's declaration in 1966 limited its effect to 'any act or decision occurring or any facts arising subsequently to the 13th of January 1966'.[30]

Acceptance of the Commission's competence under Article 24 to deal with inter-State cases was not optional, but followed automatically from acceptance of the Convention. If the respondent State had ratified the Convention, it did not matter that the applicant State was at the date of the event in issue not itself a Party to the Convention.

The point was illustrated in the *Pfunders* case,[31] brought by Austria against Italy. Six young men had been convicted of murdering an Italian customs officer in the German-speaking part of South Tyrol, an area which was the subject of a long-standing dispute between the two countries. The Austrian Government alleged that the criminal proceedings in the Italian courts were not compatible with the provisions of Article 6 of the Convention, which lays down rules concerning the proper administration of justice and the protec-tion of the rights of persons charged with criminal offences. The Italian Government objected that the Commission was not competent *ratione temporis* to deal with the case, since although Italy was a party to the Convention at the date of the proceedings in question, Austria had not ratified the Convention at that time.

The Commission, in rejecting this objection, found it inconsistent with the fundamental character of the Convention. The Convention on Human Rights is not based, as are most other treaties, on reciprocity, and does not involve a mutual exchange of rights and obligations by the Contracting Parties. Its object is to set up an independent legal order for the protection of individuals.

Relying, in particular, on the wording of the Preamble, the Commission stated that,

the purpose of the High Contracting Parties in concluding the Convention was not to concede to each other reciprocal rights and obligations in pursuance of their individual national interests but to realize the aims and ideals of the Council of Europe, as

[29] App. 6323/73, *X* v. *Italy*, 4 March 1976, (1976) 3 DR 80 and App. 9587/81, *X* v. *France*, 13 December 1982, (1983) 29 DR 228.
[30] (1966) 9 *Yearbook* 8.
[31] App. 788/60, *Austria* v. *Italy*, 11 January 1961, (1962) 4 *Yearbook* 116.

expressed in its Statute, and to establish a common public order of the free democracies
of Europe with the object of safeguarding their common heritage of political traditions,
ideals, freedom and the rule of law.[32]

Hence,

the obligations undertaken by the High Contracting Parties in the Convention are
essentially of an objective character being designed rather to protect the fundamental
rights of individual human beings from infringement by any of the High Contracting
Parties than to create subjective and reciprocal rights for the High Contracting Parties
themselves.[33]

A more recent example of the Court's approach to jurisdiction *ratione
temporis* can be found in the *Zana* case.[34] The case concerned a prosecution in
relation to remarks made by the former mayor of a Turkish town to journalists
expressing support for the Worker's Party of Kurdistan (PKK) in August 1987.
In March 1991 he was sentenced to a period of imprisonment. The Turkish
Government had accepted the jurisdiction of the Court only in relation to
facts and events subsequent to 22 January 1990, and objected to the Court's
jurisdiction to decide Zana's application on this basis. But the Court decided
that the principal fact which gave rise to the complaint of a violation of Article
10 was the judgment of the Turkish court in March 1991 rather than the
applicant's statements to journalists in August 1987. It was this event which
interfered with the applicant's freedom of speech. The Turkish objection was
rejected.

Denunciation under Article 58[35] does not have immediate effect. There is an
initial commitment for five years and thereafter six months' notice is required.
The obligations undertaken remain in full effect until the expiry of the period
of notice. So the application made by Denmark, Norway, and Sweden against
Greece in April 1970, some four months after Greece had denounced the
Convention on 12 December 1969 was admissible since the six months' notice
period did not expire until 13 June 1970.[36]

---

[32] Ibid., at 138.
[33] Ibid., at 140.
[34] *Zana* v. *Turkey* (App. 18954/91), Judgment of 25 November 1997; (1999) 27 EHRR 667.
[35] Formerly Art. 65
[36] App. 4448/70, *Denmark, Norway and Sweden* v. *Greece*, 26 May 1970, (1970) 13 *Yearbook* 108. This
application was struck out of the Commission's list in 1976 after Greece had again become a party to
the Convention: Report of 4 October 1976 (1976) 6 DR 6.

TERRITORIAL SCOPE

Under Article 1, the States Parties guarantee the rights and freedoms defined in Section I to everyone within their jurisdiction. The *Loizidou* case[37] concerned an application relating to the seizure of property in northern Cyprus, which has been occupied by Turkey since July 1974 and has been declared to be the Turkish Republic of Northern Cyprus, an entity recognized only by Turkey. Could such action be capable of falling within the jurisdiction of Turkey? The Court reiterated its earlier case-law that the concept of jurisdiction is not restricted to the national territory of a Contracting State. It went on:

Bearing in mind the object and purpose of the Convention, the responsibility of a Contracting Party may also arise when as a consequence of military action—whether lawful or unlawful—it exercises effective control of an area outside its national territory. The obligation to secure, in such an area, the rights and freedoms set out in the Convention, derives from the fact of such control whether it be exercised directly, through its armed forces, or through a subordinate local administration.[38]

The guarantee in Article 1 may be subject to certain territorial limits.[39] This follows from the so-called 'colonial' clause in Article 56[40], which provides that a State may, by means of a declaration, extend the Convention to all or any of the territories for whose international relations it is responsible. But for this Article, it would have been clear that the Convention extended, by the mere act of ratification, to all such territories. It has already been shown that the wording of Article 1 does not introduce any territorial limitation to the Convention. It is introduced, therefore, only by implication in former Article 63, which runs counter to the whole scheme of the Convention, and which can be explained by historical circumstances of little relevance today.[41]

Thus it is quite clear that the State may be responsible for the acts of its officials abroad. It is responsible, for example, for the acts of its diplomatic and consular representatives. In one case, the Commission accepted that the acts of the German consul in Morocco could make the Federal Republic liable under the Convention.[42] It justified its decision on the narrow ground that the nationals

[37] *Loizidou* v. *Turkey (Preliminary Objections)*, Judgment of 23 March 1995, Series A, No. 310; (1955) 20 EHRR 99.

[38] Para. 62 of the judgment. The *Loizidou* judgment has been confirmed in *Cyprus* v. *Turkey* (App. 25781/94), Judgment of 10 May 2001.

[39] App. 1065/61, *X* v. *Belgium*, 30 May 1961, (1961) 4 *Yearbook* 260 at 268.

[40] Formerly Art. 63.

[41] See J. G. Merrills and A. H. Robertson, *Human Rights in Europe* (Manchester, 2001), at 26–7.

[42] App. 1611/62, *X* v. *Germany*, 25 September 1965, (1965) 8 *Yearbook* 158, at 168. See also Joined Apps. 6780/74 and 6950/75, *Cyprus* v. *Turkey*, 26 May 1975, (1975) 18 *Yearbook* 82, and App. 800776, *Cyprus* v. *Turkey*, 10 July 1978, (1978) 13 DR 85, at 148–9, when Turkey was held to be responsible for acts of its armed forces, and Joined Apps. 7289/75 and 7349/79, *X and Y* v. *Switzerland*, 14 July 1977, (1977) 9 DR 57, at 73, when Switzerland was held to be responsible for official acts having effect in Liechtenstein.

of a State are, in certain respects, still within its jurisdiction, even when domiciled or resident abroad. The decision is certainly correct, but the reasoning is not satisfactory. No distinction should be made between nationals and others; it could not seriously be maintained that a State is liable under the Convention for the acts of its diplomatic and consular officials abroad towards its nationals, but not towards aliens. As we have seen, the significance of the expression 'within their jurisdiction' in Article 1 is quite different. It does not mean that a State is liable only for violations committed within its territory, or outside its territory if committed against its nationals. Such an interpretation would be contrary to the whole system of the Convention. Subject to Article 56, the State is responsible for breaches of the Convention wherever they are committed.

The United Kingdom has extended the Convention to a number of dependent overseas territories, and the Netherlands has extended it to Surinam[43] and the Netherlands Antilles.

When such territories become independent, the declaration automatically lapses, and it is unnecessary to denounce the Convention in respect of the territory concerned under Article 58(4).[44] On independence, of course, the State which has made the declaration ceases to be responsible for the international relations of the new State; and there can be no question of the new State remaining a party to the Convention by the law of State succession, since the Convention is confined, by Article 59(1),[45] to Members of the Council of Europe.[46]

A declaration under Article 56 may also lapse for a different reason. The Convention was extended by Denmark to Greenland, for whose international relations it was responsible at the time; but subsequently, in 1953, Greenland became part of metropolitan Denmark, so that the Convention automatically applied to Greenland irrespective of the declaration.

Article 56(3) provides that the provisions of the Convention apply to territories to which a declaration under Article 56(1) applies 'with due regard . . . to local requirements'. The interpretation of this phrase was considered in the *Tyrer case*[47] which concerned corporal punishment in the Isle of Man. The United Kingdom government sought to argue that public opinion on the island which supported the practice of birching was a 'local requirement' which brought the practice within Article 63(3). The Court rejected this saying that public opinion was insufficient to ground such a claim; positive and conclusive proof would be needed of the requirement.[48]

---

[43] Until its independence in 1975.   [44] Formerly Art. 65(4).   [45] Formerly Art. 66(1).

[46] See M. Eissen, 'The Independence of Malta and the European Convention on Human Rights' (1965–6) 41 BYBIL 401; and 'Malawi and the European Convention on Human Rights' (1968–9) 43 BYBIL 190. Malta subsequently became a member of the Council of Europe and a party to the Convention, as did Cyprus.

[47] *Tyrer v. United Kingdom*, Judgment of 25 April 1978, Series A, No. 26; (1980) 2 EHRR 1.

[48] Para. 38. The Court's comments suggest that corporal punishment as a preventive measure could not be taken out of the application of Article 3 by reason of being a local requirement.

A number of provisions of the Convention may have extraterritorial effect. For example, in the *Soering* case,[49] the Court took the view that the extradition of Soering to the United States where he might be exposed to the so-called 'death row phenomenon' would amount to a breach by the United Kingdom of its obligations under Article 3.

THE STATUS OF THE CONVENTION IN THE UNITED KINGDOM

The incorporation of the European Convention on Human Rights into national law in the United Kingdom is an event of major constitutional significance. Incorporation means that Convention rights can be argued and considered in national courts and tribunals alongside other issues in cases before them. There has been a renewed and energetic focus on compliance with Convention rights of many aspects of United Kingdom law following the entry into force on 2 October 2000 of the Human Rights Act 1998. This is a clever and elegant piece of legislation which sets in place a scheme which preserves the distinct roles of judges and politicians in the constitutional order of the United Kingdom.[50]

There is an improved system of pre-legislative scrutiny of legislation. Section 19 of the Act requires the Minister introducing a Bill in Parliament to state whether, in his or her view, it is compatible with the European Convention, or to decline to do so but to indicate that the Government nevertheless wishes to proceed with the Bill. Critics have expressed concern that without the support of a national Human Rights Commission, the level of scrutiny may well be inadequate to guarantee compliance with the Convention in every case.

The substantive articles of the Convention and Protocols to which the United Kingdom is party are restated in section 1 and Schedule 1 to the Act as provisions of United Kingdom law with the exception of Article 13 of the Convention.[51] The incorporated rights are known as Convention rights.

---

[49] *Soering* v. *United Kingdom*, Judgment of 7 July 1989, Series A, No. 161; (1989) 11 EHRR 439. See ch. 5 below for a discussion of this case.

[50] For a description of preparations for implementation, see generally A. Finlay, 'The Human Rights Act: The Lord Chancellor's Department's Preparations for Implementation' [1999] EHRLR 512. For a judicial comment on the impact of incorporation, see Lord Steyn, 'The New Legal Landscape' [2000] EHRLR 549.

[51] Article 13 guarantees an effective remedy before a national authority for a violation of a Convention right. Its omission is seen by some as controversial, see R. White, 'Remedies in a Multi-Level Legal Order: The Strasbourg Court and the UK' in C. Kilpatrick, T. Novitz, and P. Skidmore, *The Future of Remedies in Europe* (Oxford, 2000), at 191.

Under section 6(1) of the Act, it is unlawful for any public authority to 'act in a way which is incompatible with a Convention right'. Public authorities include a court or tribunal, and 'any person certain of whose functions are of a public nature', but does not include either House of Parliament. There remains considerable uncertainty as to the ambit of the term 'public authority', and clearly flesh will need to be given to this term under national case law. Under section 7, any person who claims that a public authority has acted in a manner which is incompatible with a Convention right, may bring proceedings against the authority in a court or tribunal as determined by rules of court made under the Act. If the act complained of is that of a court or tribunal, the matter may be raised on appeal. Furthermore, any party to proceedings can rely on a Convention right in those proceedings. Applicants bringing judicial review proceedings will have standing if they are, or would be, considered a victim of a violation under Article 34 of the Convention.[52] Convention case law has been generous over the matter of standing to raise a complaint of a violation.

Whenever Convention rights are in issue before public authorities, new rules of interpretation come into play. Firstly, in determining whether there has been a violation of a Convention right, a court or tribunal must 'take into account' case law of the Commission, Court of Human Rights, and the Committee of Ministers. In interpreting any primary or secondary legislation whenever enacted, the court or tribunal must 'so far as it is possible to do so, read and give effect to that legislation in a way which is compatible with the Convention rights.'[53]

If a court or tribunal concludes that there has been a violation of a Convention right, 'it may grant such relief or remedy, or make such order, within its jurisdiction as it considers just and appropriate.'[54] This is an enabling provision giving courts and tribunals powers based on, but going beyond, those enjoyed by the Court of Human Rights under Article 41 of the Convention to afford just satisfaction to a victim of a violation.[55] However, damages can only be awarded by those courts or tribunals which have power to award damages, or to order the payment of compensation, in civil proceedings.[56]

The failure to incorporate Article 13, which guarantees a right to a remedy in national law, may be problematic here. The Government position in Parliamentary debates was that the whole Act meets the requirements of Article 13, and there was concern that its incorporation might give all courts and tribunals sweeping powers to grant remedies which would be inappropriate.

The form of incorporation adopted in the United Kingdom has given rise to

---

[52] See ch. 24.
[53] s.3(1) of the Act.
[54] s.8(1) of the Act.
[55] See. ch. 26.
[56] s.8(2) of the Act.

a considerable debate as to whether the Convention rights can be claimed against private parties in the national legal order.[57] This matter awaits resolution through judicial decisions of the United Kingdom courts, but the preferred view is that the positive duty of courts in the United Kingdom to have regard to Convention rights in deciding matters before them is unlikely to give rise to direct horizontal effect of Convention rights in the United Kingdom. The prime responsibility for securing the guarantees in the Convention falls on public authorities, though that does not preclude their ensuring that they act to secure the positive duties imposed on them by the Court of Human Rights' case law.

Where the new rules of interpretation do not enable a court or tribunal to read and give effect to primary legislation in a way which is compatible with the Convention rights, the declaration of incompatibility comes into play. Section 4(2) of the Act provides that a court which is satisfied that a provision in primary legislation is incompatible with a Convention right 'may make a declaration of incompatibility'. For England and Wales, the following courts have power to make such a declaration: the High Court, Court of Appeal, House of Lords, Judicial Committee of the Privy Council, and the Courts Martial Appeal Court. Where a lesser court or tribunal[58] is faced with such an issue, it must apply the 'incompatible' legislation and the matter will have to be taken on appeal until a court with the power is reached. All courts and tribunals, however, have the power to rule that subordinate legislation is incompatible with Convention rights unless the primary legislation prevents removal of the incompatibility.[59] The declaration of incompatibility is the solution to the dilemma of having judges declaring primary legislation invalid, which was seen to be an interference by judges in the role of the legislature. The declaration of incompatibility does not affect the validity, continuing operation or enforcement of the provision, and is binding on the parties to the proceedings in which it is made.[60] Its effect is to prompt the legislature to consider making a remedial order under section 10 and Schedule 2 to the Act. This is a fast-track legislative procedure designed to remove the incompatibility at the heart of the court's declaration. Again critics of the Act argue that there is a role for a national Human Rights Commission to assist in ensuring that any defect is fully corrected.

The incorporation of the Convention does not in any way deprive those who believe they are victims of violations of the Convention from making applications to the Court in Strasbourg, subject to the Convention's admissibility rules.

---

[57] See S. Grosz, J. Beatson and P. Duffy, *Human Rights. The 1998 Act and the European Convention* (London, 2000), at 88–98. See also M. Hunt, 'The "horizontal effect" of the Human Rights Act' [1998] PL 423; G. Phillipson, 'The Human Rights Act, "Horizontal Effect" and the Common Law: a Bang or a Whimper' (1999) 62 MLR 824; R. Buxton, 'The Human Rights Act and Private Law' (2000) 116 LQR 48; and W. Wade, 'Horizons of Horizontality' (2000) 116 LQR 217.
[58] And there are very many of these.   [59] s.4(3) and (4) of the Act.   [60] s.4(6) of the Act.

3

PRINCIPLES OF
INTERPRETATION

INTRODUCTION

The starting point[1] for any consideration of the principles of interpretation applied by the Court is the general rules of international law on the interpretation of treaties. In the *Golder* case[2] the Court stated that Articles 31 to 33 of the Vienna Convention on the Law of Treaties of 23 May 1969, notwithstanding that the Vienna Convention was not yet in force, should guide the Court in its interpretation of the Convention on Human Rights since the principles contained in those articles were generally regarded as being declaratory of principles of customary international law. Articles 31 to 33 accordingly warrant quotation:

Article 31

General rule of interpretation

1. A treaty shall be interpreted in good faith in accordance with the ordinary meaning to be given to the terms of the treaty in their context and in the light of its object and purpose.
2. The context for the purpose of the interpretation of a treaty shall comprise, in addition to the text, including its preamble and annexes:
   (a) any agreement relating to the treaty which was made between all the parties in connection with the conclusion of the treaty;
   (b) any instrument which was made by one or more parties in connection with the conclusion of the treaty and accepted by the other parties as an instrument related to the treaty.

---

[1] The material in this chapter draws in particular on material in J. Merrills, *The Development of International Law by the European Court of Human Rights* (Manchester, 1988); M. Delmas-Marty, *The European Convention for the Protection of Human Rights. International Protection versus National Restrictions* (Dordrecht, 1992), Part III; and F. Matscher, 'Methods of Interpretation of the Convention' in R. Macdonald, F. Matscher, and H. Petzold, *The European System for the Protection of Human Rights* (Dordrecht, 1993), 63

[2] *Golder* v. *United Kingdom*, Judgment of 21 February 1975, Series A No. 18, para. 29 of the judgment; (1979–80) 1 EHRR 524.

3. There shall be taken into account, together with the context:
    (a) any subsequent agreement between the parties regarding the interpretation of the treaty or the application of its provisions;
    (b) any subsequent practice in the application of the treaty which establishes the agreement of the parties regarding its interpretation;
    (c) any relevant rules of international law applicable in the relations between the parties.
4. A special meaning shall be given to a term if it is established that the parties so intended.

Article 32

Supplementary means of interpretation

Recourse may be had to supplementary means of interpretation, including the preparatory work of the treaty and the circumstances of its conclusion, in order to confirm the meaning resulting from the application of Article 31, or to determine the meaning when the interpretation according to Article 31:
    (a) leaves the meaning ambiguous or obscure; or
    (b) leads to a result which is manifestly absurd or unreasonable.

Article 33

Interpretation of treaties authenticated in two or more languages

1. When a treaty has been authenticated in two or more languages, the text is equally authoritative in each language, unless the treaty provides or the parties agree that, in case of divergence, a particular text shall prevail.
2. A version of the treaty in a language other than one of those in which the text was authenticated shall be considered an authentic text only if the treaty so provides or the parties so agree.
3. The terms of the treaty are presumed to have the same meaning in each authentic text.
4. Except where a particular text prevails in accordance with paragraph 1, where a comparison of the authentic texts discloses a difference of meaning which the application of Articles 31 and 32 does not remove, the meaning which best reconciles the texts, having regard to the object and purpose of the treaty, shall be adopted.

The principles laid down in these articles suggest a number of propositions in addition to a general requirement that treaties are interpreted in good faith:
    (1) Terms used in the treaty should be accorded their ordinary meaning.
    (2) Regard can be had to the context in which the words appear.
    (3) Regard can be had to the object and purpose of the treaty.
    (4) The *travaux préparatoires* may be used to help resolve an ambiguity in the text, to confirm a meaning attributed by the use of other rules, or to avoid an absurdity.
    (5) The treaty is equally authentic in each authenticated language and any

differences of meaning are to be resolved by adopting the meaning which best accords with the object and purpose of the treaty.

How far do these general rules of treaty interpretation apply to the European Convention on Human Rights? While the relevant provisions of the Vienna Convention are sufficiently general to give some guidance, they must be applied with caution in view of the special features of the European Convention.

Although the European Convention on Human Rights is an international treaty, it has a special character which goes beyond merely setting out the rights and obligations of the Contracting States. The European Convention penetrates the national legal orders by requiring Contracting States to behave in a particular way towards their own citizens and those citizens of other countries who are within their jurisdiction. What was previously treated by international law as a matter within the domestic jurisdiction of States is brought within an international system of protection and supervision.

The Court has not adopted a hierarchical approach to the application of the propositions set out above to the task of interpretation. It has viewed the task of interpretation as a single complex operation, though reference to the object and purpose of the provision in the context of the Convention as a whole has been the most influential of the principles applied by the Court.

USE OF *TRAVAUX PRÉPARATOIRES*

The special nature of the European Convention means that particular caution is necessary in relying on the preparatory work of the Convention.[3] Preparatory work is notoriously unreliable as a general guide to treaty interpretation, and is hence treated only as a supplementary means of interpretation in Article 32 of the Vienna Convention. But because of the special features of the European Convention, it should be invoked, if at all, as a guide to the general intentions of the Parties, rather than to delimit strictly the scope of particular articles. This, too, is in accordance with the real purpose of the Convention. Caution is required in the use of the preparatory work because the Court has confirmed on many occasions that the Convention is a living instrument and has adopted a dynamic interpretation to the substance of its provisions.[4] In the *Sigurjonsson* case[5] the Court noted that the use of the *travaux préparatoires* in the earlier

---

[3] See the Report of the Commission of 29 August 1973 in the *Golder* case.
[4] See R. Bernhardt, 'Thoughts on the interpretation of human-rights treaties' in F. Matscher, and H. Petzold, *Protecting Human Rights: The European Dimension* (Köln, 1990), 65–71, at 68–9.
[5] *Sigurdur A. Sigurjonsson v. Iceland*, Judgment of 30 June 1993, Series A, No. 264; (1993) 16 EHRR 462.

Young, James and Webster case[6] was not decisive but merely provided a working hypothesis.[7]

The preparatory work was legitimately invoked by the Commission to show that the provision that 'Everyone shall be free to leave any country, including his own', does not entitle a convicted prisoner to leave the country in which he is lawfully detained.[8] The contrary interpretation would lead, in the words of Article 32 of the Vienna Convention, to a result which is manifestly absurd or unreasonable. On the other hand, in the *Lawless* case, the Court refused to resort to the preparatory work to interpret a provision which was sufficiently clear.[9]

Because of the limited value of the preparatory work, little account is given of it in this book. Nor is much attention paid to the provisions of national constitutions or of other international instruments which, although they may be of similar purport, are differently worded and must be construed in a different context. It may of course be valuable to refer to such instruments in certain cases: for example, to refer to the relevant Conventions of the International Labour Organization, as the Commission has done, when interpreting Article 11 of the Convention on the same matters. This may be necessary to avoid inconsistent interpretations of similar guarantees by different international institutions. In the future, efforts will also be necessary to avoid divergent interpretations of the United Nations Covenants and regional arrangements for the protection of human rights. Here, as in the application of the European Convention in those European States where it has the force of law, the work of the European Commission and Court may provide some guidance.

DIFFERENT LANGUAGE VERSIONS

The European Convention is equally authentic in the English and in the French texts. Where these texts differ, the meaning which best reconciles the texts, having regard to the object and purpose of the treaty, must be adopted.[10] In the *James* case[11] the applicants sought to challenge provisions of the United

---

[6] *Young, James and Webster v. United Kingdom*, Judgment of 13 August 1981, Series A, No. 44; (1989) 11 EHRR 439.

[7] *Sigurdur A. Sigurjonsson v. Iceland*, Judgment of 30 June 1993, Series A, No. 264; (1993) 16 EHRR 462, para. 24–5 of the judgment.

[8] See ch. 17 below.

[9] *Lawless v. Ireland*, Judgment of 1 July 1961, Series A, No.2; (1979–80) 1 EHRR 13, para. 14 of the judgment.

[10] Article 33(4) of the Vienna Convention. See also the *Wemhoff* case, Judgment of 27 June 1968, Series A, No. 7; (1979–80) 1 EHRR 55.

[11] *James and others v. United Kingdom*, Judgment of 21 February 1986, Series A, No. 98; (1986) 8 EHRR 123.

Kingdom leasehold enfranchisement legislation as being inconsistent with Article 1 of Protocol 1. The issue raised required the Court to consider whether the deprivation of property suffered by the freeholders who were compelled under the legislation to sell the freehold to their tenants could be said to be 'in the public interest'. It appeared that the French text 'pour cause d'utilité publique' carried a somewhat different connotation from the English text. The Court adopted a definition which 'best reconciles the language of the English and French texts, having regard to the object and purpose of Article 1' and referred explicitly to Article 33 of the Vienna Convention in doing so.[12]

ORDINARY MEANING

The Court has frequently used the ordinary meaning of words in order to interpret provisions of the Convention. This may involve reference to dictionaries to determine the ordinary and natural meaning of the words.[13] In the *Johnston* case[14] the Court ruled that the ordinary meaning of the words 'right to marry' did not include a right to divorce. In the *Lithgow* case[15] the Court ruled that the ordinary meaning of the reference to 'the general principles of international law' in Article 1 of the First Protocol required that the phrase be given the same meaning as under Article 38(1)(d) of the Statute of the International Court of Justice.

There is one area where the ordinary meaning of words takes on a special significance. Frequently the Convention uses terms which do not have identical scope in the national legal systems. Here a difficulty arises as to the precise scope of the Convention term. Examples are the terms 'civil rights and obligations' and 'criminal charge' in Article 6. The Court has adopted its own rules for determining the scope of such terms. This has come to be known as the independent classification of terms, or, more usually, as the autonomous meaning of terms.[16] The Court has justified this approach by the need to secure

[12] Para. 42 of the judgment. The Court had earlier taken exactly the same approach to the interpretation of the phrase 'prescribed by law' in Article 10(2) of the Convention in *Times Newspapers and others* v. *United Kingdom*, Judgment of 26 April 1979, Series A, No. 30; (1979–80) 2 EHRR 245 para. 48 of the judgment.

[13] *Luedicke, Belkacem and Koç* v. *Germany*, Judgment of 28 November 1978, Series A, No. 29; (1981) 2 EHRR 149, para. 40 of the judgment.

[14] *Johnston* v. *Ireland*, Judgment of 18 December 1986, Series A, No. 112; (1987) 9 EHRR 203.

[15] *Lithgow* v. *United Kingdom*, Judgment of 8 July 1986, Series A, No. 102; (1986) 8 EHRR 329.

[16] The Court of Justice of the European Communities has adopted a similar approach to the meaning of terms in both the EC Treaty and the Brussels Convention on Civil Jurisdiction and the Enforcement of Judgments. See generally L. Neville Brown, and F. Jacobs, *The Court of Justice of the European Communities* (London, 1994), Part Four, and A. Dashwood, R. Hacon, and R. White, *A Guide to the Civil Jurisdiction and Judgments Convention* (Deventer, 1986), chs 2 and 6.

uniformity of treatment throughout the States Parties to the Convention. Any other approach would result in the Convention's institutions having to defer to the classification adopted in the Contracting State. The issue of defining 'criminal charge' arose in the *Engel* case[17] which concerned action against persons conscripted into the Netherlands armed forces. The action was classified as disciplinary. If the matter involved consideration of a criminal charge, it was squarely within the scope of Article 6. The Court ruled that a Convention definition must be applied to the proceedings; their classification in the national legal order was only one factor to be taken into account in determining their scope. In the *König* case[18] the applicant claimed a violation arising from proceedings of an administrative nature in which he had sought to challenge the withdrawal of his right to practise medicine. The Court concluded that the proceedings involved the determination of his civil rights and obligations despite the German classification of the proceedings as administrative in nature. The need to secure a uniform interpretation of the Convention in all the States Parties clearly requires that differential application of the Convention protection arising from differences of terminology be avoided. The more controversial issue surrounds the criteria adopted by the Court for the determination of the scope of the Convention term. Here there can be opportunities for judicial creativity.

The difference between the traditional international treaty and the Convention again becomes apparent. Many of the terms used belong essentially to the domestic legal order and so the Court has used comparative law techniques in assigning the Convention meaning to the terms. Where common approaches or standards emerge from the comparative study, that meaning will be applied. Where common standards do not emerge, then a greater flexibility of standards is accepted which has come to be known as the 'margin of appreciation'.

CONTEXT

In the *Golder* case, the Court said:

In the way in which it is presented in the 'general rule' in Article 31 of the Vienna Convention, the process of interpretation of a treaty is a unity, a single combined operation; this rule, closely integrated, places on the same footing the various elements enumerated in the four paragraphs of the Article.[19]

[17] *Engel and others* v. *Netherlands*, Judgment of 8 June 1976, Series A, No. 22; (1979–80) 1 EHRR 647.
[18] *König* v. *Germany*, Judgment of 28 June 1978, Series A, No. 27; (1980) 2 EHRR 170.
[19] *Golder* v. *United Kingdom*, Judgment of 21 February 1975, Series A, No. 18; (1979–80) 1 EHRR 524, para. 30 of the judgment.

Context is defined in Article 31(2) of the Vienna Convention as the whole of the text together with its preamble and annexes, any agreement related to the treaty made by all the parties in connection with the conclusion of the treaty, and any instrument accepted by all the parties as one related to the treaty. In practice, the use of context enables a treaty to be read as a whole and assistance to be derived from the underlying objectives frequently set out in the preamble.

The use of context has most often arisen where applicants are faced with violations which are covered in some detail by provisions in a Protocol which has not been ratified by the respondent government. In such cases the respondent government often seeks to argue that the whole matter is governed by the Protocol, while applicants will argue that aspects of their claim nevertheless fall within articles of the Convention which are in force as against the respondent government. The Court has concluded in such cases that the presence of detailed rules in a Protocol does not bar the applicability of a more general provision to aspects of the case. So in the *Abdulaziz* case[20] the applicant was able to rely on the right to respect for family life in raising an issue concerning the United Kingdom immigration legislation, even though the United Kingdom is not a party to the Fourth Protocol. Similarly, the applicant in the *Rasmussen* case[21] was able to rely on Article 8 of the Convention in a case concerning paternity issues even though Denmark was not a party to the Fifth Protocol which sets out the rights of parents in relation to their children. In the *Guzzardi* case[22] the applicant was able to rely on Article 5 to challenge the requirement that he live on a small island under police supervision even though Italy had not recognized the rights of free movement contained in the Fourth Protocol.

The Court has said that interpretation of articles of the Convention 'must be in harmony with the logic of the Convention'.[23] So a finding that Article 8 did not require the disclosure of information held in a secret police register which accounted for the applicant's failure to secure employment near a naval base meant that no claim that there had been a failure to provide a remedy under Article 13 could arise. The reverse situation may also arise; if a right is not part of a more specific provision, it cannot be part of a more general provision. So, since the right to divorce is not part of the right to marry under Article 12, it cannot form part of the rights contained in Article 8, which is of more general purpose and scope.[24]

The *Maaouia* case illustrates how the Court uses context to determine the

---

[20] *Abdulaziz, Cabales and Balkandali* v. *United Kingdom*, Judgment of 28 May 1985, Series A, No. 94; (1985) 7 EHRR 471.

[21] *Rasmussen* v. *Denmark*, Judgment of 28 November 1984, Series A, No. 87; (1985) 7 EHRR 372.

[22] *Guzzardi* v. *Italy*, Judgment of 6 November 1980, Series A, No. 39; (1981) 3 EHRR 333.

[23] *Leander* v. *Sweden*, Judgment of 26 March 1987, Series A, No. 116, para. 78 of the judgment; (1988) 9 EHRR 433.

[24] *Johnston* v. *Ireland*, Judgment of 18 December 1986, Series A, No. 112; (1988) 9 EHRR 203.

meaning of terms.[25] The applicant complained at the length of the proceedings for the rescission of the deportation order made against him. The question was whether such proceedings came within the terms 'civil rights and obligation' or constituted a 'criminal charge' against him.[26] The Court stressed that these were autonomous terms and that provisions of the Convention must be construed in the light of the entire Convention system including the Protocols to the Convention. Since Protocol 7 contained certain specific guarantees relating to procedures for the expulsion of aliens, they did not constitute proceedings relating to civil rights and obligations within Article 6(1). Nor did they constitute the determination of a criminal charge against the applicant. Consequently, Article 6(1) did not apply to such proceedings.

It is easy to make too much of the use of context, whereas examination of the case law of the Court shows that the context used for reference in interpreting a term can vary considerably. In some cases, the context consists solely of paragraphs of the same article, while in others the whole Convention, including its Preamble and Protocols, is used. Selection of the context often merges into consideration of the object and purpose of the provision.

OBJECT AND PURPOSE

The Commission's Report on the *Golder* case suggests that particular account should be taken of two features of the European Convention when a question of interpretation arises. First, it provides for a system of international adjudication, while the general rules of treaty interpretation have evolved primarily as guides to interpretation by the parties themselves.[27] Hence, in the *Pfunders* case the Court stated that the Convention should be interpreted objectively:

the obligations undertaken by the High Contracting Parties in the Convention are essentially of an objective character, being designed rather to protect the fundamental rights of individual human beings from infringement by any of the High Contracting Parties than to create subjective and reciprocal rights for the High Contracting Parties themselves.[28]

Secondly, any general presumption that treaty obligations should be interpreted restrictively since they derogate from the sovereignty of States is not

---

[25] *Maaouia* v. *France* (App 39652/98), Judgment of 5 October 2000; (2001) 33 EHRR 1037.

[26] See chs 8 and 9 below.

[27] F. Jacobs, 'Varieties of Approach to Treaty Interpretation with Special Reference to the Draft Convention on the Law of Treaties before the Vienna Diplomatic Conference' (1969) 18 ICLQ 318, at 341–3.

[28] App. 788/60, *Austria* v. *Italy*, Judgment of 11 January 1961, (1962) 4 *Yearbook* 116, at 138.

applicable to the Convention. This follows indeed from the last words of Article 31(1) of the Vienna Convention which provides that a treaty is to be interpreted in good faith in accordance with the ordinary meaning to be given to the terms of the treaty in their context and *in the light of its object and purpose*. Thus the Court of Human Rights stated in the *Wemhoff* case that it was necessary 'to seek the interpretation that is most appropriate in order to realise the aim and achieve the object of the treaty, not that which would restrict to the greatest possible degree the obligations undertaken by the Parties.'[29]

These two features of the European Convention suggest that a further conclusion may be drawn as to the appropriate principles of interpretation: that the interpretation of the Convention must be 'dynamic' in the sense that it must be interpreted in the light of developments in social and political attitudes. Its effects cannot be confined to the conceptions of the period when it was drafted or entered into force. Thus the concept of degrading treatment in Article 3 may be interpreted to include racial discrimination, even though this might not have entered the minds of the drafters of the Convention;[30] and the protection of privacy under Article 8 must be developed to meet new technological developments which were not envisaged fifty years ago.[31] But the dynamic interpretation of the Convention will not justify reading new rights into the Convention. So the absence of any provision for divorce in the Convention could not be changed by reference to the increased incidence of marriage breakdown since the Convention was drafted. In the *Johnston* case, the Court said:

It is true that the Convention and its Protocols must be interpreted in the light of present-day conditions. However, the Court cannot, by means of an evolutive interpretation, derive from these instruments a right that was not included therein at the outset.[32]

Many examples of a dynamic interpretation of the Convention will be met in subsequent chapters: changes in the concept of the family, of education, of forced labour, or of trade union freedom. It cannot be objected that this approach to interpretation extends the obligations of the Contracting States beyond their intended undertakings. On the contrary, this approach is necessary if effect is to be given to their intentions, in a general sense. They did not intend solely to protect the individual against the threats to human rights which were then prevalent, with the result that, as the nature of the threats changed, the protection gradually fell away. Their intention was to protect the individual against the threats of the future, as well as the threats of the past.

[29] *Wemhoff* case, Judgment of 27 June 1968, Series A, No. 7; (1979–80) 1 EHRR 55, para. 8 of the judgment.
[30] See ch. 5 below.
[31] See ch. 10 below; and *Belgian Linguistic* case, Judgments of 9 February 1967 and 23 July 1968, Series A, Nos. 5 and 6; (1979–80) 1 EHRR 241 and 252.
[32] *Johnston* v. *Ireland*, Judgment of 18 December 1986; (1987) 9 EHRR 203, para. 53 of the Judgment.

THE PRINCIPLE OF EFFECTIVENESS

Professor Merrills rightly notes[33] that the case law of the Court of Human Rights supports the view that in interpreting the Convention, the Court seeks to give the provisions of the Convention the 'fullest weight and effect consistent with the language used and with the rest of the text and in such a way that every part of it can be given meaning.'[34] One of the most dramatic illustrations of the application of this principle arose in the *Airey* case[35]. Mrs Johanna Airey wished to seek a decree of judicial separation from her husband on the grounds of his alleged cruelty to her and their children. She is described as coming from a humble background and receiving low wages for her work. Mr Airey had left the matrimonial home, but Mrs Airey feared that he might return and wished to ensure that he had no right to do so. She was unable to find a lawyer to act for her, since no legal aid was available to assist her and she lacked the resources to fund such assistance of a fee-paying basis. She complained to the Commission which unanimously considered that there was a breach of Article 6(1) by reason of the effective denial of access to a court.

The Irish Government sought to argue, *inter alia*, that there was no bar to Mrs Airey appearing as a litigant in person before the Irish courts to seek a judicial separation. The Court, which by a majority of five to two decided that there was a violation of Article 6(1), considered it important to determine whether any remedy available to Mrs Airey was 'practical and effective' as distinct from being 'theoretical or illusory'.[36] The Court concluded that it was not 'realistic' for Mrs Airey to conduct her own case effectively.

While the *Airey* case is a dramatic illustration of an interpretation to secure effectiveness, the Court has contrasted rights which are practical and effective with those that are merely theoretical and illusory in a number of cases.[37] This principle can now be regarded as a general principle applicable whenever Convention rights are in issue.

---

[33] J. Merrills, *The Development of International Law by the European Court of Human Rights* (Manchester, 1988), ch.5.

[34] At p.98.

[35] *Airey* v. *Ireland*, Judgment of 9 October 1979, Series A, No. 32; (1979–80) 2 EHRR 305.

[36] Para. 24 of the judgment.

[37] See, e.g. *The Belgian Linguistic* case, Judgment of 23 July 1968, Series A, No. 6, paras. 3–4; (1979–80) 1 EHRR 252; *Golder* v. *United Kingdom*, Judgment of 21 February 1975, Series A, No. 18, para. 35; (1979–80) 1 EHRR 524; *Luedicke, Belkacem and Koç* v. *Federal Republic of Germany*, Judgment of 28 November 1978, Series A, No. 29, para. 42; (1980) 2 EHRR 433; *Marckx* v. *Belgium*, Judgment of 13 June 1979, Series A, No. 31, para. 31; (1979–80) 2 EHRR 330; *Artico* v. *Italy*, Judgment of 13 May 1980, Series A, No. 37, para. 33; (1981) 3 EHRR 1; *Kamasinski* v. *Austria*, Judgment of 19 December 1989, Series A, No. 168, para. 65; and *Matthews* v. *United Kingdom*, Judgment of 18 February 1999 (1999) 28 EHRR 361, para. 34.

COMPARATIVE INTERPRETATION

On the other hand, the standards adopted for interpreting the European Convention may sometimes differ from those applicable to other international instruments. This is because the interpretation of the European Convention may legitimately be based on a common tradition of constitutional law and a large measure of legal tradition common to the Member States of the Council of Europe.[38] Thus the Commission has relied as a guide to the scope of the rights guaranteed by the Convention, on comparative surveys of the laws of the Member States: the laws relating to vagrancy,[39] for example, or legislation on the right to respect for family life,[40] or on various aspects of criminal procedure,[41] or on the age of criminal responsibility.[42]

Again, to decide what is 'reasonable' or what is 'necessary'—two terms which occur frequently in the Convention—or what constitutes 'normal' civic obligations,[43] reference may be made to the general practice of the Member States of the Council of Europe. There may thus be a conflict between two legitimate aims of interpretation: to avoid inconsistencies with other international instruments, and to develop the protection of human rights in Europe on the basis of a common European law.

The yardstick of democratic standards runs through the Convention and has proved to be an important source of inspiration in delimiting the requirements of the Convention. Certain key features of a democratic society emerge from a significant case law in which the term has been relevant.[44] Democratic values require respect for the rule of law, which has been reflected in recognition by the Court of a right of access to the courts.[45] In a number of articles of the Convention, rights may be limited on grounds 'prescribed by law'[46], or 'in accordance with the law'.[47] In such cases the law which limits the rights must be accessible, clear and predictable in its application.[48] It also seems that, as a

---

[38] See generally A. Dremczewski, *European Human Rights Convention in Domestic Law* (Oxford, 1983).

[39] See Appendix IV to the Commission's Report of 19 July 1969 on the *Vagrancy Cases*, entitled 'Outline of Vagrancy legislation in force in European countries'.

[40] See ch. 11.

[41] See chs. 8 and 9.

[42] *V* v. *United Kingdom* (App. 24888/94), Judgment of 16 December 1999; (2000) 30 EHRR 121.

[43] See ch. 6.

[44] See further discussion in ch. 10. See also J. Merrills, *The Development of International Law by the European Court of Human Rights* (Manchester, 1993), ch. 6.

[45] *Golder* v. *United Kingdom*, Judgment of 21 February 1975, Series A, No. 18; (1979–80) 1 EHRR 524, para. 29 of the judgment.

[46] See e.g. Art. 10(2) of the Convention.

[47] See e.g. Art. 8(2) of the Convention.

[48] *Times Newspapers and others* v. *United Kingdom*, Judgment of 26 April 1979, Series A, No. 30; (1979–80) 2 EHRR 245, para. 48 of the judgment.

general rule, there must be procedural safeguards surrounding limitations on the freedoms laid down in the Convention.[49] The case law on freedom of expression and freedom of association indicates that democratic values require recognition of a diversity of values and the freedom to express those values without hindrance. The recognition of diversity is apparent in cases where arguments have arisen about majority and minority public opinion.[50] Democratic values require the protection of minorities against the oppression of the majority.

POSITIVE OBLIGATIONS AND *DRITTWIRKUNG*

The starting point for examining the Convention is Article 1 requiring Contracting Parties to secure to those within their jurisdiction the rights guaranteed by the Convention. More controversial is whether the securing of those rights is limited to a prohibition of State measures which interfere with them,[51] or whether the securing of those rights requires the State to take steps to ensure their observation.[52] Closely allied to these issues is the extent to which the Convention is applicable to the behaviour of private parties; this concept is known by the German word *Drittwirkung*.[53]

It is now widely accepted that the Convention does give rise to positive obligations in that the securing of certain Convention rights can only be achieved by State action to regulate certain types of conduct. So, it is now clear that the protection of the right to life in Article 2 requires State authorities to carry out an effective investigation into a death caused by actions of officials of the State,[54] or to do all that could reasonably be expected of them to avoid a real and immediate risk to life of which they have or ought to have knowledge.[55] It is also clear that the securing of the rights guaranteed by Article 8 may require positive action by States. Nowhere is this debate more sharply in focus than in

---

[49] See *Klass* v. *Germany*, Judgment of 6 September 1978, Series A, No. 28; (1979–80) 2 EHRR 214 and *Malone* v. *United Kingdom*, Judgment of 2 August 1984, Series A, No. 82; (1985) 7 EHRR 14.

[50] As in the cases concerning corporal punishment and homosexuality. See ch. 10.

[51] Negative obligations.

[52] Positive obligations.

[53] See E.A. Alkema, 'The third-party applicability or "Drittwirkung" of the European Convention on Human Rights' in F. Matscher, and H. Petzold, *Protecting Human Rights: The European Dimension. Studies in honour of Gérard J. Wiarda* (Köln, 1989), 33; and A. Clapham, 'The "Drittwirkung" of the Convention' in R. Macdonald, F. Matscher, and H. Petzold, *The European System for the Protection of Human Rights* (Dordrecht, 1993), 163.

[54] *McCann, Farrell and Savage* v. *United Kingdom*, Judgment of 27 September 1995; (1996) 21 EHRR 97.

[55] *Osman* v. *United Kingdom* (App. 23452/94), Judgment of 28 October 1998; (2000) 29 EHRR 245.

the accommodations required of States in their recognition of the issues of identity presented by transsexuals. The issue is how far the State should change its laws and administrative practices to acknowledge the 'new' gender identity of transsexuals.[56]

Consideration of positive obligations has led to suggestions that Convention rules can in some circumstances bind private parties. The better—and certainly more orthodox—view is that the Convention only impacts upon the conduct of private parties adjectivally when action is taken by the State to secure the rights protected by the Convention which requires or prohibits certain conduct by individuals. A formal analysis of the situation would, accordingly, lead to the conclusion that the duties imposed on individuals would flow from the national law implementing the State's obligations under the Convention rather than from the Convention itself. This is, of course, reflected in the fact that applications complaining of violations of the Convention can only be made against Contracting Parties to the Convention, that is, against States.

APPROACHES AND IDEOLOGIES

Fundamental differences of approach emerged in the *Golder* case. The Commission had argued that an important canon of interpretation of international treaties had only very limited application to the European Convention. A traditional starting point for the interpretation of treaty texts is consideration of the intention of the parties at the time of ratification. The Commission argued that the European Convention should not be interpreted in this subjective manner by reference to the intention of the parties, but should be interpreted objectively. The Commission argued:

The over-riding function of this Convention is to protect the rights of the individual and not to lay down as between States mutual obligations which are to be restrictively interpreted having regard to the sovereignty of these States. On the contrary, the role of the Convention and the function of its interpretation is to make the protection of the individual effective.[57]

This approach to interpretation was adopted by the majority of the Court in its 9–3 decision.

The opposing view to interpretation of the Convention was championed by Sir Gerald Fitzmaurice throughout his term as a judge at the Court and an understanding of this approach helps to explain why he was so frequently in the minority in the Court. For Sir Gerald Fitzmaurice, the objective approach to

---

[56] See ch. 11.
[57] *Golder* v. *United Kingdom*, Report of the Commission, 1 June 1973. Series B, No. 16, p.40.

interpretation was fundamentally flawed. Since the Convention made serious inroads into the domestic jurisdiction of States, a restrictive approach to its interpretation was required. He argued in his minority opinion in the *Golder* Case that it followed that a cautious and conservative approach should be adopted to the interpretation of the Convention, since extensive interpretation could impose on Contracting States obligations they have not intended to assume in ratifying the Convention. Therefore doubts should be resolved in favour of the State rather than the individual.

The resolution of doubts in favour of States has found its clearest exposition in the concept of the 'margin of appreciation' which has been used extensively by the Court. Margins of appreciation are the outer limits of schemes of protection which are acceptable under the Convention.[58] The Court will not interfere with actions which are within the margin of appreciation. So in the *Brannigan* case,[59] the Court affirmed its earlier caselaw in considering the validity of the United Kingdom's derogation under Article 15 excluding the application of Article 5(3) to the system of detention applicable under the prevention of terrorism legislation. The Court recognized that Contracting States are in a better position than the judges to decide both on the presence of an emergency threatening the life of the nation and on the nature and scope of the derogations necessary to avert it. It was therefore appropriate to leave 'a wide margin of appreciation . . . to the national authorities'.[60] However, even this wide margin of appreciation is subject to the supervision of the Convention organs, since it is for the Court to determine whether the derogation goes beyond the extent strictly required by the exigencies of the situation. It followed that 'in exercising its supervision the Court must give appropriate weight to such relevant factors as the nature of the rights affected by the derogation, the circumstances leading to, and the duration of, the emergency situation.'[61] The absence of judicial control over the extended period of detention was held not to be beyond the margin of appreciation in this case.

The use of margins of appreciation permits the Court to keep in touch with legal reality where there is scope for differential application of Convention

---

[58] See G. van der Meersch, 'Le caractère "autonome" des terms et la "marge d'appreciation" des gouvernements dans l'interprétation de la Convention européenne des Droits de l'Homme' in F. Matscher, and H. Petzold, *Protecting Human Rights: The European Dimension. Studies in honour of Gérard J. Wiarda* (Köln, 1989), 201; R. Macdonald, 'The margin of appreciation' in R. Macdonald, F. Matscher, and H. Petzold, *The European System for the Protection of Human Rights* (Dordrecht, 1993), 83; and J.G. Merrills, *The Development of International Law by the European Court of Human Rights* (Manchester, 1993), ch. 7.

[59] *Brannigan and McBride* v. *United Kingdom*, Judgment of 26 May 1993, Series A, No. 258-B; (1994) 17 EHRR 539.

[60] Para. 43, affirming *Ireland* v. *United Kingdom*, Judgment of 18 January 1978, Series A, No. 25; (1979–80) 2 EHRR 25, para. 207 of the judgment.

[61] *Brannigan and McBride* v. *United Kingdom*, Judgment of 26 May 1993, Series A, No. 258-B; (1994) 17 EHRR 539, para. 43 of the judgment.

provisions while retaining some control over State conduct. As the concept has evolved in the caselaw of the Court, it has become clear that the scope of the margin will vary according to the circumstances, subject matter, and background to the issue before the Court as well as the presence or absence of common ground among the States Parties to the Convention.[62]

The development of European Community law has also had an influence on the interpretation of the Convention. Most significantly, the EC Treaty is a framework treaty (*traité cadre*) which requires a dynamic interpretation. Courts in the Member States have become used to the teleological approach to interpretation adopted by the Court of Justice in Luxembourg and there is now general acceptance of the legitimacy of this method of interpretation in all the States Parties to the Convention.

CONCLUSION

Interpretation of the Convention builds on the rules of public international law on the interpretation of treaties and has remained consistent with those principles. At the same time the approach taken to interpretation has recognized that both the nature of the obligations contained in the Convention and the regional limitation on its application legitimately permit the giving of a particular meaning to words and phrases in the Convention.

Judge Bernhardt provides a neat summary of the principles of interpretation applicable to the Convention:

The general rules of treaty interpretation are in principle also applicable to human-rights treaties, but the object and purpose of these treaties are different and, therefore, the traditional rules need some adjustment. The notions contained in human-rights conventions have an autonomous international meaning; however, such meaning must be determined by a comparative analysis of the legal situation in the participating States. To the extent that this analysis shows considerable differences and disparities among the States, a national 'margin of appreciation' is and must be recognized. Human-rights treaties must be interpreted in an objective and dynamic manner, by taking into account social conditions and developments; the ideas and conditions prevailing at the time when the treaties were drafted retain hardly any continuing validity. Nevertheless, treaty interpretation must not amount to treaty revision. Interpretation must therefore respect the text of the treaty concerned."[63]

---

[62] See *Rasmussen* v. *Denmark*, Judgment of 28 November 1984, Series A, No. 87; (1985) 7 EHRR 372.

[63] R. Bernhardt, 'Thoughts on the interpretation of human-rights treaties' in F. Matscher, and H. Petzold, *Protecting Human Rights: The European Dimension. Studies in Honour of Gérard J. Wiarda* (Köln, 1988), at 65–71, at p.70–1.

4

THE RIGHT TO LIFE

INTRODUCTION

Article 2[1] provides:

1. Everyone's right to life shall be protected by law. No-one shall be deprived of his life intentionally save in the execution of a sentence of a court following his conviction of a crime for which this penalty is provided by law.
2. Deprivation of life shall not be regarded as inflicted in contravention of this Article when it results from the use of force which is no more than absolutely necessary:

   (a) in defence of any person from unlawful violence;
   (b) in order to effect a lawful arrest or to prevent the escape of a person lawfully detained;
   (c) in action lawfully taken for the purpose of quelling a riot or insurrection.

As the Court observed in its *McCann and others*[2] judgment, 'as a provision which not only safeguards the right to life but sets out the circumstances when the deprivation of life may be justified, Article 2 ranks as one of the most fundamental provisions in the Convention.' Given the importance of this Article, it is perhaps surprising that it was not until the *McCann* judgment, in September 1994, that the Court had the opportunity to consider it. However, since then an increasingly rich case law has developed. It emerges that the State's obligation to safeguard life consists of three main aspects: the duty to refrain, by its agents, from unlawful killing; the duty to investigate suspicious deaths; and, in certain circumstances, a positive obligation to take steps to prevent the avoidable loss of life.

---

[1] See T. Opsahl, 'The Right to Life' in R. Macdonald, F. Matscher and H. Petzold (eds), *The European System for the Protection of Human Rights* (Dordrecht, 1993), at 207.

[2] *McCann and others* v. *United Kingdom*, Judgment of 27 September 1995, Series A, No. 324; (1996) 21 EHRR 97.

PROHIBITION OF INTENTIONAL KILLING BY THE STATE

The first and most obvious element of the State's obligation under Article 2 is to refrain, through its agents, from deliberate, unjustified killing.

This aspect was considered by the Court in *McCann and others*,[3] a case brought by the relatives of three Irish republican terrorists who had been killed by members of the British security forces in Gibraltar. It was not disputed that the soldiers had intended to shoot and kill the terrorists; according to the briefing which the soldiers had been given, the terrorists had planted a car bomb in a crowded area and were likely to have been carrying a concealed detonator, which would have allowed them to explode the bomb by the touch of a button. The Government therefore claimed that the facts fell within the ambit of paragraph 2(a) of Article 2: killings resulting from the use of force which was no more than absolutely necessary to defend a number of innocent bystanders from unlawful violence. The Court held that the use of the phrase 'absolutely necessary' in paragraph 2 indicated that the force used had to be strictly proportionate to the achievement of one of the aims set out in sub-paragraphs 2(a)–(c). Given this strict test, it was not sufficient for the person administering the force honestly to believe that his or her actions were valid; this belief had also to be based on reasonable grounds, in the light of the information available at the relevant time.

The Court accepted that the soldiers were not to blame, in that they honestly and reasonably believed that it was necessary to shoot the suspects to prevent them from detonating a bomb. However, the Court widened the field of scrutiny to look at the security operation in its entirety. The identities of the three members of the terrorist squad were known to the British authorities, and it would have been possible to arrest them as they entered Gibraltar, before there was any risk of them having set a car bomb. Looking at all the facts, therefore, the Court concluded that it had not been necessary to use lethal force and that the killings amounted to a violation of Article 2.

The *McCann* case demonstrates the way in which Article 2 of the Convention can provide a much more comprehensive remedy than any otherwise available within the domestic system. For example, at the inquest in Gibraltar into the deaths of the terrorists the jury were instructed that it would be open to them to bring in a verdict of unlawful killing only if they believed (1) the soldiers had murdered the suspects (in other words, had not acted in self-defence or in the defence of others) or (2) the operation had been mounted with the

---

[3] Ibid

express purpose of bringing about the deaths.[4] Moreover, the doctrine of State immunity embodied in the Crown Proceedings Act 1947 prevented the victims' relatives from bringing civil proceedings and thereby airing in a national court their allegations that the exercise, considered as a whole, had been negligent.

It appears that the Court will itself examine the circumstances of a killing by State officials only where there is evidence that, for some reason, the domestic judicial system is inadequate or unable to uncover the truth. In the *Hugh Jordan* case,[5] it took into account the fact that civil proceedings brought by the applicant against the police regarding the killing of his son by a police officer in Northern Ireland were still pending, and explained that it would be,

inappropriate and contrary to its subsidiary role under the Convention to attempt to establish the facts of this case by embarking on a fact finding exercise of its own by summoning witnesses. Such an exercise would duplicate the proceedings before the civil courts which are better placed and equipped as fact finding tribunals.[6]

The Court distinguished the case from those brought against Turkey where the European Commission of Human Rights had embarked on fact-finding missions where there were pending proceedings against the alleged security force perpetrators of unlawful killings, on the grounds that those proceedings were criminal and had terminated, at first instance at least, by the time the Court was examining the applications. In those cases, it was an essential part of the applicants' allegations that the defects in the investigation were such as to render the criminal proceedings ineffective.[7] In the *Hugh Jordan* case, in contrast, there was no evidence to show that the civil courts would be unable to establish the facts and determine whether the killing had been lawful.

DEATH IN CUSTODY AND FORCED DISAPPEARANCE

History has shown that, in the absence of safeguards against abuse of power, it is all too easy for the State to cover up its own unlawful violence, particularly when that violence is carried out behind closed doors. The protection afforded by Article 2 would be of no value if a State could avoid international sanction by concealing the evidence of killings caused by its agents. Where an individual is known to have been taken into custody and subsequently disappears or is

[4] In *Hugh Jordan* v. *United Kingdom* (App. 24747/94), Judgment of 4 May 2001, the Court held that the Northern Irish inquest system as it applied in that case was not sufficient to comply with the procedural requirements of Art. 2: see further below.
[5] *Hugh Jordan* v. *United Kingdom* (App. 24747/94), Judgment of 4 May 2001.
[6] Para. 111 of the judgment.
[7] See further this chapter, below.

found dead, therefore, it is logical that a heavy burden should fall on the State to establish an innocent explanation.[8]

According to Amnesty International, following an analysis of the relevant international instruments, the crime of 'disappearances' has the following elements: (1) a deprivation of liberty, (2) effected by government agents or with their consent or acquiescence; followed by (3) an absence of information or refusal to acknowledge the deprivation of liberty or refusal to disclose the fate or whereabouts of the person, (4) thereby placing such persons outside the protection of the law.[9] The Inter-American Court of Human Rights has held that 'the phenomenon of disappearances is a complex form of human rights violation', including breaches of the right to life and the right not to be subjected to ill-treatment, 'that must be understood and confronted in an integral fashion'.[10] The gravity of the violations of rights attendant on a disappearance has led the United Nations Human Rights Committee to conclude in relation to Article 6 of the International Covenant on Civil and Political Rights that State Parties should take specific and effective measures to prevent them occurring and thoroughly to investigate any case of a missing of disappeared person which may involve a violation of the right to life.[11] The UN Committee has subsequently held that the disappearance of a person is inseparably linked to treatment giving rise to a violation of Article 7 of the ICCPR, which mirrors Article 3 of the European Convention.[12]

Against this background, it is arguable that the Strasbourg organs were disappointingly timid in their treatment of the first case of a disappearance to come before them.[13] The Commission and Court both accepted that it had been proved beyond reasonable doubt that the applicant's son had last been seen some four and a half years earlier surrounded by soldiers during a security operation in his village in South-East Turkey. The Court moreover conceded that in these circumstances the applicant's fears that her son might have died in unacknowledged custody at the hands of his captors could not be said to be without foundation. Nonetheless, in company with the Commission, it declined to find a breach of Article 2 in the absence of concrete evidence that the young man had been killed by the authorities. Instead, it opted for 'a particularly grave

---

[8] See the Inter-American Court of Human Rights' *Velásquez Rodríguez* v. *Honduras*, Judgment of 29–July 1988, Inter-Am. Ct. H. R. (Series C) No. 4 (1988).

[9] See Amnesty International's written submissions to the Court in connection with the case of *Kurt* v. *Turkey* (App. 24276/94), Judgment of 25 May 1998; (1999) 27 EHRR 373, paras 68–71 of the judgment.

[10] *Velásquez Rodríguez* v. *Honduras*, Judgment of 29–July 1988, Inter-Am. Ct. H. R. (Series C) No. 4 (1988).

[11] General Comment 6 (Sixteenth Session 1982), 37 UN GAOR, Supp. No. 40 (A/37/40) Annex V, para. 1.

[12] *Mojica* v. *Dominican Republic*, Decision of 15 July 1994, Committee's views under Article 5(4) of the Optional Protocol to the ICCPR concerning communication no.–449/1991; (1996) 17 HRLJ18.

[13] *Kurt* v. *Turkey* (App. 24276/94), Judgment of 25 May 1998; (1999) 27 EHRR 373.

violation of the right to liberty and security of person under Article 5 raising serious concerns about the welfare of [the applicant's son]'.

The new Court created by Protocol No. 11 has, however, shown itself more prepared to take a hard-line approach. The applicant in the case of *Timurtas* v. *Turkey*[14] alleged that his son had been taken into custody in August 1993 and had subsequently disappeared. He had filed a complaint with the Turkish authorities but the public prosecutor had decided not to investigate because the applicant was unable to substantiate his allegations and because it was likely that his son was a member of a Kurdish terrorist organization. The Government denied that the applicant's son had ever been arrested and produced in support the custody records of the local police station, army headquarters, and interrogation centre—none of which contained any mention of the young man. A delegation from the European Commission travelled to South-East Turkey to take evidence. The applicant was unable to find any eye-witness to testify to the arrest and detention of his son. He did, however, produce a photocopy of a document purporting to be an army post-operational report recording his son's arrest. The Government disputed the document's authenticity, claiming that the reference number in truth belonged to another, quite different, document, but refusing to produce this second document for security reasons.

The Court acknowledged the risk inherent in relying for proof almost entirely on a photocopy. However, it held that the Government's failure, without satisfactory explanation, to disclose evidence which it claimed to hold gave rise to an inference that the photocopied report was genuine, and that the applicant's son had been arrested. The Court next considered whether, in the absence of a body, any issue could arise under Article 2, concluding that that this would depend on all the facts of the case, in particular whether there was sufficient circumstantial evidence pointing towards death in custody. In this respect the length of time which had elapsed since the person had been placed in detention, although not decisive, was highly relevant, since the more time which passed without any news, the greater was the likelihood that he had died. Given that more than six and a half years had gone by since the applicant's son had been arrested and that the Government were unable to provide any explanation of what had happened to him, the Court found a violation of Article 2.

The same principle applies *a fortiori* where there is clear evidence of a death in custody. In *Salman* v. *Turkey*[15] the applicant's husband was arrested at midnight on 28 April 1992 on suspicion of aiding and abetting Kurdish terrorists. Twenty-four hours later he was taken to the State Hospital where he was declared dead on arrival. The hospital autopsy disclosed various marks and bruises, including a broken sternum, but did not determine the cause of death. The case was referred to the Istanbul Forensic Institute which concluded that

[14] *Timurtas* v. *Turkey* (App. 23531/94), Judgment of 13 June 2000; (2001) 33 EHRR 121.
[15] *Salman* v. *Turkey* (App. 21986/93), Judgment of 27 June 2000; (2002) 34 EHRR 425.

the applicant's husband had died of a heart attack brought on by the effect of his arrest on a pre-existing heart condition. The applicant claimed that photographs of the corpse taken by the family showed that her husband had been beaten on the soles of his feet. Ten police officers were acquitted of homicide by the Adana Aggravated Felony Court on the basis that there was inadequate evidence of any use of torture.

The Court of Human Rights observed that where a person was taken into custody in good health and then died, the obligation on the State to provide a satisfactory account was particularly stringent. Since the Government was unable to explain how the applicant's husband had come by his injuries and since the evidence did not support the contention that he had died of a heart attack caused by the stress of arrest, the Court found the State responsible under Article 2.

THE DEATH PENALTY AND THE EXTRATERRITORIAL APPLICATION OF THE RIGHT TO LIFE

The second sentence of Article 2(1) reserves the right to States to subject convicted criminals to the death penalty. However, Protocol 6 to the Convention abolishes the death penalty in peacetime. Most of the Member States of the Council of Europe[16] have ratified Protocol 6, including the United Kingdom on 20 May 1999.

If a State which has signed up to Protocol 6 wishes to extradite an accused to a country where he or she would face judicial execution[17] there will be a risk of a violation of the Protocol,[18] and it may be necessary for the sending State to secure an agreement from the receiving State that the death penalty will not be applied before the extradition can go ahead.

Furthermore, it is probable that Article 2 also has an extraterritorial application, to protect those liable to expulsion generally from serious risks to life in addition to the death penalty. Although most cases in which the applicant claims a risk to life or limb if deported or extradited have been dealt with under Article 3,[19] it is probable that the positive obligation under Article 2

---

[16] At the end of March 2002, all of the 43 Member States had ratified Protocol 6, with the exception of Armenia and Russia, which had ratified the Convention and signed but not ratified Protocol 6; and Turkey, which had not even signed the Protocol: **http://conventions.coe.int.** See also Draft Protocol No. 13 on abolition of the death penalty in all circumstances.

[17] As in *Soering* v. *United Kingdom*, see ch. 5 below.

[18] See e.g. *Nivette* v. *France*, App. 44190/98, admissibility decision of 3 July 2001.

[19] See ch. 5 below.

extends to cases where the loss of life is likely to take place outside the State's territory.[20]

THE DUTY TO INVESTIGATE SUSPICIOUS DEATHS

In the *McCann* case[21] the Court observed that any general legal prohibition of arbitrary killing by agents of the State would be ineffective in practice in the absence of a procedure for reviewing the lawfulness of the use of lethal force by State authorities:

The obligation to protect the right to life under this provision, read in conjunction with the State's general duty under Article 1 of the Convention to 'secure to everyone within their jurisdiction the rights and freedoms defined in [the] Convention', requires by implication that there should be some form of effective official investigation when individuals have been killed as a result of the use of force by, *inter alios*, agents of the State.[22]

This requirement has formed a useful part of the Court's artillery, particularly in cases where the evidence is not sufficiently clear to justify a finding of deliberate killing by the State. In *Kaya* v. *Turkey*,[23] for example, the applicant's brother was found lying dead and riddled with bullets in a field near his village in South-East Turkey. The Government claimed that he was a terrorist who had been killed during a battle with security forces. Witnesses from the village— none of whom, however, were prepared to testify before the Commission's fact-finding delegation—allegedly said that he was an ordinary, unarmed farmer who had been shot by the soldiers without justification or provocation. Only a rudimentary post-mortem had been performed before the body was handed over for burial to the villagers, and the public prosecutor who subsequently took over the inquiry appeared to have accepted without question the military's version of events, omitting to take statements from witnesses or collect any forensic evidence. In these circumstances the Commission and Court, examining the

[20] See *Tatete* v. *Switzerland* (App. 41874/98), Judgment of 6 July 2000, where a friendly settlement was reached in a case where an illegal entrant, dying of AIDS, feared deportation to the Democratic Republic of Congo where she would not be able to obtain the medical treatment she needed; cf. *D* v. *United Kingdom* (App. 30240/96), Judgment of 2 May 1997; (1997) 24 EHRR 423. and ch. 5 below. See also *Mamatkulov and Abduraulovic* v. *Turkey* (Apps. 46827/99 and 46951/99), two applications declared admissible on 31 August 1999, where the applicants, refugees from Ouzbekistan and Iran respectively, feared assassination if repatriated.
[21] See this chapter, above.
[22] *McCann and others* v. *United Kingdom*, Judgment of 27 September 1995, Series A, No. 324; (1996) 21 EHRR 97, para. 161 of the judgment.
[23] *Kaya* v. *Turkey* (App. 22729/93), Judgment of 19 February 1998; (1998) 28 EHRR 1.

case some years later and hampered by the reluctance of witnesses to come forward,[24] were unable to establish clearly what had taken place or to find for the applicant on his complaint that his brother had been deliberately killed by the soldiers. The Court did, however, find a breach of Article 2 on the basis that the domestic investigation into the death had been inadequate.

The Court has explained[25] that the essential purpose of such investigation is to secure the effective implementation of the domestic laws which protect the right to life and, in those cases involving State agents or bodies, to ensure their accountability for deaths occurring under their responsibility. What form of investigation will achieve those purposes may vary in different circumstances. However, whatever mode is employed, the authorities must act of their own motion, once the matter has come to their attention. They cannot leave it to the initiative of the next of kin either to lodge a formal complaint or to take responsibility for the conduct of any investigative procedures.

For an investigation into alleged unlawful killing by State agents to be effective and to comply with Article 2, it must be carried out by someone who is fully independent of those implicated in the events[26] on the basis of objective evidence[27]. The investigation must be capable of leading to a determination of whether the force used in such cases was justified in the circumstances and to the identification and punishment of those responsible.[28] This entails that the authorities must have taken the reasonable steps available to them to secure the evidence concerning the incident, including eye-witness testimony, forensic evidence, and, where appropriate, an autopsy which provides a complete and accurate record of injury and an objective analysis of clinical findings, including the cause of death.[29] Any deficiency in the investigation which undermines its ability to establish the cause of death or the person or persons responsible will risk falling foul of this standard. The investigation must be carried out promptly, in order to maintain public confidence in the authorities' adherence to the rule of law and to prevent any appearance of collusion in or tolerance of unlawful acts.[30] For the same reasons, the investigation must, to a certain

---

[24] See ch. 24 below for details of the Strasbourg organs' fact-finding powers.

[25] See e.g. *Hugh Jordan* v. *United Kingdom* (App. 24747/94), Judgment of 4 May 2001, paras. 105 and following of the judgment.

[26] *Güleç* v. *Turkey* (App. 21593/93), Judgment of 27–July 1998; (1999) 28 EHRR 121; *Ögur* v. *Turkey* (App. 21594/93), Judgment of 20 May 1999; (2001) 31 EHRR 912.

[27] *Ergi* v. *Turkey* (App. 23818/94), Judgment of 28 July 1998; (2001) 32 EHRR 388.

[28] *Kaya* v. *Turkey* (App. 22729/93), Judgment of 19 February 1998; (1998) 28 EHRR 1; *Ögur* v. *Turkey* (App. 21594/93), Judgment of 20 May 1999; (2001) 31 EHRR 912.

[29] *Salman* v. *Turkey* (App. 21986/93), Judgment of 27 June 2000; (2002) 34 EHRR 425; *Tanrikulu* v. *Turkey* (App. 23763/94), Judgment of 8 July 1999; (2000) 30 EHRR 950; *Gül* v. *Turkey* (App. 22676/93), Judgment of 14 December 2000; (2002) 34 EHRR 719.

[30] *Yasa* v. *Turkey* (App. 22495/93), Judgment of 2 September 1998; (1999) 28 EHRR 408; *Çakici* v. *Turkey* (App. 23657/94), Judgment of 8 July 1999; (2001) 31 EHRR 133; *Tanrikulu* v. *Turkey* (App. 23763/94), Judgment of 8 July 1999; (2000) 30 EHRR 950; *Mahmut Kaya* v. *Turkey* (App. 22535/93), Judgment of 28 March 2000.

degree, be open to public scrutiny, and the relatives of the deceased must always have the opportunity to become involved.[31]

In the United Kingdom, investigations into suspicious deaths usually take the form of inquests, which are public hearings into the facts conducted by independent judicial officers (coroners), normally sitting with a jury. Judicial review lies from procedural decisions by coroners and in respect of any mistaken directions given to the jury. In the *McCann* case[32] the Court found that the inquest held into the deaths of three terrorists shot dead by British soldiers in Gibraltar satisfied the procedural obligation contained in Article 2, as it provided a detailed review of the events surrounding the killings and gave the relatives of the deceased the opportunity to examine and cross-examine witnesses involved in the operation. More recently, however, in a series of judgments concerning killings by the security forces in Northern Ireland,[33] the Court found violations of Article 2 based on flaws in the inquests.

The son of the applicant in the *Hugh Jordan* case, for example, had been shot and killed by a British police officer. However, this police officer was not a compellable witness under the Northern Irish inquest rules, and declined to give evidence or to be cross-examined, thus seriously detracting from the inquest's power to establish the facts. Moreover, the Northern Irish system also differed from that used in Gibraltar in the *McCann* case (and applicable in England and Wales) in that the jury could not enter a verdict, such as 'unlawful killing'; all it could do was to give the identity of the deceased and the date, place, and direct cause of death. Since the inquest could not, therefore, play an effective role in the identification or prosecution of any criminal offences which might have occurred, the Court found that it fell short of the requirements of Article 2. The Court also criticized the lack of advance disclosure of witness statements to the deceased's family and the delay in the proceedings: over eight years after the death, the inquest had still not come to a conclusion.

Despite early dicta to the contrary,[34] it now appears that the obligation to investigate is not confined to cases where it can be established that the death was caused by agents of the State. In another application against Turkey,[35] the applicant's uncle, who was selling a banned Kurdish newspaper from his kiosk, was shot and killed by unknown assailants at a time when security forces were

[31] *Güleç* v. *Turkey* (App. 21593/93), Judgment of 27–July 1998; (1999) 28 EHRR 121; *Öğur* v. *Turkey* (App. 21594/93), Judgment of 20 May 1999; (2001) 31 EHRR 912.

[32] *McCann and others* v. *United Kingdom*, Judgment of 27 September 1995, Series A, No. 324; (1996) 21 EHRR 97: see above in this chapter.

[33] *Hugh Jordan* v. *United Kingdom* (App. 24747/94), Judgment of 4 May 2001; *McKerr* v. *United Kingdom* (App. 28883/94), Judgment of 4 May 2001; (2002) 34 EHRR 553; *Kelly and others* v. *United Kingdom* App. 30054/96), Judgment of 4 May 2001; and *Shanaghan* v. *United Kingdom* (App. 37715/97), Judgment of 4 May 2001.

[34] See e.g. *Kurt* v. *Turkey* (App. 24276/94), Judgment of 25 May 1998; (1999) 27 EHRR 373, para. 107 of the judgment.

[35] *Yasa* v. *Turkey* (App. 22495/93), Judgment of 2 September 1998; (1999) 28 EHRR 408.

cracking down on the newspaper and, according to the applicant, had made a number of threats against the sellers.

In that case there was, therefore, some, albeit inconclusive, evidence of State involvement in the murder. However, given that Article 2 also includes a positive obligation to protect individuals from unlawful violence from other private persons (see below), it is probable that there is a duty to establish the facts even where the killing is clearly not the work of State agents. The duty arises, moreover, where the death was caused by negligence, not just where it results from the deliberate use of force.[36]

THE POSITIVE OBLIGATION TO PROTECT LIFE

In *LCB* v. *United Kingdom*[37] the Court recognized for the first time that the first sentence of Article 2(1) enjoins the State not only to refrain from the intentional and unlawful taking of life, but also to take appropriate steps to safeguard the lives of those within their jurisdiction. This was an important statement of principle, despite the fact that the applicant was unable to prove the chain of causation which would have led to a finding of violation. Her father had served in the Royal Air Force during the United Kingdom's nuclear tests on Christmas Island in 1957–8. She claimed that he had been exposed to harmful levels of radiation during the tests, and that this had been the cause of the leukaemia she suffered in early childhood. The question whether any violation of the Convention, in relation either to the applicant or her father, had arisen from the conduct of the tests themselves was not before the Court, since the tests had taken place before the United Kingdom's acceptance of the Court's jurisdiction in 1966. The Court did, however, examine whether the authorities had done all that could be expected of them after 1966 to minimize any danger to the applicant's health, for example, by warning her parents that she might be at risk of developing leukaemia and thereby enabling them to reduce the risk by early medical intervention. Given the inconclusive evidence at that time concerning the likelihood of the Christmas Island servicemen having been exposed to radiation and of any such radiation constituting a risk to the health of subsequently conceived children, the Court did not find that the State was in breach of any duty in respect of the applicant.

It is not clear how far the principle set out in the *LCB* case should be

---

[36] See *Erikson* v. *Italy* (App. 37900/97), admissibility decision of 26 October 1999 (death caused by negligent hospital treatment) and *Ögur* v. *Turkey* (App. 21594/93), Judgment of 20 May 1999 (death caused by warning shot fired into the air by a soldier); (2001) 31 EHRR 912.

[37] *LCB* v. *United Kingdom* (App. 23413/94), Judgment of 9 June 1998; (1998) 27 EHRR 212.

extended. The applicant's father was one of a finite group who, it was argued, had been put at risk by the State's own dangerous activities. The question remains for the future, however, whether the duty to protect life places States under an obligation to provide accurate information about serious health risks to the public in general—about food contaminated by government agricultural policies, for example—and whether such a duty could also arise in connection with dangers caused by the activities of private individuals or companies, if relevant information was in the Government's possession.[38]

The nature of the positive obligation to protect life was further explored in *Osman* v. *United Kingdom*,[39] which raised questions about the State's duty to protect an individual from the criminal acts of another private person. This duty had already been accepted in its broadest form, namely the obligation to put in place effective criminal sanctions, in a ground-breaking case under Article 8, *X and Y* v. *Netherlands*.[40] In *Osman*, however, the applicants contended that in certain circumstances more specific measures were required. The applicant's schoolteacher had developed a dangerous obsession about him, which culminated in the teacher's breaking into the applicant's home and shooting and killing his father. Prior to this there had been a number of indications that the teacher posed a threat to the applicant and his family; for example, the teacher had changed his name to the applicant's, left graffiti around the school and neighbourhood, and driven his car at a van containing the applicant's school friend. The question before the Court was whether the failure by the police to take action adequate to save the applicant's father's life amounted to a breach of the duty under Article 2. Bearing in mind the difficulties in policing modern society, the unpredictability of human conduct, and the need for the police to act within the confines imposed on them by, *inter alia*, Articles 5 and 8 of the Convention, the Court defined this particular aspect of the duty to protect life rather narrowly. It considered that the authorities could be said to be in breach of Article 2 in this context only if it could be established that they knew or ought to have known at the relevant time of the existence of a real and immediate risk to the life of an identified individual or individuals from the criminal acts of a third party, and that they failed to take measures within the scope of their powers which, judged reasonably, might have been expected to avoid that risk. In the instant case, the applicants were not able to point to any decisive stage in the sequence of events leading to the shooting when it could be said that the police knew or ought or have known that the lives of the Osman family were at real and immediate risk, and the police could not be criticized for attaching weight to the presumption of

[38] For a parallel obligation under Article 8, see the *Guerra* v. *Italy* (App. 14967/89), Judgment of 19 February 1998; (1998) 26 EHRR 357; see ch. 11 below.
[39] *Osman* v. *United Kingdom* (App. 23452/94), Judgment of 28 October 1998; (1998) 29 EHRR 245.
[40] *X and Y* v. *Netherlands*, Judgment of 26 March 1985, Series A, No. 91; (1985) 8 EHRR 235.

innocence and the rights of the teacher in the absence of any concrete evidence against him.[41]

The Court has held Turkey in breach of the positive obligation to protect life in cases involving the murder of a journalist working for a Kurdish separatist newspaper and a doctor known to have treated members of the Kurdish terrorist organization, the PKK[42]. In both cases the applicants alleged that their brothers had been assassinated by members of the State security forces, but this could not be proved. The Court did, however, find that the authorities were aware that journalists, doctors, and others associated with the PKK and Kurdish separatism had been the object of a campaign of serious attacks and threats, possibly emanating from or carried out with the acquiescence of the security forces. Although there was a framework of law in place aimed at the protection of life (criminal law, police, prosecutor, and courts), at the relevant time the implementation of the criminal justice system in South-East Turkey was seriously undermined by various Emergency Rule measures (including the transfer of jurisdiction away from the courts to councils of civil servants and a series of failures to investigate allegations of wrongdoing by the members of the security forces). This situation fostered a dangerous lack of accountability amongst members of the security forces and removed the protection which the applicants' brothers should have received by law.

ABORTION, EUTHANASIA, AND THE QUALITY OF LIFE

The right to life is in an obvious sense fundamental; no derogation from the provisions of Article 2 is permitted, even in time of 'war or other emergency'.[43] Its scope, however, is uncertain in respect of laws permitting, for example, termination of pregnancy and euthanasia.

Neither the Court nor the Commission has had occasion to determine at what point, for the purposes of Article 2, human life begins and what protection, if any, the Convention affords to the foetus.[44] An early application was directed against a Norwegian law which provided for the termination of

[41] The Court also examined the question whether the impossibility under English law of bringing civil proceedings against the police gave rise to a violation of Article 6(1): see ch. 8 below.
[42] *Kiliç v. Turkey* (App. 22492/93), Judgment of 28 March 2000; (2001) 33 EHRR 1357; and *Mahmut Kaya v. Turkey* (App. 22535/93), Judgment of 28 March 2000.
[43] See ch. 21 below.
[44] *App. 6959/75, Brüggemann and Scheuten v. Federal Republic of Germany*, Report of 12 July 1977; (1978) 10 DR 100, para. 60. In *App. 8416/79, X v. United Kingdom*, 13 May 1980; (1980) 19 DR 244, the Commission suggested that the term 'everyone' did not alone extend to the unborn child, but went on to consider whether the protection of 'life' could be interpreted as including 'unborn life'.

pregnancy under certain conditions.[45] The applicant asked the Commission to decide, first, whether the 'right to beget offspring is an inalienable human right or if not, under what conditions and circumstances this right might be forfeited'; and secondly, 'whether human rights are fully applicable to the human embryo from the time of conception, or if not, at what stages in the development of the human individual' these rights arise. However, the applicant could not himself claim to be a victim of the law in question and the Commission was not competent to examine in the abstract the conformity of this law with the Convention.[46]

In its decision in an application against the United Kingdom,[47] the Commission rejected an interpretation of the Article as recognizing an unqualified right to life for an unborn child, since the right to life must also belong to the mother and there was widespread recognition of circumstances in which the life of the mother should be given priority over the life of the unborn child. Two other possibilities were suggested: first, that Article 2 did not apply at all to unborn children; and, secondly, that Article 2 recognized the right to life of the unborn child subject to certain limitations. The Commission did not form any conclusions on these questions, but instead ruled that the application was manifestly ill-founded since the case concerned a termination of pregnancy in its early stages on a medical recommendation. It is difficult to conclude other than that the Commission was anxious to sidestep a controversial case.

In the landmark judgment of the United States' Supreme Court, *Roe* v. *Wade*,[48] State laws which decriminalized abortion only where necessary to save the mother's life were held to violate the Due Process Clause of the Fourteenth Amendment of the Constitution, which protects the right to privacy, including a woman's qualified right to terminate her pregnancy (a right which carries less and less weight as the pregnancy continues). There is certainly need for more discussion under the Convention concerning ways of balancing the right to life of the unborn child and the fundamental rights of the mother. On the other hand, there is no consensus among the Member States of the Council of Europe on the legal and moral questions raised by medical termination of pregnancy and the hesitant approach of the Convention institutions in handling such cases may merely reflect this division of opinion.[49]

There is no doubt that the parents of unborn children have standing to

---

[45] App. 867/60, *X* v. *Norway*, 29 May 1961, (1961) 6 CD 34; see also App. 7045/75, *X* v. *Norway*, 10 December 1976, (1977) 7 DR 87 and App. 11045/84, *Knudsen* v. *Norway* (1985) 42 DR 247.

[46] See ch. 24 below.

[47] App. 8416/79, *X* v. *United Kingdom*, 13 May 1980, (1980) 19 DR 244.

[48] Supreme Court of the United States, Judgment of 22 January 1973, 410 US 113

[49] Compare the Court's approach in *X., Y. and Z.* v. *United Kingdom* (App. 21830/93), Judgment of 24 April 1997, (1997) 24 EHRR 143, where it held that, in view of the lack of any common European approach, States enjoyed a wide margin of appreciation in respect of the regulation of artificial insemination.

protect such rights of the unborn child as the Convention may guarantee. The issue of medical termination of pregnancy has often arisen when the father of the unborn child seeks to prevent the mother from securing a termination. Such applications often also invoke the right to respect for private and family life in Article 8 and the right to found a family under Article 12.

In an application under Article 8 relating to the right to family life,[50] the applicants complained about German legislation restricting the availability of medical termination of pregnancy; they argued that they were obliged either to renounce sexual intercourse, use methods of contraception of which they disapproved for health and other reasons, or to carry through a pregnancy against their will. The Commission indicated in its admissibility decision that the interference with the applicants' right to family life would be justifiable for the prevention of crime or for the protection of the rights and interests of others, and that 'others' under Article 8(2) 'includes the life growing in the womb'.[51] The Commission report on the merits took a somewhat different view, concluding that not every regulation of the termination of unwanted pregnancy constituted an interference with the right to respect for the private life of the mother in that Article 8(1) could not be interpreted as meaning that pregnancy and its termination were, in principle, solely a matter of the private life of the mother. They found no violation of Article 8 and this was confirmed by the Committee of Ministers.

The application of Article 2 to cases of euthanasia is equally uncertain. The legalization of euthanasia, which would seem prima facie contrary to the express terms of the first sentence of Article 2 as well as falling outside the exceptions permitted by that Article, might raise the difficult question how far the consent of a victim may negate what would otherwise be a violation of the Convention. In principle, it might seem that the absolute terms in which the right to life is expressed in Article 2, and the element of public interest, would exclude the possibility of any form of waiver of those rights. It is probable that the Court of Human Rights will take the same line as the English High Court, which recently considered an application under the Human Rights Act by a terminally ill woman who wished her husband to be permitted to assist her suicide without risk of prosecution.[52] The High Court rejected the application, observing that:

Articles 2 and 3 between them are aimed at the protection and preservation of life and the dignity of life, because of its fundamental value, not only to the individual but also

---

[50] App. 6959/75, *Brüggemann and Scheuten* v. *Federal Republic of Germany*, Decision of the Commission (admissibility) 19 May 1976, (1976) 19 *Yearbook* 382; Report of the Commission, 12 July 1977; Resolution DH(78)1 of the Committee of Ministers, 17 March 1978, (1978) 21 *Yearbook* 638.

[51] Decision of the Commission on admissibility, 19 May 1976, (1976) 19 *Yearbook* 382, at 392.

[52] *The Queen on the application of Dianne Pretty and the Director of Public Prosecutions and the Secretary of State for the Home Office*, 17 October 2001, [2001] EWHC Admin 788. At the time of writing, Ms Pretty's application was pending before the Court: no. 2346 /02. On 29 April 2002, the Court of Human Rights ruled that there had been no violation of Articles 2, 3, 8, 9, or 14 of the Convention.

to the community as a whole. It is to stand the whole purpose of these articles on its head to say that they are aimed at protecting a person's right to procure their own death.

Assisted suicide has been permitted in certain circumstances in the Nether-lands since early 2001, but so far no cases in relation to this legislation have been brought in Strasbourg.[53] The Dutch law provides that it is no longer a criminal offence for a doctor to assist a patient to die if the doctor is convinced that the patient is facing interminable and unendurable suffering and has made a volun-tary and well-considered request to die, and as long as the doctor abides by certain safeguards, such as obtaining an independent medical opinion and keeping a written record of the treatment offered.

There is no Convention case law on situations involving switching off life support machines, and the Strasbourg institutions have not, to date, given any recognition to the principle that the 'quality' of the life to be preserved is a relevant factor.

It is noteworthy in this context that in the recent case of the conjoined twins[54] the English Court of Appeal unanimously rejected any argument based on the perceived quality of life of either twin, while holding that Article 2 mirrored the English common law in including an implied defence of medical necessity.[55] The twins were born joined at the pelvis. The weaker twin, who was severely brain damaged, was dependent for life on her sister's heart, and it was predicted that the effort of pumping blood for both of them would kill the stronger twin within three to six months. If the twins were surgically separated, as proposed by the hospital in which they were born, the prognosis for the stronger sister was very good, while the weaker would be immediately killed by the operation. The twins' parents were devout Catholics who opposed the operation on religious grounds, *inter alia*. The Court of Appeal held that it was not legitimate to make any assumption about the quality of life of either twin—each had an equal right to life. However, it was necessary to weigh in the balance the likely results of each course of action (or inaction). If no operation were performed, both girls would die within a matter of months. If the operation was carried out, the weaker twin would die, but the other would have a good chance of a normal life. Performing the operation would therefore be the lesser of two evils. The Court of Appeal further ruled that the word 'intentionally' in Article 2 should be given its natural meaning and that a doctor performing the separ-ation operation could not be said intentionally to be killing the weaker twin.

---

[53] The United Nations Human Rights Committee expressed criticism of the Dutch law in a Report published on 28 July 2001.

[54] *In re A (Children) (Conjoined Twins: Surgical Separation)*, [2001] 2 WLR 489.

[55] For an interesting critique of the judgment, see J. Rogers, 'Necessity, private defence and the killing of Mary', [2001] Crim LR 515.

CONCLUDING COMMENTS

The body of judgments concerning the right to life is amongst the richest and most dynamic in all the Convention case law. It is astonishing to think that it has all developed since 1995. But there are still many unanswered questions. To date both the Court and Commission have assiduously avoided confronting the difficult questions relating to abortion and euthanasia—from what point does life deserve protection and in what circumstances should the deliberate extinction of life be authorized? As far as the prohibition on unlawful killing by the State, the broad lines have already been stated, but no doubt further detail will emerge as new and varied factual situations are placed before the Court. However, it is in connection with the positive obligations to take measures to safeguard lives—whether by providing access to reliable information about health risks or by impeding the violence of other private individuals—that the greatest scope for innovation remains, and it will be interesting to see how far the Court considers it possible to extend the protection afforded by Article 2 without placing too great a burden on the State.

5

PROHIBITION OF TORTURE

INTRODUCTION

Article 3 provides that 'No one shall be subjected to torture or to inhuman or degrading treatment or punishment.'[1] That is the extent of the Article; only in this Article are there no qualifications or exceptions, and no restrictions to the rights guaranteed. The prohibition is absolute. The fundamental character of the Article is shown also by the fact that, in common with Articles 2, 4(1), and 7, no derogation may be made from its provisions under Article 15 even in time of war or public emergency.

The absolute nature of the prohibition is well illustrated by the *Chahal* case.[2] The United Kingdom wished to deport Chahal, a Sikh separatist, to India arguing that he had been involved in terrorist activities and posed a risk to the national security of the United Kingdom. The Court emphasized the absolute nature of the prohibition in Article 3 in the following terms,

Article 3 enshrines one of the most fundamental values of democratic society. The Court is well aware of the immense difficulties faced by States in modern times in protecting their communities from terrorist violence. However, even in these circumstances, the Convention prohibits in absolute terms torture or inhuman or degrading treatment or punishment, irrespective of the victim's conduct.[3]

A number of further general introductory points can be made about the Article. In order for conduct to be embraced by the prohibition, it must 'attain a minimum level of severity'.[4] This test will apply whatever the category of

---

[1] See generally A. Cassese, 'Prohibition of Torture and Inhuman or Degrading Treatment or Punishment' in R. Macdonald, F. Matscher, and H. Petzold, *The European System for the Protection of Human Rights* (Dordrecht, 1993), at 225; and H. Danelius, 'Protection against Torture in Europe and the World' in R. Macdonald, F. Matscher, and H. Petzold, *The European System for the Protection of Human Rights* (Dordrecht, 1993), at 263,

[2] *Chahal* v. *United Kingdom* (App. 22414/93), Judgment of 15 November 1996; (1997) 23 EHRR 413.

[3] Para. 80 of the judgment. The Court has used identical language on a number of occasions and has included reference to organized crime in addition to the reference to terrorist violence: see e.g. *Egmez* v. *Cyprus* (App. 30873/96), Judgment of 21 December 2000; (2002) 34 EHRR 753, para. 77 of the judgment.

[4] *Ireland* v. *United Kingdom*, Judgment of 18 January 1978, Series A, No. 25; (1979–80) 2 EHRR 25, para. 162 of judgment; and *Tyrer* v. *United Kingdom*, Judgment of 25 April 1978, Series A, No. 26; (1979–80) 2 EHRR 1, para. 30 of judgment.

conduct in issue. The effect of setting a high threshold is that trivial complaints, and even activity which is undesirable or illegal, will not fall within the scope of the prohibition in Article 3 unless it causes sufficiently serious suffering or humiliation to the victim. In the *Selmouni* case,[5] however, the Court indicated that interpretation of the Convention as a living instrument could result in acts classified in earlier case law as inhuman or degrading treatment as distinct from torture being classified as torture in the future. Presumably, it would follow that conduct which previously had not attained the threshold for categorization as inhuman or degrading treatment might be so categorized in the future.

After addressing the issues of definition which arise under Article 3, this chapter explores evidential issues connected with proving conduct falling within the article and the extraterritorial application of Article 3, before examining a number of specific areas where Article 3 has been applied by the Commission and the Court.

DEFINING THE TERMS

THE GENERAL APPROACH

The United Nations General Assembly's definition of torture in the 1975 Declaration stated that, 'Torture constitutes an aggravated and deliberate form of cruel, inhuman and degrading treatment or punishment.'[6]

In the *Greek* case, more than three hundred pages of the Commission's Report dealt with alleged violations of Article 3 by the Greek Government after the revolution of 21 April 1967.[7] The Commission analysed the meaning of the provisions of Article 3 as follows:

It is plain that there may be treatment to which all these descriptions apply, for all torture must be inhuman and degrading treatment, and inhuman treatment also degrading. The notion of inhuman treatment covers at least such treatment as deliberately causes severe suffering, mental or physical, which, in the particular situation, is unjustifiable. The word 'torture' is often used to describe inhuman treatment, which has a purpose, such as the obtaining of information or confessions, or the infliction of punishment, and it is generally an aggravated form of inhuman treatment. Treatment or punishment of an individual may be said to be degrading if

---

[5] *Selmouni* v. *France* (App. 25803/94), Judgment of 28 July 1999; (2000) 29 EHRR 403, para. 101 of the judgment. The case is discussed below.

[6] Art. 1 of UNGA Res. 3452 (XXX) of 9 December 1975, Declaration on the protection of all persons from being subjected to torture and other cruel, inhuman or degrading treatment or punishment.

[7] *The Greek Case*, Report of 5 November 1969, (1969) 12 *Yearbook* 186–510.

it grossly humiliates him before others or drives him to act against his will or conscience.[8]

The Commission's analysis of Article 3 quoted above is at first sight questionable in referring to treatment 'which, in the particular situation, is unjustifiable'. It may be doubted whether inhuman treatment is a relative notion, dependent on the circumstances of the case, and whether inhuman treatment could ever be 'justifiable'. This, however, would be to look at the question from the wrong angle. Torture and inhuman treatment are never justifiable, and the definition is misleading if it suggests that they may be. But treatment which may be perfectly justifiable in some circumstances may, in different circumstances, be unlawful. The clearest case is of criminal punishment. A penalty which might be justified for a serious crime could constitute inhuman treatment or punishment if imposed for a petty offence. To this extent at least inhuman treatment is a relative notion.[9]

In the *Ireland* v. *United Kingdom* judgment, the Court took a narrower view than the Commission in concluding that 'it was the intention that the Convention with its distinction between torture and inhuman treatment should by the first of these terms attach a special stigma to deliberate inhuman treatment causing very serious and cruel suffering.'[10]

The starting point for the definition of inhuman and degrading treatment is the quotation from the *Greek* case cited above. The standard adopted shows the relationship between the three elements prohibited in the Article. If the distinction between torture and inhuman treatment is frequently one of degree, this may not be the case with degrading treatment, which requires the presence of gross humiliation before others or being driven to act against will or conscience.

In every case the determination of whether there has been torture, inhuman or degrading treatment must be decided in the light of all the circumstances of the case, taking account of the factors relevant to such a determination as evidenced in decisions of the Court, and to a limited extent of the Commission. The assessment of seriousness will, however, be relative. In the judgment in *Ireland* v. *United Kingdom*, the Court suggested that the following factors were relevant in determining the existence of inhuman treatment: the duration of the treatment, its physical or mental effects, and the sex, age and state of health of the victim.[11] In the *Tyrer* judgment, the Court said that the nature of and context of the punishment itself and the manner and method of its execution

---

[8] At 186.

[9] In App. 9463/78, *Kröcher and Möller* v. *Switzerland*, 16 December 1982; (1982) 34 DR 25, the Commission concluded that what would otherwise be inhuman conditions of detention and treatment might be justified where a prisoner presented a particularly high risk.

[10] *Ireland* v. *United Kingdom*, Judgment of 18 January 1978, Series A, No. 25; (1979–80) 2 EHRR 25, para. 167 of judgment.

[11] *Ireland* v. *United Kingdom*, Judgment of 18 January 1978, Series A, No. 25; (1979–80) 2 EHRR 25, para. 162 of judgment.

should be considered in determining whether a punishment constituted degrading treatment.[12]

The threshold of seriousness required and the need to consider the relative nature of the conduct in context indicate that the prohibition in Article 3 is not a static one, but receives a living interpretation and must be considered in the light of present-day circumstances.[13] It follows that too rigid a view cannot be taken of some of the older case law of the Court and decisions of the Commission in predicting the outcome of current applications. This view has been stated expressly by the Court in the *Selmouni* case.[14]

DEFINING TORTURE

In 1956 and 1957 Greece brought two cases[15] against the United Kingdom arising from the conduct of British troops in Cyprus and the use of whipping and various forms of collective punishments. Though no formal decision was made on the merits, it is clear that doubts about the compatibility of the punishments with the requirements of Article 3 were held by a majority of the Commission at the time.

Two sets of applications against Greece during the regime of the Colonels were declared admissible.[16] The Commission examined allegations of a variety of forms of ill-treatment, the commonest of which was *falanga* or *bastinado*, but which included also electric shocks, mock executions or threats to shoot or kill the victim, and other forms of beating or ill-treatment.[17] Extensive investigations were made by the Sub-Commission in Greece, and many witnesses examined in Athens, Strasbourg, and elsewhere.

The Commission concluded that torture or ill-treatment contrary to Article 3 had been inflicted in a number of cases and that there were reasons for considering that these cases were part of a practice of torture or ill-treatment of political detainees in Greece since 21 April 1967.[18]

---

[12] *Tyrer* v. *United Kingdom*, Judgment of 25 April 1978, Series A, No. 26; (1979–80) 2 EHRR 1, para. 30 of judgment.

[13] See M. Addo and N. Grief, 'Is there a policy behind the decisions and judgments relating to Article 3 of the European Convention on Human Rights?' (1995) 20 E L Rev 178.

[14] *Selmouni* v. *France* (App. 25803/94), Judgment of 28 July 1999; (2000) 29 EHRR 403, para. 101 of the judgment.

[15] App. 176/56, *Greece* v. *United Kingdom (First Cyprus Case)*, 14 December 1959 (1958–9) 2 Year-book 174, and App. 299/56, *Greece* v. *United Kingdom (Second Cyprus Case)*, 14 December 1959, (1960) 2 *Yearbook* 186; see also (1958–9) 2 *Yearbook* 186 and 196 for resolutions of Committee of Ministers.

[16] *The Greek Case*, Report of 5 November 1969 (1969) 12 *Yearbook* 186–510.

[17] At 500. *Falanga* is defined at 499 as 'the beating of the feet with a wooden or metal stick or bar, which, if skilfully done, breaks no bones, makes no skin lesions and leaves no permanent and recognisable marks but causes intense pain and swelling of the feet.'

[18] At 501.

In reaching its conclusion that there was a practice of torture, the Commission had regard to two criteria: the repetition of the acts concerned, and official tolerance of them. The notion of administrative practice, as it has come to be known, has a double significance. First, at the stage of admissibility, the Commission has held that the rule requiring the exhaustion of domestic remedies does not apply where the conduct complained of constitutes an administrative practice.[19] Secondly, on the merits, the finding of an administrative practice, implying official recognition and acceptance of that conduct is clearly far more serious than isolated instances of such conduct by individual officials.

The *Greek* case is a model case for demonstrating both the possibilities and the political limitations of the international protection of human rights. At the first stages of the proceedings the Greek Government cooperated in the examination of the merits of the case, allowing the Sub-Commission, although not without reservations, to visit Greece and to examine witnesses and some of the places where torture was alleged to have been committed. Amnesty International noted, 'This was a historic occasion for those interested in human rights, for there in Greece a body of foreign jurists heard evidence and confronted alleged torturers with their victims.'[20] Subsequently, however, the Greek Government refused access to certain witnesses, and the Sub-Commission left Greece without completing its task.

Again, in the course of negotiations with a view to reaching a friendly settlement of the case under Article 28 of the Convention, the Government signed an agreement with the International Committee of the Red Cross, giving them access to all detention places in Greece. These facilities were withdrawn after the friendly settlement talks had broken down, apparently over the question of a fixed timetable for the holding of elections and the restoration of democracy in Greece.

Shortly after the adoption of the Commission's Report, Greece felt obliged to withdraw from the Council of Europe and to denounce the Convention.

In *Ireland* v. *United Kingdom*,[21] the Irish Government alleged that persons in custody in Northern Ireland had been subjected to treatment which constituted torture and inhuman and degrading treatment and punishment within the meaning of Article 3 of the Convention and that such treatment constituted an administrative practice. In issue, in particular, were the five techniques for interrogating detained persons in depth, consisting of covering their heads with hoods, obliging them to stand for long periods against a wall with the limbs outstretched, subjecting them to intense noise, depriving them of sleep, and feeding them on a diet of bread and water. After a committee of enquiry in the United Kingdom had looked into these techniques and consideration

---

[19] See below, ch. 24.
[20] *Amnesty International Report on Torture*, 1973, at 91.
[21] *Ireland* v. *United Kingdom*, Judgment of 18 January 1978, Series A, No. 25; (1979–80) 2 EHRR 25.

by Privy Counsellors, the Prime Minister announced in March 1972 that the interrogation techniques would be discontinued. The Commission's Report of February 1976 concluded that the five techniques amounted to torture and inhuman treatment in breach of Article 3.[22] The Irish Government referred to the case to the Court which gave judgment in 1978. The Court, rather to the surprise of many, concluded that the five techniques did not amount to torture, though they did constitute inhuman and degrading treatment. The case is especially important for its contribution to the case law on the definition of the terms used in Article 3, but it contains many mixed signals. While the majority limited the finding to inhuman and degrading treatment, several judges in the minority concluded that the five techniques amounted to torture and the British judge, Sir Gerald Fitzmaurice, in a powerful, but often considered partial, dissenting opinion concluded that they did not amount even to inhuman and degrading treatment.[23]

The Court, for the first time, found a State guilty of torture in *Aksoy* v. *Turkey*.[24] The applicant had been stripped naked, with his arms tied together behind his back, and suspended by his arms; this is known as 'Palestinian hanging'. The Court considered that this form of treatment must have been deliberately inflicted, and was of such a serious and cruel nature that it could only be described as torture.[25] In coming to this conclusion, the Court had affirmed what it had said in *Ireland* v. *United Kingdom* and had noted:

In order to determine whether any particular form of ill-treatment should be qualified as torture, the Court must have regard to the distinction drawn in Article 3 between this notion and that of inhuman or degrading treatment. As it has remarked before, this distinction would appear to have been embodied in the Convention to allow the special stigma of 'torture' to attach only to deliberate inhuman treatment causing very serious and cruel suffering.[26]

Findings of torture have also been made in other cases against Turkey.[27] A greater willingness to categorize conduct as torture was signalled in the *Selmouni*

---

[22] See (1976) 19 *Yearbook* 512, at 774–6.

[23] See M. O'Boyle, 'Torture and Emergency Powers under the European Convention on Human Rights' (1977) 71 AJIL 674, and D. Bonner, '*Ireland* v. *United Kingdom*' (1978) 27 ICLQ 897.

[24] *Aksoy* v. *Turkey* (App. 21987/93), Judgment of 18 December 1996; (1997) 23 EHRR 553.

[25] Para. 64 of the judgment.

[26] Para. 63 of the judgment.

[27] *Aydin* v. *Turkey* (App. 23178/94), Judgment of 25 September 1997; (1998) 25 EHRR 251 (isolation, blindfolding, being stripped naked, being hosed with pressurized water, and rape); *Tekin* v. *Turkey* (App. 22496/93), Judgment of 9 June 1998; (2001) 31 EHRR 95 (held in a dark and cold cell, blindfolded, and subjected to beatings); *Ilhan* v. *Turkey* (App. 22277/93), Judgment of 27 June 2000; (2002) 34 EHRR 869 (beating with sticks and rifle butts while in police custody); *Salman* v. *Turkey* (App. 21986/93), Judgment of 27 June 2000; (2002) 34 EHRR 425 (beating with sticks and rifle butts while in police custody); *Dikme* v. *Turkey* (App. 20869/92), Judgment of 11 July 2000 (beatings over a considerable period of time while in custody); *Akkoç* v. *Turkey* (Apps. 22947/93 and 22948/93), Judgment of 10 October 2000 (electric shocks, hot and cold water treatment, blows to the head, and psychological pressure).

case.[28] The case concerned ill-treatment in France of persons suspected of involvement in drug-trafficking. The applicant was, over a number of days, exposed to severe beatings, was made to run along a corridor with police officers on either side to trip him up, was invited to suck a police officer's penis, was urinated upon, and was threatened with a blowlamp and then a syringe. The Court concluded, unanimously, that the physical and mental violence, considered as a whole caused severe pain and suffering that was particularly serious and cruel, and was properly categorized as torture.

INHUMAN TREATMENT

As already noted, treatment must meet a minimum level of severity in order to amount to inhuman treatment. The treatment need not necessarily be deliberate.[29] All the circumstances of the case must be considered.

The Court has recapitulated its case law in considering whether the prosecution process which led to the conviction of the killers of James Bulger in the United Kingdom constituted a violation of Article 3.[30] The Court said:

Treatment has been held by the Court to be 'inhuman' because, inter alia, it was premeditated, was applied for hours at a stretch and caused either actual bodily injury or intense physical and mental suffering, and also 'degrading' because it was such as to arouse in its victims feelings of fear, anguish and inferiority capable of humiliating and debasing them. In order for a punishment or treatment associated with it to be 'inhuman' or 'degrading', the suffering or humiliation involved must in any event go beyond that inevitable element of suffering or humiliation connected with a given form of legitimate treatment or punishment. The question whether the purpose of the treatment was to humiliate or debase the victim is a further factor to be taken into account but the absence of any such purpose cannot conclusively rule out a finding of a violation of Article 3.[31]

It seems that beating by the police will not attain the threshold to constitute torture where they occur 'over a short period of heightened tension and emotions' and where there are no aggravating factors, such as an aim to extract a confession. Such conduct will, however, constitute inhuman treatment.[32]

The following situations have been found by the Court to amount to inhuman treatment:[33] ill-treatment in detention, deportation or extradition

---

[28] *Selmouni* v. *France* (App. 25803/94), Judgment of 28 July 1999; (2000) 29 EHRR 403, para. 101 of the judgment.

[29] *Labita* v. *Italy* (App. 26772/95), Judgment of 6 April 2000, para. 120 of the judgment.

[30] *T & V* v. *United Kingdom* (Apps. 24888/94 and 24724/94), Judgment of 16 December 1999; (2000) 30 EHRR 121.

[31] Para. 71 of the judgment.

[32] See e.g. *Egmez* v. *Cyprus* (App. 30873/96), Judgment of 21 December 2000; (2002) 34 EHRR 753, para. 78 of the judgment.

[33] See below in this chapter.

where there is a real risk of inhuman treatment in the proposed country of destination, anxiety caused by failure to carry out a proper investigation into a disappearance, and destruction of personal property.

DEGRADING TREATMENT

The defining feature of degrading treatment, as noted above, is the element of humiliation or debasement; the threshold of severity would appear to require that the humiliation is gross. So the process of investigation and discharge of homosexuals in the armed forces did not reach the requisite threshold in the *Smith and Grady* case.[34] The Court, however, noted that it would not exclude the possibility of treatment 'grounded upon a predisposed bias on the part of a heterosexual majority against a homosexual minority' could fall within the scope of Article 3.

The Commission has considered that racial discrimination could constitute degrading treatment.[35] In the *Marckx* case[36] the Court ruled that legal rules discriminating against illegitimate children did not constitute degrading treatment within Article 3, though the case might be decided differently if the same situation arose today. In *Cyprus* v. *Turkey*[37] the Court found that the treatment of Greek Cypriots living in the Karpas area of northern Cyprus had been subject to discriminatory treatment which attained a level of severity which amounted to degrading treatment.[38]

Note that in *Peers* v. *Greece*[39] the Court found that the conditions of detention constituted degrading treatment where it expressly found that there was no intention to humiliate.

DISTINGUISHING TREATMENT AND PUNISHMENT

Punishment is given its ordinary meaning, but it is not normally necessary to distinguish between treatment and punishment. Treatment and punishment are often not subject to separate analysis, since in many cases punishment must involve treatment. Furthermore, whether a punishment is inhuman or

---

[34] *Smith and Grady* v. *United Kingdom* (Apps. 33985/96 and 33986/96), Judgment of 27 September 1999; (2000) 29 EHRR 493, paras 120–3 of the judgment.

[35] Apps. 4403–19/70, 4422/70, 4434/70, 4476–8/70, 4486/70, 4501/70, 4526–30/70, *East African Asians* v. *United Kingdom*, Decision of the Commission, 10 and 18 October 1970 (1970) 13 *Yearbook* 928; Report of the Commission, 14 December 1973 (1994) 78-A DR 5; Committee of Ministers Resolution DH(77)2 of 21 October 1977 (1977) 20 *Yearbook* 642; and Committee of Ministers Resolution DH(94)30 of 21 March 1994 (1994) 78-A DR 70, deciding to make the Report of the Commission public at the request of the UK Government; (1981) 3 EHRR 76, paras 207–8 of the Report.

[36] *Marckx* v. *Belgium*, Judgment of 13 June 1979, Series A, No. 31; (1979–80) 2 EHRR 330.

[37] *Cyprus* v. *Turkey* (App. 25781/94), Judgment of 10 May 2001.

[38] Paras 302–11 of the judgment.

[39] *Peers* v. *Greece* (App. 28524/95), Judgment of 19 April 2001; (2001) 33 EHRR 1192.

degrading is sometimes considered together. So birching as a punishment of a juvenile on conviction of a crime was found to be degrading but not inhuman punishment.[40] It also seems that a sentence whose severity bore no relationship to the offence could amount to an inhuman punishment.[41]

POSITIVE OBLIGATIONS

There are a number of cases which hold that a State's responsibility under Article 3 can be engaged by its failure to provide methods by which protection against torture, and inhuman and degrading treatment or punishment can be ensured, and under which incidents of torture, inhuman and degrading treatment can be verified.[42] These obligations apply regardless of whether the conduct in question is that of State agents or private parties. In *Aksoy* v. *Turkey*, the Court said:

The nature of the right safeguarded under Article 3 of the Convention has implications for Article 13. Given the fundamental importance of the prohibition of torture and the especially vulnerable position of torture victims, Article 13 imposes, without prejudice to any other remedy available under the domestic system, an obligation on States to carry out a thorough and effective investigation of incidents of torture.[43]

Though the obligation to conduct a timely and thorough investigation is well established, the precise legal basis for the obligation does not appear to have been finally settled by the Court. In the *Aksoy* case, as the quotation above indicates, Article 13 was seen to have an important role to play. In *Aydin* v. *Turkey*[44] the Court examined the complaint that there had been a failure by the authorities to carry out a proper investigation in the context of the applicant's complaints under Articles 6 and 13 rather than Article 3. The Court concluded that the prosecutor's failure to conduct a proper investigation constituted a violation of Article 6 in that it denied the applicant effective access to a court or tribunal in order to have a determination of her civil right to compensation.[45]

Assenov v. *Bulgaria*[46] concerned complaints of alleged ill-treatment by the

---

[40] *Tyrer* v. *United Kingdom*, Judgment of 25 April 1978, Series A, No. 26; (1979–80) 2 EHRR 1. See below on issues raised under Article 3 by the use of corporal punishment.

[41] *Weeks* v. *United Kingdom*, Judgment of 2 March 1987, Series A, No 114; (1988) 10 EHRR 293, para. 47 of the judgment.

[42] See also ch. 4 above; a similar approach has been adopted under Article 2.

[43] *Aksoy* v. *Turkey* (App. 21987/93), Judgment of 18 December 1996; (1997) 23 EHRR 553, para. 98 of the judgment.

[44] *Aydin* v. *Turkey* (App. 23178/94), Judgment of 25 September 1997; (1998) 25 EHRR 251.

[45] Para. 98 of the judgment.

[46] *Assenov* v. *Bulgaria* (App. 24760/94), Judgment of 28 October 1998; (1999) 28 EHRR 651.

Bulgarian police. Here the Court found that the failure to conduct an effective official investigation constituted a violation of Article 13.[47] In *Selmouni* v. *France*[48] the absence of an effective investigation was a major feature in the Court's rejection of a preliminary objection by the French Government that the applicant had not exhausted his domestic remedies, but no violation of a substantive article arose save under Article 6 in relation to the length of the time taken to deal with the applicant's complaint of police misconduct.[49]

Akkoç v. *Turkey*[50] concerned complaints under both Article 2 and Article 3. In relation to the complaint under Article 3, the Court was critical of the cursory investigations of the applicant's complaints, and commented:

The European Committee for the Prevention of Torture (CPT) has also emphasized that proper medical examinations are an essential safeguard against ill-treatment of persons in custody. Such examinations must be carried out by a properly qualified doctor, without any police officer being present and the report of the examination must include not only the detail of any injuries found but the explanations given by the patient as to how they occurred and the opinion of the doctor as to whether the injuries are consistent with those explanations. The practice of cursory and collective examinations illustrated by the present case undermines the effectiveness and reliability of this safeguard.[51]

In *Sevtap Veznedaroğlu* v. *Turkey*[52] the Court recapitulated its case law in the following terms:

[T]he Court reiterates that, where an individual raises an arguable claim that he has been seriously ill-treated by the police or other such agents of the State unlawfully and in breach of Article 3, that provision, read in conjunction with the State's general duty under Article 1 of the Convention to 'secure to everyone within their jurisdiction the rights and freedoms defined in . . . [the] Convention' requires by implication that there should be an effective official investigation capable of leading to the identification and punishment of those responsible. . . . If this were not the case, the general legal prohibition of torture and inhuman and degrading treatment and punishment, despite its fundamental importance, would be ineffective in practice and it would be possible in some cases for agents of the State to abuse the rights of those within their control with virtual impunity.[53]

The obligation is later described as a 'procedural obligation' which devolves on the State under Article 3.[54]

---

[47] Paras 117–8 of the judgment.
[48] *Selmouni* v. *France* (App. 25803/94), Judgment of 28 July 1999; (2000) 29 EHRR 403.
[49] See ch. 8 below on the requirements imposed by Article 6.
[50] *Akkoç* v. *Turkey* (Apps. 22947/93 and 22948/93), Judgment of 10 October 2000.
[51] Para. 118 of the judgment.
[52] *Sevtap Veznedaroğlu* v. *Turkey* (App. 32357/96), Judgment of 11 April 2000; (2001) 33 EHRR 1412.
[53] Para. 32 of the judgment.
[54] Para. 35 of the judgment.

Where the conduct complained of is that of private parties, rather different considerations apply. The leading authorities are the cases of *Costello-Roberts*[55] and *A*.[56] *Costello-Roberts* concerned the use of corporal punishment in private schools, while *A* concerned the beating of a child by his stepfather. The Court ruled in both cases that States had an obligation under Article 3 to ensure that those within their jurisdiction are not subjected to treatment prohibited by Article 3 even where that treatment was meted out by private individuals. Where children and other vulnerable individuals are concerned, this must take the form of effective deterrence against such serious breaches of personal integrity.

The Court has restated this view in *Z and others* v. *United Kingdom*.[57] The case concerned four children who had been subject to severe parental abuse known to the authorities in October 1987. The children had, however, not been taken into care until 1992. The United Kingdom Government did not contest the Commission's finding that the suffering of the children amounted to inhuman and degrading treatment, nor that the State had failed to provide the children with adequate protection against such treatment. The Court made clear that the positive obligation on States is to take measures:

to ensure that individuals within their jurisdiction are not subjected to torture or inhuman or degrading treatment, including such ill-treatment administered by private individuals. . . . These measures should provide effective protection, in particular, of children and other vulnerable persons and include reasonable steps to prevent ill-treatment of which the authorities had or ought to have had knowledge.[58]

EVIDENTIAL ISSUES

Because a finding that a Contracting Party is guilty of torture, or of inhuman and degrading treatment carries a certain stigma, the Convention organs have required a very high standard of proof of the conduct, even using the term 'beyond reasonable doubt' in the *Ireland* v. *United Kingdom* case.[59]

There will often be considerable dispute as to the facts where allegations of violations of Article 3 are brought before the Court. The victim may well not be in as strong a position as the State in relation to the collection and presentation

[55] *Costello-Roberts* v. *United Kingdom*, Judgment of 25 March 1993, Series A, No. 247-C; (1994) 19 EHRR 112.
[56] *A* v. *United Kingdom* (App. 25599/94), Judgment of 23 September 1998; (1999) 27 EHRR 611.
[57] *Z and others* v. *United Kingdom* (App. 29292/95), Judgment of 10 May 2001; (2002) 34 EHRR 97.
[58] Para. 73 of the judgment.
[59] *Ireland* v. *United Kingdom*, Judgment of 18 January 1978, Series A, No. 25; (1979–80) 2 EHRR 25, para. 161 of judgment.

of evidence. The Court has been sensitive to this problem, while also recognizing that there must be compelling proof of a State's failure before condemning the State under the Article.[60]

It is now clear that an obligation on the authorities to conduct a proper, timely, and conscientious investigation of allegations of ill-treatment by agents of the State is a feature of Article 3. Failure to meet this obligation also has evidential implications. The starting point is that any allegations of ill-treatment must be supported by appropriate evidence.[61] The State will then be expected to offer some explanation as to the cause of injuries of which there is cogent evidence.[62] If they cannot do so, the Court will draw appropriate inferences from evidence that an applicant had suffered unexplained injuries during, for example, a period of police custody.[63]

The application of this approach can be seen in the *Satik* case.[64] The applicants were taken from their cells in a prison in order to be taken to court. They objected to being searched. They claim that they were then subject to a beating with truncheons and wooden planks. A number of them were seriously injured. The prison officers claimed that the prisoners had formed a human chain and were making for the prison gates; there was a crush on a staircase which resulted in a fall causing the injuries. An investigation by the authorities did not result in any action being taken against the officers concerned, and the file was subsequently lost. The Court cast doubt on the integrity of the internal investigations:

In the absence of a plausible explanation on the part of the authorities, the Court is led to find that the applicants were beaten and injured by State agents as alleged.[65]

The Court's approach to internal investigations can, accordingly, have a double sting in the tail. A failure to conduct a proper and timely investigation may itself constitute a violation of the Convention, but the absence of such an investigation is likely to make it difficult to provide a plausible explanation for injuries suffered by applicants and, in effect, supports the applicants' evidence.

---

[60] For a critical discussion of evidential issues, see U. Erdal, 'Burden and standard of proof in proceedings under the European Convention' (2001) 26 E.L.Rev. HR65.

[61] Reports by the Committee for the Prevention of Torture are increasingly being referred to by the Court in its judgments. See below in this chapter on the work of the Committee.

[62] *Tomasi* v. *France*, Judgment of 27 August 1992, Series A, No. 241-A; (1993) 15 EHRR 1, para. 109 of the judgment. See also *Selmouni* v. *France* (App. 25803/94), Judgment of 28 July 1999; (2000) 29 EHRR 403, para. 87 of the judgment; and *Labita* v. *Italy* (App. 26772/95), Judgment of 6 April 2000, para. 131 of the judgment.

[63] See *Klaas* v. *Germany*, Judgment of 22 September 1993, Series A, No. 269; (1994) 18 EHRR 305, para. 30 of the judgment.

[64] *Satik and others* v. *Turkey* (App. 31866/96), Judgment of 10 October 2000.

[65] Para. 61 of the judgment.

EXTRATERRITORIAL EFFECT

In certain circumstances Article 3 can have an extra-territorial effect. In the *Soering* case,[66] the Court recognized that a State may violate the obligations in Article 3 if its action exposes a person to the likelihood of ill-treatment in a place outside the jurisdiction of the Contracting States. The case concerned possible deportation to the United States where the 'death row phenomenon' was regarded as inhuman punishment. The Court made clear that the violation of the Convention in such circumstances is that of the sending State, and, by implication, the Court is not seeking to pass any judgment on a State which is not a party to the Convention:

[T]he decision of a Contracting State to extradite a fugitive may give rise to an issue under Article 3, and hence engage the responsibility of that State under the Convention, where substantial grounds have been shown for believing that the person concerned, if extradited, faces a real risk of being subjected to torture or to inhuman or degrading treatment or punishment in the requesting country. The establishment of such responsibility inevitably involves an assessment of the conditions in the requesting country against the standards of Article 3 of the Convention. Nonetheless, there is no question of adjudicating on or establishing the responsibility of the receiving country, whether under general international law, under the Convention or otherwise. In so far as any liability under the Convention is or may be incurred, it is liability incurred by the extraditing Contracting State by reason of its having taken action which has as a direct consequence the exposure of an individual to proscribed ill-treatment.[67]

   In the *Chahal* case,[68] the United Kingdom was precluded from returning a Sikh separatist to India, because the Court concluded that there would be a very real risk that the applicant would be the victim of ill-treatment at the hands of rogue elements within the Punjab Police. In *Ahmed* v. *Austria*,[69] the Court found that the applicant, a Somali national living in Austria who was convicted of attempted robbery, would, if returned to Somalia where a civil war was raging, be exposed to a serious risk of being subjected to ill-treatment which would fall within the scope of Article 3.

   The Court in *HLR* v. *France*[70] had to consider a claim by a convicted cocaine trafficker, who was a Colombian national and who had provided information to the authorities on the instigators of the traffic, that he should not be returned

---

[66] *Soering* v. *United Kingdom*, Judgment of 7 July 1989, Series A, No. 161; (1989) 11 EHRR 439. The case is discussed further below.
[67] Para. 91 of the judgment.
[68] *Chahal* v. *United Kingdom* (App. 22414/93), Judgment of 15 November 1996; (1997) 23 EHRR 413.
[69] *Ahmed* v. *Austria* (App. 25964/94), Judgment of 17 December 1996; (1997) 24 EHRR 278.
[70] *HLR* v. *France* (App. 24573/94), Judgment of 29 April 1997; (1998) 26 EHRR 29.

to Colombia, since 'he would be exposed to vengeance by the drug traffickers who had recruited him as a smuggler.'[71] While the Court did not exclude the possibility that the extraterritorial effect of Article 3 would apply where the serious threat of ill-treatment was at the hands of private parties, they were not convinced in this case that there was such a serious risk. The six dissenting judges, in essence, disagreed with the assessment of the majority on the nature of the risk; their view is probably to be preferred.

D v. United Kingdom[72] presented a rather different set of circumstances, though the applicant was again a convicted drug smuggler. D was a national of St Kitts, who had been arrested at Gatwick Airport in possession of a large quantity of cocaine. While serving a prison sentence, he was discovered to be suffering from AIDS. As is normal, on completion of his prison sentence, he was subject to deportation back to St Kitts. He argued that medical services in St Kitts would be unable to provide treatment for his condition, and he had no relatives or friends in St Kitts who could care for him. This, he argued, would constitute treatment in breach of Article 3. The risk he had identified was, unlike the earlier cases, not a risk of intentional ill-treatment emanating from public authorities or private groups in his State of origin, but inherent inadequacies in the medical services in his home country. The Court emphasized the fundamental nature of the protection afforded by Article 3, and was clearly influenced by the consequences of the abrupt withdrawal of the medical and personal care afforded to him in the United Kingdom by the Terrence Higgins Trust, a leading AIDS charity. In the 'very exceptional circumstances'[73] of this case, the Court concluded that deportation to St Kitts would be a violation of Article 3 amounting to inhuman treatment.

However, there is no extraterritorial effect arising in circumstances where a national has been subjected to torture abroad.[74]

DISAPPEARANCES

A number of cases have addressed the application of Article 3 to situations where a person has disappeared, and the events surrounding the disappearance have not been sufficiently investigated by the authorities. The Kurt

---

[71] Para. 30 of the judgment.

[72] D v. United Kingdom (App. 30240/96), Judgment of 2 May 1997; (1997) 24 EHRR 423.

[73] Para. 54 of the judgment. Contrast Bensaid v. United Kingdom (App. 44599/98), Judgment of 6 February 2001; (2001) 33 EHRR 205, where no violation was found.

[74] Al-Adsani v. United Kingdom (App. 35763/97), Judgment of 21 November 2001; (2002) 34 EHRR 273, paras. 35–41 of the judgment.

case,[75] which was an application by a mother in relation to her disappeared son, appears to be the first consideration by the Court of this issue. The Court accepted that the uncertainty, doubt, and apprehension suffered by the applicant over a prolonged and continuing period caused her severe mental distress and anguish. The authorities failed to give serious consideration to her requests for information about his whereabouts. The Commission had concluded that this constituted inhuman and degrading treatment. The Court simply categorizes it as a breach of Article 3.

The Court in *Çakici* v. *Turkey*[76] established some general principles governing disappearance cases. The applicant claimed that his brother had been detained by the authorities in November 1993. He subsequently disappeared. The applicant said that in May 1996 he was told by the authorities that his brother had been killed in a clash with security forces in February 1995. The Government claimed that the brother had not been taken into custody, that he was a militant member of the PKK,[77] and had been killed in February 1995 in a clash with security forces. Evidence was adduced that the father of the applicant and the applicant had, in December 1993, submitted a petition to the authorities requesting information about the whereabouts of the disappearance of the brother. Enquiries continued to be made, notably by the applicant in September 1994. The response of the authorities was simply to verify whether records contained the name of the applicant's brother. The applicant complained that the lack of information about his brother's disappearance constituted inhuman treatment towards himself. The Court said:

Whether a family member is [a victim of treatment contrary to Article 3] will depend on the existence of special factors which gives the suffering of the applicant a dimension and character distinct from the emotional distress which may be regarded as inevitably caused to relatives of a victim of a serious human rights violation. Relevant elements will include the proximity of the family tie (in that context, a certain weight will attach to the parent–child bond), the extent to which the family member witnessed the events in question, the involvement of the family member in attempts to obtain information about the disappeared person and the way in which the authorities responded to those enquiries. The Court would further emphasise that the essence of such a violation does not so much lie in the fact of the 'disappearance' of the family member but rather concerns the authorities' reactions and attitudes to the situation when it is brought to their attention. It is especially in respect of the latter that a relative may claim directly to be a victim of the authorities' conduct.[78]

---

[75] *Kurt* v. *Turkey* (App. 24276/94), Judgment of 25 May 1998; (1999) 27 EHRR 373. The Court appears to have drawn some inspiration from the decision of the United Nations Human Rights Committee in *Quinteros* v. *Uruguay*, 21 July 1983, Case 107/1981, (1983) 38 UNGAOR Supp. 40 Annex XXI, para. 14.
[76] *Çakici* v. *Turkey* (App. 23657/94), Judgment of 8 July 1999; (2001) 31 EHRR 133.
[77] Workers' Party of Kurdistan.
[78] Para. 98 of the judgment.

In the particular circumstances of this case, the Court concluded that there was no violation.[79]

DESTRUCTION OF HOMES AND POSSESSIONS

In *Bilgin* v. *Turkey*[80] the Court found that destruction of the applicant's house and his possessions during operations by the security forces constituted inhuman treatment. The acts were deliberate and the operations of the security forces had been conducted with complete disregard for the safety and welfare of the applicant.

ACTS IN THE COURSE OF ARREST AND POLICE DETENTION

The use of handcuffs in connection with a lawful arrest or detention does not normally give rise to an issue under Article 3, provided that it does not entail the use of force or public exposure exceeding what is reasonably necessary in the particular circumstances of each case.[81] All the circumstances must be considered including any reasonable belief that the person concerned would resist arrest or seek to escape, or be a danger to themselves or others. But even where the arrest and detention is unlawful, the Court will not always be convinced that being handcuffed so adversely affects the applicant that the minimum level of severity is reached for Article 3 to bite.

The factually dramatic cases have tended to result in a friendly settlement following the Commission's conclusions on the merits. So in one case[82] the Swiss Government paid 14,000 Swiss francs to an applicant who was arrested on a drugs charge in circumstances where a stun grenade had been used and who had subsequently been ill-treated. The use of the stun grenade was considered to be justified, but there had been a violation when the applicant

---

[79] See also *Timurtaş* v. *Turkey* (App. 23531/94), Judgment of 13 June 2000; (2001) 33 EHRR 121, paras. 91–8 of the judgment; *Taş* v. *Turkey* (App. 24396/94), Judgment of 14 November 2000; (2001) 33 EHRR 325, paras. 77–80 of the judgment; and *Cyprus* v. *Turkey* (App. 25781/94), Judgment of 10 May 2001, paras. 154–8 of the judgment.

[80] *Bilgin* v. *Turkey* (App. 23819/94), Judgment of 16 November 2000.

[81] *Raninen* v. *Finland* (App. 20972/92), Judgment of 16 December 1997; (1998) 26 EHRR 563, paras. 52–9 of the judgment.

[82] *Hurtado* v. *Switzerland*, Judgment of 28 January 1994, Series A No. 280-A.

had had to wear soiled clothing and had been refused immediate medical treatment.

In the *Tomasi* case[83] the applicant had been subjected to considerable ill-treatment over a period of nearly two days while in police custody. He had been slapped, kicked, punched, and given forearm blows, made to stand for long periods and without support, had his hands handcuffed behind his back, been made to stand naked in front of an open window, been deprived of food, and threatened with a firearm. The Government was unable to offer any explanation for the injuries suffered by the applicant. But they argued that the injuries suffered by the applicant did not meet the level of severity necessary to constitute a violation of Article 3, and that there were particular circumstances obtaining in Corsica where there was significant terrorist activity. The Court did not accept this argument, and in concluding that there had been a violation of Article 3, said:

The requirements of the investigation and the undeniable difficulties inherent in the fight against crime, particularly with regard to terrorism, cannot result in limits being placed on the protection to be afforded in respect of the physical integrity of individuals.[84]

The *Klaas* case[85] concerned allegations by a woman social worker and her 8-year-old daughter, who found themselves in difficulties after Mrs Klaas allegedly failed to stop at a traffic light. On being stopped by the police, Mrs Klaas was requested to provide a specimen of breath. An altercation and a struggle ensued, which resulted in Mrs Klaas being handcuffed. In the scuffle, she suffered bruising, was rendered unconscious for a short period when she banged her head on a window ledge, and received a serious long-term injury to her left shoulder. She was subsequently charged with obstructing an officer in the execution of his duty and drink-driving. She complained that her treatment violated Article 3; her daughter also complained of a violation of Article 3 as a result of her witnessing the treatment accorded to her mother.

The Commission concluded that the treatment of Mrs Klaas was a disproportionate use of force and held that, when injuries were shown to arise from an arrest, it was incumbent on the Government to produce evidence casting doubt on the victim's account of events. The Commission, however, concluded that there was no violation of Article 3 in respect of the daughter; the Court agreed.

On Mrs Klaas's complaint, the Court disagreed with the Commission:

The admitted injuries sustained by the first applicant were consistent with either her or the police officers' version of events. The national courts, however, found against

---

[83] *Tomasi* v. *France*, Judgment of 27 August 1992, Series A, No. 241-A; (1993) 15 EHRR 1.
[84] Para. 11 of judgment.
[85] *Klaas* v. *Germany*, Judgment of 22 September 1993, Series A, No. 269; (1994) 18 EHRR 305.

her. In reaching the conclusion that she could have injured herself while resisting arrest and that the arresting officers had not used excessive force, the Regional Court, in particular, had the benefit of seeing the various witnesses give their evidence and of evaluating their credibility. No material has been adduced in the course of the Strasbourg proceedings which could call into question the findings of the national courts and add weight to the applicant's allegation either before the Commission or the Court.[86]

The Court expressly distinguished its findings in the *Tomasi* case. These cases highlight the difficulties of proof that will frequently arise, even where the case has been held to be admissible and where the Commission has concluded that there has been a violation.

Ribitsch v. *Austria*[87] might be regarded as the first of the modern cases on physical assault while in police custody, since it couples the failure of the authorities to provide an explanation for the applicant's injuries with its finding of a violation of Article 3. It was not disputed that the applicant's injuries had been sustained during police detention, and the Government was found not to have satisfactorily established that they were caused other than as a result of his treatment in custody. The Court found that the applicant had been the victim of inhuman and degrading treatment.[88]

CONDITIONS OF DETENTION

The fact and conditions of imprisonment are frequent sources of individual application invoking Article 3. Few have been considered by the Court, but the Commission decisions warrant consideration because of the frequency with which such issues are raised.

All those cases which have alleged that imprisonment is *per se* contrary to Article 3 because of the applicant's age or state of health have failed. In the *Bonnechaux* case[89] both the Commission and the Committee of Ministers agreed that there was no violation in the case of a 74-year-old suffering from diabetes and cardiovascular disease who had been detained on remand for thirty-five months. In none of the cases considered was it established that the detainee was denied proper medical care.[90]

---

[86] Para. 30 of judgment.

[87] *Ribitsch* v. *Austria*, Judgment of 4 December 1995, Series A, No. 336; (1996) 21 EHRR 573.

[88] See also *Aksoy* v. *Turkey* (App. 21987/93), Judgment of 18 December 1996; (1997) 23 EHRR 553.

[89] App. 8224/78, *Bonnechaux* v. *Switzerland*, 5 December 1978, (1979) 15 DR 211, and 5 December 1979, (1980) 18 DR 100; (1981) 3 EHRR 259.

[90] For a decision of the Court on admissibility addressing similar issues, see App. 64666/01, *Papon* v. *France*, Decision of 7 June 2001.

In one case that was admitted,[91] the Commission finally reached the opinion that the treatment to which the applicant was submitted did not amount to inhuman or degrading treatment within the meaning of Article 3. The applicant had been severely handled by prison officers and was finally put in a straitjacket. The Commission found that there was no evidence of any substantial physical injury as a result of the incident, and that 'Although not conclusive, this is a strong argument in favour of the opinion that the treatment had not been "inhuman" within the meaning of Article 3.'[92] It also took account of the fact that the straitjacket had been used only because of the applicant's violent behaviour.[93]

In *Simon Herold* v. *Austria*, the applicant, who was partly paralysed from poliomyelitis, made a number of serious allegations of inadequate medical treatment while he was detained on remand and complained, *inter alia*, that in the course of his treatment he was detained, although not himself mentally ill, in a closed ward of a psychiatric hospital together with a number of violent patients with mental disorders, several of whom died in his presence.[94] These complaints were declared admissible by the Commission but after extensive investigation of the facts, a friendly settlement was reached. The Austrian Federal Minister for Justice issued a directive to the Austrian judicial authorities concerning the accommodation in public hospitals of sick or injured prisoners serving sentences or remanded in custody.

In this instruction the Ministry gives notice to all these authorities that:

care must be taken to ensure that the prisoner serving his sentence or on remand is not indirectly subjected to 'inhuman or degrading treatment or punishment' when he is transferred to a hospital, since this is expressly forbidden under Article 3 of the Convention for the Protection of Human Rights and Fundamental Freedoms. . . . In the view of the Federal Minister for Justice the fact that a convicted prisoner or a prisoner on remand is admitted to a closed ward of a psychiatric hospital or to the corresponding installation in a general hospital, although there are no doubts as to his mental health, might constitute such inhuman or degrading treatment or punishment.[95]

However, in *Price* v. *United Kingdom*[96] the conditions in which a thalidomide victim was kept in prison were found to amount to degrading treatment. The applicant had been committed to prison for seven days for contempt of court;[97] she was detained both in a police cell and in prison for three and a half days. She

---

[91] App. 2686/65, *Zeidler-Kormann* v. *Federal Republic of Germany*, 3 October 1967, (1968) 11 *Yearbook* 1020.

[92] At 1026.

[93] At 1028.

[94] App. 4340/69, *Simon Herold* v. *Austria*, 2 February 1971, (1971) 14 *Yearbook* 352.

[95] Stocktaking Note, DH(73)3, at 25.

[96] *Price* v. *United Kingdom* (App. 33394/96), Judgment of 10 July 2001.

[97] Under the remission system she was only incarcerated for three and a half days.

was seriously disabled by her condition, and used a wheelchair. The Court concluded that her detention in conditions where she was dangerously cold, risked developing sores because her bed was too hard or unreachable, and was unable to get to the toilet or keep clean without the greatest of difficulties amounted to degrading treatment. Judge Bratza in a separate concurring opinion is scathing of the judicial authorities in committing the applicant to prison without determining in advance whether there were adequate facilities for meeting her special needs.

A number of cases have questioned the practice of using solitary confinement. The Commission has accepted that the use of solitary confinement may breach Article 3, stating:

In assessing whether [solitary confinement] may fall within the ambit of Article 3 of the Convention in a given case, regard must be had to the particular conditions, the stringency of the measure, its duration, the objective pursued and its effect on the person concerned. Complete sensory isolation coupled with complete social isolation can no doubt ultimately destroy the personality; this constitutes a form of inhuman treatment which cannot be justified by the requirements of security.[98]

In other cases, the Commission has held, at the stage of admissibility, that the measures complained of, even if established, were not capable of constituting violations of Article 3. Thus the Commission has rejected as being manifestly ill-founded, on the particular facts, complaints of: detention in solitary confinement;[99] the additional penalty of 'sleeping hard' (*hartes Lager*);[100] the taking of a prisoner, in the course of his trial, through a town in handcuffs and in prison uniform.[101]

The issue of prison conditions has been considered in detail by the Court in a number of recent decisions, which suggest that a more demanding view is being taken of the requirements of Article 3 in this context. *Peers* v. *Greece*[102] concerned conditions in a prison in Greece. There had been a critical report by the Committee for the Prevention of Torture[103] in relation to the prison in question. It seemed that little had been done to improve the conditions in the prison. The Court concluded that confinement in a cell with no ventilation and no window at the hottest time of the year in circumstances where the applicant had to use the toilet in the presence of another and was present while the toilet was being

---

[98] Apps. 7572/76, 7586/76 and 7587/76, *Ensslin, Baader and Raspe* v. *Federal Republic of Germany*, 8 July 1978, (1979) 14 DR 64, at 109. See also App. 14610/89, *Treholt* v. *Norway*, 9 July 1991 (1991) 71 DR 168.

[99] App. 2479/66, *De Courcy* v. *United Kingdom*, 7 October 1966, (1967) 10 *Yearbook* 368, at 382; App. 4203/69, *X* v. *Federal Republic of Germany*, 26 May 1970, (1970) 13 *Yearbook* 836, at 860, and App. 6038/73, *X* v. *Federal Republic of Germany*, 11 July 1973, (1973) 44 CD 115.

[100] App. 1502/62, not published.

[101] App. 2291/64, *X* v. *Austria*, 1 June 1967, (1967) 24 CD 20, at 31.

[102] *Peers* v. *Greece* (App. 28524/95), Judgment of 19 April 2001; (2001) 33 EHRR 1192.

[103] See below.

used by his cell mate diminished his human dignity and amounted to degrading treatment. In *Valašinas* v. *Lithuania*[104] the applicant made many claims about the shortcomings of the prison regime to which he was subject. The Court did not find that the undeniably tough regime violated Article 3 since it did not reach the minimum level of severity to amount to degrading treatment; this included a period of 15 days when the applicant was detained in a solitary confinement cell. However, a specific incident in which the applicant had been obliged to strip naked in the presence of a woman prison officer, and in which his genitals and food were handled by a prison officer with bare hands, was considered to constitute degrading treatment.

A similar approach is taken to the conditions of detention of those awaiting expulsion.[105]

It seem doubtful whether the distinctions between treatment and punishment, or even between what is inhuman and what is degrading, can be strictly applied in all these cases.

No rigid distinction, therefore, can be drawn between different forms of ill-treatment, and in particular little significance can be attached to the distinction between 'treatment' and 'punishment'. Punishment implies that an offence has been committed, but treatment which would otherwise be contrary to Article 3 is not permissible simply on that ground. Conversely, what is permissible as 'treatment' cannot go beyond what is lawful as punishment; there can plainly be no special protection for offenders. In any event, while the terms used in Article 3 can to some extent be separately analysed, the article must be read as a whole and the measures complained of, whatever their description, must be assessed in each case to see whether, in the context of the article, they constitute any of the prohibited forms of treatment.

In each case, as always, the facts must be viewed in the light of the circumstances as a whole. Thus the physical condition of the applicant may make treatment which would otherwise be lawful contrary to Article 3; conversely, the applicant's own conduct may exceptionally legitimize a degree of violence which would otherwise be prohibited. In the *McFeeley* case[106] the applicants complained of being subjected to close body searches, that is, the searching of prisoners while naked including examination of the rectum with the aid of a mirror. The Commission concluded that such searches did not amount to degrading treatment having regard to the security threat involved in the IRA killing campaign against prison officers. In the same case, the Commission concluded that a requirement to wear prison clothing was not degrading. But strip searches which have no genuine relationship to security concerns

[104] *Valašinas* v. *Lithuania* (App. 44558/98), Judgment of 24 July 2001.

[105] *Dougoz* v. *Greece* (App. 40907/98), Judgment of 6 March 2001.

[106] App. 8317/77, *McFeeley and others* v. *United Kingdom*, 15 May 1980, (1980) 20 DR 44; (1981) 3 EHRR 161.

and which are imposed on a remand prisoner can constitute degrading treatment.[107]

Again, a penalty disproportionate to the offence may constitute inhuman treatment, even though it might be justified in the case of a more serious crime. On the other hand, Article 3 must also be regarded as setting an absolute limit, based on respect for the human person, to what treatment is permissible, regardless of its label, and regardless also of the victim's own conduct. Article 3 should be considered as imposing an absolute prohibition of certain forms of punishment such as, perhaps, flogging, which are by their very nature inhuman and degrading. Within that limit, all the circumstances of the individual cases are relevant.

DETENTION AND MENTAL DISORDER

In the *Herczegfalvy* case,[108] the applicant, who had been convicted of offences of fraud and violence, complained that the medical treatment to which he had been subjected amounted to degrading treatment. He had been diagnosed as suffering from a mental illness, and was forcibly administered food and neuroleptics, isolated, and attached with handcuffs to his security bed for several weeks. The Commission concluded that there had been a violation of Article 3. Their decision was based on the conclusion that the treatment accorded to the applicant went beyond what was strictly necessary, and that it extended beyond the period necessary to serve its purpose (including the period of a week when he was handcuffed to his bed despite being unconscious).

The Court affirmed that mental patients remain under the protection of Article 3, but that the 'established principles of medicine are . . . decisive in such cases; as a general rule, a measure which is therapeutic cannot be regarded as inhuman or degrading.'[109] But the Court would need to be satisfied as to the medical necessity for any particular form of treatment. In the present case, the Court considered this test to be met. On the facts as presented, the conclusions of the Court are surprising and the opinion of the Commission is to be preferred.

In *Aerts* v. *Belgium*[110] the applicant complained about the conditions in the psychiatric wing of the prison where he was in detention pending his trial for an assault on his ex-wife with a hammer. The Committee for the Prevention of Torture[111] had reported critically on the psychiatric and therapeutic care

---

[107] *Iwańczuk* v. *Poland* (App. 25196/94), Judgment of 15 November 2001, paras. 49–60 of the judgment.

[108] *Herczegfalvy* v. *Austria*, Judgment of 24 September 1992, Series A, No. 242-B; (1993) 15 EHRR 437.

[109] Para. 82 of judgment.

[110] *Aerts* v. *Belgium* (App. 25357/94), Judgment of 30 July 1998; (2000) 29 EHRR 50.

[111] See below, this chapter.

available in the prison psychiatric wing, but did not categorize them as degrading. The Court considered that prolonged periods in the psychiatric wing would carry with them the risk of deterioration in a person's mental health. There was, however, for the Court no convincing evidence that the applicant's mental health had suffered and it was not established that the applicant had suffered treatment which could be classified as inhuman or degrading.

In the *Keenan* case,[112] the Court took a particularly robust view of the needs of a prisoner who was suffering from mental illness which included a risk of suicide. Keenan had been found hanged in his cell, and his mother as his next of kin claimed a violation of Article 3. A combination of poor medical notes, lack of effective monitoring of Keenan's health when he was a known suicide risk, and the imposition on him of seven days' segregation in the punishment block and an additional twenty-eight days added to his sentence constituted inhuman and degrading treatment.[113] He had committed suicide on his second day in segregation.

ADMISSION AND IMMIGRATION

Article 3 has also been used as the basis for challenging a refusal to admit persons to the territory of a Contracting Party. The leading Commission decision[114] concerned the immigration of East African Asians to the United Kingdom. In the first group of twenty-five cases to reach the Commission, early in 1970, the applicants had all been initially refused admission to the United Kingdom. They were subsequently and in most cases after a period of detention, admitted for a limited period. They complained, *inter alia*, of violations of Article 3 of the Convention.

The Fourth Protocol, which provides that no one shall be deprived of the right to enter the territory of the State of which he is a national, has not been ratified by the United Kingdom. The applicants could not therefore rely on any provision directly guaranteeing the right of entry. Equally, their complaint that the immigration law discriminated against them could not be examined under Article 14, since that Article prohibits discrimination only in the enjoyment of

[112] *Keenan* v. *United Kingdom* (App. 27229/95), Judgment of 3 April 2001; (2001) 33 EHRR 913.
[113] Paras. 108–15 of the judgment.
[114] Apps. 4403–19/70, 4422/70, 4434/70, 4476–8/70, 4486/70, 4501/70, 4526–30/70, *East African Asians* v. *United Kingdom*, Decision of the Commission, 10 and 18 October 1970, (1970) 13 *Yearbook* 928; Report of the Commission, 14 December 1973, (1994) 78-A DR 5; Committee of Ministers Resolution DH(77)2 of 21 October 1977 (1977) 20 *Yearbook* 642; and Committee of Ministers' Resolution DH(94)30 of 21 March 1994, (1994) 78-A DR 70, deciding to make the Report of the Commission public at the request of the UK Government. See also App. 5302/71, *X and Y* v. *United Kingdom*, 11 October 1973, (1973) 44 CD 29.

the other rights and freedoms guaranteed, which in the case of the United Kingdom did not include the right of entry.

The Commission nevertheless declared the applications admissible under Article 3, holding that 'quite apart from any consideration of Article 14, discrimination based on race could, in certain circumstances, of itself amount to degrading treatment within the meaning of Article 3 of the Convention'; that 'it is generally recognized that a special importance should be attached to discrimination based on race, and that publicly to single out a group of persons for differential treatment on the basis of race might, in certain circumstances, constitute a special form of affront to human dignity.'

Hence, 'differential treatment of a group of persons on the basis of race might be capable of constituting degrading treatment in circumstances where differential treatment on some other ground, such as language, would raise no such question.'[115]

Quite apart from the merits of this case, however, the Commission's opinion on the interpretation of 'degrading treatment' in Article 3 is important as showing that the Convention is not a static instrument, but must be interpreted in the light of developments in social and political attitudes. Racial discrimination may not have been in the minds of the drafters of Article 3 but can clearly be regarded as degrading treatment by the standards of 1970.

The Court considered similar issues in the *Abdulaziz, Cabales and Balkandali* case.[116] The applicants were married women lawfully and permanently settled in the United Kingdom, who were refused permission to be joined by their husbands who were not British nationals. A number of violations of Convention provisions were argued, including arguments that the discrimination against them based on their nationality constituted an affront to human dignity and amounted to degrading treatment. The Court concluded that the difference of treatment complained of indicated no contempt or lack of respect for the personality of the applicants but was intended solely to achieve legitimate immigration measures. There was no violation of Article 3.[117] The tenor of the judgment is such that, if the difference of treatment did indicate contempt or lack of respect for the personality of applicants, that may meet the level of severity necessary to constitute degrading treatment.

---

[115] *East African Asians* v. *United Kingdom* (1970) 13 *Yearbook* 928, at 944. See also Report of the Commission, 14 December 1973, (1994) 78-A DR 5, paras. 188–95.

[116] *Abdulaziz, Cabales and Balkandali* v. *United Kingdom*, Judgment of 28 May 1985, Series A, No. 94; (1985) 7 EHRR 471.

[117] Paras. 90 and 91 of the judgment.

DEPORTATION AND EXTRADITION

There have been many instances of complaints that imminent extradition or expulsion by one of the Parties to the Convention involves a breach of Article 3.[118] Article 3(1) of the Fourth Protocol[119] provides that no one shall be expelled from the territory of the State of which they are a national, and the next following Article prohibits the collective expulsion of aliens, but apart from these provisions there is no restriction on extradition or expulsion as such, and, in contrast to the Universal Declaration of Human Rights,[120] there is no right of asylum under the Convention. However, an issue might arise under Article 3 of the Convention if applicants were liable to suffer inhuman treatment, for example political persecution, in the country to which they are to be sent.[121]

The Commission in early cases did not accept the argument that, if the applicant is sent to a State not party to the Convention, any action which that State may take is outside its competence. Instead, the Commission recognized that the act of the sending State, which is a Contracting Party, may itself violate Article 3 in such circumstances. The underlying principle in all these cases is that,

although extradition and the right of asylum are not, as such, among the matters governed by the Convention . . . the Contracting States have nevertheless accepted to restrict the free exercise of their powers under general international law, including the power to control the entry and exit of aliens, to the extent and within the limits of the obligations which they have assumed under the Convention.[122]

In urgent cases of threatened expulsion, it was the practice of the Commission to contact the respondent Government at once, and often the Government agreed to postpone the expulsion until the Commission had had the opportunity of considering the admissibility of the application.[123] This practice protected the applicant against any precipitate or unconsidered action and warned the Government of a complaint which may later, and then too late, show a violation of the Convention.[124]

One of the best-known examples of the application of this principle is the

---

[118] See R. Vogler, 'The scope of extradition in the light of the European Convention on Human Rights' in F. Matscher and H. Petzold (eds.), *Protecting Human Rights: The European Dimension. Essays in Honour of Gérard Wiarda* (Köln, 1990), 663.

[119] See below, ch. 17.

[120] Article 14. See also American Convention on Human Rights, Article 22.7.

[121] e.g. App. 3110/67, *X v. Federal Republic of Germany*, 19 July 1968, (1968) 11 *Yearbook* 494, at 526, and cases cited there.

[122] App. 2143/64, *X v. Austria and Yugoslavia*, 30 June 1964, (1964) 7 *Yearbook* 314, at 328.

[123] For current practice on interim measures, see ch. 24 below.

[124] Rule 36 of the Commission's Rules of Procedure. See now Rule 39 of the Rules of the European Court of Human Rights. See also ch. 24 below.

Amekrane case.[125] An officer in the Moroccan Air Force, Lt.-Col. Amekrane, was convicted by court martial and executed on a charge connected with an attempt to assassinate the King of Morocco in 1972. He had arrived in Gibraltar by helicopter on the day of the attack and had asked for political asylum. The Moroccan authorities requested his extradition and on the next day he was sent back to Morocco in a Moroccan Air Force plane.

The application was introduced against the United Kingdom Government by Lt.-Col. Amekrane's widow in her own name and in the name of her late husband and of her two children, alleging violations of Articles 3, 5(4), and 8. The case was concluded by a friendly settlement, the Government agreeing to pay the applicants an ex gratia sum of £37,500.

The relationship between extradition and Article 3 has now been considered by the Court in the *Soering* case,[126] which is the leading authority in this area.[127] Jens Soering, a German national, was 18, when he and his girlfriend were alleged to have killed her parents in Virginia in the United States; the United States prosecutor subsequently appeared to accept that Soering was suffering from mental disturbance at the time which would reduce the conviction to one for manslaughter. Soering was subsequently arrested in England and his extradition was sought to the United States. The State of Virginia had the death penalty for murder, and it was usual for prisoners to spend between six and eight years on death row before being executed. Were he to be extradited, Soering might face the death penalty and the death row phenomenon. An extradition order obtained in the English courts was put into suspense pending determination of Soering's application to the Commission.[128]

The Court found that the death row phenomenon in Virginia could amount to inhuman treatment.[129] The Court also appears to have been influenced by the possibility of extradition or deportation of Soering to Germany, where he could be tried for the offences by reason of the personal jurisdiction arising from his nationality. The Court concluded:

[H]aving regard to the very long period of time spent on death row in such extreme conditions, with the ever present and mounting anguish of awaiting execution of the

---

[125] App. 5961/72, *Amekrane* v. *United Kingdom*, 11 October 1973, (1973) 44 CD 101.

[126] *Soering* v. *United Kingdom*, Judgment of 7 July 1989, Series A, No. 161; (1989) 11 EHRR 439.

[127] Note that a case such as this would now be decided having regard to Protocol 6 prohibiting the death penalty: see *Yang Chun Jin alias Yang Xiaolin* v. *Hungary* (App. 58073/00), Judgment of 15 February 2001. See ch. 4 above.

[128] The case was heard with great expedition; on 8 July 1988 the application was lodged with the Commission; on 3 August 1988 the Secretary of State signed the extradition warrant; on 11 August 1988 the President of the Commission indicated that it was desirable not to extradite the applicant; the Commission declared the application admissible on 19 January 1989 and adopted its Report on 19 January 1989; and the Court handed down its decision on 7 July 1989. The case is also notable in that Germany, in addition to the Commission and the respondent State, referred the case to the Court; this was the first time a State other than a party to the proceedings had referred a case to the Court.

[129] Paras. 100–9 of the judgment.

death penalty, and to the personal circumstances of the applicant, especially his age and mental state at the time of the offence, the applicant's extradition to the United States would expose him to a real risk of treatment going beyond the threshold set by Article 3. A further consideration of relevance is that in the particular instance the legitimate purpose of extradition could be achieved by another means which would not involve suffering of such exceptional intensity or duration.

Accordingly, the Secretary of State's decision to extradite the applicant to the United States would, if implemented, give rise to a breach of Article 3.[130]

In coming to this conclusion, the Court relied upon the principle of effectiveness[131] while recognizing as axiomatic the inability of the Convention to impose its standards on those not parties to it. It also recognized the legitimate purpose of extradition in ensuring that those alleged to have engaged in serious criminal conduct did not avoid trial on such charges. Finally, the Court noted the absolute and fundamental nature of the prohibition contained in Article 3.[132]

Extradition to a country where a person risks being sentenced to life imprisonment and where no procedure exists for release by act of grace or otherwise is not contrary to Article 3.[133]

Two important cases have concerned asylum seekers. The *Cruz Varas* case[134] concerned a family of Chilean nationality who sought political asylum in Sweden. The father was deported to Chile in the face of a request from the Commission to stay the removal. The mother and son went into hiding. The family complained to the Commission that the decision to deport violated Article 3 in that they would be at serious risk of being tortured if returned to Chile. The Commission accepted that Mr Cruz Varas had been tortured in the past, but, in the light of the political changes in Chile, did not think that there was a real risk of exposure to torture on his return to Chile and, accordingly, concluded that the expulsion did not constitute a violation of Article 3. The Court agreed. Mr Cruz Varas also argued that his expulsion involved such trauma for him that it amounted to a breach of Article 3. The Court referred to its conclusions in the *Soering* case requiring such matters to be assessed in the light of all the circumstances of the case. The Court concluded that Article 3 had not been breached, mainly because there was no substantial basis for his fears.

The *Vilvarajah* case[135] concerned the decision of the United Kingdom

---

[130] Para. 111 of judgment.

[131] See above, ch. 3.

[132] For commentaries on the case, see C. Warbrick, 'State responsibility for damage sustained in another State: Article 3' (1989) 9 YEL 387; and C. Van den Wyngaert, 'Applying the European Convention on Human Rights to Extradition: Opening Pandora's box?' (1990) 39 ICLQ 757.

[133] App. 15776/89, *B, H and L* v. *Austria*, 5 December 1989, (1990) 64 DR 264.

[134] *Cruz Varas and others* v. *Sweden*, Judgment of 20 March 1991, Series A, No. 201; (1992) 14 EHRR 1.

[135] *Vilvarajah and others* v. *United Kingdom*, Judgment of 30 October 1991, Series A, No. 215; (1993) 14 EHRR 248.

Government to deport five Sri Lankan asylum seekers. The Court reaffirmed its decision in the *Cruz Varas* case that expulsion of an asylum seeker may give rise to an issue under Article 3, where substantial grounds have been shown for believing that the person concerned faced a real risk of being subject to torture or inhuman and degrading treatment in the country of destination. The Court also confirmed its statements in *Cruz Varas* of the principles relevant to the assessment of the risk of ill-treatment. First, the Court will assess the matter in the light of all the material put before it, or obtained at the request of the Court. Secondly, the existence of the risk must be assessed primarily with reference to those facts which were known or ought to have been known by the Contracting Party at the time of the expulsion, though subsequent information which comes to light may be relevant in giving weight to the appreciation of the circumstances by the Contracting Party. Thirdly, the ill-treatment must attain a minimum level of severity if it is to fall within the scope of Article 3, and the assessment of this minimum will depend on all the circumstances of the case.[136]

Applying these principles to the particular circumstances of the applicants' cases led the Court to conclude that there had been no violation of Article 3.

The important *Chahal* case[137] has already been considered. The Court indicated that considerations of national security had no application where violations of Article 3 were in issue. The Court also indicated that the point of time for the assessment of the risk is the date of the Court's consideration of the case, and not the date when the national authorities made the decision to deport. The Court requires a high level of proof of risk in cases which are less clear-cut than the circumstances of the *Soering* case. In the *Chahal* case, a multitude of evidence was submitted. It is suggested that the Court is more likely to be persuaded by a report from a reputable, objective source rather than multiple affidavits from individuals and organizations who may be partisan in the matter. The Court concluded that the deportation of a Sikh separatist might well expose him to serious risk of treatment falling foul of Article 3 by rogue elements in the Punjab Police.[138]

In *Jabari v. Turkey*[139] the Court considered that the deportation to Iran of a woman, who had been found to have had an adulterous relationship in that country in respect of which criminal proceedings had been instituted, would violate Article 3 because she would be at serious risk of punishment by stoning there.

[136] Para. 107 of judgment.
[137] *Chahal* v. *United Kingdom* (App. 22414/93), Judgment of 15 November 1996; (1997) 23 EHRR 413.
[138] See also *Ahmed* v. *Austria* (App. 25964/94), Judgment of 17 December 1996; (1997) 24 EHRR 278; *HLR* v. *France* (App. 24573/94), Judgment of 29 April 1997; (1998) 26 EHRR 29; and *D* v. *United Kingdom* (App. 30240/96), Judgment of 2 May 1997; (1997) 24 EHRR 423 discussed earlier in this chapter.
[139] *Jabari* v. *Turkey* (App. 40035/98), Judgment of 11 July 2000.

CORPORAL PUNISHMENT

The issue of corporal punishment as degrading treatment under Article 3 has been considered by the Court in a number of cases. The *Tyrer* case[140] concerned the imposition of the penalty of birching in the Isle of Man on a 15-year-old who had been convicted of assault on a senior pupil at his school. The punishment was administered by a police constable in private in the presence of the boy's father and a doctor. In concluding that the punishment of Tyrer constituted degrading treatment, the Court had regard to its character as 'institutionalized violence', to the fact that the punishment constituted an assault on the applicant's dignity and physical integrity, which may have had adverse psychological effects, and to the anguish of anticipating the punishment.[141]

The *Campbell and Cosans* case[142] concerned the use of corporal punishment in schools. In one case, the parent was unable to obtain a guarantee that her son would not be subject to corporal punishment, and in the other the son, on his father's advice, presented himself for punishment but refused to accept it and was immediately suspended from school until such time as he was willing to accept the punishment. The form of corporal punishment in issue was the striking of the hand with a leather strap known as a 'tawse'. The Commission concluded that there was no violation of Article 3 in these cases. The Court noted that neither child had been subjected to corporal punishment. Nevertheless, 'provided it is sufficiently real and immediate, a mere threat of conduct prohibited by Article 3 may itself be in conflict with the provision.'[143] The Court, however, concluded that the suffering resulting from the treatment of the two boys did not meet the level inherent in the notion of degrading treatment as explained in the *Ireland* v. *United Kingdom* judgment.[144] The Court went on to consider whether other provisions of the Convention had been violated.[145]

In another case,[146] a friendly settlement followed the Commission's decision on admissibility and its opinion that the caning of a 15-year-old boy violated Article 3. But in the *Costello-Roberts* case[147] the Court ruled that the striking of a 7-year-old boy's clothed buttocks with a rubber-soled gym shoe as an automatic punishment for accumulating five demerit points at his boarding

---

[140] *Tyrer* v. *United Kingdom*, Judgment of 25 April 1978, Series A, No. 26; (1979–80) 2 EHRR 1.
[141] Para. 33 of judgment.
[142] *Campbell and Cosans* v. *United Kingdom*, Judgment of 25 February 1982, Series A, No. 48; (1982) 4 EHRR 293.
[143] Para. 26 of judgment.
[144] See above.
[145] See below, ch. 16.
[146] *Y* v. *United Kingdom*, Judgment of 29 October 1992, Series A, No. 247-A; (1994) 17 EHRR 238. See also App. 9471/81, *Warwick* v. *United Kingdom*, 18 July 1986 (1986) 60 DR 5.
[147] *Costello-Roberts* v. *United Kingdom*, Judgment of 25 March 1993, Series A, No. 247-C.

school had no severe long-lasting effects and did not reach the level of severity necessary to bring the matter within Article 3. The Court did, however, have some misgivings about the automatic nature of the punishment and the delay of three days between the accumulation of the demerit points and the imposition of the penalty.

As in other cases, a careful judgment needs to be applied to the particular circumstances of each case. Corporal punishments which have a long-lasting effect and reach the threshold of severity required will violate Article 3, whether imposed in a public or a private school.

The United Kingdom has responded to these judgments by passing legislation to prohibit corporal punishment in schools.

A v. United Kingdom[148] concerned the stepfather of a boy born in 1984, who in 1993 beat the boy with a garden cane using considerable force. The step-father was prosecuted for assault occasioning actual bodily harm, but a jury acquitted him, apparently not accepting that the prosecution had proved that the beatings were other than for 'lawful correction' which was a defence in English law. The Court concluded that the circumstances of this case meant that the applicant was not protected against treatment or punishment contrary to Article 3 by the United Kingdom, and consequently there was a violation of Article 3.

EUROPEAN CONVENTION FOR THE PREVENTION OF TORTURE

The European Convention for the Prevention of Torture and Inhuman and Degrading Treatment[149] came into force in February 1989. The Convention creates a surveillance mechanism in the form of a Committee which may make visits to any establishment in the territory of the Contracting Parties where persons are deprived of their liberty by a public authority. It aims at the prevention of torture rather than its repression and arises, according to the Preamble, from a conviction that,

the protection of persons deprived of their liberty against torture and inhuman and degrading treatment or punishment could be strengthened by non-judicial means of a preventive character based on visits.

---

[148] *A v. United Kingdom* (App. 25599/94), Judgment of 23 September 1998; (1999) 27 EHRR 611.

[149] European Treaty Series, No. 126. For a commentary, see M. Evans and R. Morgan, *Preventing Torture. A Study of the European Convention for the Prevention of Torture and Inhuman or Degrading Treatment* (Oxford, 1998); A. Cassese, 'A New Approach to Human Rights: The European Convention for the Prevention of Torture' (1989) 83 AJIL 128.

Examination of the *travaux préparatoires* reveals that there was considerable concern about possible conflicts between the work of the Committee for the Prevention of Torture and the Commission and Court of Human Rights.[150] Happily this has not materialized, although there have been occasions where decisions of the Commission have taken the Committee by surprise.[151]

The existence of surveillance is designed to ensure that standards of treatment meet established human rights standards. The Committee has no judicial functions, but reports its findings and makes recommendations to the State concerned. These reports are confidential. They will remain unpublished unless the State requests their publication or the Committee by a two-thirds majority decides to make a public statement on a matter in the face of a State's failure to cooperate or refusal to make changes in the light of the Committee's recommendations. The Committee submits to the Committee of Ministers each year an overview report of its activities.

The norm has very much become for publication of the reports.[152] There is a growing tendency for the Court to refer to reports by the Committee in its decision-making. So in the *Aerts* case,[153] the Commission and the Court took note of the findings of the Committee in examining the conditions of detention in a particular psychiatric hospital. In a number of other cases, the Court has noted the conclusions of a report by the Committee, and has been influenced by those findings both in coming to its own conclusions on the facts and in giving content to the requirements of Article 3.[154]

---

[150]   Evans and Morgan, n.149 above.

[151]   e.g., the decision of the Commission (subsequently reversed by the Court) that airport holding centres for aliens were not places of detention for the purposes of Article 5 ECHR in App. 19776/92, *Amuur* v. *France*, 10 January 1995, reversed by the Court, Judgment of 25 June 1996; (1996) 22 EHRR 533; see Evans and Morgan, n.149 above, 371–4.

[152]   Evans and Morgan, n.149 above, 198–203 and 339–41. For surveys of current activities under the Convention for the Prevention of Torture, see, in addition to the Committee's own reports, J. Murdoch, 'The European Convention for the Prevention of Torture and Inhuman or Degrading Treatment or Punishment: Activities in 2000'; (2001) 26 E.L. Rev. HR395.

[153]   *Aerts* v. *Belgium* (App. 25357/94), Judgment of 30 July 1998; (2000) 29 EHRR 50, para. 72 of the Commission's Report, and paras. 29–30, 42, and 62–5 of the judgment.

[154]   See e.g. *Aksoy* v. *Turkey* (App. 21987/93), Judgment of 18 December 1996; (1997) 23 EHRR 553, para. 46 of the judgment; *Aydin* v. *Turkey* (App. 23178/94), Judgment of 25 September 1997; (1998) 25 EHRR 251, paras. 49–50 of the judgment; *Dougoz* v. *Greece* (App. 40907/98), Judgment of 6 March 2001, paras. 40–1 and 46 of the judgment; and *Peers* v. *Greece* (App. 28524/95), Judgment of 19 April 2001; (2001) 33 EHRR 1192, paras. 61, and 70–2 of the judgment.

CONCLUSION

Perhaps in this area more than any other,[155] the treatment of the Convention as a living instrument has shown how wide a range of situations can potentially fall within the prohibitions in Article 3. Equally, there is a tendency on the part of applicants to attach an allegation of a violation of Article 3 to their applications in order to add weight to the complaint. Many are, unsurprisingly, held to be manifestly ill-founded. In some areas, the development of standard minimum rules would provide the means by which standards of treatment could be assessed, particularly for prisoners. Developments such as the reporting mechanisms of the European Convention on the Prevention of Torture provide a useful non-judicial system of review which supplements the provisions of Article 3, and reports under that Convention regime are increasingly providing evidence upon which the Court relies in its determination of applications complaining of torture, or inhuman or degrading treatment.

[155] But see also discussion of Article 8 in ch. 11 below.

6

PROTECTION FROM SLAVERY AND FORCED LABOUR

INTRODUCTION

Article 4 provides:

1. No one shall be held in slavery or servitude.
2. No one shall be required to perform forced or compulsory labour.
3. For the purposes of this Article the term 'forced or compulsory labour' shall not include:

    (a) any work required to be done in the ordinary course of detention imposed according to the provisions of Article 5 of this Convention or during conditional release from such detention;

    (b) any service of a military character or, in the case of conscientious objectors in countries where they are recognised, service exacted instead of compulsory military service;

    (c) any service exacted in case of an emergency or calamity threatening the life or well-being of the community;

    (d) any work or service which forms part of normal civic obligations.

Article 4(1) prohibits slavery and servitude; the wording shows that these are conceived of as questions of status. Article 4(2), by contrast, prohibits forced or compulsory labour, and is intended to protect persons who are at liberty. Slavery and servitude are continuing states, whereas forced labour may arise incidentally or on a temporary basis. The prohibitions of slavery and servitude are absolute (and outside any derogation under Article 15), but the prohibition of forced or compulsory labour is subject to the exemption for those forms of work or service expressly permitted under Article 4(3).

The exceptions in Article 4(3)(a) and (b) are genuine exceptions, while the matters listed in Article 4(3)(c) and (d) are rather examples of obligations which cannot be said to fall within the definition of forced or compulsory labour.

The infrequency with which the Court has had to deal with this article justifies closer consideration of the decisions and reports of the Commission on the scope and application of Article 4 than is found in considering other articles of the Convention.

SLAVERY OR SERVITUDE

The prohibition of slavery and servitude is governed by numerous international treaties and there is now wide recognition that both are prohibited under customary international law.[1] The distinction between slavery and servitude is one of degree.[2] Slavery connotes being wholly in the legal ownership of another person, while servitude is more limited though still connoting conditions of work or service wholly outside the control of the individual. The Commission's Report in the *Van Droogenbroeck* case[3] said that 'in addition to the obligation to provide another with certain services, the concept of servitude includes the obligation on the part of the "serf" to live on another's property and the impossibility of changing his condition.'

Happily there have been few applications alleging violations of Article 4(1) of the Convention. In *Cyprus* v. *Turkey*[4] it was argued that if any of the missing Greek Cypriots were still in Turkish custody, this would amount to a form of servitude. Both the Commission and the Court gave short shrift to this argument, refusing to speculate on the fate or whereabouts of the missing persons.[5]

FORCED OR COMPULSORY LABOUR

Article 4(2) provides that no one shall be required to perform forced or compulsory labour, but Article 4(3) provides for certain exceptions. The Court has said:

---

[1] See Article 4 of the Universal Declaration of Human Rights, and P. Sieghart, *The International Law of Human Rights* (Oxford, 1983), at 54–5. See also M. Whiteman, *Digest of International Law* (Washington, 1968), vol. 11, at 866–7.

[2] None of the major human rights instruments defines slavery and servitude. A definition of slavery can be found in Article 1 of the Slavery Convention of 1926, while servitude is defined in Article 7 of the Supplementary Convention on the Abolition of Slavery, the Slave Trade, and Institutions and Practices Similar to Slavery of 1956.

[3] *Van Droogenbroeck*, Report of 9 July 1980, Series B, No. 44.

[4] *Cyprus* v. *Turkey* (App. 25781/94), Judgment of 10 May 2001.

[5] Paras. 137–41 of the judgment.

The Court reiterates that paragraph 3 of Article 4 is not intended to 'limit' the exercise of the right guaranteed by paragraph 2, but to 'delimit' the very content of that right, for it forms a whole with paragraph 2 and indicates what 'the term "forced or compulsory labour" shall not include' (*ce qui 'n'est pas consideré comme "travail forcé ou obligatoire"'*). This being so, paragraph 3 serves as an aid to the interpretation of paragraph 2. The four sub-paragraphs of paragraph 3, notwithstanding their diversity, are grounded on the governing ideas of the general interest, social solidarity and what is normal in the ordinary course of affairs.[6]

The expression 'forced or compulsory labour' is taken over from a Convention of the International Labour Organisation, Convention No. 29 of 1930, subsequently supplemented by another ILO Convention, the Abolition of Forced Labour Convention of 1957. It seems reasonable to rely, for the interpretation of Article 4, on the work of the ILO organs in defining the term for the purposes of the ILO Conventions, and the Commission has in fact done so. The Commission has imported two key elements into the concept of forced or compulsory labour. First, the work must be performed by the worker involuntarily. Secondly, the requirement to do the work must be unjust or oppressive or the work itself involves avoidable hardship.[7]

The issue was first examined by the Commission in the *Iversen* case.[8] A law passed in Norway in 1956 provided that dentists might be required for a period of up to two years to take a position in public dental service. Some members of the Opposition had objected to the Bill on the ground that it introduced a compulsory direction of labour which was contrary to the Norwegian Constitution and to Article 4 of the Convention. The Government, however, rejected these arguments and maintained that this direction of labour was necessary to implement a public dental service. The applicant, Iversen, was directed under the Act to take up for one year the position of dentist in the Moskenes district in northern Norway. He eventually accepted the post, but after some months he gave it up and left. He was subsequently convicted and sentenced under the Act, and his appeal was dismissed by the Supreme Court.

In his application to the Commission, he alleged that the Act, and the order assigning him to the district of Moskenes, were contrary to Article 4 of the Convention. Exceptionally, the Commission's decision on admissibility records a divided vote: it held by a majority of six votes to four that the application was inadmissible. The majority considered that the service of Iversen in Moskenes was not forced or compulsory labour within the meaning of Article 4 of the Convention. However, the majority was itself divided; four members of the

---

[6] *Schmidt* v. *Germany*, Judgment of 18 July 1994, Series A, No 291-B; (1994) 18 EHRR 513, para. 22 of the judgment.

[7] See App. 4653/70, *X* v. *Federal Republic of Germany*, 1 April 1974 (1974), 17 *Yearbook* 148; App. 8410/78, *X* v. *Federal Republic of Germany*, 13 December 1979, (1980) 18 DR 216; and App. 9322/81, *X* v. *Netherlands*, 3 May 1983, (1983) 32 DR 180.

[8] App. 1468/62, *Iversen* v. *Norway*, 17 December 1963, (1963) 6 *Yearbook* 278.

majority considered that the service of Iversen in Moskenes was manifestly not forced or compulsory labour under Article 4(2), and therefore found it unnecessary to express any opinion on the applicability of Article 4(3), while the other two members of the majority considered that that service was reasonably required of him in an emergency threatening the well-being of the community and was therefore authorized under Article 4(3).

The concept of forced or compulsory labour was analysed by the four members of the majority as follows:

The concept cannot be understood solely in terms of the literal meaning of the words, and has in fact come to be regarded in international law and practice, as evidenced in part by the provisions and application of ILO Conventions and Resolutions on Forced Labour, as having certain elements . . . [namely] that the work or service is performed by the worker against his will and, secondly, that the requirement that the work or service be performed is unjust or oppressive or the work or service itself involves avoidable hardship.[9]

On this analysis the service required of Iversen was held not to be forced or compulsory labour under Article 4(2); the requirement to perform that service was not unjust or oppressive since the service, although obligatory, 'was for a short period, provided favourable remuneration, did not involve any diversion from chosen professional work, was only applied in the case of posts not filled after being duly advertised, and did not involve any discriminatory, arbitrary, or punitive application.'

However, even if the element of oppressiveness could be said to be absent in this case, it is doubtful how far it is a necessary constituent of forced labour as generally understood in international law and practice. The forced labour Convention of 1930 in fact defines the term 'forced or compulsory labour', for the purposes of that Convention, simply as 'all work or service which is exacted from any person under the menace of a penalty and for which the said person has not offered himself voluntarily'[10]; but that Convention did not prohibit such work or service if it forms part of normal civic obligations in a self-governing country, or is exacted in execution of a penal sentence, or exacted in an 'emergency requiring the mobilization of manpower for essential work of national importance'.

Article 4(3) of the European Convention, as seen above, contains similar provisions.

In the Iversen case, as already stated, the reasoning of the other two members of the Commission who voted for inadmissibility was based on Article 4(3); they held that the service of Iversen was service reasonably required of him in

[9] At 328.
[10] Art. 2(1). See Van der Mussele v. Belgium, Judgment of 23 November 1983, Series A, No. 70; (1984) 6 EHRR 163, paras. 32–3 of the judgment.

an emergency threatening the well-being of the community. The Norwegian Government had made no substantial submissions on this point but as part of the general background of the case had explained that the northern districts of Norway had a deplorable lack of social services, which seriously affected the social and health conditions of these communities; thus, while there was in Oslo in 1946 one dentist per 650 inhabitants, the ratio in three of the northern provinces was one dentist per 13,000, 6,000, and 5,500 inhabitants respectively. Moreover, adequate dental care was rendered even more difficult by the enormous distances, the difficulties of communication, and the arctic weather conditions prevailing during the winter months.

While these considerations may have made it difficult for the Norwegian authorities to find any alternative practical solution to the problem, it is by no means clear that they are relevant to the provisions of Article 4, which, unlike many of the later Articles, contains no escape clause 'for the protection of health'. The opinion of the two members of the Commission referred to above is open to criticism; for it seems doubtful whether the situation in northern Norway could be described as an 'emergency' or 'calamity' as required by Article 4(3)(c). These terms suggest some sudden overwhelming natural disaster, not the permanent social, climatic, and geographical conditions however serious they may be.

The minority of the Commission was rightly of the opinion that the application was not manifestly ill-founded, and that it should be declared admissible. The minority found that the conditions under which Iversen was required to perform his work, although it was paid and was only for a limited time, did not exclude the possibility of it being forced or compulsory labour, since it was imposed subject to penal sanctions; and that the question of the applicability of Article 4(3)(c) of the Convention required further examination.

It is hard to escape the conclusion that the Commission's decision to reject the application was influenced by political considerations. The case had caused considerable controversy in Norway and the decision coincided with a decision of the Norwegian Government to renew its declaration accepting the Commission's competence under Article 25 for a period of only one year.[11]

In the *Talmon* case,[12] the applicant complained that a requirement that he look for and accept employment deemed suitable for him as a condition of entitlement to unemployment benefit amounted to a requirement that he undertake forced or compulsory labour. He claimed that the only suitable employment for himself was work as an 'independent scientist and social critic'. The Commission declared the application manifestly ill-founded since it did

---

[11] (1963) 6 *Yearbook* 26. See also H.G. Schermers, 'European Commission of Human Rights: The Norwegian Dentist Case on Compulsory Labour' [1964] *Nederlands Tijdschrift voor International Recht* 366.
[12] App. 30300/96, *Talmon v. Netherlands*, 26 February 1997; [1997] EHRLR 448.

not raise any issues under Article 4. Though this is an unremarkable case, the question may be posed as to the severity of the sanction for non-performance before something becomes compulsory or forced labour.

PRISON LABOUR

Article 4(3)(a) excludes from the term 'forced or compulsory labour' 'any work required to be done in the ordinary course of detention imposed according to the provisions of Article 5 of this Convention or during conditional release from such detention'.

In a group of applications[13] from persons detained in various prisons in Germany, the Commission examined the scope of this provision. The applicants complained that during their detention in prison they were subjected to forced and compulsory labour without receiving adequate payment and without being insured under the social security laws.

The Commission has regularly rejected applications by prisoners claiming higher payment for their work or claiming the right to be covered by social security systems.[14] The present applicants, however, raised a new point in complaining also that part of the work required of them during their detention was performed on behalf of private firms under contracts concluded with the prison administration; this system, they alleged, constituted a state of slavery for the prisoners concerned. The Commission examined this complaint primarily, however, under Article 4(3)(a), that is, in relation to forced or compulsory labour. After an exceptionally detailed investigation of the background of this provision, and a survey of the practice in the Member States of the Council of Europe, the Commission found that the form of prison labour of which the applicants complained clearly appeared to fall within the framework of work normally required from prisoners within the meaning of Article 4(3)(a).

It may be thought that the exemption under Article 4(3)(a) of 'work required to be done in the ordinary course of detention imposed according to the provisions of Article 5' can arise only if all the provisions of Article 5 have been observed. In the *Vagrancy Cases*[15] the Commission had expressed the view that the work that the applicants were required to do was not justified under Article 4 because there had been a breach of Article 5(4). The Court, however, held that

---

[13] Apps. 3134/67, 3172/67 and 3188–3206/67, *Twenty-one Detained Persons* v. *Federal Republic of Germany*, 6 April 1968, (1968) 11 *Yearbook* 528.

[14] At 552 and the cases cited there.

[15] *De Wilde, Ooms and Versyp* v. *Belgium*, Judgment of 18 June 1971, Series A, No. 12; (1979–80) 1 EHRR 373. See ch. 7.

while there was a breach of Article 5(4), there was no breach of Article 4 because the vagrants were lawfully detained under Article 5(1)(e).[16]

This is a perplexing decision since Article 5 must be read as a whole, and it would seem that any breach of paragraphs (1) to (4) would render the arrest or detention unlawful. It is not sufficient to say that the detention is justified under one provision of the Convention if it is unlawful under another provision. Nor does Article 4(3)(a) itself differentiate between the provisions of Article 5. On this point, therefore, the view of the Commission is to be preferred to that of the Court.

MILITARY SERVICE

Article 4(3)(b) excludes 'any service of a military character' from the prohibition of forced or compulsory labour.

In the 'Sailor Boys' case[17] four applicants aged 15 and 16 had joined the British army or naval forces for a period of nine years to be calculated from the age of 18. They had subsequently applied for discharge from the service but, in spite of repeated requests, discharge had been refused. They alleged, inter alia, a violation of their right under Article 4(1) not to be held in servitude.

The Commission also considered the case under Article 4(2) but found that any complaint that the applicants' service constituted 'forced or compulsory labour' must be rejected as being manifestly ill-founded in view of the express provision of Article 4(3)(b). That provision, according to the Commission, wholly excluded voluntary military service from the scope of Article 4(2); and, by the omission of the word 'compulsory' which appeared in the ILO Convention, 'it was intended to cover also the obligation to continue a service entered into on a voluntary basis.'[18]

The United Kingdom Government submitted that the exclusion of military service in Article 4(3)(b) was to be understood as applying equally to slavery and servitude in paragraph (1). Any argument to the contrary necessarily involved the anomalous conclusion that although no service of a military character can be, under the Convention, forced or compulsory labour, military service may amount to the more oppressive condition of slavery or servitude. The applicants, however, rightly pointed out that the drafters of the article clearly intended that there should be an absolute prohibition against servitude or slavery, but only a qualified prohibition against forced or compulsory labour.

[16] Para. 89 of judgment.
[17] App. 3435–3438/67, *W, X, Y, and Z* v. *United Kingdom*, 19 July 1968, (1968) 11 *Yearbook* 562.
[18] At 594.

The Commission found that generally the duty of soldiers who enlist after the age of majority to observe the terms of their engagement, and the ensuing restriction of their freedom and personal rights, do not amount to an impairment of rights which could come under the terms 'slavery or servitude'; and that the young age at which the applicants entered the services could not in itself attribute the character of 'servitude' to the normal condition of a soldier.

With regard to the young age of enlistment, the applicants referred to the special protection of minors provided for in all legal systems in respect of 'their own possibly unconsidered engagements'. The Commission pointed out that the applicants' parents had given their consent and that 'the protection of minors in other fields of law consists exactly in the requirement of parental consent and also in the existence of the principle that an engagement entered into by the minor will be void without such consent but valid and binding if the consent has been duly given.' The Commission did not, however, refer to another element in the protection of minors, frequently found in domestic legal systems, which enables minors, in certain circumstances, to decide for themselves on reaching the age of majority whether to continue or to repudiate their undertaking.

The applications were thus finally rejected as inadmissible but subsequently revised Navy Service Regulations were introduced in the United Kingdom under which boy entrants could decide at the age of 18 to leave the navy after three years' adult service, that is, at the age of 21.

In addition to military service, Article 4(3)(b) also authorizes service required to be performed by conscientious objectors in lieu of compulsory military service.[19]

EMERGENCIES

Article 4(3)(c) takes outside the prohibition in Article 4(2) service exacted in case of an emergency or calamity threatening the life or well-being of the community. As noted above, in the *Iversen* case, some members of the Commission felt that this would encompass a shortage of dentists in remote parts of Norway. The better view is that it involves the work needed to deal with an acute and temporary emergency. Examples might be tackling a forest fire, or assisting in the evacuation of those threatened by some natural disaster. In requiring any service under this provision, the authorities would, of course, be

---

[19] Questions raised by this provision are discussed in ch. 12 in relation to App. 2299/64, *Grandrath* v. *Federal Republic of Germany*, Report of Commission, 12 December 1966; Decision of Committee of Ministers, 29 June 1967, (1967) 10 *Yearbook* 626.

required to have regard to a person's capacity for the work involved. In the absence of this exception, Contracting States would need to invoke Article 15 before the people could be required to assist in an emergency; the requirements of Article 15 are more strictly drawn than those set out in Article 4(3)(c). Nevertheless, the threshold for using the provision in Article 4(3)(c) does seem to be significant.

CIVIC OBLIGATIONS

Article 4(3)(d) authorizes 'any work which forms part of normal civic obligations'. This differs from the service encompassed within Article 4(3)(c) in that there need be no emergency. The test is one of normality in the sense of what might reasonably be expected of a particular individual in a particular situation. The distinction will usually be one of degree, but quite where the boundary is remains to be established. In one case[20] the Commission concluded that the obligation of the holder of shooting rights in a hunting district to take part in the gassing of fox holes could be justified either under paragraph (c) or (d).

The question has been raised whether the Austrian system of legal aid was compatible with Article 4 of the Convention.[21]

The applicant, a lawyer practising in Vienna, complained that he was compelled, contrary to Article 4, to act as unpaid defence counsel for a person who lacked the means to pay counsel's fees. Under the legal aid system, a lawyer was required to offer his services and was subject to disciplinary sanctions if he refused to do so. He was paid no fee and was reimbursed for practically none of his expenses. In return for these services, the Government paid annually to the Bar Association a fixed lump sum which was used for charitable purposes, especially for old-age pensions for lawyers no longer in practice; but there was no legal right to such benefits.

In the proceedings on admissibility, the Government submitted, *inter alia*, that lawyers, by voluntarily choosing their profession, accepts the obligation to act under the legal aid system, and that consequently this was not compulsory labour, but a consequence of their own free decision. Further, even if it did constitute compulsory labour it formed part of normal civic obligations under Article 4(3)(d). The applicant replied that the obligation was limited to the legal

---

[20] App. 9686/82, *S v. Federal Republic of Germany*, 4 October 1984 (1985) 39 DR 90.
[21] App. 4897/71, *Gussenbauer* v. *Austria*, 22 March 1972, (1973) 42 CD 41 and App. 5219/71, *Gussenbauer* v. *Austria*, 14 July 1972, (1973) 42 CD 94. See also App. 4653/70, *X* v. *Federal Republic of Germany*, 1 April 1974, (1974) 17 *Yearbook* 148.

profession, and within that profession applied only to counsel; consequently it could not be regarded as part of normal civic obligations. The Commission declared the application admissible, but there was subsequently a friendly settlement.

It would seem that the interpretation of 'normal' civic obligations requires a comparison with the practice in comparable professions in other Contracting Parties. Article 4(3)(d) contains the clearest invitation in the Convention to consider current practice as a standard of interpretation.

The issue of the normal incidents of professional work in the context of the free representation of indigents was considered by the Court in the *Van der Mussele* case.[22] The requirement in issue was that of Belgian law under which pupil barristers were required to represent indigent defendants without a fee or reimbursement of expenses. Failure to undertake this work could result in a refusal to admit the person to the Belgian Bar. The Court did not accept at face value the Commission's conclusion that the applicant had consented in advance to the situation. The Court's decision makes clear that the second requirement of forced or compulsory labour, namely that the character of the work to be performed must be unjust or oppressive, is very much a subsidiary criterion. The Court's approach is to have regard to all the circumstances of the case in the light of the purpose of Article 4. Having regard to the nature of the work which fell within the normal ambit of the work of an advocate, to the advantage to the pupil barrister of undertaking this work as part of professional training, and to the fact that the burden was not disproportionate, the Court concluded that there was no compulsory labour in this case for the purposes of Article 4(2) and so it did not need to consider whether the representation of indigents was a normal civic obligation for pupil barristers falling within Article 4(3)(d). The absence of any fee or reimbursement of expenses was regretted by the Court, but did not alone render the work forced or compulsory labour.

Schmidt v. *Germany*[23] concerned an application that a requirement in Germany that a person serve as a fireman or pay a fire service levy in lieu of service was discriminatory in that it applied to men but not to women, taking Article 4 together with Article 14.[24] Where the applicant lived, there was no shortage of volunteer firemen, and so the requirement was to pay the fire service levy. The court considered that compulsory fire service constituted normal civic obligations within the meaning in Article 4(3)(d), and that the compensatory charge was so closely linked to compulsory fire service that it also fell within Article 4. The court then went on to consider the issue of discrimination raised by the applicant.[25]

[22] *Van der Mussele* v. *Belgium*, Judgment of 23 November 1983, Series A, No. 70; (1984) 6 EHRR 163.
[23] *Schmidt* v. *Germany*, Judgment of 18 July 1994, Series A, No 291-B; (1994) 18 EHRR 513.
[24] See ch. 19 below on Art. 14.
[25] See ch. 19 below.

CONSENT

It seems clear that consent cannot make slavery or servitude which would otherwise be prohibited under Article 4(1) lawful. In the 'Sailor Boys' case[26] the United Kingdom Government argued that an essential feature of servitude is that it has been forced upon a person against his will, in circumstances where he has no genuine freedom of choice.[27] However, Article 4(1) should be construed as prohibiting also the voluntary acceptance of servitude. 'Personal liberty is an inalienable right which a person cannot voluntarily abandon.'[28] Indeed, a proposal to add the qualification 'involuntary' to servitude was rejected by the drafters of the Supplementary Convention on Slavery 1956 and of the United Nations Covenant on Civil and Political Rights precisely on the ground that 'It should not be possible for any person to contract himself into bondage.'[29] This interpretation is further supported by the judgment of the Court in the *Vagrancy* cases.[30]

However, it is less clear, in view of the terms 'forced' and 'compulsory', whether a voluntary undertaking would exclude the applicability of Article 4(2). It has already been seen that one of the elements of work which is prohibited is its performance by workers against their will; but the question remains whether a person who has voluntarily accepted an obligation can be compelled to continue in circumstances which, objectively viewed, would constitute forced or compulsory labour. The question raised is that of the severity of the sanction before the activity could be said to be compulsory or forced.

In the *Iversen* case the Norwegian Government contended that the applicant had freely accepted the conditions of service, that he knew of the effect of the Norwegian legislation and voluntarily entered into an agreement with the competent authorities, and in particular that by his conversations with officials in the Ministry for Social Affairs and his consent to being posted in Moskenes, the relationship between the applicant and the Ministry had assumed a contractual nature which excluded any application of Article 4 of the Convention.[31] The Commission, however, did not refer to this aspect of the case in its decision.

In the 'Sailor Boys' case, however, the Commission appeared to attach great importance to the fact that not only the applicants but also their parents

---

[26] App. 3435–3438/67, *W, X, Y, and Z* v. *United Kingdom*, 19 July 1968, (1968) 11 *Yearbook* 562.
[27] At 576.
[28] Report of the Commission in the *Vagrancy Cases*, 19 July 1969, Series B, No. 10, at 91.
[29] UN Doc. A/2929, at 33.
[30] *De Wilde, Ooms and Versyp* v. *Belgium*, Judgment of 18 June 1971, Series A, No. 12; (1979–80) 1 EHRR 373. See ch. 7.
[31] App. 1468/62, *Iversen* v. *Norway*, 17 December 1963, (1963) 6 *Yearbook* 278, at 308.

had initially given their consent. This view, again, may be open to doubt in view of the Court's judgment in the *Vagrancy* cases and the issues of principle underlying that judgment, which were not fully apparent in the Commission's reasoning.

7

PERSONAL LIBERTY AND SECURITY

INTRODUCTION

The object of Article 5 is to guarantee liberty of the person, and in particular to provide guarantees against arbitrary arrest or detention. It seeks to achieve this aim by excluding any form of arrest or detention without lawful authority and proper judicial control; by spelling out in detail, in paragraph (1), the only conditions under which a person may be deprived of his liberty; and by providing, in paragraphs (2) to (5), certain rights for persons who have been detained. Derogations from the obligations in Article 5 are permitted.[1]

Article 5 provides:

(1) Everyone has the right to liberty and security of person. No one shall be deprived of his liberty save in the following cases and in accordance with a procedure prescribed by law:

  (a) the lawful detention of person after conviction by a competent court;
  (b) the lawful arrest or detention of a person for non-compliance with the lawful order of a court or in order to secure the fulfilment of any obligation prescribed by law;
  (c) the lawful arrest or detention of a person effected for the purpose of bringing him before the competent legal authority on reasonable suspicion of having committed an offence or when it is reasonably considered necessary to prevent his committing an offence or fleeing after having done so;
  (d) the detention of a minor by lawful order for the purpose of educational supervision or his lawful detention for the purpose of bringing him before the competent legal authority;
  (e) the lawful detention of persons for the prevention of the spreading of infectious diseases, of persons of unsound mind, alcoholics or drug addicts or vagrants;
  (f) the lawful arrest or detention of a person to prevent his effecting an unauthorised entry into the country or of a person against whom action is being taken with a view to deportation or extradition.

---

[1] See ch. 21 below.

(2) Everyone who is arrested shall be informed promptly, in a language which he understands, of the reasons for his arrest and of any charge against him.

(3) Everyone arrested or detained in accordance with the provisions of paragraph (1)(c) of this article shall be brought promptly before a judge or other officer authorised by law to exercise judicial power and shall be entitled to trial within a reasonable time or to release pending trial. Release may be conditioned by guarantees to appear for trial.

(4) Everyone who is deprived of his liberty by arrest or detention shall be entitled to take proceedings by which the lawfulness of his detention shall be decided speedily by a court and his release ordered if the detention is not lawful.

(5) Everyone who has been the victim of arrest or detention in contravention of the provisions of this article shall have an enforceable right to compensation.

WHAT AMOUNTS TO A DEPRIVATION OF LIBERTY?

The Article opens by stating the general principle that 'Everyone has the right to liberty and security of person.'[2] The meaning of 'security' in this context is uncertain; the question was raised, but not resolved, in the *East African Asians* cases.[3] On the normal principles of interpretation, the term 'security' should be given a meaning independent of 'liberty', but the remainder of the Article is concerned exclusively with deprivation of liberty. The matter appears to have been finally resolved in the *Bozano* case,[4] where the Court's reasoning indicated that the primary focus of Article 5 is the deprivation of liberty.[5] In cases involving the disappearance of prisoners, however, the Court has made greater use of the terminology of 'security of person', because of uncertainty as to the continuing detention of the disappeared person and the suspicion that he or she may have been executed.[6]

It is important, therefore, to understand what 'deprivation of liberty' means in this context. It is clear that confinement to a locked prison cell constitutes such a deprivation, but less absolute forms of restriction can be more problematic. One of the optional protocols to the Convention, Article 2 of Protocol No. 4, protects the right to leave a country and to move freely within one,[7] so it has been necessary for the Court to draw a line between deprivations of liberty

---

[2] The French text reads, 'Toute personne a droit à la liberté et à la sûreté'.

[3] App. 4626/70, *East African Asians* v. *United Kingdom*, 6 March 1978, (1978) 13 DR 5.

[4] *Bozano* v. *France*, Judgment of 18 December 1986, Series A, No. 111; (1987) 9 EHRR 297.

[5] See especially para. 54 of the judgment.

[6] See e.g., *Timurtas* v. *Turkey* (App. 23531/94), Judgment of 13 June 2000; (2001) 33 EHRR 121, and ch. 4 above.

[7] See ch. 18 below.

within the meaning of Article 5, and restrictions on freedom of movement. As the case law shows, this distinction is more a matter of degree and intensity than of nature or substance.[8] In deciding whether a restriction on freedom falls within the scope of Article 5, the Court will look at such factors as the type, duration, effects, and manner of implementation of the measure in question.

Guzzardi v. *Italy*[9] is a good example of a borderline case. The applicant was ordered, on suspicion of being a member of the Mafia, to remain on a small island near Sardinia for sixteen months. Although there was no perimeter fence, he was not allowed to leave an area of two and a half square kilometres containing a village inhabited solely by other men subject to the same type of residence order, and he had to keep a curfew and report to the police twice a day. His wife and child were not prevented from living with him, but the available accommodation was cramped and dilapidated and thus unsuitable for a family. Although he was allowed to work, there were very few employers on the island and he was unable to find a job. He had to seek the permission of the police before making a telephone call or seeing an outside visitor. Any breach of these conditions was punishable by incarceration. The Court, comparing Mr Guzzardi's situation to that of a person kept in an open prison, found that there had been a deprivation of liberty for the purposes of Article 5.

Applying a similar approach, in the *Ashingdane* case[10] the Court held that, despite the applicant's transfer from a high-security mental hospital to a more relaxed regime where he was permitted to leave the hospital during the day and at weekends, his forced hospitalization under the Mental Heath Act 1959 nonetheless constituted a continuing deprivation of liberty.

The applicants in *Amuur* v. *France*[11] were refugees from Somalia who had travelled via Kenya and Syria to Paris-Orly Airport. They were refused entry to France on the ground that their passports had been falsified and for twenty days, before being sent back to Syria, they were shuttled by the police between a nearby hotel, one of the floors of which had been let as a transit zone to the Ministry of the Interior, and the '*Espace*' lounge of the airport. The Court rejected the Government's argument that, since the applicants had been free at any time to return to Syria or any other country which would have accepted them, the holding measures to which they had been subjected did not amount to a deprivation of liberty.

Cases involving members of the armed forces have also thrown up some problems of definition. The *Engel* case[12] concerned the penalties which could be

---

[8] *Guzzardi* v. *Italy*, Judgment of 6 November 1980, Series A, No. 39; (1981) 3 EHRR 333, para 93 of the judgment.

[9] *Guzzardi* v. *Italy*, Judgment of 6 November 1980, Series A, No. 39; (1981) 3 EHRR 333.

[10] *Ashingdane* v. *United Kingdom*, Judgment of 28 May 1985, Series A, No. 93; (1985) 7 EHRR 528.

[11] *Amuur* v. *France* (App. 19776/92), Judgment of 25 June 1996; (1996) 22 EHRR 533.

[12] *Engel and others* v. *Netherlands*, Judgment of 8 June 1976, Series A, No. 22; (1979–80) 1 EHRR 647.

imposed on conscripted Dutch soldiers. There were grades of arrest: the lower grades involved confinement to barracks, while 'strict arrest' involved detention in locked cells. The Court considered that 'A disciplinary penalty . . . which on analysis would unquestionably be deemed a deprivation of liberty were it to be applied to a civilian may not possess this characteristic when imposed on a serviceman.'[13] The Court went on to find that the light forms of arrest did not amount to deprivations of liberty, although strict arrest would.

Similarly, once an individual is detained in prison, additional restrictions on his or her liberty, imposed for disciplinary reasons, will not usually give rise to any issue under Article 5(1), although sufficiently severe cases could conceivably breach Article 3.[14] Thus the Court declared inadmissible an application brought under Article 5 by the relatives of a woman who committed suicide while confined in her cell during a period when other prisoners were enjoying free association.[15]

In its *Guzzardi*[16] judgment the Court acknowledged that the process of deciding where to place any particular measure on the sliding scale between a mere restriction and an all-out deprivation of liberty is not always easy and could in some cases appear subjective. While this is no doubt true, by and large, it appears to strike the right balance.

DEPRIVATIONS OF LIBERTY BY PRIVATE PERSONS AND EXTRATERRITORIALITY

One issue in connection with which the case law seems unclear and unsatisfactory relates to the State's positive obligations where a deprivation of liberty is effected by a private person. In the *Nielsen* case[17] the applicant, a 12-year-old boy, was admitted to psychiatric hospital at his mother's request. The Court held that since the hospitalization constituted an expression of the mother's parental authority, safeguarded by Article 8 of the Convention, and was justified by the applicant's mental state, and since the restrictions on his freedom were not significantly different from those which might be imposed on a child in an ordinary hospital, there had been no deprivation of liberty within the meaning of Article 5(1). This conclusion is inconsistent with the *Ashingdane* judgment; a

---

[13] Para. 59 of the Judgment.
[14] See ch. 5 above.
[15] App. 42117/98, *Bollan* v. *United Kingdom* (App. 42117/98), admissibility decision of 4 May 2000.
[16] *Guzzardi* v. *Italy*, Judgment of 6 November 1980, Series A, No. 39; (1981) 3 EHRR 333, para. 93 of the judgment.
[17] *Nielsen* v. *Denmark*, Judgment of 28 November 1988, Series A, No. 144; (1989) 11 EHRR 175.

better approach would have been to hold that the hospitalization constituted a deprivation of liberty but that it was 'lawful' and justifiable under paragraph 1(d) or (e).

In the *Koniarska* case[18] the Court distinguished the position of the applicant, a 17-year-old girl diagnosed as suffering from a psychopathic disorder and placed in local authority secure accommodation, from that of Nielsen, on the ground that Koniarska's detention was ordered by the courts, who did not have parental rights over her. This reasoning would appear to rule out the possibility of the State being bound to take measures to shield children from unjustified deprivations of liberty carried out by the parents. The grounds of the distinction might even, by extension, suggest that Article 5(1) does not incorporate any positive obligation on the State to protect against interferences with liberty carried out by private persons—a conclusion which would leave a sizeable gap in the protection from arbitrary detention and would moreover be inconsistent with the case law under Articles 2, 3, and 8.[19] However, it is perhaps unwise to read too much into this decision since, arguably, it might have been inappropriate for a single Chamber of the Court to overrule the *Nielsen* judgment in a mere admissibility decision. It will be interesting to see whether the Court adopts a more assertive position on positive obligations under Article 5 in future cases.

Similarly, it remains uncertain whether the Convention gives rise to any obligation on the State to refrain from expelling a person facing a real risk of detention in breach of Article 5 in the receiving country, in parallel with such obligations under Articles 2 and 3.[20]

THE LAWFULNESS OF THE DEPRIVATION OF LIBERTY

A deprivation of liberty which does not fall within one of the six categories listed in Article 5(1) subparagraphs (a)–(f) will, without more, be unlawful under the Convention. This was the case in *Riera Blume and others* v. *Spain*,[21] for example, where the Court found a violation of Article 5(1) arising from a court order releasing six members of a religious cult into the custody of their families who, assisted by the police, kept them confined in a hotel for ten days for 'deprogramming' by psychiatrists. Quite apart from the problems arising under Article 9 of the Convention (freedom of religious belief), 'deprogramming'

---

[18] *Koniarska* v. *United Kingdom* (App. 33670/96), admissibility decision of 12 October 2000.
[19] See chs. 4, 5, and 11.
[20] See chs. 4 and 5.
[21] *Riera Blume and others* v. *Spain* (App. 37680/97), Judgment of 9 March 1999; (2000) 30 EHRR 632.

does not fall within one of the six permitted exceptions to the right of liberty. The parameters of these exceptions are examined in more detail below.

In addition, the deprivation of liberty must be 'lawful' and carried out 'in accordance with a procedure prescribed by law'. This means, in the first place, that the particular arrest or detention must have been carried out in compliance with the procedural and substantive rules of national law. Where, for example, a warrant is required for arrest, the warrant must be in the correct form or the arrest will not be lawful under Article 5. Similarly, where force is used in order to effect an arrest, the degree of force used must not exceed that authorized in the circumstances by domestic law.

Reviewing compliance with domestic law is not normally part of the European Court's role, which tends to leave this job to the national courts in accordance with the principle of subsidiarity.[22] However, since under Article 5(1) disregard of domestic law entails a breach of the Convention, the Court must satisfy itself that national law has been followed.[23]

In order for a deprivation of liberty to be 'lawful' within the meaning of Article 5(1) it is not sufficient for it to have been carried out in accordance with national law. In addition, the Convention requires that the domestic law be of a certain quality. First, it must contain clear and accessible rules governing the circumstances in which it is permissible for the State to deprive an individual of his or liberty and the procedure which must be followed.[24] In the *Amuur* case mentioned above, there was a violation of Article 5(1) in that the only guidelines under French law concerning the holding of asylum-seekers in the international zone of an airport were contained in an unpublished Ministry of the Interior circular. This circular was not available to asylum-seekers or their lawyers, contained no guarantees against arbitrary detention, and did not permit for review by the domestic courts. Similarly, in *Baranowski* v. *Poland*[25] the Court found deficiencies in the Polish law on pre-trial detention. In 1993–4, when the applicant was arrested, it was the practice in Poland that, once a bill of indictment had been lodged, the accused could continue to be detained on remand until trial without the need for a court order. The Court found that this practice of

---

[22] Although this expression is more familiar in the context of European Community law, the principle of subsidiarity also permeates the Convention and the Strasbourg case law; see, for recent examples, *Hugh Jordan* v. *United Kingdom* (App. 24746/94), Judgment of 4 May 2001, para. 111 of the judgment; and *Z and others* v. *United Kingdom* (App. 29392/95), Judgment of 10 May 2001; (2002) 34 EHRR para. 103 of the judgment.

[23] *Benham* v. *United Kingdom* (App. 19380/92), Judgment of 10 June 1996; (1996) 22 EHRR 293, para. 40 of the judgment; *Winterwerp* v. *Netherlands*, Judgment of 24 October 1979, Series A, No. 33; (1979–80) 2 EHRR 387, para. 46 of the judgment; *Steel and others* v. *United Kingdom* (App. 24838/94), Judgment of 23 September 1998; (1998) 28 EHRR 603, para. 54 of the judgment.

[24] 'Lawfulness' in Article 5(1) thus carries the same meaning as 'in accordance with law' in Articles 8–11: see the *Steel and others* v. *United Kingdom* (App. 24838/94), Judgment of 23 September 1998; (1998) 28 EHRR 603; and ch. 10 below.

[25] *Baranowski* v. *Poland* (App. 28358/95), Judgment of 28 March 2000.

maintaining detention on the basis of the indictment was not founded on any specific legislative provision or case law but stemmed from the absence of clear rules. It did not, therefore, satisfy the test of foreseeability. Furthermore, the fact that without a court order the detention could continue for an unlimited and unpredictable period was contrary to the principle of legal certainty and open to arbitrariness and abuse.

As the *Baranowski* judgment states, even where the national law is clear and has been complied with, the deprivation of liberty will not be 'lawful' if domestic law allows for arbitrary or excessive detention. In the case of *Erkalo* v. *Netherlands*[26] the applicant was detained in a mental hospital pursuant to a court order. When the order expired there was, because of an administrative error, a period of two months during which the applicant continued to be detained before a new order was granted by the court. Although under the Dutch Code of Criminal Procedure the detention was not unlawful in these circumstances, the Court held that the lack of administrative and judicial safeguards—demonstrated by the fact that the absence of any legal basis for the detention came to light only when the applicant himself applied to court—rendered the detention arbitrary and thus unlawful under Article 5(1).

DETENTION ON REMAND

DETENTION PENDING TRIAL: ARTICLE 5(1)(C)

Article 5(1)(c) allows for the arrest and pre-trial detention of a person suspected of having committed a criminal offence. The paragraph can be broken down into a number of separate conditions, all of which must be present in order for the arrest or detention to be acceptable under the Convention. Thus the arrest or detention must be 'lawful'; it must be effected for the purpose of bringing the detainee 'before the competent legal authority'; and the detainee must reasonably be suspected of having committed an offence or of being about to commit an offence or abscond having committed an offence.

The expression 'competent legal authority' has been held to carry the same meaning as 'judge or other officer authorized by law to exercise judicial power' in paragraph 3 of Article 5;[27] this meaning is considered in more detail below in this chapter.

In the *Lawless* case[28] the Irish Government contended that Article 5(1)(c)

---

[26] *Erkalo* v. *Netherlands* (App. 23807/94), Judgment of 2 September 1998; (1999) 28 EHRR 509.

[27] *Schiesser* v. *Switzerland*, Judgment of 4 December 1979, Series A, No. 34; (1979–80) 2 EHRR 417.

[28] *Lawless* v. *Ireland*, Judgment of 1 July 1961, Series A, No. 3; (1979–80) 1 EHRR 15, paras. 13 and 14 of Judgment.

should be interpreted in such a way that if the purpose of the arrest or deten-tion was to prevent the commission of an offence, it should not be necessary also to have the intention of bringing the detainee to court. The Court of Human Rights, however, held that the phrase 'effected for the purpose of bring-ing him before the competent legal authority' qualified all the three alternative bases for arrest and detention at the end of Article 5(1)(c). It followed, therefore, that the internment of the applicant, a member of the Irish Republican Army, under a law allowing for the detention without trial of persons believed by a Minister of State to be 'engaged in activities . . . prejudicial to the preservation of public peace and order or to the security of the State' did not fall within any of the permitted categories in Article 5(1). The Court recently reached a similar conclusion in the *Ječius* case.[29] The applicant had been imprisoned under Art-icle 50 of the Lithuanian Constitution (repealed 30 June 1997), which permitted arrest and preventive detention 'having sufficient reasons to suspect that a person may commit a [specified] dangerous act'. It is not acceptable to detain someone for a crime not yet committed.

As long as, at the time of the arrest or detention, the intention to bring the suspect to court is there, it is immaterial whether or not in the event he is actually brought to court or charged,[30] although too long a period of preliminary detention without judicial control may give rise to an issue under Article 5(3).

The word 'offence' in Article 5(1)(c) carries an autonomous meaning,[31] identical to that of 'criminal offence' in Article 6.[32] Although the classification of the offence under national law is one factor to be taken into account, the nature of the proceedings and the severity of the penalty at stake are also relevant.[33] Thus, for example, detention in close arrest on charges of desertion from the British army,[34] carrying a maximum penalty of two years' imprison-ment, falls within Article 5(1)(c), although such military offences lie outside the mainstream English criminal law. The same goes for arrest for breach of the peace,[35] which English law classifies as a quasi-civil matter.

The 'offence' must be specific and concrete: preventive detention of individuals viewed by the State as generally 'undesirable' is not allowed. For this reason also the internment under consideration in the *Lawless* case would not have been covered by Article 5(1)(c). In the *Greek* case the Commission was of the opinion that administrative detention of persons considered by the military

---

[29] *Ječius* v. *Lithuania* (App. 34578/97), Judgment of 31 July 2000.

[30] *Labita* v. *Italy* (App. 26772/95), Judgment of 6 April 2000, para. 155 of the judgment.

[31] See ch. 3 above.

[32] See ch. 8 below.

[33] *Benham* v. *United Kingdom* (App. 19380/92), Judgment of 10 June 1996; (1996) 22 EHRR 293.

[34] *Hood* v. *United Kingdom* (App. 27267/95), Judgment of 18 February 1999; (2000) 29 EHRR 365.

[35] *Steel and others* v. *United Kingdom* (App. 24838/94), Judgment of 23 September 1998; (1998) 28 EHRR 603.

government then in power to be dangerous to public order and security, and the use of house arrest, fell outside any of the categories of deprivation of liberty permitted by Article 5.[36] The *Guzzardi* case[37]also makes clear that preventive detention as part of a campaign to combat organized crime cannot be brought within Article 5(1)(c). This ruling was affirmed in the *Ciulla* case[38] which concerned a residence order imposed on a person suspected of involvement in organized crime through the Mafia.

It can be seen, therefore, that there will be very few cases falling within the second two alternatives in paragraph 1(c). Since the words 'when it is reasonably considered necessary to prevent [the detained person] committing an offence' do not authorize general preventive detention, evidence of intention on the part of the detainee to commit a concrete offence will be necessary. However, in most European countries, acts preparatory to the commission of a crime are themselves categorized as offences. Such evidence would, therefore, usually be sufficient to bring the detainee within the first limb: arrest or detention upon 'reasonable suspicion of having committed an offence'. Similarly any arrest or detention falling within the third limb—'to prevent [the detainee] . . . fleeing after having [committed an offence]'—will also fall within the first.

The requirement that the arrest and detention must be dependent upon the existence of reasonable suspicion that an offence has been committed means that there must be facts or information which would satisfy an objective observer.[39] In the *Fox, Campbell and Hartley* case[40] the applicants argued that the interpretation by the courts of section 11(1) of the Northern Ireland (Emergency Provisions) Act 1978 as requiring only a subjective test of honest belief that the person detained was a terrorist was incompatible with Article 5(1)(c). The Court found that in the context of the special problems presented in combating terrorism a lower standard of 'reasonable suspicion' might be acceptable, but that some objectively realistic grounds would still be needed. Since the United Kingdom had not provided any evidence on which it could be shown that there was any basis for the suspicion that the applicants were terrorists, the Court found a violation of Article 5(1)(c). In the *Labita* case[41] it held that the uncorroborated hearsay evidence of an anonymous informant was not enough to found 'reasonable suspicion' of the applicant's involvement in Mafia-type activities.

---

[36] *The Greek Case* (1969) 22 II *Yearbook* (special volume), 134–5.

[37] *Guzzardi* v. *Italy*, Judgment of 6 November 1980, Series A, No. 39; (1981) 3 EHRR 333.

[38] *Ciulla* v. *Italy*, Judgment of 22 February 1989, Series A, No. 148; (1991) 13 EHRR 346.

[39] *Erdagöz* v. *Turkey* (App. 21890/93), Judgment of 22 October 1997; (2001) 32 EHRR 443.

[40] *Fox, Campbell and Hartley* v. *United Kingdom*, Judgment of 30 August 1990, Series A, No. 182; (1991) 13 EHRR 157; cf. *O'Hara* v. *United Kingdom*, Judgment of 16 October 2001.

[41] *Labita* v. *Italy* (App. 26772/95), Judgment of 6 April 2000.

PROTECTION WHILE ON REMAND

Article 5(3) guarantees certain rights to persons arrested or detained in accordance with the provisions of Article 5(1)(c). The first part of Article 5(3) is concerned with rights immediately on arrest; the second part deals with detention on remand.

THE RIGHT TO BE BROUGHT PROMPTLY BEFORE A JUDGE

According to Article 5(3), any person arrested on suspicion of having committed a criminal offence has the right to be brought 'promptly' before 'a judge or other officer authorized by law to exercise judicial power'. In contrast to the right to judicial review of the legality of the detention under Article 5(4), which may be conditional on the application of the detained person, the right under Article 5(3) is to be brought promptly before a judge: it is the duty of the State on its own initiative to see that this is done.[42]

There has been considerable case law on the meaning of 'promptly' in this context, particularly in connection with applicants detained on suspicion of involvement in terrorism. States as diverse as the United Kingdom and Turkey have invoked the need to hold terrorist suspects *incommunicado* for some time following arrest, because of the risk that other members of the terrorist organization could destroy evidence or put the lives of witnesses or even judges in danger. Conversely, it can of course be argued that judicial safeguards are of particular importance in connection with emotive crimes of this nature, when the police and prosecution are likely to be under pressure to secure convictions and may be tempted to use unorthodox means to force confessions.

The Court has never put a finite limit on the acceptable length of preliminary detention, since it considers that this must depend on the circumstances in each case. Some guidance is, however, provided by the *Brogan and others* v. *United Kingdom* judgment.[43] The applicants were detained under special provisions enabling the Secretary of State for Northern Ireland to extend an initial forth-eight-hour period of detention. The shortest length of detention after arrest was four days and six hours and the longest was six days and sixteen hours. All the applicants were released without charge. Even taking account of the particular situation at that time in Northern Ireland, the Court regarded all cases as violations of the requirements of Article 5(3). The United Kingdom's response to the *Brogan* judgment was not to repeal the law allowing for extended periods of pre-charge detention; instead it filed a derogation under Article 15 of the Convention, claiming that, in view of the existence of 'an emergency threatening

---

[42]   *McGoff* v. *Sweden*, Judgment of 26 October 1984, Series A, No. 83: (1986) 8 EHRR 246.
[43]   *Brogan and others* v. *United Kingdom*, Judgment of 29 November 1988, Series A, No. 145-B; (1989) 11 EHRR 117.

the life of the nation' this part of Article 5(3) should be disapplied in Northern Ireland. When the same extended detention provisions came before the Court in the *Brannigan and McBride* case[44] the Government conceded that they were not consistent with Article 5(3), but the Court found that the derogation was valid and that there was no violation.[45]

Even where a Government has derogated from its Article 5(3) obligations the Court retains a power of review. The applicant in the case of *Aksoy* v. *Turkey*[46] was arrested on suspicion of involvement with the Kurdish terrorist organization, the PKK, and detained *incommunicado* for fourteen days under emergency provisions in force in South-East Turkey. The Government claimed that there was no violation because it had filed an Article 15 derogation in view of Kurdish separatist violence which had given rise to an 'emergency threatening the life of the nation'. The Court accepted that there was such an emergency, but ruled that, even taking into account the difficulty of investigating terrorist offences, fourteen days was too long to hold a suspect without judicial supervision and without access to a lawyer, doctor or friend.

A number of cases have considered the character of the 'other officer authorized by law to exercise judicial power'. The 'officer' need not be a judge but must display judicial attributes sufficient to protect the rights of the detained person. Most importantly, he or she must be independent of the executive and the parties to the case.[47] Thus a District Attorney who has been involved in indicting and prosecuting the accused cannot fulfil the role of judicial 'officer' under Article 5(3).[48] When assessing independence, the appearance of the situation from the viewpoint of an outside observer is decisive: if it appears that the 'officer' may intervene in subsequent criminal proceedings on behalf of the prosecution, his or her independence and impartiality may be open to doubt. In a case against Bulgaria the Court therefore held that the prosecutor who authorized the applicant's continued detention on remand could not provide sufficient guarantees of independence since he could in theory have taken over the prosecution of the subsequent criminal proceedings.[49] Military disciplinary regimes in several countries have led to violations of Article 5(3), since the Court's autonomous interpretative approach brings many military offences within the scope of Article 5 paragraphs (1)(c) and (3). In the *Hood* case,[50] for

---

[44] *Brannigan and McBride* v. *United Kingdom*, Judgment of 26 May 1993, Series A, No. 258-B; (1994) 17 EHRR 539.

[45] In February 2001 the UK Government lifted the derogation, in the light of the Northern Irish peace process. A new derogation to Art. 5 (1)(f) was filed on 18 December 2001 following the September 11 attacks.

[46] Aksoy v. *Turkey* (App. 21987/93), Judgment of 18 December 1996; (1997) 23 EHRR 553.

[47] *Schiesser* v. *Switzerland*, Judgment of 4 December 1979, Series A, No. 34; (1979–80) 2 EHRR 417.

[48] *Huber* v. *Switzerland*, Judgment of 23 October 1990, Series A, No. 188.

[49] *Assenov* v. *Bulgaria* (App. 24760/94), Judgment of 28 October 1998; (1998) 28 EHRR 652.

[50] *Hood* v. *United Kingdom* (App. 27267/95), Judgment of 18 February 1999; (2000) 29 EHRR 365.

example, the Court found that the British system whereby the accused soldier's commanding officer remanded him in close arrest was incompatible with Article 5(3) since the same officer was likely to play a central role in the ensuing prosecution and trial by court martial. Similarly, the lack of complete impartiality of the Dutch *auditeur militeur* and the Belgian counterpart took them outside the provision.[51]

The 'officer' must adopt a procedure which meets the normal requirements of due process. This includes hearing representations from the detainee at an oral hearing and deciding, by reference to legal criteria, whether or not the detention is justified.[52] If it is not justified, the 'officer' must have the power to order release.[53]

TRIAL WITHIN A REASONABLE TIME OR RELEASE

Article 5(3) next provides that 'Everyone arrested or detained in accordance with the provisions of paragraph (1)(c) of this Article . . . shall be entitled to trial within a reasonable time or to release pending trial.'

The drafting of this provision is ambiguous. Read together with Article 5(1) it appears to permit the detention on remand of any person reasonably suspected of having committed an offence—that is, any person likely to stand trial—as long as the trial takes place within a reasonable time, a right in any case guaranteed by Article 6(1). Such an interpretation would, however, be at odds with the purpose of Article 5 which is, broadly, to limit detention to those circumstances where it is strictly necessary in the public interest and to provide guarantees to detainees against arbitrariness. Moreover, it would mean that the Convention allowed for pre-trial detention in many more cases than most national European legal systems, where it is usually necessary to show some ground such as a risk of absconding or tampering with evidence before it is possible to lock up a person who, although accused of an offence, is innocent until proved guilty.

The Court has therefore rejected this reading and, in a clear example of the purposive interpretative approach, has held in a series of judgments that not only the initial arrest, but also the continuing *detention* must be justified, as long as it lasts, by adequate grounds; and that, independently of those grounds, its *duration* must also not exceed a reasonable time.

[51] *De Jong, Baljet and Van den Brink* v. *Netherlands*, Judgment of 22 May 1984, Series A, No. 77; (1986) 8 EHRR 20, *Van der Sluijs, Zuiderfeld and Klappe* v. *Netherlands*, Judgment of 22 May 1984, Series A, No. 78; (1991) 13 EHRR 461; *Duinhoff and Duif* v. *Netherlands*, Judgment of 22 May 1984, Series A, No. 79; (1991) 13 EHRR 478, and *Pauwels* v. *Belgium*, Judgment of 26 May 1988, Series A, No. 135; (1989) 11 EHRR 238. See also *Brincat* v. *Italy*, Judgment of 26 November 1992, Series A, No. 249-A; (1993) 16 EHRR 591, concerning the Italian deputy public prosecutor.

[52] *Assenov* v. *Bulgaria* (App. 24760/94), Judgment of 28 October 1998; (1998) 28 EHRR 652, para. 146; *Caballero* v. *United Kingdom* (App. 32819/96), Judgment of 8 February 2000; *Sabeur ben Ali* v. *Malta* (App. 35892/97), Judgment of 29 June 2000.

[53] See e.g. *Aquilina* v. *Malta* (App. 25642/94), Judgment of 29 April 1999; (1999) 29 EHRR 185.

The standard paragraphs setting out the Court's approach which appear in almost every judgment concerned with this part of Article 5(3) provide:

[W]hether a period of pre-trial detention can be considered 'reasonable' must be assessed in each case according to its special features. . . .

Continued detention can be justified in a given case only if there are specific indications of a genuine requirement of public interest which, notwithstanding the presumption of innocence, outweighs the rule of respect for individual liberty. It falls in the first place to the national judicial authorities to examine all the circumstances arguing for or against the existence of such a requirement and to set them out in their decisions on the applications for release. It is essentially on the basis of the reasons given in these decisions and of the facts stated by the applicant in his appeals that the Court is called upon to decide whether or not there has been a violation of Article 5(3).

The persistence of reasonable suspicion that the person arrested has committed an offence is a condition *sine qua non* for the lawfulness of the continued detention, but after a certain lapse of time it no longer suffices: the Court must then establish whether the other grounds given by the judicial authorities continued to justify the deprivation of liberty. Where such grounds were 'relevant' and 'sufficient', the Court must also ascertain whether the competent national authorities displayed 'special diligence' in the conduct of the proceedings. The complexity and special characteristics of the investigation are factors to be considered in this respect.[54]

Thus, as far as the need for pre-trial detention is concerned, it can be seen that the Court understands its role essentially as one of reviewing whether the reasons given by the national courts for refusing release are adequate and sufficient. In each case, the national courts must assess the need for detention with reference to the particular facts. For this reason a British law which automatically denied release on bail to a person charged with a serious violent crime if he had already been convicted of such a crime was incompatible with Article 5(3).[55]

The Court has never elaborated an exhaustive list of grounds which could justify pre-trial detention; each case is to be judged on its own particular merits.

As previously stated, suspicion that the detained person has committed an offence, while a necessary condition, does not suffice to justify detention continuing beyond a short initial period, even where the accused is charged with a particularly serious crime and the evidence against him is strong.[56]

The ground most frequently relied upon by national courts is the risk of

---

[54] This particular extract was taken from *Scott* v. *Spain* (App. 21335/93), Judgment of 18 December 1996; (1997) 24 EHRR 391, para. 74 of the judgment.

[55] *Caballero* v. *United Kingdom* (App. 32819/96), Judgment of 8 February 2000.

[56] *Tomasi* v. *France*, Judgment of 27 August 1992, Series A, No. 241-A; (1993) 15 EHRR 309; *Ječius* v. *Lithuania* (App. 34578/97), Judgment of 31 July 2000.

absconding. But the risk must be substantiated in each case: it is not sufficient, for example, for the national authorities simply to point to the fact that the accused would receive a long prison sentence if convicted as evidence that he or she would be likely to disappear,[57] although this may be a relevant consideration. The applicant in the case of *Barfuss* v. *Czech Republic*[58] was charged with fraudulently obtaining a number of large bank loans and faced a heavy sentence. The decisions of the Czech courts refusing his applications for bail referred in addition to the fact that he had contacts in Germany, and that if he fled there it would be impossible to continue with the prosecution because there was no extradition agreement between Germany and the Czech Republic. This reasoning was held by the Court of Human Rights to be sufficient for the purposes of Article 5(3).

Where the danger of absconding can be avoided by bail or other guarantees, the accused must be released, and there is an obligation on the national authorities to consider such alternatives to detention.[59] Moreover, in those countries which have the system of bail on financial sureties, the amount of the sureties must not be excessive, and must be fixed by reference to the purpose for which they are imposed, namely to ensure that this particular defendant appears for trial.[60] The sum must never be set exclusively by reference to the seriousness of the charge without considering the accused's financial circumstances.

Another common ground invoked to justify pre-trial detention is the risk of re-offending prior to trial. Again, the domestic court judgments must show that this risk was substantiated: reference to past crimes may not be sufficient.[61] In an early case, *Matznetter* v. *Austria*, the applicant was an accountant charged with committing a number of serious company frauds. The Court held that it was compatible with Article 5(3) for the national court to rely on the risk of reoffending as a ground for refusing bail, since Matznetter had the skill and experience 'such as to make it easy for him to resume his unlawful activities'.[62] Similarly, in the *Assenov* case[63] the Bulgarian authorities were entitled to rely on this ground since the applicant was charged with a long series of thefts, some of which had allegedly been committed subsequent to his initial arrest and questioning by the police.

[57] See e.g. *Muller* v. *France* (App. 21802/93), Judgment of 17 March 1997.
[58] *Barfuss* v. *Czech Republic* (App. 35848/97), Judgment of 31 July 2000; (2002) 34 EHRR 948.
[59] *Wemhoff* v. *Germany*, Judgment of 27 June 1968, Series A. No. 7; (1979–80) 1 EHRR 55, para. 15 of 'The Law'; and see, more recently, *Jablonski* v. *Poland* (App. 33492/96), Judgment of 21 December 2000.
[60] *Neumeister* v. *Austria*, Judgment of 27 June 1968, Series A, No. 8; (1979–80) 1 EHRR 91, paras. 13–14 of 'The Law', and see more recently e.g. *Punzelt* v. *Czech Republic* (App. 31315/96), Judgment of 25 April 2000; (2001) 33 EHRR 1159.
[61] *Muller* v. *France* (App. 21802/93), Judgment of 17 March 1997.
[62] *Matznetter* v. *Austria*, Judgment of 10 November 1969, Series A, No. 10; (1979–80) 1 EHRR 198, para. 9 of 'The Law'.
[63] *Assenov* v. *Bulgaria* (App. 24760/94), Judgment of 28 October 1998; (1998) 28 EHRR 652.

Other grounds which have been accepted by the Court as capable of justifying detention are the risk of suppression of evidence[64] and of collusion, that is, contacting other defendants or witnesses to agree on a false version of events.[65]

The right to trial within a reasonable time under Article 5(3) can be invoked only by those detained until trial. If a person is released at any stage before the trial, the situation is governed by Article 6(1) alone. Provided the relevant periods are sufficiently long, there is nothing to prevent a detainee from making claims under both provisions.

The relevant period under Article 5(3) begins with arrest or detention. The question when the Article ceases to apply is more complicated, since some European legal systems regard all detention as provisional until the conviction and sentence are confirmed by the final appeal court. In the *Wemhoff* case the Court held that the relevant period ended with the delivery of the judgment at first instance,[66] and that the protection of Article 5(3) did not, therefore, extend to the date on which German law considered the conviction to have become final, that is, after appeal or upon the expiry of the time-limit for appeal. The Court found it decisive in favour of this interpretation that a person convicted at first instance was in the position provided for by Article 5(1)(a), which authorizes deprivation of liberty 'after conviction'. This last phrase could not be interpreted as being restricted to the case of a final conviction, for this would exclude the detention immediately on conviction of those who appear for trial while still at liberty.

In the *Ringeisen* case the Commission requested the Court to review its *Wemhoff* decision or at least to interpret it in such a way that detention after conviction might be considered as remaining subject to Article 5(3) until the conviction became final. Ringeisen had been detained on two charges and separate proceedings were pending in each. His detention after conviction on the first charge ran concurrently with his remand in custody pending trial on the second charge. In these circumstances the Court did not consider it necessary to pronounce on the issues raised by the Commission; Article 5(3) applied throughout Ringeisen's detention.[67]

The point was finally resolved in the case of *B* v. *Austria*,[68] where the Court confirmed its *Wemhoff* judgment to hold that, despite the rule of Austrian law that sentence becomes final only with the determination of any appeal,

[64] *Wemhoff* v. *Germany*, Judgment of 27 June 1968, Series A, No. 7; (1979–80) 1 EHRR 55, paras. 13–14 of 'The Law'.

[65] *Ringeisen* v. *Austria*, Judgment of 16 July 1971, Series A, No. 13; (1979–80) 1 EHRR 455, para. 107 of Judgment.

[66] *Wemhoff* v. *Germany*, Judgment of 27 June 1968, Series A, No. 7; (1979–80) 1 EHRR 55, paras 6–9 of 'The Law'.

[67] *Ringeisen* v. *Austria*, Judgment of 16 July 1971, Series A, No. 13; (1979–80) 1 EHRR 455, para. 109 of Judgment.

[68] *B* v. *Austria*, Judgment of 28 March 1990, Series A, No. 175; (1991) 13 EHRR 20.

the applicant's detention on remand came to an end for the purposes of the Convention with the finding of guilt and sentencing at first instance.

Just as the start and end points of the period to be considered under Article 5(3) are different from those relevant for Article 6(1), so the assessment of what length of time is 'reasonable' differs for the two Articles. In its *Wemhoff* judgment the Court said:

Article 5, which begins with an affirmation of the right of everyone to liberty and security of person, goes on to specify the situations and conditions in which derogations from this principle may be made, in particular with a view to the maintenance of public order, which requires that offences shall be punished. *It is thus mainly in the light of the fact of the detention* of the person being prosecuted that national courts, possibly followed by the Court [of Human Rights], must determine whether the time that has elapsed, for whatever reason, before judgment is passed on the accused has at some stage exceeded a reasonable limit, that is to say imposed a greater sacrifice than could, in the circumstances of the case, reasonably be expected of a person presumed to be innocent.[69]

Consequently Article 5(3) requires that there must be 'special diligence' in bringing the case to trial if the accused is detained.[70] A detained person is entitled to have the case given priority and conducted with particular expedition.[71]

The Court applies a broad two-stage approach. It will first determine whether the grounds relied upon by the national authorities were adequate, until the very end, to justify remanding the accused in custody. If the detention was justified in principle, the Court will then examine the conduct of the prosecution to ensure that the pre-trial detention was not unnecessarily prolonged. Periods of inactivity by the national authorities lasting more than a few months are usually taken by the Court as a sign of lack of diligence, particularly if the overall duration of the detention was long. By way of example, the Court has recently found excessive periods of pre-trial detention lasting from two and a half[72] to nearly five years.[73]

[69] *Wemhoff* v. *Germany*, Judgment of 27 June 1968, Series A, No. 7; (1979–80) 1 EHRR 55, para. 5 of 'The Law' (emphasis added).

[70] *Stögmüller* v. *Germany*, Judgment of 10 November 1969, Series A, No. 9; (1979–80) 1 EHRR 155, para. 5 of 'The Law'.

[71] *Wemhoff* v. *Germany*, Judgment of 27 June 1968, Series A, No. 7; (1979–80) 1 EHRR 55, para. 17 of 'The Law'.

[72] *Punzelt* v. *Czech Republic* (App. 31315/96), Judgment of 25 April 2000; (2001) 33 EHRR 1159.

[73] *P.B.* v. *France* (App. 38781/97), Judgment of 1 August 2000.

DETENTION AFTER CONVICTION BY A COMPETENT COURT: ARTICLE 5(1)(a)

Article 5(1)(a) permits 'the lawful detention of a person after conviction by a competent court'. It is important to note that it is the *detention* which must be 'lawful', not the *conviction*. Although many applicants to Strasbourg allege that they have been convicted of crimes they did not commit, the Court has no power under Article 5(1)(a) to examine whether the evidence adduced before the domestic courts was sufficient for a finding of guilt.[74] Similarly, if an appeal against conviction is successful, the quashing of the conviction does not render the previous detention unlawful; and the same applies to acquittal following a retrial.[75]

As long as the detention was one of the sentences permitted by domestic law, and as long as the sentencing court followed the procedure provided by that law, the detention will usually be 'lawful' within the meaning of Article 5.[76]

The sentencing body must be a 'competent court'. 'Competent' means that it must have the power under domestic law to order the detention in question and 'court' carries the same meaning as in Article 5(4): the body must possess a judicial character and follow a fair procedure.[77]

It does not, however, appear necessary that the 'court' must have followed the strict requirements of Article 6 of the Convention when making the order for detention, although very grave breaches amounting to arbitrariness would, presumably, be sufficient to render the detention 'unlawful'.

In the *Drozd and Janousek* case,[78] for example, the two applicants, respectively nationals of Spain and Czechoslovakia, had been convicted of robbery and sentenced to imprisonment in Andorra, which was not, at that time, a signatory to the European Convention. Under the Andorran Code of Criminal Procedure, such sentences were to be served in a French or Spanish prison. The applicants elected to serve their sentences in France.

It was argued before the Court of Human Rights that the detention in France was unlawful because the French courts had not carried out any review of the judgments of the courts in Andorra to determine whether their composition and procedure met the requirements of Article 6 in providing a fair trial. The Court concluded that the Andorran court was the 'competent court' referred to in Article 5(1)(a), but that, in order to facilitate international cooperation in

---

[74] In accordance with the 'fourth instance doctrine'.

[75] App. 3245/67, *X* v. *Austria*, 4 February 1969, (1969) 12 *Yearbook* 206, 236.

[76] Although an excessively long period of detention might raise an issue under Article 3: see ch. 5.

[77] *De Wilde, Ooms and Versyp* v. *Belgium*, Judgment of 18 November 1970, Series A, No. 12, para 78; *Engel and others* v. *Netherlands*, Judgment of 8 June 1976, para. 68.

[78] *Drozd and Janousek* v. *France*, Judgment of 26 June 1992, Series A, No. 240; (1992) 14 EHRR 745.

criminal justice, the Convention did not require Contracting Parties to impose Convention standards on third States. The situation would be different if the conviction was the result of a flagrant denial of justice.[79] The Court accordingly held by twelve votes to eleven that there had been no violation of Article 5(1). The dissenting judges expressed considerable disquiet that the majority were unwilling to impose upon France the obligation to check that the procedure by which the conviction had been imposed met the minimum requirements of the Convention. One of the joint dissenting opinions tellingly cites the Explanatory Report on the European Convention on the International Validity of Criminal Judgments, which provides that a condition for the enforcement of a foreign judgment is that it has been rendered in full observance of the fundamental principles of the Convention, notably Article 6.[80]

'Conviction', like 'court', carries an autonomous meaning under the Convention, and can include a finding of guilt in respect of what is classified as a disciplinary or administrative offence under domestic law.[81] The 'offence' in question must, however, be specific and concrete: preventive detention of individuals suspected generally of wrongdoing is not permitted under this, or any other, provision of Article 5(1).[82]

The deprivation of liberty must flow directly from the conviction. In the *Van Droogenbroeck* case[83] the sentence of the court involved imprisonment for two years followed by a further ten years following release during which the convicted person was 'placed at the Government's disposal', meaning that he could be detained by executive order. The Court considered that there was a sufficient causal connection between the original conviction and the recall during the ten-year period. Similarly in the *Weeks* case[84] the Court considered that the deprivation of liberty which arose when Weeks was recalled on revocation of the licence under which he had been released was sufficiently closely linked to the original conviction to meet the requirements of Article 5(1)(a).

The English provision permitting the Court of Appeal to determine that the time spent in prison pending an unmeritorious appeal shall not form part of the sentence being served was in issue in the *Monnell and Morris* case.[85] The Commission concluded that there had been a breach of Article 5, but the Court disagreed. The rule created a disincentive to unmeritorious appeals, thereby

---

[79] Para. 110 of the Judgment.

[80] Joint dissenting opinion of Judges Pettiti, Valticos, and Lopes Rocha, approved by Judges Walsh and Spielmann, p.39.

[81] *Engel and others* v. *Netherlands*, Judgment of 8 June 1976; (1979–80) 1 EHRR 647, and see ch. 8 below.

[82] *Lawless* v. *Ireland*, Judgment of 1 July 1961, Series A, No. 3; (1979–80) 1 EHRR 15.

[83] *Van Droogenbroeck* v. *Belgium*, Judgment of 24 June 1982, Series A, No. 50; (1982) 4 EHRR 443.

[84] *Weeks* v. *United Kingdom*, Judgment of 2 March 1987, Series A, No. 114; (1988) 10 EHRR 293. A separate complaint of a violation of Article 5(4) was successful: see below.

[85] *Monnell and Morris* v. *United Kingdom*, Judgment of 2 March 1987, Series A, No. 115; (1988) 10 EHRR 205.

assisting the speedier handling of deserving cases; and trial within a reasonable time is one of the objectives of Article 6.[86] Possible loss of time was therefore an integral part of the criminal appeal process following conviction of an offender and so was permissible under Article 5(1)(a). The case indicates that the requirement for a causal connection between conviction and the period of imprisonment will be very broadly construed.

Again, as part of the 'fourth instance doctrine', the Court will not substitute its own views on the appropriateness of a sentence for those of the national authorities. Thus, the applicants in the cases of *T. and V. v. United Kingdom*[87] failed to persuade the Court that their detention following their convictions, aged 11, for murdering a toddler when they were 10, was contrary to Article 5(1). In common with all children convicted of murder in England and Wales they were sentenced to an indeterminate period of detention ('during Her Majesty's pleasure'). It was argued on their behalf that to impose the same sentence on all child murderers, regardless of their age or circumstances, was arbitrary and therefore 'unlawful'. The Court, however, held that since the applicants' sentences complied with English law and followed conviction by a competent court, no issue arose under Article 5, although it did indicate that very long periods of detention in respect of juveniles might be inconsistent with Article 3 of the Convention.[88]

DETENTION OF A PERSON FOR FAILURE TO COMPLY WITH AN OBLIGATION PRESCRIBED BY LAW: ARTICLE 5(1)(b)

The first limb of paragraph (1)(b) authorizes detention for 'non-compliance with the lawful order of a court'. This could mean, *inter alia*, arrest to secure attendance in court following a failure to comply with a summons,[89] or imprisonment for failure to pay a fine[90] or to comply with an injunction or a custody or maintenance order.[91] In the *Steel and others* case,[92] the applicant hunt

---

[86] See ch. 8 below.

[87] *T. v. United Kingdom* (App. 24724/94); and *V. v. United Kingdom* (App. 24888/94) Judgments of 16 December 1999; (2000) 30 EHRR 121.

[88] See ch. 5 above.

[89] App. 32206/96, *GK v. Austria*, Commission's decision on admissibility of 16 October 1996.

[90] App. 28188/95, *Tyrell v. United Kingdom*, Commission's decision on admissibility of 4 September 1996.

[91] App. 26109/95, *Santa Cruz Ruiz v. United Kingdom*, decision of the Commission on admissibility of 22 October 1997.

[92] *Steel and others* v. *United Kingdom* (App. 24838/94), Judgment of 23 September 1998; (1998) 28 EHRR 603

saboteurs had been ordered by the magistrates' court to agree to be bound over to keep the peace for a period of twelve months. Their imprisonment for refusing to enter into this promise of future good conduct was held by the Court to fall within the scope of the first limb of Article 5(1)(b).

The second limb authorizes detention 'to secure the fulfilment of any obligation prescribed by law'. In the *Benham* case[93] the applicant's imprisonment for failing to pay the community charge was held to fall within this part of Article 5(1)(b).

The wording of this paragraph, and in particular this second limb, is problematic in that it arguably authorizes preventive detention. In the *Lawless* case the Irish Government submitted before the Commission (but not before the Court) that detention of a suspected terrorist to prevent the possible commission of an offence might be legitimate under Article 5(1)(b) 'to secure the fulfilment of an obligation prescribed by law'. The Commission considered, however, that this provision does not allow arrest or detention generally for the prevention of offences against public order or against the security of the State; so wide an interpretation would undermine the whole basis of Article 5. The obligation prescribed by law must be specific.[94] This reasoning was confirmed in the *Engel* case;[95] detention to secure the performance of general obligations could not fall within the terms of Article 5(1)(b).

Imprisonment for debt may be permitted by Article 5(1)(b). However, within the jurisdiction of the States which have ratified the Fourth Protocol to the Convention, a restriction on detention in such cases is introduced by Article 1 of that Protocol, which provides: 'No one shall be deprived of his liberty merely on the ground of inability to fulfil a contractual obligation.'

This Article was conceived to prohibit 'as contrary to the concept of human liberty and dignity, any deprivation of liberty for the sole reason that the individual had not the material means to fulfil his contractual obligations'.[96] The Article applies only to contractual debts, and not to obligations arising from legislation in public or private law.[97] Further, it does not apply if a debtor acts with malicious or fraudulent intent; or if a person deliberately refuses to fulfil an obligation, irrespective of his reasons; or if inability to meet a commitment is due to negligence. In these circumstances, the failure to fulfil a contractual obligation may legitimately constitute a criminal offence.[98]

The scope of Article 1 was examined *ex officio* by the Commission in a case

[93] *Benham* v. *United Kingdom* (App. 19380/92), Judgment of 10 June 1996; (1996) 22 EHRR 293.

[94] *Lawless* v. *Ireland*, Report of the Commission, 19 December 1959.

[95] *Engel and others* v. *Netherlands*, Judgment of 8 June 1976, Series A, No 22; (1979–80) 1 EHRR 647, para. 69 of Judgment.

[96] Explanatory Reports on the Second to Fifth Protocols to the Convention, Strasbourg 1971, at 39. For a list of the states which have ratified the protocol see: http://conventions.coe.int

[97] Ibid.

[98] Ibid.

where the applicant was detained in civil proceedings brought by a creditor. The German Code of Civil Procedure enables a court, at the request of a creditor, to order the detention of a debtor who fails to make an affidavit of his possessions. The Commission found that the applicant was lawfully detained under Article 5(1)(b), since there was a specific obligation under German law to make an affidavit.[99] Nor was the complaint admissible under the Fourth Protocol. The applicant had been detained in order to secure the fulfilment of his obligation to swear an affidavit. Consequently, his detention was not based merely on the ground of inability to fulfil a contractual obligation.

DETENTION OF MINORS: ARTICLE 5(1)(d)

This clause authorizes detention in two distinct sets of circumstances: the detention of minors by lawful order for the purposes of educational supervision and the lawful detention of minors for the purpose of bringing them before a competent legal authority. The paragraph clearly authorizes the exercise of the jurisdiction of juvenile courts in non-criminal cases.

The first limb covers orders requiring compulsory attendance at school which might amount to a deprivation of liberty under Article 5(1), even if the person affected is not in full-time detention. There is no requirement that the order should be that of a court; the making of such orders by an administrative authority is not excluded. In such cases however the person subject to the order will be entitled under paragraph (4) 'to take proceedings by which the lawfulness of his detention shall be decided speedily by a court and his release ordered if the detention is not lawful.'[100]

The second limb of paragraph (1)(d) allows the minor to be brought before the judicial or administrative authority which is to decide whether or not to order his or her detention.

It has not been clearly established at what age a person ceases to be a minor. The Council of Europe has adopted a resolution recommending Member States in principle to reduce the age of majority from 21 to 18,[101] but the adoption of the age of 18 as the age of majority has not been universal under national legal systems. In its decision on admissibility in the case of *Koniarska* v. *United Kingdom*,[102] the Court held that the applicant was a minor until the age of 18 and that Article 5(1)(d) permitted her detention for educational supervision up to that age, even though the school-leaving age in the United Kingdom is 16. It

[99] App. 5025/71, *X* v. *Federal Republic of Germany*, 18 December 1971 (1971) 14 *Yearbook* 692.
[100] See below in this chapter.
[101] Resolution CM(72) 29 of the Committee of Ministers of the Council of Europe.
[102] *Koniarska* v. *United Kingdom* (App. 33670/96), admissibility decision of 12 October 2000.

would appear, therefore, that 'minor' is to be given an autonomous meaning under the Convention, independent of the age of majority under national law.

The *Bouamar* case[103] concerned the detention of a 16-year-old boy with a disturbed personality. He had displayed behavioural problems and was detained in an adult prison for nine periods each of up to fifteen days because the authorities had been unable to find a suitable juvenile institution able to accept him immediately. The Belgian Government sought to argue that the detention was for educational supervision, but this argument failed since no genuine educational facilities had been made available for him. The Court concluded that an interim custody measure prior to placement involving supervised education was not precluded by Article 5(1)(d) but that the shuttling between prison and other arrangements totalling 119 days of detention in a 291-day period did violate the provision.[104]

In contrast in the *Koniarska* case,[105] the applicant was a 17-year-old girl who had been diagnosed as suffering from a psychopathic disorder and was placed in a specialist, secure, residential facility for seriously disturbed young people. She submitted that this detention was not for the purpose of educational supervision but was instead ordered as a containment measure, any education offered being purely incidental. However, the Court held that the words 'educational supervision' should not be equated rigidly with notions of classroom teaching but could also be seen as embracing other aspects of local authority care, particularly where, as was the case with the applicant, an extensive range of classes was made available.

The specific provisions relating to minors in Article 5(1)(d) do not preclude the application to them of arrest and detention under any of the other sub-paragraphs of Article 5(1), such as detention consequent upon conviction or as persons of unsound mind.

VULNERABLE GROUPS: ARTICLE 5(1)(e)

Article 5(1)(e) draws together a disparate group whose detention might be justified on grounds of social protection: those with infectious diseases, persons of unsound mind, alcoholics, drug addicts, and vagrants.

There is no requirement that the detention should be imposed by a court; it may be ordered by an administrative authority, although such an order will be subject to judicial control under paragraph (4).

---

[103] *Bouamar* v. *Belgium*, Judgment of 29 February 1988, Series A, No. 129; (1989) 11 EHRR 1.
[104] Paras. 51–3 of the Judgment.
[105] *Koniarska* v. *United Kingdom* (App. 33670/96), admissibility decision of 12 October 2000.

VAGRANTS

One of the leading authorities on Article 5(1)(e) is the judgment of the Court in the *Vagrancy* cases in 1971,[106] which concerned three applicants detained in vagrancy centres in Belgium by order of a magistrate under legislation then in force. The Court examined the definition of 'vagrant' in Belgian law, namely that 'vagrants are persons who have no fixed abode, no means of subsistence and no regular trade or profession' and held that this definition was not irreconcilable with the usual understanding of the term 'vagrant' or with its meaning under Article 5(1)(e). It then went on to find that, on the facts before the magistrates, the applicants were 'vagrants' and that there had been no breach of Article 5(1).[107] The Court thus not only examined the compatibility of the domestic law with the Convention, but also decided, in effect, that it had been correctly interpreted and applied.

This approach is unsustainable. Given the large number of applications received in Strasbourg from individuals claiming to have been wrongly detained and the practical difficulties involved in obtaining and assessing independent expert evidence, it would not be possible for the Court in each case itself to decide whether the detained person was, in fact, mentally ill or an alcoholic, for example. As will be seen below, in connection with the detention of persons of 'unsound mind', the case law generally places the emphasis on procedural safeguards and affords a large margin to the national authorities in assessing the medical evidence.

Another issue raised in the *Vagrancy* cases was whether the voluntary acts of the applicants could operate to waive their rights under the Convention. The Government argued that the applicants could not be regarded as having been 'deprived of liberty' within the meaning of Article 5, since they reported voluntarily to the police and since each man's admission to the vagrancy institution had been the result of an express or implicit request. The Court rejected this argument, holding:

[T]he right to liberty is too important in a 'democratic society' within the meaning of the Convention for a person to lose the benefit of the protection of the Convention for the single reason that he gives himself up to be taken into detention. Detention might violate Article 5 even although the person concerned might have agreed to it. When the matter is one which concerns *ordre public* within the Council of Europe, a scrupulous supervision by the organs of the Convention of all measures capable of violating the rights and freedoms which it guarantees is necessary in every case.[108]

There is no provision in Article 5 governing the length of detention

---

[106] *De Wilde, Ooms and Versyp v. Belgium*, Judgment of 18 June 1971, Series A, No. 12; (1979–80) 1 EHRR 438.
[107] Para. 68 of Judgment.
[108] Para. 65 of Judgment.

permissible under paragraph (1)(e). In the *Vagrancy* cases, two of the applicants had been placed at the disposal of the Government for the astonishingly long period of two years (they were both released earlier), while the third was placed at its disposal indefinitely (although in practice under Belgian law this meant one year). The case of vagrancy is exceptional because the 'vagrant' is detained for his or her previous rather than present condition, so that there is no obvious trigger for release. Unless a general limit to the length of detention can be inferred from the practice of the contracting States, so as to render longer periods 'arbitrary', the only control in the Convention would appear to be that the detention must not be so lengthy as to constitute inhuman or degrading treatment under Article 3.

It is, however, possible that if another such case were to come before the Court today, it would have regard to the fact that social attitudes in Europe have progressed and, in line with the case law on the detention of mental patients and alcoholics,[109] read into this provision an implied requirement that the detention be proved necessary for the welfare of the vagrant or the public.

MENTAL ILLNESS

The approach adopted by the Court to provide protection for persons detained by reason of mental illness has been to establish a framework of procedural tests which must be satisfied. In the *Winterwerp* case[110] the Court established three tests. First, the presence of 'unsound mind' must be determined by objective medical evidence; secondly, the mental illness must result in a condition making detention necessary for the protection of the patient or others; thirdly, the detention must be justified on a continuing basis.

In the case of *Varbanov* v. *Bulgaria*,[111] the Court found a violation based on the fact that the applicant, who had a history of threatening behaviour, had been committed to psychiatric hospital for a period of twenty days on the order of a prosecutor in the absence of any medical evidence of mental illness. Although the Court observed that in an urgent case where immediate committal was believed to be necessary for safety reasons it might be acceptable under Article 5(1)(e) to arrest the patient first and get a medical appraisal shortly thereafter, in Varbanov's case there was no evidence of danger and no psychiatric evaluation was ever undertaken throughout the time of his detention.

The developing nature of medical understanding of mental illness, together with the fact that individuals suffering from certain psychiatric conditions, if released, may pose a danger not only to themselves but also to the community,

---

[109] See below.
[110] *Winterwerp* v. *Netherlands*, Judgment of 24 October 1979, Series A, No. 33; (1979–80) 2 EHRR 387.
[111] *Varbanov* v. *Bulgaria* (App. 31365/96), Judgment of 5 October 2000.

has meant that there is a certain deference to national authorities in their evaluation of the medical evidence in connection with the second and third limbs of the *Winterwerp* test.[112] Even where the evidence shows that the detained person is no longer suffering from mental illness, it does not automatically follow that he or she should immediately and unconditionally be released back into the community.

The Court made this approach clear in the *Johnson* case,[113] although it also emphasized that the exercise of official caution cannot justify delaying release indefinitely. The applicant had been charged with assaulting a pregnant woman and diagnosed as suffering from a psychotic mental illness exacerbated by drug and alcohol abuse. Following his conviction in 1984 the court had made an order committing him to a secure psychiatric hospital. By 1989 the Mental Health Review Tribunal, which carried out an annual review of the continuing need for his detention, found on the medical evidence before it that the applicant was no longer mentally ill, although it did not consider that he was ready to live on his own in the community, and therefore ordered his discharge from hospital to be conditional on his residence under supervision in a hostel. However, because of a combination of the limited number of hostel places and the applicant's negative attitude, which deterred the few available hostels from taking him, no place was found for him and his release from hospital was delayed for four years, until the Tribunal ordered his unconditional release.

Before the Court the applicant argued that from the time of the 1989 review, when the Tribunal found that he was no longer suffering from mental illness, his detention had not been in conformity with Article 5(1)(e) and he should have been immediately and unconditionally released. The Court rejected this submission, declaring that such a rigid approach to the interpretation of the third *Winterwerp* condition would place an unacceptable degree of constraint on the national authorities' discretion, given that the assessment of full recovery from mental illness was not a certain science and that premature, unsupervised release might be risky in some cases. The Tribunal had based its decision on the medical evidence before it and it had not been unreasonable to make the applicant's release conditional on residence in a hostel.

However, once this condition had been imposed, the onus was on the authorities to make sure that a hostel place was available. In fact, the lack of a hostel place and the continuing insistence that the applicant could only be released to a hostel led to the indefinite deferral of his release, until he was unconditionally discharged four years after the Tribunal had first found him free of mental illness. This delay, together with the lack of adequate procedural safeguards—it

[112] See *Luberti v. Italy*, Judgment of 23 February 1984, Series A, No. 75; (1984) 6 EHRR 440, para. 27 of the Judgment. The criteria apply to recall of patients who have been detained in mental hospitals: see *X v. United Kingdom*, Judgment of 24 October 1981, Series A, No. 46; (1982) 4 EHRR 188.

[113] *Johnson v. United Kingdom* (App. 22520/93), Judgment of 24 October 1997; (1997) 27 EHRR 296.

was not possible for the applicant to petition the Tribunal between annual reviews—gave rise to a violation of Article 5(1).

It is perhaps fair to say that because of the need for specialist expertise and the near impossibility of the Court itself attempting to assess medical evidence, the requirement of procedural 'lawfulness' is particularly important in connection with the detention of the mentally ill. In the above-mentioned *Varbanov* case, as well as finding the applicant's detention unlawful for lack of supporting medical opinion, the Court found an additional ground of violation in that, at the time of the committal, Bulgarian law did not contain any express provision empowering a prosecutor to order compulsory confinement for the purpose of psychiatric evaluation. There was an instruction issued by the Minister of Health, implying that prosecutors had such powers, but this lacked the requisite clarity to conform with the standard of 'lawfulness' under the Convention.

There have also been findings of violations of Article 5 where the domestic law has been sufficiently clear and accessible but has simply not been complied with, which will, of course, render the deprivation of liberty unlawful under the Convention. So in the *Van der Leer* case[114] the absence of the hearing required by national law tainted the legality of the detention and in the *Wassink* case[115] the absence of participation by the court registrar (whose task it was to draw up a record of the proceedings) in the hearing which resulted in the detention violated the requirements of Article 5(1)(e).

The focus of Article 5 on the issue of deprivation of liberty has already been mentioned. The consequence of this for the mental patient is that Article 5(1)(e) provides no basis for raising questions about the conditions of detention or treatment afforded to a person detained as a mental patient,[116] although such issues could conceivably be raised under Articles 3 or 8.[117] The Court has however made it clear that there must be some relationship between the ground of detention relied upon under Article 5(1) and the place and conditions of detention. Thus, if a person is detained because of mental illness, he must be held in a hospital or clinic, and not in a prison where the treatment and therapy he requires is unavailable.[118]

Persons detained as being mentally unsound are normally detained for an indefinite period, although often with a right to periodical review.[119] Article

---

[114] *Van der Leer* v. *Netherlands*, Judgment of 21 February 1990, Series A, No. 170; (1990) 12 EHRR 567.
[115] *Wassink* v. *Netherlands*, Judgment of 27 September 1990, Series A, No. 185-A.
[116] See *Ashingdane* v. *United Kingdom*, Judgment of 28 May 1985, Series A, No. 93; (1985) 7 EHRR 528, para. 44 of the judgment. See also App. 10448/83, *Dhoest* v. *Belgium*, 14 May 1987, (1988) 55 DR 5.
[117] See chs. 5 and 11.
[118] *Aerts* v. *Belgium* (App. 25357/94), Judgment of 30 July 1998; (1999) 29 EHRR 50.
[119] See App. 2518/65, *X* v. *Denmark*, 14 December 1965, (1965) 8 *Yearbook* 370. Contrast App. 4625/70, *X* v. *Belgium*, 20 March 1972 (1972) 40 CD 21.

5(4), discussed below, is therefore of great importance for mental patients, for it will frequently be the case that initial detention in hospital is justified, but the need for continuing detention may be more questionable.

ALCOHOLICS AND THOSE SUFFERING FROM INFECTIOUS DISEASES

As with all the other terms describing vulnerable groups in Article 5(1)(e), the word 'alcoholic' carries an autonomous Convention meaning. The Court gave some indication as to how it should be interpreted in the first case to come before it concerning detention for drunkenness, *Litwa* v. *Poland*.[120] The applicant, a partially sighted pensioner, was apprehended by the police at a post office where he was complaining that his post box had been opened and emptied. He was taken to a sobering-up centre, where he was certified by a doctor as being 'moderately intoxicated' and held for six and a half hours. The Court observed that in common usage the word 'alcoholic' denotes a person who is addicted to alcohol. There was, however, a link with the other categories in sub-paragraph (e), in that the detention of individuals in these groups could be justified only where it was necessary for medical treatment or on grounds of social policy to prevent a risk of danger to themselves or to the public. Having regard to the rule in the Vienna Convention on the Law of Treaties that in interpreting a treaty it is necessary to look at its object and purpose,[121] the Court found that this purpose would be defeated if the provision allowed for the detention only of those suffering from the clinical condition of alcoholism, but not for non-alcoholics whose conduct under the influence of drink gave rise to a danger to the safety of themselves or others. This approach was confirmed by the *travaux préparatoires*, which included reference to 'drunkenness'. The applicant's arrest and detention therefore in principle fell within the scope of Article 5(1)(e). However, the Court found that there had been a violation of Article 5(1) because there was no evidence that the applicant had behaved in such a way as to pose a threat to himself or others or that the draconian measure of detention was necessary in the light of the rather trivial facts of the case. It is to be presumed that a similar approach should be followed in relation to the detention of 'drug addicts', but no case has yet come before the Court.

There has not, to date, been any judgment concerning detention 'for the prevention of the spreading of infectious diseases'. Under the Swedish Infectious Diseases Act, the compulsory isolation was permitted of HIV carriers who failed to comply with certain statutory measures designed to prevent the spread of AIDS. In October 2000 a case concerning the hospitalization under

---

[120] *Witold Litwa* v. *Poland* (App. 26629/95) Judgment of 4 April 2000; (2001) 33 EHRR 1267.
[121] See ch. 3 above.

the Act of an HIV-positive man who transmitted the virus to a 15-year-old boy was communicated for observations to the Swedish Government.[122]

DETENTION IN CONNECTION WITH DEPORTATION OR EXTRADITION: ARTICLE 5(1)(f)

The Court has so far declined to read into the words of Article 5(1)(f) any implied protection for persons facing expulsion, and, apart from the requirement of 'lawfulness', this paragraph therefore provides only limited assistance to detainees.

In order to comply with this provision, the detained person must be the object of action 'with a view to deportation or extradition'. There is no need for the State to establish that the detention was reasonably considered necessary in order to prevent the proposed expulsee from absconding or from committing an offence—in contrast to the position of a person detained under Article 5(1)(c), for example.[123]

In addition, as long as the *detention* is 'lawful', it is immaterial for the purposes of Article 5(1)(f) whether the underlying *decision to expel* can be justified under national or Convention law.[124] This interpretation follows from the wording of Article 5(1)(f) and can also be seen as an extension of the 'fourth instance' doctrine, corresponding, for example, to the principle that in assessing compliance with Article 5(1)(a) the Court of Human Rights will not itself examine whether there was sufficient evidence to support the applicant's conviction. Thus in the *Chahal* case,[125] even though the Court found that the decision to expel the applicant to India was contrary to Article 3 of the Convention because he would run a real risk of torture or illegal killing, his detention for six years prior to the Court's judgment was permissible under Article 5(1)(f).

It follows that, in the absence of any procedural irregularity or official arbitrariness such as to render the detention unlawful, the only way for an applicant to establish a breach of this provision is to show that, throughout or for some part of his detention, he was not truly the object of deportation or extradition action. One way of establishing this is to show that the State authorities did not pursue the expulsion proceedings with 'due diligence' and that

---

[122] *E.E. v. Sweden* (App. 56529/00).
[123] *Chahal v. United Kingdom* (App. 22414/93), Judgment of 15 November 1996: (1997) 23 EHRR 413, para. 112 of the judgment.
[124] Ibid.
[125] Ibid.

they thereby allowed the detention to be unnecessarily prolonged. In the *Kolompar* case[126] delays of over two years and eight months awaiting deportation were found not to constitute a violation of Article 5 since the delays were not attributable to the action of the authorities. Even more strikingly, as mentioned above, the Court found no violation of Article 5(1) in the *Chahal* case[127] where the applicant, a Sikh separatist accused of terrorism by the British Government, had been detained for over six years pending the completion of the domestic and Strasbourg proceedings. This period included a delay of over seven months while the Home Office considered and rejected an application for refugee status and a further six months for the Home Office to make a fresh decision after the first had been quashed by judicial review. The Court found that these delays were justified in view of the importance of the issues in the case—the Government alleged that intelligence information showed that Mr Chahal's continued residence in England raised a threat to British national security, whereas Mr Chahal denied these accusations and claimed that he would run a risk of torture or illegal execution if returned to India. Hasty decision-making in such a case would not, in the Court's view, benefit either the applicant or the general public. However, perhaps the *Chahal* case should be regarded as exceptional—six years does seem a very long time to imprison a person who has not been proved to have committed even the most insignificant criminal offence, and in such circumstances it is arguable that a high standard of speed and diligence should be expected of the State authorities.

NOTIFICATION OF THE REASONS FOR ARREST OR DETENTION

In the words of the Court:

[Article 5(2)] contains the elementary safeguard that any person arrested should know why he is being deprived of his liberty. This provision is an integral part of the scheme of protection afforded by Article 5: by virtue of paragraph 2 any person arrested must be told, in simple, non-technical language that he can understand, the essential legal and factual grounds for his arrest, so as to be able, if he sees fit, to apply to a court to challenge its lawfulness in accordance with paragraph 4. Whilst this information must be conveyed 'promptly' (in French: 'dans le plus court délai'), it need not be related in its entirety by the arresting officer at the very moment of the arrest. Whether the

---

[126] *Kolompar* v. *Belgium*, Judgment of 24 September 1992, Series A, No. 235-C; (1993) 16 EHRR 197, paras. 37–43 of the Judgment.

[127] *Chahal* v. *United Kingdom* (App. 22414/93), Judgment of 15 November 1996; (1997) 23 EHRR 413.

content and promptness of the information conveyed were sufficient is to be assessed in each case according to its special features.[128]

This provision applies in respect of *everyone* who is arrested or detained. It may be compared with Article 6(3)(a), which provides that everyone charged with a criminal offence must be informed promptly, in a language which they understand and in detail, of the nature and cause of the accusation against them. The information to which a person is entitled under Article 6 is more specific and more detailed than that required by Article 5, because it is necessary to enable him or her to prepare a defence. For the purposes of Article 5(2), on the other hand, it is sufficient if detainees are informed in general terms of the reasons for the arrest and of any charge against them.[129]

The question of the timing of notification was raised in the *Murray* case.[130] The Court noted that whether the content and promptness of the information given to the detainee were sufficient depended on the special features of each case. An interval of a matter of hours between arrest and interrogation, during which the reasons for her arrest were brought to her attention, could not be regarded as not being prompt notification.

On occasion, however, the circumstances of the arrest may speak for themselves, as the Court found to have been the case in *Dikme* v. *Turkey*.[131] The applicant had presented false identity papers to the police and had been arrested immediately the police discovered the forgery. Whether or not the police gave reasons, the Court found that the applicant could not complain under Article 5(2) that he had been ignorant of the grounds for his arrest.

In the *Kerr* case[132] the applicant was informed at the time of his arrest of the provision of domestic law under which he was detained (the Prevention of Terrorism Act). The Court held that a bare indication of the legal basis for an arrest could not, on its own, be sufficient for the purposes of Article 5(2), but that since, immediately after his arrest, the applicant was questioned about his suspected involvement in a recent bomb explosion at a military barracks, his membership of a proscribed organization, and about the use he had made of items seized by the police from his house, in particular computer equipment and the information stored on the computer, the reasons for his detention must have been sufficiently clear to him for the purposes of Article 5(2).

The requirement that the information should be given 'in a language which he understands' may create difficulties, particularly in view of the numbers of

---

[128] *Kerr* v. *United Kingdom* (App. 40451/98), admissibility decision of 7 December 1999.

[129] *App. 343/57, Nielsen* v. *Denmark*, 2 September 1959 (1958–9) 2 *Yearbook* 412, 462.

[130] *Murray* v. *United Kingdom*, Judgment of 28 October 1994, Series A, No. 300-A; (1995) 19 EHRR 193.

[131] *Dikme* v. *Turkey* (App. 20869/92), Judgment of 11 July 2000.

[132] *Kerr* v. *United Kingdom* (App. 40451/98), admissibility decision of 7 December 1999.

migrant workers in Europe and in the absence of a multilingual police force. However, the Commission has held that this requirement is satisfied if, immediately after the arrest, a person is interrogated by the investigating judge in his or her mother tongue.[133]

It is not clear whether the expression 'informed in a language (*une langue*) which he understands' requires that suspects should in fact understand the charge or that it should be explained if necessary at a level within their comprehension. Having regard to the purpose of the provision, it is arguable that the information should at least be given in language which would be understood by a person of only average intelligence.[134]

TESTING THE LEGALITY OF THE DETENTION

Article 5(4) provides that: 'Everyone who is deprived of his liberty by arrest or detention shall be entitled to take proceedings by which the lawfulness of his detention shall be decided speedily by a court and his release ordered if the detention is not lawful.'

Unlike the right to be 'brought promptly before a judge or other officer' in Article 5(3) which applies only to those detained on suspicion of having committed a criminal offence, the right to judicial control under Article 5(4) covers all forms of arrest and detention.

THE NATURE OF THE JUDICIAL REVIEW

The scope of the proceedings required by Article 5(4) was the subject of comment in *E* v. *Norway*:

Article 5(4) does not guarantee a right to judicial review of such a scope as to empower the court on all aspects of the case, including questions of pure expediency, to substitute its own discretion for that of the decision-making authority. The review should, however, be wide enough to bear on those conditions which are essential for the 'lawful' detention of a person according to Article 5(1).[135]

It follows, therefore, that if a person is detained under Article 5(1)(c) of the Convention, the 'court' must be empowered to examine whether or not there is sufficient evidence to give rise to a reasonable suspicion that he or she has committed an offence, because the existence of such a suspicion is essential if

---

[133] App. 2689/65, *Delcourt* v. *Belgium*, 7 February 1967 (1967) 10 *Yearbook* 238, 270.

[134] App. 8098/77, *X* v. *Federal Republic of Germany*, 13 December 1978 (1979) 16 DR 111.

[135] *E* v. *Norway*, Judgment of 29 August 1990, Series A, No. 181; (1990) 17 EHRR 30, para. 50 of the Judgment.

detention on remand is to be 'lawful' under the Convention.[136] Similarly, in the case of a person detained on grounds of mental ill-health, the reviewing 'court' must assess the legality of the detention in the light of the *Winterwerp* criteria discussed above.

The scope of review required with regard to a person detained under paragraph 5(1)(f) appears uncertain. In the *Chahal* judgment,[137] as has been seen, the Court held that all that was needed to ensure that the detention was 'lawful' under this provision was proof that action was being taken with a view to deportation; it was immaterial for the purposes of Article 5(1) whether or not the underlying decision to expel was justified or whether there was any evidence that the detention was necessary to prevent the proposed deportee from absconding or committing a crime, for example.[138] It might be assumed, therefore, that all that could be expected from the 'court' reviewing the legality of the detention under Article 5(4) would be a determination of the fact that deportation proceedings were genuinely underway. However, the Court went on to hold in the *Chahal* judgment that the bail and *habeas corpus* proceedings brought by the applicant in the English courts were deficient under Article 5(4) because the courts were unable to look behind the Secretary of State's assertions that national security would be at risk if Mr Chahal was at liberty so as to determine the question themselves in the light of all the available evidence. The Court went so far as to refer to a procedure used in Canada in such cases, which it suggested would ensure compliance with Article 5(4), whereby all evidence relating to national security was aired before the court deciding on the legality of the detention in the presence of a security-cleared counsel instructed by the detainee.

As noted above, the Court's case law under Article 5(1)(f) is anomalous, in that it provides a much lower level of protection to persons detained with a view to deportation than to persons detained under the other subparagraphs of Article 5(1). In the *Chahal* case, the Court's approach under Article 5(4) is greatly to be preferred to its ruling under Article 5(1), and it is to be hoped that any future decisions removing this inconsistency do so by increasing the safeguards for aliens deprived of their liberty.

The 'court' to which the detained person has access for the purposes of Article 5(4) does not have to be a 'court of law of the classic kind integrated within the standard judicial machinery of the country'.[139] It must,

---

[136] See e.g. *Nikolova* v. *Bulgaria* (App. 31195/96), Judgment of 25 March 1999; and *Grauslys* v. *Lithuania* (App. 36743/97), Judgment of 10 October 2000.

[137] *Chahal* v. *United Kingdom* (App. 22414/93), Judgment of 15 November 1996; (1997) 23 EHRR 413.

[138] Para. 112 of the Judgment.

[139] *Weeks* v. *United Kingdom*, Judgment of 2 March 1987, Series A, No. 254; (1988) 10 EHRR 293, para. 61 of the Judgment.

however, be a body of a 'judicial character' offering certain procedural guarantees.[140]

Thus the 'court' must be independent both of the executive and of the parties to the case.[141] It must have the power to order release if it finds that the detention is unlawful; a mere power of recommendation is insufficient.[142]

As far as procedural requirements are concerned, Article 5(4) does not always require the same guarantees as would be necessary under Article 6(1) for criminal or civil litigation. The proceedings must generally be capable of commencement on the application of the person deprived of his or her liberty, though automatic reference to review of a judicial character will also suffice. The form of procedure followed may vary depending on the nature of the detention under review and the relevant issues before the 'court'.[143] An adversarial oral hearing with legal representation is always required, however, in cases of detention under Article 5(1)(c) or where the continued legality of the detention depends on an assessment of the applicant's character or mental state.[144] In the *Lamy* case,[145] the Court considered that the failure to make documents available promptly to the applicant's lawyer precluded the possibility of an effective challenge to statements which formed the basis of the decision to detain, giving rise to a violation of Article 5(4).

The requirement for review by a 'court' has prompted a spate of applications from former Communist countries where under the old regime it was common for the prosecuting authorities to be empowered to decide virtually all questions relating to pre-trial detention, with the possibility of only limited recourse to a court. In Bulgaria, for example, in the mid-1990s, a person detained on remand on the decision of the prosecutor was entitled to contest his detention in court only once, even if the detention continued for two years or more. Since the frequency of this periodic review was inadequate, and since the prosecution was not an independent 'court' for the purposes of Article 5(4), the Court found a violation in the *Assenov* case.[146] During the same period in Poland, although a person detained on remand could apply to a court, neither the detained person nor his lawyer was entitled to attend the hearing or be informed

---

[140] *De Wilde, Ooms and Versyp v. Belgium*, Judgment of 18 June 1971, Series A, No. 12; (1979–80) 1 EHRR 438.

[141] *Neumeister v. Austria*, Judgment of 27 June 1968, Series A, No. 8; (1979–80) 1 EHRR 91, para. 24 of 'The Law'.

[142] See e.g. *Singh v. United Kingdom* (App. 23389/94), Judgment of 21 February 1996, para. 65 of the judgment; and *Curley v. United Kingdom* (App. 32340/96), Judgment of 28 March 2000.

[143] See e.g. *Niedbala v. Poland* (App. 27915/95), Judgment of 4 July 2000, para. 66 of the judgment.

[144] *Assenov v. Bulgaria* (App. 24760/94), Judgment of 28 October 1998; (1998) 28 EHRR 652; *Niedbala v. Poland* (App. 27915/95), Judgment of 4 July 2000; *Grauzlys v. Lithuania* (App. 36743/97), Judgment of 10 October 2000; *Wloch v. Poland*, Judgment of 19 October 2000; (2002) 34 EHRR 229.

[145] *Lamy v. Belgium*, Judgment of 30 March 1989, Series A, No. 151; (1989) 11 EHRR 529.

[146] *Assenov v. Bulgaria* (App. 24760/94), Judgment of 28 October 1998; (1998) 28 EHRR 652.

of the prosecutor's reasons for opposing release, leading the European Court to find violations in a number of cases.[147]

WHEN ARE REVIEWS REQUIRED?

Article 5(4) provides that 'the lawfulness of [the] detention shall be decided *speedily*' (emphasis added). There are two aspects to this requirement: first, the opportunity for legal review must be provided soon after the person is taken into detention (and thereafter, as discussed below, at reasonable intervals if necessary); secondly, the review proceedings must be conducted with due diligence.

In each case, the question whether the review has been completed sufficiently 'speedily' depends on all the circumstances. In a case of a straightforward bail application by a man detained on suspicion of drug-trafficking, for example, the Court held that three weeks was too long.[148] Longer periods might be acceptable in more complex cases—for example, where it is necessary to seek medical reports in respect of a detained mental patient—but, given the importance of the right to liberty, there is still a pressing obligation on the authorities to deal quickly with such applications for release. In the *Baranowski* case,[149] for example, the fact that it took a court deciding a bail application six weeks to obtain a report from a cardiologist and a further month to obtain evidence from a neurologist and a psychiatrist was evidence of lack of due diligence and gave rise to a violation of Article 5(4).

In many cases, the examination carried out by the court which first makes the order for detention is sufficient for the purposes of Article 5(4). This is so, for example, where a person convicted of a criminal offence is sentenced to a determinate term of imprisonment.

Where, however, the justification for a prolonged period of detention is liable to vary over time, the detained person is entitled under Article 5(4) to apply for judicial review of the detention's continued legality at intervals. This proposition was first enunciated in cases of indefinite detention under mental health legislation, but has been extended to cases where continuing detention is conditioned upon a view that the person is dangerous in a broader sense, and even to cases of detention on remand.[150]

[147] *Niedbala* v. *Poland* (App. 27915/95), Judgment of 4 July 2000; *Trzaska* v. *Poland* (App. 25792/94), Judgment of 11 July 2000; *Wloch* v. *Poland* (App. 27785/95); Judgment of 19 October 2000, (2002) 34 EHRR 229; and see the *Grauzinis* v. *Lithuania* (App. 37975/97), Judgment of 10 October 2000 for a similar problem in Lithuania.

[148] *Rehbock* v. *Slovenia* (App. 29462/95), Judgment of 28 November 2000; and see also *G.B.* v. *Switzerland* (App. 27426/95), Judgment of 30 November 2000; (2002) 34 EHRR 265 (32 days to decide the bail application of terrorist suspect was too long).

[149] *Baranowski* v. *Poland* (App. 28358/95), Judgment of 28 March 2000.

[150] *De Jong, Baljet and van der Brink* v. *Netherlands*, Judgment of 22 May 1984, Series A, No. 77; (1986) 8 EHRR 20 and *Bezicheri* v. *Italy*, Judgment of 25 October 1989; Series A, No. 164 (1990) 12 EHRR 210.

Thynne, Wilson and Gunnell[151] concerned applicants serving indeterminate life sentences for sex offences, who had not been released, despite having served periods of imprisonment in excess of the normal sentence for their offences. The Court ruled that they were entitled to periodic review of the continuing existence of grounds for their detention, since the circumstances which originally justified the indeterminate sentence might well have changed. The review had to be effective, in the sense of taking proper account of the original concerns which led to the detention, and it should also be conducted judicially, in a procedurally fair manner, and speedy. In the *Oldham* case[152] the Court held that a two-year interval between reviews of detention following the applicant's recall to prison was too long to be 'speedy'.

In the *Wynne* case[153] the Court made it clear that a prisoner serving a life sentence for murder is not entitled to periodic review, because the sentence (which is mandatory in the United Kingdom for murder) is imposed as punishment in recognition of the seriousness of the offence, and does not include any indeterminate element based on a characteristic of the offender, such as dangerousness, which was liable to change over time. In such a case, therefore, the requirements of Article 5(4) were met by the original trial and appeal proceedings.[154] The applicability of Article 5(4) to mandatory life prisoners will be considered again by the Grand Chamber in the case of *Stafford* v. *United Kingdom.*[155]

In the *Hussain* and *Singh* cases[156] the Court held that the sentence of 'detention during Her Majesty's pleasure', automatically imposed on juveniles convicted of murder in the United Kingdom, was closer to an adult discretionary, rather than a mandatory, life sentence. After the expiry of an initial 'tariff' period of imprisonment, served to satisfy the public requirement of retribution, the juvenile's continued detention could be justified only on grounds of dangerousness, and periodic review was therefore necessary under Article 5(4). In the cases of *T. and V.* v. *United Kingdom,*[157] which also concerned children detained during Her Majesty's pleasure, the Court found that Article 5(4) had been violated because there had never been a judicial control of the applicants' detention. Following their conviction for murder, the Home Secretary, rather than a judge, had decided on the length of the 'tariff' to be served, and there had

---

[151] *Thynne, Wilson and Gunnell* v. *United Kingdom,* Judgment of 25 October 1990, Series A, No. 190; (1991) 13 EHRR 666.

[152] *Oldham* v. *United Kingdom* (App 36273/97), Judgment of 26 September 2000; (2001) 31 EHRR 34.

[153] *Wynne* v. *United Kingdom,* Judgment of 18 July 1994, Series A, No. 294-A; (1995) 19 EHRR 333.

[154] Para. 38 of the judgment.

[155] *Stafford* v. *United Kingdom* (App. 46295/99), admissibility decision of 29 May 2001.

[156] *Hussain* v. *United Kingdom* (App. 21928/93), Judgment of 21 February 1996; (1996) 22 EHRR 1; *Singh* v. *United Kingdom* (App. 23389/94), Judgment of 21 February 1996.

[157] *T.* v. *United Kingdom* (App. 24724/94); and *V.* v. *United Kingdom* (App. 24888/94) Judgments of 16 December 1999; (2000) 30 EHRR 121.

been no subsequent review because, at the time the case was considered by the Court of Human Rights, the tariffs had not yet expired.

AN ENFORCEABLE RIGHT TO COMPENSATION

Article 5(5) provides that: 'Everyone who has been the victim of arrest or detention in contravention of the provisions of this Article shall have an enforceable right to compensation.' It is not clear why special provision is made for compensation for a breach of Article 5(1) to (4), when there is no such special provision in relation to the other rights guaranteed by the Convention, and when there is a general provision under Article 13 requiring an effective remedy for any violation.

Although any breach of Article 5 established by domestic courts or by Convention organs will, in the absence of an enforceable right to compensation under national law, give rise in addition to a breach of Article 5(5), relatively few applicants invoke this provision before the Court, perhaps because by the time they get to Strasbourg most applicants are more interested in seeking damages under Article 41.

However, the fact that in the United Kingdom it is virtually impossible to obtain compensation for unlawful detention without evidence either of bad faith on the part of the court making the order for detention[158] or a miscarriage of justice,[159] has led to several findings of violation of Article 5(5). In the *Fox, Campbell and Hartley*[160] and *Brogan*[161] cases, for example, the Court found this provision to have been breached since there was no rule of Northern Irish law which would have provided compensation for the arrest and prolonged initial detention of the applicants under the prevention of terrorism legislation. More recently, the Court came to the same conclusion in the *Hood* case,[162] where the applicant, a soldier, was unable to claim compensation before the English courts in respect of the fact that his commanding officer, who was not sufficiently independent for the purposes of Article 5(3), had authorized his detention in close arrest.

---

[158] See e.g. section 108 of the Courts and Legal Services Act 1990, considered in *Benham* v. *United Kingdom* (App. 19380/92), Judgment of 10 June 1996; (1996) 22 EHRR 293.

[159] Criminal Justice Act 1988, section 133.

[160] *Fox, Campbell and Hartley* v. *United Kingdom*, Judgment of 30 August 1990, Series A, No. 182; (1991) 13 EHRR 157.

[161] *Brogan and others* v. *United Kingdom*, Judgment of 29 November 1988, Series A, No. 145-B; (1989) 11 EHRR 117.

[162] *Hood* v. *United Kingdom* (App. 27267/95), Judgment of 18 February 1999; (2000) 29 EHRR 365.

CONCLUDING COMMENTS

The right to liberty is of fundamental importance. As well as the value to the individual of liberty in itself, many of the other rights protected by the Convention are to a certain extent conditional upon it, since once a person is held within the custody of the State it becomes possible to interfere with and place limitations on his or her autonomy in every imaginable way; the detainee may only send and receive letters if this is allowed by those holding him, for example, and his detention may leave him vulnerable to torture and execution.[163] It is, therefore, regrettable that the text of Article 5 of the Convention is rather confused and unclear. Instead of using a multiplicity of expressions— 'competent court' in 5(1)(a), 'court' in 5(1)(b) and 5(4), 'competent legal authority' in 5(1)(c), and 'judge or other office authorized by law to exercise judicial power' in 5(3)—would it not have been possible for those drafting this Article to use one term consistently? And what is to be made of the apparent overlap of limitations on pre-trial detention in paragraphs 1(c) and 3, and of the rights to judicial review in paragraphs 3 and 4?

In their approach to the interpretation of this Article the Strasbourg organs have done much to overcome these problems. However, there remains scope to improve the protection of detainees still further. It seems anomalous, for example, that whereas the alleged necessity of detaining criminal suspects and the mentally ill is subjected to the strictest scrutiny, under the case law as it stands States are free to deprive asylum-seekers of their liberty as long as deportation proceedings are in progress, regardless of any need to show that the detention is required to prevent avoidance of immigration controls. The extent to which States are required to take action to prevent unlawful detention by third parties—either within national jurisdiction or extraterritorially—is another area where clarification from the Court would be welcome.

[163] See *Aksoy* v. *Turkey* (App. 21987/93), Judgment of 18 December 1996; (1997) 23 EHRR 553, para. 76 of the judgment.

8

THE RIGHT TO A FAIR TRIAL IN CIVIL AND CRIMINAL CASES

INTRODUCTION

Article 6 is an omnibus provision, which has been described as 'a pithy epitome of what constitutes a fair administration of justice'.[1] The rights protected by the Article occupy a central place in the Convention system. A fair trial, in civil and criminal cases alike, is a basic element of the notion of the rule of law and part of the common heritage, according to the Preamble, of the Contracting States.

While Article 6(2) and (3)[2] contain specific provisions setting out 'minimum rights' applicable only in respect of those charged with a criminal offence, Article 6(1) applies both to civil and criminal proceedings.

The text of Article 6(1) reads:

In the determination of his civil rights and obligations or of any criminal charge against him, everyone is entitled to a fair and public hearing within a reasonable time by an independent and impartial tribunal established by law. Judgment shall be pronounced publicly but the press and public may be excluded from all or part of the trial in the interests of morals, public order or national security in a democratic society, where the interests of juveniles or the protection of the private life of the parties so require, or to the extent strictly necessary in the opinion of the court in special circumstances where publicity would prejudice the interests of justice.

Article 6 is the provision of the Convention most frequently invoked by applicants to Strasbourg.[3] As with other provisions of the Convention, many of the terms used in Article 6(1) bear 'autonomous' meanings and require interpretation. It is therefore hardly surprising that there is substantial case law on the provision's application. It would not be possible, within the scope of this book, to give a comprehensive account of this case law, and the present chapter

---

[1] J. Cremona, 'The public character of trial and judgment in the jurisprudence of the European Court of Human Rights' in F. Matscher and H. Petzold, *Protecting Human Rights: The European Dimension: Studies in Honour of Gérard J. Wiarda* (Köln, 1990), at 107.

[2] Considered in ch. 9 below.

[3] Of the 10,486 new applications registered by the Court in 2000, 7,264 included a complaint under Art. 6.

is intended only to provide an overview of some of the more important and interesting aspects.[4]

THE SCOPE OF ARTICLE 6(1)

THE 'FOURTH INSTANCE' DOCTRINE

Every month the Court of Human Rights receives many hundreds of letters complaining about the decisions reached by national courts in civil and criminal trials. These applications are, however, based on a fundamental misconception of the Convention system. The Court has no jurisdiction under Article 6 to reopen domestic legal proceedings or to substitute its own findings of fact or national law for the findings of domestic courts.[5] The Court's task with regard to a complaint under Article 6 is to examine whether the proceedings, taken as a whole, were fair and complied with the specific safeguards stipulated by the Convention. Unlike a national court of appeal, it is not concerned with the questions whether the conviction was safe, the sentence appropriate, the award of damages in accordance with national law, and so on. And a finding by the Court that an applicant's trial fell short of the standards of Article 6 does not have the effect of quashing the conviction or overturning the judgment, as the case may be.[6]

The Court calls this principle the 'fourth instance' doctrine, because it is *not* to be seen as a third or fourth instance of appeal from national courts. It is important to bear the doctrine in mind when considering whether a particular factual situation based on criminal or civil proceedings raises any issue under Article 6.

WHAT IS A 'CRIMINAL CHARGE'?

Article 6(1) applies 'in the determination of [a person's] civil rights and obligations or of any criminal charge against him'. As with other key expressions used in the Convention, the Court has ruled that the concept of a 'criminal charge' must bear an 'autonomous' meaning, independent of the categorizations employed by the national legal systems of the Member States.[7] In this way, it is

---

[4] See e.g. J. Simor and B. Emmerson (eds.), *Human Rights Practice* (London, 2000) for a more detailed account.

[5] It follows, therefore, that an application pending before the Court of Human Rights is not a ground for a stay of execution in domestic proceedings: see *Locabail (UK) Ltd* v. *Waldorf Investment Corp and others* [2000] HRLR 623, 25 May 2000, Chancery Division.

[6] See ch. 25 below.   [7] See ch. 3 above.

possible to achieve uniformity of approach throughout Europe and prevent States from avoiding Convention controls by classifying offences as disciplinary, administrative or civil matters.

The *Engel* case[8] concerned action taken against members of the armed forces in respect of offences, such as insubordination, classified in the Netherlands as disciplinary in nature. The Court stated that relevant considerations in establishing whether the matter should be seen as involving the determination of a 'criminal charge' for the purposes of Article 6 included the nature of the offence charged, the severity of the sanction at stake (having regard in particular to any loss of liberty, a characteristic of criminal liability), and the group to whom the legislation applied (small and closely defined groups of potential offenders are suggestive of a disciplinary or administrative rather than a mainstream criminal offence). Short periods of imprisonment are not sufficient in themselves to bring Article 6 into play: Engel's punishment of two days of strict arrest was insufficiently severe, in the absence of other criminal characteristics, to be regarded as a criminal penalty. The domestic classification is important, however, since if a matter is classed as criminal under national law this will be enough to bring it within the scope of Article 6, even if it is relatively trivial.

In the *Campbell and Fell* case,[9] the Court used this methodology to rule that the parallels between the jurisdiction of prison Boards of Visitors to order substantial loss of remission for disciplinary matters within the prison, and that of the criminal courts, were sufficient for the Boards' jurisdiction to be considered as involving the determination of a criminal charge.

Rather more problematic are situations in which lesser offences are involved and where a policy of decriminalization is in operation. The situation in the *Öztürk* case[10] concerned the imposition of a fine by a German court for a minor motoring offence. The European Court was called upon to consider whether these proceedings attracted the full protection of the rights contained in Article 6 governing the determination of criminal charges. It reaffirmed its earlier case law that the nature and severity of the offence and penalty were relevant: the purpose of the fine was both deterrent and punitive and this sufficed to show the criminal nature of the matter for Convention purposes. The process of decriminalization in the national law did not affect the classification under the Convention.[11]

[8] *Engel and others* v. *Netherlands*, Judgment of 8 June 1976, Series A, No. 22; (1979–80) 1 EHRR 647; see also *Findlay* v. *United Kingdom* (App. 22107/93), Judgment of 25 February 1997; (1997) 24 EHRR 221; *Hood* v. *United Kingdom* (App. 27267/95), Judgment of 18 February 1999; (2000) 29 EHRR 365.

[9] *Campbell and Fell* v. *United Kingdom*, Judgment of 28 June 1984, Series A, No. 80; (1985) 7 EHRR 165; see also *Ezeh and Conners* v. *United Kingdom* (Apps. 39665/98 and 40086/98), admissibility decisions of 30 January 2001.

[10] *Öztürk* v. *Germany*, Judgment of 21 February 1984, Series A, No. 73; (1984) 6 EHRR 409.

[11] The Court has similarly found, against other States, that motoring offences, despite local classification as 'administrative', are 'criminal' for the purposes of Article 6: *Lutz* v. *Germany*, Judgment of 25 August 1987, Series A, No. 123; (1988) 10 EHRR 163; *Schmautzer* v. *Austria*, Judgment of 23 October 1995,

A strong dissenting group of five felt that the decision did not adequately reflect the trend towards decriminalization of minor offences in several European countries and the fact that it was in the interests of the accused to remove certain types of conduct from the stigma of criminality. Recognizing the legitimacy of these significant changes would, for them, take such matters outside the ambit of criminal charges.

The Court has not, to date, ruled whether contempt of court proceedings in the United Kingdom are 'criminal' within the meaning of Article 6. Some guidance can, however, be drawn from the case law concerning parallel pro- cedures in other countries. The applicant in the *Weber* case[12] had been engaged in defamation proceedings in Switzerland. He held a press conference in which, contrary to the Code of Criminal Procedure which protected the confidentiality of court proceedings, he disclosed some of the details of the case, and was fined 300 Swiss francs. The Court of Human Rights, holding that this was 'a determination of a criminal charge', found it significant that the rule in the Code potentially applied to the whole population (rather than, for example, lawyers) and made provision for a punitive measure. Moreover, the fine could in certain circumstances be converted into a prison sentence.[13]

It would appear to be a different matter, however, where the contempt has no wide, public ramifications, but relates entirely to maintaining respectful and disciplined conduct of litigants towards the court. The applicant in the *Ravnsborg* case[14] was a university law lecturer engaged in civil proceedings about the care of his mother, had been fined 1,000 Swedish kroner for making defama- tory statements about public officials in his written court pleadings. The Court noted that it was not established that provisions on sanctions for disturbing the good order of court proceedings fell within the criminal law of Sweden. Using the three criteria established in the earlier cases, it held that the circumstances of this case were distinguishable from those in *Weber*, principally because the nature of the offence was closely allied to the maintenance of good order in civil proceedings, and was in essence disciplinary:

Rules enabling a court to sanction disorderly conduct in proceedings before it are a common feature of the legal systems of the Contracting States. Such rules and sanctions derive from the indispensable power of a court to ensure the proper and orderly func- tioning of its own proceedings. Measures ordered by courts under such rules are more

---

Series A, No. 328-A; (1995) 21 EHRR 511; *Malige* v. *France* (App. 27812/95), Judgment of 23 September 1998; (1999) 28 EHRR 578; and see also *Lauko* v. *Slovakia* (App. 26138/95), Judgment of 2 September 1998 (nuisance); and *Bendenoun* v. *France*, Judgment of 24 February 1994, Series A, No. 284; (1994) 18 EHRR 54; *AP, MP and TP* v. *Switzerland* (App. 19958/92), Judgment of 29 August 1997; (1998) 26 EHRR 541 (tax offences).

[12] *Weber* v. *Switzerland*, Judgment of 22 May 1990, Series A, No. 177; (1990) 12 EHRR 508.
[13] See also *Demicoli* v. *Malta*, Judgment of 27 August 1991, Series A, No. 210; (1992) 14 ECHR 47.
[14] *Ravnsborg* v. *Sweden*, Judgment of 23 March 1994, Series A, No. 283-B; (1994) 18 EHRR 38.

akin to the exercise of disciplinary powers than to the imposition of a punishment for commission of a criminal offence.

The Court did not consider that the fact that the applicant faced the 'theoretical possibility' of imprisonment if he failed to pay the fine imposed for his misconduct was enough to make the proceedings 'criminal'. The position might perhaps have been different had Mr Ravnsborg stood a real risk of a substantial period of detention. The *Benham* case[15] concerned proceedings in an English magistrates' court for committal to prison for non-payment of community charge ('poll tax'). The proceedings were classified as civil under English law but the Court held that they were 'criminal' for the purposes of Article 6. It attached significance to the facts that the obligation to pay the charge applied to all adults; that there was a punitive element to the imprisonment, which could be imposed only following a finding of 'wilful refusal to pay or culpable neglect'; and that the maximum penalty was three months' imprisonment.

AT WHAT STAGES OF CRIMINAL PROCEEDINGS DOES ARTICLE 6(1) APPLY?

The protection of Article 6 starts from the time when a person is charged with a criminal offence. This is not, however, necessarily the moment when formal charges are first made against a person suspected of having committed an offence. For, as previously noted, the protection of Article 6 does not depend on the particular features of the system of criminal investigation and prosecution, which may and do vary considerably between the Contracting Parties. Moreover, as the object of Article 6 is to protect a person throughout the criminal process, and since formal charges may not be brought until a fairly advanced stage of an investigation, it is necessary to find a criterion for the opening of criminal proceedings which is independent of the actual development of the procedure in a specific case.

The Court has defined a 'charge' for the purposes of Article 6(1) as 'the official notification given to an individual by the competent authority of an allegation that he has committed a criminal offence.'[16] It may, however, 'in some instances take the form of other measures which carry the implication of such an allegation and which likewise substantially affect the situation of the suspect.'[17]

Article 6(1) covers the whole of the proceedings in issue, including appeal proceedings and the determination of sentence.[18]

---

[15] *Benham* v. *United Kingdom* (App. 19380/92), Judgment of 10 June 1996; (1996) 22 EHRR 293; see also *Steel and others* v. *United Kingdom* (App. 24838/94), Judgment of 23 September 1998; (1998) 28 EHRR 603.

[16] *Eckle* v. *Germany*, Judgment of 15 July 1982, Series A, No. 51; (1983) 5 EHRR 1, para. 73 of judgment.

[17] *Foti* v. *Italy*, Judgment of 10 December 1982, Series A, No. 56; (1983) 5 EHRR 313, para. 52 of judgment.

[18] *Eckle* v. *Germany*, Judgment of 15 July 1982, Series A, No. 51; (1983) 5 EHRR 1, paras. 76–7; *Phillips* v. *United Kingdom* (App. 41087/98), Judgment of 5 September 2001.

Thus, in the *Delcourt* case,[19] Article 6(1) was found to be applicable to proceedings before the Belgian Court of Cassation. The Government had argued that the Court of Cassation did not deal with the merits of cases submitted to it, but the Court found that although the judgment of the Court of Cassation could only confirm or quash a decision, and not reverse or replace it, it was still 'determining' a criminal charge.

The cases of *T* and *V* v. *United Kingdom*[20] raised questions about the applicability of Article 6(1) to a sentencing procedure. The applicants had been convicted at the age of 11 of murdering a toddler the year before. As with all children convicted in England and Wales of murder, they were sentenced to be detained 'during Her Majesty's pleasure'. This is an indeterminate sentence: a period of detention, 'the tariff', is served to satisfy the requirements of retribution and deterrence, and thereafter it is legitimate to continue to detain the offender only if this appears to be necessary for the protection of the public. At the time of the applicants' conviction, the tariff was set by the Home Secretary. The Court held that the tariff-fixing procedure amounted to the fixing of a sentence and that there had been a violation of Article 6(1) since the Home Secretary was not 'an independent and impartial tribunal'.[21]

Proceedings which take place after conviction and sentence have become final fall outside Article 6. Thus this provision does not cover an application by a convicted prisoner for release on probation or parole,[22] or for a new trial,[23] or for review of his sentence after the decision has become *res judicata*.[24] Nor does Article 6(1) apply on an application for provisional release pending trial.[25]

WHAT ARE 'CIVIL RIGHTS AND OBLIGATIONS'?

The definition of 'civil rights and obligations' has proved more problematic.

First, it is clear that there must be a '*right*' (or an 'obligation'). Thus, for example, questions relating to the making of an *ex gratia* payment by the State

---

[19] *Delcourt* v. *Belgium*, Judgment of 17 January 1970, Series A, No. 11; (1979–80) 1 EHRR 355.

[20] *T* v. *United Kingdom* (App. 24724/94); and *V* v. *United Kingdom* (App. 24888/94) Judgments of 16 December 1999; (2000) 30 EHRR 121.

[21] The position may be different as regards the fixing of the tariff for adult offenders serving mandatory life sentences: see *Wynne* v. *United Kingdom*, Judgment of 18 July 1994, Series A, No. 294-A; (1994) 19 EHRR 333, para. 35 of the judgment, shortly to be reconsidered by the Grand Chamber in *Stafford* v. *United Kingdom* (App. 46295/99), admissibility decision of 29 May 2001.

[22] App. 606/59, *X* v. *Austria*, 19 September 1961 (1961) 4 *Yearbook* 340; App. 1760/63, *X* v. *Austria*, 23 May 1966, (1966) 9 *Yearbook* 166; App. 4133/69, *X* v. *United Kingdom*, 13 July 1970, (1970) 13 *Yearbook* 780.

[23] App. 864/60, *X* v. *Austria*, 10 March 1962, (1963) 9 CD 17; App. 4429/70, *X* v. *Federal Republic of Germany*, 1 February 1971, (1971) 37 CD 109.

[24] App. 1237/61, *X* v. *Austria*, 5 March 1962 (1962) 5 *Yearbook* 96, at 102.

[25] *Neumeister* v. *Austria*, Judgment of 27 June 1968, Series A, No. 8; (1979–80) 1 EHRR 91, paras. 22 and 23 of The Law; *Matznetter* v. *Austria*, Judgment of 10 November 1969, Series A, No. 10; (1979–80) 1 EHRR 198, para. 13 of The Law.

would not attract the protection of Article 6 because there is no *right* to such a payment. Secondly, the right (or obligation) must exist under national law: this point is dealt with in more detail below in the section on 'access to court'. Thirdly, the right (or obligation) must be *'civil'* in nature, and it is in connection with this aspect of the definition that the real difficulties arise.

It is evident that this phrase covers ordinary civil litigation between private individuals, relating, for example, to actions in tort, contract, and family law. It is more difficult, however, to determine whether Article 6(1) should apply also to disputes between individuals and the State concerning rights which, under some systems of law, fall under administrative rather than private law. If, for example, a public authority expropriates my land, do I have the right to a court hearing? Does the term cover only private rights to the exclusion of public law matters?[26]

From the start, the Court and Commission took the view that, as with the definition of 'criminal charge', the question whether a dispute relates to 'civil rights and obligations' could not be answered solely by reference to the way in which it is viewed under the domestic law of the respondent State; the concept has an 'autonomous' meaning under the Convention.[27] Any other approach would have allowed States to circumvent fair trial guarantees under Article 6(1) simply by classifying various areas of the law as 'public' or 'administrative' and would have risked creating disparity in the protection of human rights throughout Europe.

Whilst this refusal to be tied by national law definitions is no doubt correct, it does give rise to uncertainty as to whether a particular type of dispute is included. Although the Court has, from time to time, appeared to base itself on various elements such as the economic nature of the right concerned, it has never attempted to elaborate universal criteria, comparable to the *Engel* criteria for a 'criminal offence',[28] by which to identify 'civil rights and obligations', preferring instead to decide the matter on a case-by-case basis. The closest it has come to giving general guidance is to repeat that whilst the domestic law position is not totally without importance, the substantive content, character, and effects of the right concerned are more decisive.

The Court first considered the interpretation of 'civil rights and obligations' in the *Ringeisen* case.[29] The dispute in question involved an application by

---

[26] For a detailed consideration of the legislative history of the provision, see P. Van Dijk, 'The interpretation of "civil rights and obligations" by the European Court of Human Rights—One more Step to Take' in F. Matscher and H. Petzold, *Protecting Human Rights: The European Dimension: Studies in Honour of Gérard J. Wiarda* (Köln, 1990), at 131–43.

[27] App. 1931/63, *X v. Austria*, 2 October 1964, (1964) 7 *Yearbook* 212 at 222; *König v. Germany*, Judgment of 28 June 1978, Series A, No. 27; (1979–80) EHRR 170; and see, more recently, *Maaouia v. France* (App. 39652/98), Judgment of 5 October 2000; (2001) 33 EHRR 1037, para. 34 of the judgment.

[28] See above in this chapter.

[29] *Ringeisen v. Austria*, Judgment of 16 July 1971, Series A, No. 13; (1979–80) 1 EHRR 455.

Ringeisen for approval of the transfer to him, from a private person, of certain plots of land in Austria. He alleged that the Regional Real Property Transactions Commission which had heard his appeal against the decision of the District Commission, was biased, and consequently that it was not an impartial tribunal as required by Article 6(1).

The majority of the Commission concluded that Article 6(1) did not apply because the expression 'civil rights and obligations' should be construed restrictively as including only disputes between private individuals and not any proceedings in which the citizen is confronted by a public authority. In contrast, the Court held that Article 6(1) was applicable (although it had not been violated because there was no evidence of bias). As to the interpretation of Article 6(1), it held as follows:[30]

For Article 6, paragraph (1), to be applicable to a case ('contestation') it is not necessary that both parties to the proceedings should be private persons, which is the view of the majority of the Commission and of the Government. The wording of Article 6, paragraph (1), is far wider; the French expression 'contestations sur (des) droits et obligations de caractère civil' covers all proceedings the result of which is decisive for private rights and obligations. The English text, 'determination of . . . civil rights and obligations', confirms this interpretation.

The character of the legislation which governs how the matter is to be determined (civil, commercial, administrative law, etc.) and that of the authority which is invested with jurisdiction in the matter (ordinary court, administrative body, etc.) are therefore of little consequence.

In the present case, when Ringeisen purchased property from the Roth couple, he had a right to have the contract for sale which they had made with him approved if he fulfilled, as he claimed to do, the conditions laid down in the Act. Although it was applying rules of administrative law, the Regional Commission's decision was to be decisive for the relations in civil law ('de caractère civil') between Ringeisen and the Roth couple. This is enough to make it necessary for the Court to decide whether or not the proceedings in the case complied with the requirements of Article 6, paragraph (1), of the Convention.

Following its decision in the *Ringeisen* case, the Court adopted an increasingly liberal interpretation of the concept of civil rights and obligations. Thus, in another early case, *König*,[31] it held that proceedings which involved the withdrawal of an authority to run a medical clinic and an authorization to practise medicine were within the scope of Article 6(1). This was so even though the function of the body which had taken the decision was to act in the interests of public health and to exercise responsibilities borne by the medical profession towards society at large. Similarly, in the *Pudas* case,[32] where the applicant's

---

[30] Para. 94 of the judgment.
[31] *König* v. *Germany*, Judgment of 28 June 1978, Series A, No. 27; (1979–80) 2 EHRR 170. See also *Kraska* v. *Switzerland*, Judgment of 19 April 1993, Series A, No. 254-B; (1994) 18 EHRR 188.
[32] *Pudas* v. *Sweden*, Judgment of 27 October 1987, Series A, No. 125; (1988) 10 EHRR 380.

licence to operate a taxi on specified routes was revoked as part of a programme of rationalization which would have involved the replacement of one of his routes by a bus service, the Court rejected the Swedish Government's argument that, since the revocation of the licence depended essentially on an assessment of policy issues not capable of, or suited to, judicial control, the matter did not involve the determination of civil rights and obligations. Instead the Court held, unanimously, that the public law features of the case did not exclude the matter from the scope of Article 6(1), which applied since the revocation of the licence affected the applicant's business activities.

Questions relating to children taken into public care;[33] the expropriation of property by public authorities;[34] objections to and the enforcement of planning decisions;[35] the withdrawal of licences to serve alcohol[36] and to work a gravel pit;[37] and disciplinary proceedings resulting in suspension from medical[38] and legal[39] practice have all been held to be sufficiently 'civil' in nature to fall within the scope of Article 6(1).

Disputes concerning liability to tax, despite their pecuniary consequences, have been held to be public law issues to which Article 6(1) does not apply.[40] It might be thought that social security is another such issue. However, in the *Feldbrugge* case,[41] which concerned a claim for sickness benefits, the Court concluded by a majority of ten to seven that Article 6(1) applied. It considered that, although the character of the legislation, the compulsory nature of insurance against certain risks, and the assumption by public bodies of responsibility for ensuring social protection were public law characteristics, these were outweighed by the personal and economic nature of the asserted right by Mrs Feldbrugge, the connection with a contract of employment, and the similarities with insurance under ordinary law. In the *Deumeland* case,[42] decided the same

[33] *McMichael* v. *United Kingdom*, Judgment of 24 February 1995, Series A, No. 307-B; (1995) 20 EHRR 205.

[34] *Sporrong and Lönnroth* v. *Sweden*, Judgment of 23 September 1982, Series A, No. 52; (1983) 5 EHRR 35; and *Bodén* v. *Sweden*, Judgment of 27 October 1987, Series A, No. 125; (1988) 10 EHRR 36; *Zanatta* v. *France* (App. 38042/97), Judgment of 28 March 2000.

[35] *Mats Jacobsson* v. *Sweden*, Judgment of 28 June 1990, Series A, No. 180-A; (1991) 13 EHRR 79; *Bryan* v. *United Kingdom*, Judgment of 9 September 1997, Series A, No. 335-A; (1995) 21 EHRR 342.

[36] *Tre Traktörer AB* v. *Sweden*, Judgment of 7 July 1989, Series A, No. 159; (1991) 13 EHRR 309.

[37] *Fredin* v. *Sweden*, Judgment of 18 February 1991, Series A, No. 192; (1991) 13 EHRR 784.

[38] *Le Compte, van Leuven and de Meyere* v. *Belgium*, Judgment of 23 June 1981, Series A, No. 43; (1982) 4 EHRR 1.

[39] *H* v. *Belgium*, Judgment of 30 November 1987, Series A, No. 127; (1988) 10 EHRR 339; *WR* v. *Austria* (App. 26602/95), Judgment of 21 December 1999. See also *De Moor* v. *Germany*, Judgment of 23 June 1994, Series A, No. 292-A; (1994) 18 EHRR 372, on decisions on admission to the profession.

[40] *Charalambos* v. *France* (App. 49210/99), admissibility decision of 8 February 2000; *Vidacar S.A. and Obergrup S.L.* v. *Spain* (Apps. 41601/98, 41775/98), admissibility decision of 20 April 1999.

[41] *Feldbrugge* v. *Netherlands*, Judgment of 29 May 1986, Series A, No. 99; (1986) 8 EHRR 425.

[42] *Deumeland* v. *Germany*, Judgment of 29 May 1986, Series A, No. 100; (1986) 8 EHRR 448. See also *Schouten and Meldrum* v. *Netherlands*, Judgment of 9 December 1994, Series A, No. 304; (1995) 19 EHRR 432.

day, the Court reached the same conclusion as regards the right to a widow's supplementary pension following the death of her husband in an industrial accident.[43]

Until the *Salesi* judgment,[44] it was not clear whether this interpretation would extend to non-contributory types of social assistance, such as income support, which are not based on any 'contract' between the State and the individual and are harder to compare to private law insurance schemes.[45] In *Salesi*, however, which concerned a dispute over entitlement to a disability allowance financed entirely from public funds and not dependent on the payment of contributions, the Court found that Article 6(1) applied.[46] It appeared to rely on two factors: first, the fact that entitlement to the allowance was an *assertable right*, derived from statute, and was not dependent on an exercise of State discretion; secondly, the fact that, as a result of being denied the allowance, the applicant had suffered an interference with her means of subsistence. This second factor was sufficient to make the right *civil* for the purposes of the Convention.

The same arguments could perhaps be applied to certain rights of aliens to enter and stay in States of which they are not nationals. Rights such as the right to asylum are governed by international and domestic law and are not within the discretion of the State to withhold; moreover, a decision to expel an alien can have the most serious consequences on his or her economic and personal welfare. However, the Commission consistently rejected all such applications as inadmissible under Article 6(1),[47] and this approach was recently confirmed by the Court in the *Maaouia* case.[48] The applicant, a Tunisian national, complained about the length of the proceedings he had brought to overturn an order excluding him from France. In this case the Court did not consider the economic or personal effect of exclusion on the individual concerned, but instead attempted to determine the intention of the States Parties who had drafted and signed the Convention. Despite the fact that Protocol 7 to the Convention was adopted only in November 1984, after the Commission had already expressed the view that a decision to deport a person does 'not involve a determination of his civil rights and obligations or of any criminal charge against him' within the meaning of Article 6(1), the Court decided that the creation of this Protocol, which contains procedural guarantees applicable to the expulsion of aliens,

[43] See also, similarly, *Schuler-Zgraggen* v. *Switzerland*, Judgment of 24 June 1993, Series A, No. 263; (1993) 16 EHRR 405, relating to invalidity p ension.

[44] *Salesi* v. *Italy*, Judgment of 23 February 1993, Series A, No. 257-A; (1998) 26 EHRR 187, para. 19 of the judgment.

[45] See the discussion in the 2nd edn. of this book at 131–2.

[46] See also *Mennitto* v. *Italy* (App. 33804/96), Judgment of 3 October 2000.

[47] See the citations in the *Maaouia* v. *France* (App. 39652/98), Judgment of 5 October 2000; (2001) 33 EHRR 1037, para. 35 of the judgment.

[48] *Maaouia* v. *France* (App. 39652/98), Judgment of 5 October 2000; (2001) 33 EHRR 1037.

indicated that the States did not regard such proceedings as being governed by Article 6.

The Court's emphasis on the character of the right in question and its effects on the individual has created difficulties in classifying employment-related claims brought by civil servants against their employer, the State. The Court initially held that 'disputes relating to the recruitment, careers and termination of service of civil servants are as a general rule outside the scope of Article 6(1)'.[49] This principle was soon perceived as unsatisfactory, however, since it left everyone working in the public sector without the protection of Article 6(1) and led to disparity between the Member States of the Council of Europe because the type of employees categorized as 'civil servants' varies from State to State; in some countries, for example, teachers are 'civil servants' whereas they are assimilated with private sector employees in others.

The Court's case law, therefore, witnessed a gradual whittling away of this sweeping exclusion. In a series of cases involving, for example, pension[50] and salary[51] disputes, it was held that where the claim in issue related to a 'purely' or 'essentially' economic right, Article 6(1) applied. Where, however, the claim principally called into question the authorities' discretionary powers, Article 6(1) did not apply.

Once again, the Court's approach proved unworkable. Almost any employment dispute will have economic consequences for the employee and it proved difficult to draw the line between cases falling within Article 6(1) and those excluded without creating uncertainty and injustice. In the *Neigel* case,[52] for example, the proceedings brought by the applicant centred on the authorities' refusal to reinstate her to a permanent post in the civil service, but the Court held that it concerned her recruitment and career and that Article 6(1) was not applicable; her claim for lost salary was insufficient to bring it within the scope of that provision because in order to succeed with this claim she needed first to prove that the refusal to reinstate her had been unlawful.

One of the first acts of the new Court was to attempt to rectify this situation. In the *Pellegrin* judgment[53] the Grand Chamber set out a new test for determining the application of Article 6(1) to civil service employment disputes, based on the nature of the employee's duties and responsibilities. The only disputes now excluded from the scope of Article 6(1) are 'those which are raised by public servants whose duties typify the specific activities of the public service in

---

[49] *Massa* v. *Italy*, Judgment of 24 August 1993, Series A, No. 265-B; (1994) 18 EHRR 266, para. 26 of the judgment.

[50] *Massa* v. *Italy*, Judgment of 24 August 1993, Series A, No. 265-B; (1994) 18 EHRR 266; *Francesco Lombardo* v. *Italy*, Judgment of 26 November 1992, Series A, No. 249-B; (1996) 21 EHRR 188.

[51] *De Santa* v. *Italy* (App. 25574/94); *Lapalorcia* v. *Italy* (App. 25586/94); *Abenavoli* v. *Italy* (App. 25587/94), Judgments of 2 September 1997.

[52] *Neigel* v. *France* (App. 18725/91), Judgment of 17 March 1993.

[53] *Pellegrin* v. *France* (App. 28541/95), Judgment of 8 December 1999.

so far as the latter is acting as the depository of public authority responsible for protecting the general interests of the State or other public authorities'.[54] This principle allows the State to protect its interests by giving it virtually a free hand (as far as Article 6 is concerned) in hiring and firing core civil servants, such as diplomats, policy-makers, policemen, and soldiers,[55] whilst protecting the rights of the thousands of others (cleaners, nurses, teachers, and so on) whose jobs, to all intents and purposes, are identical to their counterparts in the private sector.[56]

In conclusion, then, it can be seen that the expression 'civil rights and obligations' has come to encompass many areas which are frequently regarded by national systems as part of public or administrative law. While this extension of the protection offered by Article 6(1) can only be welcomed, it is on occasion difficult to discern any consistent principle in the Court's case law. This lack of principle can make it difficult for States to determine the extent of their obligations under Article 6(1) and for citizens to know their rights. Moreover, certain inconsistencies can appear difficult to defend. What, for example, is the fundamental difference between entitlement to a tax allowance and entitlement to a social security benefit which could justify holding the latter to fall within the scope of 'civil rights and obligations' but not the former?

THE NEED FOR A DISPUTE

Article 6(1) requires not only that the matter concern civil rights or obligations, but that there be a dispute (*contestation*, from the French text of Article 6(1)) concerning the particular rights or obligations. In the *Benthem* judgment[57] the Court reviewed the case law on this requirement and summarized its content as follows:

(a) Conformity with the spirit of the Convention requires that the word '*contestation*' (dispute) should not be 'construed too technically' and should be 'given a substantive rather than a formal meaning' . . .

(b) The '*contestation*' (dispute) may relate not only to 'the actual existence of a . . . right' but also to its scope or the manner in which it may be exercised . . . It may concern both 'questions of fact' and 'questions of law' . . .

---

[54] Para. 66 of the judgment.

[55] See e.g. *Batur* v. *Turkey* (App. 38604/97), admissibility decision of 4 July 2000.

[56] See e.g. *Frydlender* v. *France* (App. 30979/96), Judgment of 27 June 2000; *Procaccini* v. *Italy* (App. 31631/96), Judgment of 30 March 2000; *Satonnet* v. *France* (App. 30412/96), Judgment of 2 August 2000; *Castanheira Barros* v. *Portugal* (App. 36945/97), Judgment of 26 October 2000; *Lambourdière* v. *France* (App. 37387/97), Judgment of 2 August 2000; *Martinez-Caro de la Concha Casteneda and others* v. *Spain* (App. 42646/98), admissibility decision of 7 March 2000; *Kajanen and Tuomaala* v. *Finland* (App. 36401/97), admissibility decision of 18 October 2000.

[57] *Benthem* v. *Netherlands*, Judgment of 23 October 1985, Series A, No. 97; (1986) 8 EHRR 1, para. 32 of the judgment.

(c) The 'contestation' (dispute) must be genuine and of a serious nature . . .

(d) . . . 'the . . . expression 'contestations sur (des) droits et obligations de caractère civil'
[disputes over civil rights and obligations] covers all proceedings the result of
which is decisive for [such] rights and obligations' . . . However, 'a tenuous connection or remote consequences do not suffice for Article 6(1) . . . : civil rights and
obligations must be the object—or one of the objects—of the 'contestation' (dispute); the result of the proceedings must be directly decisive for such a right.

Thus, for example, in the *Fayed* case,[58] the Court held that an investigation by
inspectors appointed by the Department of Trade and Industry into the applicants' take-over of Harrods did not attract the protection of Article 6, despite
the applicants' argument that their reputations (a civil right) had been at stake.
The Court found that the purpose of the inquiry had been to ascertain and
record facts which might subsequently be used as the basis for action by other
competent authorities—prosecuting, regulatory, disciplinary or even legislative.
It was satisfied that the functions performed by the inspectors were essentially
investigative and that they had not been empowered to make any legal
determination as to criminal or civil liability concerning the Fayed brothers.

Article 6(1) continues to apply to all stages of legal proceedings for the
'determination of . . . civil rights and obligations', not excluding stages subsequent to judgment on the merits. For example, in the *Robins* case[59] the Court
held that proceedings to determine the costs liability of the unsuccessful party
to civil litigation should be seen as a continuation of the principal dispute, and
had therefore to be decided within a reasonable time.

RIGHT OF ACCESS TO COURT

One of the rights which has been developed out of the provisions of Article 6 is
the right to access to a court for the determination of a particular civil issue.
There is no right under Article 6 to have criminal proceedings brought against a
suspected offender.

The Court first recognized this right in the *Golder* case in 1975.[60] In a clear
application of the 'effective rights' interpretation technique,[61] it held that the
detailed fair trial guarantees under Article 6 would be useless if it were impossible to commence court proceedings in the first place. The applicant was
detained in an English prison where serious disturbances broke out. He was

[58] *Fayed* v. *United Kingdom*, Judgment of 21 September 1994, Series A, No. 294-B; (1994) 18 EHRR 393.
[59] *Robins* v. *United Kingdom* (App. 22410/93), Judgment of 23 September 1997; (1998) 26 EHRR 527.
[60] *Golder* v. *United Kingdom*, Judgment of 21 February 1975, Series A, No. 18; (1979–80) 1 EHRR 524.
[61] See ch. 3 above.

accused of assault by a prison officer and wished to bring proceedings for defamation in order to have his record cleared, but this was precluded by the Prison Rules. Though not without limitation, the Court concluded that Article 6(1) contained an inherent right of access to a court, observing:

In civil matters one can scarcely conceive of the rule of law without there being a possibility of access to the courts. . . . The principle whereby a civil claim must be capable of being submitted to a judge ranks as one of the universally recognised fundamental principles of law; the same is true of the principle of international law which forbids the denial of justice. Article 6(1) must be read in the light of these principles.[62]

The right of access to court is not absolute: it is open to States to impose restrictions on would-be litigants, as long as these restrictions pursue a legitimate aim and are not so wide-ranging as to destroy the very essence of the right.[63] For example, orders preventing vexatious litigants from commencing or pursuing claims without leave are not usually in breach of Article 6(1), since such orders pursue the aim of preserving court time and resources for deserving cases and since the litigant would be granted leave to pursue a meritorious action.[64]

Similarly, the Court found in the *Stubbings* case[65] that the provisions of the Limitation Act 1960, requiring actions for damages for trespass against the person to be commenced within three years of the alleged injury or the victim's eighteenth birthday, were not a disproportionate restriction on the right of access to court, even though the applicants, victims of child sexual abuse, had been unable to bring proceedings within the time-limit because of the effects of repressed memory syndrome. Limitation periods were held to pursue the legitimate aim of ensuring legal certainty and finality, whilst still allowing litigants some opportunity to come to court.[66]

The right of access to a court must not only exist in theory, it must also be effective. This means, for example, that if a poor litigant wishes to bring court proceedings which are meritorious but so complex as to be impossible to pursue without professional legal assistance, the State must provide legal aid if this is 'indispensable for an effective access to court'.[67]

---

[62] *Golder* v. *United Kingdom*, Judgment of 21 February 1975, Series A, No. 18; (1979–80) 1 EHRR 524, paras. 34–5 of the judgment.

[63] *Ashingdane* v. *United Kingdom*, Judgment of 28 May 1985, Series A, No. 93; (1985) 7 EHRR 528.

[64] App. 11559/85, *H* v. *United Kingdom* (1985) 45 DR 281.

[65] *Stubbings and others* v. *United Kingdom* (Apps. 22083/93 and 22095/93), Judgment of 24 September 1996; (1997) 23 EHRR 213.

[66] In its report published 10 July 2001, *Limitation of Actions* (Law Com. 270) the Law Commission recommended, in view *inter alia* of the problems faced by victims of childhood sexual abuse, a three-year limit, running from the date the claimant knew or should reasonably have known the facts, for most types of legal claim, with a discretion for the judge to extend it.

[67] *Airey* v. *Ireland*, Judgment of 9 October 1979, Series A, No 32; (1979–80) 3 EHRR 592, para. 26 of the judgment.

The right to bring a claim to court applies only in respect of rights provided for by the domestic law; it is not possible through Article 6(1) to challenge the substantive *content* of domestic law. Sometimes, however, it can be difficult to decide whether a particular rule of domestic law negates a substantive right, or simply forms a procedural impediment to access to court such as to raise an issue under Article 6(1). This has been the case with the rules under English law providing that certain professions are immune from civil suit. In the *Osman* case[68] a member of the applicants' family was shot and killed by a stalker. The applicants claimed that the police had negligently failed to protect them, despite the presence of clear warning signs from the killer. They commenced negligence proceedings against the police in the English courts, but these were struck out by the Court of Appeal which held that, in light of House of Lords case law, no action could lie against the police in negligence in the investigation and suppression of crime because public policy (the desire to save police resources for fighting crime rather than fighting court cases) required an immunity from suit. Before the European Court, the Government argued that Article 6(1) did not apply, because the exclusionary rule applied by the Court of Appeal meant that the applicants had no substantive right under domestic law against the police.

In a controversial decision, the Court held that Article 6(1) was applicable. It observed that English common law had long accorded a plaintiff the right to bring proceedings in negligence. Faced with such a claim, it was for the domestic court to determine whether the defendant owed the plaintiff a duty of care; in other words, whether the damage caused had been foreseeable, whether there existed a relationship of proximity between the parties, and whether it was fair, just, and reasonable to impose a duty of care in the circumstances. The rule applied by the Court of Appeal—giving the police a certain, limited immunity from suit on policy grounds—did not automatically doom the proceedings to failure from the start, but instead in principle allowed the domestic court to make a considered assessment as to whether or not the rule should be applied in that particular case. The Court therefore concluded that that applicants had a right under English law, derived from the law of negligence, to seek an adjudication on the admissibility and merits of their claim against the police.

The Court then went on to consider whether the restriction on the applicants' right of access to court had been proportionate. Its findings under this head appear somewhat to contradict its ruling on applicability. Although it accepted that the exclusionary rule pursued a legitimate aim, since it was directed at maintaining the efficiency of the police, the Court decided that it was disproportionate, because:

---

[68] *Osman* v. *United Kingdom* (App. 23452/94), Judgment of 28 October 1998; (2000) 29 EHRR 245. See ch. 4 above for the Court's findings under Article 2 in this case.

While the Government have contended that the exclusionary rule of liability is not of an absolute nature . . . and that its application may yield to other public-policy considerations, it would appear to the Court that in the instant case the Court of Appeal proceeded on the basis that the rule provided a watertight defence to the police and that it was impossible to prise open an immunity which the police enjoy from civil suit in respect of their acts and omissions in the investigation and suppression of crime.

The Court would observe that the application of the rule in this manner without further enquiry into the existence of competing public-interest considerations serves to confer a blanket immunity on the police for their acts and omissions during the investigation and suppression of crime and amounts to an unjustifiable restriction on the applicant's right to have a determination on the merits of his or her claim against the police in deserving cases.[69]

In a later case, *Z and others* v. *United Kingdom*,[70] the Court, while not expressly overruling its judgment in *Osman*, conceded that its reasoning there 'was based on an understanding of the law of negligence . . . which has to be reviewed in the light of the clarifications subsequently made by the domestic courts'.[71]

The applicants in *Z and others* were five children who had been badly neglected and abused by their parents. During a period of over five years, despite being aware of the situation, the local authority took no steps to remove the children from their parents' care. The applicants subsequently commenced proceedings against the local authority, claiming damages for negligence and/or breach of statutory duty and arguing that the local authority's failure to act had resulted in their psychological damage. The proceedings were struck out as revealing no cause of action, and the applicants appealed to the Court of Appeal and, finally, the House of Lords. In its judgment[72] the House of Lords examined, *inter alia*, whether the local authority had owed the applicants a duty of care. It was accepted that the damage to the applicants had been foreseeable, and that there was a relationship of proximity between the parties. The House of Lords did not, however, consider that it would be just and reasonable to impose a duty of care in the circumstances, in view of the interdisciplinary nature of the statutory system of child protection, and the extraordinarily difficult and delicate task faced by social services in such situations. If liability in damages were to be imposed, it was feared that local authorities would adopt a more cautious and defensive approach to their duties, which would not be in the interests of children generally.

---

[69] Paras 150–151 of the judgment.
[70] *Z and others* v. *United Kingdom* (App. 29392/95), Judgment of 10 May 2001; (2002) 34 EHRR 97.
[71] Para. 100 of the judgment.
[72] *X and others* v. *Bedfordshire County Council* [1995] 3 All ER 353.

The Court of Human Rights found that Article 6(1) applied, since prior to the House of Lords' judgment there had been no domestic decision indicating whether or not a local authority owed children a duty of care in such circumstances; until that judgment, therefore, the applicants had had an arguable claim to a civil right under English law. This aspect of the Court's reasoning alone would appear to contradict its *Osman* judgment, since by the time the applicants in *Osman* commenced proceedings the House of Lords had already established that no negligence action could lie against the police in respect of their acts and omissions in the investigation and suppression of crime. Moreover, when the Court in *Z and others* went on to examine whether there had been a violation of Article 6, it found that the applicants had not in fact been deprived of access to court, since they had been able to bring their claims before the domestic courts, culminating in a detailed consideration by the House of Lords as to whether a novel category of negligence actions should be developed.[73]

THE OVERALL REQUIREMENTS OF A FAIR HEARING

Much of what will be said later in this chapter will deal with the specific features of a fair trial set out in Article 6(1), but there is also an overriding requirement that the proceedings should be fair. Compliance with specific rights set out in Article 6 will not alone guarantee that there has been a fair trial. It is not possible to state in the abstract the content of the requirement of a fair hearing; this can be considered only in the context of the proceedings as a whole.[74] The Court has said,

The effect of Article 6(1) is, *inter alia*, to place the 'tribunal' under a duty to conduct a proper examination of the submissions, arguments and evidence adduced by the parties, without prejudice to its assessment of whether they are relevant to its decision.[75]

A number of specific features have emerged from the case law, which can now be regarded as ingredients of a fair trial.

---

[73] The Court did, however, find violations of Articles 3 and 13 based on the local authority's failure to act and the lack of any effective domestic remedy.

[74] *Kostovski* v. *Netherlands*, Judgment of 20 November 1989, Series A, No. 166; (1990) 12 EHRR 434.

[75] *Kraska* v. *Switzerland*, Judgment of 19 April 1993, Series A, No. 254-B; (1994) 18 EHRR 188, para. 30 of the judgment.

PROCEDURAL EQUALITY

The concept of 'equality of arms' (*égalité des armes*) was first mentioned in the *Neumeister* case,[76] and has been a feature of Article 6(1) ever since. It requires a fair balance between the parties and applies to both civil and criminal cases. In the context of civil cases between private parties, the Court has said,

The Court agrees with the Commission that as regards litigation involving opposing private interests, 'equality of arms' implies that each party must be afforded a reasonable opportunity to present his case—including his evidence—under conditions that do not place him at a substantial disadvantage *vis-à-vis* his opponent.[77]

The *Borgers* case not only illustrates the application of equality of arms but also demonstrates the dynamic nature of the Convention.[78] Borgers was tried and convicted of forgery offences. He appealed successfully to the Court of Cassation, which remitted the case for retrial, at which he was again convicted. He again appealed to the Court of Cassation, but was unsuccessful. At this appeal, the Court had heard submissions from the *avocat général*, who subsequently participated in its deliberations. In the *Delcourt* case[79] the Court had found the role of the *procureur général* entirely acceptable, since he or she was totally impartial. In the *Borgers* case, the Court reconsidered that view, stressing the development of the its case law on the requirements of a fair trial 'notably in respect of the importance attached to appearances and to the increased sensitivity of the public to the fair administration of justice'.[80] The role of the *avocat général* compromised the principle of equality between the parties and constituted a violation of Article 6(1).

AN ADVERSARIAL PROCESS AND DISCLOSURE OF EVIDENCE

Closely related to equality of arms is the concept of a judicial process, sometimes referred to as the right to have an adversarial trial:

The right to have an adversarial trial means the opportunity for the parties to have knowledge of and comment on the observations filed or evidence adduced by the other party.[81]

In order for the adversarial process to work effectively, it is important, in civil

---

[76] *Neumeister* v. *Austria*, Judgment of 27 June 1968, Series A, No. 8; (1979–80) 1 EHRR 91.
[77] *Dombo Beheer BV* v. *Netherlands*, Judgment of 27 October 1993, Series A, No. 274-A; (1994) 18 EHRR 213, para. 33 of the judgment.
[78] *Borgers* v. *Belgium*, Judgment of 30 October 1991, Series A, No. 214; (1993) 15 EHRR 92.
[79] *Delcourt* v. *Belgium*, Judgment of 17 January 1970, Series A, No. 11; (1979–80) 1 EHRR 355.
[80] *Borgers* v. *Belgium*, Judgment of 30 October 1991, Series A, No. 214; (1993) 15 EHRR 92, para. 24 of the judgment.
[81] *Ruiz-Mateos* v. *Spain*, Judgment of 23 June 1993, Series A, No. 262; (1993) 16 EHRR 505, para. 63 of the judgment.

and criminal proceedings, that relevant material is available to both parties. The Court explained the principle as it applies in criminal proceedings in its *Rowe and Davis* judgment:[82]

It is a fundamental aspect of the right to a fair trial that criminal proceedings, including the elements of such proceedings which relate to procedure, should be adversarial and that there should be equality of arms between the prosecution and defence. The right to an adversarial trial means, in a criminal case, that both prosecution and defence must be given the opportunity to have knowledge of and comment on the observations filed and the evidence adduced by the other party. . . . In addition Article 6(1) requires . . . that the prosecution authorities should disclose to the defence all material evidence in their possession for or against the accused.

The entitlement to disclosure of relevant evidence is not, however, an absolute right. In criminal (and sometimes also in civil) proceedings there may be competing factors, such as national security, or the need to protect witnesses at risk of reprisals, or to keep secret police methods of investigation of crime, which must be weighed against the rights of the accused. In some cases it may be necessary to withhold certain evidence from the defence so as to preserve the fundamental rights of another individual or to safeguard an important public interest. However, as the Court emphasized in *Rowe and Davis*, only such measures restricting the rights of the defence which are strictly necessary are permissible under Article 6(1).

In accordance with the 'fourth instance' doctrine, the Court will not itself review whether or not an order permitting non-disclosure was justified in any particular case. Instead, it examines the decision-making procedure to ensure that it complied, as far as possible, with the requirements of adversarial proceedings and equality of arms and incorporated adequate safeguards to protect the interests of the accused.

In the *Rowe and Davis* case the prosecution had unilaterally decided, without consulting the trial judge, to withhold evidence in its possession about the existence and role of an informer. This man, who was one of the main prosecution witnesses at the applicants' trial on charges of armed robbery and murder, had, unbeknown to the defence or the judge, received a substantial reward for assisting the prosecution authorities. The applicants were convicted and appealed, and at this stage the prosecution notified the Court of Appeal about the withheld material. The Court of Appeal inspected it and held a hearing to decide whether it should be disclosed, but the defence were not permitted to attend this hearing and were never allowed to see the evidence or informed of its nature or content.

The Human Rights Court decided that the procedure before the Court of

---

[82] *Rowe and Davis* v. *United Kingdom* (App. 28901/95), Judgment of 16 February 2000; (200) 30 EHRR 1, para. 60 of the judgment.

Appeal was not sufficient to satisfy the requirements of Article 6(1). The rights of the defence would have been adequately protected if the trial judge had had the opportunity to examine the withheld evidence and make the decision on disclosure.[83] However, the Court took the view that, unlike the trial judge, who saw the witnesses give their testimony and was fully versed in all the evidence and issues in the case, the judges in the Court of Appeal were dependent for their understanding of the possible relevance of the undisclosed material on transcripts of the Crown Court hearings and on the account of the issues given to them by prosecuting counsel. In addition, the first instance judge would have been in a position to monitor the need for disclosure throughout the trial, assessing the importance of the undisclosed evidence at a stage when new issues were emerging, when it might have been possible through cross-examination seriously to undermine the credibility of key witnesses and when the defence case was still open to take a number of different directions or emphases. In contrast, the Court observed, the Court of Appeal was obliged to carry out its appraisal *ex post facto* and might even, to a certain extent, have unconsciously been influenced by the jury's verdict of guilty into underestimating the significance of the undisclosed evidence.

A REASONED DECISION

A reasoned decision, while not expressly required by Article 6, is implicit in the requirement of a fair hearing, which has been recognized by the Court.[84] If a court gives some reasons, then prima facie the requirements of Article 6 in this respect are satisfied, and this presumption is not upset simply because the judgment does not deal specifically with one point considered by an applicant to be material. On the other hand, if, for example, an applicant were to show that the court had ignored a fundamental defence, which had been clearly put before it and which, if successful, would have discharged him in whole or in part from liability, then this would be sufficient to rebut the presumption of a fair hearing.

This analysis applies a fortiori to criminal proceedings. Thus, where a convicted person has the possibility of an appeal, the lower court must state in detail the reasons for its decision, so that on appeal from that decision the accused's rights may be properly safeguarded.[85]

---

[83] As occurred in the cases of *Jasper* v. *United Kingdom* (App. 27052/95), Judgment of 16 February 2000; (2000) 30 EHRR 97; and *Fitt* v. *United Kingdom* (App. 29777/96), Judgment of 16 February 2000; (2000) 30 EHRR 223, where the Court found no violation.

[84] *Van de Hurk* v. *Netherlands*, Judgment of 19 April 1994, Series A, No. 288; (1994) 18 EHRR 481, para. 61 of the judgment. See also *Ruiz-Torija* v. *Spain*, Judgment of 9 December 1994, Series A, No. 303-A; (1994) 19 EHRR 553; and *Hiro Balani* v. *Spain*, Judgment of 9 December 1994, Series A, No. 303-B; (1994) 19 EHRR 566.

[85] App. 1035/61, *X* v. *Federal Republic of Germany*, 17 June 1963 (1963) 6 *Yearbook* 180, at 192.

APPEARANCE IN PERSON

It depends on the nature of the proceedings whether a failure to allow the individual accused or civil litigant to attend in person will constitute a violation of Article 6(1).[86] In the *Kremzow* case,[87] the applicant was represented by a lawyer at the hearing of his appeal against sentence, but was not himself brought to court from prison. The Court made it clear that, as a general rule, an accused should always be present at first instance trial. It further held that the applicant should have been enabled to attend the hearing of his appeal against sentence, since an increase from twenty years to life imprisonment was in issue, and an assessment of the applicant was to take place. The Court said,

These proceedings were thus of crucial importance for the applicant and involved not only an assessment of his character and state of mind at the time of the offence but also his motive. In circumstances such as those of the present case, where evaluations of this kind were to play such a significant role and where their outcome could be of major detriment to him, it was essential to the fairness of the proceedings that he be present during the hearing of the appeals and afforded the opportunity to participate in it together with his counsel.[88]

In contrast, no issue arose under Article 6 by virtue of Kremzov's absence during the appeal court's consideration of his plea of nullity, since he was represented and the nature of the hearing did not require him to be there.

The same principles apply in civil proceedings. Thus the individual concerned should be allowed to attend where, for example, an assessment of his or her character is directly relevant to the formation of the court's opinion, as in the case of a parent seeking access to a child.[89]

EFFECTIVE PARTICIPATION

It is not, however, sufficient that the criminal defendant or civil party is present in court. He or she must, in addition, be able effectively to participate in the proceedings. In one criminal case,[90] the applicant was slightly deaf and had not been able to hear some of the evidence given at trial. The Court did not, however, find a violation of Article 6(1) in view of the fact that the applicant's counsel, who could hear all that was said and was able to take his client's instructions at all times, chose for tactical reasons not to request that the accused be seated closer to the witnesses. The applicants in the cases of *T* and *V*

---

[86] And, in criminal cases, Article 6(3)(c): see ch. 9 below.
[87] *Kremzow* v. *Austria*, Judgment of 21 September 1993, Series A, No. 268-B; (1994) 17 EHRR 322.
[88] Para. 67 of the judgment.
[89] *App. 434/58, X* v. *Sweden*, 30 June 1959 (1958–9) 2 *Yearbook* 354, at 370.
[90] *Stanford* v. *United Kingdom*, Judgment of 23 February 1994, Series A, No. 282-A.

v. *United Kingdom*[91] were 11 years old at the time of their trial for the murder of a toddler. The proceedings were held in a blaze of publicity, in a packed court-room, and there was medical evidence to show that both boys were suffering from post-traumatic stress at the time. The Court found violations of Article 6(1), commenting that it was highly unlikely that the applicants would have felt sufficiently uninhibited, in the tense courtroom and under public scrutiny, to have consulted with their lawyers during the trial.

THE SPECIFIC REQUIREMENTS OF ARTICLE 6(1)

AN INDEPENDENT AND IMPARTIAL TRIBUNAL ESTABLISHED BY LAW

Article 6(1) guarantees the right to a fair trial before 'an independent and impartial tribunal established by law'. There cannot be a fair criminal or civil trial before a court which is, or appears to be, biased against the defendant or litigant, and the fair trial guarantees are meaningless if the tribunal's decision is liable to be overturned by some other authority which does not offer such guarantees.[92]

The Court is concerned both with the subjective and objective elements of independence and impartiality. The subjective element involves an enquiry into whether the personal conviction of a judge in a particular case raises doubts about his or her independence or impartiality. The judge's lack of bias is presumed unless there is evidence to the contrary and there are few cases where subjective bias has been established since in practice such evidence can be very hard to come by. The objective element involves determination of whether, in terms of structure or appearance, the accused's doubts about the tribunal's independence and impartiality may be legitimate.[93]

In a recent case[94] the Court was called upon to consider the effect of a judge's membership of the Freemasons. The applicant had brought proceedings to challenge the codicil of a will, made by a Freemason, which revoked an earlier will in favour of the applicant and left the property instead to a man claimed by the applicant also to be a Freemason. The applicant referred before the European Court to popularly held suspicions about the secretive, pervasive, and

---

[91] *T* v. *United Kingdom* (App. 24724/94); and *V* v. *United Kingdom* (App. 24888/94) Judgments of 16 December 1999; (2000) 30 EHRR 121.

[92] *Van de Hurk* v. *Netherlands*, Judgment of 19 April 1994, Series A, No. 288; (1994) 18 EHRR 481.

[93] See generally *Piersack* v. *Belgium*, Judgment of 1 October 1982, Series A, No. 53; (1983) 5 EHRR 169, and *Hauschildt* v. *Denmark*, Judgment of 24 May 1989, Series A, No. 154; (1990) 12 EHRR 266.

[94] *Salaman* v. *United Kingdom* (App. 43505/98), admissibility decision of 15 June 2000; and see also *Kiiskinen and Kovalainen* v. *Finland* (App. 26323/95), admissibility decision of 3 June 1999.

corrupting nature of Freemasonry. The Court, however, did not consider that membership of a judge in the Freemasons in the United Kingdom could in itself raise doubts as to his impartiality where a witness or party in a case was also a Freemason; in particular, there was no reason to fear that a judge would not regard his oath on taking judicial office as taking precedence over any other social commitments or obligations. The applicant's doubts as to the lack of impartiality of the judge were not objectively justified.

The Court commented that whether or not a problem could arise, for example, due to a judge's personal acquaintance with a fellow Freemason or due to the interests of a Freemason institution being in issue in a case would depend on all the circumstances. The same applies whenever a member of a tribunal knows one of the parties to or witnesses at a trial. In the *Pullar* case,[95] for example, by sheer coincidence one of the jurors selected to try a case of corruption had previously been employed by the leading prosecution witness. The Court did not consider that this gave rise to a problem under Article 6(1), because a detailed examination of the juror's relationship with the witness— who had dismissed him from his job—did not demonstrate that the juror would be predisposed to believe his testimony.[96]

Care is also required, particularly in Continental criminal justice systems, where a judge has had some involvement in the pre-trial stages of the process. If this is routine pre-trial supervision of the case, there will be no breach of Article 6(1), but if the nature of the decision could suggest some pre-judging of the substantive issue, a violation of Article 6(1) could arise.[97]

In one case,[98] five of the nine jurors who served in the trial of a defamation action brought by way of private prosecution were members of the political party which was the principal target of the allegedly defamatory material. The jury selection procedures complied with the requirements of Swedish law; attempts by the applicant to have those jurors disqualified who were members of the political party failed. The Court found that the links between the defendants and the five jurors could give rise to misgivings as to their objective independence and impartiality; this in turn rendered the independence and impartiality of the court questionable and there was a violation of Article 6(1).

This judgment may be less far-reaching than at first sight appears. In essence, there was a failure by the national procedures to achieve their objective of

---

[95] *Pullar* v. *United Kingdom* (App. 22399/93), Judgment of 10 June 1996; (1996) 22 EHRR 391.

[96] See also *Langborger* v. *Sweden*, Judgment of 22 June 1989, Series A, No. 155; (1990) 12 EHRR 416.

[97] As in *Hauschildt* v. *Denmark*, Judgment of 24 May 1989, Series A, No. 154; (1990) 12 EHRR 266; see also *De Cubber* v. *Belgium*, Judgment of 26 October 1984, Series A, No. 86; (1985) 7 EHRR 236; *Ben Yaacoub* v. *Belgium*, Judgment of 27 November 1987, Series A, No. 127-A; (1991) 13 EHRR 418; *Fey* v. *Austria*, Judgment of 24 February 1993, Series A, No. 255; (1993) 16 EHRR 387; *Nortier* v. *Netherlands*, Judgment of 24 August 1993, Series A, No. 267; (1993) 17 EHRR 273.

[98] *Holm* v. *Sweden*, Judgment of 25 November 1993, Series A, No. 279-A; (1994) 18 EHRR 79.

removing from the jury those with an interest in the outcome of the litigation. Wider applications, such as complaints about trial by a jury whose composition does not correspond to the ethnic origin of the defendant, are unlikely to succeed unless the particular facts of the case show that the defendant's concerns about racism in the tribunal are objectively justified.

In the *Sander* case,[99] for example the defendant was Asian. In the course of his trial in the Crown Court a member of the jury sent a note to the judge alleging that two fellow jurors had been making openly racist remarks and jokes and expressing the fear that the defendant would be convicted, not on the evidence, but because he was Asian. The judge adjourned the case, asking each member of the jury to consider overnight whether he or she felt able to try the case without prejudice. The following morning the judge received two letters from the jury. The first, signed by all the jurors including the one who had sent the complaint, refuted the allegation of racism. The second letter was written by a single juror who explained that he might have been the one responsible for making the racist jokes. He apologized for causing offence and declared that, in truth, he was not in the slightest racially biased. The judge decided not to dismiss the jury—despite a request from the defence—but instead redirected them on the importance of their task and the trial continued, culminating in the applicant's conviction.

The Court of Human Rights, finding a violation of Article 6(1), held that, viewed objectively, the collective letter from the jury could not have been sufficient to dispel the applicant's fears, because the jurors would have been unlikely openly to admit to racism. Nor could his fears have been allayed by the judge's redirection, however trenchant, because racist views could not be changed overnight. This judgment demonstrates, perhaps, that the new Court has a more realistic understanding of racism than its predecessor: in an earlier case, *Gregory* v. *United Kingdom*,[100] with almost identical facts, the old Court found that the judge's redirection had been adequate to guarantee the jury's impartiality.

In other cases, the defect in the tribunal derives not from the personality, behaviour or prior involvement of one particular member, but from more formal concerns about the body's structure, powers, and composition. Relevant factors here are the manner of appointment and duration of office of the adjudicators[101] and the existence of guarantees against outside interference,[102] as well as the appearance of independence.[103]

---

[99] *Sander* v. *United Kingdom* (App. 34129/96), Judgment of 9 May 2000; (2001) 31 EHRR 1003.

[100] *Gregory* v *United Kingdom* (App. 22299/93), Judgment of 25 February 1997; (1998) 25 EHRR 577.

[101] *Le Compte, van Leuven and de Meyere* v. *Belgium*, Judgment of 23 June 1981, Series A, No. 43; (1982) 4 EHRR 1, para. 55 of the judgment.

[102] *Piersack* v. *Belgium*, Judgment of 1 October 1982, Series A, No. 53; (1983) 5 EHRR 169, para. 27 of the judgment.

[103] *Delcourt* v. *Belgium*, Judgment of 17 January 1970, Series A, No. 11; (1979–80) 1 EHRR 355.

In the *Findlay* case[104] the Court examined the independence and impartiality of an army court martial. Under the legislation then in force, a court martial in the United Kingdom was convened on an ad hoc basis by a senior officer in the defendant's regiment. The convening officer not only appointed all the officers who sat as judges in the court martial, he also appointed the prosecuting and defending officers, prepared the evidence against the accused, and had the power to quash or vary the court's decision. It is not, therefore, surprising that European Court found that the court martial was not 'independent and impartial'.[105]

The case of *Incal v. Turkey*[106] was also concerned with the effect of the participation of military personnel in the criminal justice system. The applicant, a civilian, was convicted of disseminating Kurdish separatist propaganda by a National Security Court. These courts, composed of two civilian judges and a legally trained army officer, were set up specifically to deal with offences against Turkey's territorial integrity and national security. The Court of Human Rights found a violation of Article 6(1) on the basis that, given the nature of the charges against him and the fact that he was a civilian, the applicant could legitimately fear that the reason for including a military judge on the tribunal was to lead it to be unduly influenced by considerations which had nothing to do with the evidence in the case.

The requirements of independence and impartiality apply equally in civil cases. In a group of related cases,[107] the Court found that the presence of civil servants on adjudicating tribunals did not, of itself, taint the tribunal provided that there were appropriate guarantees of their independence, including a prohibition on public authorities from giving them instructions concerning the exercise of the judicial function.

PUBLIC HEARINGS

Publicity is seen as one guarantee of the fairness of trial; it offers protection against arbitrary decisions and builds confidence by allowing the public to see justice being administered.[108] To answer the question whether there has been a public hearing within the meaning of Article 6(1), it is necessary to consider the

---

[104] *Findlay v. United Kingdom* (App. 22107/93), Judgment of 25 February 1997; (1997) 24 EHRR 221.

[105] The legislation on courts martial was amended by the Armed Forces Act 1995, but in *Morris v. United Kingdom*, Judgment of 26 February 2002, the Court found that the presence of two army officers in a court martial under the new Act made it insufficiently 'independent'.

[106] *Incal v. Turkey* (App. 22678/93), Judgment of 9 June 1998; (2000) 29 EHRR 449.

[107] *Ettl and others v. Austria*, Judgment of 23 April 1987, Series A, No. 117; (1988) 10 EHRR 255; *Erkner and Hoffauer v. Austria*, Judgment of 23 April 1987, Series A, No. 117; (1987) 9 EHRR 464; and *Poiss v. Austria*, Judgment of 23 April 1987, Series A, No. 117; (1988) 10 EHRR 231; cf. *Sramek v. Germany*, Judgment of 22 October 1984, Series A, No. 84; (1985) 7 EHRR 351.

[108] *Pretto and others v. Italy*, Judgment of 8 December 1983, Series A, No. 71; (1984) 6 EHRR 182.

proceedings as a whole. For example, the absence of a public hearing on appeal or cassation raises an issue under Article 6(1) only if the superior court is 'determining' an issue, which is not the case in legal systems where the appeal or cassation court carries out a supervisory role, in the sense that decisions of earlier hearings can be overturned only on points of law, requiring a further hearing in the court below.[109] In the *Axen* case,[110] for example, there was a public first instance hearing of a personal injuries claim, but the appeal was heard *in camera*, pursuant to a scheme to reduce the workload of the courts. This did not violate Article 6(1), since the proceedings taken as a whole could be regarded as public. The role of the appeal court was limited to dismissal of the appeal on points of law, thus making the decision of the first instance court final.[111]

In England and Wales, applications for leave to appeal against conviction or sentence are normally heard in private, and the position is similar in other countries. It would seem that this is permissible if such applications can be regarded as a step in the appellate process, and if there is a right to an appeal, heard in public, against the refusal of the application. Similarly, in civil cases, interlocutory proceedings which are held in private may be permissible subject to corresponding conditions.[112]

Article 6(1) contains a list of limitations to the right to a public hearing on grounds of public policy, national security, privacy, or where strictly necessary in the interests of justice. The *Campbell and Fell* case[113] concerned the hearings of prison disciplinary offences by Boards of Visitors, which were held in private. The Government relied on public order, national security grounds, and the interests of justice to justify the lack of publicity. The Court concluded that there were 'sufficient reasons of public order and security justifying the exclusion of the press and the public'.[114] This reasoning is not wholly convincing, and no real explanation is given for the distinction drawn between criminal proceedings leading to the imposition of a sentence of imprisonment and the proceedings of Boards of Visitors. The case appears implicitly to have been overruled by the Court in its *Riepan* v. *Austria* judgment,[115] where the applicant was tried for offences committed in prison in a special hearing room in the prison. The public was not excluded, but no steps were taken to let anyone know that the hearing would take place. The Court held that only in rare cases could security concerns justify excluding the public. It observed that a trial would comply with the requirement of publicity only if the public was able to

---

[109] Ibid.

[110] *Axen* v. *Germany*, Judgment of 8 December 1983, Series A, No. 72; (1984) 6 EHRR 195.

[111] See also *Sutter* v. *Switzerland*, Judgment of 22 February 1984, Series A, No. 74; (1984) 6 EHRR 272.

[112] App. 3860/68, *X* v. *United Kingdom*, 16 May 1969 (1970) 30 CD 70.

[113] *Campbell and Fell* v. *United Kingdom*, Judgment of 28 June 1984, Series A, No. 80; (1985) 7 EHRR 165.

[114] Para. 88 of the judgment.

[115] *Riepan* v. *Austria* (App. 35115/97), Judgment of 14 November 2000, para. 34 of the judgment.

obtain information about its date and place and if this place was easily access-ible. In many cases these conditions would be fulfilled by holding the hearing in a normal courtroom large enough to accommodate spectators. The holding of a trial outside a regular courtroom, in particular in a place like a prison to which the general public usually has no access, presented a serious obstacle to its public character, and the State was under an obligation to take compensatory measures to ensure that the public and the media were informed and granted effective access.

The cases of *P and B* v. *United Kingdom*[116]concerned hearings to determine the residence of children. According to the Family Proceedings Rules applicable in England and Wales, the presumption is that such hearings should be held in chambers, although the judge has a discretion to hold a public hearing if one of the parties requests this and shows that there are strong grounds for doing so. The Government relied on the proviso in Article 6(1) that 'the press and public may be excluded from all or part of the trial . . . where the interests of juveniles or the private life of the parties so require, or to the extent strictly necessary in the opinion of the court in special circumstances where publicity would prejudice the interests of justice.' The Court held the proceedings concerning the residence of children were:

prime examples of cases where the exclusion of the press and public may be justified in order to protect the privacy of the child and parties and to avoid prejudicing the interests of justice. To enable the deciding judge to gain as full and accurate a picture as possible of the advantages and disadvantages of the various residence and contact options open to the child, it is essential that the parents and other witnesses feel able to express themselves candidly on highly personal issues without fear of public curiosity or comment.

PUBLIC JUDGMENTS

Article 6(1) also gives a right, in civil and criminal cases, to the public pro-nouncement of the judgment. There have been a number of cases concerning the precise meaning to be given to the words 'pronounced publicly'.[117] Fairly early on, the Court decided that it was not necessary for the judgment actually to be read out in open court and that States enjoyed a discretion as to the manner in which judgments would be made public. In the leading case of *Pretto*,[118] for example, the applicant complained that the judgment of the Court of Cassation on appeal had not been pronounced at a public hearing. The Court of Human Rights stressed the need to take account of the entirety of the proceedings. Furthermore, although the Court of Cassation's decision had not

---

[116] *P and B* v. *United Kingdom* (Apps. 36337/97 and 35974/97), Judgment of 24 April 2001.
[117] In the French text, '*doit être rendu publiquement.*'
[118] *Pretto and others* v. *Italy*, Judgment of 8 December 1983, Series A, No. 71; (1984) 6 EHRR 182.

been pronounced in open court, anyone could consult or obtain a copy of it. There had therefore been no violation of Article 6(1). The Court said:

The form of publicity to be given to a judgment must be assessed in the light of the special features of the proceedings in question and by reference to the object and purpose of Article 6(1).[119]

The requirement in Article 6(1) for public pronouncement of judgments, unlike that for a public hearing, is not expressed to be subject to any limitations. In the *P and B* cases,[120] however, the Court agreed with the Government that it would frustrate the purpose of holding child residence hearings in private— namely, to protect the privacy of the children and their families and to promote justice—if judgments were freely available to the public. It held that the requirements of Article 6(1) were satisfied in child residence cases by the facts that anyone who could establish an interest could, with the leave of the court, consult or obtain a copy of the full text of the orders and/or judgments of first instance courts, and that the judgments of the Court of Appeal and of first instance courts in cases of special interest were routinely published, thereby enabling the public to study the manner in which the courts generally approach such cases and the principles applied in deciding them.

JUDGMENT IN A REASONABLE TIME

The right under Article 6(1) to 'a fair and public hearing within a reasonable time' may be compared with the right under Article 5(3) to trial within a reasonable time. However, while the right guaranteed under Article 5(3) applies only to persons detained on remand on a criminal charge, the scope of Article 6(1) is wider, extending to civil and criminal cases alike, and in criminal cases it applies whether the accused is detained or at liberty. The latter factor is important in assessing the reasonableness of the period, since, as stated above, Article 5(3) requires that there must be 'special diligence' in bringing the case to trial if the accused is detained. The object of the provision in Article 6(1) is to protect the individual concerned from living too long under the stress of uncertainty and, more generally, to ensure that justice is administered without delays which might jeopardize its effectiveness and credibility.[121]

In civil cases there is usually no problem in deciding when the period to be taken into consideration commenced: this is usually the date on which proceedings were initiated, for example by the issuing of a summons or writ. In criminal cases, time begins to run as soon as the accused is officially notified of an

---

[119] Para. 26 of the judgment.
[120] *P and B* v. *United Kingdom* (Apps. 36337/97 and 35974/97), Judgment of 24 April 2001; see also above, in relation to 'public hearings'.
[121] *Bottazzi* v. *Italy* (App. 34884/97), Judgment of 28 July 1999.

allegation that he has committed a criminal offence; this may occur on a date prior to the case coming before the trial court, such as the date of arrest, the date when the person concerned was officially notified that he would be prosecuted, or the date when preliminary investigations were opened.[122] The suspect may live for a long period in the knowledge that investigations are proceeding, although no formal charge is brought. In the *Neumeister* case, the accused was first examined by the investigating judge on 21 January 1960, but the indictment was not preferred until 17 March 1964. He was charged on 23 February 1961, and the Court took this date as the beginning of the period to be considered under Article 6(1).[123] In the *Wemhoff* case, however, the Court considered that the period began on the date when Wemhoff was arrested. On the following day a warrant of arrest was issued, stating that he was under grave suspicion of an offence, but the indictment was not filed until the preliminary investigation was completed more than two years later.[124]

The period to be taken into consideration lasts until the final determination of the case, and therefore includes appeal or cassation proceedings,[125] proceedings to assess damages or sentence, and enforcement proceedings. The State can be held responsible only for delays which are attributable to it; if the parties to the litigation or the defendant in a criminal case have caused or contributed to the delay, those periods of time are not taken into account.[126]

The reasonableness of the length of proceedings is assessed in the light of all the circumstances of the case, having regard in particular to the complexity of the issues before the national courts, the conduct of the parties to the dispute and of the relevant authorities, and what was at stake for the applicant. For example, in a case where the applicant sought compensation from the State for having negligently infected him with HIV, 'special diligence' was required in view of the fact that the applicant was dying of AIDS.[127] Similarly, delays are less likely to be tolerable where the dispute concerns access between a parent and child, given the irreversible damage which can be done to such a relationship through lack of contact.[128]

The Court is called upon to determine more complaints about the unreasonable length of proceedings than any other type of case under the Convention.[129]

---

[122] *Eckle* v. *Germany*, Judgment of 15 July 1982, Series A, No. 51; (1983) 5 EHRR 1.
[123] *Neumeister* v. *Austria*, Judgment of 27 June 1968, Series A, No. 8; (1979–80) 1 EHRR 91, para. 18 of The Law.
[124] *Wemhoff* v. *Germany*, Judgment of 27 June 1968, Series A, No. 7; (1979–80) 1 EHRR 55.
[125] *Neumeister* case, para. 19 of The Law; *Wemhoff* case, para. 18 of The Law.
[126] *Deumeland* v. *Germany*, Judgment of 29 May 1986, Series A, No. 100; (1986) 8 EHRR 448.
[127] *A and others* v. *Denmark* (App. 20826/92), Judgment of 8 February 1996; (1996) 22 EHRR 458.
[128] *H* v. *United Kingdom*, Judgment of 8 July 1987, Series A, No. 120: (1988) 10 EHRR 95
[129] In 2000, approximately two-thirds of the judgments delivered by the Court related to length of domestic proceedings.

Certain States are 'repeat offenders',[130] and seemingly lack the capacity or resources to organize their justice systems efficiently. The Court has repeatedly held that backlogs of judicial business will not excuse unreasonable delays.[131] In the *Bottazzi* case[132] in 1999 it observed that the frequency with which violations of this provision were found against Italy reflected a continuing situation that had not been remedied, constituting a practice of systematic human rights breaches incompatible with the Convention.[133]

Entrenched problems of this kind, as in Italy, mean not only that the rights of litigants in the offending countries are continually violated; these failures also damage the efficiency of the whole system of human rights protection in Europe, since the time and money spent by the Court in dealing with these cases obviously reduce the resources available for examining other applications, and they therefore contribute towards increasing the backlog of cases pending in Strasbourg. In what was described by the President of the Court[134] as 'perhaps the most significant judgment' of 2000, *Kudła* v. *Poland*,[135] the Court departed from existing case law and held that, even where it had already found a violation of the reasonable time requirement of Article 6(1), it could further examine whether there had, in addition, been a violation of the right to an effective remedy under Article 13. In the past the Court had always considered that the right to an effective remedy was absorbed by the stricter procedural guarantee provided for in Article 6(1). The change in its case law was prompted by the increasing burden of length of proceedings cases, and the desire to bring home to States their obligation to protect human rights first and foremost within their own legal systems. It remains to be seen, however, whether the requirement to create a separate, presumably judicial, remedy will assist in resolving the problem or whether it will only serve to place a further burden on underfunded, badly organized and overstretched national justice systems.

---

[130] For example, in 2000 the Court delivered 375 judgments in length of proceedings cases against Italy, out of a total of 695 judgments delivered that year.

[131] See e.g. *Hentrich* v. *France*, Judgment of 22 September 1994, Series A, No. 296-A; (1994) 18 EHRR 440, para. 61 of the judgment.

[132] *Bottazzi* v. *Italy* (App. 34884/97), Judgment of 28 July 1999.

[133] The Court referred in its judgment to the Committee of Ministers' Resolution DH (97) 336 of 11 July 1997: see ch. 25 below

[134] In his speech in Strasbourg at the opening of the judicial year, 25 January 2001.

[135] *Kudła* v. *Poland* (App. 30210/96), Judgment of 26 October 2000.

APPEALS

Article 6 does not include the right to an appeal, although if an appeal procedure is provided by domestic law it must conform with the requirements of Article 6.[136] The Court generally looks at the totality of the domestic proceedings in determining whether there has been a violation[137] and, depending on the nature of the proceedings and of the defect under Article 6, it may be possible for a fair appeal procedure to remedy unfairness at first instance.[138]

WAIVING RIGHTS

A question which has arisen in a number of cases is whether it is possible to waive any of the rights set out in Article 6. There is case law to suggest that certain rights can be waived. The right to a public hearing would appear to be an example.[139] Similarly, it is obvious that a person can waive their right to be assisted by a lawyer.[140]

In the *Zumtobel* case,[141] the applicant complained that there had been no oral hearing before an administrative court. The usual practice of that court was not to hear the parties unless an application to do so was made. No such application had been made. The Court deemed the applicant to have unequivocally waived the right to a hearing and there was no compelling reason of public interest requiring such a hearing.

It is much more doubtful whether those defending criminal proceedings can waive all their rights, though there will always be a difficulty in balancing actions made through the genuine choice (or lack of conscious effort) on the part of defendants, and actions which are the result of the pressures of the process.

---

[136] *Delcourt* v. *Belgium*, Judgment of 17 January 1970, Series A, No. 11; (1979–80) 1 EHRR 355.

[137] *Fedje* v. *Sweden*, Judgment of 26 September 1991, Series A, No. 212-C; (1994) 17 EHRR 14.

[138] Compare e.g. *Edwards* v. *United Kingdom*, Judgment of 16 December 1992, Series A, No. 247-B; (1993) 15 EHRR 417, and *Rowe and Davis* v. *United Kingdom* (App. 28901/95), Judgment of 16 February 2000; (2000) 30 EHRR 1; or *Bryan* v. *United Kingdom*, Judgment of 22 November 1995, Series A, No. 335-A; (1996) 21 EHRR 342, with *Kingsley* v. *United Kingdom* (App. 35605/97), Judgment of 7 November 2000; (2001) 33 EHRR 288.

[139] *Le Compte, van Leuven and de Meyere* v. *Belgium*, Judgment of 23 June 1981, Series A, No. 43; (1982) 4 EHRR 1, pp. 25–46; *H* v. *Belgium*, Judgment of 30 November 1987, Series A, No. 127; (1988) 10 EHRR 339, p.36.

[140] *Melin* v. *France*, Judgment of 22 June 1993, Series A, No. 261-A; (1994) 17 EHRR 1, paras. 22–25 of the judgment.

[141] *Zumtobel* v. *Austria*, Judgment of 21 September 1993, Series A, No. 268-A; (1994) 17 EHRR 116.

CONCLUDING COMMENTS

The Court's case law on the right to a fair trial is extensive and has had a significant impact. For the individual concerned, a finding of a violation by the Court can lead to criminal proceedings being reopened or, in civil cases, the award of damages.[142] Perhaps more importantly, States all over Europe have amended and improved their legal procedures to comply with the Court's rulings.

There are, however, limitations to the scope of the Court's review under Article 6. First, like the rest of the Convention, this provision protects only against violations imputable to the State;[143] if unfairness is caused in legal proceedings by the negligence or misconduct of a lawyer (a private person), rather than, for example, the courts, no issue can arise.[144] Secondly, in accordance with the principle of subsidiarity and the 'fourth instance' doctrine, the Court has no power under Article 6 to substitute its own assessment of the evidence in a case for that of the domestic courts, and in connection with certain procedural matters, such as the need to call a particular witness, it will take issue with the domestic courts only in exceptional circumstances. Article 6 cannot be used as a vehicle to criticize the *content* of domestic law. And the Court's interpretation of the expressions 'criminal charge' and 'civil rights and obligations', though extensive, does not embrace all types of legal proceedings.

Some of these lacunae are filled by other provisions in the Convention and Protocols. Article 1 of Protocol No. 7, for example, provides certain procedural rights to an alien lawfully resident in the territory of a State and facing expulsion. In addition, the Court has read procedural guarantees into some of the substantive rights under the Convention—the right to family life under Article 8, for example, requires that a fair procedure be followed when a child is taken into public care and, in accordance with Article 13, an effective domestic remedy must be provided in respect of all arguable breaches of the Convention.[145]

The following chapter is concerned with certain additional rights which arise in the context of criminal law and procedure.

---

[142] See ch. 24 below.

[143] Art. 34 of the Convention.

[144] *Tripodi* v. *Italy*, Judgment of 22 February 1994, Series A, No. 281-B; (1994) 18 EHRR 295.

[145] See *Z and others* v *United Kingdom* (App. 29392/95), Judgment of 10 May 2001; (2002) 34 EHRR 97, and, in respect of the procedural guarantees available to asylum seekers, *Chahal* v. *United Kingdom* (App. 22414/93), Judgment of 15 November 1996: (1997) 23 EHRR 413.

9
ASPECTS OF THE CRIMINAL PROCESS

INTRODUCTION

This chapter examines the fair trial guarantees specific to criminal proceedings. These are principally contained in paragraphs (2) and (3) of Article 6, although certain aspects of the right to a fair trial in Article 6(1) which apply only in criminal proceedings are also considered here. The second part of the chapter is concerned with the rule against retrospective legislation in Article 7 of the Convention, and a number of additional rights connected with the criminal process introduced by Articles 2 to 4 of Protocol 7.

THE SCOPE OF ARTICLE 6 PARAGRAPHS (2) AND (3)

Article 6, paragraphs (2) and (3) provide:

2. Everyone charged with a criminal offence shall be presumed innocent until proved guilty according to law.
3. Everyone charged with a criminal offence has the following minimum rights:
   (a) to be informed promptly, in a language which he understands and in detail, of the nature and cause of the accusation against him;
   (b) to have adequate time and facilities for the preparation of his defence;
   (c) to defend himself in person or through legal assistance of his own choosing or, if he has not sufficient means to pay for legal assistance, to be given it free when the interests of justice so require;
   (d) to examine or have examined witnesses against him and to obtain the attendance and examination of witnesses on his behalf under the same conditions as witnesses against him;
   (e) to have the free assistance of an interpreter if he cannot understand or speak the language used in court.

Articles 6(2) and (3) apply to 'everyone charged with a criminal offence'. As with the expression 'in the determination ... of any criminal charge against him' in Article 6(1),[1] the Court has adopted an autonomous interpretation, independent of the categorization of legal proceedings under national law.

In order to decide whether a person can be said to be 'charged with a criminal offence' within the meaning of Article 6, paragraphs (2) and (3), the Court has regard to the same '*Engel* criteria'[2] that it applies when assessing whether proceedings are 'in the determination of any criminal charge' in paragraph (1). Indeed, there does not appear to be any significant difference between the scope of the two expressions except as regards the duration of the proceedings covered. In the *Phillips* case[3] the Court explained:

[W]hilst it is clear that Article 6(2) governs criminal proceedings in their entirety, and not solely the examination of the merits of the charge[4] ... the right to be presumed innocent under Article 6(2) arises only in connection with the particular offence 'charged'. Once an accused has properly been proved guilty of that offence, Article 6(2) can have no application in relation to allegations made about the accused's character and conduct as part of the sentencing process, unless such accusations are of such a nature and degree as to amount to the bringing of a new 'charge' within the autonomous Convention meaning.

It can be presumed that the same is true of the application of Article 6(3). In contrast, Article 6(1) applies throughout criminal proceedings in their entirety, including sentencing.[5]

FAIR TRIAL GUARANTEES IN CRIMINAL CASES

In addition to the safeguards discussed in the preceding chapter, which are necessary to a greater or lesser degree in both civil and criminal proceedings, the Court has held that a person charged with a criminal offence enjoys, *inter alia*, certain additional rights considered below. The five rights set out in Article 6(3) are stated to be minimum rights in criminal cases.

---

[1] See ch. 8 above.
[2] *Engel and others* v. *Netherlands*, Judgment of 8 June 1976, Series A, No. 22; (1979–80) 1 EHRR 647; and see ch. 8 above.
[3] *Phillips* v. *United Kingdom* (App. 41087/98), Judgment of 5 September 2001.
[4] The Court referred here to *Minelli* v. *Switzerland*, Judgment of 25 March 1983, Series A, No. 62; (1983) 5 EHRR 554, para. 30 of the judgment; *Sekanina* v. *Austria*, Judgment of 25 August 1993, Series A, No. 266-A; (1994) 17 EHRR 221; and *Allenet de Ribemont* v. *France*, Judgment of 10 February 1995, Series A, No. 308.
[5] See ch. 8 above.

POLICE METHODS OF INVESTIGATION

Even before charges are brought against an accused, unfairness on the part of the police responsible for the investigation against him or her may be sufficient to give rise to a violation of Article 6(1). In the *Teixeira de Castro* case,[6] for example, the applicant was offered money by undercover police officers to supply them with heroin. Although he had no previous criminal record, the applicant did have contacts who were able to get hold of drugs, and, tempted by the money, he complied with the officers' request. He was subsequently charged and convicted of a drugs offence. There was no evidence that the trial proceedings in themselves were unfair, but the Court held that, since the police officers appeared to have instigated the offence, which would not otherwise have been committed, from the outset the applicant was deprived of a fair trial in breach of Article 6(1). The Court contrasted the officers' actions with those of 'true' undercover agents, who conceal their identities in order to obtain information and evidence about crime, without actively inciting it; the second type of situation would not normally in itself give rise to any issue under Article 6.[7]

Incitement is regarded as an offence in many criminal law systems, in recognition of human susceptibility to temptation and pressure. It is surely inappropriate for the police to use their resources actively to incite crime, although perhaps their behaviour in the *Teixeira de Castro* case could better be analysed as an interference with the applicant's right to private life rather than a breach of his Article 6(1) rights, since, apart from the initial incitement, there was no evidence of any unfairness in the criminal proceedings.

The Court has taken a much less hard-line approach where the police have relied upon other forms of unlawful activity in order to gain evidence subsequently used against the accused at trial. In *Khan v. United Kingdom*[8] the police had installed a hidden listening device in a hotel and obtained a recording of the applicant discussing a drugs deal. At the time of the investigation and trial there was no legislation in the United Kingdom governing the use of such apparatus by the police; in consequence, the Court found that Article 8 of the Convention had been violated.[9] It declined, however, the applicant's invitation to find that Article 6(1) had also been breached by virtue of the unlawful methods employed during the investigation. Instead, the Court examined the fairness of the proceedings as a whole and found no violation of Article 6(1), referring to the fact that the applicant had had the opportunity to contest the authenticity of the recording and its admission in evidence. It reached a similar conclusion in *Schenk v. Switzerland*[10] where the obtaining of a tape recording by

[6] *Teixeira de Castro* v. *Portugal* (App. 25829/94), Judgment of 9 June 1998; (1999) 28 EHRR 101.
[7] See *Ludi* v. *Switzerland*, Judgment of 15 June 1992, Series A, No. 238; (1993) 15 EHRR 440.
[8] *Khan* v. *United Kingdom* (App. 35294/97), Judgment of 12 May 2000; (2001) 31 EHRR 1016.
[9] The procedure was not 'in accordance with law': see ch. 11 below.
[10] *Schenk* v. *Switzerland*, Judgment of 12 July 1988, Series A, No. 140; (1991) 13 EHRR 242.

the police was unlawful not only according to the Convention, but also under domestic law.

THE RIGHT TO SILENCE, THE PRINCIPLE AGAINST SELF-INCRIMINATION, AND THE PRESUMPTION OF INNOCENCE

Although it is not specifically mentioned in Article 6 of the Convention, the Court has held[11] that the right to silence and the right not to incriminate oneself are generally recognized international standards which lie at the heart of the notion of a fair criminal procedure under Article 6(1). These rights are closely linked to the principle enshrined in Article 6(2), that a person accused of a crime is innocent until proved guilty according to law.

As Lord Mustill observed in *R. v. Director of Serious Fraud Office, ex parte Smith*,[12] the 'right to silence' is a composite term which in fact encompasses a number of separate rights. He identified the following as protected, to a greater or lesser degree, by English law:

(1) A general immunity, possessed by all persons and bodies, from being compelled on pain of punishment to answer questions posed by other persons or bodies.

(2) A general immunity, possessed by all persons and bodies, from being compelled on pain of punishment to answer questions the answers to which may incriminate them.

(3) A specific immunity, possessed by all persons under suspicion of criminal responsibility whilst being interviewed by police officers or others in similar positions of authority, from being compelled on pain of punishment to answer questions of any kind.

(4) A specific immunity, possessed by accused persons undergoing trial, from being compelled to give evidence, and from being compelled to answer questions put to them in the dock.

(5) A specific immunity, possessed by persons who have been charged with a criminal offence, from having questions material to the offence addressed to them by police officers or persons in a similar position of authority.

(6) A specific immunity . . . possessed by accused persons undergoing trial, from having adverse comment made on any failure (a) to answer questions before the trial, or (b) to give evidence at the trial.

The case of *JB v. Switzerland*[13] concerned, broadly, the right included in points (2) and (4) of Lord Mustill's analysis, not to be compelled to provide self-incriminating evidence. The applicant was the subject of tax evasion proceedings brought by the District Tax Commission, which requested him to

---

[11] *Saunders* v. *United Kingdom* (App. 19187/91), Judgment of 17 December 1996; (1997) 23 EHRR 313.

[12] [1992] 3 WLR 66

[13] *JB* v. *Switzerland* (App. 31827/96), Judgment of 3 May 2001. See also *Funke and others* v. *France*, Judgment of 25 February 1993, Series A, No. 256-A; (1993) 16 EHRR 297.

submit all documents in his possession relating to investments in a number of companies. He admitted that he had made investments without properly declaring the income, but he refused to submit the documents requested. As a result of his continuing refusal, three separate disciplinary fines were imposed on him, totalling 3,000 Swiss francs. The Court of Human Rights held that, given the amount of the fine imposed and its punitive character, the proceedings could be characterized as 'criminal' for the purposes of Article 6(1). It appeared that the authorities were attempting to compel the applicant to submit documents which would have provided information about his income and thus his liability to tax, and it could not be excluded that the documents would have provided evidence which could have been used against the applicant in a prosecution for tax evasion. The fines imposed for non-production of possibly incriminating documents violated the right to silence and the privilege against self-incrimination, included in the right to a fair trial under Article 6(1).

In the *Saunders* case[14] the applicant had been forced, through the threat of imprisonment for failure to answer questions, to give evidence to government-appointed investigators about an allegedly illegal share-support scheme. Transcripts of his interviews with the inspectors were subsequently used by the prosecution in criminal proceedings against him. The Court, which had found in an earlier judgment[15] that Article 6 did not apply to investigations of this kind, did not find any breach of the Convention arising from the inspectors' compulsory powers *per se* – a result which might be said to contradict the position in the *JB* case. However, it held that the subsequent use by the prosecution at the applicant's criminal trial of transcripts of the interviews violated his right to silence.

In its *Saunders* judgment the Court observed that the rationale of the right to silence and the principle against self-incrimination lies in the protection of the accused against improper compulsion by the authorities, thereby contributing to the avoidance of miscarriages of justice. The right not to incriminate oneself, in particular, presupposes that the prosecution in a criminal case should seek to prove its case against the accused without resort to evidence obtained through methods of coercion or oppression in defiance of the will of the accused. On the basis of this explanation, the Court drew a distinction between the right of an accused person to remain silent, which is protected by the Convention, and the use in criminal proceedings of material which might be obtained from the accused through the use of compulsory powers but which has an existence independent of the will of the suspect, such as documents acquired pursuant to a warrant, breath, blood and urine samples, and bodily tissue for the purpose of DNA testing, which is not inconsistent with Article 6.

---

[14] *Saunders* v. *United Kingdom* (App. 19187/91), Judgment of 17 December 1996; (1997) 23 EHRR 313.
[15] *Fayed* v. *United Kingdom*, Judgment of 21 September 1994, Series A, No. 294-B; (1994) 18 EHRR 393.

This distinction was adopted and applied by the Privy Council in *Brown* v. *Stott*,[16] where it held that a statutory requirement to provide a breath specimen when suspected of driving with excess alcohol, with a maximum penalty of a £1,000 fine or six months' imprisonment for non-compliance, was not incompatible with Article 6(2).[17] It does not, however, appear that the European Court is entirely consistent in its application of this principle.[18] In the *JB* case, for example, the documents which the tax authorities sought to compel the applicant to disclose were presumably created before the investigation was initiated and thus had an 'independent existence'.

There is also considerable case law under paragraphs (1) and (2) of Article 6 on the extent to which a criminal court may draw an inference of guilt from an accused's silence. This is the aspect of the right to silence referred to at point (6) in Lord Mustill's list above, and the question is also relevant to the presumption of innocence, which requires that the burden of proving an offence lies on the prosecution.

The applicant in *Telfner* v. *Austria*[19] was convicted of an offence involving a hit-and-run driving incident. The victim of the incident had been able to give the police the make and registration number of the car, but could not identify the driver. The applicant elected not to give evidence at trial, and the prosecution case relied almost entirely on the findings of the police that the applicant was the principal user of the car (registered in his mother's name) and had not been at home at the time of the accident. The Court of Human Rights held that, although it might be permissible for a court to draw an inference of guilt from an accused's silence, where the evidence adduced was so strong that the only common-sense inference to be drawn was that the accused had no answer to the case against him, in the instant case the evidence for the prosecution was extremely weak. In requiring the applicant to provide an explanation, without having first established a convincing prima-facie case against him, the courts in effect shifted the burden of proof from the prosecution to the defence, giving rise to a violation of Article 6(2).

In contrast in the *John Murray* case[20] the Court found that it was compatible with Article 6(1) for the trial judge (who sat alone, without a jury) to draw an inference of guilt from the fact that the applicant had remained silent under police questioning and at trial. The evidence against him was strong and, in accordance with Article 3 of the Criminal Evidence (Northern Ireland) Order

---

[16] [2001] 2 WLR 817.

[17] See also App. 8239/78, *X* v. *Netherlands* (1979) 16 DR 184, where the Commission came to a similar conclusion.

[18] See Professor Andrew Ashworth's commentary on *Heaney and Guinness* v. *Ireland* [2001] Crim LR 482.

[19] *Telfner* v. *Austria* (App. 33501/96), Judgment of 20 March 2001.

[20] *Murray (John)* v. *United Kingdom* (App. 18731/91), Judgment of 8 February 1996; (1996) 22 EHRR 29.

1988, he had been warned at the time of his arrest that he did not have to say anything, but that his failure to mention any fact which he subsequently relied on in his defence might be treated in court as supporting the case against him.

It is clear, therefore, that the Court does not consider that the drawing of inferences from an accused's silence is in itself incompatible with Article 6, as long as judicial safeguards operate to ensure fairness. In *Condron* v. *United Kingdom*[21] it found a violation of Article 6(1), because the trial judge failed to direct the jury that they could draw an adverse inference only if satisfied that the applicants' silence at the police interview could only sensibly be attributed to their having no answer to the accusations against them, or none that would stand up to cross-examination. The applicants were heroin addicts and suffering from withdrawal at the time of their interviews with the police on suspicion of drug dealing. Although they were cautioned by the investigating officers that it might harm their defence if they failed to mention something which they might later rely on in court, and were found by a police doctor to be fit for questioning, they made no comment on the advice of their solicitor, who disagreed with the doctor's assessment.

This case illustrates the Court's tendency to assess the fairness of proceedings looked at as a whole, rather than to formulate rigid procedural rules. If the trial judge had exercised his discretion properly, no unfairness would have been caused to the accused. It was, however, impossible for the Court of Appeal to rectify the problem (without ordering a retrial) because of the difficulty of assessing the extent to which the jury had been influenced by the misdirection.

In *Salabiaku* v. *France*,[22] the Court was asked to consider the compatibility with Article 6(2) of a law reversing the burden of proof in respect of certain elements of an offence. The applicant had been found in possession of illegal drugs at a Paris airport. He was not, however, charged with and convicted of an offence of simple possession, but instead with offences of smuggling and importation, which include an element of knowledge or intent. The French Customs Code setting out the offences stated generally that 'the person in possession of contraband goods shall be deemed liable for the offence.' The Court rejected the Commission's opinion that Article 6(2) merely provided a procedural guarantee to be observed by the courts, and held that the provision also placed a duty on legislators to respect the rights of the accused when framing offences. It observed, generally, that:

Presumptions of fact or of law operate in every legal system. Clearly, the Convention does not prohibit such presumptions in principle. It does, however, require the Contracting States to remain within certain limits in this respect as regards criminal law.

---

[21] *Condron* v. *United Kingdom* (App. 35382/97), Judgment of 2 May 2000; (2001) 31 EHRR 1.
[22] Judgment of 7 October 1988, Series A, No. 141-A; (1991) 13 EHRR 379. See also *Hoang* v. *France*, Judgment of 25 September 1992, Series A, No. 243; (1993) 16 EHRR 53.

The Court underlined that it was not its task to consider legislation *in abstracto*, and instead examined the facts of the particular case. It found that the presumption created by the Code and applied to the applicant was not irrebuttable, since the courts which had dealt with the applicant had followed case law to the effect that once the fact of possession had been established by the prosecution, the burden shifted to the defence to prove, if they could, that the accused was the victim of '*force majeure*' or for some reason could not have been expected to know about the goods in his possession, in which case he would have been acquitted. The courts had examined all the evidence, including evidence that the applicant had shown no surprise when the drugs were discovered in his suitcase, and had found him guilty without relying on the statutory presumption. In these circumstances, there had been no violation of Article 6(2).

The Court was again called upon to examine legal presumptions of guilt in the case of *Phillips* v. *United Kingdom*.[23] Following his conviction of a drug-trafficking offence, the applicant was subjected to proceedings under the Drug Trafficking Act 1994, which required the Crown Court to make a confiscation order against him if it found that he had received at any time any payment or other reward in connection with drug-trafficking. The Act provided that the confiscation order should be set at a sum corresponding to the proceeds of drug-trafficking assessed by the court to have been gained by the defendant, unless the court was satisfied that, at the time the confiscation order was made, only a lesser sum could be realized. In determining whether and to what extent the applicant had benefited from drug-trafficking, the Act required the court to assume that any property appearing to have been held by him at any time since his conviction or during the period of six years before the date on which the criminal proceedings were commenced was received as a payment or reward in connection with drug-trafficking, and that any expenditure incurred by him during the same period was paid for out of the proceeds of drug-trafficking. This statutory assumption could be set aside in relation to any particular property or expenditure if the applicant could show, on the balance of probabilities, that it was incorrect or that there would be a serious risk of injustice if it were applied.

The Court did not deal with the applicant's complaint about the operation of the statutory assumption under Article 6(2), because of its finding that the confiscation procedure was analogous to sentencing, and that Article 6(2) ceased to apply once an accused had been properly convicted of the offence charged. Instead, it examined the fairness of the presumption under Article 6(1), applying a test derived from the *Salabiaku* judgment quoted above.

The Court noted that there was no direct evidence that the applicant had

---

[23] *Phillips* v. *United Kingdom* (App. 41087/98), Judgment of 5 September 2001.

engaged in drug-trafficking prior to the events which led to his conviction and that in calculating the amount of the confiscation order based on the benefits of drug-trafficking, the judge had expressed himself to be reliant on the statutory assumption. In reality, however, and looking in detail at the steps taken by the judge to reach the final figure, the Court observed that in respect of every item taken into account the judge was satisfied, on the basis either of the applicant's admissions or evidence adduced by the prosecution, that the applicant owned the property or had spent the money. Since he did not appear to have been employed during the relevant period, the obvious inference was that it had come from an illegitimate source. In addition, the Court noted that, had the applicant's account of his financial dealings been true, it would not have been difficult for him to rebut the statutory assumption. It concluded that the application to the applicant of the relevant provisions of the Drug Trafficking Act 1994 was confined within reasonable limits given the importance of what was at stake, that the rights of the defence were fully respected, and that there had been no breach of Article 6(1).

It is interesting to speculate as to what type of reversed burden of proof the Court would find inconsistent with Article 6.[24] The *Telfner, John Murray* and *Condron* cases underline that Article 6(1) and (2) require the prosecution at least to establish prima-facie that the accused has committed an offence, and that it is permissible for a court to draw an inference of guilt from the accused's failure to provide an explanation only where this is the sole common-sense conclusion to be drawn. The legislation under examination in *Salabiaku* placed the onus on the prosecution to establish possession of prohibited goods, and then required the court to infer that the accused had knowledge of them, in the absence of proof to the contrary. Again, particularly having regard to the way in which this law was actually applied in the applicant's case, it might be said that the reversal of the burden of proof only went so far as to permit the court to draw a 'common-sense' inference.

In the *Phillips* case, the statutory presumption came into operation once the prosecution had established (1) that the accused had derived some benefit from drug-trafficking (which must in many cases follow almost automatically from his or her conviction for the offence which triggers the confiscation procedure); and (2) that the accused had owned property or incurred expenditure at any time since his conviction or during the period of six years before the date on which the criminal proceedings were commenced. The burden then passed to the accused to prove that the property or expenditure did not represent the proceeds of drug-trafficking.

Owning property and spending money are activities undertaken by almost

---

[24] See also on this question the judgments of the House of Lords in *R. v. DPP, ex parte Kibilene and others* [1999] 3 WLR 972 and the Court of Appeal in *R. v. Lambert, Ali and Jordan, The Times,* 5 September 2000.

everyone in Western society and, unlike possessing illegal drugs, are not prima-facie unlawful. In finding no violation of Article 6(1), the Court appears to have influenced by the fact that had the applicant's account of his financial dealings been true, it would not have been difficult for him to rebut the statutory assumption; most people who, for example, buy a house, are able to show where the money came from without great difficulty. The Court indicated that 'an issue relating to the fairness of the procedure might arise in circumstances where the amount of a confiscation order was based on the value of assumed hidden assets', presumably because of the difficulty which would be involved in disproving the existence and source of unspecified and unsubstantiated articles. The Court's acceptance of the reversed burden of proof in this case might also be explained by the fact that it operated in the context of a procedure analogous to sentencing, to enable the national court to assess the amount at which a confiscation order should properly be fixed. It is possible that if a similarly sweeping presumption were applied to facilitate a court in finding a person guilty of an offence, this might give rise to a violation of Article 6(1) and (2).

OTHER ASPECTS OF THE PRESUMPTION OF INNOCENCE

Is it contrary to Article 6(2) for the court to be informed, in the course of the trial, of the previous convictions of the accused? Early in its history, the Commission examined this question under paragraphs (1) and (2) of Article 6 in the light of the practice of the Contracting States. Having found that, in a number of these countries, information as to previous convictions is regularly given during the trial before the court has reached a decision as to the guilt of accused, the Commission concluded that such a procedure does not violate any provision of Article 6,[25] even when the information is given to a jury.[26] Nevertheless, while this practice may not as such be contrary to Article 6(2), it may be that, having regard to the doctrine that the question of 'fair hearing' must be viewed in the context of the trial as a whole, it could in a particular case support a conclusion that the accused has not had a fair trial under Article 6.

Article 6(2) is not merely concerned with the burden of proof. It also pro-hibits the authorities from saying or doing anything which indicates that they believe a person is guilty of an offence, unless or until guilt is proven. This does not prevent the authorities from informing the public about criminal investiga-tions in progress, but it does require them to be discreet and circumspect in order to preserve the presumption of innocence. So reference, without qualifi-cation, at a press conference conducted by senior officials that a person was an

[25] App. 2742/66, X v. *Austria*, 1 April 1966 (1966) 9 *Yearbook* 550.
[26] App. 2518/65, X v. *Denmark*, 14 December 1965 (1965) 8 *Yearbook* 370.

accomplice to murder amounted to a declaration of guilt in breach of Article 6(2).[27] In this case the Court for the first time indicated that the protection of Article 6(2) may be infringed not only by a judge or a court, but also by other public authorities.

In a group of related cases,[28] statements were made, after criminal proceedings had been discontinued and where the defendants were seeking reimbursement of expenses, indicating some probability that the defendants were guilty. On close analysis, the Court concluded that the terms used by the judges described a state of suspicion rather than a finding of guilt. Article 6(2) had not been violated. This issue was taken up in the *Sekanina* case.[29] Sekanina had been tried and acquitted for the murder of his wife, then brought proceedings for reimbursement of costs and compensation for detention on remand for just over a year. The claim for compensation was dismissed on the ground that his acquittal had not dispelled the suspicion of his having committed the murder. The Government argued that the indications given by the court merely referred to the continued existence of suspicion, which had been accepted in earlier cases, and did not reflect the opinion that Sekanina was guilty. The Court unanimously distinguished the earlier cases which concerned the discontinuance of proceedings before a final determination, whereas the present case concerned proceedings following an acquittal. The statements made by the national courts were inconsistent with the presumption of innocence.

PROMPT NOTIFICATION OF THE CHARGES AND INTERPRETATION

The possibility for an accused to know the case against him is essential to the preparation of a defence. The duty on the State under Article 6(3)(a) is more explicit than the requirement of notification of the reason for detention in Article 5(2), and demands prompt information in a language the accused understands and in detail. Article 6(3)(e) grants the right to free interpretation if a person cannot understand or speak the language used in court. This issue has often been raised in conjunction with the right to notification of the charges and the two issues will be considered together.

Whereas the right to publicly funded legal assistance does not arise in every case, interpretation, where necessary, must be provided free regardless of the means of the defendant and must extend to the translation or interpretation of all documents or statements in the proceedings which it is

---

[27] *Allenet de Ribemont* v. *France*, Judgment of 10 February 1995, Series A, No. 308; (1996) 22 EHRR 582.

[28] *Lutz* v. *Germany, Nölkenbockhoff* v. *Germany, Englert* v. *Germany*, Judgments of 25 August 1987, Series A, No. 123; (1988) 10 EHRR 163.

[29] *Sekanina* v. *Austria*, Judgment of 25 August 1993, Series A, No. 266-A; (1994) 17 EHRR 221.

essential for the defendant to understand in order to have the benefit of a fair trial.[30]

In the *Brozicek* case,[31] the applicant, a German national, was charged in Italy with resisting the police and assault and wounding. He was sent notification of the proceedings in Germany, but these were drafted in Italian. Because he could not understand the notification, he did not attend the trial, and was convicted in his absence. The Court concluded that there had been a violation of Article 6(3)(a) because the Italian authorities had not provided the information in a language which Brozicek understood, nor had they taken any steps to ascertain whether he understood Italian.

The *Kamasinski* case[32] concerned an American charged with offences in Austria. He was provided with an interpreter during the pre-trial stages of the criminal process and a lawyer who was a registered English language interpreter was appointed to represent him at his trial. He nevertheless complained that he had not received English translations of the indictment. The Court held that Article 6(3)(a) did not require that the notification of the charge be given in writing nor translated in written form. In some cases, a difficulty could arise under the provision if no written translation of the indictment was provided, but in the circumstances of the present case, it was clear that the oral explanations provided to the applicant in his first language constituted sufficient information of the charges against him.

An accused person whose own conduct has been the principal cause of his not receiving notification of the charges against him cannot complain under Article 6(3)(a).[33] Discrepancies resulting from a clerical error in the statement of the provision which is the basis of the charge will not amount to a violation of the provision.[34]

TIME AND FACILITIES TO RUN A DEFENCE

The obligation in Article 6(3)(b) that those charged with a criminal offence are to have adequate time and facilities for the preparation of a defence is linked to the right in Article 6(3)(c) to personal representation or legal assistance. There are comparatively few cases in which Article 6(3)(b) alone has resulted in a violation of the Convention.

A pragmatic view is taken of the nature of the right. For example, where an

---

[30] *Luedicke, Belkacem and Koç v. Germany*, Judgment of 28 November 1978, Series A, No. 29; (1979–80) 2 EHRR 149. See also *Öztürk v. Germany*, Judgment of 21 February 1984, Series A, No. 73; (1984) 6 EHRR 409 and *Kamasinski v. Austria*, Judgment of 19 December 1989, Series A, No. 168; (1991) 13 EHRR 36.

[31] *Brozicek v. Italy*, Judgment of 19 December 1989, Series A, No. 167; (1990) 12 EHRR 371.

[32] *Kamasinski v. Austria*, Judgment of 19 December 1989, Series A, No. 168; (1991) 13 EHRR 36.

[33] *Hennings v. Germany*, Judgment of 16 December 1992, Series A, No. 215-A; (1993) 16 EHRR 83, para. 26 of the judgment.

[34] *Gea Catalán v. Spain*, Judgment of 10 February 1995, Series A, No. 309; (1995) 20 EHRR 266.

accused person's lawyer has access to documentation, but not the accused himself, there will be no breach of the provision,[35] and a failure by the court to comply with a procedural request will not give rise to a breach if it seems that the procedure would not have served a useful purpose.[36]

The applicant in the *Hadjianastassiou* case[37] wished to challenge in the Court of Cassation the legality of proceedings in the Court of Appeal. The Court of Appeal's decision had been read out in summary form on 22 November 1985, but the full reasons were not disclosed until 10 January 1986. The time-limit for applying to the Court of Cassation was five days from the date of the Court of Appeal's judgment (in November), and after the expiry of the time-limit applicants were barred from expanding upon any legal argument. The Court concluded that the rights of the defence had been restricted to such a degree that there had been a violation of Article 6(3)(b) taken in conjunction with Article 6(1).

LEGAL ASSISTANCE

Article 6(3)(c) provides that 'everyone charged with a criminal offence' has three minimum rights: (1) to defend himself in person, or (2) to defend himself through legal assistance of his own choosing, and (3) if he has not sufficient means to pay for legal assistance, to be given it free when the interests of justice so require. The aim of this provision is to ensure that defendants have the possibility of presenting an effective defence.[38]

Only shortcomings in legal representation which are imputable to the State authorities can give rise to a violation of Article 6(3)(c). In the *Tripodi* case,[39] the applicant's lawyer was ill and unable to attend a hearing before the Court of Cassation, which refused his request for an adjournment and determined the matter in his absence, on the basis of written pleadings. It appeared that the lawyer had done little to ensure that he was replaced for the day of the hearing and the European Court, looking at the proceedings as a whole, found no violation.

The rights in Article 6(3)(c) are capable of applying pre-trial, since absence of legal representation at this stage could in certain circumstances affect the fairness of the proceedings as a whole.[40] In the *John Murray* case,[41] for example,

---

[35] *Kamasinski* v. *Austria*, Judgment of 19 December 1989, Series A, No. 168; (1991) 13 EHRR 36.

[36] *Bricmont* v. *Belgium*, Judgment of 7 July 1989, Series A, No. 158; (1990) 12 EHRR 217.

[37] *Hadjianastassiou* v. *Greece*, Judgment of 16 December 1992, Series A, No. 252-A; (1993) 16 EHRR 219.

[38] *Goddi* v. *Italy*, Judgment of 9 April 1984, Series A, No. 76; (1984) 6 EHRR 457.

[39] *Tripodi* v. *Italy*, Judgment of 22 February 1994, Series A, No. 281-B; (1994) 18 EHRR 295.

[40] *Imbrioscia* v. *Switzerland*, Judgment of 24 November 1993, Series A, No. 275; (1994) 17 EHRR 441.

[41] *Murray (John)* v. *United Kingdom* (App. 18731/91), Judgment of 8 February 1996; (1996) 22 EHRR 29.

the Court found that the denial of access to a solicitor in the first forty-eight hours of police questioning had breached the applicant's rights under Article 6(1) and (3)(c). The right to see a lawyer in the early stages of a police investigation is not absolute, and, where there is a good reason, can be subjected to restrictions. The Government argued that the problems involved in investigating terrorist offences justified the denial of access, but the Court disagreed. Since Northern Irish law permitted an inference of guilt to be drawn from the applicant's silence under police questioning (see above), the refusal of a lawyer had deprived him of a fair trial.

Poitrimol v. *France*[42] concerned a rule of criminal procedure which allowed the appeal courts to refuse to hear an appeal against conviction where the accused was a fugitive from justice and declined to attend. The Human Rights Court ruled that a person does not lose his right to the benefit of legal assistance by virtue of his own absence from court. Although it was permissible to have sanctions to secure the attendance of the accused in court, in Poitrimol's case the refusal to hear his lawyer was disproportionate and there was a violation of Article 6(1) and 6(3)(c) taken together.

The Court has held that 'where the deprivation of liberty is at stake, the interests of justice in principle call for legal representation', and if the defendant cannot afford to pay for this himself, public funds must be available as of right.[43] It will normally be in the interests of justice for a person to receive representation on an appeal where a substantial prison sentence is involved and there is a real issue to be considered.[44] Where an initial refusal of legal aid has taken place, and such an issue emerges, there should be a procedure for further considering the grant of legal assistance.[45]

The *Croissant* case[46] raised issues of the relationship between the choice of a lawyer and entitlement to free legal aid. The court had appointed three lawyers to assist in the defence of the applicant, who was charged with various criminal offences arising out his activities as lawyer to various members of the Red Army Faction; the trial had political overtones. Croissant objected to the assignment of one of the lawyers, whom he alleged had been assigned to ensure that the trial proceeded without interruption rather than to protect his interests. There was no evidence to show that the relationship was so strained as to make a

---

[42] *Poitrimol* v. *France*, Judgment of 23 November 1993, Series A, No. 277-A; (1994) 18 EHRR 130. See also *Lala* v. *Netherlands*, Judgment of 22 September 1994, Series A, No. 297-A; (1994) 18 EHRR 586 and *Pelladoah* v. *Netherlands*, Judgment of 22 September 1994, Series A, No. 297-B; (1994) 19 EHRR 81.

[43] *Bentham* v. *United Kingdom* (App. 19380/92), Judgment of 10 June 1996; (1996) 22 EHRR 293.

[44] *Granger* v. *United Kingdom*, Judgment of 28 March 1990, Series A, No. 174; (1990) 12 EHRR 469; *Boner* v. *United Kingdom*, Judgment of 28 October 1994; (1995) 19 EHRR 246; and *Maxwell* v. *United Kingdom*, Judgment of 28 October 1994, Series A, No. 300-C; (1995) 19 EHRR 97. See also *Quaranta* v. *Switzerland*, Judgment of 24 May 1991, Series A, No. 205.

[45] Ibid.

[46] *Croissant* v. *Germany*, Judgment of 25 September 1992, Series A, No. 237-B; (1993) 16 EHRR 135.

proper defence impossible. The Court found no violation of Article 6(3)(c) either in the appointment of multiple counsel nor in the appointment of counsel against the wishes of the defendant, though it did recognize that a 'court should, as a rule, endeavour to choose a lawyer in whom the defendant places confidence.'[47]

WITNESSES

Article 6(3)(d) grants a number of rights in respect of witnesses: to secure the attendance of witnesses to give evidence and to examine them on the same basis as the witnesses against the accused. This provision must be considered in the context of both the accusatorial system—where it is for the parties, subject to the control of the court, to decide which witnesses they wish to call—and the inquisitorial system—where the court decides for itself which witnesses it wishes to hear. In the former system, the witnesses are examined and cross-examined by the parties or their representatives, although additional questions may be put by the judge, while in the latter system witnesses are examined by the court.

Article 6(3)(d) is intended to ensure, under each system, that the accused is placed on a footing of equality with the prosecution as regards the calling and examination of witnesses,[48] but it does not give defendants a right to call witnesses without restriction. Moreover, in accordance with the 'fourth instance' doctrine, it is normally for the national courts to decide whether it is necessary or advisable to call a witness, and, provided the principle of equality has been respected, the Court would find a violation only in exceptional circumstances.[49] A court can therefore refuse to hear a witness for the reason that his statement would be irrelevant,[50] and, even where the evidence is relevant, the court fulfils its obligation if it takes all appropriate steps to try to ensure the appearance of the witness.[51]

The *Unterpertinger* case[52] provides an example of the kind of 'exceptional circumstances' where the Court would find a violation based on the failure to call a witness. The trial court relied on witness statements because the witnesses in question (who were members of the defendant's family) declined to attend and give evidence in person. The Court observed that the use of such statements would not always breach Article 6(3)(d), but in this case, since they were

---

[47] Para. 7 of the judgment.

[48] *Bönisch v. Austria*, Judgment of 6 May 1985, Series A No 92; (1987) 9 EHRR 191.

[49] *Bricmont v. Belgium*, Judgment of 7 July 1989, Series A, No. 158; (1990) 12 EHRR 217.

[50] App. 1404/62, *Wiechert v. Federal Republic of Germany*, 7 March 1964 (1964) 7 *Yearbook* 104, at 112; App. 4119/69, 35 CD 127.

[51] App. 3566/68, *X v. Federal Republic of Germany*, 15 December 1969 (1970)31 CD 31, at 34–5; App. 4078/69, 35 CD 121, at 125.

[52] *Unterpertinger v. Austria*, Judgment of 24 November 1986, Series A, No. 110; (1991) 13 EHRR 175.

relied on by the prosecution to prove the central elements of the case against the accused, the fact that the evidence could not be tested in the normal way compromised the rights of the defence to an extent which resulted in a breach of Article 6(1) taken together with Article 6(3)(d).

The Court has been called upon to decide a number of cases in which the prosecution in criminal trials has relied upon the evidence of anonymous witnesses. The applicant in the case of *Doorson* v. *Netherlands*[53] had been convicted of drugs offences on the evidence of a number of anonymous witnesses. He had not been permitted to see these witnesses since they claimed to be frightened of reprisals, but during the course of the appeal proceedings his lawyer had been present while they were questioned by the investigating judge and had had an opportunity to put questions to them himself, and the investigating judge had drawn up a full report for the Court of Appeal explaining her reasons for considering that the witnesses could be relied upon. The Court found that it was justifiable to protect the rights of the witnesses to respect for their life, liberty, and security of person (as secured by various provisions in the Convention) by preserving their anonymity and that the difficulties this caused for the defence had been adequately counterbalanced by the procedures followed by the investigating judge. Nonetheless, the Court observed that it would never be acceptable for a conviction to be based solely or to a decisive extent on anonymous statements.[54]

A similar issue arose in *Van Mechelen and others* v. *Netherlands*.[55] Here the applicants were convicted of attempted murder and robbery after a trial at which the prosecution evidence included the uncorroborated statements of several police officers who refused to reveal their names and were identified only by numbers. The defence were given a chance to question the officers in the following conditions: each officer was confined in a closed room with the investigating judge and a registrar, while the defendants, their lawyers, and an advocate general sat in another room. There was a sound-link between the two rooms, so that the defence could hear all the questions put to the officers and their answers, but they could not observe their demeanour under questioning and thus test their reliability.

The Court distinguished this case from *Doorson* in view of the particular problems which arise where police officers give evidence anonymously. Although their interests—and those of their families—also deserved protection under the Convention, it had to be recognized that their position was different from an ordinary disinterested witness or a victim, since they owed a general duty of obedience to the State's executive authorities and usually had links to

[53] *Doorson* v. *Netherlands* (App. 20524/92), Judgment of 26 March 1996; (1996) 22 EHRR 330.

[54] See also *Saidi* v. *France*, Judgment of 20 September 1993, Series A, No. 261-C; (1994) 17 EHRR 251.

[55] *Van Mechelen and others* v. *Netherlands* (Apps 21363/94, 21364/94, 21427/93, and 22056/93), Judgment of 23 April 1997; (1998) 25 EHRR 647.

the prosecution. The Court was not satisfied that the measures in question had been strictly necessary—for example, the domestic court had not made a sufficient effort to assess whether the threat of reprisals which had been made against the police officers could be taken seriously. It therefore found a violation of Articles 6(1) and 3(d) taken together.

THE PRINCIPLE OF LEGALITY

The Convention is not merely concerned with the procedural fairness of criminal trials. Article 7 is concerned with the substantive criminal law and embodies the principle of legality, which stipulates that no one should be convicted or punished except in respect of a breach of a pre-existing rule of law.[56] There are two main aspects to this principle. First, Article 7 prohibits legislatures and courts from creating or extending the law so as to criminalize acts or omissions which were not illegal at the time of commission or omission, or to increase a penalty retroactively. Secondly, it requires that the criminal law should be clearly defined; this second aspect of the principle is almost a precondition of the first, since the more precisely drafted an offence is, the less scope there is for creative judicial interpretation and nasty court-room surprises for defendants.

Article 7 states:

1. No one shall be held guilty of any criminal offence on account of any act or omission which did not constitute a criminal offence under national or international law at the time when it was committed. Nor shall a heavier penalty be imposed than the one that was applicable at the time the criminal offence was committed.
2. This Article shall not prejudice the trial and punishment of any person for any act or omission which, at the time when it was committed, was criminal according to the general principles of law recognised by civilised nations.

APPLICABILITY OF ARTICLE 7

The terms 'criminal offence' and 'penalty' in Article 7 carry autonomous meanings independent of the characterization under domestic law. The question whether any particular act amounts to a conviction for a 'criminal offence' is determined by reference to the '*Engel* criteria':[57] principally the classification in

---

[56] *Nullum crimen, nulla poena sine lege*; best paraphrased in English as: only the law can define a crime and prescribe a penalty.

[57] See ch. 8 above.

domestic law, the nature of the offence itself, and the nature and severity of the sentence which can be imposed.[58] Similar considerations apply in deciding whether a measure amounts to a 'penalty'. As the Court observed in the *Welch* case:[59]

The wording of Article 7(1), second sentence, indicates that the starting point in any assessment of the existence of a penalty is whether the measure in question is imposed following conviction for a 'criminal offence'. Other factors that may be taken into account as relevant in this connection are the nature and purpose of the measure in question; its characterisation under national law; the procedures involved in the making and implementation of the measure; and its severity.

The applicant in that case was arrested for drugs offences committed in November 1986. The Drug Trafficking Offences Act 1986 came into force in January 1987; it introduced confiscation orders intended to ensure that those convicted of drugs offences could not retain the profits of drugs-related activity. The retroactive effect of the confiscation order imposed on the applicant was not in dispute; the only question before the Court was whether such an order could properly be described as a 'penalty'.

The Court rejected the Government's argument that the order was preventive, rather than punitive, observing that 'the aims of prevention and reparation are consistent with a punitive purpose and may be seen as constituent elements of the very notion of punishment.' It concluded that Welch faced more 'far-reaching detriment' as a result of the confiscation order than that to which he would have been exposed at the time he committed the offences, and that there had, therefore, been a violation of Article 7.

In the *Adamson* case[60] the Court was called upon to decide whether inclusion on a register of known sex offenders constituted a 'penalty'. Under the Sex Offenders Act 1997, which entered into force on 1 September 1997, any person convicted after that date of one of the sexual offences listed in the Act, or any person already serving a sentence of imprisonment for such an offence at the date of commencement, was required, after his release, to register with the police and keep them informed of any change of name or address.

In holding that this requirement did not amount to a 'penalty', the Court found it relevant that its purpose was not to punish sex offenders, but to contribute towards a lower rate of reoffending. It noted that the obligation to register was imposed as a matter of law, with no additional procedure, following conviction of a sexual offence. Although failure to register constituted a criminal offence, punishable by imprisonment, independent proceedings would have to be brought against a defaulter in which his degree of culpability in

---

[58] *Brown* v. *United Kingdom* (App. 38644/97), admissibility decision of 24 November 1998.
[59] *Welch* v. *United Kingdom*, Judgment of 9 February 1993, Series A, No. 307-A.
[60] *Adamson* v. *United Kingdom* (App. 42293/98), admissibility decision of 26 January 1999.

defaulting would be taken into account in sentencing. Finally, the Court did not consider that the obligation to notify the police of the information required by the Act could, in itself, be regarded as severe. The applicant had expressed the fear that his inclusion on the register would lead to vigilante-style attacks on him or his family, but the Court dismissed this concern because it had not been provided with any evidence to suggest that the applicant would be put at risk in this way.

RETROACTIVE CRIMINALIZATION

The Convention was drafted in the aftermath of the Second World War, and presumably those responsible for framing Article 7 had in mind events in Germany and other parts of Europe in the 1930s, when newly imposed totalitarian regimes promulgated retroactive laws, making criminal without warning acts which had been lawful under democratic rule. Following the fall of the Berlin Wall in November 1989, the change of administration in many Eastern and Central European countries was almost as extreme, with democratic governments being elected in the place of Communist dictatorships. Quite naturally, these changes were frequently accompanied by a strong desire to bring to justice those responsible for the worst excesses of the old regimes.

Faced with a similar situation following the fall of Nazi Germany in 1945, the international community developed the 'Nuremburg principles', which permitted individuals to be prosecuted for acts so heinous as to be classified as 'crimes against humanity', even if these same acts had not been criminal according to Nazi legislation and practice. These principles are reflected in the second paragraph of Article 7.

In two applications against Germany the Court was required to examine whether it was compatible with Article 7(1) for the courts of the unified Federal Republic to convict men in respect of acts which, in the submission of the applicants, had not been criminal according to the law and practice of the German Democratic Republic.

The three applicants in the case of *Streletz, Kessler and Krenz* v. *Germany*[61] had occupied senior positions in the GDR State apparatus. After unification, the first two applicants were convicted of incitement to commit intentional homicide and the third applicant was convicted of intentional homicide as an indirect principal on the grounds that, as they had participated in high-level decisions on the GDR's border-policing regime, they shared responsibility for the deaths of a number of young people who had attempted to flee to West Berlin between 1971 and 1989 and had been killed by landmines or by shots fired

---

[61] *Streletz, Kessler and Krenz* v. *Germany* (Apps. 34044/96, 35532/97, and 44801/98), Judgment of 22 March 2001; (2001) 33 EHRR 751.

by East German border guards. The applicant in the case of *K-HW*.[62] had served as a soldier in the GDR border guard and, in 1973, when he was 20 years old, had shot and killed a fugitive attempting to swim to West Berlin.

The German courts which convicted the applicants did not rely on the argument that the acts in question had amounted to 'crimes against humanity' or had been criminal according to the general principles of international law. Instead they held that the acts had been prohibited by GDR law on the dates they were committed.

They relied on the fact that the GDR had ratified the United Nations' International Covenant on Civil and Political Rights (which guarantees, *inter alia*, the right to life and the right to freedom of movement) and enacted a number of statutory provisions protecting the right to life and restricting the use of lethal force to the prevention of serious crime. The practice of the East German authorities, however, for which the applicants in the *Streletz* case had been partly responsible, was to encourage border guards to disregard the legislation and to annihilate border violators. In the event of a successful crossing, the guards on duty could expect to be the subject of an investigation by the military prosecutor.

In the *Streletz* case the Court of Human Rights observed that GDR statute law, together with the provisions of the international treaties ratified by it, had provided a clear prohibition on disproportionate and arbitrary killing. It was not open to the applicants to argue that, in the light of GDR State practice, their convictions as accessories to murder had not been foreseeable, since they themselves had to a large extent been responsible for the disparity between the legislation and the practice.

The Court's finding of no violation of Article 7 in the *K-HW*. case appears somewhat harsher (and three of the seventeen judges in the Grand Chamber dissented from it). The applicant had been a young and junior soldier; he had undergone a process of indoctrination and had been ordered to protect the border 'at all costs'; he knew that he would be subject to investigation if he allowed a fugitive successfully to escape from East Germany. However, the Court held that the GDR statute law was accessible to all, and that 'even a private soldier could not show total, blind obedience to orders which flagrantly infringed not only the GDR's own legal principles but also internationally recognised human rights'.[63]

Perhaps more convincing is the argument put by Sir Nicolas Bratza in his concurring opinion:

I accept . . . that the situation in the GDR was such that the applicant could hardly have foreseen at the time that his actions would result in his prosecution for the offence of intentional homicide. But this is a very different question from the one facing the

---

[62] *K-HW*. v. *Germany* (App. 32701/97), Judgment of 22 March 2001.
[63] Para. 75 of the judgment.

Court, namely whether the applicant could reasonably have foreseen that his actions amounted to such an offence. While this question may be open to differing opinions, I can find no reason to depart from the considered opinion of the national courts that opening fire on a defenceless person, who was attempting to swim away from East Berlin and who posed no threat to life or limb, so clearly breached any principle of proportionality that it was foreseeable that it violated the legal prohibition on killing.

CLARITY OF CRIMINAL LEGISLATION

It follows from the rule against retrospective legislation under Article 7 that legal provisions which interfere with individual rights must be adequately accessible and formulated with sufficient precision to enable the citizen to regulate his conduct. The Court's approach towards such cases under Article 7 is identical to that used to determine whether a provision authorizing an inter-ference with the right to private and family life under Article 8 or to freedom of religion or expression under Articles 9 and 10 is sufficiently precise as to render the interference 'in accordance with the law'.[64] The condition is satisfied where the individual can know from the wording of the relevant provision and, if need be, with the assistance of the national courts' interpretation of it, what acts and omissions will make him liable.[65]

Whilst it is possible that certain offences known to English law, such as those based on dishonesty, public mischief or conspiring to corrupt public morals may be inconsistent with Article 7,[66] the Strasbourg case law shows that a crime has to be very loosely defined indeed before the Court will find a violation of this provision.

In the *Kokkinakis* case,[67] for example, the applicant, a Jehovah's witness, was convicted under a Greek law which prohibited proselytism. 'Proselytism' was defined in the statute as meaning,

in particular, any direct or indirect attempt to intrude on the religious beliefs of a person of a different religious persuasion, with the aim of undermining those beliefs, either by any kind of inducement or promise of an inducement or moral support or material assistance, or by fraudulent means or by taking advantage of his inexperience, trust, need, low intellect or naïvety.

The applicant contended that this provision was so widely defined that it

[64] See ch. 10 below.

[65] *Kokkinakis v. Greece*, Judgment of 25 May 1993, Series A, No. 260-A; (1994) 17 EHRR 397, para. 52 of the judgment.

[66] See *Shaw* v. *Director of Public Prosecutions*, [1962] AC 220; *Knuller (Publishing, Printing and Promotions) Limited* v. *Director of Public Prosecutions*, [1973] AC 435; *R.* v. *Pattni, Dhunna, Soni and Poopalarajah*, [2001] Crim LR 570; and discussion at D. Feldman, *Civil Liberties and Human Rights in England and Wales* (Oxford, 1993), at 706–8.

[67] *Kokkinakis* v. *Greece*, Judgment of 25 May 1993, Series A, No. 260-A; (1994) 17 EHRR 397, para. 52 of the judgment.

could encompass almost any attempt to convert a person to another religious faith. The Court noted that the wording of many statutes is not absolutely precise and that the need to avoid excessive rigidity and to keep pace with changing circumstances means that many laws were inevitably couched in fairly vague terms. However, the settled national case law interpreting the statute was sufficiently clear to enable Kokkinakis to regulate his conduct in the matter.[68]

Article 7 does not merely prohibit retrospective law-making by the legislature or executive, it also prohibits extension of the application of the criminal law by the judiciary.[69] Nonetheless, the European Court has shown itself prepared to give national courts considerable leeway in this respect, recognizing that:

however clearly drafted a legal provision may be, in any system of law, including criminal law, there is an inevitable element of judicial interpretation. There will always be a need for elucidation of doubtful points and for adaptation to changing circumstances. Indeed, in the . . . Convention States, the progressive development of the criminal law through judicial law-making is a well entrenched and necessary part of legal tradition. Article 7 of the Convention cannot be read as outlawing the gradual clarification of the rules of criminal liability through judicial interpretation from case to case, provided that the resulting development is consistent with the essence of the offence and could reasonably be foreseen.[70]

The applicant in the case of *CR* v. *United Kingdom*[71] was convicted of the attempted rape of his wife. At the time he tried to force her to have sex, and indeed until the judgments of the Court of Appeal and House of Lords in his case, it was an established rule of common law that a man could not rape his wife, because in getting married a woman was deemed to have consented once and for all to intercourse with her husband. A number of exceptions to this principle had been developed—for example, where the couple had separated by court order or deed of agreement—but these did not apply in the applicant's case. The Court of Appeal and House of Lords both refused his appeal against conviction, holding that the rule was unacceptable in modern Britain and should be held inapplicable.

Despite the fairly overwhelming evidence that the domestic courts' judgments represented a reversal, rather than a clarification, of the law, the Court of Human Rights rejected the applicant's complaint under Article 7, holding that 'judicial recognition of the absence of immunity had become a reasonably foreseeable development of the law'.

Perhaps the true explanation for the Court's decision was its understandable

---

[68] See also, more recently, *Baskaya and Okçuoglu* v. *Turkey* (Apps. 23536/94 and 24408/94), Judgment of 8 July 1999; (2001) 31 EHRR 292.

[69] App. 1852/63, *X* v. *Austria*, 22 April 1965 (1965) 8 *Yearbook* 190, at 198.

[70] *CR* v. *United Kingdom*, Judgment of 2 November 1995, Series A, No. 335-C; (1996) 21 EHRR 363, para. 34 of the judgment.

[71] Para. 34 of the judgment.

repugnance for the rule conferring immunity from rape charges to husbands. As it observed:

> The essentially debasing character of rape is so manifest that the result of the decisions of the Court of Appeal and the House of Lords—that the applicant could be convicted of attempted rape, irrespective of his relationship with the victim—cannot be said to be at variance with the object and purpose of Article 7 of the Convention, namely to ensure that no one should be subjected to arbitrary prosecution, conviction or punishment. . . . What is more, the abandonment of the unacceptable idea of a husband being immune against prosecution for rape of his wife was in conformity not only with a civilised concept of marriage but also, above all, with the fundamental objectives of the Convention, the very essence of which is respect for human dignity and human freedom.[72]

The Court's reasoning appears to overlook the fact that most criminal laws are directed at behaviour which offends against human dignity and freedom. Whilst the removal of the immunity from English law is to be welcomed, the rule of law would have been better respected if Parliament had carried out the reform with purely prospective effect.

THE IMPACT OF INTERNATIONAL LAW

The Court's reasoning in the *CR* case comes close to an application of Article 7(2), which provides that: 'This Article shall not prejudice the trial and punishment of any person for any act or omission which, at the time when it was committed, was criminal according to the general principles of law recognised by civilised nations.'

According to the preparatory work on the Convention, the purpose of Article 7(2) is to make it clear that Article 7 'does not affect laws which, under very exceptional circumstances at the end of the Second World War, were passed in order to suppress war crimes, treason and collaboration with the enemy.'[73]

Thus, Article 7(2) is designed to meet objections such as those levelled against the war crimes tribunals, that they applied retrospective legislation. It is interesting to note, however, that the German courts, which were the courts mainly concerned with the prosecution of war crimes, did not rely on the doctrine that a person may be convicted for an offence which is criminal according to the general principles of law. On the contrary, the Federal Government made a reservation to Article 7 according to which: 'it will only apply the provisions of Article 7 paragraph 2 of the Convention within the limits of Article 103 clause 2 of the Basic Law of the German Federal Republic. This provides that "any act is only punishable if it was so by law before the offence was committed".'[74]

---

[72] Para. 42 of the judgment.
[73] App. 1038/61, *X* v. *Belgium*, 18 September 1961 (1961) 4 *Yearbook* 324, at 336.
[74] This was the rule applied by the German Courts in *Streletz, Kessler and Krenz* v. *Germany* (Apps. 34044/96, 35532/97, and 44801/98), Judgment of 22 March 2001; (2001) 33 EHRR 751.

This reservation, instead of restricting the Government's obligations under the Convention, appears actually to extend them.[75] The Government undertook not to take advantage of the authorization to apply retrospective legislation since to do so would be unconstitutional. Rather than rely on retrospective legislation, the German courts generally preferred to rely on the doctrine that acts which were committed under Nazi 'law' were illegal because that 'law' was invalid under a higher, unwritten law.

Article 7(2) was also applied by the Commission in cases from countries occupied during the Second World War, such as Belgium and Denmark, which subsequently introduced retrospective legislation to punish collaborators.[76] While this practice may be in accordance with the intention of Article 7(2), it is doubtful whether its terms cover the various offences of collaboration to which it has been applied. Not all forms of collaboration with a de facto government, however abhorrent they may be, are criminal according to the general principles of law recognized by civilized nations.

The expression 'national or international law' in Article 7(1) raises the question whether, under the rules of conflict of laws, a State can enforce the law of another State even where the conduct concerned is not contrary to its own law. The Commission has held that a State may include on a person's police record an offence committed abroad if the acts concerned constituted a criminal offence at the place where, and the time when, he was convicted.[77] The decision raises some doubts. If action relating to a police record comes within Article 7 at all, should not the conduct constituting the offence abroad also be criminal at home, before any criminal consequence should attach to it?

The fact that the acts were criminal in the place where the person was convicted may show that the foreign court had jurisdiction and consequently be relevant under private international law. But this is not sufficient under Article 7. What the principle of legality requires is that if the national law prescribes penal consequences, the conduct in question must be an offence under the substantive law of that State. The inclusion in Article 7 of the term 'international law' shows that this condition may be satisfied if the conduct in question constitutes a crime against international law; for it is of the essence of international criminal law, as it has been developed since 1945, that national courts have jurisdiction over crimes against international law. But this has no bearing on the enforcement by one State, under the rules of private international law, of the criminal law of another State.

Article 7 should therefore be interpreted as excluding the enforcement of a foreign criminal judgment in respect of acts which were not an offence in the

---

[75] See the Commission's comment cited in J. E. S. Fawcett, *The Application of the European Convention on Human Rights* (Oxford, 1987), at 209.

[76] See e.g. App. 214/56, *De Becker* v. *Belgium*, 9 June 1958 (1958–59) 2 *Yearbook* 214, at 226.

[77] App. 448/59, X v. *Federal Republic of Germany*, 2 June 1960 (1960) 3 *Yearbook* 254, at 270.

enforcing State. This interpretation is confirmed by State practice. Thus, in accordance with this principle, Article 4(1) of the European Convention on the International Validity of Criminal Judgments,[78] which allows the enforcement in one Contracting State of sanctions imposed in another, provides that: 'The sanction shall not be enforced by another Contracting State unless under its law the act for which the sanction was imposed would be an offence if committed on its territory and the person on whom the sanction was imposed would be liable to punishment if he had committed the act there.'

Similarly, Article 2(1) of the European Convention on Extradition,[79] embodies a general rule of international law known as the rule of double criminality; this provides that the offence in respect of which extradition is granted must be punishable under the law of both the requesting State and the requested State.

If it is correct to interpret the provisions of the Convention, within certain limits, by reference to the domestic practice of the Contracting Parties,[80] it must be legitimate to interpret them by reference to other Conventions between Member States of the Council of Europe which may be presumed to embody a consensus on the proper limits of public authority. Conversely, these Conventions must themselves be interpreted by the Contracting parties so as to avoid any conflict with their obligations under the Human Rights Convention.

PROTOCOL 7

Protocol 7 includes a number of additional rights in respect of the criminal process: a rule against double jeopardy, the right to an appeal, and the right to compensation following a miscarriage of justice. However, since very few States have signed and ratified this Protocol,[81] the case law concerning it is limited.

THE FINALITY OF FINAL ACQUITTALS

Article 4 of Protocol 7 provides,

1. No one shall be liable to be tried or punished again in criminal proceedings under the jurisdiction of the same State for an offence for which he has already been finally acquitted or convicted in accordance with the law and penal procedure of that State.

---

[78] European Treaty Series, No. 70.
[79] European Treaty Series, No. 24.
[80] See ch. 3 above.
[81] The UK is not one of them: see the updated list of Council of Europe treaty ratifications: conventions.coe.int/treaty/EN/cadreprincipal.htm

2. The provisions of the preceding paragraph shall not prevent the reopening of the case in accordance with the law and penal procedure of the State concerned, if there is evidence of new or newly discovered facts, or if there has been a fundamental defect in the previous proceedings, which could affect the outcome of the case.
3. No derogation from this Article shall be made under Article 15 of the Convention.

The Explanatory Memorandum to Protocol 7 resolves some aspects of the wording of the provision. A conviction or acquittal becomes final, according to the Memorandum, when 'no further ordinary remedies are available or when the parties have exhausted such remedies or have permitted the time-limit to expire without availing themselves of these.'

There is no intention in the wording of the Article to preclude cases being reopened in favour of the convicted person, but the prohibition on double jeopardy does not preclude a person being subject to several different types of procedure in relation to the same conduct, for example, to civil proceedings for compensation in addition to a criminal trial.

The application of the Article is limited to proceedings in a single State. The Explanatory Memorandum notes that the international application of the prohibition is adequately covered in the European Convention on Extradition of 1957, the European Convention on the International Validity of Criminal Judgments of 1970, and the European Convention on the Transfer of Proceedings in Criminal Matters of 1972.

THE RIGHT TO AN APPEAL

Article 2 of Protocol 7 provides:

1. Everyone convicted of a criminal offence by a tribunal shall have the right to have his conviction or sentence reviewed by a higher tribunal. The exercise of this right, including the grounds on which may be exercised, shall be governed by law.
2. This right may be subject to exceptions in regard to offences of a minor character, as prescribed by law, or in cases in which the person concerned was tried in the first instance by the highest tribunal or was convicted following an appeal against acquittal.

The explanatory report indicates that the reference to a tribunal in paragraph (1) is designed to exclude from its ambit any conviction resulting from a decision of a non-judicial organ. There is no explanation as to the relationship of this provision with Article 6, which would seem to require that the determination of criminal charges is by an independent tribunal. Paragraph (2) allows limitations to be placed on the right, and excludes it altogether in certain situations. It is unclear how the provision accommodates systems, like that of England and Wales, which in many cases require leave to be obtained before an appeal may be pursued. The explanatory report indicates that the intention was to view application for leave to appeal as a form of review under the provision, though it is at least arguable that the words of the text do not achieve this.

COMPENSATION FOR A MISCARRIAGE OF JUSTICE

Article 3 of Protocol 7 provides,

When a person has by final decision been convicted of a criminal offence and when subsequently his conviction has been reversed, or he has been pardoned, on the ground that a new or newly discovered fact shows conclusively that there has been a miscarriage of justice, the person who has suffered punishment as a result of such conviction shall be compensated according to the law or the practice of the State concerned, unless it is proved that the non-disclosure of the unknown fact in time is wholly or partly attributable to him.

The right to compensation is narrowly drafted, but the provision is reasonably self-explanatory. It is intended only to cover the clearest cases of miscarriages of justice where the miscarriage cannot be said to be wholly or partly the fault of the person punished. The scope of the reference to the 'practice' of the State in the provision is unclear. It suggests that ex gratia arrangements may be permissible. The right to compensation for victims of arrest or detention in breach of the requirements of Article 5 refers to 'an enforceable right to compensation', which is an altogether clearer phrase.

10

LIMITATIONS COMMON TO ARTICLES 8-11

INTRODUCTION

This chapter is about the express limitations to be found in the second paragraphs of Articles 8 to 11, but it also reports the historical debate on whether there are inherent limitations to some of the rights protected by the Convention arising as a consequence of particular circumstances in which individuals might find themselves. Brief consideration of the restrictions on the political activities of aliens which may arise under Article 16 is also included in this chapter.

Each of Articles 8–11 sets out a Convention right in the first paragraph, but then qualifies it by listing limitations in the second paragraph. Though there are some differences of detail in the nature of the limitations arising under each article, there is sufficient commonality of approach to justify a collective consideration of these limitations before examining the substantive rights protected under each of these articles.

INHERENT LIMITATIONS

The principle that only the restrictions expressly provided by the Convention are allowed has not always been accepted. In the early days the Commission appeared to accept that there were certain situations, notably those involving prisoners and other detained persons, in which there were inherent limitations arising from the applicant's situation.[1] The notion has also been supported by some writers on the Convention.[2] The Court did not follow the Commission in this regard, and the Commission abandoned the notion many years ago.

The Commission's doctrine that certain restrictions are an 'inherent feature'

---

[1] For more detail, see the 2nd edn. of this book, at 297–301.

[2] J. Fawcett, *The Application of the European Convention on Human Rights* (Oxford, 1987), at 232–3.

of detention seems to have been disapproved by the Court in the *Vagrancy* cases.[3] In that case, the Court held:

[I]n the light of the information given to it, that the competent Belgian authorities did not transgress in the present cases the limits of the power of appreciation which Article 8(2) of the Convention leaves to the Contracting States: even in cases of persons detained for vagrancy, those authorities had sufficient reason to believe that it was 'necessary' to impose restrictions for the purpose of the prevention of disorder or crime, the protection of health or morals, and the protection of the rights and freedoms of others.[4]

In the *Golder* case, the Court held that there was unquestionably an interference with the right to respect for correspondence; it thus rejected the notion that there was no need to find justification under paragraph (2), and went on to say explicitly that the restrictive formulation of Article 8(2) 'leaves no room for the concept of implied limitations'.[5] The same conclusion applies in relation to Articles 9–11 of the Convention.

The current position is that any limitation on the rights guaranteed by Articles 8–11 must be justified under the provisions of the second paragraph of the article in issue. The notion of inherent limitations is of purely historical interest.

EXPRESS LIMITATIONS: SOME GENERAL POINTS

The second paragraphs of Articles 8–11 allow for interference by the authorities with the protected rights under certain prescribed conditions. There are two basic principles concerning the restrictions on the rights guaranteed. The first principle is that only the restrictions expressly authorized by the Convention are allowed. That principle is nowhere stated in the Convention, but it is presupposed by the whole system of the Convention. Further, it is presupposed, in particular, by the second basic principle, which is expressly stated by Article 18. This principle is that 'the restrictions permitted under this Convention to the said rights and freedoms shall not be applied for any purpose other than those for which they have been prescribed.'

Table 10.1 maps the common elements to be found in the second paragraphs of Article 8–11 of the Convention. Article 10 on freedom of expression has the

[3] *De Wilde, Ooms & Versyp* v. *Belgium*, Judgment of 18 June 1971, Series A, No. 12; (1979–80) 1 EHRR 373.

[4] Para. 93 of the judgment.

[5] See also *Golder* v. *United Kingdom*, Judgment of 21 February 1975, Series A, No. 18; (1979–80) 1 EHRR 524, para. 44 of the judgment.

Table 10.1 Express limitations in Aricles 8–11

Article 8	Article 9	Article 10	Article 11
Right to respect for private and family life	Freedom of thought, conscience, and religion	Freedom of expression	Freedom of assembly and association
in accordance with law	prescribed by law	prescribed by law	prescribed by law
necessary in a democratic society	necessary in a democratic society	necessary in a democratic society	necessary in a democratic society
interests of national security		interests of national security	interests of national security
		interests of territorial integrity	
interests of public safety	interests of public safety	interests of public safety	interests of public safety
interests of economic well-being of the country			
prevention of disorder or crime	protection of public order	prevention of disorder or crime	prevention of disorder or crime
protection of health or morals	protection of health or morals	protection of health or morals	protection of health or morals
		protection of the reputation of others	
protection of the rights and freedoms of others	protection of the rights and freedoms of others	protection of the rights of others	protection of the rights and freedoms of others
		preventing the disclosure of information received in confidence	
		maintaining the authority and impartiality of the judiciary	

longest list of limitations, and Article 9 on freedom of thought, conscience, and religion the shortest list of limitations.

The importance of requiring that restrictions must, in every case, be justified by an express provision of the Convention is very great. It enables the Court to control the alleged interference by reference to those express provisions. In dealing with exceptions to Convention rights, the Court adopts a narrow interpretation.[6]

The Court adopts a three-part questioning where a State seeks to rely on a limitation in one of the Convention articles. First, it determines whether the interference is in accordance with, or prescribed by, law, then it looks to see whether the aim of the limitation is legitimate in that it fits one of the expressed heads in the particular article, and finally it asks whether the limitation is in all the circumstances necessary in a democratic society. Central to this determination is the proportionality of the interference in securing the legitimate aim. Only the minimum interference with the right which secures the legitimate aim will be permitted. The essence of each of the restrictions is that the interests of society as a whole override the interests of the individual. In such cases, the difficulty the Court will experience is in determining whether the interference goes beyond what is necessary in a democratic society.

A REQUIRED LEGAL BASIS FOR THE INTERFERENCE

First it must be shown that the restriction was in each case 'in accordance with the law',[7] or 'prescribed by law'.[8] The difference in the language used in Article 8 when compared with Articles 9–11 is immaterial; the French text of the Convention reads *prévue(s) par la loi* in all cases.[9]

The Court, building on the Commission's case law, has established a threefold test for determining whether an interference is in accordance with law. First, it must be established that the interference with the Convention right has some basis in national law. Secondly, the law must be accessible; and, thirdly, the

---

[6] See e.g. *Klass* v. *Germany*, Judgment of 6 September 1978, Series A, No. 28; (1979–80) 2 EHRR 214, para 42 of the judgment; and *The Observer and The Guardian* v. *United Kingdom*, Judgment of 26 November 1991; Series A, No. 216; (1992) 14 EHRR 153, para. 59 of the judgment.

[7] Art. 8(2) of the Convention. The same language is used in Arts. 2(3) and (4) of Protocol 4, and Art. 1(1) of Protocol 7. What is said here is relevant to consideration of those provisions of the Convention.

[8] Arts. 9(2), 10(2), and 11(2). The same language is used in Art. 2(2) of Protocol 7. What is said here is relevant to consideration of those provisions of the Convention.

[9] Art. 1 of the Protocol 1 requires interferences to be 'subject to the conditions provided for by law', which raises similar issues to those discussed in this section.

law must be formulated in such a way that a person can foresee, to a degree that is reasonable in the circumstances, the consequences which a given action will entail. This is known as the test of foreseeability.

The references to 'law' are, of course, to national law, and the Court must accept the interpretation of national law adopted by the national courts. This is not because the Court is not a 'fourth instance', or higher court of appeal above the national courts. It is rather because questions of national law are for the Court simply questions of fact.

There is no requirement that the law be statutory; it can be unwritten law. In the *Sunday Times* case[10] it was the common law of contempt that was in issue. In the *Barthold* case[11] it was the rules of the Veterinary Surgeons' Council, which had authority to make professional rules.

The character of the law imposing the limitations was considered in the *Sunday Times* case.[12] It is not alone enough that the law qualifies as such in the national legal system (though if it does not, any defence the State seeks to mount is certain to fail), it must also display additional qualities,

Firstly, the law must be adequately accessible: the citizen must be able to have an indication that is adequate in the circumstances of the legal rules applicable to a given case. Secondly, a norm cannot be regarded as 'law' unless it is formulated with sufficient precision to enable the citizen to regulate his conduct: he must be able—if need be with appropriate advice—to foresee, to a degree that is reasonable in the circumstances, the consequences which a given action may entail.[13]

The Court went on to explain that the requirement of foreseeability was not designed to secure absolute certainty, so that no interpretation would be required in determining the scope of application of the law. However, a certain level of clarity is required. In *Vogt* v. *Germany*[14] the Court said that the level of precision required 'depends to a considerable degree on the content of the instrument in question, the field it is designed to cover and the number and status of those to whom it is addressed.'[15]

These requirements can be problematic in cases where they relate to the interests of national security. In the *Malone* case,[16] the Court stressed that the law must indicate the scope of any discretion of the executive with regard to the interception of communications and the manner of its exercise with sufficient clarity to give the individual protection against arbitrary interference. The law

---

[10] *Sunday Times* v. *United Kingdom*, Judgment of 26 April 1979, Series A, No. 30; (1979–80) 2 EHRR 245.

[11] *Barthold* v. *Germany*, Judgment of 23 March 1985, Series A, No. 90; (1985) 7 EHRR 383.

[12] *Sunday Times* v. *United Kingdom*, Judgment of 26 April 1979, Series A, No. 30; (1979–80) 2 EHRR 245.

[13] Para. 49 of the judgment.

[14] *Vogt* v. *Germany* (App. 17851/91), Judgment of 26 September 1995; (1996) 21 EHRR 205.

[15] Para. 48 of the judgment.

[16] *Malone* v. *United Kingdom*, Judgment of 2 August 1984, Series A, No. 82; (1985) 7 EHRR 14.

of England and Wales was so obscure and subject to such differing interpretations, particularly in respect of the dividing line between conduct covered by
legal rules and that covered by executive discretion that it lacked the minimum
degree of legal protection required to qualify as 'law' for the purposes of the
Convention. In the *Halford* case,[17] there was no regulation of interceptions
of calls made on telecommunications systems outside the public network.
Telephone calls made on a private network by Alison Halford when Assistant
Chief Constable with the Merseyside Police were intercepted; this constituted a
violation of Article 8, since the interference with respect for her private life and
correspondence was not in accordance with the law.

In the *Leander* case,[18] which concerned security checks on certain government personnel, the Court recognized that the requirement of foreseeability
could not be the same in the context of security checks on personnel as in other
fields. Nevertheless, the law had to be sufficiently clear in regard to the circumstances and conditions which justified secret checks. The Swedish law met these
standards.

Two modern cases against the United Kingdom illustrate the application
of the requirement of identifiability, accessibility and foreseeability in determining whether an interference is 'prescribed by law'. *Steel and others* v. *United
Kingdom* concerned the imposition of a requirement to be bound over to keep
the peace on those charged with, and convicted of, breaches of the peace.
The Court concluded that a liability to be bound over to keep the peace was
sufficiently clear where such a requirement was imposed after a finding that
a person had committed a breach of the peace, despite its being couched in
vague and general terms. In the particular circumstances it would be clear that
those bound over were agreeing to refrain from causing further, similar,
breaches of the law for the period for which they agreed to be bound over.[19] The
facts before the Court in the *Hashman and Harrup* case[20] were, arguably, significantly different. The applicants had been involved in activities designed to
disrupt a fox-hunt. They were brought before the magistrates' court by way of
complaint that they should be required to enter into a recognizance to keep
the peace and be of good behaviour. They were so bound over. On a complaint
that the measures constituted an interference with their freedom of expression,
the Court considered whether binding over to keep the peace as a means of
controlling anti-social behaviour was 'prescribed by law'. Here the Court
regarded the law as being too vague; the binding over orders were not in the
nature of a sanction for past unlawful conduct; the notion of conduct *contra*

---

[17] *Halford* v. *United Kingdom* (App. 20605/92), Judgment of 25 June 1997; (1997) 24 EHRR 523.
[18] *Leander* v. *Sweden*, Judgement of 26 March 1987, Series A, No. 116; (1987) 9 EHRR 433.
[19] Paras. 76 and 94 of the judgment.
[20] *Hashman and Harrup* v. *United Kingdom* (App. 25594/94), Judgment of 25 November 1999; (2000)
30 EHRR 241.

bonos mores[21] was too vague to meet the requirement of predictability of application. It could not be said that what the applicants were being bound over not to do must have been apparent to them. The dissenting judge disagreed, noting that the binding over order placed an 'unmistakable obligation on the applicants, namely to refrain from any offensive and deliberate action which would disturb the lawfully organised activity of others engaged in fox-hunting.'[22] The distinction between a case where there is conduct of which the applicants were convicted which rendered the binding over foreseeable, and one where there is conduct leading to a complaint but no conviction, is a particularly narrow one.

SPECIFIED LEGITIMATE AIMS

Once the Court is satisfied that any restriction has a legal basis which meets the requirements of 'law' under the Convention provisions, it will go on to consider whether the restriction is for one of the specified legitimate aims. The justifications set out in the Convention provisions are exhaustive. That said, it is relatively easy for a Contracting State to bring its action within one of the stated exceptions, and the Court seldom has to spend much time analysing the nature of the limitation to satisfy itself that it falls within one of them. The Court does, however, adopt a rigorous approach to the issues of necessity and proportionality in relation to the measures taken to secure the legitimate aim. What follows are simply some illustrations of cases in which reliance has been placed on a particular ground.

THE INTERESTS OF NATIONAL SECURITY

In *Zana* v. *Turkey*[23] the Court had no difficulty in regarding measures taken by Turkey to deal with the security situation in South-East Turkey as measures for the protection of national security.

The *Klass* case[24] concerned the legitimacy of secret surveillance. The Court accepted that the German measures fell within the national security exception,

---

[21] Defined as behaviour which is 'wrong rather than right in the judgment of contemporary fellow citizens': para. 38 of the judgment

[22] Dissenting opinion of Judge Baka.

[23] *Zana* v. *Turkey* (App. 18954/91), Judgment of 25 November 1997; (1999) 27 EHRR 667, para. 49 of the judgment.

[24] *Klass* v. *Germany*, Judgment of 6 September 1978, Series A, No. 28; (1979–80) 2 EHRR 214.

since democratic societies found themselves threatened by highly sophisticated forms of espionage and by terrorism, and needed to undertake secret surveillance to counter such threats.

In *Rekvényi* v. *Hungary*[25] the Court accepted, in the context of a challenge that the provisions violated Article 10, that a constitutional ban on political activities and party affiliation by police officers could be imposed 'for the protection of national security and public safety and the prevention of disorder'.

THE INTERESTS OF TERRITORIAL INTEGRITY

This ground is often linked to national security as in *Zana* v. *Turkey*.[26] The Court has chosen to couple territorial integrity closely with issues of national security. This would seem to require some threat of violence or disorder before resort can be made to this ground. Turkish arguments that a limitation justified on grounds of territorial integrity involved issues relating to the preservation of national unity as an idea[27] were rejected.

THE INTERESTS OF PUBLIC SAFETY

Few cases have raised questions of limitations based solely on public safety, and the Court does not appear to have relied exclusively on this head, though frequently, as in the *Rekvényi* case above, reliance is placed on public safety alongside national security and the prevention of disorder. In one case,[28] the Commission upheld resort to public safety in a case where it was argued that married people should be able to continue their married life in prison. A more easily sustained case could be made under the prevention of public disorder head.

The ground was raised and accepted in the *Buckley* case,[29] which concerned

---

[25] *Rekvényi* v. *Hungary* (App. 25390/94), Judgment of 20 May 1999; (2000) 30 EHRR 519, para. 41 of the judgment.

[26] *Zana* v. *Turkey* (App. 18954/91); Judgment of 25 November 1997; (1999) 27 EHRR 667, para. 49 of the judgment.

[27] And so justifying restrictions on freedom of expression, see e.g. *Arslan* v. *Turkey* (App. 23462/94), Judgment of 8 July 1999; (2001) 31 EHRR 264.

[28] App. 8166/78, *X and Y* v. *Switzerland*, 3 October 1978 (1979) 13 DR 241, at 243.

[29] *Buckley* v. *United Kingdom* (App. 20348/92), Judgment of 25 September 1996; (1997) 23 EHRR 101, paras. 62–3 of the judgment.

the refusal of planning permission to a gypsy for caravans to be used as homes. The requirement of planning permission was said in this case to be 'aimed at furthering highway safety, the preservation of the environment and public health'. The Court accepted that these came within the exceptions relating to public safety, the economic well-being of the country, the protection of health, and the protection of the rights of others.

FOR THE ECONOMIC WELL-BEING OF THE COUNTRY

The *Miailhe* case[30] concerned the exercise of search and seizure powers of people's homes by customs authorities. The applicants argued that there had been a violation of Article 8. The Court considered that the interferences with the rights protected in Article 8 were in the interests of the economic well-being of the country.

Similarly in the *Funke* case[31] the Court was faced with a complaint of a violation of Article 8 arising from searches of the applicant's home in connection with enquiries into financial dealings with foreign countries contrary to French law. The Court concluded that the interferences pursued a legitimate aim of being in the interest of the economic well-being of the country.

THE PREVENTION OF DISORDER OR CRIME

This justification for interferences is the most frequently raised before the Court and the most frequently accepted by it. This is unsurprising since many complaints involve penal measures, whose underlying purpose is the prevention of disorder or crime.

In the *Otto-Preminger Institute* case[32] the Court accepted that the provisions of the Austrian Penal Code which permitted seizure of a film considered to offend the religious sensibilities of Roman Catholics were 'intended to suppress behaviour directed against objects of religious veneration that is likely to cause "justified indignation"'[33] and so operated to prevent public disorder.

---

[30] *Miailhe* v. *France*, Judgment of 25 February 1993, Series A, No. 256-C; (1993) 16 EHRR 332.
[31] *Funke* v. *France*, Judgment of 25 February 1993, Series A, No. 256-A; (1993) 16 EHRR 297.
[32] *Otto-Preminger Institute* v. *Germany*, Judgment of 20 September 1994, Series A, No. 295-A; (1995) 19 EHRR 34.
[33] Para. 48 of judgment.

THE PROTECTION OF HEALTH OR MORALS

Again this limitation is frequently cited as the justification for interferences with Convention rights. The classic example is the seizure of *The Little Red Schoolbook* which gave rise to the *Handyside* case.[34] The Court was called upon to consider whether the conviction of individuals who had published a reference book targeted at children of school age containing advice on sexual and other matters violated the guarantee of freedom of expression in Article 10. The Court readily accepted that the issues raised here related to the protection of morals. A similar view was taken in a case involving the confiscation of a number of sexually explicit paintings.[35]

THE PROTECTION OF THE RIGHTS OR FREEDOMS OF OTHERS

This is also a frequently raised limitation, which covers a wide range of matters. Articles 8 and 9 refer to the protection of the rights and freedoms of others, while Article 10 refers to the protection of the reputation or rights of others. Little seems to turn on the different form of wording, but the subordination of freedom of expression for the protection of the reputation of others probably justifies specific reference in Article 10.

The limitation was used in the *Otto-Preminger Institute* case[36] where the showing of the offending film was considered to breach the right to respect for religious feelings when the rights in Articles 9 and 10 were read together.[37]

This limitation has also been applied frequently in child-care cases, where it is readily accepted that national legislation for placing children in care serves the purpose of 'protecting the rights and freedoms of other': in this case the child.[38]

Rather more controversially this ground was used as the basis for upholding the German Unfair Competition Act in the *Jacubowski* case.[39] A provision

---

[34] *Handyside* v. *United Kingdom*, Judgment of 7 December 1976, Series A, No. 24; (1979–80) 1 EHRR 737.

[35] *Müller and others* v. *Switzerland*, Judgment of 24 May 1988, Series A, No. 132; (1991) 13 EHRR 212.

[36] *Otto-Preminger Institute* v. *Germany*, Judgment of 20 September 1994, Series A, No. 295-A; (1995) 19 EHRR 34.

[37] Paras 46 to 48 of the judgment.

[38] See e.g. *Johansen* v. *Norway* (App. 17383/90), Judgment of 7 August 1996 (1997) 23 EHRR 33.

[39] *Jacubowski* v. *Germany*, Judgment of 23 June 1994, Series A, No. 291; (1995) 19 EHRR 64. See also *Barthold* v. *Germany*, Judgment of 23 March 1985, Series A, No. 90; (1985) 7 EHRR 383, and *Markt Intern Verlag GmbH and Klaus Beermann* v. *Germany*, Judgment of 20 November 1989, Series A, No. 165; (1990) 12 EHRR 161. See discussion of these cases in ch. 13.

seeking to protect the reputation and rights of others does not at first sight appear to have anything to do with protecting commercial interests.

THE PREVENTION OF THE DISCLOSURE OF INFORMATION RECEIVED IN CONFIDENCE

Article 10(2) contains two additional limitations. The first relates to measures for preventing the disclosure of information received in confidence. Interestingly in the *Weber* case,[40] where the applicant had been fined for breaching the confidentiality of the judicial investigation, the Court regarded the limitation as designed to protect the authority and impartiality of the judiciary, rather than on this ground. This suggests that this limitation is seen as rather more concerned with material received in confidence outside the courtroom.

Further examples of the use of this ground can be found in the *Spycatcher* cases.[41]

MAINTAINING THE AUTHORITY AND IMPARTIALITY OF THE JUDICIARY

Article 10(2) also permits limitations justified as maintaining the authority and impartiality of the judiciary. Resort to this ground for interferences with the rights contained in Article 10 is rare. Where the interests of the judiciary are concerned it is more usual to rely upon the protection of the reputation or rights of others. In one case,[42] the applicant company complained that the grant of injunctions by the Austrian authorities prohibiting the publication of a photograph of a suspect violated the rights in Article 10. The injunctions were granted on the basis that they were intended to protect the suspect against insult and defamation and against violations of the presumption of innocence. The Court concluded that this met the aim of protecting the reputation of others and also served to maintain the authority and impartiality of the

---

[40] *Weber* v. *Switzerland*, Judgment of 22 May 1990, Series A, No. 177; (1990) 12 EHRR 508.
[41] *Observer and Guardian* v. *United Kingdom*, Judgment of 26 November 1991, Series A, No. 216; (1992) 14 EHRR 153; and *Sunday Times* v. *United Kingdom (No. 2)*, Judgment of 26 November 1991, Series A, No. 217; (1992) 14 EHRR 229. See below ch. 13.
[42] *News Verlags GmbH and CoKG* v. *Austria* (App. 31457/96), Judgment of 11 April 2000; (2001) 31 EHRR 246.

judiciary.[43] In the *Schöpfer* case,[44] the Court accepted that a penalty imposed upon a lawyer by a professional body in respect of a lawyer's inflammatory criticisms of the judiciary pursued the legitimate aim of maintaining the authority and impartiality of the judiciary. But in *Wille v. Liechtenstein*,[45] the Court appears to have been uncertain. The case concerned a complaint by a former politician that, following a lecture he had given on constitutional law, the monarch of Liechtenstein had written to him announcing his intention not to appoint the applicant to political office again. The applicant complained that this was a violation of Article 10. The Court appears somewhat hesitant both over whether the measure was prescribed by law and over the underlying objective of the measure. It was argued that the measure was required to maintain public order and to promote civil stability, and to preserve judicial independence and impartiality. The Court did not find it necessary to consider these issues but proceeded on the assumption that the measure was prescribed by law and pursued a legitimate aim in deciding that such a measure was not necessary in a democratic society.[46]

THE LIMITATION MUST BE NECESSARY IN A DEMOCRATIC SOCIETY

THE BASIC TEST

In addition to being lawful, the restriction must be 'necessary in a democratic society'[47] for one of the purposes there prescribed. Establishing that the measure is necessary in a democratic society involves showing that the action taken is in response to a pressing social need, and that the interference with the rights protected is no greater than is necessary to address that pressing social need. The latter requirement is referred to as the test of proportionality. This test requires the Court to balance the severity of the restriction placed on the individual against the importance of the public interest. The classic formulation of the test is to be found in the *Silver* case:

(a) the adjective 'necessary' is not synonymous with 'indispensable', neither has it the flexibility of such expressions as 'admissible', 'ordinary' 'reasonable' or 'desirable';

(b) the Contracting States enjoy a certain but not unlimited margin of appreciation in

---

[43] Paras. 44–5 of the judgment.

[44] *Schöpfer* v. *Switzerland* (App. 25054/94), Judgment of 20 May 1998; (2001) 33 EHRR 845.

[45] *Wille* v. *Liechtenstein* (App. 28396/95), Judgment of 28 October 1999; (2000) 30 EHRR 558.

[46] Paras. 53–6 of the judgment.

[47] Articles 8(2) to 11(2).

the matter of the imposition of restrictions, but it is for the Court to give the final ruling on whether they are compatible with the Convention;

(c) the phrase 'necessary in a democratic society' means that, to be compatible with the Convention, the interference must, *inter alia*, correspond to a 'pressing social need' and be 'proportionate to the legitimate aim pursued';

(d) those paragraphs of Articles of the Convention which provide for an exception to a right guaranteed are to be narrowly construed.[48]

THE MARGIN OF APPRECIATION

In deciding whether action is necessary in a democratic society, the notion of the State's margin of appreciation has arisen and can often be troublesome. To what extent should the Strasbourg organs defer to the State's interpretation of the situation it faces in allowing a limitation on the rights guaranteed by the Convention? In the *Handyside* case[49] the Court said:

By reason of their direct and continuous contact with the vital forces of their countries, State authorities are in principle in a better position than the international judge to give an opinion on the exact content of these requirements as well as on the 'necessity' of a 'restriction' or 'penalty' intended to meet them.[50]

In considering whether a State has gone beyond what the situation requires,

The Court's supervisory functions oblige it to pay the utmost attention to the principles characterizing a 'democratic society'.[51]

Surprisingly, the Court has not discussed in any sort of detail the qualities of a democratic society,[52] but it is clear that the Court regards the qualities of pluralism, tolerance, broadmindedness, equality, liberty, and encouraging self-fulfilment as important ingredients of any democracy. This leads to the search for a balance between the competing interests that are presented in any case which reaches this stage of deliberation. At the heart of this consideration is the margin of appreciation referred to above.

The scope of the margin of appreciation will sometimes be broad and sometimes narrow depending on the nature of the rights in issue, or on the balancing of competing rights. The doctrine is of relevance both in considering the scope of a State's choices when interfering with a right protected by Articles 8–11,[53]

---

[48] *Silver* v. *United Kingdom*, Judgment of 25 March 1983, Series A, No. 61; (1983) 5 EHRR 347, para. 97 of the judgment.

[49] *Handyside* v. *United Kingdom*, Judgment of 7 December 1976, Series A, No. 24; (1979–80) 1 EHRR 737.

[50] Para. 48 of the judgment.

[51] Para. 26 of the judgment.

[52] See J. Merrills, *The Development of International Law by the European Court of Human Rights* (Manchester, 1993), ch. 8, 'Human rights and democratic values' at 125–50.

[53] Negative obligations.

and in considering the steps which a State must take to guarantee the rights protected for individuals within their jurisdiction.[54]

Where a particularly important facet of an individual's existence or identity is in issue under Article 8, the Court will be less likely to accept that the State should be afforded a broad discretion.

One example is the *X and Y* case,[55] which concerned a young mentally handicapped girl who had been seriously sexually assaulted. Because of a lacuna in Dutch law, it was not possible for criminal proceedings to be instituted, although she could have brought a civil claim for damages. While recognizing that in principle States enjoyed a margin of appreciation when it came to the choice of means calculated to secure respect for private life between individuals, the Court ruled that the precise nature of the State's obligation would depend on the particular aspect of private life in issue. This was a case where 'fundamental values and essential aspects of private life' (that is, a woman's right to physical integrity and freedom from sexual assault) were at stake. Since it was of vital importance to protect women from interference of this kind, the State could not be allowed a great deal of discretion: effective deterrence, in the form of criminal sanctions, was indispensable.[56]

Similarly, in *Z* v. *Finland*,[57] while accepting that individual interests could sometimes be outweighed by the public interest in the investigation and prosecution of crime, the Court emphasized the fundamental importance of protecting the confidentiality of medical data, for the sake of personal privacy and to preserve confidence in the medical profession and health services. It found that measures including the disclosure of the applicant's medical records without her consent in the course of criminal proceedings against her husband amounted to a violation of Article 8.

A similar balancing exercise was undertaken in *Dudgeon* v. *United Kingdom*,[58] where the complaint was that certain forms of homosexual activity were prohibited by the criminal law. Although the tendency is to allow a wide margin to the State where questions of morality are in issue, the applicable criminal law inhibited the applicant from enjoying 'a most intimate aspect of private life' and the therefore Court required particularly serious reasons to be shown before it would accept that this interference was 'necessary'.

In areas of morality, the scope of the margin is likely to be wide, since there is among the Contracting States no uniform conception of morals. This is illustrated by the *Handyside* case concerning *The Little Red Schoolbook*,[59] and

---

[54] Positive obligations.

[55] *X and Y* v. *Netherlands*, Judgment of 26 March 1985, Series A, No. 91; (1986) 8 EHRR 235.

[56] Paras. 24 and 27 of the judgment.

[57] *Z* v. *Finland* (App. 22009/93), Judgment of 25 February 1997; (1998) 25 EHRR 371

[58] *Dudgeon* v. *United Kingdom*, Judgment of 22 October 1981, Series A, No. 45; (1982) 4 EHRR 149.

[59] *Handyside* v. *United Kingdom*, Judgment of 7 December 1976, Series A, No. 24; (1979–80) 1 EHRR 737.

also explains how its publication could be accepted in some Contracting States but not others. It may also explain the decision in the *Otto-Preminger Institute* case.[60] The location of the cinema in a predominantly Roman Catholic area, where a film was shown that would be deeply offensive to devout Roman Catholics, appears to have been an important factor in the Court's decision that the interference with the rights in Article 10 was justified.

Though at first sight, the Court may appear to grant a wider margin of appreciation where positive obligations are in issue, this is often more apparent than real, since it will often be the case that the nature of the right in respect of which positive obligations are argued is finely balanced against the wider interests of the whole community. In the cases involving transsexuals which have come before it, the Court has allowed States a wide margin of appreciation, despite the fact that the same 'intimate aspect of private life' (an individual's sexual identity) was in issue here as in *Dudgeon*.

In *Rees* v. *United Kingdom*,[61] for example, the Court was asked to decide whether the respondent Government was under a positive obligation to allow the entry in the register of births relating to the applicant and his birth certificate to be altered to reflect his change of sex from female to male. In the view of the Court, since the 'particular features [of transsexualism] [had] been identified and examined only fairly recently' and there was no European consensus to how such individuals should be treated, a wide margin of appreciation was permitted. In contrast, as the Court had observed in *Dudgeon*:

[I]n the great majority of the member States of the Council of Europe it is no longer considered necessary or appropriate to treat homosexual practices of the kind now in question as in themselves a matter to which the sanctions of the criminal law should be applied; the Court cannot overlook the marked changes which have occurred in this regard in the domestic law of the member States.

In *X, Y and Z* v. *United Kingdom*,[62] the Court again pointed to the lack of any common European standard, when it ruled that the State's failure to allow a female-to-male transsexual to be registered as the father of a child born by artificial insemination to his female partner did not violate Article 8. Although in the past it had held that Article 8 required States to establish legal mechanisms to reinforce a child's stability within the family, these earlier cases had been concerned with family ties between biological parents and their children. Since there was no generally shared approach amongst the High Contracting Parties with regard to either the granting of parental rights to transsexuals or the

---

[60] *Otto-Preminger Institute* v. *Austria*, Judgment of 20 September 1994, Series A, No. 295-A; (1995) 19 EHRR 34.

[61] *Rees* v. *United Kingdom*, Judgment of 17 October 1986, Series A, No. 106; (1987) 9 EHRR 56, paras. 37–38 of the judgment; and see also the *Cossey* v *United Kingdom*, Judgment of 27 September 1990, Series A, No. 184; (1991) 13 EHRR 622.

[62] *X, Y and Z* v. *United Kingdom* (App. 21830/93), Judgment of 22 April 1997; (1997) 24 EHRR 143.

manner in which the social relationship between a child conceived by artificial insemination by donor and the 'social father' should be reflected in law, and since the law in these fields at national level appeared to be in a transitional stage, it was not for the Court to adopt or impose any single viewpoint; in other words, the respondent State had to be afforded a wide margin of appreciation.

Other examples of cases where the Court has recognized a wide margin of appreciation because of the variety of practice in Europe arise from differing cultural traditions and economic resources,[63] and considerations of the appropriateness of intervention by public authorities in the care of children.[64]

These cases, where a wide margin of appreciation is allowed because of a lack of common ground in Europe, can be seen as further examples of the principle that the nature of the individual right determines the breadth of the margin, since a divergence in national law may indicate that the nature and degree of importance of the individual interest is still in the process of being understood, recognized, and accepted.

In some cases, the width of the margin allowed to States depends not so much on the importance to the individual of the rights concerned, but rather on the nature of the general interest with which they conflict. As the Court remarked in the *Dudgeon* judgment, 'the scope of the margin of appreciation is not identical in respect of each of the aims [set out in the second paragraph of Article 8] justifying restrictions on a right.'[65]

Thus, in *Laskey, Jaggard and Brown* v. *United Kingdom*,[66] where the applicants complained of having been prosecuted and convicted for offences of assault and wounding arising from consensual sado-masochistic activities, the Court held that States were entitled to seek to regulate practices involving the infliction of physical harm:

The determination of the level of harm that should be tolerated by the law in situations where the victim consents is in the first instance a matter for the State concerned since what is at stake is related, on the one hand, to public health considerations and to the general deterrent effect of the criminal law, and, on the other, to the personal autonomy of the individual.

National security is another area where States are allowed a wide margin, since the protection of large numbers of people is in issue and the information on which such decisions are based is frequently highly sensitive. Thus, in *Klass* v.

---

[63] *Stjerna* v. *Finland*, Judgment of 25 November 1994, Series A, No. 299-B; (1997) 24 EHRR 195, concerning legal restrictions on changing surname.

[64] *Johansen* v. *Norway* (App. 17383/90), Judgment of 7 August 1996; (1997) 23 EHRR 33.

[65] *Dudgeon* v. *United Kingdom*, Judgment of 22 October 1981, Series A, No. 45; (1982) 4 EHRR 149, paras. 52 of the judgment.

[66] *Laskey, Jaggard and Brown* v. *United Kingdom* (Apps. 21627/93, 21826/93, and 21974/93), Judgment of 19 February 1997; (1997) 24 EHRR 39.

Germany,[67] the Court, which accepted that the sophistication of modern terrorism entailed that some system of secret surveillance over post and telecommunications might in exceptional circumstances be necessary, allowed a certain discretion to the national legislature as to how such a system should be organized and controlled: it was 'certainly not for the Court to substitute for the assessment of the national authorities any other assessment of what might be the best policy in this field.' Nonetheless, in view of the encroachment on individual rights inherent in such a system, States could not be afforded an unlimited licence but had to satisfy the Court that adequate and effective safeguards were in place.

In *Leander* v. *Sweden*,[68] the applicant complained that he had been excluded from employment in the civil service because he had been registered as a security risk by the police. Since it was undoubtedly necessary, for security reasons, for States to have laws enabling the secret collection and storage of information and to use it when assessing the suitability of candidates for employment in sensitive posts, and since Mr Leander's private life was not affected except in so far as he was prevented from gaining employment as a civil servant (a right which was not as such enshrined in the Convention),

the Court accepted that the State should enjoy a wide margin of appreciation, both in assessing the existence of a pressing social need and in choosing the means for achieving the legitimate aim of protecting national security.

It is not only in cases involving national security that the Court allows a wide margin in recognition of the practical realities of certain types of State activity. In child-care cases, for example, the national authorities may frequently be called upon to make extremely difficult and delicate decisions rapidly, for the benefit of the child. In these circumstances, the scope of the discretion allowed to the State will vary, depending both on the urgency of the case and the competing interests at stake. Thus, the Court recognizes that the authorities enjoy a wide margin of appreciation in assessing the necessity of taking a child into care. In such cases it considers that it would not be appropriate for it to substitute its own judgment, reached with the benefit of hindsight but without direct contact with the individuals concerned or the prevailing social and cultural conditions.[69] On the other hand, decisions taken in this area often prove to be irreversible: a child who has been taken away from his parents may in the course of time establish new bonds which should not be disrupted by renewed parental contact. There is, accordingly, an even greater call than usual

---

[67] *Klass* v. *Germany*, Judgment of 6 September 1978, Series A, No. 28 (1979–80) 2 EHRR 214, paras 48–50 of the judgment.

[68] *Leander* v. *Sweden*, Judgment of 26 March 1987, Series A, No. 116; (1987) 9 EHRR 433.

[69] *Olsson* v. *Sweden (No. 2)*, Judgment of 27 November 1992, Series A, No. 250 (1994) 17 EHRR 134, para. 90 of the judgment.

for protection against arbitrary interferences.[70] The Court therefore sees its role predominantly as one of reviewing the quality of the decision-making process, including whether relevant and sufficient reasons were given[71] and the parents were consulted if possible.[72] A stricter scrutiny is, however, called for in relation to any further measures such as restrictions on access, not only because these could eradicate the family life shared between parent and child,[73] but also because the public interest in protecting the child carries less weight once the child is in a safe place.

Another area where the Court in principle allows a wide margin to the national authorities is town and country planning. As with the national security and child-care cases, the reasons for this are twofold. First, the public interest, in safeguarding a pleasant environment, is weighty. Secondly, such measures require an appreciation of local, social, economic, and environmental conditions, which the national authorities are best placed to assess.[74] Thus, in *Gillow* v. *United Kingdom*,[75] the Court took the view that 'the Guernsey legislature is better placed than the international judge to assess the effects of any relaxation of the housing controls.' However, State discretion in this field is not unlimited, particularly where important Convention rights, such as the right to respect for a 'home', are in issue. As in the child-care cases referred to above, the Court will pay particular attention to the procedural safeguards in the decision-making process in determining whether the impugned measure falls within the margin of appreciation.[76]

The significance of the margin of appreciation in examining the requirement that any restriction be necessary in a democratic society cannot be underestimated. It will be at the heart of nearly all the cases coming before the Court.[77]

---

[70] *W.* v. *United Kingdom*, Judgment of 8 July 1987, Series A, No. 121; (1988) 10 EHRR 29.

[71] *Hokkanen* v. *Finland*, Judgment of 23 September 1994, Series A, No. 299-A; (1994) 19 EHRR 139, para. 55 of the judgment.

[72] *W.* v. *United Kingdom*, Judgment of 8 July 1987, Series A, No. 121; (1988) 10 EHRR 29.

[73] *Johansen* v. *Norway* (App. 17383/90), Judgment of 7 August 1996; (1997) 23 EHRR 33, para. 64 of the judgment.

[74] And see also *Powell and Rayner* v. *United Kingdom*, Judgment of 21 February 1990, Series A, No. 172; (1990) 12 EHRR 355, para. 44 of the judgment, where the Court ruled that it should not 'substitute for the assessment of the national authorities any other assessment of what might be the best policy in this difficult social and technical sphere [the regulation of aircraft noise]. This is an area where the Contracting States are to be recognised as enjoying a wide margin of appreciation.'

[75] *Gillow* v. *United Kingdom*, Judgment of 24 November 1986, Series A, No. 109; (1986) 11 EHRR 355, para. 56 of the judgment.

[76] *Buckley* v. *United Kingdom* (App. 20348/92), Judgment of 25 September 1996; (1997) 23 EHRR 101, para. 76 of the judgment.

[77] MacDonald, 'The margin of appreciation in the jurisprudence of the European Court of Human Rights' in A. Giuffré (ed.), *Le Droit International à l'heure de sa Codification: études en l'honneur de Roberto Ago* (Milan, 1987), at 187–208.

THE POLITICAL ACTIVITIES OF ALIENS

Article 16 provides:

Nothing in Articles 10, 11 and 14 shall be regarded as preventing the High Contracting Parties from imposing restrictions on the political activity of aliens.

This is potentially a very restrictive provision, which could be used to exclude from the application of the Convention those within the jurisdiction of the Contracting States who otherwise enjoy the protection of the Convention. It is not a blanket derogation from the requirements of Articles 10, 11, and 14, but merely permits derogation from those rights contained in those articles which relate to political activity. It is not easy to see how objectionable conduct by those who are not nationals of the State might fall outside the widely drafted limitations discussed earlier in this chapter. This may explain why the provision does not appear to have been used. It has certainly never been considered by the Court.

The Parliamentary Assembly has recommended that the permitted derogation be removed from the Convention.[78]

---

[78] Recommendation 799 (1977) on the political rights and positions of aliens, 25 January 1977. Council of Europe, Parliamentary Assembly, texts adopted at the 28th ordinary session.

11

PROTECTION OF PRIVATE AND FAMILY LIFE

INTRODUCTION

Article 8 is one of the most open-ended provisions of the Convention.[1] Though there is an abundant case law under the article and there has been much development in particular of the notion of private life, there remains much potential for development of the rights protected by Article 8.

Article 8 provides:

1. Everyone has the right to respect for his private and family life, his home and his correspondence.
2. There shall be no interference by a public authority with the exercise of this right except such as is in accordance with the law and is necessary in a democratic society in the interests of national security, public safety or the economic well-being of the country, for the prevention of disorder or crime, for the protection of health or morals, or for the protection of the rights and freedoms of others.

The right to marry and found a family may be considered as a particular form of family life, but it is separately protected in Article 12, which provides:

Men and women of marriageable age have the right to marry and found a family, according to the national laws governing the exercise of this right.

Article 5 of Protocol 7 adds to the rights in Article 12 by providing:

Spouses shall enjoy equality of rights and responsibilities of a private law character between them, and in their relations with their children, as to marriage, during marriage and in the event of its dissolution. This Article shall not prevent States from taking such measures as are necessary in the interests of children.

The rights protected by Articles 8 and 12, and Article 5 of Protocol 7, are somewhat disparate. However, the fact that the rights in Article 8 are grouped together in the same article strengthens the protection given by that article,

---

[1] See generally D. Feldman, 'The developing scope of Article 8 of the European Convention on Human Rights' [1997] EHRLR 265; and C. Warbrick, 'The structure of Article 8', [1998] EHRLR 32

since each right is reinforced by its context. Thus, the right to respect for family life, the right to privacy, and the right to respect for the home and correspondence may be read together as guaranteeing collectively more than the sum of their parts. This method of interpretation is justified even in the case of rights protected by separate articles,[2] but it is all the more necessary where a single article is concerned.

It is quite clear, for example, that wire-tapping, unless it can be justified in a particular case under paragraph (2), is prohibited by Article 8, and it matters little whether it is considered as interference with correspondence, or with privacy, or even with the home if it takes place there, since these notions should be considered together rather than in isolation. Hence, in the following pages, it will sometimes be necessary to take together, as the Strasbourg organs have frequently done, privacy and the home, or family life and the home, or privacy and correspondence.

The scope of the protection of private life, or privacy, under the Convention is being increasingly explored in the Court's case law. It was suggested[3] some years ago that the Convention protects the individual, under this head, against attacks on physical or mental integrity or moral or intellectual freedom, attacks on honour and reputation and similar torts, the use of a person's name, identity, or likeness, being spied upon, watched, or harassed, and the disclosure of information protected by the duty of professional secrecy. This has proved to be the case.

Since there is no single or embracing concept contained in Article 8, the issues which have arisen under Article 8 need to be classified under a number of headings, which at first sight appear to have little in common. As with a number of articles, the rights contained in the first paragraph are subject to the limitations set out in the second paragraph. In many cases, the interference will be justifiable on the basis of these limitations.[4]

POSITIVE OBLIGATIONS UNDER ARTICLE 8

The wording of Article 8(1) differs from the wording of Articles 2 to 7. It refers to a right to respect for private and family life, home, and correspondence. The notion of 'respect' is a relatively imprecise one, but the Commission and the Court have applied an interpretation which serves to give effect to the

---

[2] See ch. 3.

[3] C. Velu, 'The European Convention on Human Rights and the Right to Respect for Private Life, the Home and Communications' in A. H. Robertson, *Privacy and Human Rights* (Manchester, 1973), at p.12.

[4] For a discussion of the limitations in Articles 8–11, see ch. 10 above.

continuing evolution of concepts of privacy and family life.[5] Article 8 prohibits arbitrary interferences by the State into respect for family and private life, the home, and correspondence.

However, the sources of infringements of privacy are not only State agencies but also bodies which may be independent of the State: the Press and other media, or private electronic data banks. It remains unclear just how far the activities of such bodies can be brought within the scope of the Convention,[6] though the case law is beginning to suggest that few areas of activity will escape scrutiny where Article 8 rights are legitimately in issue. What is clear is that Article 8 does not merely require the State to abstain from interferences in the rights protected; there is a positive element to the protection required by Article 8. This presupposes the existence of rules in the national legal order protecting the essential features of family and private life, and to afford protection to the home and correspondence. A law which fails to meet this test may violate Article 8(1) without the need to examine the limitations in Article 8(2).[7] A failure to intervene by the State which results in a failure to secure respect for the rights protected by the article amounts to a breach of Article 8 even though the interference is not caused directly by the State. However, the Court frequently carries out a balancing exercise between the rights of the individual and the rights of the community in deciding whether a positive obligation exists.

Positive obligations under Article 8 can arise in two types of situations. The first is where the State must take some action to secure respect for the rights included in the article, as distinct from simply refraining from interfering with the rights protected. Examples of this type of case are the immigration cases where the State must allow a person to enter or remain in the country, or changing the law to recognize the new gender identity of transsexuals, or operating a night-flying scheme at a major airport which did not interfere with the quality of life of those living in the vicinity of the airport.[8] The second type of situation is where a duty arises for the State to protect an individual from interferences by other individuals. Examples of this type of case are ensuring effective sanctions against personal violence or regulating activities which cause pollution.

In a case against the Netherlands,[9] the Court considered an application made on behalf of a mentally handicapped girl aged 16, who had been raped while in a privately run home for the those with special needs. The law of the Netherlands did not recognize a complaint unless made by the victim in person.

---

[5] See G. Cohen-Jonathan, 'Respect for private and family life' in R. Macdonald, F. Matscher, and H. Petzold, *The European System for the Protection of Human Rights* (Dordrecht, 1993), 405.

[6] See A. Clapham, *Human Rights in the Private Sphere* (Oxford, 1993), at 211–22.

[7] *Marckx* v. *Belgium*, Judgment of 13 June 1979, Series A, No. 31; (1979–80) 2 EHRR 330.

[8] *Hatton and others* v. *United Kingdom* (App. 36022/97), Judgment of 2 October 2001; (2002) 34 EHRR 1, discussed later in this chapter.

[9] *X and Y* v. *Netherlands*, Judgment of 26 March 1985, Series A, No. 91; (1986) 8 EHRR 235.

If she lacked capacity, the criminal law could take no cognizance of the alleged offence. It appeared that there was no similar bar on the use of the civil law. The family argued that this violated respect for the private life of their daughter, and there was no dispute as to the applicability of the article, since the concept of private life covers the physical and moral integrity of the person, including their sexual life.[10] The absence of protection by the criminal law in so serious a case was found to be a violation of Article 8, and the Court confirmed that:

[A]lthough the object of Article 8 is essentially that of protecting the individual against arbitrary interference by the public authorities, it does not merely compel the State to abstain from such interference: in addition to this primarily negative undertaking, there may be positive obligations inherent in an effective respect for private or family life.[11]

But it seems clear that, where positive obligations are in issue, there is a considerable margin of appreciation to the State as to how it regulates a particular area.[12] In the *Hatton* case in 2001, the Court went on to indicate that the approach to positive obligations was essentially the same as where there were interferences,

Whatever analytical approach is adopted—the positive duty or an interference—the applicable principles regarding justification under Article 8(2) are broadly similar. In both contexts, regard must be had to the fair balance that has to be struck between the competing interests of the individual and of the community as a whole. In both contexts the State enjoys a certain margin of appreciation in determining the steps to be taken to ensure compliance with the Convention. Furthermore, even in relation to the positive obligations flowing from Article 8(1) in striking the required balance the aims mentioned in Article 8(2) may be of a certain relevance.[13]

DEFINING 'PRIVATE LIFE', 'FAMILY LIFE', 'HOME', AND 'CORRESPONDENCE'

PRIVATE LIFE

In 1976, the Commission defined private life as follows:

For numerous Anglo-Saxon and French authors the right to respect for 'private life' is the right to privacy, the right to live as far as one wishes, protected from publicity. . . . In the opinion of the Commission however, the right to respect for private life does

---

[10] Para. 22 of judgment.
[11] Para. 23 of judgment.
[12] See *Rees* v. *United Kingdom*, Series A, No. 106; (1987) 9 EHRR 56, paras 37 and 44 of the judgment, and the discussion of this issue in ch. 10.
[13] *Hatton and others* v. *United Kingdom* (App. 36022/97), Judgment of 2 October 2001; (2002) 34 EHRR 1, para. 96 of the judgment.

not end there. It comprises also, to a certain degree, the right to establish and develop relationships with other human beings especially in the emotional field, for the development and fulfilment of one's own personality.[14]

Cohen-Jonathan observes:

One can consider anything having to do with personal health, philosophical, religious or moral beliefs, family and emotional life, friendships and, subject to reservations, professional and material life as part of private life.[15]

The Court had occasion to comment on the meaning of 'private life' in the *Niemetz* case,[16] which concerned the question of whether a search of law offices violated Article 8. The Court observed:

The Court does not consider it possible or necessary to attempt an exhaustive definition of the notion of 'private life.' However, it would be too restrictive to limit the notion to an 'inner circle' in which the individual may live his own personal life as he chooses and to exclude therefrom entirely the outside world not encompassed within that circle. Respect for private life must also comprise to a certain degree the right to establish and develop relationships with other human beings.

There appears, furthermore, to be no reason of principle why this understanding of the notion of 'private life' should be taken to exclude activities of a professional or business nature since it is, after all, in the course of their working lives that the majority of people have a significant, if not the greatest, opportunity of developing relationships with the outside world. . . . Thus, especially in the case of a person exercising a liberal profession, his work in that context may form part and parcel of his life to such a degree that it becomes impossible to know in what capacity he is acting at a given moment of time.[17]

Clayton and Tomlinson helpfully suggest that respect for private life involves respect for a person's moral and physical integrity, personal identity, personal information, personal sexuality, and personal or private space.[18] In concluding that mental health must also be regarded as a crucial part of private life associated with the aspect of moral identity, the Court confirmed that private life is a broad term 'not susceptible to exhaustive definition' but will protect such important elements of the personal sphere as 'gender identification, name and sexual orientation and sexual life'.[19]

[14] App. 6825/74, *X* v. *Iceland*, 18 May 1976 (1976) 5 DR 86. See also L. Doswald-Beck, 'The Meaning of the "Right to respect for Private Life" under the European Convention on Human Rights' (1983) 4 HRLJ 283, and L. Loucaides, 'Personality and Privacy under the European Convention on Human Rights' (1990) 61 BYIL 175.
[15] Cohen-Jonathan, 'Respect for private and family life' in Macdonald, Matscher, and Petzold, *The European System for the Protection of Human Rights* (Dordrecht, 1993), 405, at 407.
[16] *Niemetz* v. *German*, Judgment of 16 December 1992 Series A, No. 251-B; (1993) 16 EHRR 97.
[17] Para. 29 of the judgment.
[18] R. Clayton, and H. Tomlinson, *The Law of Human Rights* (Oxford, 2000), para. 12.85–12.94.
[19] *Bensaid* v. *United Kingdom* (App. 44599/98), Judgment of 6 February 2001; (2001) 33 EHRR 205, para. 47 of the judgment.

The Court uses the term 'physical and moral integrity of the person' as within the concept of private life.[20] Where conduct, such as child sexual abuse, is in issue, there is a positive obligation on the State to provide protection from such grave interferences with private life. This will not, however, require unlimited civil actions where the conduct is adequately covered by criminal law sanctions.

FAMILY LIFE

Respect for family life requires identification of what constitutes a family. The protection of the family, as the fundamental unit of society, figures at more than one place in the Convention. Article 12 guarantees the right to marry and to found a family, while Article 8 prohibits in principle, and subject to the provisions of paragraph (2), interference with an existing family unit. Article 2 of the First Protocol deals with an important aspect of the rights of parents in relation to their children's education. It provides for the right of parents to ensure such education in conformity with their own religious and philosophical convictions.[21]

The right to respect for family life, as guaranteed by Article 8 of the Convention, has as its principal element the protection of the integrity of the family. What then constitutes a 'family', and under what conditions is interference authorized under the Convention?[22] Generally, the Commission and the Court have considered the family to include husband and wife and children who are dependent on them, including illegitimate and adopted children. Indeed, the Court has said that 'the mutual enjoyment by parent and child of each other's company constitutes a fundamental element of family life.'[23] Relationships between brothers and sisters, taken together with those between parents and children are also covered.[24] It seems that de facto family ties can arise where parties are living together outside marriage[25] and children born out of such relationships form part of the family unit from the moment of birth and by the very fact of it. The family ties exist even where the parents are not living

---

[20] *Stubbings and others* v. *United Kingdom* (Apps. 22083/93 and 22095/93), Judgment of 22 October 1996; (1997) 23 EHRR 213, para. 59 of the judgment.

[21] See ch. 16.

[22] See J. Liddy, 'The concept of family life under the ECHR' [1998] EHRLR 15; and U. Kilkelly, *The Child and the European Convention on Human Rights* (Ashgate, 1999), ch.7.

[23] *B.* v. *United Kingdom*, Judgment of 8 July 1987, Series A, No. 121; (1988) 10 EHRR 87, para. 60 of the judgment.

[24] *Moustaquim* v. *Belgium*, Judgment of 18 February 1991, Series A, No. 193; (1991) 13 EHRR 802, para. 36 of the judgment. See also *X, Y and Z* v. *United Kingdom* (App. 21830/93), Judgment of 22 April 1997; (1997) 24 EHRR 143, paras. 36–7 of the judgment.

[25] *Johnston and others* v. *Ireland*, Judgment of 18 December 1986, Series A, No. 112; (1987) 9 EHRR 203, para. 25 of the judgment.

together at the time of the child's birth.[26] It is a violation of Article 8 to deny a mother the opportunity to enable recognition of the biological father of her child, as where a legal presumption that the husband is the father of a child born in wedlock exists which cannot be denied by the mother.[27]

In some circumstances, relations with grandparents may be protected under Article 8.[28] More remote relationships are generally not close enough to constitute family relationships protected by Article 8. There is, however, some slender evidence to suggest that a broader view is being taken of what constitutes the family. In a friendly settlement on an application against the United Kingdom,[29] the relationship was that of uncle and nephew. The uncle had complained that, prior to the Children Act 1989, the local authority had denied him access to his nephew and there was no procedure for him to apply to the courts for access. The Commission had found a violation of Article 8 by fourteen votes to four.

Engagement does not in itself constitute family life, but the relationship between a prisoner and his fiancée falls within private life.[30] The same is true of homosexual couples.[31]

The question whether there is a violation of the right to respect for family life where a person cannot obtain legal recognition of her factual domestic situation arose in the *Airey* case.[32] Here the inability to obtain legal recognition arose not from any lacuna in the substantive law but in the absence of provision for legal aid; it was therefore, so to speak, a lacuna at one remove. Nonetheless the Court held that Mrs Airey, being unable to seek recognition in law of her de facto separation from her husband (and therefore being deprived of access to a court contrary to Article 6(1)),[33] was also the victim of a violation of Article 8. Judge Evrigenis's dissenting opinion is perhaps to be preferred on this point; he was unable to perceive a violation of a right protected directly or indirectly by Article 8. In his view the violation related to the 'procedural superstructure' of Article 8 and was covered by Article 6(1).

The Court's pronouncements on the nature of the family suggest that there is a hierarchy of relationships. At the top of the hierarchy is the traditional heterosexual relationship of married couples, moving through parenting between

---

[26] *Berrehab* v. *Netherlands*, Judgment of 21 June 1988, Series A, No. 138; (1989) 11 EHRR 322, para. 21 of the judgment, and *Keegan* v. *Ireland*, Judgment of 26 May 1994, Series A, No. 290; (1994) 18 EHRR 342, para. 44 of the judgment.

[27] *Kroon and others* v. *Netherlands*, Judgment of 27 October 1994, Series A, No. 297-C; (1995) 19 EHRR 263.

[28] See *Vermeire* v. *Belgium*, Judgment of 29 November 1991, Series A, No. 214-C; (1993) 15 EHRR 488, which concerned exclusion of a granddaughter from the estate of a grandparent because of the illegitimate nature of the kinship.

[29] *Boyle* v. *United Kingdom*, Judgment of 28 February 1994, Series A, No. 282-B; (1995) 19 EHRR 179.

[30] App. 15817/89, *Wakeford* v. *United Kingdom*, 1 October 1990 (1990) 66 DR 251.

[31] App. 11716/85, *X* v. *United Kingdom*, 14 May 1986, (1986) 47 DR 274.

[32] *Airey* v. *Ireland*, Judgment of 9 October 1979, Series A, No. 32; (1979–80) 2 EHRR 305.

[33] See ch. 8.

non-married heterosexual couples down to more removed family relationships at the bottom of the hierarchy.

HOME

Article 8 requires States to guarantee respect for the home.[34] This does not appear to include a right to a home,[35] nor to a particular home.[36] But it does cover a requirement that the State protect the physical security of a person's actual home and belongings there. So deliberate destruction of homes by the security forces is a particularly grave and unjustified interference with the rights in Article 8.[37] In *Cyprus* v. *Turkey*,[38] the refusal of the authorities in northern Cyprus to allow displaced Greek Cypriots to return to their homes there constituted a continuing violation by Turkey of Article 8.[39] The 'multitude of adverse circumstances' which attended the daily lives of Greek Cypriots living in the Karpas region of northern Cyprus violated their right to respect for their private and family life and home under Article 8.[40]

A broad view is taken of what is a person's home. It can include the business premises of a professional person,[41] or a caravan site used as a home in breach of planning permission.[42]

Applications relating specifically to this aspect of Article 8 have not been numerous; many issues have involved a combination of private life and home. Also, many issues which might otherwise have fallen within its provisions have been considered under Article 1 of Protocol 1.[43]

In the *Greek* case, Article 8 was violated by the suspension of the right to respect for the home in the Greek Constitution, and by 'the consequent disregard of this right, in particular by the practice of the Greek authorities of carrying out arrests at night.'[44]

---

[34] For the substantive nature of the guarantee, see below in this chapter.

[35] See Commission's decision in *X* v. *Germany* (1956) 1 *Yearbook* 202, concerning a claim that the Article required a State to provide a home for a refugee.

[36] See Commission's decision in *Burton* v. *United Kingdom*, 15 September 1996, (1996) 22 EHRR CD135 concerning a claim by a gypsy to be permitted to live her last days in a caravan according to gypsy tradition.

[37] *Selçuk and Asker* v. *Turkey* (Apps. 23184/94 and 23185/94), Judgment of 24 April 1998; (1998) 26 EHRR 477, para. 86 of the judgment.

[38] *Cyprus* v. *Turkey* (App. 25781/94), Judgment of 10 May 2001.

[39] Para. 175 of the judgment.

[40] Para. 296 of the judgment.

[41] *Niemetz* v. *Germany*, Judgment of 16 December 1992, Series A, No. 251-B; (1993) 16 EHRR 97, paras. 30–1 of the judgment.

[42] *Buckley* v. *United Kingdom* (App. 20348/92), Judgment of 25 September 1996; (1997) 23 EHRR 101, para. 54 of the judgment. See also *Gillow* v. *United Kingdom*, Judgment of 24 November 1986, Series A, No. 109; (1989) 11 EHRR 335, para. 46 of the judgment.

[43] See ch. 15.

[44] (1969) 12 *Yearbook* 152–3.

CORRESPONDENCE

Correspondence includes written materials including materials sent through the post, as well as telephonic communications. What appears to characterize 'correspondence' as distinct from materials constituting 'expression' within Article 10 is direct communication to another. Applications concerning interference with correspondence have mainly been brought by those in prison,[45] and in relation to various surveillance techniques, most notably telephone tapping.[46]

THE RIGHT TO MARRY AND FOUND A FAMILY

Article 12 guarantees the right to marry and to found a family. These rights are not subject to limitations of the kind set out in paragraph (2) of Articles 8 to 11. Instead, limitations are to be found in the provision that men and women of marriageable age have the right to marry and to found a family, 'according to the national laws governing the exercise of this right'.

The scope of this qualification is not clear. It is evident that the exercise of the rights guaranteed cannot be wholly governed by national law. In that case, the protection of Article 12 would extend only to cases where there was a breach of national law. But the purpose of the Convention, here as elsewhere, is to guarantee certain human rights irrespective of the provisions of national law.[47]

The correct view, therefore, would seem to be that Article 12 imposes an obligation to recognize, both in principle and in practice, the right to marry and to found a family. This obligation implies that the restrictions placed on these rights by national law must be imposed for a legitimate purpose, for example, to prevent polygamy or incest, and must not go beyond a reasonable limit to attain that purpose. On the other hand, the precise scope of the restrictions may vary among the Contracting States, as does, for example, the marriageable age.

Article 14 is also of special importance in relation to Article 12, since it prohibits discrimination not only, for example, on racial or religious grounds, but also on grounds of sex. Thus, in relation to marriage and the founding of a family, there must be no discrimination between men and women. Not all forms of differential treatment, of course, constitute discrimination so that there is no requirement that marriageable age, for example, should be the same

---

[45] See below, this chapter.

[46] See below, this chapter.

[47] See Opsahl, 'The Convention and the right to respect for family life, particularly as regards the unity of the family and the protection of the rights of parents and guardians in the education of children' in A. H. Robertson, *Privacy and Human Rights* (Manchester, 1973) at 182.

for both men and women but all differential treatment must be examined by reference to its purpose and justification to ensure that it is not unlawful.

While the right to marry and the right to found a family are two separate rights, it seems from the wording of the Article that only married heterosexual couples can claim the right to found a family. If the Article had been worded 'Everyone has the right to marry and to found a family', it might have been easier to infer that unmarried people or same sex couples also had the right to found a family.

It may be significant, also, that the Article ends with a reference to 'this right', rather than 'these rights', thus apparently envisaging a close connection between the two.[48]

But while the unmarried may have no right under Article 12 to found a family, the term 'family' in Article 8 has a wider meaning, and the relations of a parent with an illegitimate child are protected under that Article. It cannot be argued that the meaning of 'family' in Article 8 is as restricted as in Article 12, for it is necessary to give it a wider interpretation in other respects also. 'Family' in Article 8 must include the family into which a person is born, as well as the family which he or she founds. Otherwise the absurd conclusion would follow that only parents, and not children, could claim the right to respect for family life. It is therefore reasonable to interpret Article 8, as the Commission and the Court have done, as extending in principle to any close relationship, whether by blood or marriage, and whether legitimate or not.

National laws may restrict the right of prisoners to marry. In an application against the Federal Republic of Germany, the Commission held that not merely a convicted prisoner, but a person detained on remand, may be refused permission to marry. The applicant, who had been arrested on charges of theft, was refused permission to marry by the German authorities and objected in particular to the reasons given for their decision. The courts had taken into account the applicant's criminal record and the probability that, if he were convicted, he would be given a long prison sentence and perhaps an indefinite period of detention. This the applicant complained infringed his right to be presumed innocent until convicted. The authorities had also considered the applicant's personality, and the fact that the marriage of prisoners inevitably affected the maintenance of order within prison establishments. The Commission appears to have approved all these grounds.[49]

In another case,[50] a man sentenced to prison in England and later deported to Pakistan complained that the authorities had refused to allow him to marry,

---

[48] Contrast the wording of the European Union Charter of Fundamental Rights which provides in Article 9, 'The right to marry and the right to found a family shall be guaranteed in accordance with the national laws governing the exercise of these rights. See also C. McGlynn, 'Families and the European Union Charter of Fundamental Rights: progressive change or entrenching the status quo?' (2001) 26 ELRev 582.

[49] App. 892/60, X v. Federal Republic of Germany, 13 April 1961, (1961) 4 Yearbook 240, at 256.

[50] App. 3898/68, X v. United Kingdom, 2 February 1970, (1970) 13 Yearbook 666.

while in prison, a woman living in England who was the mother of his child. After obtaining observations from the Government and the applicant, then in Pakistan, the Commission found that, according to the information available at the time at which the prison authorities refused the applicant's petition to marry, he already had a wife and children in Pakistan. The applicant subsequently stated that he had been divorced from his wife before his deportation, but this statement was only made during the proceedings before the Commission and after he had already been deported. The Commission also observed that the applicant's submissions had not been substantiated by any evidence and that the applicant had not shown that he made it clear to the United Kingdom authorities, before his deportation that he no longer had a wife in Pakistan. The Commission accordingly rejected the application as manifestly ill-founded.

The right of men and women, once married, to found a family may be subject to increasing strain in a society preoccupied with the dangers of over-population. Article 12 plainly does not preclude the provision of family planning services; at the other extreme, sterilization, according to the Commission, may even, in certain circumstances, involve a violation of Articles 2 and 3 of the Convention.[51] Fiscal and other non-coercive disincentives are probably not contrary to Article 12. A temporary prohibition on remarriage within three years after divorce imposed under Swiss law applicable at the time on the spouse held responsible for the breakdown of the marriage was held to violate Article 12 as being disproportionate to the legitimate aim being pursued, namely protecting the institution of marriage and the rights of others.[52]

Several applications have sought to read into the provisions of Articles 8 and 12 a right to divorce. In the *Johnston* case[53] the Court concluded that the right to divorce cannot be derived from the provisions of Article 12, and it would accordingly be inconsistent to interpret the extent of the positive obligations flowing from Article 8 to include a right to divorce.

EQUALITY BETWEEN SPOUSES

Article 5 of Protocol 7 provides:

Spouses shall enjoy equality of rights and responsibilities of a private law character between them, and in their relations with their children, as to marriage, during marriage and in the event of its dissolution. This article shall not prevent States from taking such measures as are necessary in the interests of children.

---

[51] App. 1287/61, not published.
[52] *F. v. Switzerland*, Judgment of 18 December 1987, Series A, No. 128; (1988) 10 EHRR 411.
[53] *Johnston and others* v. *Ireland*, Judgment of 18 December 1986, Series A, No. 112; (1987) 9 EHRR 203.

The rights protected under this article are of a private law character, and the articles have no application to public law areas, such as tax, social security, labour laws, or the criminal law. It is only spouses who are protected, so the position of those about to marry remains governed wholly by Article 12. The article should not be regarded as having any application to the disposition of property in the event of a dissolution of the marriage, nor does it imply any obligation on the State to provide for dissolution of the marriage.[54]

CUSTODY, ACCESS, AND CARE PROCEEDINGS

Many applications under Article 8 have concerned the relationship of parents and children on marriage breakdown, or other family crises. The issue may arise after the separation or divorce of the parents, when the courts make an order concerning the custody of, or access to, the children of the marriage. Or it may arise, although less often, when the children of an existing marriage are taken into the care of the public authorities.

It should be noted that Article 8 imports a notion of a fair procedure for determining issues relating to the care and custody of children. In one case, the Court said:

The Court would point to the difference in the nature of the interests protected by Article 6(1) and 8. Thus, Article 6(1) affords a procedural safeguard, namely the 'right to a court' in the determination of one's 'civil rights and obligations' . . . whereas not only does the procedural requirement inherent in Article 8 cover administrative procedures as well as judicial proceedings, but it is ancillary to the wider purpose of ensuring proper respect for, *inter alia*, family life. . . . The difference between the purpose pursued by the respective safeguards afforded by Article 6(1) and 8 may, in the light of the particular circumstances, justify the examination of the same set of facts under both Articles.[55]

So a procedure which denied the applicants a sight of the social work reports on children the subject of care proceedings failed to afford them the requisite protection of their interests as parents of the child to which the proceedings related. The Court found a violation of Article 8(1).

Most of the other cases on family life which have been brought before the Commission and the Court concern the rights of parents in relation to their children. The situations giving rise to these cases have been extremely varied, but certain principles can be found in the case law.

[54] Explanatory memorandum to Protocol 7, Council of Europe Document H(84)5, at 12.
[55] *McMichael* v. *United Kingdom*, Judgment of 24 February 1995, Series A, No. 307-B; (1995) 20 EHRR 205, para 91 of the judgment.

First, the family life of parents with their children does not cease owing to the separation or divorce of the parents,[56] or other intervening circumstances, such as where a father agreed to his daughter being looked after by her maternal grandparents, who subsequently refused to return her to his custody.[57]

Where the courts award custody of the children to one parent, there is inevitably an interference with the family life of the other parent. However, in these cases, 'it may be legitimate, or even necessary, for the national law to provide rules governing the relationship between parents and children which differ from the rules which are applicable when the family unit is still maintained.'[58]

In *K & T* v. *Finland*,[59] the Grand Chamber recapitulated its case law on the impact of Article 8 on cases where the public authorities take a child into care. The Court stressed that the mutual enjoyment by parent and child of each other's company constitutes a fundamental element of family life. Any interference with this enjoyment will constitute an interference with family life respect for which is guaranteed in Article 8.[60] Any interferences will, accordingly have to be in accordance with law and for a legitimate aim. In many cases, these requirements will be readily satisfied. Care proceedings will normally be taken in order to protect the child and so will meet the legitimate aim of being for the protection of health or morals, or for the protection of the rights of the child. Most cases will turn on whether the interference is necessary in a democratic society. Referring to its earlier case law,[61] the Court said:

154. In determining whether the impugned measures were 'necessary in a democratic society', the Court will consider whether in the light of the case as a whole, the reasons adduced to justify these measures were relevant and sufficient for the purpose of paragraph 2 of Article 8 of the Convention. . . .

In so doing, the Court will have regard to the fact that perceptions as to the appropriateness of intervention by public authorities in the care of children vary from one Contracting State to another, depending on such factors as traditions relating to the role of the family and to State intervention in family affairs and the availability of resources for public measures in this particular area. However, consideration of what is in the best interests of the child is in every case of crucial importance. Moreover, it must be borne in mind that the national authorities have the benefit of direct contact with all the persons concerned . . ., often at the very stage when care measures are being

---

[56] *Hoffmann* v. *Austria*, Judgment of 23 June 1993, Series A, No. 255-C; (1994) 17 EHRR 293, where Article 8 was considered in conjunction with Article 14.

[57] *Hokkanen* v. *Finland*, Judgment of 23 September 1994, Series A, No. 299-A; (1995) 19 EHRR 139.

[58] App. 2699/65, *X* v. *Federal Republic of Germany*, 1 April 1968, (1968) 11 *Yearbook* 366, at 376.

[59] *K & T* v. *Finland* (App. 25702/94), Judgment of 12 July 2001.

[60] Para. 151 of the judgment.

[61] Notably *Olsson* v. *Sweden* (*No. 1*), Judgment of 24 March 1988, Series A, No 130; (1989) 11 EHRR 259; *Olsson* v. *Sweden* (*No. 2*), Judgment of 30 October 1992, Series A, No 250; (1994) 17 EHRR 134; *Hokkanen* v. *Finland*, Judgment of 23 September 1994, Series A, No. 299-A; (1995) 19 EHRR 139; and *Johansen* v. *Norway* (App. 17383/90), Judgment of 7 August 1996; (1997) 23 EHRR 33

envisaged or immediately after their implementation. It follows from these considerations that the Court's task is not to substitute itself for the domestic authorities in the
exercise of their responsibilities for the regulation of the public care of children and the
rights of parents whose children have been taken into care, but rather to review under
the Convention the decisions taken by those authorities in the exercise of their power of
appreciation . . .

The margin of appreciation so to be accorded to the competent national authorities
will vary in the light of the nature of the issues and the seriousness of the interests at
stake, such as, on the one hand, the importance of protecting a child in a situation
which is assessed to seriously threaten his or her health or development and, on the
other hand, the aim to reunite the family as soon as circumstances permit. After a
considerable period of time has passed since the child was originally taken into public
care, the interest of a child not to have his or her *de facto* family situation changed again
may override the interests of the parents to have their family reunited. The Court thus
recognises that the authorities enjoy a wide margin of appreciation in assessing the
necessity of taking a child into care. However, a stricter scrutiny is called for in respect
of any further limitations, such as restrictions placed by those authorities on parental
rights of access, and of any legal safeguards designed to secure an effective protection of
the right of parents and children to respect for their family life. Such further limitations
entail the danger that the family relations between the parents and a young child are
effectively curtailed.[62]

In a case against the United Kingdom[63] the applicant complained that she
had been denied access to her child who had subsequently been adopted. She
also complained that access had been denied during a strike by social workers
which had lasted for six months. She argued that both matters were a violation
of respect for her family life. The issues in the case concerned whether the
procedures surrounding the decisions in relation to her child had gone beyond
what was necessary in a democratic society. The Court recognized that the
involvement of the natural parents may be limited, but the principle of
involvement of natural parents in decisions about the future of their children
was an important one which should not lightly be dispensed with. In this case
the lack of involvement of the mother at key stages of the decision-making
process resulted in a violation of respect for her family life.[64]

In another case against the United Kingdom[65] a decision on the adoption
of, and access to, the applicant's daughter was determined in essence by the
effluxion of time where there had been delays in proceedings to determine these

---

[62] *K & T* v. *Finland* (App. 25702/94), Judgment of 12 July 2001, paras. 154 and 155 of the judgment. See
also *TP and KM* v. *United Kingdom* (App. 28945/95), Judgment of 10 May 2001; (2002) 34 EHRR 42.

[63] *B* v. *United Kingdom*, Judgment of 8 July 1987, Series A, No. 121; (1988) 10 EHRR 87.

[64] See also *O* v. *United Kingdom*, Judgment of 8 July 1987, Series A, No. 120; (1988) 10 EHRR 82; *R.* v.
United Kingdom, Judgment of 8 July 1987, Series A, No. 121; (1988) 10 EHRR 74; and *W.* v. *United
Kingdom*, Judgment of 8 July 1987, Series A No. 121; (1988) 10 EHRR 29. Contrast *Olsson* v. *Sweden (No.
1)*, Judgment of 24 March 1988, Series A, No. 130; (1989) 11 EHRR 259.

[65] *H* v. *United Kingdom*, Judgment of 8 July 1987, Series A, No. 120; (1988) 10 EHRR 95.

questions. The Court considered that effective respect for family life required that such decisions were determined on their merits. Where this did not happen there was a violation of Article 8.

Where a care order is implemented in an inappropriate manner, as, for example, where children are dispersed over some distance which renders the objective of reuniting the family difficult to achieve, there may be a violation of respect for family life by such action.[66] A similar conclusion was reached where, for a period of six years, a mother's access to her daughter was restricted and she had no enforceable visiting rights under a regime designed ultimately to reunite the family.[67] There may also be a violation of Article 8 if no adequate steps are taken to enable a non-custodial parent to have access to a child.[68]

The protection of Article 8 extends also to illegitimate children. The mother of an illegitimate child may in some cases be entitled to custody, and the rights of the mother, as well as the child, must be respected.[69] The *Marckx* case[70] concerned aspects of Belgian law which disadvantaged an unmarried mother in relation to the manner of establishing affiliation, the extent of the child's family relationships, and the property rights of the child and the mother. The Court considered that no distinction should be drawn between the 'legitimate' and the 'illegitimate' family, relying in part on a Council of Europe resolution to this effect[71] and in part on the evolution of public opinion in this regard. Legal certainty, however, required the effects of the decision to be limited to events post-dating the judgment.

A similar approach is taken where it is grandparents rather than parents who are taking issue with the decisions of the public authorities.[72]

[66] *Olsson* v. *Sweden (No. 1)*, Judgment of 24 March 1988, Series A, No. 130; (1989) 11 EHRR 259.

[67] *Eriksson* v. *Sweden*, Judgment of 22 June 1989, Series A, No. 156; (1990) 12 EHRR 183. See also *Margareta and Roger Andersson* v. *Sweden*, Judgment of 25 February 1992, Series A, No. 226-A; (1992) 14 EHRR 615. Contrast *Rieme* v. *Sweden*, Judgment of 22 April 1992, Series A, No. 226-B; (1992) 16 EHRR 155, and *Olsson* v. *Sweden (No.2)*, Judgment of 27 November 1992, Series A, No. 250. See also *Johansen* v. *Norway* (App. 17383/90), Judgment of 7 August 1996; (1997) 23 EHRR 33; and *L* v. *Finland* (App. 25651/94), Judgment of 27 April 2000; (2001) 31 EHRR 737.

[68] *Nuutinen* v. *Finland* (App. 32842/96), Judgment of 27 June 2000; (2002) 34 EHRR 358.

[69] App. 514/59, *X* v. *Austria*, 5 January 1960 (1960) 3 *Yearbook* 197.

[70] *Marckx* v. *Belgium*, Judgment of 13 June 1979, Series A, No. 31; (1979–80) 2 EHRR 330.

[71] Resolution (70)15 of 15 May 1970 on the social protection of unmarried mothers and their children.

[72] *Bronda* v. *Italy* (App. 22430/93), Judgment of 9 June 1998, para. 59 of the judgment.

ADOPTION

The leading case is *Keegan* v. *Ireland*,[73] which concerned the adoption of a child against the wishes of the natural father who complained that this violated his rights under Article 8. The applicant was the father of a daughter by his unmarried partner. The relationship had broken down shortly after the mother had become pregnant. The father visited the newborn baby at the nursing home where she was born, but was subsequently denied access when he tried to visit the child at the home of his former partner's parents. The mother made arrangements for the child to be adopted, and she was subsequently placed by a registered adoption society with prospective adoptive parents. The applicant was advised of these actions by letter from his former partner after the child had been placed with the prospective adoptive parents.

The applicant sought appointment from the courts as guardian of the child, and to be granted custody of the child. A decision by the courts to appoint the applicant guardian and to award him custody of the child was appealed by the mother and the prospective adoptive parents. In the meantime the child remained with the adoptive parents. Following a decision in favour of the father, a case was stated for the opinion of the Irish Supreme Court. The majority decision of the Supreme Court was that only married fathers were entitled to apply to be appointed as guardian, and the matter was referred back to the High Court. The decision was that the child should remain with the adoptive parents. An adoption order was subsequently made in respect of the child.

Noting that the birth of the child was not the result of casual sex but 'was the fruit of a planned decision taken in the context of a loving relationship' the Court concluded that there was family life in this case.[74] The question was whether a process of adoption which allowed no involvement by the father could be justified.

The Court said:

The fact that Irish law permitted the secret placement of the child for adoption without the applicant's knowledge or consent, leading to the bonding of the child with the proposed adopters and to the subsequent making of the adoption order, amounted to an interference with his right to respect for family life. Such interference is permissible only if the conditions set out in paragraph 2 of Article 8 are satisfied.[75]

The Court had little difficulty in concluding that the procedure could not be justified by the limitations in paragraph (2). The Court was clearly influenced

---

[73] *Keegan* v. *Ireland*, Judgment of 26 May 1994, Series A, No. 290; (1994) 18 EHRR 342.
[74] Paras. 44–5 of the judgment.
[75] Para. 51 of the judgment.

by the existence of a sequence of events the outcome of which 'was likely to prove to be irreversible'.[76]

IMMIGRATION ISSUES

Action by the authorities, such as expelling a person from a country, or refusing to admit someone, may result in separation of husband and wife, or of parents and children. In the first type of situation, when expulsion or refusal of admission is the source of the complaint, that action in itself cannot constitute a breach of the Convention. The Convention does not guarantee, at any rate outside the Fourth Protocol, any right to reside in a particular country.[77] But, as in the *East African Asians* cases,[78] the question may arise whether, for example, a refusal of admission does not infringe some other right which is guaranteed. Thus, while the right to reside in a particular country is not, as such, guaranteed by the Convention, it is necessary to examine complaints of expulsion or of refusal of admission in relation to Article 8 where such a measure might disrupt the family unit.

There have, for example, been many cases where the applicant complains of being separated from his wife as a result of his expulsion from the country where they lived together, or as a result of his not being allowed entry or permanent admission to the country in which she lives. In such cases the Court (and, in its time, the Commission) has first examined whether there existed an effective family life between the members of the family concerned. This normally requires two elements: a close relationship; and one between persons who have been living together at the time of, or shortly before, the alleged interference.

The relationship between an uncle and a nephew or niece is not sufficiently close, at least in a case where they are not and have not been living in the same household.[79] The only cases which have been regarded as constituting a close relationship for this purpose are the relationship of husband and wife;[80] and of parent and child where there is some situation of dependence.

[76] Para. 55 of the judgment.

[77] See ch. 7.

[78] Apps. 4403–19/70, 4422/70, 4434/70, 4476–8/70, 4486/70, 4501/70, 4526–30/70, *East African Asians* v. *United Kingdom*, Decision of the Commission, 10 and 18 October 1970, (1970) 13 *Yearbook* 928; Report of the Commission, 14 December 1973, (1994) 78-A DR 5; Committee of Ministers' Resolution DH(77)2 of 21 October 1977, (1977) 20 *Yearbook* 642; and Committee of Ministers' Resolution DH(94)30 of 21 March 1994, (1994) 78-A DR 70, deciding to make the Report of the Commission public at the request of the UK Government.

[79] App. 3110/67, *X* v. *Federal Republic of Germany*, 19 July 1968, (1968) 11 *Yearbook* 494, at 518.

[80] As in Apps. 4403–19/70, 4422/70, 4434/70, 4476–8/70, 4486/70, 4501/70, 4526–30/70, *East African Asians* v. *United Kingdom*, Decision of the Commission, 10 and 18 October 1970, (1970) 13 *Yearbook* 928;

However, even if a sufficiently close relationship exists, it does not follow that expulsion, or refusal of admission, will constitute an interference with the right to respect for family life.

The Court will consider whether the family unit could not be preserved by establishing the family's residence in the country to which the member of the family is to be expelled, or from which he seeks admission. If it could, then the State has not interfered with the right to respect for family life. Such a limitation on the notion of interference is necessary; for otherwise there would be an effective prohibition on expulsion, and on refusal of admission, whenever family life was established.

If, however, it is doubtful whether the family could establish itself elsewhere, then the complaint must be examined on the merits. This was the situation in two applications in the first group of *East African Asians* cases.[81] In each of the two, the applicant had been refused permission to enter the United Kingdom from Uganda to join his wife, who had lawfully entered the United Kingdom, in one case with six children, some time previously. The complaints were declared admissible, but shortly afterwards all the applicants in this group of cases were admitted for permanent residence.

The conclusion seems to be that the Convention does not *guarantee* the right to family life in a particular country, but only an effective family life as such, no matter where. This principle, however, appears to be modified in the case of the relationships between parents and their children if the latter are not admitted to the country where the former have their residence.

It would seem to follow that, while the admission of a person to permanent residence may not imply any obligation to admit the spouse (present or future), it may imply an obligation to admit any dependent children. The issue of the admission of spouses of those permanently settled was raised by the Court in the *Abdulaziz, Cabales and Balkandali* cases[82] where three women applicants lawfully and permanently settled in the United Kingdom who had subsequently married husbands from their countries of origin complained that the refusal of the British authorities to permit their husbands to join them in the United Kingdom constituted a violation of Article 8. In the face of a submission from

Report of the Commission, 14 December 1973 (1994) 78-A DR 5; Committee of Ministers' Resolution DH(77)2 of 21 October 1977, (1977) 20 *Yearbook* 642; and Committee of Ministers' Resolution DH(94)30 of 21 March 1994, (1994) 78-A DR 70, and App. 5269/71, *X and Y* v. *United Kingdom*, 8 February 1972, (1972) 39 CD 104.

[81] Apps. 4403–19/70, 4422/70, 4434/70, 4476–8/70, 4486/70, 4501/70, 4526–30/70, *East African Asians* v. *United Kingdom*, Decision of the Commission, 10 and 18 October 1970, (1970) 13 *Yearbook* 928, at 1004; see also Report of the Commission, 14 December 1973, (1994) 78-A DR 5; Committee of Ministers Resolution DH(77)2 of 21 October 1977, (1977) 20 *Yearbook* 642; and Committee of Ministers Resolution DH(94)30 of 21 March 1994, (1994) 78-A DR 70.

[82] *Abdulaziz, Cabales and Balkandali* v. *United Kingdom*, Judgment of 28 May 1985, Series A, No. 94; (1985) 7 EHRR 471.

the United Kingdom that the issue raised concerned immigration control for which Protocol 4 (to which the United Kingdom is not a party) alone made provision, the Court stated that the Convention and its Protocols must be read as a whole; it did not follow that because a State had not ratified a part of the Convention concerned with immigration that those parts of the Convention to which they were a party and which touched on measures taken in that field would not be applicable. The Court noted that the nature of the application was that the wives (who were settled in the United Kingdom) were complaining that they were threatened with deprivation of the society of their spouses.

The United Kingdom advanced two further arguments. First, there was no family life to protect, since the couples had never established homes together; and, secondly, there was no obstacle to the couples living together in the countries of their husband's residence and the claim was, in effect, a claim to choose their country of residence. The Court recalled that it had said in the *Marckx* case[83] that Article 8 presupposes the existence of a family, but considered that marriage established a family life between husband and wife that was protected by the Convention even if the couple had not yet set up home together. Cohabitation was seen as a normal incident of marriage; all three couples had cohabited, and one had a son. This was sufficient to establish the family life protected by the article. The Court, differing from the Commission, went on to consider whether there was a violation of Article 8 taken alone in these circumstances. The Court confirmed that in the circumstances presented by the applicants, there was no violation of Article 8 taken alone:

The duty imposed by Article 8 cannot be considered as extending to a general obligation on the part of a Contracting State to respect the choice by married couples of the country of their matrimonial residence and to accept the non-national spouses for settlement in that country.[84]

A final point that has arisen in some of these cases is whether the immigration laws involve an element of discrimination based on sex which might raise an issue under Article 14 taken together with Article 8. In the United Kingdom, as in other European countries, the rule is frequently applied that a woman may normally be admitted to join her husband, but that only exceptionally may a man be admitted to join his wife. In the *East African Asians* cases, the Government submitted that the place of residence of a family is normally the place of residence of the husband, and that Article 8 does not safeguard any right for husband and wife to live together permanently in any other place than the place of residence of the husband, or at a place where he is entitled to be.[85] The

---

[83] *Marckx* v. *Belgium*, Judgment of 13 June 1979, Series A, No. 31; (1979–80) 2 EHRR 330.
[84] *Abdulaziz, Cabales and Balkandali* v. *United Kingdom*, Judgment of 28 May 1985, Series A, No. 94; (1985) 7 EHRR 471, para. 68 of the judgment.
[85] (1970) 13 *Yearbook* 928, at 978, cf. 1004.

question is whether such differential treatment of men and women in this field is justifiable under Article 14, or whether it constitutes discrimination under that Article.

The question of discrimination on grounds of sex was also raised in the *Abdulaziz, Cabales and Balkandali* cases[86] since it was easier for a man settled in the United Kingdom to be joined by his wife than for a woman to be joined by her husband. The Court found a violation of Article 8 taken together with Article 14.

Where a marriage ends, immigration issues can arise. In the *Berrehab* case[87] a Moroccan national became divorced from his Dutch wife; the couple had a daughter who was born after the couple had ceased living together, though Mr Berrehab saw her regularly over a number of years. Following the divorce, he was then refused a residence permit and complained that this violated his family life under Article 8. The Court held that Article 8 was applicable and rejected an argument that Berrehab could travel from Morocco to the Netherlands to see his daughter. The Dutch authorities relied on the exception in paragraph (2) in the interests of public order. The Court concluded that the exclusion of Berrehab in these circumstances was excessive in protecting public order and so constituted a violation of Article 8.

The interests of preserving family life may also be relevant when decisions to deport someone arise. In the *Moustaquim* case[88] the applicant, a Moroccan national who had lived in Belgium since the age of 2, was successful in arguing that deportation would interfere with his family life by depriving him of contact with his parents and brothers and sisters.[89]

The Court's case law has been recapitulated in *Gül* v. *Switzerland.*[90] The applicant was a Turkish national who unsuccessfully sought political asylum in Switzerland. While the application was under consideration, his wife was permitted to join him on humanitarian grounds and received medical treatment in Switzerland. Subsequently a daughter was born in Switzerland; this child was placed in a home because the mother's medical condition was such that she could not care for her. Indeed, her medical condition was such that a Swiss doctor considered that a return to Turkey by the mother might prove fatal to her. The applicant, his wife, and their daughter were permitted to remain in Switzerland on humanitarian grounds. The applicant asked for his two sons to

[86] *Abdulaziz, Cabales and Balkandali* v. *United Kingdom,* Judgment of 28 May 1985, Series A, No. 94; (1985) 7 EHRR 471.
[87] *Berrehab* v. *Netherlands,* Judgment of 21 June 1988, Series A, No. 138; (1989) 11 EHRR 322.
[88] *Moustaquim* v. *Belgium,* Judgment of 18 February 1991, Series A, No., 193; (1991) 13 EHRR 802.
[89] See also *Beldjoudi* v. *France,* Judgment of 26 March 1992, Series A, No. 234-A; (1992) 14 EHRR 801; *Djeroud* v. *France,* Judgment of 23 January 1991, Series A, No. 191-B; (1992) 14 EHRR 68; and *Boughanemi* v. *France* (App. 22070/93) Judgment of 24 April 1996; (1996) 22 EHRR 228.
[90] *Gül* v. *Switzerland* (App. 23218/94), Judgment of 19 February 1996; (1996) 22 EHRR 93, para. 38 of the judgment.

be permitted to join the family in Switzerland; one son was over 18 and did not come within the Swiss rules governing family reunion. The younger son had lived in Turkey since his birth in January 1983, and, after his mother moved to Switzerland in 1987, had lived with his grandfather. He had been visited several times by his father. The applicant claimed that the refusal to permit the younger son to join the family in Switzerland violated his right to respect for his family life under Article 8. The Court recalled that the essential object of Article 8 was to protect the individual against arbitrary action by public authorities, and noted that this might involve both positive as well as negative obligations. The boundary between these two types of obligations does not lend itself to precise definition; in both contexts, however, the objective was to strike a fair balance between the competing interests of the individual and of the community as a whole. The Court continued:

The present case concerns not only family life but also immigration and the extent of a State's obligation to admit to its territory relatives of settled immigrants will vary according to the particular circumstances of the persons involved and the general interest. As a matter of well-established international law and subject to its treaty obligations, a State has the right to control the entry of non-nationals into its territory.

Moreover, where immigration is concerned, Article 8 cannot be considered to impose on a State a general obligation to respect the choice by married couples of the country of their matrimonial residence and to authorise family reunion in its territory.

The majority of the Court concluded that there had been no breach of Article 8(1) in this case. The minority concluded that there was an interference with family life, that the interference was in accordance with law in the interests of the economic well-being of the country, but that the refusal to permit the son to join the family in Switzerland was not proportionate. The couple and their daughter had become integrated in Switzerland, and the balance of humanity required that the son be permitted to come to Switzerland rather than that the family in Switzerland return to Turkey.

Where migrants have become integrated into their countries of residence as part of a family, the ability of the host country to deport them is, however, likely to become heavily circumscribed.[91] *Lamguindaz v. United Kingdom*[92] was a friendly settlement in which the United Kingdom withdrew a threat of deportation in the case of a Moroccan citizen who had lived since the age of 7 with his parents in the United Kingdom and who had acquired a string of convictions for offences of violence at the lesser end of the spectrum of seriousness. The Commission had concluded that the deportation order was a violation of

---

[91] See R. Cholewinski, 'Strasbourg's "Hidden Agenda"? The Protection of Second-Generation Migrants from Expulsion under Art. 8 of the ECHR' (1994) 3 NQHR 287.

[92] *Lamguindaz v. United Kingdom*, Judgment of 28 June 1993, Series A, No.258-C; (1994) 17 EHRR 213.

Article 8 since the hardship its execution would involve was such that it could only be justified as proportionate in exceptional circumstances.

Perhaps more significantly in *Nasri* v. *France*,[93] the Court ruled that execution of a deportation order against an Algerian national who was deaf and without speech from birth, who had lived virtually all his life in France with his parents and eight siblings, who was illiterate, could not read and did not know a recognized sign language, but who had been convicted of gang rape, would be disproportionate in the exceptional circumstances of the particular case. But in the *Bensaid* case,[94] the Court found no violation of Article 8 in a case involving a person with a mental illness who argued that removal would necessarily result in the loss of the treatment he was receiving under the public health system in the United Kingdom with serious adverse consequences for his mental health. The Court accepted that mental health is an element of private life, but concluded that the risk of damage to the applicant's health by his removal to Algeria was based largely on hypothetical factors and it was not established that his moral integrity would be substantially effected to a degree falling within the scope of Article 8.[95]

PERSONAL INTEGRITY

NAMES

Some international conventions make explicit reference to names.[96] The European Convention is silent on this issue, but both the Commission and the Court have held that regulation of names falls within the ambit of family and private life. In the *Burghartz* case,[97] the applicants were Swiss nationals who had married in Germany. They chose the wife's last name, Burghartz, as their family name under the provisions of the German Civil Code. On returning to Switzerland, they applied to use Burghartz as their family name, and Mr Burghartz sought to use the name Schnyder Burghartz. The applications were turned down. Under Swiss law, the wife was permitted to use her family name

[93] *Nasri* v. *France*, Judgment of 13 July 1995, Series A, No 324; (1996) 21 EHRR 458. See also *Ezzouhdi* v. *France* (App. 47160/99), Judgment of 6 February 2001; and *Boultif* v. *Switzerland* (App. 54273/00), Judgment of 2 August 2001; (2001) 33 EHRR 1179.
[94] *Bensaid* v. *United Kingdom* (App. 44599/98), Judgment of 6 February 2001; (2001) 33 EHRR 205.
[95] Paras. 46–9 of the judgment.
[96] Art. 24(2) of the International Covenant on Civil and Political Rights, Articles 7 and 8 of the Convention on the Rights of the Child, and Art. 18 of the American Convention on Human Rights. For a Community law case concerning names, see Case C-168/91, *Konstantinidis* v. *Altensteig-Standesamt*, [1993] ECR I-2755.
[97] *Burghartz* v. *Switzerland*, Judgment of 22 February 1994, Series A, No 280-B; (1994) 18 EHRR 101.

before that of her husband. An appeal in respect of the use of the name Burghartz as the family name succeeded, but Mr Burghartz was denied the use of his family name before Burghartz.

The Court ruled that a person's name as a means of personal identification and of linking to a family concerns family and private life under Article 8. Nevertheless the State has an interest in regulating the use of names. In this case, the different treatment accorded to men and women in the use of names constituted a violation of Article 8 taken in conjunction with the non-discrimination provision in Article 14.[98]

In another case[99] a Finnish national challenged the refusal of the Finnish authorities to permit him to change his last name. The Court considered whether there was an interference in this case, and noted that there is a distinction between a situation in which the State refuses to permit a name to be changed and in which the State requires a name to be changed. The distinction is between the positive and negative obligations of States under the Convention. The Court went on:

Despite the increased use of personal identity numbers in Finland and in other Contracting States, names retain a crucial role in the identification of people. Whilst therefore recognizing that there may exist genuine reasons prompting an individual to wish change his or her name, the Court accepts that legal restrictions on such a possibility may be justified in the public interest; for example in order to ensure accurate population registration or to safeguard the means of personal identification and of linking the bearers of a given name to a family.[100]

In the absence of common ground between the Contracting States, the Court allowed Finland a wide margin of appreciation. There was no interference with the rights in Article 8(1) in this case because the sources of inconvenience to the applicant were not sufficient to raise an issue of failure to respect his private life; there were also alternative names which the authorities would have permitted him to use.

SCHOOL DISCIPLINE

The use of corporal punishment in schools has been examined by the Court in a number of complaints of violations of Article 3.[101] But comments in the *Costello-Roberts* case[102] suggest that certain aspects of schooling and school discipline might attract protection under Article 8 additional to that afforded

---

[98] See ch. 18.
[99] *Stjerna* v. *Finland*, Judgment of 25 November 1994, Series A, No. 299-B; (1997) 24 EHRR 195.
[100] Para. 39 of the judgment.
[101] See ch. 5, above.
[102] *Costello-Roberts* v. *United Kingdom*, Judgment of 25 March 1993, Series A, No. 247-C; (1994) 19 EHRR 112.

by Article 3. The Court recognized that even the act of 'sending a child to school necessarily involved some degree of interference with his or her private life', though it is not clear that such interference would entail adverse effects for the person's physical or moral integrity. Indeed, in this case the Court concluded that the disciplinary regime at the independent preparatory boarding school, which included the possibility of being beaten on the bottom with a rubber-soled gym shoe, did not come within the scope of the prohibition in Article 8. The dissenting opinions of four judges took the view that 'the protection afforded by Article 8 to the applicant's physical integrity is not wider than that contemplated by Article 3. In view of the division of opinion within the Court, it must be seriously doubted whether, in relation to questions of physical integrity, Article 8 affords a wider protection than that afforded by Article 3.'[103]

HOMOSEXUALITY

In early decisions the Commission recognized that laws prohibiting homosexual behaviour constituted an interference with the right to respect for private life; it considered, however, that such interference was justified under paragraph (2) as being 'for the protection of health and morals'. The Commission further held that Article 14 of the Convention, which prohibits discrimination between men and women in the enjoyment of the rights guaranteed, did not preclude treating men in this area differently from women. In later cases, the Commission has held that homosexual relationships fall within the ambit of private life.[104]

In the *Dudgeon* case[105] the applicant complained that under the law in force in Northern Ireland he was liable to criminal prosecution on account of his homosexual conduct and that he had experienced fear, suffering, and psychological distress directly caused by the very existence of the laws in question, including fear of harassment and blackmail. He further complained that, following a search of his house, he was questioned by the police about certain homosexual activities and that personal papers belonging to him were seized during the search and not returned until more than a year later.

Dudgeon alleged that, in breach of Article 8, he had thereby suffered, and

---

[103] Though the statement in *Costello-Roberts* was repeated in *Raninen* v. *Finland* (App. 20972/92), Judgment of 16 December 1997; (1998) 26 EHRR 563, para. 63 of the judgment. The applicant's complaint was that he had been handcuffed while being transported from prison to a military hospital and argued that the only purpose of the handcuffing was to degrade and frighten him. The application under Art. 8 was dismissed.

[104] App. 11716/85, *X* v. *United Kingdom*, 14 May 1986, (1986) 47 DR 274.

[105] *Dudgeon* v. *United Kingdom*, Judgment of 22 October 1981, Series A, No. 45; (1982) 4 EHRR 149.

continued to suffer, an unjustified interference with his right to respect for his private life. In Northern Ireland, but not, as a result of changes in the law, elsewhere in the United Kingdom, the offences were committed whether the act took place in public or in private, whatever the age or relationship of the participants involved, and whether or not the participants consented. The Court said:

[T]he maintenance in force of the impugned legislation constitutes a continuing interference with the applicant's right to respect for his private life (which includes his sexual life) within the meaning of Article 8, paragraph (1). In the personal circumstances of the applicant, the very existence of this legislation continuously and directly affects his private life . . . either he respects the law and refrains from engaging—even in private with consenting male partners—in prohibited sexual acts to which he is disposed by reason of his homosexual tendencies, or he commits such acts and thereby become liable to criminal prosecution.[106]

The question was whether the interference was justified under paragraph (2). There was no doubt that the limitation was in accordance with the law, but a more contentious issue was whether the prohibition in the law of Northern Ireland was 'necessary in a democratic society' as for 'the protection of morals' or the 'protection of the rights and freedoms of others'. The Court accepted that some degree of regulation of male homosexual conduct, as indeed of other forms of sexual conduct, by means of the criminal law can be justified as 'necessary in a democratic society', and recalled that the national authorities have a margin of appreciation in assessing this necessity. Nevertheless, any restriction must be proportionate to the legitimate aim pursued. This was particularly striking in a situation where the law of Great Britain and Northern Ireland differed, even though they were constituent parts of the same State. Despite the acknowledged conservatism of society in Northern Ireland, as compared to other parts of the United Kingdom, the Court did not consider that there remained any justification for keeping the prohibitory law on the statute book. The Court did not consider that decriminalization implied approval of the conduct regulated previously by the criminal law. Taking all the circumstances into account, the maintenance in force of the criminal sanctions for homosexual conduct between adult males in private was disproportionate to the aims sought to be achieved and violated Article 8 of the Convention.[107]

A similar approach was taken in the *Norris* case[108] which concerned similar legislation in effect in Ireland, and in the *Modinos* case,[109] which concerned the law of Cyprus.[110]

---

[106] Para. 41 of the judgment.   [107] Paras. 60–1 of the judgment.
[108] *Norris* v. *Ireland*, Judgment of 26 October 1988, Series A, No. 142; (1991) 13 EHRR 186.
[109] *Modinos* v. *Cyprus*, Judgment of 22 April 1993, Series A No. 259; (1994) 16 EHRR 485.
[110] See also P. van Dijk, 'The Treatment of Homosexuals under the European Convention on Human Rights' in K. Waaldijk and A. Clapham, *Homosexuality: A European Community Issue* (Dordrecht, 1993), at p. 179.

Two cases decided in 1999 addressed the issue of whether a discharge from the Royal Navy solely on the grounds of the applicants' homosexuality and in pursuance of the Ministry of Defence policy to exclude homosexuals from the armed forces violated their right to a private life.[111] The Court found that the exclusion of homosexuals from the armed forces was in accordance with law, and could be said to be in the interests of national security and for the prevention of disorder, but concluded that the exclusion in the case of the applicants was not necessary in a democratic society. A detailed consideration of the issue had been conducted by the British Government by its Homosexuality Assessment Policy Team (HAPT) which concluded that the policy should be maintained. The Court was clearly influenced by the policies of other Contracting Parties to the Convention. Although the margin of appreciation to the State was acknowledged, the Court considered that, where the restrictions concerned 'a most intimate part of an individual's private life', particularly serious reasons would be required before such interferences would fall within the limitations in Article 8(2).[112] These decisions are to be welcomed and show that the Court's assessment of a State's margin of appreciation requires substantiated specific examples of the risks asserted by the State which are claimed to justify an interference with private life.

In *Sutherland* v. *United Kingdom*[113] the applicant successfully argued before the Commission that United Kingdom legislation which fixed the minimum age of consent for homosexual conduct by men at the age of 18 rather than at the age of 16 which was the age of consent applicable to a woman constituted a violation of Article 8 when read with Article 14 prohibiting discrimination.[114] The Commission concluded that this was so. The case was subsequently struck out of the list following amendment of the United Kingdom legislation on the age of consent for homosexuals.[115]

The issue of the criminalization of specific sexual practices of some homosexual men was considered in the *Laskey, Jaggard and Brown* case.[116] Three men were convicted of assault and wounding arising from sadomasochistic practices between consenting adults and taking place wholly in private. The men argued that the decision of the House of Lords refusing a defence of consent to the practices in which they had engaged constituted violations of their right to respect for their private life. No justification for the interference could be

---

[111] *Smith and Grady* v. *United Kingdom* (Apps. 33985/96 and 33986/96), Judgment of 27 September 1999; (2000) 29 EHRR 493; and *Lustig-Prean and Beckett* v. *United Kingdom* (Apps. 31417/96 and 32377/96), Judgment of 27 September 1999; (2000) 29 EHRR 548.

[112] *Smith and Grady*, para. 89 of the judgment; *Lustig-Prean*, para. 82 of the judgment.

[113] *Sutherland* v. *United Kingdom* (App. 25186/94), Judgment of 27 March 2001.

[114] On Article 14, see ch. 19.

[115] Sexual Offences (Amendment) Act 2000 which entered into force on 8 January 2001.

[116] *Laskey, Jaggard and Brown* v. *United Kingdom* (Apps. 21627/93, 21826/93 and 21974/93), Judgment of 19 February 1997; (1997) 24 EHRR 39.

sustained under the Convention. They also argued that there was discrimination in comparison to other acts likely to cause greater harm and cited the availability of the defence of consent in the sport of boxing as an example.

The Court accepted that the regulation of the conduct in question was in accordance with law, and that it could be said to be for the protection of health or morals. Some hesitation can be detected in the decision of the majority, which noted that, although sexual orientation and activity concern an intimate aspect of private life, 'not every sexual activity carried out behind closed doors necessarily falls within the scope of private life'.[117] However, the Court proceeded on the assumption that the activities in issue formed part of private life. Given the nature of the activities, the Court allowed the State a wider margin of appreciation since the activities involved the infliction of physical harm; it did not matter that the context was in the course of sexual conduct. The Court rejected the suggestion by the applicants that they had been singled out because they were homosexuals, noting the comment of the trial judge that the unlawful conduct would be dealt with equally whether it arose between homosexuals, heterosexuals or bisexuals.[118] The Court of Human Rights concluded that the measures were necessary in a democratic society for the protection of health, and did not find it necessary to address the issue of whether the interference could also be justified for the protection of morals.

The case may usefully be contrasted with *ADT* v. *United Kingdom*.[119] This case involved the prosecution for gross indecency of a male homosexual arising from sexual conduct[120] involving up to four other men which had been recorded on videotape for the private use of the applicant. Here the Court has no difficulty categorizing the activity as falling within the private life of those involved. It was appropriate to apply a narrow margin of appreciation; 'the absence of any public health considerations and the purely private nature of the behaviour'[121] did not justify the application of criminal sanctions. The Court was unanimous in finding that there had been a violation of Article 8.

Whereas the Court has found it relatively easy to require the decriminalization of homosexual conduct between consenting adults in private because of the general consensus on this issue among the Contracting Parties, they felt less comfortable when dealing with the extreme forms of sexual gratification in issue in the *Laskey* case, and can be criticized for responding with extreme caution.[122] In so far as the fact that the conduct was recorded on videotape may

---

[117] Para. 36 of the judgment. In a short and trenchant concurring opinion, Judge Pettiti concludes that Article 8 was not applicable in this case.

[118] Para. 47 of the judgment.

[119] *ADT* v. *United Kingdom* (App. 35765/97), Judgment of 31 July 2000; (2001) 31 EHRR 33.

[120] Oral sex and mutual masturbation.

[121] *ADT*, para. 38 of the judgment.

[122] See L. Moran, '*Laskey* v. *The United Kingdom*: Learning the Limits of Privacy' (1998) 61 MLR 77.

have been relevant, that seems not now to be significant in the light of the decision in *ADT*. That must be right.

TRANSSEXUALS

INTRODUCTION

Transsexuals[123] have long sought to use Article 8 to secure more favourable treatment in some of the Contracting States. This line of cases provides an excellent case study of both the interpretation of the Convention as a living instrument and the development of positive obligations for Contracting Parties under the European Convention.

The first case to come to the Court was the *Van Oosterwijck* case,[124] in which the Commission had found a violation of Article 8 resulting from the refusal of the Belgian authorities to make changes to his birth certificate. The Court, however, concluded that Van Oosterwijck had not exhausted his domestic remedies and declared the application inadmissible for this reason.

The non-recognition for legal purposes of a post-operative transsexual's new sexual identity was next raised in the *Rees* case.[125] The applicant had been born with the physical and biological characteristics of a girl and was named Brenda Margaret. Following drug therapy which accentuated the male characteristics which had become apparent, the applicant changed his name to Brendan Mark Rees, and later to Mark Nicholas Alban Rees. He underwent gender reassignment surgery. He sought unsuccessfully on several occasions to obtain a passport showing his new gender identity[126] and to have an alteration made in the register of births. The Court faced the difficulty that the case concerned the positive duty of the State to set in place legislation recognizing certain rights for transsexuals. The Court said:

In determining whether or not a positive obligation exists, regard must be had to the fair balance that has to be struck between the general interest of the community and the interest of the individual, the search for which balance is inherent in the whole of the Convention.[127]

---

[123] See Council of Europe and the International Commission on Civil Status, *Transsexualism in Europe* (Strasbourg, 2000).

[124] *Van Oosterwijck v. Belgium*, Judgment of 6 November 1980, Series A, No. 40; (1981) 3 EHRR 557.

[125] *Rees v. United Kingdom*, Judgment of 17 October 1986, Series A, No. 106; (1987) 9 EHRR 56.

[126] He was allowed to use his new names, but denied the title 'Mr'.

[127] *Rees v. United Kingdom*, Judgment of 17 October 1986, Series A, No. 106; (1987) 9 EHRR 56, para. 37 of the judgment. See also App. 10622/83, *J v. United Kingdom*, Report of the Commission, 15 December 1988, (1989) 61 DR 37, confirmed by the Committee of Ministers, Resolution DH(89)17, 15 June 1989, (1989) 61 DR 49.

In the absence of any common ground between the Contracting States, the Court did not feel able to conclude that the treatment accorded to Mark Rees constituted a violation of Article 8. The Court revisited this issue four years later in the *Cossey* case[128] whose facts were not materially distinguishable from those of the *Rees* case (save that this case concerned a male-to-female gender reassignment). The outcome and reasoning were essentially the same as in the *Rees* case, though the majorities had shifted. In the *Rees* case, the Court had held by twelve votes to three that there was no violation. By 1990 the majority had become ten votes to eight, and offered a ray of hope to transsexuals:

[The Court] is conscious of the seriousness of the problems facing transsexuals and the distress they suffer. Since the Convention always has to be interpreted and applied in the light of current circumstances, it is important that the need for appropriate legal measures in this area should be kept under review.[129]

In a case brought against France[130] a male-to-female transsexual sought rectification of the civil status register and her official identity documents. She also experienced difficulties in her business life in that many invoices and cheques indicated her original gender. The accommodation by France of the difficulties faced by transsexuals was much less than that of the United Kingdom, which provided a ground for distinguishing the *Rees* and *Cossey* cases. The Court considered that the totality of the situation in which B found herself was not consistent with respect for family life. Since the case concerned positive obligations, the Court was not willing to specify the ways in which the French Government should take action to remedy the violations which had been found by changes to its laws.

The most recent case is *Sheffield and Horsham* v. *United Kingdom*.[131] The applicants were male-to-female transsexuals who complained of the many situations in the United Kingdom in which disclosure of the gender recorded at birth would be required. These it was argued constituted interferences in their private lives contrary to Article 8. It was common ground that the issue in the case was whether the United Kingdom had failed to comply with its positive obligation to ensure respect for private life. Though the applications were couched in wider terms than in the *Rees* and *Cossey* cases, the Court did not find that there had been 'noteworthy scientific developments in the area of transsexualism' nor were they fully satisfied that legislative trends established the existence of a common European approach to the problems created by the

---

[128] *Cossey* v. *United Kingdom*, Judgment of 27 September 1990, Series A, No. 184; (1991) 13 EHRR 622.

[129] Para. 42 of the judgment.

[130] *B.* v. *France*, Judgment of 25 March 1992, Series A, No. 232-C; (1994) 16 EHRR 1.

[131] *Sheffield and Horsham* v. *United Kingdom* (Apps. 22885/93 and 23390/94), Judgment of 30 July 1998; (1999) 27 EHRR 163. See also *X, Y and Z* v. *United Kingdom* (App. 21830/93), Judgment of 22 April 1997; (1997) 24 EHRR 143.

recognition of post-operative gender status.[132] For these reasons the Court did not depart from its decisions in *Rees* and *Cossey*. Examination of the State's margin of appreciation led to the conclusion that the indignities suffered by the applicants as a result of the position adopted by the United Kingdom were not of sufficient seriousness to call into question the position of the United Kingdom. There was no violation of Article 8. The Court did, however, criticize the United Kingdom for failing to keep the need for appropriate legal measures in this area under review in the light of scientific and societal developments, and stressed the importance of all States doing so.[133] Strong and detailed dissenting judgments took a different view and would have found a violation of Article 8 in this case.

MARRIAGE AND TRANSSEXUALS

Both the *Rees* and *Cossey* cases had raised the issue of the right of transsexuals to marry and had alleged a violation of Article 12. In the *Rees* case, the Court said:

The right to marry guaranteed by Article 12 refers to the traditional marriage between persons of opposite biological sex. This appears also from the wording of the Article which makes it clear that Article 12 is mainly concerned to protect marriage as the basis of the family.[134]

The formulation of reasons had changed somewhat by 1990 in the *Cossey* case, but not enough to produce a different result:

Although some Contracting States would now regard as valid a marriage between a person in Miss Cossey's situation and a man, the developments which have occurred to date ... cannot be said to evidence any general abandonment of the traditional concept of marriage. .... Attachment to the traditional concept of marriage provides sufficient reason for the continued adoption of biological criteria for determining a person's sex for the purpose of marriage, this being encompassed within the power of the Contracting State to regulate by national law the exercise of the right to marry.[135]

The issue was also raised in the *Sheffield and Horsham* case, which constitutes a reaffirmation of the position stated in the *Cossey* case.

---

[132] Paras. 55–7 of the judgment.
[133] Para. 60 of the judgment.
[134] *Rees* v. *United Kingdom*, Judgment of 17 October 1986, Series A, No. 106; (1987) 9 EHRR 56, para. 49 of the judgment.
[135] *Cossey* v. *United Kingdom*, Judgment of 27 September 1990, Series A, No. 184; (1991) 13 EHRR 622, para. 46 of the judgment.

RECOGNITION OF PARENTHOOD

X, Y and Z v. *United Kingdom*[136] concerned X, a female-to-male transsexual, who lived in a permanent stable relationship with Y. Y underwent artificial insemination by an anonymous donor and gave birth to a child, Z. X sought registration as the father of the child. The Registrar-General advised that only a biological man could be regarded as the father for the purposes of registration, though the child could bear X's last name and that X would be entitled to a personal tax allowance in respect of the child provided he could show that he maintained the child. X went ahead and sought to register himself as the father of the child but was not permitted to do so.

In considering the complaint of a violation of Article 8, the Court considered that de facto family ties linked the three applicants and so Article 8 was applicable. The Court noted that the issues raised in this case were different from those raised in the earlier transsexual cases, and concerned recognition of parenthood in cases where there had been artificial insemination by donor. Since there was no common ground on these issues among the Member States of the Council of Europe, a wide margin of appreciation should be accorded to individual States. Had a fair balance been struck between the competing interests of the individual and those of the community as a whole? After considering the arguments on both sides, the Court concluded that there was no obligation falling on the United Kingdom formally to recognize X as the father of Z, and there was no violation of Article 8. Four dissenting judges would have found a violation of Article 8, while one further judge would have found a violation of Article 14 taken in conjunction with Article 8, and one further judge would have found violations of Article 8 and Article 14.

PRISONERS

GENERAL

Article 8 has been used as a vehicle for addressing a number of prisoners' rights, particularly the rights of correspondence of those detained in prison.[137] This justifies treating a number of issues affecting them separately from the consideration of the application of Article 8 in other contexts.

---

[136] *X, Y and Z* v. *United Kingdom* (App. 21830/93), Judgment of 22 April 1997; (1997) 24 EHRR 143.

[137] See also European Prison Rules 1987; see generally N. Loucks, *A Working Guide to Prison Rules* (London, 1993).

CORRESPONDENCE

'Correspondence' refers primarily to communication in writing.[138] Article 8 prohibits, subject to the exceptions in paragraph (2), any form of interference with correspondence, whether by censorship or otherwise. Prisoners' letters may be stopped or intercepted. There may be censorship of incoming and of outgoing letters. Or there may be a restriction on the number of letters that may be written.

The subject may be treated in two parts: restrictions on the correspondence of prisoners, and other detained persons; and restrictions on correspondence with defence counsel.

DETAINEES' CORRESPONDENCE

Often, of course, interference with prisoners' letters can be justified on one of the grounds stated in paragraph (2), as being necessary, for example, for the prevention of crime, or for the protection of the rights of others.[139]

The leading case is the *Golder* case.[140] Golder was serving a term of imprisonment for robbery. There was a riot in Parkhurst Prison and Golder was wrongly accused of being involved in it. Certain letters he wrote concerning the consequences of the allegation were stopped by the prison governor because he had not raised his complaints internally first; his petition to the Home Secretary asking for a transfer and requesting permission to consult a lawyer with a view to bringing civil proceedings in respect of the allegations against him were rejected. The effect of this was to bar him from communicating with a lawyer about his complaints. The Court concluded that there was an interference with the applicant's correspondence, and went on to consider whether the interference could be justified under the second paragraph of Article 8. The issue was whether the interference was 'necessary' for one of the grounds set out in the paragraph. This must, said the Court be considered 'having regard to the ordinary and reasonable requirements of imprisonment'.[141] The Court concluded that there was no justification for a restriction on Golder's right to communicate with a lawyer with a view to seeking advice in connection with possible civil proceedings.[142]

The position which appears to have emerged from the case law is that

---

[138] See J. E. S. Fawcett, *The Application of the European Convention on Human Rights* (Oxford, 1987), at 228.

[139] App. 3717/68, *X* v. *Ireland*, 6 February 1970, (1970) 31 CD 96.

[140] *Golder* v. *United Kingdom*, Judgment of 21 February 1975, Series A, No. 18; (1979–80) 1 EHRR 524.

[141] Para. 45 of judgment. See also *Campbell and Fell* v. *United Kingdom*, Judgment of 28 June 1984, Series A, No. 80; (1985) 7 EHRR 165.

[142] See also *Silver and others* v. *United Kingdom*, Judgment of 25 March 1983, Series A, No. 61; (1983) 5 EHRR 347.

freedom of correspondence for prisoners will be protected to a high degree. The Court requires the national law authorizing the interference to be drafted with precision in order to meet the requirement that the interference is in accordance with law.[143] The Court will also require the clearest evidence that the action taken is proportional to the aim of the limitation of freedom of correspondence. So stopping or censoring letters containing what are regarded as derogatory remarks about the prison authorities will not be justified.[144] The position is neatly summarized in the words of the Court.

The Court recognises that some measures of control over prisoners' correspondence is not of itself incompatible with the Convention, but the resulting interference must not exceed what is required by the legitimate aim pursued.[145]

In the *Campbell* case[146] Campbell, who had been convicted of assault and murder and sentenced to life imprisonment with a recommendation that he serve not less than twenty years in prison, complained that his correspondence with his lawyer concerning a number of civil matters was opened and read by the prison authorities. The Court had no difficulty in concluding that there had been an interference nor that it was in accordance with law with the aim of preventing disorder or crime. Once again the consideration came down to determining whether the interference was necessary in a democratic society. The Court saw

no reason to distinguish between the different categories of correspondence with lawyers which, whatever their purpose, concern matters of a private and confidential character. In principle, such letters are privileged under Article 8.[147]

The opening of mail might be justified to determine whether it contained any illicit enclosure, but that would not extend to reading the letter. This could be guaranteed by opening the letter in the presence of the prisoner. The reading of any letters between lawyer and prisoner could only be justified where the authorities have reasonable cause to believe that the privilege is being abused. In the *Campbell* case, the Court concluded that there was no pressing social need for the opening and reading of Campbell's correspondence with his solicitor.

It is vital to distinguish the different elements involved in 'control' of correspondence, and to differentiate quite clearly the grounds of exception permitted under Article 8(2).

Some aspects of the control of prisoners' correspondence would present no

---

[143] For examples of cases where the national law left the authorities too much latitude and so did not meet the requirement, see *Domenichini v. Italy* (App. 15943/90, Judgment of 21 October 1996; and *Petra v. Romania* (App. 27273/95), Judgment of 24 August 1998.
[144] *Pfeifer and Plankl v. Austria*, Judgment of 25 February 1992, Series A, No. 227; (1992) 14 EHRR 692.
[145] Para. 46 of judgment.
[146] *Campbell v. United Kingdom*, Judgment of 25 March 1992, Series A, No. 223; (1993) 15 EHRR 137.
[147] Para. 48 of judgment.

difficulties on this analysis. The stopping of a particular letter could obviously be justified in a particular case on one of the grounds mentioned in paragraph (2) (for example, 'for the prevention of crime') if the object of the letter were for example to effect an escape from prison. This in turn would justify, on the same ground, the reading by prison authorities of all letters, both incoming and outgoing. Finally, the fact that all letters may have to be read by prison authorities, who are responsible for good order in prisons, might in turn be said to justify the imposition of a limit to the number of letters which a prisoner may send or receive. In each case, however, the interference would have to be properly justified on one of the grounds stated in paragraph (2), and the reasons given by the authorities ascertained and assessed on this basis.

CORRESPONDENCE WITH DEFENCE COUNSEL

The correspondence of detained persons with their defence counsel is specially privileged. This follows from Article 6(3)(b) of the Convention which guarantees to everyone charged with a criminal offence the right to have adequate time and facilities for the preparation of his defence. This provision applies equally to proceedings on appeal.

The *Schönenberger and Durmaz* case[148] concerned the stopping of a letter from a lawyer instructed by the wife of Durmaz, who had been arrested and was being held in custody. Despite the letter's having been received, the district prosecutor kept it from Durmaz, who then had a lawyer assigned to him as an indigent. The lawyer's letter had urged Durmaz to make no statement to the authorities. The issue before the Court was whether the interference which had taken place was necessary in a democratic society. The Government argued that the stopping of the letter was necessary because the advice jeopardized the proper conduct of pending criminal proceedings by inviting the suspect not to make a statement. The Court noted that the advice contained in the letter was not to take any action which was not lawful; it did not pose a threat to the normal conduct of the prosecution. Nor was it relevant that the lawyer had at the time of sending the letter been instructed by Durmaz's wife. The Court was unanimous in finding that there was a violation of Article 8.

THE FAMILY LIFE OF PRISONERS

Applicants detained in prison have frequently complained of interference with the right to respect for family life. Some have complained that they have been refused permission to have visits from their children. The Commission frequently rejected such complaints under paragraph (2), for example on the

---

[148] *Schönenberger and Durmaz* v. *Switzerland*, Judgment of 20 June 1988, Series A, No. 137; (1989) 11 EHRR 202.

ground that such interference with family life was necessary for the prevention of crime.[149]

The issue was raised before the Court in the *Boyle and Rice* case in the context of a complaint of a violation of Article 13.[150] The Court said:

When assessing the obligations imposed on the Contracting States by Article 8 in relation to prison visits, regard must be had to the ordinary and reasonable requirements of imprisonment and to the resultant degree of discretion which the national authorities must be allowed in regulating a prisoner's contact with his family.[151]

The Court found that there was no arguable complaint where a prisoner in the lowest security category was allowed twelve visits a year of one hour's duration.[152]

HOUSING, PLANNING, AND ENVIRONMENTAL MATTERS

Many cases involving housing and the home will fall to be considered under Article 1 of Protocol 1.[153] But it is clear that aspects of security of tenure under landlord and tenant laws can involve issues touching on respect for the home.[154]

The leading case on housing rights under Article 8 is the *Gillow* case.[155] Mr and Mrs Gillow sought to challenge under Article 8 the restrictive system of licences for the occupation of housing on Guernsey. The couple had acquired a house on Guernsey during a period of employment there, which had subsequently been let while the couple were working elsewhere than Guernsey. They returned to occupy it, but were refused the requisite licence and were prosecuted and convicted for unlawful occupation under Guernsey law.

The Court considered that there was an interference with respect for the home, which was in accordance with law. The legislation restricting who could live on the island was accepted as having a legitimate aim. Was the interference necessary in a democratic society? The Court concluded that on its terms, there was no violation of Article 8 as far as the contested legislation *per se* was concerned. But the Court went on to consider whether the manner of its

---

[149] App. 1983/63, *X v. Netherlands*, 13 December 1965, (1966) 18 CD 19; cf. App. 2515/65, *X v. Federal Republic of Germany*, 23 May 1966, (1966) 20 CD 28.

[150] *Boyle and Rice* v. *United Kingdom*, Judgment of 27 April 1988, Series A, No 131; (1988) 10 EHRR 425.

[151] Para. 74 of the judgment.

[152] See also *Messina* v. *Italy (No. 2)* (App. 25498/94), Judgment of 28 September 2000.

[153] See ch. 15 below.

[154] See *Larkos* v. *Cyprus* (App. 29515/95), Judgment of 18 February 1999; (2000) 30 EHRR 597.

[155] *Gillow* v. *United Kingdom*, Judgment of 24 November 1986, Series A, No. 109; (1989) 11 EHRR 335.

application to Mr and Mrs Gillow violated Article 8. On the particular facts of the case, the Court concluded that the refusal of both temporary and permanent licences to occupy their home and the conviction and fine imposed were disproportionate to the legitimate aim of the legislation and so constituted a violation of Article 8.

A further series of cases has concerned the rights of gypsies. The *Buckley* case[156] concerned the refusal of planning permission to enable a gypsy to live in caravans on her own land. The Court rejected a suggestion that respect for the home was only engaged where the home had been established lawfully. A refusal of planning permission constituted an interference which was in accordance with law, and planning legislation was accepted to serve the interests of the economic well-being of the country, the protection of health, and the protection of the rights of others. In considering whether the interference is necessary in a democratic society, the Court noted, in concluding that there was no violation of Article 8, that the process by which decisions were made had to be fair:

Whenever discretion capable of interfering with the enjoyment of a Convention right such as the one at issue in the present case is conferred on national authorities, the procedural safeguards available to the individual will be especially material in determining whether the respondent State has, when fixing the regulatory framework, remained within the margin of its appreciation. Indeed, it is settled case law that, whilst Article 8 contains no explicit procedural requirements, the decision-making process leading to measures of interference must be fair and such as to afford due respect to the interests safeguarded to the individual by Article 8.[157]

Judgment was given in January 2001 in five further cases against the United Kingdom concerning planning and enforcement measures taken against gypsies in respect of their occupation on their land of caravans as their homes.[158] The cases contain a wealth of information on domestic and international texts on gypsies. The facts of the four cases were broadly similar. The applicants were gypsies by birth and had lived a travelling lifestyle. They bought land with the intention of living on it in a caravan; they moved onto the land and applied for planning permission, which was refused. Enforcement notices were served requiring the use of the land for residential purposes to cease. The Court referred to its decision in *Buckley* and noted that 'in the interests of legal certainty, foreseeability and equality before the law that it should not depart, without good reason, from precedents laid down in previous cases' though due

---

[156] *Buckley* v. *United Kingdom* (App. 20348/92), Judgment of 25 September 1996; (1997) 23 EHRR 101.
[157] Para. 76 of the judgment.
[158] *Beard* v. *United Kingdom* (App. 24882/94); (2001) 33 EHRR 442; *Chapman* v. *United Kingdom* (App. 27238/95); (2001) 33 EHRR 399; *Coster* v. *United Kingdom* (App. 24876/94); (2001) 33 EHRR 479; *Lee* v. *United Kingdom* (App. 25289/94); (2001) 33 EHRR 677; and *Smith (Jane)* v. *United Kingdom* (App. 25154/94); (2001) 33 EHRR 712; all Judgments of 18 January 2001.

regard should be had to changing conditions and any emerging consensus among the Member States of the Council of Europe.[159] The Court considered the measures in issue to affect the applicants' private and family life, and home. There had been an interference with those rights which was in accordance with law, and in the interests of protecting the rights of others. The question was therefore whether the interference was necessary in a democratic society. The applicant relied heavily on the growing international consensus about the importance of providing legal protection of the rights of minorities, and an obligation to protect their security, identity, and lifestyle. The British Government stressed the importance of planning controls in balancing the needs of the individual and the community, and that national authorities were better placed to make the necessary judgments on these issues. The Court came down in favour of the British Government; the decisions on planning matters had been taken after weighing the various competing interests, and there were adequate procedural safeguards for the applicants. The Court was influenced by the fact that the homes were initially established unlawfully, that is, without the required planning permission.[160] A dissenting opinion of seven judges would have found a violation of Article 8 on the grounds that there is an international consensus which is sufficiently concrete that gypsies require special protection in respect of their right to respect for home, private and family life, which has a dimension beyond environmental concerns. Such concerns when weighed against the interference in the applicants' rights did not disclose a pressing social need. The dissenting judges denied that their decision was tantamount to excluding gypsies from the system of planning control.

A number of complaints arising from nuisance caused by adjacent commercial activity has been made under Article 1 of Protocol 1,[161] but a better basis for complaint may be Article 8. In the *López Ostra* case[162] the applicant complained that the operations of a liquid and solid waste management plant operated by a group of tanneries 12 metres from her home which released 'gas fumes, pestilential smells and contamination' harmful to health violated respect for her home guaranteed by Article 8. The Court found that Article 8 was applicable and stressed the need to strike a fair balance between the competing interests of the individual and of the community as a whole. Despite the relatively wide margin of appreciation enjoyed by the State, this was a case where the level of nuisance borne by the applicant exceeded that which would be viewed as reasonable when weighing the competing interests.

The *Hatton* case[163] concerned complaints that the noise from night flights for

[159] *Chapman*, para. 70 of the judgment.
[160] *Chapman*, para. 102 of the judgment.
[161] See ch. 15.
[162] *López Ostra* v. *Spain*, Judgment of 9 December 1994, Series A, No. 303-C; (1995) 20 EHRR 277.
[163] *Hatton and others* v. *United Kingdom* (App. 36022/97), Judgment of 2 October 2001; (2002) 34 EHRR 1. The case has been referred for reconsideration by a Grand Chamber.

those living in the vicinity of Heathrow Airport constituted a violation of their rights under Article 8. The Court considered that this was a case in which they had to consider whether the United Kingdom Government had met its positive obligations to take reasonable and appropriate measures to secure the applicants' rights under Article 8. The Court considered the arguments put forward by the Government based on the economic benefits of night flying, but noted that 'mere reference to the economic well-being of the country is not sufficient to outweigh the rights of others' in the sensitive context of environmental questions.[164] The Court is also influenced by the absence of 'any serious attempt to evaluate the extent or impact of the interferences with the applicants' sleep patterns' and of any comprehensive and completed study aimed at finding a solution to flying needs and the needs of people for quiet at night.[165] A violation of Article 8 was found.

Guerra and others v. *Italy*[166] established that the right to respect for family life requires the State to disclose to those living in the area the dangers of serious environmental pollution which might arise from an accident at a factory classified as a high risk.

SEARCHES, SURVEILLANCE, AND PERSONAL RECORDS

A number of Article 8 cases concern respect for the home in the context of the legitimacy of searches of either the home or professional premises.

The *Chappell* case[167] challenged the use of Anton Piller orders under English law. Anton Piller orders represent a common law development of interlocutory measures in civil proceedings, *inter alia*, enabling a search of premises to take place often with the object of seizing material produced in breach of a copyright or trademark. The Court concluded that the search of the applicant's home authorized by the order constituted an interference with respect for his home. The aim, namely, to protect the rights of others, was legitimate and the order met the requirements of Article 8 as being in accordance with law. The necessary safeguards existed to ensure that action was only taken where it was necessary in a democratic society. The undertaking given by solicitors for plaintiffs seeking such an order was sufficient to ensure the proper supervision of the implementation of any order granted by the court.

The *Niemetz* case[168] concerned a search of a lawyer's office under warrant

---

[164] Paras. 97 and 101–2 of the judgment.
[165] Paras. 106–7 of the judgment.
[166] *Guerra and others* v. *Italy* (App. 14967/89), Judgment of 19 February 1998; (1998) 26 EHRR 357.
[167] *Chappell* v. *United Kingdom*, Judgment of 30 March 1989, Series A, No. 152; (1990) 12 EHRR 1.
[168] *Niemetz* v. *Germany*, Judgment of 16 December 1992, Series A, No. 251-B; (1993) 16 EHRR 97.

from the court in order to establish the true identity of a person who had signed himself Klaus Wegner which was believed to be a pseudonym. As is common in Article 8 cases, the Court concluded that the interference was in accordance with law and pursued the legitimate aid of being for the prevention of crime and the protection of the rights of others, but went on to consider whether it was necessary in a democratic society. The Court found that the interference was out of all proportion to the aim pursued, in that it impinged on professional secrecy and that searches of lawyer's offices in Germany are not surrounded by any special procedural safeguards.

The *Funke* case[169] involved consideration of the legitimacy of search of the applicants' homes by customs officers in France in connection with alleged exchange control irregularities. The Court ducked considering whether the provisions in the Customs Code violated the French Constitution, since 'the interferences complained of are incompatible with Article 8 in other respects.'[170] The aim was legitimate in that it could be said to be for the economic well-being of the country and the prevention of crime. Once again the issue came down to determination of whether the interferences were necessary in a democratic society. There must always be adequate safeguards against abuse, but this was not so in the present case. The customs authorities had very wide powers, including exclusive competence to assess the expediency, number, length, and scale of searches. There was no requirement to obtain a judicial warrant. This resulted in a situation in which the restrictions and limitations provided for in the law were too lax and full of loopholes for the interferences to be strictly proportionate to the legitimate aim pursued. The situation in the case of Funke was made worse in that the customs authorities never lodged any complaint against him alleging an offence against the exchange control regulations.

Entries and searches, including recording and retaining personal details and photographing individuals under anti-terrorist legislation are unlikely to give rise to successful complaints under Article 8, since they will normally be easily justified as measures for the prevention of crime.[171]

A group of cases has concerned the extent to which Article 8 protects the citizen from various forms of surveillance, which might include the opening or correspondence or listening to telephone communications. The *Klass* case[172] raised the question of the compatibility of German law with Article 8. The applicants objected that the German law on surveillance did not oblige the authorities to notify the persons subject to the surveillance after the event and did not provide any system of remedies for the ordering and execution of such

---

[169] *Funke and others* v. *France*, Judgment of 25 February 1993, Series A, No. 256-A; (1993) 16 EHRR 297.
[170] Para. 51 of the judgment.
[171] *Murray* v. *United Kingdom*, Judgment of 28 October 1994, Series A, No. 300-A; (1995) 19 EHRR 193.
[172] *Klass and others* v. *Germany*, Judgment of 6 September 1978, Series A, No. 28; (1979–80) 2 EHRR 214.

measures. The Court agreed with the Commission that the applicants could claim to be victims of a violation of the Convention as required under Article 25.[173] On the substantive complaint, the Court considered that telephone conversations came within the ambit of 'private life' and the concept of 'correspondence'. As in so many cases under Article 8, the Court concluded that surveillance could constitute an interference, that it was in accordance with law, and that it could serve a legitimate aim, but was the interference so arising necessary in a democratic society? The answer to this question turned on the existence and adequacy of safeguards against possible abuse. The German conditions were considered to be appropriately restrictive and to be within the State's margin of appreciation. The test laid down by the Court was as follows:

The Court must be satisfied that, whatever system of surveillance is adopted, there exist adequate and effective guarantees against abuse. This assessment has only a relative character: it depends on all the circumstances of the case, such as the nature, scope and duration of the possible measures, the grounds required for ordering such measures, the authorities competent to permit, carry out and supervise such measures, and the kind of remedy provided by the national law.[174]

The Court expressed mild concern that supervisory control was not exercised by a judge, but noted that initial control under the German legislation was effected by an 'official qualified for judicial office and by the control provided by the Parliamentary Board and the G 10 Commission'.[175] The Court concluded that, taking judicial notice of technical advances in the means of espionage and surveillance, and of the development of terrorism in Europe, the German system for controlling covert surveillance met the requirements of Article 8 of the Convention.

The *Malone* case[176] concerned the law of England and Wales on the interception of communications on behalf of the police for the purposes of the prevention and detection of crime. Interception involved both postal and telephonic communication. The practice of 'metering' also came under scrutiny. Metering involves the use of a meter check printer which registers the number dialled on a particular telephone and the time and duration of each call. It does not record speech. James Malone was an antique dealer, who was charged and convicted of handling stolen goods. The investigation had involved the interception of Malone's telephone calls. He also complained that his telephone line had been metered. At the time there was no overall statutory code governing the interception of postal and telephone communications. Metering was essentially a system by which the Post Office checked that customers were correctly

---

[173] See ch. 26.
[174] *Klass and others* v. *Germany*, Judgment of 6 September 1978, Series A, No. 28; (1979–80) 2 EHRR 214, at para. 50 of the judgment.
[175] Para. 56 of the judgment.
[176] *Malone* v. *United Kingdom*, Judgment of 2 August 1984, Series A, No. 82; (1985) 7 EHRR 14.

charged, though it was admitted in the proceedings that the Post Office did on occasion cooperate with the police in metering a telephone line if 'the information is essential to police enquiries in relation to serious crime and cannot be obtained from other sources.'[177] The absence of a proper statutory code governing interception of communications proved fatal to the Government's defence of the case. The Court said:

[I]t cannot be said with any reasonable certainty what elements of the powers to intercept are incorporated in legal rules and what elements remain within the discretion of the executive. In view of the attendant obscurity and uncertainty as to the state of the law in this essential respect, . . . the law of England and Wales does not indicate with reasonable clarity the scope and manner of exercise of the relevant discretion conferred on the public authorities. To that extent, the minimum degree of legal protection to which citizens are entitled under the rule of law in a democratic society is lacking.[178]

The interferences with James Malone's communications were therefore in breach of Article 8 in that they were not 'in accordance with the law'. The Court came to a similar conclusion in relation to the practice of metering.

The examination of the French system for authorizing telephone-tapping in the *Huvig* and *Kruslin* cases[179] revealed a system midway between that of Germany and the United Kingdom in the two cases already examined. Since the French Courts had consistently viewed various provisions of the Code of Criminal procedure as authorizing the carrying out of telephone-tapping by a senior police officer on a warrant issued by an investigating judge, the Court regarded the practice as being in accordance with law. But the Court went on to say that to be fully in accordance with the law, the quality of the law must be such as to provide safeguards against what is a serious interference with private life. The French system was very short on processes to prevent abuse, with key aspects of the process not adequately defined, such as the categories of person liable to have their telephones tapped or the nature of the offences which warranted such measures. There was consequently a violation of Article 8.[180]

Obviously a telephone tap without obtaining legal authority where such a procedure is provided for will amount to a violation of Article 8, as in one case, where a senior police officer colluded in obtaining a recording of a telephone conversation in a manner inconsistent with the requirements of French law.[181]

In two cases since the *Klass* case, the Court has decided that surveillance did

---

[177] Para. 56 of the judgment.
[178] Para. 79 of the judgment.
[179] *Huvig* v. *France*, Judgment of 24 April 1990, Series A, No. 176-B; (1990) 12 EHRR 528; and *Kruslin* v. *France*, Judgment of 24 April 1990, Series A, No. 176-B; (1990) 12 EHRR 547. See also *Valenzuela Contreras* v. *Spain* (App. 27671/95); (1999) 28 EHRR 483 for a recapitulation of the case law.
[180] See also *Herczegfalvy* v. *Austria*, Judgment of 24 September 1992, Series A, No. 242-B; (1993) 15 EHRR 437, para. 91 of the judgment.
[181] *A* v. *France*, Judgment of 23 November 1993, Series A, No. 277-B; (1994) 17 EHRR 462.

not constitute a violation of Article 8. The *Leander* case[182] concerned the 'personnel control procedure' applicable to navy employees in Sweden, which had resulted in his being found unsuitable for particular employment. That procedure involved the maintenance of a secret police register containing information concerning his private life. The Court found the Swedish law setting up the system sufficiently clear and precise as to its ambit to meet the requirements of the Convention that interferences with private life be in accordance with law. This left the question of whether the system was necessary in a democratic society in the interests of national security. Where national security is involved the margin allowed to the Contracting Party is a wide one, but there must nevertheless be safeguards for the citizen. There was, in fact, in this case an elaborate system of safeguards, which met the requirements of the Convention.

In the *Lüdi* case[183] the applicant complained that his telephone had been tapped and that he had been tricked by an undercover agent. Both actions had been undertaken following information received by the police that he had sought to arrange to borrow 200,000 Swiss francs while in detention in order to fund the purchase of cocaine. The Court confirmed the opinion of the Commission that the telephone interception met all the requirements of the Convention. But the Commission had considered the introduction of the undercover agent as more problematic, since it moved from passive interception to active generation of the material to be intercepted. This activity did not, in the view of the Commission, have a sufficient legal basis. The reasoning of the Court in coming to a different conclusion can be considered somewhat scanty:

The aim of the operation was to arrest the dealers when the drugs were handed over. Toni [the undercover agent] thereupon contacted the applicant, who said that he was prepared to sell him 2 kg of cocaine worth 200,000 Swiss francs. . . . Mr Lüdi must therefore have been aware from then on that he was engaged in a criminal act punishable under Article 19 of the Drugs Law and that consequently he was running the risk of encountering an undercover police officer whose task would in fact be to expose him.[184]

The *Halford* case[185] concerned the interception of telephone calls made by Alison Halford, Assistant Chief Constable of the Merseyside Police both in her office and at home. The Court rejected an argument by the British Government that Article 8 did not apply because the applicant could have no reasonable expectation of privacy in relation to calls made from her office, recalling its earlier case law as set out above. The Court concluded that telephone

---

[182] *Leander* v. *Sweden*, Judgment of 26 March 1987, Series A, No. 116; (1987) 9 EHRR 433; see also *Rotaru* v. *Romania* (App. 28341/95), Judgment of 4 May 2000; and *Khan* v. *United Kingdom* (App. 35394/97), Judgment of 12 May 2000; (2001) 31 EHRR 1016.
[183] *Lüdi* v. *Switzerland*, Judgment of 15 June 1992, Series A, No. 238; (1993) 15 EHRR 173.
[184] Para. 40 of the judgment.
[185] *Halford* v. *United Kingdom* (App. 20605/92), Judgment of 25 June 1997; (1997) 24 EHRR 523.

conversations came within the scope of 'private life' and 'correspondence' in Article 8. The interception of office telephone calls was not in accordance with law since there was no regulation of interception of calls outside the public network. The Court was not satisfied that the applicant had not proved on the balance of probabilities that there was interception of calls made from home. Accordingly there was no violation. The Court noted that the applicant was complaining of measures of surveillance actually applied to her, and not, as in *Klass*, that the very possibility of telephone interceptions violated her Article 8 rights.

The whole area of covert surveillance is one where advances in technology present increasing threats to the private life of the individual. The Court is not unaware of the need for vigilance in the light of an increasingly sophisticated technology.[186] The Court has decided that it is not only the party whose telephone line is tapped who has standing to complain, but also third parties whose conversations are intercepted.[187]

There is, however, no doubt that the storing of information concerning a person's private life in a secret police register interferes with the right to respect for private life guaranteed by Article 8.[188] The potentially pervasive extent of telephone surveillance and data collection by the State is illustrated by the facts and judgment in the *Amman* case.[189] The applicant is a businessman living in Switzerland. Among the products he sells is 'Perma Tweez', a battery-operated depilatory appliance. In October 1981 a woman telephoned the applicant from the former Soviet embassy in Berne enquiring about the product. The telephone call was intercepted by the Federal Public Prosecutor's Office, and was noted in its national security card index. The Intelligence Service was asked to carry out an investigation into the applicant and his business. The applicant learned of this in 1990, but certain passages in the copy sent to him had been deleted. It transpired that the telephone lines at the former Soviet embassy had been systematically monitored for counter-intelligence reasons. The Court found a violation of Article 8 in relation to the interception of the telephone call since it was not conducted in accordance with law. Similar conclusions were reached in relation to the creation and storage of the index card.

The *Foxley* case[190] concerned a rather different set of circumstances. Foxley had been convicted of serious offences of corruption committed while he worked as an ammunition procurement officer for the Ministry of Defence. A confiscation order for £1.5 million was made against him as his total assessed

---

[186] *Kopp* v. *Switzerland* (App. 23224/94), Judgment of 25 March 1998; (1999) 27 EHRR 91, para. 72 of the judgment. See also *PG and JH* v. *United Kingdom* (App. 44787/98), Judgment of 25 September 2001.

[187] *Lambert* v. *France* (App. 23618/94), Judgment of 24 August 1998; (2000) 30 EHRR 346.

[188] *Hewitt and Harman* v. *United Kingdom* (App. 12175/86), Judgment of 9 May 1989; (1992) 14 EHRR 657.

[189] *Amman* v. *Switzerland* (App. 27798/95), Judgment of 16 February 2000; (2000) 30 EHRR 843.

[190] *Foxley* v. *United Kingdom* (App. 33274/96), Judgment of 20 June 2000; (2001) 31 EHRR 25.

realizable assets in respect of his having benefited in the sum of £2 million from the offences. The applicant did not pay. Subsequently a Receiver and Trustee in Bankruptcy were appointed, and an order was obtained from the court for the interception of all postal packets for a three-month period. The applicant's mail was intercepted under the order for a period of nearly four months. Among the intercepted mail were communications by the applicant with his legal advisers; these letters were read and copied to the file before being forwarded to the applicant. He complained that the interception of his mail violated Article 8.

Unsurprisingly, the Court found that there was a proper legal base for the interception until the expiry of the order but not for the period of nearly one month thereafter when the applicant's mail continued to be intercepted. The applicant accepted that the interception of his mail was for a legitimate reason: the protection of the rights of others. But the applicant argued strongly that the interception and retention of copies of his correspondence with his legal advisers was not necessary in a democratic society. Even where the State is facing a situation where a person may be concealing assets to the detriment of his creditors,

the implementation of the measures must be accompanied by adequate and effective safeguards which ensure minimum impairment of the right to respect for his correspondence. This is particularly so where . . . correspondence with the bankrupt's legal advisers may be intercepted. The Court notes in this connection that the lawyer–client relationship is, in principle, privileged and correspondence in that context, whatever its purpose, concerns matters of a private and confidential nature.[191]

The duty of confidentiality in relation to records lawfully held has also been the subject of proceedings before the Court.[192] Though the disclosure of which the applicant complained (of her health records in connection with a social security claim) was found not to be a violation of Article 8, the Court noted:

The Court reiterates that the protection of personal data, particularly medical data, is of fundamental importance to a person's enjoyment of his or her right to respect for private and family life as guaranteed by Article 8 of the Convention. Respecting the confidentiality of health data is a vital principle in the legal systems of all the Contracting Parties to the Convention. It is crucial not only to respect the sense of privacy of a patient but also to preserve his or her confidence in the medical profession and in the health services in general. The domestic law must afford appropriate safeguards to prevent any such communication or disclosure of personal health data as may be inconsistent with the guarantees in Article 8 of the Convention.[193]

---

[191] Para. 43 of the judgment.
[192] *MS* v. *Sweden* (App. 20837/92), Judgment of 27 August 1997; (1999) 28 EHRR 313. See also *Z* v. *Finland* (App. 22009/93), Judgment of 25 February 1997; (1998) 25 EHRR 371.
[193] *MS* v. *Sweden*, para. 41 of the judgment.

ACCESS TO PERSONAL RECORDS

Article 8 may assist children to know and understand their childhood. Though there is no right of access to case records and a refusal of complete access does not amount to an interference with family life, nevertheless a system which allows disclosure of care records to children formerly in care only with the consent of contributors but makes no provision for considering the reasonableness of any refusal of consent will go beyond the margin permitted by the article.[194]

In the *Guerra* case,[195] the Court found a violation of a positive obligation to provide information to local residents of the dangers to those living about one kilometre away from a factory producing fertilizers which had been classified as presenting a high risk of causing severe environmental pollution with attendant health hazards. There is, in such circumstances, a positive obligation of the State to provide essential information which would enable individuals to assess the risks they and their families might face if they continued to live so close to the source of the risk.

Access to records and to personal information may well prove to be an area where the requirements of Article 8 increasingly impose positive obligations on a State. An interesting set of circumstances was presented to the Court in the *McGinley and Egan* case.[196] The applicants had been stationed on or near Christmas Island and took part in the line-up procedure[197] during atmospheric nuclear tests. They sought increases of their war pensions on the basis that they had developed medical conditions caused by their exposure to radiation. They believed that documents in the possession of the Government would assist them, but were refused access to them. They claimed that non-disclosure of records constituted an unjustifiable interference with their private lives. The Court concluded that Article 8 did apply:

Where a Government engages in hazardous activities, such as those in issue in the present case, which might have hidden adverse consequences on the health of those involved in such activities, respect for private and family life under Article 8 requires that an effective and accessible procedure be established which enables such persons to seek all relevant and appropriate information.[198]

There was, however, in this case no violation, since there was a procedure

---

[194] *Gaskin* v. *United Kingdom*, Judgment of 7 July 1989, Series A, No. 160; (1990) 12 EHRR 36.

[195] *Guerra and others* v. *Italy* (App. 14967/89), Judgment of 19 February 1998; (1998) 26 EHRR 357.

[196] *McGinley and Egan* v. *United Kingdom* (Apps. 21825/93 and 23414/94), Judgment of 9 June 1998; (1999) 27 EHRR 1.

[197] Service personnel were ordered to line up in the open and to face away from the explosions with their eyes closed and covered until twenty seconds after the blast.

[198] *McGinley and Egan* v. *United Kingdom* (Apps. 21825/93 and 23414/94), Judgment of 9 June 1998; (1999) 27 EHRR 1, para. 101 of the Judgment

under the Pension Appeal Tribunal Rules of Procedures under which the applicants could have requested the documents which had not been used.[199]

PRIVACY

It is surprising that there is so little direct authority under Article 8 on media intrusion into the private life of individuals. There would appear to be no decision of the Court directly in point. The issue was raised before the Commission by Earl and Countess Spencer in relation to press publicity surrounding the Countess's eating disorder and other matters.[200] The Press Complaints Committee subsequently found that some of the publicity breached the Code of Practice relating to privacy. The complaint of a violation of Article 8 was that the United Kingdom had failed to fulfil its obligations to protect the right to respect for private life in that it had failed to prohibit the publication and republication of information and photographs relating to the private life of the applicants. Though the applications were found to be inadmissible because of the applicants' failure to exhaust domestic remedies,[201] the Commission noted that the absence of an appropriate remedy within the national legal order to restrain publication of matters relating to private life could constitute a violation of Article 8's protection of private life. The Commission was obviously conscious in this case of the tension between the right to private life under Article 8 and freedom of expression under Article 10 of the Convention. This is, no doubt, an area where future case law from the Court of Human Rights will provide further guidance.

CONCLUDING COMMENT

The length of this chapter is testament to the very broad range of circumstances covered by the right protected by Article 8, and related provisions of the Convention. What does emerge is the primacy of family life in terms of

---

[199] A subsequent request for revision on the basis that the procedure under the Pension Appeals Tribunal rules would not have secured the relevant documents failed by 5 votes to 2: see *McGinley and Egan* v. *United Kingdom* (Apps. 21825/93 and 23414/94) (Revision request), Judgment of 28 January 2000.

[200] Apps. 28851/95 and 28852/95 *Earl Spencer and Countess Spencer* v. *United Kingdom*, 16 January 1998; (1998) 25 EHRR CD105.

[201] An action for breach of confidence.

the depth of protection afforded. In other areas, such as private life, there is much more scope for the balancing of the rights of society as a whole against the rights of the individual. Where this is the case, the existence of safeguards within the national legal order which address this balance are likely to be needed if any interference is to be regarded as being necessary in a democratic society. Cases under the article also show the operation of the Convention as a living instrument able to reflect the changing and developing attitudes and values of the Contracting Parties. It is certain that new lines of case law will emerge from the rights protected under Article 8.

12

FREEDOM OF THOUGHT, CONSCIENCE, AND RELIGION

INTRODUCTION

Article 9[1] provides:

1. Everyone has the right to freedom of thought, conscience and religion; this right includes freedom to change his religion or belief and freedom, either alone or in community with others and in public or private, to manifest his religion or belief, in worship, teaching, practice and observance.
2. Freedom to manifest one's religion or beliefs shall be subject only to such limitations as are prescribed by law and are necessary in a democratic society in the interests of public safety, for the protection of public order, health or morals, or for the protection of the rights and freedoms of others.

The freedoms guaranteed are closely related to the freedom of opinion guaranteed by Article 10. Religious education, which is a subject of special difficulty, is also dealt with by Article 2 of the First Protocol.[2]

In the first case under Article 9 to come before it,[3] the Court underlined the importance of the rights protected:

[F]reedom of thought, conscience and religion is one of the foundations of a 'democratic society' within the meaning of the Convention. It is, in its religious dimension, one of the most vital elements that go to make up the identity of believers and their conception of life, but it is also a precious asset for atheists, agnostics, sceptics and the unconcerned. The pluralism indissociable from a democratic society, which has been dearly won over the centuries, depends on it.

However, as will be seen, the Convention organs have allowed States a fairly wide margin of appreciation when it comes to placing limitations on the manifestation of religion and belief.

---

[1] See C. Evans, *Freedom of Religion under the European Convention on Human Rights* (Oxford, 2001).
[2] See *Kjedlsen and others* v. *Denmark*, Judgment of 7 December 1976, Series A, No. 23; (1979–80) 1 EHRR 711, discussed in ch. 16.
[3] *Kokkinakis* v. *Greece*, Judgment of 25 May 1993, Series A, No. 260-A; (1994) 17 EHRR 397, para. 31.

WHAT IS A 'BELIEF'?

As the above quotation from the *Kokkinakis* judgment demonstrates, the protection of Article 9 extends to a wide range of convictions and philosophies, not limited to, for example, religious belief. However, for the Article to apply, a belief must 'attain a certain level of cogency, seriousness, cohesion and importance'.[4] The borderline can frequently be difficult to draw, since belief is, of course, inherently subjective. In a case brought by an association providing legal information to prisoners on a non-commercial basis, for example, the Commission took the view that 'aims of an idealistic nature' were not within the rights protected by Article 9, making the application manifestly ill-founded.

A distinction must be drawn between the holding and communication of a belief, and acts motivated by the belief but not central to its expression. Thus although pacifism has been held by the Commission to fall within the scope of Article 9, it did not consider that an applicant was able to challenge her conviction and sentence resulting from the distribution of leaflets indicating opposition to the policy of the United Kingdom Government in Northern Ireland, since the leafleting 'did not manifest her belief in the sense of Article 9(1).'[5] In another case, the Commission received a complaint that a decision of the Market Court in Sweden, restricting the terms used in advertisements for the sale by the Church of Scientology of the Hubbard Electrometer, violated Article 9. The Hubbard Electrometer was described by the applicants as a religious artefact used to measure the electrical characteristics of the 'static field' surrounding the body. The Commission distinguished between words in publicity material related to the beliefs of the sect and words aimed at selling, which were not within Article 9(1) since they were 'more a manifestation of a desire to market goods for profit than the manifestation of a belief in practice'.[6]

---

[4] *Campbell and Cosans* v. *United Kingdom*, Judgment of 25 February 1982, Series A, No. 48; (1982) 4 EHRR 293, para. 36.

[5] App. 7050/75, *Arrowsmith* v. *United Kingdom*, 12 October 1978 (1980) 19 DR 5.

[6] App. 7805/77, *Pastor X and the Church of Scientology* v. *Sweden*, 5 May 1979, (1979) 22 *Yearbook* 244, at 250.

THE MANIFESTATION OF RELIGION OR BELIEF

Freedom of thought, conscience, and religion includes freedom to manifest one's religion or belief.[7] Again, to quote from the Court's judgment in the *Kokkinakis* case:

While religious freedom is primarily a matter of individual conscience, it also implies, *inter alia*, freedom to 'manifest [one's] religion'. Bearing witness in words and deeds is bound up with the existence of religious convictions.

According to Article 9, freedom to manifest one's religion is not only exercisable in community with others, 'in public' and within the circle of those whose faith one shares, but can also be asserted 'alone' and 'in private'; furthermore, it includes in principle the right to try to convince one's neighbour, for example through 'teaching', failing which, moreover, 'freedom to change [one's] religion or belief', enshrined in Article 9, would be likely to remain a dead letter.[8]

The general right to freedom of thought, conscience, and religion protected by Article 9(1) is absolute. The manifestation of religion or belief is, however, subject to the limitations set out in paragraph (2), where 'necessary in a democratic society in the interests of public safety, for the protection of public order, health or morals, or for the protection of the rights and freedoms of others'.

The applicants in the case of *Kokkinakis* v. *Greece*[9] were Jehovah's Witnesses engaged in evangelical activity, including calling at houses to persuade the occupiers to join the sect. They had the misfortune to call upon the wife of an Orthodox priest, who reported them to the police, since in Greece proselytism (defined as attempting to convert believers away from the Orthodox religion)[10] is a criminal offence. The applicants were arrested, charged, and subsequently convicted and fined.

The Court concluded that the Greek law against proselytism was sufficiently clearly drafted for the purposes of Article 9(2) and that it pursued the legitimate aim of protecting the rights and freedoms of others. This left consideration of whether the limitation was necessary in a democratic society. A fine distinction is made in this part of the majority's judgment. Bearing Christian witness—an interesting phrase—is described as true evangelism, and is contrasted with 'improper proselytism', described as 'a corruption or deformation of it which was not compatible with respect for freedom of thought, conscience and religion'. The Greek action violated Article 9 because there was no evidence that

---

[7] Thus, liberty of conscience has been defined as 'the right to hold and profess what principles we choose, and to live in accordance with them', J. Plamenatz, *Man and Society* (London: Longmans, 1963), 49.

[8] *Kokkinakis* v. *Greece*, Judgment of 25 May 1993, Series A, No. 260-A; (1994) 17 EHRR 397, para. 31.

[9] Ibid.

[10] Ibid.

the applicants had attempted to convince the householder by improper means. The conviction was accordingly not justified by a pressing social need.

An example of what the Court considers 'improper proselytism' was provided by the *Larissis and others* case.[11] The applicants were officers in the Greek air force who were convicted of proselytism after complaints from soldiers under their command that they had attempted to persuade the soldiers to become Jehovah's Witnesses. The Court decided that the Greek authorities had been justified in taking measures to protect the junior airmen from the applicants, in view of the fact that the hierarchical and claustrophobic nature of life within the armed forces might make it difficult for a subordinate to rebuff the approaches of an individual of superior rank or to withdraw from a conversation initiated by him.

The Court emphasized that not every discussion about religion or other sensitive matters between individuals of unequal rank would justify a State in taking repressive measures under Article 9(2). However, such justification would arise wherever there was evidence of harassment or the application of undue pressure in abuse of power.

Schools are similarly hierarchical structures, and teachers are in a powerful position to influence the children in their charge. The applicant in the *Dahlab* case[12] was a teacher in a Swiss state school for 4-to-8-year-olds. She converted to Islam and began wearing a veil to school. Although there was no evidence that she had spoken about religion to her pupils, the Court considered that the Swiss authorities were justified in forbidding her from wearing the veil at work, consistent with their policy of maintaining religious neutrality in schools. The Court held that seeing their teacher wearing the veil might have a 'proselytizing effect' on children at a young and impressionable age, and would transmit negative messages to them about lack of equality between the sexes. It does not appear to have given much weight to the argument that the experience of being taught by a woman in traditional Islamic dress might have passed on to the children positive messages about the equality of different religious and cultural groups.

Compliance with dietary laws is another aspect of the manifestation of religious belief, and was considered by the Court in the case of *Cha'are Shalom Ve Tsedek* v. *France*.[13] The applicant association represented a group of ultra-orthodox Jews who refused to eat any meat which was not certified as '*glatt*', meaning that the animal had been ritually slaughtered and that the lungs had been examined for impurities. The French authorities authorized a number of slaughterhouses administered by a body representing the majority of Jews in France, which ensured that meat was prepared in such a way as to be kosher, but

---

[11] *Larissis and others* v. *Greece* (Apps. 23772/94, 26377/94, and 23678/94), Judgment of 24 February 1998; (1999) 27 EHRR 329.

[12] *Dahlab* v. *Switzerland* (App. 42393/98), admissibility decision of 15 February 2001.

[13] *Cha'are Shalom Ve Tsedek* v. *France* (App. 27417/95), Judgment of 27 June 2000.

not 'glatt', but the Government refused to allow the applicant to set up its own slaughterhouses. In the event, the Court was not required to examine the question whether the Government's refusal was 'necessary in a democratic society', because it found that, since 'glatt' meat imported from Belgium was available in France, there had been no interference with the applicant association's members' right to freedom to manifest their religion.

EXPRESSION OF RELIGION AND BELIEF BY PRISONERS

There have been a number of complaints by prisoners of interference with religious liberty. It remains doubtful how far a prisoner can claim under Article 9 facilities to practise a religion which is not generally practised in that State. Where a British prisoner complained of the absence of the services of a Church of England priest in a German jail, the Commission appears to have considered that a German Protestant pastor might have been sufficient to comply with Article 9 in such a case.[14] The Commission has stated that a refusal by the prison authorities to provide special food required by a religion which was not a religion usually practised in that State was permitted under Article 9(2).[15] Nor, in the Commission's opinion, does Article 9 impose any obligation to put at the disposal of prisoners books which they consider necessary for the exercise of their religion or for the development of their philosophy of life.[16] The Commission might, however, have considered this complaint under Article 10 of the Convention, or even under Article 2 of the First Protocol. In the same case, the applicant's complaint that the prison authorities had refused him permission to grow a beard, as prescribed by his religion, was rejected under Article 9(2). The respondent Government had submitted, somewhat curiously, that the refusal was justified as being necessary in order to be able to identify the prisoner. The decision is not satisfactory.

One application[17] concerned a Buddhist prisoner who was refused permission to send out articles for publication in a Buddhist magazine. He claimed that the exchange of ideas with his fellow Buddhists was an element in the exercise of his religion, and alleged a violation of Article 9. The Commission noted that the prison authorities had tried to find a Buddhist minister for him and, when they had been unable to do so, allowed him an extra letter each

---

[14] App. 2413/65, X v. Federal Republic of Germany, 16 December 1966, (1967) 23 CD 1, at 8.
[15] Not published. See Case Law Topics No. 1, Human Rights in Prison, 31.
[16] App. 1753/63, X v. Austria, 15 February 1965, (1965) 8 Yearbook 174, at 184.
[17] App. 5442/72, X v. United Kingdom, 20 December 1974, (1975) 1 DR 41.

week to communicate with a fellow Buddhist. The Commission found that the applicant had failed to prove that communication with other Buddhists was a necessary, as distinct from important, part of the practice of his religion. Consequently the application was manifestly ill-founded.

In another application[18] the prison authorities refused to allow a prisoner to retain a copy of *Tai Chi Ch'ua and I Ching (A Choreography of Body and Mind)* because it contained an illustrated section on the martial arts and self-defence, which they considered would be dangerous if used against others. The Commission concluded that there had been an interference with the applicant's freedom of religion, but that it was justified under the limitations in Article 9(2). Again the application was manifestly ill-founded.

In one extraordinary case, an Indian, of Sikh ethnic origin and religion, found himself imprisoned for breaking nine windows in a University Senate House during a degree ceremony. He refused to wear prison clothes and spent twenty-three months dressed only in a towel or a blanket. His refusal to wear clothes led to his isolation from other prisoners and he refused to clean out his cell. He complained, *inter alia*, of violations of Article 9. The Commission ruled that Article 9 does not imply any right for prisoners to wear their own clothes and that the applicant had failed to show any reason within Article 9 why he should not wear prison clothes. The Commission was prepared to accept that his religion might require a practice of high-class Sikhs of not cleaning floors and that an interference with his rights under Article 9 in this respect might have arisen. However, the Commission went on to hold that any such interference would be justified as 'necessary in a democratic society' under the limitations recognized by Article 9(2).[19] Accordingly the application was in this respect manifestly ill-founded.

The reported cases taken together give the impression that the Commission was somewhat unsympathetic to complaints of interference with religious freedom by prisoners. The Court has not yet been called upon to decide any such case since, as has been seen, under the old system most were declared in admissible by the Commission. It will be interesting to see whether the new Court takes a less pragmatic stand.

PARTICIPATION IN NATIONAL LIFE

Article 9 also prevents the State from imposing obligations on the citizen which offend his or her religious beliefs, unless these obligations are 'necessary in a democratic society'.

[18] App. 6886/75, *X v. United Kingdom*, 18 May 1976, (1976) 5 DR 100.
[19] App. 8121/78, *X v. United Kingdom*, 6 March 1982 (1982) 28 DR 5, at 38.

A State-imposed obligation found not to serve a pressing social need was examined in the case of *Buscarini and others*.[20] The applicants had been elected as Members of the San Marino Parliament. Before taking office they were required to swear an oath 'on the Holy Gospels' to uphold the Constitution. The Court held that this was tantamount to requiring elected representatives of the people to swear allegiance to a particular religion, and was not, therefore, compatible with Article 9.

CONSCIENTIOUS OBJECTORS

Greater problems arise in balancing the competing interests where the State requires a citizen to behave in a manner contrary to his beliefs in pursuit of a more obviously useful social aim. Compulsory military service is a prime example, since in a number of European States it is still considered necessary to safeguard national security even in peacetime, whilst many pacifists find it objectionable in the extreme. Moreover, Article 4(3)(b) expressly excludes from the prohibition on forced or compulsory labour, 'any service of a military character or, in the case of conscientious objectors where they are recognised, service exacted instead of compulsory military service'.

Two conclusions seem to follow from the wording of Article 4(3)(b). First, since it speaks of conscientious objectors 'in countries where they are recognised', it seems that States are not obliged, under Article 9, to recognize a right to conscientious objection. Secondly, since it makes express provision for substitute service, it follows that where conscientious objectors are permitted to perform substitute service in lieu of military service, they cannot claim, under Article 9, exemption from substitute service. Hence no one is entitled under Article 9 to exemption on grounds of conscience either from military service or from substitute service.[21] The issue was examined by the Commission in the *Grandrath* case.[22] The applicant was a Jehovah's Witness and exercised within this sect the function of Bible study leader. Like other Jehovah's Witnesses he objected, for reasons of conscience and religion, not only to performing military service but also to any kind of substitute service. The German authorities recognized him as a conscientious objector but required him to perform substitute civilian service. When he refused to do so, criminal proceedings were

---

[20] *Buscarini and others* v. *San Marino* (App. 24645/94), Judgment of 18 February 1999, (2000) 30 EHRR 208.

[21] App. 17086/90, *Autio* v. *Finland*, 6 December 1991, (1992) 72 DR 245.

[22] App. 2299/64, *Grandrath* v. *Federal Republic of Germany*, Report of Commission, 12 December 1966; Decision of Committee of Ministers, 29 June 1967, (1967) 10 *Yearbook* 626; see also App. 5591/72, *X* v. *Austria*, 2 April 1973 (1973) 43 CD 161, and App. 7705/76, *X* v. *Federal Republic of Germany*, 5 July 1977, (1978) 9 DR 196.

instituted and he was convicted and sentenced to eight months' imprisonment, a sentence which was reduced on appeal to six months. In addition to the applicant's complaint under Article 9, the Commission considered of its own motion the question whether, under Article 14 in conjunction with Article 9 or Article 4, he had been subject to discrimination as compared with Roman Catholic or Protestant ministers.

In the Commission's opinion, there were two aspects to be considered under Article 9.[23] First, the question whether civilian service would have restricted the applicant's right to manifest his religion. The Commission considered that, given the nature of the service in question, it would not in fact have interfered either with the private and personal practice of his religion or with his duties to his religious Community, which were in any case a spare-time activity. Secondly, the Commission examined whether Article 9 had been violated by the mere fact that the applicant had been required to perform a service which was contrary to his conscience or religion. It concluded that, having regard to the provisions of Article 4, objections of conscience did not, under the Convention, entitle a person to exemption from substitute service.

Under the German legislation, an ordained Evangelical or Roman Catholic minister was exempt from military service, and therefore also from substitute service, while a minister of another religion was exempt if the ministry was his principal occupation and if his functions were equivalent to those of an ordained Evangelical or Roman Catholic Minister. The Commission, finding that this difference in treatment did not amount to discrimination in violation of Article 14 taken in conjunction with Article 9, noted that the legislation had been drafted in such a way in order to prevent a large-scale evasion of the general duty to perform military service. If the limitation were abandoned, the result might well be to exempt an entire religious community.

While the Commission's analysis of Article 14 is persuasive, its application of the Article to the facts of this case is more questionable. It would have been acceptable if exemption from compulsory service had been based solely on the criterion of the minister's function; but it was not. There was the additional requirement in the case of a minister who was neither Roman Catholic nor Evangelical that his ministry must be his principal occupation. The Commission's finding with regard to the reason for the distinction made by German law also raises some doubts. Even if this were in fact the reason, and even if differential treatment can be justified in some cases by the objects of the legislation, as the Court held in the *Belgian Linguistic* case,[24] it seems doubtful whether this would be adequate justification for this distinction. For it would have been

---

[23] App. 2299/64, *Grandrath v. Federal Republic of Germany*, Report of Commission, 12 December 1966; Decision of Committee of Ministers, 29 June 1967, (1967) 10 *Yearbook* 626, at p. 672.

[24] *Belgian Linguistic Case (No. 2)*, Judgment of 23 July 1968, Series A, No. 6; (1979–80) 1 EHRR 252.

open to the legislature simply to provide that any minister of religion should be exempt whose ministry was his principal occupation.[25]

Whilst the Court has not, to date, found that the obligation to perform military service breaches Article 9,[26] it has been prepared to examine the proportionality of sanctions imposed against conscientious objectors, and to find violations of Article 9 if they are excessive.

In the *Thlimmenos* case[27] the applicant, another Greek Jehovah's Witness, had been convicted of the criminal offence of 'insubordination' as a result of his refusal to wear a military uniform. He was subsequently refused permission to practise as an accountant, in accordance with a law excluding anyone with a criminal record from the profession. The Court did not examine the proportionality of the criminal measures—since the applicant did not complain about them—but it did find that the accountancy ban amounted to a violation of Articles 9 and 14 taken together. The Court recognized that:

[A]s a matter of principle, States have a legitimate interest to exclude some offenders from the profession of chartered accountant. However, the Court also considers that, unlike other convictions for serious criminal offences, a conviction for refusing on religious or philosophical grounds to wear the military uniform cannot imply any dishonesty or moral turpitude likely to undermine the offender's ability to exercise this profession. Excluding the applicant on the ground that he was an unfit person was not, therefore, justified. The Court takes note of the Government's argument that persons who refuse to serve their country must be appropriately punished. However, it also notes that the applicant did serve a prison sentence for his refusal to wear the military uniform. In these circumstances, the Court considers that imposing a further sanction on the applicant was disproportionate.

---

[25] See also Committee of Ministers Recommendation No. R(87)8 of 9 April 1987, reproduced in Council of Europe *Information Sheet No. 21*, H/INF(87)1, at 160.

[26] See *Tsirlis and Kouloumpas* v. *Greece* (Apps. 19233/91 and 19234/91), Judgment of 29 May 1997; (1998) 25 EHRR 198, where the Court found a violation of Art. 5(1) arising from the imprisonment of two Jehovah's Witnesses' ministers for refusing to do military service, on the basis that the detention was 'unlawful' under Greek law. It did not find it necessary to examine the complaint under Art. 9 and 14 of the Convention. See also *Valsamis* v. *Greece* (App. 21787/93), Judgment of 18 December 1996; (1997) 24 EHRR 294, where the Court decided that requiring the children of Jehovah's Witnesses to attend a military parade did not offend against their pacifist beliefs.

[27] *Thlimmenos* v. *Greece* (App. 34369/97), Judgment of 6 April 2000; (2001) 31 EHRR 411, para 62 of the judgment.

STATE INTERFERENCE IN ORGANISED RELIGION

In the *Hasan and Chaush* case[28] the Court observed that '[w]ere the organisational life of the [religious] community not protected by Article 9 of the Convention, all other aspects of the individual's freedom of religion would become vulnerable.'

For some time it was uncertain whether a church was itself capable of exercising the right contained in Article 9. An apparently serious interference with religious freedom was brought before the Commission in an early application against the United Kingdom by the Church of Scientology of California.[29] The authorities considered that the applicant church was a dangerous sect and accordingly took certain measures, including the denial or withdrawal of visas, to prevent its members from entering and remaining in the country. Rejecting the application under Article 9, the Commission held that a legal, as opposed to a natural, person was incapable of having or exercising the rights mentioned in Article 9(1).[30] In any event, it considered that the impugned measures did not prevent Scientologists, whether resident or coming from abroad, from attending the college of the church or its other branches in the United Kingdom, or otherwise manifesting their religious beliefs—despite the fact that this was precisely what the restrictions were designed to prevent.

In 1979 the Commission reversed this case law, holding that a church or association with religious or philosophical objects could exercise the right to manifest religion under Article 9, since it was really no more than the collection of its members.[31] By contrast, it seems to be established that an association is not capable of exercising the right of freedom of conscience,[32] since this would be a metaphysical impossibility.

Whether the application is brought by the church or one or more of its members, the Court treats attempts by the State to interfere in the running of mainstream religious organizations very seriously:

Where the organisation of the religious community is at issue, Article 9 must be interpreted in the light of Article 11 of the Convention which safeguards associative life against unjustified State interference. Seen in this perspective, the believer's right to freedom of religion encompasses the expectation that the community will be

[28] *Hasan and Chaush* v. *Bulgaria* (App. 30985/96), Judgment of 26 October 2000.
[29] App. 3798/68, *Church of X* v. *United Kingdom*, 17 December 1968 (1969) 12 *Yearbook* 306.
[30] The Commission revised this conclusion in App. 7805/77, *Pastor X and the Church of Scientology* v. *Sweden*, 5 May 1979, (1979) 22 *Yearbook* 244, at 250. See above.
[31] App. 7805/77, *Pastor X and the Church of Scientology* v. *Sweden*, 5 May 1979 (1979), 22 *Yearbook* 244 and App. 12587/86, *Chappell* v. *United Kingdom*, 14 July 1987, (1987) 53 DR 241.
[32] App. 11308/84, *Vereniging Rechtswinkels Utrecht* v. *Netherlands*, 13 March 1986, (1986) 46 DR 200. See also App. 11921/86, *Kontakt-Information-Therapie and Hagen* v. *Austria*, 12 October 1988, (1988) 57 DR 81.

allowed to function peacefully free from arbitrary State intervention. Indeed, the autonomous existence of religious communities is indispensable for pluralism in democratic society and is thus an issue at the very heart of the protection which Article 9 affords.[33]

The applicant in the case of *Serif* v. *Greece*[34] enjoyed the support of part of the Muslim community in Thrace, and was elected Mufti (religious leader), despite the fact that another Mufti had already been appointed by the State. The applicant was subsequently convicted of the criminal offences of having usurped the functions of a minister of a 'known religion' and having publicly worn the uniform of such a minister without having the right to do so. The Government argued before the European Court that the authorities had had to intervene in order to avoid the creation of tension between different religious groups in the area. The Court, finding a violation of Article 9, observed that tension between competing religious groups was an unavoidable consequence of pluralism, but that the role of the authorities in such a situation was not to remove the cause of the tension, thereby eliminating pluralism, but instead to ensure tolerance between the rival factions. In a democratic society, it commented, there was no need for the State to take measures to ensure that religious communities remained or were brought under a unified leadership. In the *Hasan and Chaush* case,[35] where the Bulgarian authorities were found to have similarly interfered in the affairs of the Muslim community, the Court declared a violation of Article 9 based on the arbitrary nature of the relevant legislation, which gave an almost unfettered power to the executive to appoint the person of its choice as Chief Mufti.

CONCLUDING COMMENTS

History—and sadly, very recent history at that—shows that differences in religious belief are a potent source of conflict and bloodshed. Thus, while most would agree with the Court's view, expressed in the *Serif* judgment, that in circumstances of religious tension governments should work to promote pluralism and 'ensure tolerance between the rival factions', it may frequently be the case that allowing one person complete freedom to manifest his religion or belief would be to impinge—sometimes with dangerous consequences—on the rights of others. It would therefore perhaps be understandable if, in dramatic

---

[33] *Hasan and Chaush* v. *Bulgaria* (App. 30985/96), Judgment of 26 October 2000, para. 62 of the judgment.
[34] *Serif* v. *Greece* (App. 38178/97), Judgment of 4 December 1999; (2001)31 EHRR 561.
[35] *Hasan and Chaush* v. *Bulgaria* (App. 30985/96), Judgment of 26 October 2000.

cases, the Court were to allow a wide margin of appreciation to place restrictions of the freedom to manifest religion or belief. However, it is in the more mundane cases—the teacher who wishes to wear the Islamic veil to school, the children whose Jehovah's Witness parents do not wish them to attend a militaristic parade—that the Court has demonstrated a certain lack of empathy for the believer, and has appeared only to pay lip-service to the commitment to religious freedom proclaimed in such judgments as *Kokkinakis* v. *Greece*.

13

FREEDOM OF EXPRESSION

INTRODUCTION

Article 10 provides,

1. Everyone has the right to freedom of expression. This right shall include freedom to hold opinions and to receive and impart information and ideas without interference by public authority and regardless of frontiers. This article shall not prevent States from requiring the licensing of broadcasting, television or cinema enterprises.
2. The exercise of these freedoms, since it carries with it duties and responsibilities, may be subject to such formalities, conditions, restrictions or penalties as are prescribed by law and are necessary in a democratic society, in the interests of national security, territorial integrity or public safety, for the prevention of disorder or crime, for the protection of health or morals, for the protection of the reputation or rights of others, for preventing the disclosure of information received in confidence, or for maintaining the authority and impartiality of the judiciary.

In the leading case, *Handyside* v. *United Kingdom*,[1] the Court emphasized the importance of the right protected by Article 10, which, it said, 'constitutes one of the essential foundations of a democratic society, one of the basic conditions for its progress and for the development of every man.'

The right to freedom of expression set out in the article's first paragraph, including freedom to hold opinions and to receive and impart information and ideas[2] without interference by the State, is extremely broad. All forms of expression are included, through any medium (for example, paintings,[3] books,[4] films,[5] statements in radio interviews,[6] and information

---

[1] *Handyside* v. *United Kingdom*, Judgment of 7 December 1976, Series A, No. 24; (1979–80) 1 EHRR 737, para. 48.

[2] *Autronic AG* v. *Switzerland*, Judgment of 22 May 1990, Series A, No. 178; (1990) 12 EHRR 485.

[3] *Müller* v. *Switzerland*, Judgment of 24 May 1988, Series A, No. 133; (1991) 13 EHRR 212.

[4] *Handyside* v. *United Kingdom*, Judgment of 7 December 1976, Series A, No. 24; (1979–80) 1 EHRR 737.

[5] *Otto-Preminger Institute* v. *Austria*, Judgment of 20 September 1994, Series A, No. 295-A; (1994) 19 EHRR 34.

[6] *Barthold* v. *Germany*, Judgment of 23 March 1985, Series A, No. 90; (1985) 7 EHRR 383.

pamphlets)[7] and with any content, including racist hate speech[8] and pornography.[9]

To quote again from the *Handyside* case, Article 10

is applicable not only to 'information' or 'ideas' that are favourably received or regarded as inoffensive or as a matter of indifference, but also those that offend, shock or disturb the State or any sector of the population. Such are the demands of that pluralism, tolerance and broadmindedness without which there is no 'democratic society'. [10]

However, as is explicitly recognized in the text of Article 10(2), and by the Court in its case law, free expression, particularly by way of the mass media, is a powerful tool, carrying special duties and responsibilities. If it is vital to protect the right to free speech because of its power to promote democracy, uncover abuses, and advance political, artistic, scientific, and commercial development, it is also important to recognize that free speech can equally be used to incite violence, spread hatred, and impinge on individual privacy and safety. The Court's case law is an attempt to strike the proper balance between these competing interests.[11]

WHAT CONSTITUTES AN 'INTERFERENCE' WITH FREE EXPRESSION?

The Court takes a broad view of what constitutes an 'interference'. At its most obvious this includes executive orders preventing publication[12] or the confiscation of published material.[13] Post-publication measures are also likely to come within the category of interference because of the chilling effect which they have on future speech. Article 10(2) in any case makes clear that 'penalties' as well as 'restrictions' must be justified. Consequently if, as a result of the exercise of free expression, a person finds himself facing criminal proceedings[14] or

---

[7] *Open Door Counselling and Dublin Well Woman* v. *Ireland*, Judgment of 29 October 1992, Series A, No. 246; (1993) 15 EHRR 244.

[8] *Jersild* v. *Denmark*, Judgment of 24 September 1994, Series A, No. 298; (1994) 19 EHRR 1.

[9] *Wingrove* v. *United Kingdom* (App. 17419/90), Judgment of 25 November 1996; (1997) 24 EHRR 1.

[10] Para. 48 of the judgment.

[11] For an interesting study of the approaches taken by national courts in the UK and Austria, see M. Oetheimer '*L'Harmonisation de la Liberté d'Expression en Europe*' (Paris, 2001).

[12] See the 'Spycatcher' cases: *The Observer and Guardian Newspapers Ltd* v. *United Kingdom*, Judgment of 26 November 1991, Series A, No. 216; (1992) 14 EHRR 153 and *Sunday Times* v. *United Kingdom (No 2)* Judgment of 26 November 1991, Series A, No. 217; (1992) 14 EHRR 229.

[13] *Vereniging Weekblad Bluf!* v. *Netherlands*, Judgment of 9 February 1995, Series A, No. 306-A; (1995) 20 EHRR 189.

[14] *Zana* v. *Turkey* (App. 18954/91), Judgment of 25 November 1997; (1999) 27 EHRR 667.

paying vast sums of damages in a civil action,[15] the State will have to justify its national law under Article 10(2).

An even wider meaning was given to 'interference' in the *VDSÖ and Gubi* case,[16] where the Austrian military authorities, which usually distributed newspapers and magazines free of charge to soldiers, refused to distribute a satirical and critical magazine, *der Igel*. The Court held that Article 10(1) did not impose an obligation on States to distribute magazines but it did prevent discriminatory treatment of one particular publication unless this could be justified under Article 10(2).

LIMITATIONS ON FREEDOM OF EXPRESSION

Certain restrictions are expressly allowed. Article 10(1) itself provides that States may require the licensing of broadcasting, television or cinema enterprises. Moreover, in common with Articles 8, 9, and 11, Article 10 includes a second paragraph which permits the State to limit the right set out in the first paragraph, provided that such limitations are 'prescribed by law', and 'necessary in a democratic society' in pursuit on one of the specified aims.[17]

The situations in which a restriction may be justifiable include the need to protect important public interests—such as national security, territorial integrity, freedom from crime and disorder, health and morality, and the authority and impartiality of the judiciary—and also other individual rights, such as a person's right to privacy or reputation. The margin of appreciation allowed to the Contracting State in restricting freedom of expression will vary depending on the purpose and nature of the limitation and of the expression in question. As the Court made clear in the *Handyside* judgment, 'every "formality", "condition", "restriction" or "penalty" imposed in this sphere must be proportionate to the legitimate aim pursued.'[18]

On the other side of the balance, to be weighed against the importance of the aim pursued by the restriction, is the nature of the expression restricted. The

---

[15] *Tolstoy Miloslavsky* v. *United Kingdom*, Judgment of 13 July 1997, Series A, No. 316-B.

[16] *Vereinigung Demokratischer Soldaten Österreichs and Gubi* v. *Austria*, Judgment of 19 December 1994, Series A, No. 302; (1995) 20 EHRR 55. See also *Vereniging Weekblad 'Bluf'* v. *Netherlands*, Judgment of 9 February 1995, Series A, No. 306-A; (1995) 20 EHRR 189.

[17] See ch. 10 above.

[18] *Handyside* v. *United Kingdom*, Judgment of 7 December 1976, Series A, No. 24; (1979–80) 1 EHRR 737, para. 48

Court takes into account the fact that, in the context of effective political democracy and respect for human rights mentioned in the Preamble to the Convention, freedom of expression is not only important in itself, but also plays a central role in the protection of the other rights under the Convention.[19] Thus the Court consistently gives a higher level of protection to publications and speech which contribute towards social and political debate, criticism and information—in the broadest sense. Artistic and commercial expression, in contrast, receive a lower level of protection.

POLITICAL SPEECH, DEFAMATION, AND PRIVACY

Since democracy cannot function unless it is possible to scrutinize the acts of politicians and other powerful figures, the Court has held that the interests of such individuals in retaining their privacy weighs less heavily in the balance.

In the *Lingens* case,[20] the applicant published in a magazine two articles strongly criticizing certain attitudes of the Federal Chancellor, Bruno Kreisky. The Chancellor brought a private prosecution for defamation in the press. Lingens was convicted and fined. The Court commented that 'freedom of the press affords the public one of the best means of discovering and forming an opinion of the ideas and attitudes of political leaders.' It followed that the limits of acceptable criticism were wider when the target was a politician rather than a private individual; politicians knowingly lay themselves open to the scrutiny of the press and public.[21]

The same principle applies to other public figures, such as prominent businessmen, who should expect their business dealings to be the subject of public debate.[22] Even public figures are entitled to some privacy, however, and since there is little public benefit to be derived from exposing certain aspects of a politician's private life, the national authorities may be justified in taking preventive measures.[23]

The Court upholds the right of the press to impart ideas and information on

---

[19] See e.g. D. Feldman, *Civil Liberties and Human Rights in England and Wales* (Oxford, 1993), at 547–52.

[20] *Lingens* v. *Austria*, Judgment of 8 July 1986, Series A, No. 103; (1986) 8 EHRR 103.

[21] Paras 41–42 of the judgment; see also *Oberschlick* v. *Austria*, Judgment of 23 May 1991, Series A, No. 204: (1994) 19 EHRR 389.

[22] *Fayed* v. *United Kingdom*, Judgment of 21 September 1994, Series A, No. 294-B; (1994) 18 EHRR 393.

[23] *Tammer* v. *Estonia* (App. 41205/98), Judgment of 6 February 2001.

matters of public interest, even when this involves the publication of untrue and damaging statements about private individuals. The *Bladet Tromsø* case[24] concerned a newspaper and its editor ordered to pay damages for defamation following the publication of statements made by a third party concerning alleged violations by named individuals of seal-hunting regulations in Norway. The Court found a violation of Article 10, observing that the newspaper had acted in good faith and that it had been reasonable for it to rely on an official report without having to carry out its own verification of the facts reported.

HATE SPEECH AND SPEECH WHICH INCITES VIOLENCE

Although all forms of expression, including racist and hate speech, fall within the right set out in paragraph (1) of Article 10, it is obviously easier for the State to justify interference when the expression is likely to incite disorder or crime or undermine the security of minority groups within society.

Thus the Court, and the Commission in its time, relying either on Article 17 of the Convention[25] or on the limitations set out in Article 10(2), have frequently declared inadmissible applications from individuals and groups complaining about restrictions placed on hate speech.[26]

The position may be different, however, when the intention behind the publication of hate speech is to inform the public or illuminate debate. The *Jersild* case[27] concerned the broadcast on Danish television of a programme in which a group of self-confessed racist youths made extremely offensive remarks about black people. The youths, the presenter, and the head of the news section were prosecuted and convicted. The journalists complained to the Commission of a breach of Article 10. The only point in issue in the case was whether the limitations were necessary in a democratic society. The Court stressed the foundational nature of freedom of expression, but also noted that the potential impact of the medium should be considered, since it is commonly acknowledged that radio and television have a much more immediate and powerful

---

[24] *Bladet Tromsø and Stensaas* v. *Norway* (App. 21980/97), Judgment of 20 May 1999; (2000) 29 EHRR 125.

[25] See ch. 20 below.

[26] See e.g., App. 21128/92, *Walendy* v. *Germany*, Decision of 11 January 1995, (1995) 80 DR 94; App. 25096/94, *Remer* v. *Germany*, Decision of 6 September 1995, (1995) 82 DR 117; App. 25062/94, *Honsik* v. *Austria*, Decision of 18 October 1995, (1995) 83 DR 77; App. 31159/96, *Marais* v. *France*, Decision of 24 June 1996, (1996) 86 DR 184; *Witzsch* v. *Germany* (App. 32307/96), Decision of 20 April 1999, unpublished; *Schimanek* v. *Austria* (App. 41448/98), Decision of 1 February 2000, unpublished.

[27] *Jersild* v. *Denmark*, Judgment of September 24, 1994, Series A, No. 298; (1994) 19 EHRR 1.

effect than the printed word. The Court was satisfied that the presentation of the item was not intended to propagate racist views, but to address an issue of some public interest. The broadcast was part of a serious Danish news programme and was intended for a well-informed audience. Taking account of all these factors, the penalties imposed on the presenter and the head of the news section were not necessary in a democratic society for the protection of the rights of others.

In a series of recent judgments the Court has noted that journalists bear special responsibilities and duties in situations of political conflict and tension, because they can become 'a vehicle for the dissemination of hate speech and violence'.[28] In all the cases the applicants were editors or owners of newspapers in Turkey which published articles or letters criticizing government policy in the south-east of the country and were prosecuted and convicted of offences against the integrity of the State. The Court examined each item and the editorial context in which it had been published. It stressed the importance of safeguarding the right and duty of the press to impart information and ideas on political issues, including controversial ones, and the right of the public to be informed of a different perspective on the Kurdish conflict, and found no violation of Article 10 only in those cases[29] where it considered that the publication genuinely amounted to an incitement to separatist violence.

The *Surek (No. 1)* case, for example, concerned the owner of a newspaper who was prosecuted and fined for publishing readers' letters about the Kurdish conflict. These letters condemned the military actions of the authorities in south-east Turkey and accused them of brutal suppression of the Kurdish people in their struggle for independence and freedom. One of the letters alleged that the State had connived in imprisonment, torture, and killing of dissidents in the name of the protection of democracy and the Republic. The other letter referred to two massacres which the writer claimed were intentionally committed by the authorities as part of a strategic campaign to eradicate the Kurds, and concluded:

[T]he struggle of our people for national freedom in Kurdistan has reached a point where it can no longer be thwarted by bloodshed, tanks and shells. Every attack launched by the Turkish Republic to wipe out the Kurds intensifies the struggle for freedom. The bourgeoisie and its toadying press, which draw attention every day to the brutalities in Bosnia-Herzegovina, fail to see the brutalities committed in Kurdistan. Of

---

[28] *Erdogdeu and Ince v. Turkey* (Apps. 25067/94 and 25068/94); *Sürek and Özdemir v. Turkey* (Apps. 23927/94 and 24277/94); *Sürek v. Turkey (No. 1)* (App. 26682/95); *Sürek v Turkey (No. 2)* (App. 24122/94); *Sürek v. Turkey (No. 4)* (App. 24762/94), Judgments of 8 July 1999; and see also *Ceylan v Turkey* (App. 23556/94) and *Okçuoglu v Turkey* (App. 24246/94), Judgments of 8 July 1999. Politicians and other public figures must also act responsibly, because of their power to influence the public mood: *Zana v. Turkey* (App. 18954/91), Judgment of 25 November 1997; (1999) 27 EHRR 667.

[29] *Sürek v. Turkey (No. 1)* (App. 26682/95) and *Sürek v. Turkey (No 3)* (App. 24735/94), Judgments of 8 July 1999.

course, one can hardly expect reactionary fascists who call for a halt in the brutalities in Bosnia-Herzegovina to call for a halt in the brutalities in Kurdistan.

The Kurdish people, who are being torn from their homes and their fatherland, have nothing to lose. But they have much to gain.

The Court emphasized that there was limited scope under Article 10(2) for restrictions on political speech or on debate on matters of public interest, and that the boundaries of permissible criticism were wider with regard to the government than in relation to a private citizen or even a politician.[30] Governments should display restraint in resorting to criminal proceedings, particularly where other means were available for replying to unjustified criticism. Nevertheless, in the Court's view, the letters amounted to 'an appeal to bloody revenge by stirring up base emotions and hardening already embedded prejudices which have manifested themselves in deadly violence'. In view of the tense security situation in south-east Turkey, the authorities were justified in penalizing the publisher.

The case was by no means clear-cut. Six of the eighteen judges in the Grand Chamber dissented, on the ground, broadly, that it had not been established that there was a real risk of the letters inciting hatred or violence. Judge Palm referred to the facts that the newspaper was published in Istanbul rather than in the south-east, the letters page formed only a fraction of the whole, and that the views expressed in the letters were not endorsed by editorial comment. Judge Bonello advocated a test based on American case law, requiring proof of a 'clear and present danger' of violence before placing any limitation on free speech.

OFFICIAL SECRETS, NATIONAL SECURITY, AND 'WHISTLE-BLOWING'

Article 10 guarantees the freedom to receive as well as impart information, but it does not confer a right of access to information.[31] Although the Court appears increasingly ready to find an obligation on the State to provide information to concerned individuals included in the right to respect for private life under Article 8,[32] Article 10, in contrast, is directed at proscribing interference by a public authority between a willing giver and a willing recipient.

---

[30] Para. 61 of the judgment.
[31] *Leander* v. *Sweden*, Judgment of 26 March 1987, Series A, No. 116; (1987) 9 EHRR 433; and *Gaskin* v. *United Kingdom*, Judgment of 7 July 1989, Series A, No. 160; (1990) 12 EHRR 36. Compare Art. 19 of the Covenant on Civil and Political Rights.
[32] See ch. 11 above.

In the *Hadjianastassiou* case[33] the Court made it clear that the State was to be afforded a very wide margin of appreciation when the protection of national security was in issue. The applicant had been convicted and sentenced for having disclosed military secrets. The leaked information was of very minor importance, but the Court concluded that any disclosure of State secrets was apt to compromise national security and found no violation.

In two cases concerning the publication of Peter Wright's book, *Spycatcher*,[34] the newspapers concerned complained of a violation of Article 10 arising from the action by the Attorney General in bring breach of confidence actions and seeking injunctions restraining publication of extracts of the book. Of particular significance was a decision of the Court of Appeal that the injunctions against *The Observer* and *The Guardian* bound all the media within the jurisdiction of the English courts and that any publication or broadcast of the *Spycatcher* material would constitute a criminal contempt of court.

Despite the arrival in the United Kingdom of copies of the book imported from outside the country, the injunctions were kept in force until October 1988. For the first period[35] the Court ruled by 14–10 that the risk of material prejudicial to the security services existed and that this justified the imposition of injunctions. For the remaining period, the decision was unanimous that there was a violation of Article 10; the material could no longer be regarded as likely to prejudice the security services since the book was freely circulating in the United States.

The Court has recognized that dismissal, of a public sector employee at least, can constitute an 'interference' with freedom of expression.[36] In a number of cases where civil servants had publicly criticized their employers and suffered disciplinary measures,[37] the Commission accepted that State employees and service personnel have a special 'duty of discretion', meaning that their freedom to criticize government policies in a public manner is curtailed. Nonetheless, restrictive measures must be proportionate, and the 'whistle-blower's' motives and ability to substantiate his or her criticisms are relevant considerations. Criticisms which are made to a more limited audience, for example the commanding officer of military personnel, require a greater degree of tolerance, even if expressed in strong terms.[38]

---

[33] *Hadjianastassiou* v. *Greece*, Judgment of 16 December 1992, Series A, No. 252-A; (1993) 16 EHRR 219, paras. 38 to 47 of the judgment.

[34] *Observer and Guardian* v. *United Kingdom*, Judgment of 26 November 1991, Series A, No. 216; (1992) 14 EHRR 153; and *Sunday Times* v. *United Kingdom (No. 2)*, Judgment of 26 November 1991, Series A, No. 217; (1992) 14 EHRR 229.

[35] From July 1986 to July 1987.

[36] *Vogt* v. *Germany*, Judgment of 26 September 1995, Series A, No. 323; (1996) 21 EHRR 205.

[37] See, for example, App. 18597/92, *Haseldine* v. *United Kingdom*, admissibility decision of 13 May 1992.

[38] *Grigoriades* v. *Greece* (App. 24348/94), Judgment of 25 November 1997; (1999) 27 EHRR 464.

BROADCASTING

Broadcasting is subject to greater regulation than the written word, since Article 10(1) includes the power to license broadcasting, cinema, and television enterprises. The purpose of the licensing can be broad,[39] but there is a duty to ensure that the rights under Article 10 remain protected.[40]

In the *Groppera Radio* case,[41] Groppera Radio broadcast radio programmes from Italy to listeners in Switzerland. They failed to comply with a Swiss Ordinance prohibiting cable retransmission of such programmes. The Court ruled that the object, purpose, and scope of the third sentence of Article 10(1) had to be considered in the context of the article as a whole, and in particular the limitations in Article 10(2). No violation was found in the case.

The *Informationsverein Lentia* case[42] concerned five applications for broadcasting licences (one for television and four for radio) which were refused, because the Austrian Broadcasting Corporation held a monopoly. The Austrian Government relied on the third sentence of paragraph (1), or, in the alternative, on the limitations in paragraph (2), and argued that the monopoly enabled the State to regulate the technical aspects of audio-visual activities and to determine their place and role in modern society. The Court found a violation of Article 10, observing that the State is the 'ultimate guarantor' of pluralism, and that a public broadcasting monopoly could be not be justified.

In regulating broadcasting, a State must take care not to infringe the right of a person to receive information. In the *Autronic* case,[43] the Swiss Government had refused permission for a company specializing in home electronics to receive programmes from a Soviet satellite. There was a violation of Autronic's rights under Article 10.

---

[39] App. 4515/70, *X and the Association of Z v. United Kingdom*, 12 July 1971, (1971) 14 *Yearbook* 538.

[40] App. 9297/81, *X Association v. Sweden*, 1 March 1982, (1982) 28 DR 204.

[41] *Groppera Radio AG and others v. Switzerland*, Judgment of 28 March 1990, Series A, No. 173; (1990) 12 EHRR 321.

[42] *Informationsverein Lentia v. Austria*, Judgment of November 24, 1993, Series A, No. 276; (1994) 17 EHRR 93.

[43] *Autronic AG v. Switzerland*, Judgment of 22 May 1990, Series A, No. 178; (1990) 12 EHRR 485.

OBSCENITY AND BLASPHEMY

In the *Handyside* case the Court noted that there was no uniform European concept of 'morality' and made it clear that States would enjoy a wide margin of appreciation in assessing whether measures were required to protect moral standards.[44]

This approach was followed in the *Müller* case,[45] which concerned an exhibition of contemporary art including three paintings depicting sexual acts, seized by the authorities on the grounds that they were obscene. The Court found that it was not unreasonable for the Swiss courts to have found the paintings liable to offend the sense of sexual propriety of persons of ordinary sensitivity. The imposition of fines did not violate Article 10. In coming to a similar conclusion on the issue of confiscation, the Court noted that the deprivation of the items restricted the artist's use of them. But there was a procedure under which the artist could apply for their restitution, and the confiscation order would be varied if appropriate measures to protect the interests of public morals could be put in place.

The expression under consideration in the *Wingrove* case[46] was a video made by the applicant portraying a woman, dressed as a nun and described in the credits as 'Saint Teresa' (of Avila), having an erotic fantasy involving the crucified figure of Christ. The video was refused a certificate for distribution by the British Board of Film Classification on the grounds that it appeared to contravene the British blasphemy law, in that the Board considered that its public distribution would outrage and insult the feelings of believing Christians.

The Court observed that blasphemy legislation was still in force in various European countries, although the application of these laws had become increasingly rare—in the United Kingdom, for example, there had been only two prosecutions concerning blasphemy in the preceding seventy years. Strong arguments had been advanced in favour of the abolition of blasphemy laws, which the applicant accused of discriminating against different faiths or denominations. However, the Court did not consider that there was yet sufficient common ground in the legal and social orders of the member States of the Council of Europe to conclude that a system allowing a State to impose restrictions on the propagation of material on the basis that it was blasphemous was, in itself incompatible with the Convention. Whereas there was little scope

[44] *Handyside* v. *United Kingdom*, Judgment of 7 December 1976, Series A, No. 24; (1979–80) 1 EHRR 737, para. 43 of the judgment.

[45] *Müller and others* v. *Switzerland*, Judgment of 24 May 1988, Series A, No. 133; (1991) 13 EHRR 212. See also *Otto-Preminger Institute* v. *Austria*, Judgment of 20 September 1994, Series A, No. 295-A; (1995) 19 EHRR 34.

[46] *Wingrove* v. *the United Kingdom* (App. 17419/90), Judgment of 25 November 1996; (1997) 24 EHRR 1.

under Article 10(2) the Court considered that for restrictions on political speech or on debate of questions of public interest, a wider margin of appreciation was generally available to States when regulating freedom of expression in relation to matters liable to offend intimate personal convictions within the sphere of morals or, especially, religion, since the State authorities were in a better position that the international judge to assess what was likely to cause offence to believers in each country.

Having viewed the film itself, the Court concluded that the reasons given by the British authorities to justify the measures taken could be considered as both relevant and sufficient for the purposes of Article 10(2).

PROFESSIONAL AND COMMERCIAL SPEECH

A series of cases has concerned the limitations that may be imposed on freedom of expression in the context of regulated professions. Dr Barthold,[47] a veterinary surgeon, published an article explaining the treatment he had given to a cat outside normal office hours and arguing that a regular night service should be provided in Hamburg. His name and clinic address was given. A private association against unfair competition complained that the article breached the professional rules on advertising of veterinary surgeons. An injunction restraining future similar publications was obtained against him.

The Court ruled that Article 10 applied, that there had been an interference prescribed by law for the legitimate purpose of protecting the rights of others by preventing the applicant from obtaining a commercial advantage over professional colleagues. The Court noted that the issue raised in the article was one of genuine public interest, that Dr Barthold had always campaigned within the Veterinary Surgeons' Council for compulsory night duty for veterinary surgeons. The national court had been wrong to suggest that there was an intent to act for commercial purposes as long as that intent was not completely over-ridden by other motives; this was too rigid a test. It operated to deny the possibility of members of regulated professions from entering into public debate on matters affecting the life of the community if there was any risk of their contributions being regarded as entailing some element of advertising.

Similar issues arose in a different context in another case.[48] Restraining orders were issued in respect of articles published in a journal whose aim was to defend the interests of small and medium enterprises against large enterprises

[47] *Barthold* v. *Germany*, Judgment of 25 March 1985, Series A, No. 90; (1975) 7 EHRR 383.
[48] *Markt Intern verlag GmbH and Klaus Beermann* v. *Germany*, Judgment of 20 November 1989, Series A, No. 165; (1990) 12 EHRR 161.

which criticized the refund policies of a large organization. The journal and its editor complained of violations of Article 10. The reasoning of the Court in finding no violation is not easy to follow. There was no suggestion that the information published was inaccurate, but it was felt that it was inappropriate to publish an account of something which the large organization had agreed to investigate. The basis for this is that an isolated incident could give the false impression that it was evidence of a general practice. The granting of the injunction was within Germany's margin of appreciation.

The same German legislation[49] was considered by the Court in the *Jacubowski* case.[50] Jacubowski had been dismissed as editor of a news agency, which issued a press release concerning its own reorganization and criticizing Jacubowski's management in blunt terms. The news agency was later ordered to publish his reply. In the meantime Jacubowski had sent newspapers articles critical of his former employers. An injunction had been obtained to restrain him from sending out such material. He complained of a violation of Article 10.

The Commission was unanimous in holding that there was a violation of Article 10, but the Court by 6 votes to 3 concluded that there had been no violation. The Court allows the Contracting State a considerable margin of appreciation, strangely noting that other forms of expression remained open to Jacubowski to put forward his case. The minority opinion attacks this approach head on:

In our opinion, the majority judgment makes it appear as though this case involves simply a choice between two conflicting principles of equal weight. It relies too heavily on the findings of fact by the national courts. In doing so, it gives an excessive significance to the doctrine of margin of appreciation.

In our view, freedom of expression is the guiding principle in the instant case. Exceptions to this fundamental principle must be interpreted narrowly.[51]

The Court appears to have got itself into difficulties in this area because it has not addressed the fundamental question whether the Convention permits Contracting States to limit freedom of expression in order to protect private commercial interests. It is certainly arguable that the limitation justified for the protection of the reputation and rights of others was not intended to protect commercial interests. Until this issue is faced squarely by the Convention organs, there remains the likelihood of unsatisfactory decisions emerging.[52]

This is not to say that restrictions on advertising speech will always fall foul of Article 10. The restrictions in Spain on lawyers' advertising were upheld in the *Casado Coca* case,[53] though professional advertising is in a state of flux in the

---

[49] The Unfair Competition Act of 7 June 1909 (*Gesetz gegen den unlautern Wettbewerb*).

[50] *Jacubowski* v. *Germany*, Judgment of June 24, 1994, Series A, No. 291; (1994) 19 EHRR 64.

[51] Dissenting opinion of Judges Walsh, MacDonald, and Wildhaber.

[52] M. Merieux, 'The German Competition Law and Article 10 ECHR' (1995) 20 E L Rev. 388.

[53] *Casado Coca* v. *Spain*, Judgment of 24 February 1994, Series A, No. 285; (1994) 18 EHRR 1.

Contracting States. In the *Colman* case[54] the Court struck out of its list an application by a British doctor who complained about the advertising ban applicable to the medical profession. The application became moot when the General Medical Council changed its rules to permit the publication of factual information about medical practices, and the United Kingdom Government made a payment without admission of liability which was acceptable to the applicant.

While in some areas advertising can be restricted, in others it cannot. It might be thought that the interests of the regulated professions are rather less weighty than matters of constitutional significance, but in the *Open Door Counselling* case[55] the Court was prepared to give priority to freedom of expression in the form of advice about the availability of medical terminations of pregnancy in the United Kingdom and about the addresses of clinics in London lawfully offering this service over the constitutional protection of the right to life of the unborn child in the Irish Constitution. The Court did note that the absolute and perpetual nature of the injunctions against the organizations offering advice was, of itself, disproportionate. The Court was also at pains to state that the case was not about the right to life. The case is undoubtedly rightly decided, particularly as the information being disseminated was already widely available from other sources, but the contrast with the cases concerning the German competition law becomes all the more striking set in this context.

THE JUDICIARY

Article 10(2) expressly authorizes limitations for maintaining the authority and impartiality of the judiciary. However, as with most cases under Article 10, the Court will consider carefully the tone, context, and intent of the speech or publication in question. It will be more difficult for the State to justify restrictions placed on criticisms of judges where these form part of a reasonable public debate on the functioning of the judicial system.

Thus, the Court found a violation in a case[56] where the applicant journalists had criticized in virulent terms the Court of Appeal judges who had awarded custody of two children to their father, a notary who had been accused by his ex-wife of child abuse. The journalists had been sued in defamation by the judges and ordered to pay nominal damages.

[54] *Colman* v. *United Kingdom*, Decision of 28 June 1983, Series A, No. 258-D; (1994) 18 EHRR 119.
[55] *Open Door Counselling and Dublin Well Woman* v. *Ireland*, Judgment of 29 October 1992, Series A, No. 246; (1993) 15 EHRR 244.
[56] *De Haes and Gijsels* v. *Belgium* (App. 19983/92), Judgment of 24 February 1997.

The Court of Human Rights recognized that, in order to maintain public confidence in the judiciary, judges should be protected from unjustified, destructive and untrue attacks. However, in the applicants' case the articles had been well researched and had formed part of a public debate which had been taking place in Belgium at the time on incest, child abuse, and judicial reactions to these problems. In contrast, in the *Barfod* case,[57] where the applicant had been convicted of criminal defamation following his publication of an article questioning the impartiality of two lay judges, the Court found no violation of Article 10. The attack on the judges had been personal and destructive, and the applicant had not been prevented from voicing criticism of the judgment, rather than of the judges themselves.

CONCLUDING COMMENT

The interpretation of many of the substantive Articles of the Convention and the delineation of the rights protected frequently involves a balancing exercise between the interests of the applicant and those of other individuals or the public as a whole. This is particularly true of the right to freedom of expression, given the power of the media in modern society. It is possible to argue, in relation to many judgments and decisions, that the Commission and the Court have not struck the balance correctly. Some commentators will consider that the Convention case law allows the State too wide a discretion to place limitations on free speech, while others will criticize judgments such as *Jersild* or *Bladet Tromsø*[58] as overly media-friendly, to the detriment of individual rights to privacy and freedom from racist hate speech.

Since the expansion of the Council of Europe in the last ten years, the importance and sensitivity of the rights protected by Article 10 have become even more apparent. The media in Central and Eastern Europe were instrumental in bringing down totalitarianism, and continue to form a vital safeguard in the new democracies, and throughout Europe.

In addition to the work of the Court and Committee of Ministers under the Convention, the Council of Europe is involved in a number of projects to support and encourage the independent media. Amongst its other activities, the Media Division of the Human Rights Directorate publishers regularly updated booklets summarizing the case law on freedom of expression.[59]

---

[57] *Barfod* v. *Denmark*, Judgment of 22 February 1989, Series A, No. 149; (1991) 13 EHRR 493.
[58] See above in this chapter
[59] 'Case Law concerning Art. 10 of the European Convention on Human Rights' (2001), Council of Europe Publishing, F-67075 Strasbourg Cedex.

14

FREEDOM OF ASSEMBLY
AND ASSOCIATION

INTRODUCTION

Article 11 guarantees the right to freedom of peaceful assembly and to freedom of association with others.

1. Everyone has the right to freedom of peaceful assembly and to freedom of association with others, including the right to form and to join trade unions for the protection of his interests.
2. No restrictions shall be placed on the exercise of these rights other than such as are prescribed by law and are necessary in a democratic society in the interests of national security or public safety, for the protection of health or morals or for the protection of the rights and freedoms of others. This article shall not prevent the imposition of lawful restrictions on the exercise of these rights by members of the armed forces, of the police or of the administration of the state.

FREEDOM OF ASSEMBLY

Article 11 guarantees the right to freedom of peaceful assembly. This right is closely associated with Articles 9 and 10 and will frequently need to be considered in the light of the rights guaranteed in those Articles.[1]

In the *Plattform 'Ärzte für das Leben'* case,[2] an association of doctors which campaigned against abortion with a view to securing changes in the Austrian legislation complained of violations of Article 11 when two demonstrations were disrupted by counter-demonstrations, despite a significant police presence. One issue which arose in the case was the extent to which a State is required

---

[1] *Young, James and Webster v. United Kingdom,* Judgment of 13 August 1981, Series A, No. 44; (1982) 4 EHRR 38.

[2] *Plattform 'Ärzte für das Leben' v. Austria,* Judgment of June 21 1988, Series A, No. 139; (1991) 13 EHRR 204.

under Article 11 to intervene to secure conditions permitting the exercise of the right. The Court said:

Genuine, effective freedom of peaceful assembly cannot . . . be reduced to a mere duty on the part of the State not to interfere: a purely negative conception would not be compatible with the object and purpose of Article 11. . . . Article 11 sometimes requires positive measures to be taken, even in the sphere of relations between individuals, if need be.[3]

On the substantive point, the Court found that the Austrian authorities had not failed in their duty to take positive measures to protect the exercise of the right.

The *Ezelin* case[4] concerned an application by a lawyer, who was Vice-Chairman of the Trade Union of the Guadeloupe Bar, complaining that the French courts had imposed a disciplinary penalty by way of reprimand on him because he had taken part in a demonstration protesting at the use of the Security and Freedom Act in Guadeloupe, and had failed to express his disapproval of insults uttered by other demonstrators against the judiciary.

In assessing the proportionality of the sanction, the Court noted that it was to a certain extent symbolic, because it did not prevent the applicant from practising as a lawyer. However, it observed that:

The proportionality principle demands that a balance be struck between the requirements of the purposes listed in Article 11(2) and those of the free expression of opinions, by word, gesture or even silence by persons assembled on the streets or in other public places. The pursuit of a just balance must not result in *avocats* being discouraged, for fear of disciplinary sanctions, from making clear their beliefs on such occasions.[5]

The penalty exceeded that which was necessary in a democratic society, since Ezelin had not himself committed any reprehensible act at all during the demonstration.

FREEDOM OF ASSOCIATION

Article 11 protects the right to 'freedom of association with others'. Put broadly, and subject to the provisos set out in the second paragraph, this constitutes the right to choose whether or not to form and join associations such as political

---

[3] Para. 32 of the judgment.
[4] *Ezelin* v. *France*, Judgment of 26 April 1991, Series A, No. 202; (1992) 14 EHRR 362.
[5] Para. 52 of the judgment.

parties and trade unions, and also other organizations, such as lodges of Free-masons[6] or hunting clubs.[7]

In the industrial or professional context, the right to freedom of association applies only to private-law organizations. Professional and other associations established by the State and governed by public law in principle fall outside the scope of this provision, since such associations are part of the regulatory framework and act in the public interest to ensure the maintenance of professional standards. The distinction was invoked for the first time in relation to the Belgian *Ordre des Médecins*,[8] which had been established by the State to regulate the medical profession. It could not, therefore, be regarded as an 'association' within the meaning of Article 11.[9]

In contrast, an Icelandic body representing taxi-drivers known as '*Frami*' which enjoyed some measure of regulation of the conduct of the business was held to be an association within Article 11,[10] since it was established under private law and enjoyed full autonomy in determining its own organization, procedure, and aims, which included the protection of the professional interests of its members.

POLITICAL PARTIES

In the case of the *United Communist Party of Turkey*[11] the Court rejected the Government's argument that Article 11 applied only to trade union-type associations, and held that political parties also fell within its scope.

The United Communist Party had been dissolved as unconstitutional by the Turkish authorities. The Court emphasized the essential role of political parties in ensuring pluralism and the proper functioning of democracy; many of the fundamental Convention rights, such as the right to elections under Article 3 of Protocol No. 1, would be

inconceivable without the participation of a plurality of political parties representing the different shades of opinion to be found within a country's population. By relaying this range of opinion, not only within political institutions but also—with the help of the media—at all levels of social life, political parties make an irreplaceable

---

[6] *N.F.* v. *Italy; Grande Oriente d'Italia di Palazzo Giustiniani* v. *Italy* (App. 35972/97), Judgments of 2 August 2001.

[7] *Chassagnou and others* v. *France* (Apps. 25088/94, 28331/95, and 28443/95), Judgment of 29 April 1999; (2000) 29 EHRR 615.

[8] *Le Compte, van Leuven and de Meyere* v. *Belgium*, Judgment of 23 June 1981, Series A, No. 43; (1982) 4 EHRR 1.

[9] See also *Barthold* v. *Federal Republic of Germany*, 25 March 1985, Series A, No. 90; (1985) 7 EHRR 383, concerning veterinary surgeons, paras. 60–1 of the judgment.

[10] *Sigurdur A Sigurjónsson* v. *Iceland*, Judgment of 30 June 1993, Series A, No. 264-A; (1993) 16 EHRR 462.

[11] *United Communist Party of Turkey and others* v. *Turkey* (App. 19392/92), Judgment of 30 January 1998; (1998) 26 EHRR 121.

contribution to political debate, which is at the very core of the concept of a democratic society.[12]

Consequently, where political parties were concerned, the exceptions set out in Article 11 were to be construed strictly; only convincing and compelling reasons could justify restrictions on such parties' freedom of association and the State was to enjoy only a very limited margin of appreciation. Having made this point, however, the Court explained that its task was not to substitute its own view for that of the relevant national authorities:

but rather to review under Article 11 the decisions they delivered in the exercise of their discretion. This does not mean that [the Court] has to confine itself to ascertaining whether the respondent State exercised its discretion reasonably, carefully and in good faith; it must look at the interference complained of in the light of the case as a whole and determine whether it was 'proportionate to the legitimate aim pursued' and whether the reasons adduced by the national authorities to justify it are 'relevant and sufficient'. In so doing, the Court has to satisfy itself that the national authorities applied standards which were in conformity with the principles embodied in Article 11 and, moreover, that they based their decisions on an acceptable assessment of the relevant facts.[13]

The Court therefore examined the reasons invoked by the Turkish Constitutional Court for dissolving the United Communist Party. The first ground of dissolution had been the inclusion of the word 'Communist' in the title. The Court of Human Rights considered that a political party's choice of name could not in principle justify a measure as drastic as dissolution, in the absence of other relevant and sufficient circumstances. Secondly, the Constitutional Court had relied upon the fact that the Party had drawn a distinction in its manifesto between the Turkish and the Kurdish nations; in Turkey, the promotion of separatism is unconstitutional. The Court of Human Rights noted, however, that the Party had advocated a political solution to the Kurdish problem and had repudiated violence. Since one of the principal characteristics of democracy was the possibility of resolving a country's problems through dialogue, there could be no justification for hindering a political group solely because it sought to debate in public the situation of part of the State's population and to take part in the nation's political life in order to find, according to democratic rules, solutions capable of satisfying everyone concerned. The dissolution of the Party was, therefore, disproportionate and contrary to Article 11.[14]

In contrast, in the case of *Refah Partisi (Prosperity Party) and others* v. *Turkey*,[15] the Court took the view that it had not been incompatible with Article 11 to

[12] Para. 44 of the judgment. [13] Para. 47 of the judgment.
[14] The Court reached similar conclusions in relation to the dissolution of Turkish political parties in the following cases: *Socialist Party and others* v. *Turkey* (App. 21237/93), Judgment of 25 May 1998; (1999) 27 EHRR 51; *Freedom and Democracy Party* v. *Turkey* (App. 23885/94), Judgment of 8 December 1999.
[15] *Refah Partisi (Prosperity Party) and others* v. *Turkey* (Apps. 41340/98, 41342/98, and 41344/98), Judgment of 31 July 2001.

dissolve the applicant political party, which at the time of dissolution had actually been in power for one year as part of a coalition government. The Court observed that, when campaigning for changes in legislation or to the legal or constitutional structures of the State, political parties would enjoy the protection of Article 11 only if (1) the means used to those ends were lawful and democratic from all standpoints, and (2) the proposed changes were compatible with fundamental democratic principles.

The leaders of the Refah Partisi had declared their intention to establish a plurality of legal systems in Turkey based on differences in religious belief and to establish Islamic (*Sharia*) law, a system of law which was in marked contrast to the values embodied in the Convention. Even if the State's margin of appreciation was limited when it came to the dissolution of political parties, it was reasonable to allow a State to take measures to prevent the implementation of a political programme which was incompatible with Convention norms, before it was given effect through specific acts that might jeopardize civil peace and the country's democratic regime.

TRADE UNION RIGHTS

The right to form and join trade unions is an aspect of the wider right to freedom of association set out in Article 11(1). It includes a positive obligation on the State to protect, through legislation, the union rights of workers in the private sector, as well as those employed by the State.[16]

The Court has held that the words in that paragraph, 'for the protection of his interests' cannot be devoid of meaning, and that it follows therefore that members of a trade union have a right, in order to protect their interests, that the union be heard.[17] It also follows that, in principle, Article 11 safeguards freedom to protect the occupational interests of trade union members by collective action, such as strikes.[18] The Court has, however, adopted an extremely cautious attitude in relation to these rights, allowing a very wide margin of appreciation to the State to decide the extent to which union rights should be recognized and protected under national law.[19]

Thus, Article 11 does not include a right for a union to be consulted or

---

[16] *Gustafsson* v. *Sweden* (App. 15573/89), Judgment of 25 April 1996; (1996) 22 EHRR 409, para. 45.

[17] *National Union of Belgian Police* v. *Belgium*, Judgment of 22 October 1975, Series A, No. 19; (1979–80) 1 EHRR 578.

[18] *Schmidt and Dahlström* v. *Sweden*, Judgment of 6 February 1976, Series A, No. 21; (1979–80) 1 EHRR 637.

[19] The question will be considered again by the new Court in 2002 in *Wilson and the National Union of Journalists and others* v. *United Kingdom* (Apps. 30668/96, 30671/96, and 30678/96) (see the admissibility decision of 16 September 1997).

recognized for collective bargaining.[20] In one case, the Swedish Engine Drivers' Union[21] complained that the National Collective Bargaining Office, a government body, refused to enter into collective agreements with it to the disadvantage of its members. The Court concluded that Article 11 did not encompass specifically any obligation on the part of the employer to enter into collective agreements with unions.

The right to strike and the consequences of doing do were considered in the *Schmidt and Dahlström* case[22] in which the applicants were a professor of law at the University of Stockholm and an officer in the Swedish army. They were members of unions which called selective strikes after the expiry of a collective agreement and the negotiation of its replacement. Neither went on strike, but as members of the 'belligerent' unions, they were denied certain retrospective benefits which were paid to members of other trade unions and to non-union employees who had not participated in the strikes. The Court concluded, first, that the rights enshrined in Article 11 did not include any rights to retroactivity of benefits, such as salary increases, resulting from a new collective agreement. Secondly, though the right to strike represents one of the most powerful means of protecting the interests of its members, such a right is to 'regulation of a kind that limits its exercise in certain instances'. There was thus no violation of Article 11 in the treatment accorded to the applicants.

FREEDOM NOT TO JOIN AN ASSOCIATION

Article 11 does not prohibit the 'closed shop' system, whereby workers cannot be employed in a particular trade unless they are members of a particular union. The preparatory work on the Convention shows that, on account of the difficulties raised by the 'closed shop' system, it was considered undesirable to include the principle set out in Article 20(2) of the Universal Declaration of Human Rights, that no one may be compelled to belong to an association.[23]

The Court has wrestled with the notion of the 'closed shop'. In the *Young, James and Webster* case[24] the applicants complained that they had lost their jobs when they refused to join any of the trades unions within the closed shop

---

[20] *National Union of Belgian Police* v. *Belgium*, Judgment of 22 October 1975, Series A, No. 19; (1979–80) 1 EHRR 578.

[21] *Swedish Engine Drivers' Union* v. *Sweden*, Judgment of 6 February 1976, Series A, No. 20; (1979–80) 1 EHRR 617.

[22] *Schmidt and Dahlström* v. *Sweden*, Judgment of 6 February 1976, Series A, No. 21; (1979–80) 1 EHRR 637.

[23] But see App. 4072/69, *X* v. *Belgium*, 3 February 1970, (1970) 13 *Yearbook* 708, at 718, where it seems to have been assumed *per incuriam* that freedom of association implies freedom not to join an association.

[24] *Young, James and Webster* v. *United Kingdom*, Judgment of 13 August 1981, Series A, No. 44; (1982) 4 EHRR 38.

agreement and that this amounted to a violation of Article 11. The arrangement had been introduced after they had begun their employment with British Rail. In this case, the Court sidestepped the question whether Article 11 encompassed the right not to be compelled to join an association, though it noted that the *travaux préparatoires* suggested that such a right had been deliberately excluded from the Convention. The closed shop agreement at British Rail did, however, interfere with the applicants' right to form or join a trade union, since

a threat of dismissal involving loss of livelihood is a most serious form of compulsion and, in the present instance, it was directed against persons engaged by British Rail before the introduction of any obligation to join a particular trade union.

In the Court's opinion, such a form of compulsion, in the circumstances of the case, strikes at the very substance of the freedom guaranteed by Article 11. For this reason alone, there has been an interference with that freedom as regards each of the three applicants.[25]

The issue was revisited in the *Sigurjónsson* case[26] where the applicant complained that the obligation on him to become a member of '*Frami*' in order to retain his licence to operate a taxicab violated his rights under Article 11. The Court reviewed the current statements on the right *not* to join an association and noted a 'growing measure of common ground' both within the Council of Europe and internationally. This led it to conclude:

[T]he Convention is a living instrument which must be interpreted in the light of present-day conditions. . . . Accordingly, Article 11 must be viewed as encompassing a negative right of association. It is not necessary for the Court to determine in this instance whether this right is to be considered on an equal footing with the positive right.[27]

The Court clearly disliked the degree of compulsion embedded in the provision and was not convinced that membership of '*Frami*' was necessary in order to achieve its objectives. It concluded, that notwithstanding Iceland's margin of appreciation, the measures complained on were disproportionate to the legitimate aim pursued.

The *Sibson* case[28] concerned an employee who resigned from his union following allegations of dishonesty and joined another union. His fellow employees voted in favour of a closed shop and threatened strike action if he continued to work at their depot. The employers sought to resolve the problem by transferring the applicant to another place of work. Another option was that

---

[25] Para. 55 of the judgment.
[26] *Sigurdur A Sigurjónsson* v. *Iceland*, Judgment of 30 June 1993, Series A, No. 264-A; (1993) 16 EHRR 462.
[27] Para. 35 of the judgment.
[28] *Sibson* v. *United Kingdom*, Judgment of 20 April 1993, Series A, No. 258-A; (1994) 17 EHRR 193.

he rejoin the union from which he had initially resigned. The applicant refused both options and resigned with immediate effect. The Court distinguished the *Young, James and Webster* case and found no violation of Article 11: the applicant had no strong objection to rejoining the union (he simply wanted an apology), and could, in any event, have kept his job by moving to another depot.

In the *Gustafsson* case[29] the applicant was an employer, a restaurant owner, who refused to join one of the employers' associations established in Sweden for the purposes of collective bargaining with employees. Because of his refusal to enter into a collective agreement, his restaurant was the object of a union blockade which had a negative effect on his business. He complained that the Government should have provided some mechanism under national law whereby he could have terminated the union action.

The Court observed that in order to comply with the Swedish law on collective bargaining, it would not have been necessary for the applicant to join an employers' association. The law would have been satisfied, and the union action called off, if he had consented to sign a substitute agreement with his employees, recognizing their right to collective bargaining. The Court noted the special role and importance of collective agreements in the regulation of labour relations in Sweden, and the recognition of the legitimate character of collective included in a number of international instruments, including Article 6 of the European Social Charter, Article 8 of the 1966 International Covenant on Economic, Social and Cultural Rights, and Conventions nos. 87 and 98 of the International Labour Organisation. It concluded that the requirement on an employer to enter into a collective wage agreement fell within the Swedish Government's margin of appreciation under Article 11.

RESTRICTIONS ON PARTICULAR GROUPS OF WORKERS

Paragraph (2) of Article 11 contains the standard limitations which are common to Articles 8 to 11.[30] Additionally, it provides that 'This article shall not prevent the imposition of lawful restrictions on the exercise of these rights by members of the armed forces, of the police or of the administration of the State.'

The concept of 'lawfulness' in this provision is the same as that elsewhere in the Convention,[31] requiring, in addition to conformity with domestic law, that the domestic law must be accessible, certain, and not arbitrary.[32]

---

[29] *Gustafsson* v. *Sweden* (App. 15573/89), Judgment of 25 April 1996; (1996) 22 EHRR 409.
[30] See generally ch. 10.   [31] See ch.10 above.
[32] *Rekvényi* v. *Hungary* (App. 25390/94), Judgment of 20 May 1999; (2000) 30 EHRR 519.

It is not clear, however, whether interferences with the rights of association of civil servants in the specified groups must pursue a legitimate aim and be proportionate. The Commission, examining an application arising from the prohibition of trade union membership among civilian workers at the United Kingdom Government Communications Headquarters (GCHQ) in Cheltenham,[33] took the view that the sole requirements in such cases were that the restrictions be in accordance with national law and be free from arbitrariness.[34] In the *Vogt* case[35] the Court appeared to imply that such a measure would need to be proportionate, but left the question open, as it did in a recent case brought by a Hungarian police officer, who complained about an amendment to the Constitution prohibiting the police and members of the armed forces from joining political parties or engaging in political activities.[36] The Court did not need to consider the question under Article 11(2) since it had already determined that the restriction was proportionate under Article 10, given in particular the problems Hungary had suffered in the past with a politicized police force.

The Court has held that it is permissible for a State to restrict the political activity of local government officials,[37] but not to require them to renounce Freemasonry.[38] In the *Vogt* case,[39] it found violations of Articles 10 and 11 where a West German teacher had been dismissed for membership of the Communist Party, given that she had not let her political beliefs affect her professional conduct in any way.

CONCLUDING COMMENTS

The case law under Article 11 can, very broadly, be divided into two categories. The first, concerned with 'political' or 'democratic' rights—such as the freedom to take part in a demonstration or to join a political party—which are closely linked to freedom of expression, draws heavily on the principles developed by the Court under Article 10. The second type of case which arises under Article 11 relates to the employment-based rights to join, or refuse to join, a trade union.

---

[33] App. 11603/85, *Council of Civil Service Unions and others* v. *United Kingdom*, 20 January 1987, (1987) 50 DR 228.
[34] At 240 and 241.
[35] *Vogt* v. *Germany*, Judgment of 26 September 1995, Series A, No. 323, para. 67; (1996) 21 EHRR 205.
[36] *Rekvényi* v. *Hungary* (App. 25390/94), Judgment of 20 May 1999; (2000) 30 EHRR 519.
[37] *Ahmed and others* v. *United Kingdom* (App. 22954/93), Judgment of 2 September 1998; (2000) 29 EHRR 1.
[38] *Grande Oriente d'Italia di Palazzo Giustiniani* v. *Italy* (App. 35972/97), Judgment of 2 August 2001.
[39] *Vogt* v. *Germany*, Judgment of 26 September 1995, Series A, No. 323; (1996) 21 EHRR 205.

Here the Court appears slightly less confident, sometimes allowing the Contracting States such a wide margin of appreciation that it is difficult to discern any real content to the rights for practical purposes.

It must be remembered, however, that there is other international machinery for dealing with complaints concerning trade union rights, in particular under the conventions of the International Labour Organisation and under the European Social Charter. The provisions of the other international instruments are naturally more detailed, and within the International Labour Organisation, in particular, a substantial body of law has been developed.

The Court of Human Rights could react to this in one of two ways. Either it could decide that it does not have the expertise, and that the Convention is not the most appropriate vehicle, for settling complex socio-economic labour law questions.[40] In this case, the Court will continue to interpret Article 11 as affording a wide margin of appreciation to the State, and disgruntled trade unionists might be better advised to address their complaints to another forum. Alternatively, the Court might begin to look more closely at the case law built up under other treaties, and apply the principles developed to promote uniformity of international law in this field.

[40] See the seperate opinions in the *Gustafsson* v. *Sweden* case, Judgment of 25 April 1996; (1996) 22 EHRR 409.

15

PROTECTION OF PROPERTY

INTRODUCTION

Protecting property rights as human rights presents particular problems[1] and it is therefore not surprising that agreement could not be reached on its inclusion in the Convention as originally drafted. A right to property of sorts is included in Article 1 of Protocol 1, but its content is broadly framed and the permissible restrictions are very widely drawn indeed.

All the provisions of the Convention, including Articles 13 to 18, apply equally to the rights guaranteed by the First Protocol.[2] These rights are also subject in the same way to the control of the organs set up by the Convention.

Article 1 of the First Protocol provides:

Every natural or legal person is entitled to the peaceful enjoyment of his possessions. No one shall be deprived of his possessions except in the public interest and subject to the conditions provided for by law and by the general principles of international law.

The preceding provisions shall not, however, in any way impair the right of a State to enforce such laws as it deems necessary to control the use of property in accordance with the general interest or to secure the payment of taxes or other contributions or penalties.

Though drafted rather differently, the structure of the provision is similar to that found in Articles 8 to 11. There is a general right to peaceful enjoyment of possessions. Interferences can, however, be justified on the conditions set out in the article which include references both to the 'public interest' and the 'general interest'; this is the test of proportionality that pervades the Convention's consideration of interferences and requires the balancing of the interests of the individual against the collective interest.

There is also a requirement in the article that deprivations are 'subject to the

---

[1] See generally, H.G. Schermers, 'The international protection of the right of property' in F. Matscher and F. Petzold (eds.), *Protecting Human Rights: The European Dimension. Essays in honour of Gérard J. Wiarda* (Köln, 1988), at 565; J. Frowein, 'The Protection of Property' in R. Macdonal, F. Matscher, and H. Petzold, *The European System for the Protection of Human Rights* (Dordrecht, 1993) at 515; and J. McBride, 'The Right to Property' (1996) 21 E L Rev HRC/40.

[2] Protocol No. 1, Art. 5.

conditions provided for by law'[3] and so the discussion of the notion of inter-ferences being in accordance with law in relation to Articles 8 to 11 will also be relevant here.[4]

The article makes express provision for certain deprivations of property, though these must be in accordance with national law, in accordance with the general principles of international law, and in the public interest. It is also acknowledged that public authorities can control the use of property either in the general interest, or specifically to secure the payment of taxes or other contributions or penalties.

The Court has repeatedly said that the article comprises three distinct rules.[5]

The first rule, which is of a general nature, enounces the principle of peaceful enjoy-ment of property; it is set out in the first sentence of the first paragraph. The second rule covers deprivation of possessions and subjects it to certain conditions; it appears in the second sentence of the same paragraph. The third recognises that the States are entitled, amongst other things, to control the use of property in accordance with the general interest, by enforcing such laws as they deem necessary for the purpose; it is contained in the second paragraph.

These three distinct rules have been reaffirmed in a number of cases, but they should not be viewed as unconnected.

However, the three rules are not 'distinct' in the sense of being unconnected: the second and third rules are concerned with particular instances of interference with the right to peaceful enjoyment of property and should therefore be construed in the light of the general principle enunciated in the first rule.[6]

The beneficiaries of the guarantees in the article are said to be every natural or legal person, thus making it clear that the protections are afforded not only to individuals but also to business entities, including corporations. The article has, consequently, taken on a commercial character and been used extensively by business in the advancement of its interests.

The first judgment of the Court to consider Article 1 of Protocol 1 arose in the context of the illegitimacy laws in Belgium.[7] In its judgment, the Court stated some general propositions on the scope of Article 1 of Protocol 1. The article applies only to a person's existing possessions and gives no guarantee of a right

---

[3] *Prévues par la loi* in the French text.

[4] See ch. 10 above; see also the discussion in relation to this issue under Art. 5 in ch. 7.

[5] *Sporrong and Lönnroth v. Sweden*, Judgment of 23 September 1982, Series A, No. 52; (1983) 5 EHRR 35, para. 61 of judgment. See, more recently, *Holy Monasteries v. Greece*, Judgment of 9 December 1994, Series A, No. 301-A; (1995) 20 EHRR 1, para. 56 of the judgment; and *Carbonara and Ventura v. Italy* (App. 24638/94), Judgment of 30 May 2000, para. 58 of the judgment.

[6] *AGOSI v. United Kingdom*, Judgment of 24 October 1986, Series A, No. 108; (1987) 9 EHRR 1, para. 48 of judgment.

[7] *Marckx v. Belgium*, Judgment of 13 June 1979, Series A, No. 31; (1979–80) 2 EHRR 330.

to acquire possessions.[8] But the right to property does include the right to dispose of one's property.[9]

The general approach of the Court in considering cases where a violation of Article 1 of Protocol 1 is claimed is to consider first whether there has been a deprivation of possessions, followed by consideration of whether there has been a control of the use of possessions, since these are matters specifically dealt with by the article. Only if there has been neither deprivation of possessions nor a control of their use does the Court consider, as a separate issue, whether there has been some other interference with the peaceful enjoyment of possessions. Such interferences will, however, only be unlawful if they are not in the general interest. In its more recent case law, the Court has brought together the tests it applies in relation to both deprivations, the control of the use of property, and to other interferences with property, so that the questions the Court will ask in each of these circumstances are now very similar.

POSITIVE OBLIGATIONS

Perhaps because the exceptions to the right to property in Article 1 of Protocol 1 are so sweeping, there is little case law of the Court on the positive obligations of the State which arise under the Article. But it is clear that positive obligations may arise. The *Gustafson* case[10] concerned a union boycott of the applicant's restaurant, and the termination of membership of his youth hostel in the Swedish Touring Club because of his refusal to accede to certain collective labour agreements. The applicant argued that the Government was in breach of Article 1 of Protocol 1 in not protecting him from such action. Though the Court concluded that, in the particular circumstances of the case, no such duty arose, it did comment that 'the State may be responsible under Article 1 for interferences with peaceful enjoyment of possessions resulting from transactions between private individuals.'[11]

The complex facts of the *Loizidou* case[12] also gave rise to claims of a violation of the right to protection of property. The claims arose in connection with the partition of Cyprus and the difficulties experienced by Greek Cypriots in the south gaining access to their property in the north. Though it is nowhere expressly stated, it follows from the Court's finding of a continuing violation of

---

[8] Para. 50 of the judgment.
[9] Para. 63 of the judgment.
[10] *Gustafsson* v. *Sweden* (App. 15573/89), Judgment of 25 April 1996; (1996) 22 EHRR 409.
[11] Para. 60 of the judgment.
[12] *Loizidou* v. *Turkey* (App. 15318/89), Judgment of 18 December 1996; (1996) 23 EHRR 513.

Article 1 of Protocol 1[13] that a State has a positive obligation to ensure that the owner of real property has access to it so that it can be enjoyed.[14]

DEFINING THE TERM 'POSSESSIONS'

THE BASIC APPROACH

The scope of the protection in Article 1 of Protocol 1 turns on what constitutes possessions. Possessions have been defined in broad terms by both the Commission and the Court. In this context, it is worth noting that French text of the Convention uses the term 'biens' which connotes a very broad range of property rights. The Court has said:

The Court recalls that the notion 'possession' (in French: biens) in Article 1 of Protocol 1 has an autonomous meaning which is certainly not limited to ownership of physical goods: certain other rights and interests constituting assets can also be regarded as 'property rights' and thus as 'possessions', for the purposes of this provision.[15]

It follows that it is for the Strasbourg organs to determine what falls within the concept of possessions in the article having regard to the classification of the matter under national law. Clearly both real and personal property[16] are within the notion of possessions, but the concept extends far beyond to all manner of things which have an economic value. So the Commission has held that company shares are possessions.[17] A patent is also a possession.[18] Goodwill in a business constitutes possessions,[19] as does a licence to serve alcoholic beverages where this is vital to an applicant's business.[20] Similarly a licence to extract gravel was regarded by the Court as a possession.[21] Fishing rights are

---

[13] Paras. 58–64 of the judgment.

[14] See also *Cyprus* v. *Turkey* (App. 25781/94), Judgment of 10 May 2001.

[15] *Gasus Dosier- und Fördertechnik GmbH* v. *Netherlands*, Judgment of 23 February 1995, Series A, No. 306-B; (1995) 20 EHRR 403, para. 53 of the judgment.

[16] Often referred to as immovable and movable property.

[17] Apps. 8588/79 and 8589/79, *Bramelid & Malmström* v. *Sweden*, 12 October 1982, (1982) 29 DR 64, and App. 11189/84, *Company S & T* v. *Sweden*, 11 December 1988, (1987) 50 DR 121.

[18] App. 12633/87, *Smith Kline and French Laboratories Ltd* v. *Netherlands*, 4 October 1990, (1990) 66 DR 70.

[19] *Van Marle and others* v. *Netherlands*, Judgment of 26 June 1986, Series A, No. 101; (1986) 8 EHRR 483, para. 41 of the judgment. But see also App. 10438/83, *Batelaan & Huiges* v. *Netherlands*, 3 October 1984, (1985) 41 DR 170 to the effect that expectations lack the degree of certainty needed to constitute possessions.

[20] *Tre Traktörer Aktiebolag* v. *Sweden*. Judgment of 7 July 1989, Series A, No. 159; (1991) 13 EHRR 309, para. 53 of the judgment.

[21] *Fredin* v. *Sweden*, Judgment of 18 February 1991, Series A, No. 192 (1991) 13 EHRR 784, para. 40 of the judgment.

possessions.[22] A planning permission is a possession.[23] But a driving licence is not a possession.[24]

It may be that a title to property which is null and void under national law is sufficient to constitute a possession for the purposes of raising a complaint under Article 1 of Protocol 1. In one case,[25] the Commission was willing to consider a complaint made by a couple who had purchased an apartment, but had subsequently been deprived of it under the Restitution Law in Bulgaria when it was returned to the son of its former owners before the property's nationalization some time between 1947 and 1952. The Commission said it would be unreasonable to accept that a State might enact legislation allowing nullification of title and so avoid responsibility for an interference with property rights under the Convention. The Court appears to have taken a similar approach in a case in which the ownership of a cinema site had been in dispute for many years.[26]

LEASES AND LICENCES TO OCCUPY PROPERTY

Rights flowing from leases are accepted as possessions. In *Mellacher* v. *Austria*,[27] it was not disputed that reductions in contractually agreed rents under rent control legislation constituted an interference with the applicants' enjoyment of their rights as owners of the rented properties.

Somewhat inconsistently with the broad interpretation of possessions taken in other contexts, the Court has drawn a narrow distinction between the basis on which individuals occupy property as their homes. In an admissibility decision[28] the Court was faced with a situation in which a soldier in the provisional reserve force was allocated housing by the army. Following a change in the system for housing members of the military, the applicant was required to vacate the property and was evicted. The Court observed that the applicant did not have a lease, and that the arrangement could not be equated to 'an agreement under private law'. The Court went on to say:

[The Court] points out that a right to live in a particular property not owned by the applicant does not constitute a 'possession' within the meaning of Article 1 of Protocol 1. . . . Furthermore, allowing a 'user' such as the applicant (who was not even a tenant)

---

[22] App. 11763/85, *Banér* v. *Sweden*, 9 March 1989, (1989) 60 DR 128.
[23] *Pine Valley Developments Ltd and others* v *Ireland*, Judgment of 29 November 1991, Series A, No. 222; (1992) 14 EHRR 319.
[24] App. 9177/80, *X* v. *Federal Republic of Germany*, 6 October 1981, (1982) 26 DR 255.
[25] App. 29583/96, *Panikian* v *Bulgaria*, Decision of 10 July 1999, (1997) 24 EHRR CD63.
[26] *Iatridis* v. *Greece* (App. 31107/96), Judgment of 25 March 1999; (2000) 30 EHRR 97, para. 54 of the judgment.
[27] *Mellacher* v. *Austria*, Judgment of 19 December 1989, Series A, No. 169; (1990) 12 EHRR 391, para. 43 of the judgment.
[28] *JLS* v. *Spain* (App. 41917/98), Decision of 27 April 1999.

to remain indefinitely in premises belonging to the State would prevent the authorities from performing their obligation to administer State property in accordance with their statutory and constitutional duties.[29]

The Court accordingly found the application to be inadmissible. It is suggested that a more satisfactory approach would have been to recognize the applicant's property right in his housing, but to find that the interference was justified in the general interest.[30]

In *Larkos* v *Cyprus*[31] the Court sidestepped the issue when faced with a complaint by a government tenant that the differences in the levels of protection afforded under national law to private tenants and government tenants on termination of the lease violated Article 1 of Protocol 1 when read with Article 14 of the Convention.[32] The Cypriot Government had argued that the applicant did not possess any interest in the property which constituted a possession falling within the scope of Article 1 of Protocol 1. The Court disposed of the case by finding a violation of Article 14 when read in conjunction with Article 8.

The English law of property makes a clear distinction between tenants and licensees, but would regard licensees as entitled to protection of their property rights, though to a lesser extent than tenants. It is accordingly odd that the Court should seemingly draw a distinction between a mere (lawful) user[33] who has nothing which constitutes a possession within the article, and a tenant who has a possession.

SOCIAL SECURITY PAYMENTS AND PENSIONS

Entitlements arising under pension and social security schemes have proved difficult to classify; the position remains unclear. Where a fund is created in which a person has an individual share and where a value can be placed on it at any given moment, there is a possession.[34] But where the relationship between contributions and ultimate benefits is not closely related, no possession exists.[35]

In an application against the United Kingdom, the applicant complained that she did not receive a widow's pension to which she claimed she was entitled by virtue of her own and her late husband's contributions.[36] The Commission recognized that a question might arise under Article 1 if contributions made

---

[29] Para. 2 of the decision.

[30] The applicant does not appear to have complained of a violation of his right to a home under Art. 8, presumably because an alternative home was made available to him.

[31] *Larkos* v. *Cyprus* (App. 29515/95), Judgment of 18 February 1999; (2000) 30 EHRR 597.

[32] Art. 14 provides protection against discrimination in matters within the scope of the Convention: see ch. 19 below.

[33] Likely to be characterized as a licensee under English law.

[34] App. 5849/72, *Müller* v. *Austria*, 16 December 1974, (1975) 1 DR 46.

[35] App. 10094/82, *G* v. *Austria*, 14 May 1984, (1984) 38 DR 84.

[36] App. 4288/69, *X* v. *United Kingdom*, 17 March 1970, (1970) 13 *Yearbook* 892.

many years before to a compulsory contributory pensions scheme, which had subsequently been replaced by a comprehensive National Insurance system, could be regarded as creating a vested interest in a pension which might be described as 'possessions' within the meaning of Article l.

The Commission found, however, after examining the legislation in force at the time, that the applicant had not acquired any such vested interest. A widow's pension was payable under that legislation only in respect of her late husband's contributions; and at the relevant period the applicant had not been married.

The Commission also left open the question whether even contributions to a general national insurance system might give rise to acquired rights capable of coming within Article l. The better view probably is that while Article 1 may protect rights arising out of compulsory contributory pension schemes, where the amount of the pension is directly related to the amount of contributions, it has no application to general social security systems where there is no direct correlation of contributions and benefits. This view was adopted by the Commission in a subsequent case concerning pension schemes in the Netherlands.[37] Hence, the benefits accruing under the schemes did not constitute a property right which could be described as 'possessions' under Article l.

Similar issues came before the Court in the *Gaygusuz* case.[38] Gaygusuz was a Turkish national who had worked in Austria, where he had paid contributions under the Austrian social security scheme. He had experienced periods of unemployment and periods when he was unfit for work. He applied for an advance on his retirement pension as a form of emergency assistance, but was refused because he was not an Austrian national. He complained that there had been a violation of Article 14 when read in conjunction with Article 1 of Protocol 1. The first question was whether the substance of the claim was a matter within the scope of the article, since otherwise Article 14 could not be brought into play. Both the Commission and the Court concluded that the article was applicable but for different reasons. The Commission concluded that the article was brought into play because the obligation to pay 'taxes or other contributions' falls within its field of application.[39] The Court, however, said:

The Court considers that the right to emergency assistance—in so far as provided for in the applicable legislation—is a pecuniary right for the purposes of Article 1 of Protocol 1. That provision is therefore applicable without it being necessary to rely solely on the link between entitlement to emergency assistance and the obligation to pay 'taxes or other contributions'.[40]

[37] App. 4130/69, *X v. Netherlands*, 20 July 1971, (1972) 38 CD 9.
[38] *Gaygusuz v. Austria* (App. 17371/90), Judgment of 16 September 1996; (1997) 23 EHRR 364.
[39] Para. 47 of the Commission Opinion.
[40] Para. 41 of the judgment.

That was sufficient to engage the anti-discrimination provision in Article 14 and to found a violation since the discrimination between nationals and non-nationals was blatant.

LEGAL CLAIMS AS POSSESSIONS

Various types of legal claims have been treated as possessions. Some of these cases are complex in their factual situations, making it difficult to draw general principles from them. What is clear is that there must be something which can be regarded as a legal claim. So in the *Van der Mussele* case,[41] the Court found that the absence of remuneration for legal services where a pupil lawyer had been required to represent a client without payment did not constitute an interference with possessions because no legal duty to pay remuneration ever arose, and the client's indigence meant that no assessment of fees could take place.

In the *Gasus* case[42] the Court was faced with a situation in which the Dutch tax authorities had seized a concrete mixer from a buyer in order to enforce tax debts. The buyer had not yet paid the full price to the applicant company, which had the benefit of a retention of title clause. The Court considered that it made no difference whether the applicant company's right to the concrete mixer was a right of ownership or a 'security right *in rem*'. Whatever view was taken, there was an interference with the peaceful enjoyment of its possessions.

The *Stran Greek Refineries* case[43] involved very large sums of money arising in connection with disputes surrounding the building of an oil refinery. Arbitration proceedings eventually took place, and an award was made. The arbitration award was subsequently declared void. The applicants complained of a violation of, among other articles, Article 1 of Protocol 1, in that they had been deprived of the benefit of the award made in the arbitration proceedings. The Greek Government argued that there was no 'possession' involved here, since the arbitration award had a precarious legal basis and the award could not be equated with any right which might be recognized by such an award. The Court felt that the test was whether 'the arbitration award had given rise to a debt . . . that was sufficiently established to be enforceable.'[44] In the particular circumstances of the case, the Court concluded that the arbitration award was a final and binding award and did give rise to an enforceable debt, even though that right was revocable through the process of annulment of the award. There was therefore a possession within the meaning of Article 1 of Protocol 1.[45]

[41] *Van der Mussele* v. *Belgium*, Judgment of 23 November 1983, Series A, No. 70; (1984) 6 EHRR 163.
[42] *Gasus Dosier- und Fördertechnik GmbH* v. *Netherlands*, Judgment of 23 February 1995, Series A, No. 306-B; (1995) 20 EHRR 403.
[43] *Stran Greek Refineries and Stratis Andreadis* v. *Greece*, Judgment of 9 December 1994, Series A, No. 301-B; (1994) 19 EHRR 293.
[44] Para. 59 of the judgment.
[45] Paras 60–2 of the judgment.

The *Pressos Compania Naviera* case revisited the issue in the context of claims in tort.[46] The dispute centred around claims arising following a collision at sea. Various parties concluded that the collision had arisen as the result of the negligence of the Belgian pilots on board the ships in question. A number of proceedings were brought. Legislation subsequently removed their causes of action retrospectively. The applicants claimed that this constituted an interference with their 'possessions'. The Commission concluded that there was nothing which constituted a possession; an action for damages simply raised the possibility of securing payment. Until there was an enforceable judgment, there was no debt and so no possession within the meaning of Article 1 of Protocol 1.

The Court disagreed, ruling that, having regard to the national law in issue, under the rules of tort, claims to compensation come into existence as soon as the damage occurs, and that a claim constituted an asset which was a possession within the meaning of Article 1 of Protocol 1.[47] The Court does not refer to its decision in *Stran Greek Refineries*, and it is difficult to see a distinction between the two cases which would justify different decisions. The mere expectation that a claim in tort will be determined in accordance with the general law of tort and give rise to an award of damages was sufficient to constitute a possession. A mere expectation is usually not sufficient to constitute a possession.

The Court could have resolved the uncertainty in the *National & Provincial Building Society* case,[48] but did not do so. The case concerned claims that changes to the system for the taxation of interest paid to savers with building societies deprived them of the possibility of securing refunds of taxation paid by them when the regulations were invalidated. Certain regulations were declared invalid, giving rise in the view of the building societies to claims for restitution of tax paid to the Government. These regulations were later retrospectively validated by subsequent legislation, which deprived the building societies of their claims for restitution.

The issue was whether undetermined claims to restitution of monies paid constituted a possession. The Court, clearly aware of the case law in the two earlier cases, sidesteps the definitional problem, and expresses 'no concluded view as to whether any of the claims asserted by the applicant societies could properly be considered to constitute possessions'.[49] The Court, however proceeds 'on the working assumption that . . . the applicant societies did have possessions in the form of vested rights to restitution'.[50] Ultimately no breach of Article 1 of Protocol 1 was found.

---

[46] *Pressos Compania Naviera SA and others* v. *Belgium*, Judgment of 20 November 1995, Series A, No. 332; (1996) 21 EHRR 301.

[47] Para. 31 of the judgment.

[48] *The National & Provincial Building Society, the Leeds Permanent Building Society and the Yorkshire Building Society* v. *United Kingdom* (Apps. 21319/93, 21449/93, and 21675/93), Judgment of 23 October 1997; (1998) 25 EHRR 127.

[49] Para. 70 of the judgment.   [50] Ibid.

Where does this leave the authorities? The best that can be hazarded in response to this question is that a legally acknowledged and enforceable debt is an asset (and so constitutes a possession within Article 1 of Protocol 1),[51] and that a legitimate expectation that an award of damages will be forthcoming on the application of the general law of obligations will also fall within the notion. Distinguishing the *Pressos Compania Naviera* case from the *National & Provincial Building Society* case requires the conclusion that in the former the expectation was 'legitimate' whereas in the latter it was not.

DEPRIVATION OF PROPERTY

WHAT CONSTITUTES DEPRIVATION?

The essence of deprivation of property is the extinction of the legal rights of the owner. This can arise in a number of circumstances. Where a claim is made that there has been a deprivation of property in the absence of a formal transfer of ownership, the Court will:

look behind the appearances and investigate the realities of the situation complained of. Since the Convention is intended to guarantee rights that are 'practical and effective', it has to be ascertained whether that situation amounted to a *de facto* expropriation.[52]

In the *Sporrong and Lönnroth* case,[53] the presence of expropriation permits had the effect of imposing a long-term planning blight on the property in question and of reducing the selling price below normal market prices, but the Court concluded that the adverse impact on the property rights was not such as to make them disappear. There was accordingly no deprivation of property in this case. The *Holy Monasteries* case has complex facts relating to the ownership of monasteries in Greece.[54] Many monasteries in Greece date their foundations to periods between the ninth and thirteenth centuries, and over the centuries they have accumulated considerable landholdings. In May 1987 a Greek law provided that the State would become the owner of the monasteries' property unless the monasteries proved their title to it in one of a number of specified ways. In some cases, the requirements would have been difficult for the monasteries to meet. In effect, there was a presumption that the property belonged to

[51] See *Almeida Garrett, Mascarenhas Falcão and others* v. *Portugal* (Apps. 29813/96 and 30229/96), Judgment of 11 January 2000; (2002) 34 EHRR 642.
[52] *Sporrong and Lönnroth* v *Sweden*, Judgment of 23 September 1982, Series A, No. 52; (1983) 5 EHRR 35, para. 63 of the judgment.
[53] Ibid.
[54] *Holy Monasteries* v. *Greece*, Judgment of 9 December 1994, Series A, No. 301-A; (1995) 20 EHRR 1.

the State unless this was rebutted by the monasteries. One essential issue before the Court was whether this was a procedural device, as the Greek Government argued, relating to the burden of proof of title to property, or whether it was, as the monasteries argued, a substantive provision whose effect is to transfer full ownership of the land in question to the Greek State.[55] The Court concluded that there had been a deprivation.[56]

In the *Pressos Compania Naviera* case,[57] retrospective legislation which operated to deny the claimants an opportunity to sue in respect of claimed negligence by pilots which had led to collisions at sea was treated as a deprivation of property.

DESTRUCTION

Destruction of property will clearly constitute a deprivation of property. A whole series of cases against Turkey related to the destruction of property in the course of clashes between the security forces and PKK[58] sympathizers. A friendly settlement was reached on 22 March 2001 in 201 applications.[59] There can be no doubt that destruction of property constitutes a deprivation of property.[60]

EXPROPRIATIONS

It will be clear from what has been said above that no formal expropriation is required for a deprivation of property to arise. But the distinction between deprivation and interference will be subtle. For a de facto deprivation through expropriation to arise, there must effectively be an extinction of property rights. As noted above, that did not arise in the *Sporrong and Lönnroth* case.[61] A similar conclusion was reached where rent control legislation limited the rental income of the owners of the property in question.[62]

The *Papamichalopoulos* case[63] is a good example of a de facto deprivation.

---

[55]   Para. 61 of the judgment.
[56]   Para. 66 of the judgment.
[57]   *Pressos Compania Naviera SA and others* v. *Belgium*, Judgment of 20 November 1995, Series A, No. 332; (1996) 21 EHRR 301; and see discussion of this case earlier in this chapter.
[58]   Turkish People's Party.
[59]   Court of Human Rights, Information Note No. 28, March 2001, at 33.
[60]   See also *Handyside* v. *United Kingdom*, Judgment of 7 December 1976, Series A, No. 24; (1979–80) 1 EHRR 737, paras. 62–3 of the judgment (destruction of a book); and *Akdivar* v. *Turkey* (App. 21893/93), Judgment of 16 September 1996; (1997) 23 EHRR 143, para. 88 of the judgment (destruction of a home).
[61]   *Sporrong and Lönnroth* v *Sweden*, Judgment of 23 September 1982, Series A, No. 52; (1983) 5 EHRR 35.
[62]   *Mellacher* v. *Austria*, Judgment of 19 December 1989, Series A, No. 169; (1990) 12 EHRR 391, para. 44 of the judgment.
[63]   *Papamichalopoulos and others* v. *Greece*, Judgment of 24 June 1993, Series A, No. 260-B; (1993) 16 EHRR 440.

The Greek Government had transferred land to the Greek Navy. Court proceedings had resulted in decisions that the land was not for disposal, but the Navy nevertheless established a naval base and holiday resort for officers on the land. The whole area was designated as a 'naval fortress'. The Court considered that the applicants remained the lawful owners of the land, but that there had been a de facto expropriation. Despite attempts to make amends after the restoration of democracy in Greece, no substitute land had been allocated to the applicants and this continued the violation of the right to peaceful enjoyment of their land.

Similarly in the *Hentrich* case,[64] a French law which permitted the revenue authorities to buy property which had been sold at below market value in order to discourage the practice was a de facto expropriation.

TEMPORARY OR PROVISIONAL DEPRIVATION

The *Handyside* case[65] makes it clear that temporary seizures do not constitute deprivation of property, though they may well constitute controls on the use of the property seized. In this case the material seized was a book which was considered to be obscene. Other examples of temporary seizures are provisional property confiscations in criminal proceedings;[66] provisional transfers of land as part of agricultural land consolidation proceedings;[67] and the seizure of an aircraft in which a consignment of cannabis had been found with a view to its forfeiture.[68]

CONDITIONS FOR PERMITTED DEPRIVATIONS

A deprivation falling within the first paragraph of Article 1 of Protocol 1 must meet three conditions to be justifiable under the provision:

- The measure providing for the deprivation must be in accordance with the conditions provided for by national law.
- The general principles of international law must be respected.
- The deprivation must be in the public interest, and this will require a balancing of the public interest against individual rights.

---

[64] *Hentrich* v. *France*, Judgment of 22 September 1994, Series A, No. 296-A; (1994) 18 EHRR 440.

[65] *Handyside* v *United Kingdom*, Judgment of 7 December 1976, Series A, No. 24; (1979–80) 1 EHRR 737, para. 62 of the judgment.

[66] *Raimondo* v. *Italy*, Judgment of 22 February 1994, Series A, No. 281-A; (1994) 18 EHRR 237, paras. 29–30 of the judgment.

[67] *Erkner and Hofauer* v. *Austria*, Judgment of 23 April 1987, Series A, No. 117; (1987) 9 EHRR 464, para. 74 of the judgment, and *Wiesinger* v. *Austria*, Judgment of 24 September 1991, Series A, No. 213; (1993) 18 EHRR 258, para. 72 of the judgment.

[68] *Air Canada* v. *United Kingdom*, Judgment of 5 May 1995, Series A, No. 316; (1995) 20 EHRR 150, paras 28–33 of the judgment.

The requirement that the measure must be in accordance with the conditions provided for by national law raises issues similar to those raised in relation to Articles 8 to 11.[69] This does not merely involve the identification of a national law authorizing the taking, but also involves some consideration of the quality of that law, so that there is protection against arbitrary action. In considering the United Kingdom's Leasehold Reform Act 1967, which entitled certain tenants to require the landlord to transfer the freehold of the property to them, the Court said:

The Court has consistently held that the terms 'law' or 'lawful' in the Convention '[do] not merely refer back to domestic law but also [relate] to the quality of the law, requiring it to be compatible with the rule of law.'[70]

The law must accordingly be sufficiently precise and foreseeable in its consequences, and the deprivation must be surrounded by appropriate procedural guarantees. So in the *Hentrich* case,[71] which concerned the State's power to buy property sold at an undervalue, the absence of adversarial proceedings to challenge the State's right of pre-emption constituted a violation of Article 1 of Protocol 1.[72]

Of course, any taking which is in breach of national law will amount to a violation of Article 1 of Protocol 1.[73]

Deprivations of property must also evince respect for the general principles of international law, which require that non-nationals are protected against arbitrary expropriations and, in the case of lawful expropriations, are entitled to compensation for the loss of their property. The rule provides no protection for nationals of a State deprived of property by that State.[74] Once the Court had adopted this position, this requirement has proved to have little application in cases involving Article 1 of Protocol 1.

The public interest test will be at the heart of many cases arising under Article 1 of Protocol 1 as it is under many other claims of violations of Convention rights. In property cases, there is almost a presumption that a national measure is in the public interest. In the *James* case,[75] which concerned United Kingdom leasehold enfranchisement legislation, the Court said:

---

[69]   See in general ch. 10 above

[70]   *James* v. *United Kingdom*, Judgment of 21 February 1986, Series A, No. 98; (1986) 8 EHRR 123, para. 67 of the judgment.

[71]   *Hentrich* v. *France*, Judgment of 22 September 1994, Series A, No. 296-A; (1994) 18 EHRR 440.

[72]   Para. 42 of the judgment.

[73]   As in *Iatridis* v. *Greece* (App. 31107/96), Judgment of 25 March 1999; (2000) 30 EHRR 97.

[74]   Affirmed in *James* v. *United Kingdom*, Judgment of 21 February 1986, Series A, No. 98; (1986) 8 EHRR 123, paras. 61–3 of the judgment; and in *Lithgow* v. *United Kingdom*, Judgment of 8 July 1986, Series A, No. 102; (1986) 8 EHRR 329, paras. 111–19 of the judgment.

[75]   *James* v. *United Kingdom*, Judgment of 21 February 1986, Series A, No. 98; (1986) 8 EHRR 123, para. 46 of the judgment.

The Court, finding it natural that the margin of appreciation available to the legislature in implementing social and economic policies should be a wide one, will respect the legislature's judgment as to what is 'in the public interest' unless that judgment be manifestly without reasonable foundation. In other words, although the Court cannot substitute its own assessment for that of the national authorities, it is bound to review the contested measures under Article 1 of Protocol 1 and, in doing so, to make an enquiry into the facts with reference to which the national authorities acted.

In this case, the Court concluded that the United Kingdom system of lease-hold enfranchisement under the Leasehold Reform Act 1967 was compatible with Article 1 of Protocol 1. Indeed, it is difficult to find a case in which the Court has not recognized the policy preferences of a State as providing a legitimate goal. But the Court has gone further than merely requiring the identification of a legitimate goal in determining whether a deprivation of property is in the public interest. The test of proportionality is also brought into play:

Not only must a measure depriving a person of his property pursue, on the facts as well as in principle, a legitimate aim 'in the public interest', but there must also be a reasonable relationship of proportionality between the means employed and the aim sought to be realised. This latter requirement was expressed in other terms in the *Sporrong and Lönnroth* judgment by the notion of the 'fair balance' that must be struck between the demands of the general interest of the community and the requirements of the protection of the individual's fundamental rights. The requisite balance will not be found if the person has had to bear 'an individual and excessive burden.' . . . The Court considers that a measure must be both appropriate for achieving its aim and not disproportionate thereto.[76]

The *Pine Valley Developments* case[77] concerned the impact of the annulment of a planning permission.[78] The Court in determining that there had been no violation of Article 1 of Protocol 1 was influenced by the element of risk inherent in a commercial venture in considering the proportionality of the State action which had resulted in the annulment of an earlier planning permission relating to an area 'zoned for the further development of agriculture so as to preserve a green belt'.[79]

The offering of compensation has come to play a crucial part of the consideration of proportionality, and is discussed in some detail below.

---

[76] Para. 50 of the judgment.

[77] *Pine Valley Developments Limited and others* v. *Ireland*, Judgment of 29 November 1991, Series A, No. 222; (1992) 14 EHRR 319.

[78] It was an interference case rather than a deprivation case.

[79] *Pine Valley Developments Limited and others* v. *Ireland*, Judgment of 29 November 1991, Series A, No. 222; (1992) 14 EHRR 319, para. 59 of the judgment. See also *Håkansson and Sturesson* v. *Sweden*, Judgment of 21 February 1990, Series A, No. 171; (1991) 13 EHRR 1, para. 53 of the judgment.

THE ISSUE OF COMPENSATION

Where there has been a deprivation of property, there is now at least an expectation that compensation will be paid if the taking is to constitute a fair balance between the individual interest and the general interest. In the *Holy Monasteries* case,[80] the Court restated the position established in its case law,

Compensation terms under the relevant legislation are material to the assessment whether the contested measure respects the requisite fair balance and, notably, whether it does not impose a disproportionate burden on the applicants. In this connection, the taking of property without payment of an amount reasonably related to its value will normally constitute a disproportionate interference and a total lack of compensation can be considered justifiable under Article 1 only in exceptional circumstances. Article 1 does not, however, guarantee a right to full compensation in all circumstances, since legitimate objectives of 'public interest' may call for less than reimbursement of the full market value.[81]

The existence of safeguards by which the reasonableness of the compensation can be checked can be important in showing that the burden on the individual is not excessive. In a group of cases against Greece[82] an irrefutable presumption of benefit as a result of the compulsory purchase of property needed to build a new road which reduced the compensation payable was considered to place a disproportionate burden on the property owners. They were unable to argue that the work was of less, or even no, benefit to them.[83] Consideration of individual circumstances will not, however, always be a required feature of the calculation of compensation. In the *Lithgow* case,[84] the Court accepted that major nationalization programmes may require a standardized rather than an individual approach to the calculation of compensation, and, subject to the securing of a fair balance, a wide margin of appreciation will be allowed in the method for determining the calculation of the compensation payable.

Long delays in the payment of compensation, particularly where there is high inflation or an inadequate payment of interest on the late payment, will also impose an excessive burden on the individual. In a line of cases against Turkey, violations were found where the land valuation was at price obtaining at the

---

[80] *Holy Monasteries* v. *Greece*, Judgment of 9 December 1994, Series A, No. 301-A; (1995) 20 EHRR 1.

[81] Para. 71 of the judgment.

[82] *Katikaridis and others* v. *Greece* (App. 19385/92), Judgment of 15 November 1996; *Tsomtsos and others* v. *Greece* (App. 20680/92), Judgment of 15 November 1996; and *Papachelas* v. *Greece* (App. 31423/96), Judgment of 25 March 1999; (2000) 30 EHRR 923.

[83] *Papachelas* v. *Greece* (App. 31423/96), Judgment of 25 March 1999; (2000) 30 EHRR 923, para. 54 of the judgment.

[84] *Lithgow and others* v. *United Kingdom*, Judgment of 8 July 1986, Series A, No. 102; (1986) 8 EHRR 329, paras. 121–2 of the judgment.

date of the taking and where inflation was running at 70 per cent, but this had not been taken into account in the payments eventually made.[85]

CONTROLLING THE USE OF PROPERTY

SCOPE

The second paragraph of Article 1 of Protocol 1 preserves the power of the State to control the use of property whether in the general interest or 'to secure the payment of taxes or other contributions or penalties'. Many of the examples discussed earlier in this chapter on what constitutes a deprivation of property (and which fall short of deprivation) are examples of control on the use of property. So, seizure of obscene publications,[86] rent controls,[87] planning restrictions,[88] temporary seizure of property in criminal proceedings,[89] temporary seizure of an aircraft in connection with drugs enforcement legislation,[90] the withdrawal of a licence,[91] retrospective tax legislation,[92] and refusal to register applicants as certified accountants with adverse effects for their business,[93] all constitute measures of control on the use of property.

JUSTIFYING THE CONTROLS

Some of the early case law suggested that, where a State can bring its actions within the scope of the second paragraph, there is no need for the balancing of interests to take place.[94] But later case law has moved to a position where the fair

---

[85] *Akkuş v. Turkey* (App. 19263/92), Judgment of 9 July 1997; (2000) 30 EHRR 365; literally dozens of other cases have been taken on this ground: see e.g. 21 judgments issued by the Court on 5 June 2001.

[86] *Handyside* v. *United Kingdom*, Judgment of 7 December 1976, Series A, No. 24; (1979–80) 1 EHRR 737.

[87] *Mellacher* v. *Austria*, Judgment of 19 December 1989, Series A, No. 169; (1990) 12 EHRR 391.

[88] *Pine Valley Developments Limited and others* v. *Ireland*, Judgment of 29 November 1991, Series A, No. 222; (1992) 14 EHRR 319.

[89] *Raimondo* v. *Italy*, Judgment of 22 February 1994, Series A, No. 281-A; (1994) 18 EHRR 237; and *Venditelli* v. *Italy*, Judgment of 18 July 1994, Series A, No. 293-A; (1994) 19 EHRR 464.

[90] *Air Canada* v. *United Kingdom*, Judgment of 5 May 1995, Series A, No. 316; (1995) 20 EHRR 150

[91] *Tre Traktörer Aktiebolag* v. *Sweden*. Judgment of 7 July 1989, Series A, No. 159; (1991) 13 EHRR 309; and *Fredin* v. *Sweden*, Judgment of 18 February 1991, Series A, No. 192; (1991) 13 EHRR 784.

[92] *The National & Provincial Building Society, the Leeds Permanent Building Society and the Yorkshire Building Society* v. *United Kingdom* (Apps. 21319/93, 21449/93, and 21675/93), Judgment of 23 October 1997; (1998) 25 EHRR 127.

[93] *Van Marle and others* v. *Netherlands*, Judgment of 26 June 1986, Series A, No. 101; (1986) 8 EHRR 483.

[94] *Handyside* v. *United Kingdom*, Judgment of 7 December 1976, Series A, No. 24; (1979–80) 1 EHRR 737, para. 62 of the judgment.

balance test which applies to deprivations and other interferences is also applied to matters within the second paragraph of Article 1 of Protocol 1.[95]

The forfeiture and destruction of obscene materials is a justifiable measure within this second paragraph of Article 1.[96]

A similar view was taken of the forfeiture within the United Kingdom of Krügerrands.[97] In this case, the company had the misfortune to engage in business transactions in which they sold Krügerrands in exchange for a dishonoured cheque. They had the transaction declared void under German law and sought the recovery of the gold coins from the British customs authorities which had seized them. The Court considered the case one in which forfeiture did constitute a deprivation of property but was essentially a consequence of their illegal importation, the prohibition of which was a constituent element in a measure for the control of their use in the United Kingdom. Therefore it was necessary to consider only whether there had been compliance with the second paragraph of Article 1.

Finally, the *Gasus* case[98] concerned the seizure by the Dutch tax authorities of property from a company the title in which remained with its seller in Germany, since a retention of title clause prevented the passing of the property until all instalments of the purchase price had been paid. Such seizure was in accordance with the provisions of Dutch tax law. The complaint of the applicant company was that they had been deprived of their property in payment of a tax debt owed by a third party, that they were in no way responsible for causing the tax debt, and that they could not have been aware of it in agreeing to accept the price of the concrete mixer and ancillary equipment by instalments. Nevertheless, the Court concluded that this was a deprivation falling within the second paragraph of Article 1 of Protocol 1.

More recent case law has placed greater emphasis on the need to secure a fair balance between the individual interest and the general interest, though it has been acknowledged that a wide margin of appreciation will be accorded to States.[99] The modern approach can be illustrated by the *Chassagnou* case.[100] The applicants were opposed to hunting on ethical grounds. They had, nevertheless,

[95] See *Pine Valley Developments Limited and others v. Ireland*, Judgment of 29 November 1991, Series A, No. 222; (1992) 14 EHRR 319, paras. 57–59.

[96] See *Handyside v United Kingdom*, Judgment of 7 December 1976, Series A, No. 24; (1979–80) 1 EHRR 737, para. 63 of the judgment.

[97] *AGOSI v. United Kingdom*, Judgment of 24 October 1986, Series A, No. 108; (1987) 9 EHRR 1.

[98] *Gasus Dosier-und Fördertechnik GmbH v. Netherlands*, Judgment of 23 February 1995, Series A, No. 306-B.

[99] *The National & Provincial Building Society, the Leeds Permanent Building Society and the Yorkshire Building Society v. United Kingdom* (Apps. 21319/93, 21449/93, and 21675/93), Judgment of 23 October 1997; (1998) 25 EHRR 127, para. 80 of the judgment; and *Mellacher v. Austria*, Judgment of 19 December 1989, Series A, No. 169; (1990) 12 EHRR 391, para. 53 of the judgment.

[100] *Chassagnou and others v. France* (Apps. 25088/94, 28331/95, and 28443/95), Judgment of 29 April 1999; (2000) 29 EHRR 615.

been obliged to transfer hunting rights over their land to local hunters' associations, had been made members of the local association, and had been unable to prevent hunting on their land. The measures were treated as falling within the second paragraph of Article 1, and are categorized as 'an interference with the . . . enjoyment of their rights as owners of property'.[101] The Court restates its established case law that the second paragraph must be construed in the light of the principle laid down in the first sentence of Article 1, and goes on to say that the interference must achieve a fair balance between the demands of the general interest of the community and the requirements of the protection of individuals' fundamental rights. The Court continues:

The search for this balance is reflected in the structure of Article 1 as a whole, and therefore also in the second paragraph thereof: there must be a reasonable relationship of proportionality between the means employed and the aim pursued. In determining whether this requirement is met, the Court recognises that the State enjoys a wide margin of appreciation with regard both to choosing the means of enforcement and to ascertaining whether the consequences of enforcement are justified in the general interest for the purpose of achieving the object of the law in question.[102]

A violation of Article 1 of Protocol 1 was found in the case since the measures lacked proportionality.

The *Spadea and Scalabrino* case[103] concerned the Italian system of postponing, suspending or staggering the enforcement of eviction orders in order to avoid an upsurge in tenants having to find alternative homes because of the large number of leases which expired in 1982 and 1983. The Court concluded that the system operated as a control on the use of the property by the freeholders, but accepted that the legislation authorizing the delays in the enforcement of the eviction orders served the social purposes of protecting tenants on low incomes and of avoiding a risk of public disorder. A fair balance had been struck between the interests of the individual and the collective interest. But where the delays imposed an excessive burden amounting to some eleven years when the freeholders were kept out of their property, and where there was no possibility of getting compensation for the losses arising from their inability to gain possession of their property, that balance was not met and a breach of Article 1 of Protocol 1 was found.[104]

In summary, three conditions need to be satisfied for a control on the use of property to be permissible under Article 1:

---

[101] Para. 74 of the judgment.
[102] Para. 75 of the judgment.
[103] *Spadea and Scalabrino* v. *Italy*, Judgment of 28 September 1995, Series A, No. 315-B; (1996) 21 EHRR 481.
[104] *Immobiliare Saffi* v. *Italy* (App. 22774/93), Judgment of 28 July 1999. See also *Lunari* v. *Italy* (App. 21463/93), Judgment of 11 January 2001; *PM* v. *Italy* (App. 24650/94), Judgment of 11 January 2001; and *Tanganelli* v. *Italy* (App. 23424/94), Judgment of 11 January 2001.

- The measure must have the character of law.
- The measure must be in the general interest, or be for the purpose of securing the payment of taxes or other contributions or penalties.
- The measure must be deemed necessary by the State.

This modern approach has blurred somewhat the distinction between those measures constituting control of the use of property and those measures which are in the residual category of other interferences with peaceful enjoyment of possessions. It is also very close to the test for the permissibility of deprivation of property. Thus a unity of approach has developed in relation to all interferences with property rights.

OTHER INTERFERENCES WITH PEACEFUL ENJOYMENT OF POSSESSIONS

An increasingly small group of cases falls for consideration under a residual category of other interferences with peaceful enjoyment of possession. Although this right is guaranteed in the first sentence of the article, the practice of the Court is to consider first whether there has been a deprivation, and then whether there has been a control on the use of property before considering whether there has been some other interference with the peaceful enjoyment of possessions. As indicated above, the Court has come to adopt a broad approach to the concept of the control of the use of property, leaving comparatively few cases to be considered under this head. The earlier case law in which certain measures were considered to fall within this head would now almost certainly be considered as measures of control of the use of property. This is because the earlier case law on the second paragraph of Article 1 did not require the State to show that the measure of control struck a fair balance between the individual and the collective interest.

For example, the system of expropriation permits in issue in the *Sporrong and Lönnroth* case[105] was considered to be an interference with the peaceful enjoyment of possessions, whereas now it would probably be regarded as a measure for the control of the use of property. A similar view would probably now be taken of land use plans,[106] though perhaps land consolidation plans might still be regarded as interferences with peaceful possession rather than

---

[105] *Sporrong and Lönnroth* v. *Sweden*, Judgment of 23 September 1982, Series A, No. 52; (1983) 5 EHRR 35.
[106] *Katte Klitsche de la Grange* v. *Italy*, Judgment of 27 October 1994, Series A, No. 293-B; (1994) 19 EHRR 368

measures for the control of use.[107] In a recent case against Greece,[108] the applicants bought a plot of land and proposed to develop it by building a shopping centre, but the local authority decided to block the development though it did not have the funds to expropriate the land. A freeze on new building licences followed. Eventually the land was expropriated. The Court did not consider the early stages to constitute a deprivation of the property, since the owners' rights remained unaffected, nor was it a control of the use of property since the measures did not pursue such an aim. What was in issue was an interference with the peaceful use of possessions. There was no reasonable balance in this case between the rights of the owners and the environmental concerns of the local authority. Consequently, there was a violation of Article 1 of Protocol 1.

In determining whether an interference with the peaceful enjoyment of possessions is permissible, the Court now applies the same test that it has developed in relation to cases involving a deprivation of property.

CONCLUDING COMMENT

The early case law suggested a need to define with some precision the nature of the interference with property rights, because there were differences in the standards demanded of States, but the more modern case law takes a very similar approach to all forms of interferences with property rights. Though the conditions for a lawful interference with the rights protected by Article 1 of Protocol 1 are perhaps not as stringent as those arising in relation to the rights protected by Articles 8 to 11, the Court has been influenced by the approach adopted there, and has required any measures of interference to meet a legitimate aim and to be proportionate in that it strikes a fair balance between the individual interest and the collective interest.

[107] See *Erkner and Hofauer* v. *Austria*, Judgment of 23 April 1987, Series A, No. 117; (1987) 9 EHRR 464; and *Wiesinger* v. *Austria*, Judgment of 24 September 1991, Series A, No. 213; (1993) 18 EHRR 258.
[108] *Pialopoulos and others* v. *Greece* (App. 37095/97), Judgment of 15 February 2001.

16

THE RIGHT TO EDUCATION

INTRODUCTION

Article 2 of the First Protocol provides:

No person shall be denied the right to education. In the exercise of any functions which it assumes in relation to education and teaching, the State shall respect the right of parents to ensure such education and teaching in conformity with their own religious and philosophical convictions.

The article contains a right to education which is enjoyed primarily by the student. In many cases, however, these will be children and the right is likely to be exercised on their behalf by their parents. But the second sentence of the article contains a specific right for parents, who are entitled to respect for their religious and philosophical convictions in the delivery of education and teaching of their children.

As with the right to property,[1] the inclusion of a right to education among the Convention rights proved to be controversial and complicated.[2] Even when agreement could be reached on the inclusion of the right in Article 2 of Protocol 1, a large number of reservations were entered in respect of it.[3]

All the provisions of the Convention, including Articles 13 to 18, apply equally to the rights guaranteed by the First Protocol.[4] These rights are also subject in the same way to the control of the organs set up by the Convention.

Article 2 of Protocol 1 has resulted in comparatively few decisions of the Court, but is not infrequently invoked in applications to Strasbourg. A number of general propositions can be made by way of introduction to the right enshrined in this article. Though drafted as a negative formulation, it has been

---

[1] See ch.15 above.

[2] A.H. Robertson, 'The European Convention on Human Rights—Recent Developments' (1951) BYBIL 359; and L. Wildhaber, 'Right to Education and Parental Rights' in R. Macdonald, F. Matscher and H. Petzold (eds.), *The European System for the Protection of Human Rights* (Dordrecht, 1993), at 531.

[3] Including a reservation by the United Kingdom. Even today there are reservations to the Article by Bulgaria, Germany, Greece, Ireland, Malta, Moldova, The Netherlands, Portugal, Romania, Sweden, the former Yugoslav Republic of Macedonia, Turkey and the United Kingdom. See www.conventions.coe.int for a current list of reservations of Council of Europe instruments.

[4] Protocol No. 1, Art. 5.

accepted that there is a right to education within existing provision, which applies to primary, secondary, and further or higher education. The concept of education is considered broadly. Most of the rights are enjoyed by the pupil or student, but parents have a separate right to respect for their own religious and philosophical convictions in the education of their children.

The main focus of the case law has been on primary education, but it is now clear that the rights also relate to secondary and higher education.[5] The Court has recognized that the right to education has links with the rights protected by Articles 8 to 10 of the Convention and needs to be interpreted consistently with the general spirit of the Convention as an instrument designed to maintain and promote the ideals and values of a democratic society.[6]

In the *Campbell and Cosans* case,[7] the Court noted that the rights enshrined in the article involved a duty on the State to regulate the provision of education.

The right to education guaranteed by the first sentence of Article 2 by its very nature calls for regulation by the State, but such regulation must never injure the substance of the right nor conflict with other rights enshrined in the Convention or its Protocols.[8]

Where there is differential treatment in the provision of education, the anti-discrimination provision in Article 14 frequently comes into play.[9]

POSITIVE OBLIGATIONS

Despite its somewhat broad-brush approach and accommodation to the concerns of States, Article 2 can, nevertheless, give rise to positive obligations on the State. In the *Valsamis* case,[10] the Court said that the obligation in the second sentence of the article implies 'some positive obligations on the part of the State'. So, it would seem that States must strive to accommodate parental wishes flowing from religious or philosophical convictions. Whether that would extend to the funding, or even partial funding, of private schools where this is the only way in which respect for particular convictions could be secured is, as

[5] See e.g. App. 24515/94, *Sulak* v. *Turkey*, Decision of 17 January 1996; (1996) 84-A DR 98.
[6] *Kjeldsen, Busk Madsen and Pedersen* v. *Denmark*, Judgment of 7 December 1976, Series A, No. 23; (1979–80) 1 EHRR 711, para. 54 of the judgment. See also *Valsamis* v. *Greece* (App. 21787/93), Judgment of 18 December 1996; (1997) 24 EHRR 314, para. 25 of the judgment.
[7] *Campbell and Cosans* v. *United Kingdom*, Judgment of 25 February 1982, Series A, No. 48; (1982) 4 EHRR 293.
[8] Para. 41 of the judgment.
[9] See below ch. 19.
[10] *Valsamis* v. *Greece* (App. 21787/93), Judgment of 18 December 1996; (1997) 24 EHRR 294, para. 27 of the judgment.

yet, an unanswered question. In a number of cases, the reservation filed in respect of the article would, if found to be legitimate, protect the State.[11]

In relation to the first sentence of Article 2, a discontinuance of provision may constitute a violation. This means that there may be a positive obligation to continue educational provision in, for example, the language of a minority once that has been provided, even though there is no obligation to provide education in minority languages.[12]

THE RIGHT TO EDUCATION

Although the wording of the article is that 'no person shall be denied the right to education', the Court stated in the merits phase of the *Belgian Linguistic* case[13] that the negative formulation meant that there was no obligation for the Contracting Parties to 'establish at their own expense, or to subsidise, education of any particular type or at any level'.[14] The Court went on to note that all the Contracting Parties have public education systems, and that Article 2 guaranteed the right, in principle, to 'avail themselves of the means of instruction existing at a given time'.[15] What this means is that the article guarantees a right of access to existing educational provision, but the State has a wide margin of appreciation as to the resources it devotes to the system of education and as to its organization.

In a group of cases involving the removal of gypsies from land where they had set up homes in breach of planning laws,[16] it was argued that the refusal to allow the families to remain on their own land resulted in their children being denied access to satisfactory education. In all three cases the Court found that the applicants had failed to substantiate their claims under this provision of the Convention and so there was no violation. The applications, however, signal the potential linkage between provisions of the Convention, though in most cases a requirement that a family moves its home would not result in schooling being

---

[11] Where the reservation indicated that the provision of education was subject to national resource constraints.

[12] See *Cyprus* v. *Turkey* (App. 25781/94), Judgment of 10 May 2001, paras. 273–80 of the judgment.

[13] *Case relating to certain aspects of the laws on the use of languages in education in Belgium (Belgian Linguistic Case (No. 2))*, Judgment of 23 July 1968, Series A, No. 6; (1979–80) 1 EHRR 252 (cited in this chapter as the '*Belgian Linguistic* case').

[14] Para. 3 of the judgment under the heading 'B. Interpretation adopted by the Court'.

[15] Ibid.

[16] *Coster* v. *United Kingdom* (App. 24876/94), (2001) 33 EHRR 479; *Lee* v. *United Kingdom* (App. 25289/94), (2001) 33 EHRR 677; and *Smith (Jane)* v. *United Kingdom* (App. 25154/94), (2001) 33 EHRR 712, all Judgments of 18 January 2001.

unavailable to them if they were within the age range for which attendance at school was required by the State.

In the *Belgian Linguistic* case, the Court defined the scope of the right to education in the following terms:

The first sentence of Article 2 of the Protocol consequently guarantees, in the first place, a right of access to educational institutions existing at a given time, but such access constitutes only a part of the right to education. For the 'right to education' to be effective, it is further necessary that, *inter alia*, the individual who is the beneficiary should have the possibility of drawing profit from the education received, that is to say, the right to obtain, in conformity with the rules in force in each State, and in one form or another, official recognition of the studies which he has completed.[17]

In the *Belgian Linguistic* case,[18] six groups of applicants claimed that various aspects of the Belgian legislation governing the use of languages in schools were inconsistent with the Convention. The applicants, who were French-speaking residents in the Dutch-speaking part of Belgium and in the Brussels periphery, wanted their children to be educated in French. The Court decided that Article 2 did not include a right to be taught in the language of parents' choice, nor a right of access to a particular school of the parents' choice. Ultimately, the Court found that the Belgian legislation failed to comply with the provisions of the Convention and Protocol in only one respect. It infringed Article 14 of the Convention,[19] read in conjunction with the first sentence of Article 2 of the First Protocol, in so far as it prevented certain children, solely on the basis of the residence of their parents, from having access to the French-language schools in certain communes on the periphery of Brussels. The law provided that the language of instruction in these communes was Dutch, but that French-speaking classes should be provided at the nursery and primary levels, on condition that it was asked for by sixteen heads of family. However, this education was not available to children whose parents lived outside these communes, even though there were no French-speaking schools in the communes where they lived. The Dutch classes, on the other hand, accepted all children, whatever the place of residence of the parents. Applying the criteria of discrimination which it elaborated in this case, the Court held that this differential treatment could not be justified under Article 14.

---

[17] Para. 4 of the judgment under the heading 'B. Interpretation adopted by the Court'.

[18] *Case relating to certain aspects of the laws on the use of languages in education in Belgium (Preliminary objections) Belgian Linguistic Case (No. 1)*, Judgment of 9 February 1967, Series A, No. 5, (1979–80) 1 EHRR 241; *Case relating to certain aspects of the laws on the use of languages in education in Belgium (Merits) Belgian Linguistic Case (No. 2)*, Judgment of 23 July 1968, Series A, No. 6; (1979–80) 1 EHRR 252.

[19] The prohibition on discrimination; see ch. 19 below.

ACCESS TO EDUCATION

The right of access is to the educational provision existing at any given time. The choice of provision is a matter for the State, though it would seem that there is a right of persons to establish private schools.[20] Commission decisions establish that there is no obligation on the State to provide selective education,[21] or schools offering education in the context of particular religious affiliations,[22] single-sex schools,[23] or separate schools for those with special educational needs.[24]

EFFECTIVE EDUCATION

Comments in the *Belgian Linguistic* case to the effect that the right to education involves a right to an effective education would seem to require States to maintain certain standards in education. This means that, whereas there may be universal entitlement to education up to a certain age, education beyond that age may be dependent upon the attainment of qualifications deemed necessary for the pursuit of more advanced education.[25]

The *Belgian Linguistic* case recognized that effective education may require the State to regulate education by requiring compulsory attendance at school. The Strasbourg organs have, however, consistently accorded to the Contracting States a wide margin of appreciation in the measures of regulation taken.[26] However, where the regulation operates as a denial of education, there will be a violation of the article. So a provision in Scotland excluding a pupil from a State school because of a refusal to submit to corporal punishment exceeded the scope for reasonable regulation of education and amounted to a violation of the right to education in the first sentence of the article.[27]

[20] *Kjeldsen, Busk Madsen and Pedersen* v. *Denmark*, Judgment of 7 December 1976, Series A, No. 23; (1979–80) 1 EHRR 711, para. 50 of the judgment. See also App. 11533/85, *Jordebo Foundation of Christian Schools and Jordebo* v. *Sweden*, Decision of 6 March 1987; (1987) 51 DR 125; and App. 23419/94, *Verein Gemeinsam Lernen* v. *Austria*, Decision of 6 September 1995; (1995) 82-A DR 41.

[21] Apps 10228/92 and 10229/82, *W and others* v. *United Kingdom*, Decision of 6 March 1984; (1984) 37 DR 96.

[22] App. 7728/77, *X* v. *United Kingdom*, Decision of 2 May 1978; (1979) 14 DR 179.

[23] Apps 10228/92 and 10229/82, *W and others* v. *United Kingdom*, Decision of 6 March 1984; (1984) 37 DR 96.

[24] App. 14688/89, *Simpson* v. *United Kingdom*, Decision of 4 December 1989; (1989) 64 DR 188; and App. 28915/95, *SP* v. *United Kingdom*, Decision of 17 January 1997.

[25] See Commission decision in App. 11655/85, *Glasewska* v. *Sweden*, Decision of 10 October 1985; (1985) 45 DR 300.

[26] e.g. as to the setting of the curriculum: see *Kjeldsen, Busk Madsen and Pedersen* v. *Denmark*, Judgment of 7 December 1976, Series A, No. 23; (1979–80) 1 EHRR 711, para. 53 of the judgment.

[27] *Campbell and Cosans* v. *United Kingdom*, Judgment of 25 February 1982, Series A, No. 48; (1982) 4 EHRR 293.

SAFEGUARDING PLURALISM IN EDUCATION

The scope of the second sentence of the article is much wider than the first, although it must be recalled that the Court has indicated that the two sentences of the article must be read in the light of each other and of other provisions of the Convention.[28] Indeed the Court has said that Article 2 is 'dominated' by its first sentence.[29] Its scope is wide because it is delimited by reference to the functions which a State assumes in relation to education; many governments assume wide functions in relation to the regulation of education offered by the State and by the private sector. The Court has described the purpose of the second sentence of Article 2 as follows:

The second sentence of Article 2 aims in short at safeguarding the possibility of plural- ism in education, which possibility is essential for the preservation of the 'democratic society' as conceived by the Convention.[30]

The rights protected by the second sentence are rights of parents, and so the focus will be on education provided before the children reach adulthood and can make their own decisions. The Court has also indicated that one of the purposes of the provision is to operate as a check against possible indoctrination:

The State is forbidden to pursue an aim of indoctrination that might be considered as not respecting parents' religious and philosophical convictions. That is the limit that must not be exceeded.[31]

The effect of the second sentence of the article on parental choice allows parents either to enrol their children in State education, to withdraw their children from the State system, and educate them privately whether at a private school or at home,[32] or to enforce respect for their religious and philosophical convictions by alleging a violation of the second sentence of Article 2. It allows a significant parental influence on the both the organization and content of educational provision.

The Court has ruled that the duty applies not to education viewed narrowly, but to the performance of all the functions assumed by the State, which will include the internal administration of the school.[33]

[28] *Kjeldsen, Busk Madsen and Pedersen* v. *Denmark*, Judgment of 7 December 1976, Series A, No. 23; (1979–80) 1 EHRR 711, para. 53 of the judgment.

[29] Ibid.

[30] Para. 50 of the judgment.

[31] Para. 53 of the judgment.

[32] Though this may be regulated by the State, see App. 10233/83, *Family H* v. *United Kingdom*, Decision of 6 March 1984; (1984) 37 DR 105.

[33] *Campbell and Cosans* v. *United Kingdom*, Judgment of 25 February 1982, Series A, No. 48; (1982) 4 EHRR 293, para. 33 of the judgment.

THE NATURE OF RELIGIOUS AND PHILOSOPHICAL CONVICTIONS

The leading authority on the nature of religious convictions is the *Valsamis* case,[34] which arose in the context of objections raised by a family of Jehovah's Witnesses. The Court recalled its case law under Article 9 and acknowledged that Jehovah's Witnesses 'enjoy both the status of a "known religion" and the advantages flowing from that as regards observance'.[35] Thus, any person whose convictions can be described as those of a 'known religion' will be able to argue that they have religious convictions.

The leading authority on the nature of philosophical convictions is the *Campbell and Cosans* case.[36] The Court said,

In its ordinary meaning the word 'convictions', taken on its own, is not synonymous with the words 'opinions' and 'ideas', such as are utilised in Article 10 of the Convention, which guarantees freedom of expression; it is more akin to the term 'beliefs' . . . appearing in Article 9—which guarantees freedom of thought, conscience and religion—and denotes views that attain a certain level of cogency, seriousness, cohesion and importance.

As regards the adjective 'philosophical', it is not capable of exhaustive definition and little assistance as to its precise significance is to be gleaned from the *travaux préparatoires*. . . .

Having regard to the Convention as a whole . . ., the expression 'philosophical convictions' in the present context denotes, in the Court's opinion, such convictions as are worthy of respect in a 'democratic society' and are not incompatible with human dignity; in addition, they must not conflict with the fundamental right of the child to education, the whole of Article 2 being dominated by its first sentence.[37]

THE NATURE OF THE DUTY TO RESPECT RELIGIOUS AND PHILOSOPHICAL CONVICTIONS

In the *Valsamis* case,[38] the Court explained its view of the nature of the duty to respect religious and philosophical convictions. The duty arose in relation not only to the contents of education and the manner of its provision but also to the performance of all of the functions assumed by the State.[39] Respect, said the Court, involves more than acknowledgement. Quite how this will convert into

[34] *Valsamis* v. *Greece* (App. 21787/93), Judgment of 18 December 1996; (1997) 24 EHRR 294. See also *Efstratiou* v. *Greece* (App. 24095/94), Judgment of 18 December 1996.

[35] *Valsamis* v. *Greece* (App. 21787/93), Judgment of 18 December 1996; (1997) 24 EHRR 294, para. 25 of the judgment.

[36] *Campbell and Cosans* v. *United Kingdom*, Judgment of 25 February 1982, Series A, No. 48; (1982) 4 EHRR 293.

[37] Para. 36 of the judgment.

[38] *Valsamis* v. *Greece* (App. 21787/93), Judgment of 18 December 1996; (1997) 24 EHRR 294. See also *Efstratiou* v. *Greece* (App. 24095/94), Judgment of 18 December 1996.

[39] *Valsamis* v. *Greece* (App. 21787/93), Judgment of 18 December 1996; (1997) 24 EHRR 294, para. 27 of the judgment.

practice will involve the judgment of national authorities, but it would seem to require that genuine consideration is made to the possibility of accommodations which will avoid conflicts in the delivery and organization of education with the religious or philosophical convictions of parents.

The Court reaffirmed its earlier case law that respect for democratic values did not mean that the views of the majority must always prevail. Although individual interests had to be subordinated to the views of the majority in some circumstances, a balance had to be achieved which ensured the fair and proper treatment of minorities and avoided any abuse of the position of the majority group.[40]

APPLICATION OF THE DUTY

The *Kjeldsen* case[41] concerned compulsory sex education in Denmark. Sex education had been an optional subject in Danish state schools for many years. In 1970 a law was enacted to make it obligatory in these schools. According to the law, sex education would not be presented as a separate subject, but would be integrated with the teaching of other subjects. The parents of a number of children objected that this law infringed their right to ensure education and teaching in conformity with their own religious and philosophical convictions. The Court concluded that compulsory sex education did not violate Article 2 in failing to respect the wishes of the parents. The Court stressed that there must be no attempt at indoctrination that might be regarded as not respecting the parents' religious or philosophical convictions. The information must be presented in 'an objective, critical and pluralistic manner'. The sex education programme in Denmark was considered to be 'within the bounds of what a democratic State may regard as the public interest'.

A different view was taken in relation to parents' objections to corporal punishment in the *Campbell and Cosans* case.[42] At issue here was what, at best, was a philosophical belief. The Court stated that a philosophical belief must relate to 'a weighty and substantial aspect of human life and behaviour'. The parental objection to corporal punishment met this standard since it concerned 'the integrity of the person, the propriety or otherwise of the infliction of corporal punishment and the exclusion of the distress which risk of such punishment entails'. The Court concluded that the United Kingdom had violated Article 2 of the Protocol when the school offered the parents in question no guarantee that their son would not be beaten, and no alternative education was available for him.

[40] Ibid.

[41] *Kjeldsen, Busk Madsen and Pedersen v. Denmark*, Judgment of 7 December 1976, Series A, No. 23; (1979–80) 1 EHRR 711.

[42] *Campbell and Cosans v. United Kingdom*, Judgment of 25 February 1982, Series A, No. 48; (1982) 4 EHRR 293.

Compulsory attendance at a school parade to mark National Day in Greece[43] was at issue in the *Valsamis* case.[44] The applicants were a family of Jehovah's Witnesses; part of their religious beliefs involved opposition to events with military overtones. The daughter was punished by the school for not attending the school parade, despite having been advised that attendance would be inconsistent with her religious beliefs. Her parents complained that their wishes in respect of the family's religious convictions had not been respected. Though there is little that can be criticized in the Court's discussion of the content of religious convictions, their application to the facts of this case, which resulted in a finding that there was no violation of the article, is unsatisfactory. The Court noted that the school had exempted the daughter from religious classes at the school, and went on to express surprise that 'pupils can be required on pain of suspension . . . to parade outside the school precincts on a holiday.'[45] It concluded that there was nothing in the requirement to attend the school parade which 'could offend the applicants' pacifist convictions to an extent prohibited by the second sentence of Article 2 of Protocol 1', because such celebrations serve both pacifist objectives and the public interest.[46] Perhaps the Court wished to send out a signal in this case that respect for religious and philosophical convictions would depend on an objective assessment of the situation, rather than simply seeking to ascertain whether the beliefs and the consequences of them were genuinely held.

The view of the two dissenting judges is to be preferred. They indicated that there was nothing to suggest that the beliefs of the family were unfounded and unreasonable. In the light of those beliefs the requirement of attendance was disturbing to the family and humiliating to the daughter. The applicant family was under no obligation to share the views of the majority on the value of the commemorative events of 28 October. Participation was not a neutral act, and it could not be said that attendance formed part of the usual school curriculum. The minority concluded that there had been a violation of the article.

The case law is now rather muddled and it is not easy to provide a rational explanation for the outcomes. In the *Belgian Linguistic* case, the Court declined to guarantee education in a particular language. In the *Kjeldsen* case, the Court declined to strike down compulsory sex education in the light of parental objections. In the *Valsamis* and *Efstratiou* cases, the Court declined to strike down compulsory attendance at a national commemorative occasion with military overtones found to be objectionable to those with religious beliefs a

---

[43] On 28 October each year, which marks the outbreak of war between Greece and Fascist Italy on 28 October 1940, and so recognizes Greek attachment to values of democracy, liberty, and human rights.

[44] *Valsamis* v. *Greece* (App. 21787/93), Judgment of 18 December 1996; (1997) 24 EHRR 294. See also *Efstratiou* v. *Greece* (App. 24095/94), Judgment of 18 December 1996.

[45] Para. 31 of the judgment.

[46] Ibid.

central part of which included pacifism. However, in the *Campbell and Cosans* case, the Court upheld the parental objections to corporal punishment. One possible explanation is that corporal punishment involves the physical integrity of the individual, whereas sex education reflects the duty of the State to provide children with information, language education arouses great political and constitutional sensitivities in some regions of Europe, and parading as part of a national commemoration was not considered inconsistent with pacifist beliefs when the overall objectives of the National Day were taken into consideration.

EDUCATION FOR CONVICTED PRISONERS

Special difficulties may arise in relation to the right to education of convicted prisoners, especially since Article 2 contains no escape clause allowing inter-ference in the interests of public order, security, or otherwise. The question has not yet been fully examined. In the *Golder* case,[47] the applicant referred to certain examination facilities which he was trying to obtain, but did not make any specific complaint in this respect. An application against Austria[48] which put the question clearly was rejected for non-exhaustion of domestic remedies. The applicant alleged that his right to further education was being denied by the prison authorities. Although the Austrian law on the Execution of Sentences provided that prisoners should be given the opportunity for further education, such provisions were ineffective because they were required to pay for their books and other educational material, which they could not afford out of their prison earnings.

Again, it may be possible to apply by analogy the reasoning of the Court in the *Belgian Linguistic* case and to argue that States have no positive obligation to subsidize prisoners' education, but may not take steps to interfere with it. In this sense, the obligation under the first sentence of Article 2 may be much less susceptible to positive obligations on the State than the obligation in the second sentence of the article.

[47] *Golder* v. *United Kingdom*, Judgment of 21 February 1975, Series A, No. 18; (1979–80) 1 EHRR 524. For a discussion of the case in relation to Article 8, see ch. 11 above.

[48] App. 4511/70, *X* v. *Austria*, Decision of 24 May 1971, (1972) 38 CD 84.

CONCLUDING COMMENT

The decision in the *Belgian Linguistic* case may have set back the development by the Strasbourg organs of the right to education. There are undoubtedly political and constitutional sensitivities of language in national life. In such a content, the decision is unsurprising. But if provision of education in a language widely spoken in a country but which is not the official language of the State falls outside the scope of Article 2 of Protocol 1, then few aspects of educational policy choice by a Contracting State are likely to violate the guarantee in the article. The current President of the Court, writing in a personal capacity, has opined that there might be an arbitrary restriction of education if it is only available in the national language and not the territorial language.[49] This could render the provision of education ineffective to those whose first language was the territorial language.

Some support for this view may be found in the decision of the Court in the *Cyprus* v. *Turkey* case.[50] One of the complaints of the Cyprus Government was that the provision of secondary education through the medium of the Greek language in the northern part of Cyprus had been discontinued. The only secondary education available was in Turkish. Those wishing to have their children educated in Greek could transfer to the southern part of the island. A violation of Article 2 was found since no appropriate secondary-school facilities were available to them. It is important to note that the discontinuance of the provision appears to have been a crucial issue in this case. The failure to continue Greek-language teaching constituted a denial of the substance of the right to education.

The interpretation of the Convention as a living instrument may result in significant developments in the scope and protection of the article in the future. To date, the germination of the seeds of this change cannot yet be observed.

---

[49] L. Wildhaber, 'Right to Education and Parental Rights' in R. Macdonald, F. Matscher, and H. Petzold (eds.), *The European System for the Protection of Human Rights* (Dordrecht, 1993), 531, at 541.

[50] *Cyprus* v. *Turkey* (App. 25781/94), Judgment of 10 May 2001. See specifically paras. 273–80 of the judgment.

17
THE RIGHT TO FREE ELECTIONS

INTRODUCTION

Article 3 of the First Protocol provides:

The High Contracting Parties undertake to hold free elections at reasonable intervals by secret ballot, under conditions which will ensure the free expression of the opinion of the people in the choice of the legislature.

All the provisions of the Convention, including Articles 13 to 18, apply equally to the rights guaranteed by the First Protocol.[1] Article 3, like Articles 1 and 2 of the First Protocol, but to a lesser extent, reflects the difficulties which prevented these rights from being incorporated in the text of the Convention. Those difficulties are preserved in an unsatisfactory draft, the result of a compromise, and continue to give rise to problems of interpretation.

Article 3 of the First Protocol 'presupposes the existence of a representative legislature, elected at reasonable intervals, as the basis of a democratic society'.[2] It goes further than requiring free elections; it requires that the exercise of political power be subject to a freely elected legislature. Examination of the rights and freedoms guaranteed by the Convention has shown the importance of all those rights and freedoms being guaranteed by law, and of all restrictions on them being subject to the law. Article 3 of the First Protocol underpins the whole structure of the Convention in requiring that laws should be made by a legislature responsible to the people. Free elections are thus a condition of the 'effective political democracy' referred to in the Preamble, and of the concept of a democratic society which runs through the Convention. The Court has repeatedly stated that Article 3 of Protocol 1 'enshrines a characteristic of an effective political democracy.'[3]

Free elections imply a genuine choice. Hence, as the Commission stated in

[1] Protocol No. 1, Art. 5.
[2] *The Greek Case*, Report of the Commission, 5 November 1969, (1969) 12 *Yearbook* 179.
[3] *Mathieu-Mohin and Clerfayt* v. *Belgium*, Judgment of 2 March 1987, Series A, No. 113; (1988) 10 EHRR 1, para. 47 of the judgment; *United Communist Party of Turkey and others* v. *Turkey* (App. 19392/92), Judgment of 30 January 1998; (1998) 26 EHRR 121, para. 45 of the judgment; and *Matthews* v. *United Kingdom* (App. 24833/94), Judgment of 18 February 1999; (1999) 28 EHRR 361, para. 42 of the judgment.

the *Greek* case, the suspension of political parties is also contrary to Article 3.[4] On the other hand, it is consistent with the Convention, in accordance with Article 17, to prohibit political parties with totalitarian aims.[5]

The obligation in Article 3 is expressed as an undertaking by the Contracting Parties rather than in the form of a right or prohibition. This had led to suggestions that, unlike other provisions of the Convention, it was intended that it should only be invoked by States and not by individuals. The Court has now stated:

Accordingly—and those appearing before the Court were agreed on this point—the inter-State colouring of the wording of Article 3 does not reflect any difference of substance from the other substantive clauses in the Convention and Protocols. The reason for it would seem to lie rather in the desire to give greater solemnity to the commitment undertaken and in the fact that the primary obligation in the field concerned is not one of abstention or non-interference, as with the majority of the civil and political rights, but one of adoption by the State of positive measures to 'hold' democratic elections.[6]

WHAT IS THE LEGISLATURE?

The wording of Article 3 only encompasses elections to the legislature. This raises the question of what constitutes the legislature. The Commission consistently stated that the term must be interpreted in the light of both the institutions established by the constitutions of the Contracting Parties and the international undertakings affecting the legislative powers of the legislative body under consideration.[7] The Court takes a similar view.[8]

The Article does not apply to elections to organs of a professional body, such as the Royal Society for the Cultivation of Flower Bulbs, even if certain legislative power has been conferred on it.[9] Nor to the appointment of the Head of State, such as the Federal President of Austria.[10]

---

[4] *The Greek Case*, Report of the Commission, 5 November 1969, (1969) 12 *Yearbook* 179, at 180.

[5] See below, ch. 23.

[6] *Mathieu-Mohin and Clerfayt* v. *Belgium*, Judgment of 2 March 1987, Series A, No. 113; (1988) 10 EHRR 1.

[7] e.g. in App. 11123/84, *Tête* v. *France*, 9 December 1987, (1987) 54 DR 52.

[8] *Mathieu-Mohin and Clerfayt* v. *Belgium*, Judgment of 2 March 1987, Series A, No. 113; (1988) 10 EHRR 1, para. 53 of judgment; and *Matthews* v. *United Kingdom* (App. 24833/94), Judgment of 18 February 1999; (1999) 28 EHRR 361, para. 40 of the judgment.

[9] App. 9926/82, *X* v. *Netherlands*, 1 March 1983, (1983) 32 DR 274.

[10] App. 15344/89, *C-L and L Habsburg-Lothringen* v. *Austria*, 14 December 1989, (1990) 64 DR 210, at 219.

Much more problematic are issues of whether regional authorities constitute the legislature.

Of the Member States of the Council of Europe, Switzerland is the clearest proof that Article 3 cannot be confined to the central power. It must extend to the Swiss cantons, which have a very high degree of autonomy, and to all provincial legislatures where there is a measure of decentralization of power. The only federal States apart from Switzerland in the Council of Europe are Germany and Austria, the German *Länder* having more power than the Austrian *Bundesländer*.

In a case referred to above, where a convicted prisoner was refused permission to vote, his complaints related both to *Land* elections and to federal elections in Germany, and the Commission did not distinguish between them.[11] It would certainly be incorrect to exclude *Land* elections from the scope of Article 3.

However, local government in the non-federal States may lack the necessary autonomy to constitute the legislature. However, it should be noted that the Court's decision in the *Ahmed* case is expressly stated to be without prejudice to the question of whether local government elections in the United Kingdom are within the scope of Article 3.[12]

A distinction can be drawn in all modern States between the legislative bodies which have supreme legislative powers, and subordinate authorities which are empowered only to enact subordinate legislation, however general it may be in its application. The term 'legislature', used without qualification in Article 3, should be interpreted as extending to a provincial legislature which has a degree of autonomy, but not to such subordinate authorities. This was the view taken by the Commission in the case of English Metropolitan county councils[13] which could not be considered the legislature, since their powers are derivative and are defined by legislation with certain activities requiring approval or consent. They did not 'possess an inherent primary rulemaking power'.[14]

The status of the European Parliament and the application of Article 3 to elections to it arose in the *Matthews* case.[15] The applicant was a British citizen living in Gibraltar, which is a dependent territory of the United Kingdom with its own legislature. The EC Treaty applies to Gibraltar, although the operation of parts of the EC Treaty is excluded in relation to Gibraltar under the terms of the Treaty of Accession. Elections to the European Parliament are governed

---

[11] App. 2728/66, *X v. Federal Republic of Germany*, 6 October 1967, (1967) 10 *Yearbook* 336.
[12] *Ahmed and others* v. *United Kingdom* (App. 22954/93), Judgment of 2 September 1998; (2000) 29 EHRR 1, para. 76 of the judgment.
[13] App. 11391/85, *Booth-Clibborn and others* v. *United Kingdom*, 5 July 1985, (1985) 43 DR 236.
[14] Ibid., at 248.
[15] *Matthews* v. *United Kingdom* (App. 24833/94), Judgment of 18 February 1999; (1999) 28 EHRR 361

by the Act Concerning the Election of the Representatives of the European Parliament by Universal Suffrage of 20 September 1976; this was signed by the ministers of foreign affairs of the Member States and attached to Council Decision 76/787. The Act provided for elections to take place only in the territory of the United Kingdom but not in Gibraltar.

The Court rejected the argument of the United Kingdom Government that the European Parliament should be excluded from the ambit of elections within the scope of Article 3 on the ground that it is a supranational rather than a national representative organ. The Government then argued that it lacked the attributes of a legislature, which they defined as the power to initiate and adopt legislation.[16] After analysing the powers of the European Parliament and their impact upon Gibraltar, the Court concluded that the European Parliament constitutes 'part of the legislature of Gibraltar for the purposes of Article 3 of Protocol 1'.[17]

ELECTORAL SYSTEMS

Although Article 3, in contrast to Article 21(3) of the Universal Declaration of Human Rights, does not refer expressly to universal suffrage, the Commission, reversing an earlier position, expressed the view that the Article implies recognition of universal suffrage.[18] The Court has agreed.[19] On the other hand, its form is different from that in which the other rights in the Convention and Protocol are expressed. It does not provide in absolute terms that everyone has the right to vote. If a person complains that he is disqualified from voting, the Court's task is to consider whether such disqualification affects the free expression of the opinion of the people under Article 3.[20]

The formulation is important if only because of the question of the effect of Article 14. The Commission accepted that certain categories of citizen may be excluded from voting, without the free expression of the opinion of the people being prejudiced. Thus, Belgians resident in the Congo complained

[16] The Parliament's most extensive legislative functions arise under the co-decision procedure set out in Article 251 (ex 189b) EC, under which the European Parliament can block the progress of legislative measures proposed by the Commission and supported by the Council.

[17] *Matthews* v. *United Kingdom* (App. 24833/94), Judgment of 18 February 1999; (1999) 28 EHRR 361, para. 54 of the judgment.

[18] App. 2728/66, *X* v. *Federal Republic of Germany*, 6 October 1967, (1967) 10 *Yearbook* 336, at 338; see also App. 5302/71, *X & Y* v. *United Kingdom*, 11 October 1973, (1973) 44 CD 29, at 48.

[19] *Mathieu-Mohin and Clerfayt* v. *Belgium*, Judgment of 2 March 1987, Series A, No. 113; (1988) 10 EHRR 1, para. 51 of judgment.

[20] *Gitonas and others* v. *Greece* (Apps. 18747/91, 19376/92, 19379/92, 28208/95, and 27755/95), Judgment of 1 July 1997; (1998) 26 EHRR 691, para. 39 of the judgment.

unsuccessfully that they were denied the right to vote in the metropolis.[21] Convicted prisoners may also be refused permission to vote.[22]

On the other hand, wider disqualifications, such as, for example, the disqualification of women, might be considered as affecting the free expression of the opinion of the people, even without regard to Article 14. An argument to this effect might be based on the general spirit of the Convention as well as the modern understanding of a democratic society.

In any event, it is clear that Switzerland regarded as an obstacle to ratification of the Convention and First Protocol the fact that women had only recently acquired the right to vote in federal legislative elections and did not have this right in certain of the cantons.[23] The former disability was removed by revision of the federal constitution.

The scope of the rights embedded in Article 3 was considered in the *Mathieu-Mohin and Clerfayt* case.[24] The case concerned the complex rules operating in Belgian elections to ensure appropriate representation of the French- and Dutch-speaking communities. Before considering the application of Article 3 to the particular facts of the case, the Court provided authoritative guidance on the scope of the rights protected by the Article. The Court approved the Commission's decisions in which it had held that the provision included a right of universal suffrage,[25] which embraced both the right to vote and the right to stand for election to the legislature.[26] But the Court went on to confirm that these rights are not absolute and that there is room for implied limitations. States enjoy a wide margin of appreciation as to the conditions they attach to the exercise of the right. However, the Court

has to satisfy itself that the conditions do not curtail the rights in question to such an extent as to impair their very essence and deprive them of their effectiveness; that they are imposed in pursuance of a legitimate aim; and that the means employed are not disproportionate.... In particular, such conditions must not thwart 'the free expression of the opinion of the people in the choice of the legislature'.[27]

The Court went on to declare that Article 3 does not create any obligation to introduce a specific system of elections and States enjoy a wide margin of appreciation in the choice of voting system. The key test is whether the chosen

[21] App. 1065/61, *X* v. *Belgium*, 18 September 1961, (1961) 4 *Yearbook* 260.

[22] App. 2728/66, *X* v. *Federal Republic of Germany*, 6 October 1967, (1967) 10 *Yearbook* 336.

[23] Federal Council's Report to the Federal Assembly on the Convention, (1969) 12 *Yearbook* 502, at 509–10.

[24] *Mathieu-Mohin and Clerfayt* v. *Belgium*, Judgment of 2 March 1987, Series A, No. 113; (1988) 10 EHRR 1.

[25] App. 2728/66, *X* v. *Federal Republic of Germany*, 6 October 1967, (1967) 10 *Yearbook* 336.

[26] Apps. 6745–46/76, *W, X, Y and Z* v. *Belgium*, 30 May 1975, (1975) 18 *Yearbook* 244.

[27] *Mathieu-Mohin and Clerfayt* v. *Belgium*, Judgment of 2 March 1987, Series A, No. 113; (1988) 10 EHRR 1, para. 52 of judgment.

system provides for the free expression of the opinion of the people in the choice of the legislature.

The dissenting opinions related to the specific facts of the case, but a concurring opinion of Judge Pinheiro Farinha expressed reservations about the Court's approach to legislative systems which have two chambers. The majority had said that Article 3 applies 'to the election of the "legislature", or at least one of its chambers if it has two or more'.[28] Judge Pinheiro Farinha considered this wording 'inadequate and dangerous'.

As it stands, it would allow of a system at variance with 'the opinion of the people in the choice of the legislature' and might even lead to a corporative, elitist or class system which did not respect democracy.

In my opinion, we should say 'or at least of one of its chambers if it has two or more, on the twofold condition that the majority of the membership of the legislature is elected and that the chamber or chambers whose members are not elected does or do not have greater powers than the chamber that is freely elected by secret ballot,

Some years ago the Liberal Party in the United Kingdom sought to challenge the simple majority voting system used in British elections on the grounds that it violated Article 3 when read in conjunction with Article 14 in that the effect of the chosen voting system was to give less weight to votes cast for Liberal Party candidates than for the Conservative or Labour Party candidates.[29] It was conceded by the applicants that the simple majority voting system could not be a violation of Article 3 when read alone, and the Commission noted that this concession was rightly made. But the Commission, in deciding that the application was manifestly ill-founded, also concluded that Article 3 when read in conjunction with Article 14 did not admit of the argument that there was any entitlement to the protection of equal voting influence for all voters.

THE RIGHT TO VOTE

It has long been the position of the Commission that the right to vote and the right to stand for election to the legislature may be subject to legitimate restrictions imposed by the State.[30] The Court has adopted the same position.[31]

---

[28] Ibid., para. 53 of judgment.

[29] App. 8765/79, *Liberal Party, R and P* v. *United Kingdom*, Decision of 18 December 1980, (1981) 21 DR 211.

[30] App. 6850/74, *X, Y and Z* v. *Federal Republic of Germany*, 18 May 1976, (1976) 5 DR 90 and App. 11391/85, *Booth-Clibborn and others* v. *United Kingdom*, 5 July 1985, (1985) 43 DR 236.

[31] *Mathieu-Mohin and Clerfayt* v. *Belgium*, Judgment of 2 March 1987, Series A, No. 113; (1988) 10 EHRR 1, para. 52 of judgment.

Depriving persons abroad of the right to vote in their country of origin is permissible;[32] nor does restricting voting rights of those in prison[33] violate the Convention even if the conviction is for conscientious objection to military service by a person who has refused to comply with the formalities for acquiring objector status.[34]

THE RIGHT TO STAND FOR ELECTION

The Court, in the *Mathieu-Mohin and Clerfayt* case,[35] confirmed the long-held view of the Commission that States may impose certain restrictions on the right to stand for election. So a requirement that a certain number of signatures be obtained as qualification to stand as a candidate is a reasonable requirement.[36] A system of deposits will not violate the Convention.[37] Nor will restriction on the return of deposits and the reimbursement of election expenses in a system of proportional representation where the lists do not obtain 5 per cent. of the vote.[38]

The Greek rules prohibiting public officials from standing for election within a period of thirty-three months of holding such office were considered by the Court in the *Gitonas* case.[39] The applicants had stood for election, been elected, and had their election annulled by the Greek courts. The applicants argued that the Greek rules were imprecise and incoherent, and that far more senior posts did not carry the exclusion which applied to them. In a strongly factually based judgment, the Court disagreed with the Commission[40] in finding that there was no violation of Article 3.

Restrictions on the ability of certain local government officials to stand in local government elections in the United Kingdom were challenged in the *Ahmed* case.[41] In order to retain their posts in local government, the applicants all had to give up their political activities on behalf of political parties. They

---

[32] App. 7730/76, *X v. United Kingdom*, 28 February 1979, (1979) 15 DR 137.

[33] App. 2728/66, *X v. Federal Republic of Germany*, 6 October 1967, (1967) 10 *Yearbook* 336.

[34] App. 9914/82, *H v. Netherlands*, 4 July 1983, (1983) 33 DR 274.

[35] *Mathieu-Mohin and Clerfayt v. Belgium*, Judgment of 2 March 1987, Series A, No. 113; (1988) 10 EHRR 1, para. 52 of judgment.

[36] App. 6850/74, *X, Y and Z v. Federal Republic of Germany*, 18 May 1976, (1976) 5 DR 90.

[37] App. 12897/87, *Desmeules v. France*, 3 December 1990, (1991) 67 DR 166.

[38] App. 11406/85, *Fournier v. France*, 10 May 1988, (1988) 55 DR 130.

[39] *Gitonas and others v. Greece* (Apps. 18747/91, 19376/92, 19379/92, 28208/95, and 27755/95), Judgment of 1 July 1997; (1998) 26 EHRR 691.

[40] Which had found a violation of Art. 3 by 9 votes to 8.

[41] *Ahmed and others v. United Kingdom* (App. 22954/93), Judgment of 2 September 1998; (2000) 29 EHRR 1

claimed that the requirement to do so breached, among other provisions, their right to full participation in the electoral process as guaranteed by Article 3 of Protocol 1. The regulations, they argued, had the effect of limiting without justification the electorate's choice of candidates. The language used by the Court in unanimously rejecting the applicants' claims is significant, since the Court imports the sort of language it would use in considering violations of Articles 8 to 11 into a conclusion in respect of Article 3:

The Court considers that the restrictions imposed on the applicants' rights to contest seats at elections must be seen in the context of the aim pursued by the legislature in enacting the Regulations namely, to secure political impartiality. That aim must be considered legitimate for the purposes of restricting the exercise of the applicants' subjective rights to stand for election under Article 3 of Protocol No.1; nor can it be maintained that the restrictions limit the very essence of their rights under that provision having regard to the fact that they only operate for as long as the applicants occupy politically restricted posts.[42]

Where the right to stand for election touches on the issue of individuals forming a political party, the Court has determined these issues under Article 11 and has avoided addressing the question of whether the right to form and maintain a political party falls within the scope of Article 3 of Protocol 1.[43]

CONCLUDING COMMENT

After some initial uncertainty about the availability of individual petitions under Article 3 of Protocol 1, a significant case law is building both on the nature of the legislature to which the article refers and of the right to free elections.

There remain issues relating to which bodies within the national legal order fall within the scope of the term 'legislature', and there may be some narrowing of the wide margin of appreciation referred to in the early cases now that the Court seems to be adopting a more robust test for interferences which States impose.

---

[42] Para. 75 of the judgment.

[43] See discussion of cases involving political parties in ch. 14. For examples of cases where the Court has not felt the need to consider applications under Art. 3 of Protocol 1, see *United Communist Party of Turkey and others* v. *Turkey* (App. 19392/92), Judgment of 30 January 1998; (1998) 26 EHRR 121; *The Socialist Party and others* v. *Turkey* (App. 21237/93), Judgment of 25 May 1998; (1999) 27 EHRR 51; and *Refah Partisi (Prosperity Party) and others* v. *Turkey* (Apps. 41340/98 and 41342/98), Judgment of 31 July 2001.

18

FREEDOM OF MOVEMENT

INTRODUCTION

Provisions of the Fourth and Seventh Protocols concern freedom of movement in the broadest sense. Article 2 of Protocol 4 concerns liberty of movement and freedom to choose a residence. Article 3 of the same Protocol prohibits the expulsion of nationals and enshrines the right of nationals to enter their own country, while Article 4 prohibits the collective expulsion of aliens. Finally, Article 1 of Protocol 7 provides that aliens are not to be expelled without due process of law. These provisions, which are controversial in some States since they touch on issues of immigration policy, have not been ratified by all the parties to the Convention.[1] There is little case law of the Court of Human Rights on the articles considered in this chapter, and so the decisions of the Commission take on greater significance than in other areas.

As between the States parties to Protocol 4, its provisions are to be regarded as additional Articles of the Convention, and all the provisions of the Convention are to apply accordingly.[2] Article 5 of Protocol 4 and Article 6 of Protocol 7 make provision for a declaration concerning the application of the Protocol to dependent territories on the model of Article 57 of the Convention.[3]

In addition, however, Article 5(4) of Protocol 4 provides that, for the purposes of Articles 2 and 3 of the Protocol, the territory of a State to which the Protocol applies by virtue of ratification, and each territory to which it applies by a declaration under Article 5, shall be treated as separate territories. The effect of this provision is that a State which ratifies the Protocol, and extends its application under Article 5 to its dependent territories, guarantees freedom of movement within each of those territories without also guaranteeing freedom of movement from one territory to another. The Committee of Experts explains paragraph 4 as follows:

The Committee decided to add a paragraph 4 to Article 5 in order to take account of a problem which may arise in connection with States which are responsible for the

---

[1] Notably, Greece, Spain, Switzerland, Turkey, and the United Kingdom.
[2] Article 6(1) of Protocol 4.
[3] See above ch. 2.

international relations of overseas territories. Thus, for example, insofar as nationality is concerned, there is no distinction between the United Kingdom and most of the territories for whose international relations it is responsible; in relation to these territories and the United Kingdom there is a common citizenship, designated as 'citizenship of the United Kingdom and Colonies'.

Persons who derive the common nationality from a connection with one such territory do not, however, have the right to admission to, or have immunity from expulsion from, another such territory. Each territory has its own laws relating to admission to and expulsion from its territory. Under these laws admission can be refused to persons who, though they possess the common nationality, do not derive it from connection with the territory in question, and in certain circumstances such persons can be expelled from that territory. Equally, persons who derive the common nationality from a connection with a dependent territory can in certain circumstances be refused admission to the United Kingdom or, if admitted, be expelled from the United Kingdom. What is said above is relevant to Article 3 of this Protocol, but a similar situation would arise as regards the interpretation of 'territory' for the purposes of Article 2.

Accordingly, it is desirable that the references in Articles 2 and 3 to the territory of a State should relate to the metropolitan territory and each non-metropolitan territory separately, and not to a single geographical entity comprising the metropolitan and other territories.

This interpretation would apply only to Article 2, paragraph 1, and to Article 3 of Protocol 4.[4]

Article 6(5) of Protocol 7 contains similar provisions.

MOVEMENT AND RESIDENCE

Article 2 of Protocol 4 provides:

1. Everyone lawfully within the territory of a State shall, within that territory, have the right to liberty of movement and freedom to choose his residence.
2. Everyone shall be free to leave any country, including his own.
3. No restrictions shall be placed on the exercise of these rights other than such as are in accordance with law and are necessary in a democratic society in the interests of national security or public safety, for the maintenance of the *ordre public*, for the prevention of crime, for the protection of health or morals, or for the protection of the rights and freedoms of others.
4. The rights set forth in paragraph 1 may also be subject, in particular areas, to restrictions imposed in accordance with law and justified by the public interest in a democratic society.

[4] Explanatory Reports on the Second to Fifth Protocols to the Convention, Strasbourg 1971, at 55.

These provisions are based on Article 13(1) and (2) of the Universal Declaration of Human Rights, whose wording they follow closely. The right to return to the country of nationality, which is also included in Article 13(2) of the Universal Declaration, is dealt with separately by Article 3 of Protocol 4. While Article 2 deals with freedom of movement within a country, and the right to leave it, Article 3 precludes a State from expelling, or refusing to admit, its own nationals. Thus, Article 2 applies to everyone, in relation to any country, but Article 3 applies only to nationals in relation to their own State.

The reference, in Article 2(1), to 'Everyone lawfully within the territory of a State' includes all that State's nationals present within its territory, since it follows from the provisions of Article 3 that, subject to the possible exception of extradition, the presence of persons in the State of which they are a national cannot be unlawful. As for persons who are not nationals, they are lawfully within the territory so long as they comply with any conditions of entry that may have been imposed. Such conditions may, of course, include restrictions as to the length of stay, after the expiry of which their presence will be unlawful. But it is argued that, subject to the limitations permitted under paragraphs 3 and 4, these conditions cannot, under Article 2(1), include any restrictions on their liberty of movement, or on their freedom to choose their residence.[5]

The freedom to leave a country, under Article 2(2), is subject to the restrictions set out in paragraph 3. These restrictions are, of course, sufficient to preclude convicted prisoners from leaving the country in which they are detained. The reference to 'the maintenance of *ordre public*' in paragraph 3 was included, as is shown by the preparatory work, expressly to allow for the case of persons lawfully detained under Article 5.[6] Similarly, a person who has been detained with a view to deportation or extradition under Article 5(1)(f)[7] cannot claim the right to leave the country freely.[8]

In one case,[9] an applicant who was subject to a compulsory residence order which involved placing him under special police supervision complained of a violation of the provision. The Commission ruled that the measures were an interference with his right of freedom of movement, but they were measures provided by law, which were necessary in a democratic society for the prevention of crime and maintenance of the *ordre public*. The measures were proportionate to a legitimate aim and the application was declared inadmissible.

---

[5] See to the contrary, Explanatory Reports on the Second to Fifth Protocols to the Convention, Strasbourg 1971, at 41.

[6] App. 4256/69, *X v. Federal Republic of Germany*, 14 December 1970, (1971) 37 CD 67; App. 10893/84, *C v. Federal Republic of Germany*, 2 December 1985, (1986) 45 DR 198.

[7] See ch. 9 above.

[8] App. 4436/70, *X v. Federal Republic of Germany*, 26 May 1970, (1970) 13 *Yearbook* 1029.

[9] App. 12541/86, *Ciancimino v. Italy*, 27 May 1991, (1991) 70 DR 103.

In the *Raimondo* case,[10] the applicant, who was suspected of being a member of the Mafia, had been put under house arrest and placed under special police supervision. He complained that the special police supervision breached his rights under Article 2 of Protocol 4. The Court concluded that the measures fell short of a deprivation of liberty within the meaning of Article 5(1) and fell to be considered under Article 2 of the Protocol. The measures were, however, in its view justified as serving the aim of maintaining public order and for the prevention of crime; there was no lack of proportionality. However, for reasons which are not explained, there was a delay of eighteen days before the revocation of the special police supervision was notified to the applicant. For this period the interference with his rights under Article 2 of the Protocol was not in accordance with law nor was it necessary. There was to this extent a violation of the article.[11]

The *Labita* case is a more dramatic example of a violation.[12] The applicant had been tried and acquitted of certain offences connected with Mafia-type activities. But the Government continued in place special police supervision notwithstanding the acquittal, arguing that these were preventive measures to guard against the risk of future offences.[13] The Court concluded:

[T]he Court considers that it is legitimate for preventive measures, including special supervision, to be taken against persons suspected of being members of the Mafia, even prior to conviction, as they are intended to prevent crimes being committed. Furthermore, an acquittal does not necessarily deprive such measures of all foundation, as concrete evidence gathered at trial, though insufficient to secure a conviction, may nonetheless justify reasonable fears that the person concerned may in the future commit criminal offences.[14]

However, in this case, the Court of Human Rights concluded that there was no such basis for the continuation of the measures, which were, consequently, a breach of Article 2 of Protocol 4.

The monitoring of movements and expulsion to a specific part of the national territory will be a violation of Article 2 of Protocol 4. The *Denizci* case[15] concerned restrictions on the movement of the applicants in the southern part of Cyprus and subsequent expulsion to the northern part of Cyprus. No lawful basis for the restrictions on the applicants' movements was put forward by the Cyprus Government, and the Court concluded that there was an interference with the rights in Article 2 which were neither provided by law nor necessary.[16]

---

[10] *Raimondo* v. *Italy*, Judgment of 22 February 1994, Series A, No. 281-A; (1994) 18 EHRR 237.
[11] See paras. 37–40 of the judgment.
[12] *Labita* v. *Italy* (App. 26772/95), Judgment of 6 April 2000.
[13] As in the *Raimondo* judgment above.
[14] *Labita* v. *Italy* (App. 26772/95), Judgment of 6 April 2000, para. 195 of the judgment.
[15] *Denizci and others* v. *Cyprus* (Apps. 25316–25321/94, and 27207/95), Judgment of 23 May 2001.
[16] Paras. 400–6 of the judgment. The Court decided that its conclusions on the violation of Article 2 of Protocol 4 made it unnecessary to consider the complaint as a violation of Art. 3 of Protocol 4.

THE PROHIBITION OF EXPULSION OF NATIONALS

As already stated, Article 3 precludes a State from expelling, or refusing to admit, its own nationals. Article 3(1) provides:

No one shall be expelled, by means either of an individual or of a collective measure, from the territory of the State of which he is a national.

There is no provision for any restrictions to the rights guaranteed by Article 3, which is curious since the provision makes no exception for the practice of extradition. It is extraordinary that the explanatory report on Protocol 4 merely says that 'It was understood that extradition was outside the scope of this paragraph.'[17] Such understandings are not an adequate basis for drafting a legal text. In any event, on the accepted principles of treaty interpretation, this explanatory report cannot be invoked to interpret the text, since the text is clear and unambiguous.[18]

The European Convention on Extradition does not preclude the extradition of nationals, but provides that a Contracting Party shall have the right to refuse extradition of its nationals.[19] The extradition of nationals is prohibited by the law of many Member States of the Council of Europe.[20] But the Convention on Extradition permits a State to refuse the extradition of its nationals even if this would not be contrary to its own law. It would seem that States Parties to Protocol 4 are precluded from extraditing their nationals in the absence of a reservation to the contrary.[21]

The Commission has defined what constitutes expulsion, which occurs when a 'person is obliged permanently to leave the territory of the State . . . without being left the possibility of returning later'.[22] This definition neatly excludes extradition from the compass of expulsion under the Article.

It appears that the Committee of Experts which drafted Protocol 4 also considered the hypothesis of a State expelling one of its nationals after first depriving them of their nationality, but 'thought it was inadvisable in Article 3 to touch on the delicate question of the legitimacy of measures depriving individuals of nationality'.[23]

However, the effect of Article 3(1) must be to preclude a State from depriving

---

[17] Explanatory Reports on the Second to Fifth Protocols to the Convention, Strasbourg 1971, at 47.

[18] Art. 31, Vienna Convention on the Law of Treaties, and see generally ch. 3 above.

[19] European Treaty Series No. 24, Art. 6(1).

[20] For example, Cyprus, Germany, the Netherlands, and Switzerland.

[21] This view is not supported by J. Merrills and A. Robertson, *Human Rights in Europe* (Manchester, 2001), at 256, nor by P. van Dijk and G. van Hoof, *Theory and Practice of the European Convention on Human Rights* (Deventer, 1999) at 672.

[22] App. 6189/73, *X v. Federal Republic of Germany*, 13 May 1974, (1974) 46 CD 214.

[23] Explanatory Reports on the Second to Fifth Protocols to the Convention, Strasbourg 1971, at 47–8.

persons of their nationality in order to expel them. Otherwise it would offer no adequate protection. The Commission, indeed, has gone further, and has considered whether it may be contrary to Article 3(1) to refuse to grant a person nationality if the object of the refusal is to be able to expel them. An applicant complained both of his imminent expulsion, and of the refusal of the German authorities to recognize him as a German citizen. The Commission stated that, although the Convention confers no right to a nationality as such, the question arose whether there existed, between the decision to refuse him nationality and the order for his expulsion, a causal relation creating the presumption that the refusal had as its sole object his expulsion from German territory. There was no evidence of that, however, in the present case.[24]

THE RIGHT OF ENTRY TO THE TERRITORY OF THE STATE OF NATIONALITY

Similar considerations relating to the withdrawal of nationality apply to paragraph 2, which provides that:

No one shall be deprived of the right to enter the territory of the State of which he is a national.

A State could not refuse persons nationality if they fulfil the conditions laid down by its law, or deprive such persons of their nationality, in order to be able to refuse them admission.

PROHIBITING THE COLLECTIVE EXPULSION OF ALIENS

Article 4 simply states, 'Collective expulsion of aliens is prohibited.' The Article does not regulate in any way the individual expulsion of aliens. Its scope is thus extremely limited. The reasons given for this omission by the Committee of Experts are set out in the explanatory report.[25] One reason was that the matter had already been dealt with in the European Convention on Establishment. However, that Convention does not deal with the expulsion of aliens in general; it deals only with the expulsion of nationals of other States parties to that Convention.[26] Possibly a difficulty for the Governments was that if any

---

[24] App. 3745/68, X v. *Federal Republic of Germany*, 15 December 1969, (1970) 31 CD 107.
[25] Explanatory Reports on the Second to Fifth Protocols to the Convention, Strasbourg 1971, at 50–1.
[26] European Treaty Series No. 19, Art. 3.

rights were recognized in the Protocol in relation to the expulsion of aliens generally, then the rights granted on a reciprocal basis, under the Establishment Convention or under other treaties, to the nationals of other State parties to those instruments might have had to be extended, through the effect of Article 14, to all aliens.

One issue which remains is what constitutes a collective expulsion. This poses the question of when a series of individual expulsions can be regarded as a collective expulsion. The Commission appears to have concluded that where persons are expelled with others without their cases having received individual treatment, the expulsion will be collective.[27]

EXPULSION ONLY TO FOLLOW DUE PROCESS

Article 1 of Protocol 7 provides:

1. An alien lawfully resident in the territory of a State shall not be expelled therefore except in pursuance of a decision reached in accordance with law and shall be allowed:

    a.   to submit reasons against his expulsion
    b.   to have his case reviewed; and
    c.   to be represented for these purposes before the competent authority or a person or persons designated by that authority.

2. An alien may be expelled before the exercise of his rights under paragraph 1.a, b and c of this article, when such expulsion is necessary in the interests of public order or is grounded on reasons of national security.

This Article provides certain limited procedural guarantees for those who are lawfully resident in one of the States which has ratified this provision in respect of decisions to expel them. Expulsion, according to the Explanatory Memorandum, is any measure compelling the departure of the person from the territory except extradition.[28] To be lawfully resident, a person must have passed through the necessary immigration procedures and have been admitted for residence rather than some more limited purpose, such as, perhaps a person admitted for a limited period as a student or a visitor. Residence in the sense of the Protocol appears to equate to the notion of settlement under the British immigration rules.

---

[27] App. 7011/75, *Becker* v. *Denmark*, 30 October 1975, (1976) 19 *Yearbook* 416; App. 14209/88, *A and others* v. *Netherlands*, 16 December 1988, (1989) 59 DR 274.
[28] Explanatory Memorandum on the Seventh Protocol, p.7.

The procedural guarantees are set out in self-explanatory manner in the Article,[29] which provides no protection of substance,[30] that is, relating to the grounds on which their expulsion might be sought. Nevertheless, the due process requirements themselves almost certainly operate to preclude arbitrary decisions to expel.

[29] For further explanation, see Explanatory Memorandum on the Seventh Protocol.
[30] Other provisions of the Convention might assist, such as Arts. 3, 5(1)(f), 8, and 13.

19

FREEDOM FROM DISCRIMINATION

INTRODUCTION

Article 14 of the Convention contains a general prohibition of discrimination in relation to the rights guaranteed by the Convention and Protocols.[1] It provides that:

The enjoyment of the rights and freedoms set forth in this Convention shall be secured without discrimination on any ground such as sex, race, colour, language, religion, political or other opinion, national or social origin, association with a national minority, property, birth or other status.

The term 'Convention' in this Article must be understood as including the First, Fourth, Sixth, and Seventh Protocols, which themselves provide that all the provisions of the Convention apply to them.[2]

The enunciation of the principle of equality, and the prohibition of discrimination, were considered so fundamental as to be placed at the beginning of the Universal Declaration of Human Rights,[3] and of the United Nations Covenants on Economic, Social and Cultural Rights and on Civil and Political Rights.[4] These principles also have a prominent place in many national constitutions, for example in Article 3 of the German Basic Law, in the 'equal protection' clauses of the United States Constitution, and in the constitutions of many Commonwealth countries. Several international instruments prohibiting particular forms of discrimination, or discrimination in particular fields, have been drawn up, in the United Nations, in the International Labour Organisation, in UNESCO, and elsewhere. There is thus a substantial body of law on the subject.

Article 14 of the European Convention is very frequently cited by applicants,

---

[1] See K. Partsch, 'Discrimination' in R. Macdonald, F. Matscher, and H. Petzold, (eds.) *The European System for the Protection of Human Rights* (Dordrecht, 1993), at 571.

[2] Art. 5 of Protocol 1; Art. 6(1) of Protocol 4; Art. 6 of Protocol 6; and Art. 7 of Protocol 7.

[3] Arts. 1 and 2.

[4] Arts. 2 and 3.

but in very many cases the Court does not determine whether there has been a violation of Article 14 in conjunction with a substantive article where it has first decided that there is a violation of the substantive article.[5] In the *Chassagnou* case,[6] the Court said,

Where a substantive Article of the Convention has been invoked both on its own and together with Article 14 and a separate breach has been found of the substantive Article, it is not generally necessary for the Court to consider the case under Article 14 also, though the position is otherwise if a clear inequality of treatment in the enjoyment of the right in question is a fundamental aspect of the case.[7]

This approach addresses a criticism which could be levelled at some early decisions of the Court where clear inequality of treatment had been ignored to the detriment of the development of the case law on the prohibition of discrimination.

CONCEPTUAL ISSUES

Before the judgment of the Court in the *Belgian Linguistic* case, there was some doubt as to the relation between Article 14 and the articles which define the other rights and freedoms guaranteed. Article 14 does not prohibit discrimination as such, in any context, but only in 'the enjoyment of the rights and freedoms set forth in this Convention'. On the other hand, does Article 14 only come into play if there has been a violation of one of those rights? The view that Article 14 has such a subsidiary role, advanced by the Belgian Government before the Court in the *Belgian Linguistic* case, derived some support from certain earlier decisions of the Commission.[8]

However, this interpretation would, as the Commission itself argued in the *Belgian Linguistic* case, have deprived Article 14 of its effectiveness, and it was rejected by the Court. The breach of Article 14 does not presuppose the violation of the rights guaranteed by other Articles of the Convention.

While it is true that this guarantee has no independent existence in the sense that under the terms of Article 14 it relates solely to 'rights and freedoms set forth in the Convention', a measure which in itself is in conformity with the requirements of the Article

---

[5] Described by Partsch, n.1 above at 583 as being for 'reasons of procedural economy'.

[6] *Chassagnou and others* v. *France* (Apps. 25088/94, 28331/95, and 28443/95), Judgment of 29 April 1999; (2000) 29 EHRR 615.

[7] Para. 89 of the judgment.

[8] M. Eissen, 'L'autonomie de l'article 14 de la Convention européenne des droits de l'homme dans la jurisprudence de la Commission', in *Mélanges Modinos* (Paris, 1968), at 122; *Belgian Linguistic* case, Judgment of 23 July 1968, Series A, No. 6; (1979–80) 1 EHRR 252.

enshrining the right or freedom in question may however infringe this Article when read in conjunction with Article 14 for the reason that it is of a discriminatory nature.

Thus, persons subject to the jurisdiction of a Contracting State cannot draw from Article 2 of the Protocol the right to obtain from the public authorities the creation of a particular kind of educational establishment; nevertheless, a State which had set up such an establishment could not, in laying down entrance requirements, take discriminatory measures within the meaning of Article 14.

To recall a further example, cited in the course of the proceedings, Article 6 of the Convention does not compel States to institute a system of appeal courts. A State which does set up such courts consequently goes beyond its obligations under Article 6. However it would violate that Article, read in conjunction with Article 14, were it to debar certain persons from these remedies without a legitimate reason while making them available to others in respect of the same type of actions.

In such cases there would be a violation of a guaranteed right or freedom as it is proclaimed by the relevant Article read in conjunction with Article 14. It is as though the latter formed an integral part of each of the Articles laying down rights and freedoms. No distinctions should be made in this respect according to the nature of these rights and freedoms and of their correlative obligations, and for instance as to whether the respect due to the right concerned implies positive action or mere abstention. This is, moreover, clearly shown by the very general nature of the terms employed in Article 14 'the enjoyment of the rights and freedoms set forth in this Convention shall be secured'.[9]

Thus, to put the matter differently, while there can never be a violation of Article 14 considered in isolation, there may be a violation of Article 14, considered together with another Article of the Convention, in cases where there would be no violation of that other Article taken alone.

The example selected by the Court emphasizes the potential scope of Article 14. It might have selected, as an example of an 'independent' violation of Article 14, the type of situation considered by the Commission in the *Grandrath* case.[10] Here a limitation on a right is expressly authorized, for example by paragraph (2) of one of Articles 8 to 11. However, a State may not limit the right in a discriminatory way. Although to do so would not violate the substantive article, it would infringe that article taken in conjunction with Article 14.

The right of appeal, however, in the example given by the Court, is as such outside the scope of the Convention altogether, whether in civil or in criminal cases. Nevertheless, Article 14 together with Article 6 prohibits discrimination in access to the courts throughout the whole of the judicial system.

The conclusion is, therefore, that discrimination is prohibited, not only in the restrictions permitted, but also in laws implementing the rights guaranteed,

[9] *Belgian Linguistic* case, Judgment of 23 July 1968, Series A, No. 6; (1979–80) 1 EHRR 252, Section I B, para. 9 of the judgment.
[10] App. 2299/64, *Grandrath v. Federal Republic of Germany*, Report of Commission, 12 December 1966; Decision of Committee of Ministers, 29 June 1967, (1967) 10 *Yearbook* 626.

even if those laws go beyond the obligations expressly provided by the Convention.

A second, and more difficult, major problem of interpretation raised by Article 14 was also dealt with by the Court in the *Belgian Linguistic* case. What forms of differential treatment constitute 'discrimination'?

To argue that Article 14 prohibits all inequalities of treatment based on the grounds stated would lead to manifestly unreasonable results, since the inequality might actually be designed to benefit the less privileged class. For example, the provision of additional educational facilities for the children of poorer families would not necessarily constitute discrimination. On the other hand, if only certain forms of inequality are prohibited, by what objective criteria can they be identified? On this issue, the Court said:

> In spite of the very general wording of the French version ('*sans distinction aucune*'), Article 14 does not forbid every difference in treatment in the exercise of the rights and freedoms recognized. This version must be read in the light of the more restrictive text of the English version ('without discrimination'). In addition, and in particular, one would reach absurd results were one to give Article 14 an interpretation as wide as that which the French version seems to imply. One would, in effect, be led to judge as contrary to the Convention every one of the many legal or administrative provisions which do not secure to everyone complete equality of treatment in the enjoyment of the rights and freedoms recognised. The competent national authorities are frequently confronted with situations and problems which, on account of differences inherent therein, call for different legal solutions; moreover, certain legal inequalities tend only to correct factual inequalities. The extensive interpretation mentioned above cannot consequently be accepted.

> It is important, then, to look for the criteria which enable a determination to be made as to whether or not a given difference in treatment, concerning of course the exercise of one of the rights and freedoms set forth, contravenes Article 14. On this question the Court, following the principles which may be extracted from the legal practice of a large number of democratic States, holds that the principle of equality of treatment is violated if the distinction has no objective and reasonable justification. The existence of such a justification must be assessed in relation to the aim and effects of the measure under consideration, regard being had to the principles which normally prevail in democratic societies. A difference of treatment in the exercise of a right laid down in the Convention must not only pursue a legitimate aim: Article 14 is likewise violated when it is clearly established that there is no reasonable relationship of proportionality between the means employed and the aim sought to be realised.[11]

The Court thus adopted, and applied in its examination of the legislation in question, the weaker of two alternative theses on the meaning of

[11] *Belgian Linguistic* case, Judgment of 23 July 1968, Series A, No. 6; (1979–80) 1 EHRR 252, Section I B, para. 10 of the judgment.

discrimination. On this weaker thesis, differential treatment is justified if it has an objective aim, derived from the public interest, and if the measures of differentiation do not exceed a reasonable relation to that aim.

A stronger thesis would be that differential treatment is justified only if, *without regard to the purpose of the measures in question*, the facts themselves require or permit differential treatment. This view of Article 14 was clearly formulated by a member of the Commission, Mr Balta, in an individual opinion in the *Grandrath* case.[12] He stated,

In my view, the intention of Article 14 is to establish the principle of complete equality in the enjoyment of the rights and freedoms set forth in the Convention. This being so, enjoyment of those rights and freedoms may not be made subject to any kinds of discrimination other than those which are either inherent in the nature of the right in question or are designed to remedy existing inequalities.

The two theses both start from the idea that a difference of status, of sex, race, language, and so on, cannot of itself justify differential treatment; but whereas on the first thesis differential treatment might be justified by the purpose of the measures in question, on the second thesis it could only be justified if the difference of status implied certain objective factual differences which required or permitted different legal treatment.

The distinction is of considerable practical importance, since on the thesis adopted by the Court it found a violation on only one aspect of the Belgian legislation; on the stronger thesis, other provisions might also have been inconsistent with the Convention.

A difficult question is the scope of the domestic remedies rule in relation to complaints of discrimination. The difficulty here is that there may be no remedy against the exercise of a power which is lawful in itself, and unlawful through the effect of Article 14. An example would be measures to prohibit political meetings on the ground that they would lead to breaches of the peace. Such a measure might be justified under Article 11(2), but it would be contrary to Article 14 if only the meetings of the opposition parties were banned, while the Government's supporters continued to hold public meetings. Yet it would be difficult to challenge the banning of a particular meeting without consideration of the general policy; and where national law contained no prohibition of discrimination, corresponding to Article 14, which could be invoked in the courts, it would probably be impossible to succeed. More generally, it may be said that whenever the executive has a discretionary power, it may be difficult to secure, by an action in an isolated case, that this power is not exercised in a discriminatory manner.

Discrimination on certain of the grounds referred to in Article 14 has already

---

[12] App. 2299/64, *Grandrath* v. *Federal Republic of Germany*, Report of Commission, 12 December 1966; Decision of Committee of Ministers, 29 June 1967, (1967) 10 *Yearbook* 626.

been discussed: in relation to sex, under Article 8;[13] to race, under Article 3;[14] to language, under Article 2 of Protocol 1;[15] and to religion, under Article 9.[16]

Finally, it should be noted that the grounds listed in Article 14 are not exhaustive. Discrimination based on any 'other status' is prohibited. The French text, *toute autre situation*, seems to go even further in this respect.

Discrimination may also arise where there is a failure to treat different individuals or groups differently. The *Thlimmenos* case concerned a conviction for refusal to serve in the armed forces by a Jehovah's witness.[17] The applicant complained that, as a result of his conviction for the offence, he had been excluded from the profession of chartered accountant, and that the law failed to make any distinction between those convicted of a result of their religious beliefs and those convicted on other grounds. The applicant complained of a violation of Article 14 when taken together with Article 9 on freedom of thought, conscience, and religion. The Court, in finding a violation of Article 14 taken in conjunction with Article 9, extended its earlier case law to situations where, without any objective and reasonable justification, a State fails to treat differently persons whose situations are significantly different.

THE COURT'S METHODOLOGY

In practice, the Court appears to ask a number of questions in addressing complaints of discrimination:[18]

- Does the complaint of discrimination fall within the sphere of a protected right?
- Is there a violation of the substantive provision?
- Is there different treatment?
- Does the treatment pursue a legitimate aim?
- Are the means employed proportionate to the legitimate aim?
- Does the difference of treatment go beyond a State's margin of appreciation?

Each of these questions will now be considered.

---

[13] See above, ch. 10.

[14] See above, ch. 5.

[15] See above, ch. 15.

[16] See above, ch. 11.

[17] *Thlimmenos* v. *Greece* (App. 34369/97), Judgment of 6 April 2000; (2001) 31 EHRR 411.

[18] See e.g. *Rasmussen* v. *Denmark*, Judgment of 28 November 1984, Series A, No. 87; (1985) 7 EHRR 371; and *Chassagnou and others* v. *France* (Apps 25088/94, 28331/95, and 28443/95), Judgment of 29 April 1999; (2000) 29 EHRR 615, para. 91 of the judgment.

DOES THE COMPLAINT OF DISCRIMINATION FALL WITHIN THE SPHERE
OF A PROTECTED RIGHT?

Article 14 only applies in respect of 'the enjoyment of the rights and freedoms
as set forth' in the Convention. The standard formula used by the Court is that
stated in the *Abdulaziz, Cabales and Balkandali* case,[19]

According to the Court's established case-law, Article 14 complements the other
substantive provisions of the Convention and the Protocols. It has no independent
existence, since it has effect solely in relation to 'the enjoyment of the rights and
freedoms' safeguarded by those provisions. Although the application of Article 14 does
not necessarily presuppose a breach of those provisions—and to this extent it is
autonomous—there can be no room for its application unless the facts at issue fall
within the ambit of one or more of the latter.[20]

As noted earlier in this chapter, it will not always be easy to see where the
boundary lies between a violation occurring in conjunction with a substance
provision and one which falls outside the ambit of a substantive provision. In
one case,[21] an Irish loyalist prisoner complained that he was the victim of
discrimination in that he was not segregated from British loyalist prisoners,
whereas such segregation existed in other prisons in Northern Ireland. The
Commission ruled the application inadmissible because the Convention
contained no right of detention under segregated conditions.

IS THERE A VIOLATION OF THE SUBSTANTIVE PROVISION?

In very many cases, the Court first addresses whether there has been a violation
of the substantive provision. If a violation is found, the Court does not always
consider separately the allegation of a violation under Article 14 in conjunction
with the substantive provision. So, in the *Dudgeon* case,[22] the Court considered
the complaint of a violation of Article 8 in respect of the legislation on
homosexual conduct in Northern Ireland[23] and found a violation. In addition
the applicant complained that there was discrimination arising in particular
from the different ages of consent for different forms of sexual relations. The
Court said:

Where a substantive Article of the Convention has been invoked both on its own and in
conjunction with Article 14 and a separate breach has been found of the substantive
Article, it is not generally necessary for the Court also to examine the case under Article

---

[19] *Abdulaziz, Cabales and Balkandali* v. *United Kingdom*, Judgment of 28 May 1985, Series A, No. 94;
(1985) 7 EHRR 471.
[20] Para. 71 of judgment.
[21] App. 11208/84, *McQuiston* v. *United Kingdom*, 4 March 1986, (1986) 46 DR 182.
[22] *Dudgeon* v. *United Kingdom*, Judgment of 22 October 1981, Series A, No. 45; (1982) 4 EHRR 149.
[23] See above ch. 11.

14, though the position is otherwise if a clear inequality of treatment in the enjoyment of the right in question is a fundamental aspect of the case.[24]

The Court found that the complaint under Article 14 was 'in effect, the same complaint, albeit seen from a different angle' to the complaint under Article 8 and so did not require separate consideration under Article 14.

By contrast, in the *Marckx* case,[25] the Court found violations of Article 8 taken alone in the process of recognition required of an unmarried mother to establish her maternity, and then went on to consider whether violations had occurred under Article 8 taken in conjunction with Article 14. It is difficult to see how these complaints were not in substance the same as those taken under Article 8 alone, but this was presumably one of those cases in which a 'clear inequality of treatment in the enjoyment of the right in question' arose as 'a fundamental aspect of the case'.

In the *Burghartz* case,[26] the applicants complained under Article 8 taken alone and in conjunction with Article 14 that they had been refused consent to change their family surname and the husband's surname. The Court considered whether there had been a violation of Article 8 taken in conjunction with Article 14 first. The basis for doing so was said to be 'the nature of the complaints',[27] which was essentially a difference of treatment on the grounds of sex in relation to the use of names. The Court found a violation.

Where the applicant complains of a violation of a substantive provision, and of Article 14 taken together with that substantive provision, and where the Court finds a violation of the substantive provision, the modern approach is to consider a complaint of a violation of Article 14 read together with the substantive provision if there is a clear inequality of treatment in the enjoyment of the right in question which is a fundamental aspect of the case.[28] This will, of course, require an exercise of judgment by the Court.[29]

---

[24] *Dudgeon* v. *United Kingdom*, Judgment of 22 October 1981, Series A, No. 45; (1982) 4 EHRR 149, para. 67 of the judgment. See also *Chassagnou and others* v. *France* (Apps 25088/94, 28331/95, and 28443/95), Judgment of 29 April 1999; (2000) 29 EHRR 615.

[25] *Marckx* v. *Belgium*, Judgment of 13 June 1979, Series A, No. 31; (1979–80) 2 EHRR 330.

[26] *Burghartz* v. *Switzerland*, Judgment of 22 February 1994, Series A, No. 280-B.

[27] Ibid., para. 21 of the judgment.

[28] *Chassagnou and others* v. *France* (Apps. 25088/94, 28331/95, and 28443/95), Judgment of 29 April 1999; (2000) 29 EHRR 615, para. 89 of the judgment.

[29] For a recent example, see *Sahin* v. *Germany* (App. 30943/96), Judgment of 11 October 2001.

IS THERE DIFFERENT TREATMENT?

The practice of the Court is that it is for the applicant to show that there has been a difference of treatment, but that it is then for the respondent Government to show that the difference in treatment can be justified.[30]

In the *Lithgow* case,[31] the Court stated that Article 14 'safeguards persons ... who are "placed in analogous situations" against discriminatory differences of treatment.'[32] The applicant will need to identify the group which is treated differently. This will involve considerations of whether the situations are comparable. In the *Fredin* case, the Court said that for a claim to succeed, it has to be 'established, *inter alia*, that the situation of the alleged victim can be considered similar to that of persons who have been better treated.'[33]

The problem of comparing like with like is illustrated in the *Van der Mussele* case,[34] where the applicant argued unsuccessfully that the comparators were different professional groups. The Court considered that there were fundamental differences in the regulation of different professions that precluded their use as comparators in the case.

The starting point is to consider whether applicants can show that they have been treated less favourably than the comparator group by reason of the characteristics identified. However, Article 14 also applies where there is indirect discrimination. This occurs where the same requirement applies to both groups, but where a significant number of one group is unable to comply with the requirement. As early as the *Belgian Linguistic* case, the Court indicated that the existence of discrimination might relate to the *effects* of State measures.[35] The Court's analysis does not use the terms direct and indirect discrimination, but rather focuses on whether the differential treatment alleged has no objective and reasonable justification.[36]

Where the differential treatment is between men and women,[37] on grounds

[30] *Chassagnou and others* v. *France* (Apps. 25088/94, 28331/95, and 28443/95), Judgment of 29 April 1999; (2000) 29 EHRR 615, paras 91 and 92 of the judgment.

[31] *Lithgow and others* v. *United Kingdom*, Judgment of 8 July 1986, Series A, No. 102; (1986) 8 EHRR 329.

[32] Para. 177 of judgment.

[33] *Fredin* v. *Sweden*, Judgment of 18 February 1991, Series A, No. 192; (1991) 13 EHRR 784.

[34] *Van der Mussele* v. *Belgium*, Judgment of 23 November 1983, Series A, No. 70; (1984) 6 EHRR 163.

[35] *Belgian Linguistic* case, Judgment of 23 July 1968, Series A, No. 6; (1979–80) 1 EHRR 252, para. 10 of Section IB.

[36] See e.g. *Abdulaziz, Cabales and Balkandali* v. *United Kingdom*, Judgment of 28 May 1985, Series A, No. 94; (1985) 7 EHRR 471, para. 72 of the judgment.

[37] *Abdulaziz, Cabales and Balkandali* v. *United Kingdom*, Judgment of 28 May 1985, Series A, No. 94; (1985) 7 EHRR 471, para. 78 of the judgment. See also *Van Raalte* v. *Netherlands* (App. 20060/92), Judgment of 21 February 1997; (1997) 24 EHRR 503, para. 39 of the judgment.

of nationality,[38] on grounds of religion,[39] on grounds of legitimacy,[40] and on grounds of sexual orientation,[41] very weighty reasons are required to justify the differential treatment.[42]

DOES THE DIFFERENT TREATMENT PURSUE A LEGITIMATE AIM?

In the *Lithgow* case,[43] the Court said

for the purposes of article 14, a difference of treatment is discriminatory if it 'has no objective or reasonable justification', that is, if it does not pursue a 'legitimate aim'.[44]

In asserting a legitimate aim for the differential treatment, the respondent State must not only show the nature of the legitimate aim it is pursuing, but must also show by convincing evidence the link between the legitimate aim pursued and the differential treatment challenged by the applicant.[45]

Obvious groups where comparisons will be made are men and women. The Court is taking an increasingly robust view of discrimination on grounds of sex:

The Court reiterates that the advancement of the equality of the sexes is today a major goal in the member States of the Council of Europe; this means that very weighty reasons would have to be put forward before a difference of treatment on the sole ground of sex could be regarded as compatible with the Convention.[46]

It follows that the nature of the justification presented will vary with the nature of the differential treatment in issue. Generally, however, it will be reasonably easy for a State to show that a difference of treatment pursues a legitimate aim. In the *Gillow* case,[47] the Court considered that preferential treatment for those with a strong attachment to Guernsey reflected in the island's restrictive housing laws was a legitimate aim. In the *Darby* case,[48] the Court concluded

---

[38] *Gaygusuz* v. *Austria* (App. 17371/90), Judgment of 16 September 1996; (1997) 23 EHRR 364, para. 42 of the judgment.

[39] *Hoffmann* v. *Austria*, Judgment of 23 June 1993, Series A, No. 255-C; (1994) 17 EHRR 293, para. 36 of the judgment.

[40] *Inze* v. *Austria*, Judgment of 28 October 1987, Series A, No. 126; (1988) 10 EHRR 394, para. 41 of the judgment. See also *Mazurek* v. *France* (App. 34406/97), Judgment of 1 February 2000, para. 49 of the judgment.

[41] *Salgueiro da Silva Mouta* v. *Portugal* (App. 33290/96), Judgment of 21 December 1999; (2001) 31 EHRR 1055, para. 35 of the judgment.

[42] A similar view would almost certainly be taken by the Court in relation to differential treatment on grounds of race.

[43] *Lithgow and others* v. *United Kingdom*, Judgment of 8 July 1986, Series A, No. 102; (1986) 8 EHRR 329.

[44] Para. 177 of the judgment.

[45] *Larkos* v. *Cyprus* (App. 29515/95), Judgment of 18 February 1999; (2000) 30 EHRR 597, para. 31 of the judgment.

[46] *Burghartz* v. *Switzerland*, Judgment of 22 February 1994, Series A, No. 280-B, para 27 of the judgment; see also *Schuler-Zgraggen* v. *Switzerland*, Judgment of 24 June 1993, Series A, No. 263; (1993) 16 EHRR 405, para. 67 of the judgment.

[47] *Gillow* v. *United Kingdom*, Judgment of 24 November 1986, Series A, No. 109; (1989) 11 EHRR 335.

[48] *Darby* v. *Sweden*, Judgment of 23 October 1990, Series A, No. 187; (1991) 13 EHRR 774.

that the refusal to grant exemption from a church tax to a claimant not formally registered as a resident in Sweden on the grounds that their case for exemption was less strong than for those registered as formally resident and would give rise to administrative inconvenience, did not meet the requirement of being a legitimate aim.

Where the basis for the difference of treatment is grounds of sex, the States enjoy no margin of appreciation and it will be difficult to avoid a finding of a violation. This can be illustrated by the *Karlheinz Schmidt* case.[49] The applicant complained that the system of requiring men to serve in the fire brigade or to pay a fire service levy in lieu violated Article 4 taken together with Article 14. The Court looked at the practicalities of the situation which was that men were not in practice required to serve, since there was no shortage of volunteers. But there remained the liability to pay the levy, which bore only on men and not on women. This difference of treatment on grounds of sex could hardly be justified.

ARE THE MEANS EMPLOYED PROPORTIONATE TO THE LEGITIMATE AIM?

In the *Lithgow* case,[50] the Court identified two aspects to the determination of the presence of discrimination. In addition to the requirement that the measure pursues a legitimate aim, a difference of treatment will be discriminatory if

there is no 'reasonable relationship of proportionality between the means employed and the aim sought to be realised'.[51]

The Court has said that the test of proportionality requires that consideration be given to whether the disadvantage suffered by the applicant in pursuit of a legitimate aim is excessive. If it is, Article 14 is likely to be breached.[52] Because of the infrequency with which transsexuals who had undergone gender reassignment surgery would be required to disclose their preoperative gender in the United Kingdom, the differential treatment they experienced was held not to have a disproportionate interference with their private lives.[53]

In the *Abdulaziz, Cabales and Balkandali* case,[54] the Court concluded that the construction of immigration rules in such a way as to protect the domestic

[49] *Karlheinz Schmidt* v. *Germany*, Judgment of 18 July 1994, Series A, No. 291-B; (1994) 18 EHRR 513.

[50] *Lithgow and others* v. *United Kingdom*, Judgment of 8 July 1986, Series A, No. 102; (1986) 8 EHRR 329.

[51] Para. 177 of the judgment.

[52] *National Union of Belgian Police* v. *Belgium*, Judgment of 27 October 1975, Series A, No. 9; (1979–80) 1 EHRR 578, para 49 of the judgment.

[53] *Sheffield and Horsham* v. *United Kingdom* (Apps. 22885/93 and 23390/94), Judgment of 30 July 1998; (1999) 27 EHRR 163, para. 76 of the judgment.

[54] *Abdulaziz, Cabales and Balkandali* v. *United Kingdom*, Judgment of 28 May 1985, Series A, No. 94; (1985) 7 EHRR 471.

labour market was 'without doubt legitimate'[55] but that in its application the need to apply rules for this purpose which discriminated on grounds of sex could not be regarded, in fact, as sufficiently important to justify the difference of treatment.[56]

DOES THE DIFFERENCE OF TREATMENT GO BEYOND A STATE'S MARGIN OF APPRECIATION?

The final question asked by the Court relates to the State's margin of appreciation. How wide the State's choice is to regulate a particular area by introducing rules which could be regarded as discriminatory will vary according to the context.

The Contracting States enjoy a certain margin of appreciation in assessing whether and to what extent differences in otherwise similar situations justify a different treatment in law; the scope of this margin of appreciation will vary according to the circumstances, the subject matter and its background.[57]

So, as has been seen, there is little room for choice where the discrimination is based on sex, race, nationality, religion, legitimacy of children, and sexual orientation. However, in matters of, for example, housing policy designed to ensure an adequate supply of housing for the poorer section of the community, there will be a wide margin.[58] There is a similarly wide margin of appreciation in relation to policies in the area of taxation.[59]

PROTOCOL 12: A GENERAL PROHIBITION OF DISCRIMINATION

Protocol 12[60] adds a general prohibition of discrimination to the prohibition of discrimination in relation to rights within the ambit of the Convention currently to be found in Article 14 of the Convention. Protocol 12 will enter into force when it has been ratified by ten Contracting States.

---

[55] Ibid., para. 78 of the judgment.
[56] Ibid., para. 79 of the judgment.
[57] *Inze* v. *Austria*, Judgment of 28 October 1987, Series A, No. 126; (1988) 10 EHRR 394.
[58] *Gillow* v. *United Kingdom*, Judgment of 24 November 1986, Series A, No. 109; (1989) 11 EHRR 335, para. 66 of the judgment.
[59] *National & Provincial Building Society and others* v. *United Kingdom* (Apps. 21319/93, 21449/93, and 21675/93), Judgment of 23 October 1997; (1998) 25 EHRR 127, para. 88 of the judgment.
[60] For some background to Protocol 12, see G. Moon, 'The Draft Discrimination Protocol to the European Convention on Human Rights: A Progress Report' [2000] EHRLR 49. The Protocol was opened for signature on 4 November 2000.

Article 1 of Protocol 12 reads,

1. The enjoyment of any right set forth by law shall be secured without discrimination on any ground such as sex, race, colour, language, religion, political or other opinion, national or social origin, association with a national minority, property, birth or other status.
2. No one shall be discriminated against by any public authority on any ground such as those mentioned in paragraph 1.

The emphasis under Protocol 12 moves from a prohibition of discrimination to a recognition of a right of equality. The preamble to the Protocol refers to all persons being equal before the law and being entitled to the equal protection of the law, and expresses a commitment to the promotion of the equality of all persons through the collective prohibition of discrimination.

The Explanatory Report[61] states that the additional scope of the protection of Protocol 12 when compared with Article 14 relates to cases where a person is discriminated against,

i. in the enjoyment of any right specifically granted to an individual under national law;
ii. in the enjoyment of a right which may be inferred from a clear obligation of a public authority under national law, that is, where a public authority is under an obligation under national law to behave in a particular manner.
iii. by a public authority in the exercise of discretionary power (for example, granting certain subsidies);
iv. by any other act or omission by a public authority (for example, the behaviour of law enforcement officers when controlling a riot.

The Explanatory Report goes on to note that it is unnecessary to specify which of the four examples given above comes within the first or second paragraph of Article 1 of Protocol 12, since the two paragraphs are complementary and their combined effect is to include all the circumstances listed. The Explanatory Report goes on to note that the emphasis on acts or omissions of public authorities should not be taken to exclude the possibility of positive obligations emerging from the new rights protected, just as it has emerged under many articles of the current Convention.

Though there is significant overlap between the provisions, Article 1 of Protocol 12 is not drafted as a replacement for Article 14, and there is intended to be harmony of interpretation across the two provisions. Article 14 requires the applicant to show that there is differential treatment in an area within the ambit of the Convention rights. Article 1 of Protocol 12 requires the applicant to show that there is differential treatment in the enjoyment of any right set forth

---

[61] Explanatory Report to Protocol No. 12 to the Convention for the Protection of Human Rights and Fundamental Freedoms. See also administrative opinion of the European Court of Human Rights of 6 December 1999 on the Protocol.

in national law. This will include rights granted by legislative measures, as well as rights granted by common law rules and by international law.[62] As with Article 14, the list of comparators given in the article is illustrative only and not exhaustive.

[62] The Explanatory Report states that, in the case of international law, this does mean that the Court of Human Rights will sit in judgment on compliance with international treaties.

20

ABUSES

INTRODUCTION

This chapter concerns two provisions of the Convention which ensure that the provisions of the Convention are not used to undermine the scheme of protection set out in the Convention.

Article 17 reflects a concern for the defence of democratic society and its institutions, and precludes actions which might undermine those principles. It is concerned with protection against totalitarian activities. Article 17 may be of special significance where an article of the Convention contains no limitations, since in such a case Article 17 can provide the basis for a limitation on the rights protected. But the Court has consistently, and rightly, taken a very restrictive view of its application.

Article 18 prohibits the use of the limitations permitted by the Convention provisions for any purpose other than that for which the Convention allows.

PROHIBITION OF ABUSE OF RIGHTS

Article 17 provides:

Nothing in this Convention may be interpreted as implying for any State, group or person any right to engage in any activity or perform any act aimed at the destruction of any of the rights and freedoms set forth herein or at their limitation to a greater extent than is provided for in the Convention.

THE EARLY COMMISSION DECISIONS

The Commission stated that Article 17 is designed to safeguard the rights listed in the Convention, by protecting the free operation of democratic institutions.[1]

---

[1] App. 250/57, *Parti Communiste* v. *Federal Republic of Germany*, 20 July 1957, (1955–7) 1 *Yearbook* 222, at 224.

In an early case introduced by the German Communist Party, the Commission quoted, from the preparatory work, the statement that the object was to prevent adherents to totalitarian doctrines from exploiting the rights guaranteed by the Convention for the purpose of destroying human rights.[2]

The object of Article 17, therefore, is to limit the rights guaranteed only to the extent that such limitation is necessary to prevent their total subversion, and it must be quite narrowly construed in relation to this object.

In the above case, the German Communist Party had, in 1956, been declared 'anti-constitutional' by the Federal Constitutional Court. The Court had consequently dissolved it and ordered the confiscation of its property. The Party challenged this decision as contrary to Articles 9, 10, and 11 of the Convention. The Commission, applying Article 17, rejected the application as incompatible with the provisions of the Convention. The avowed aim of the Communist Party, according to its own declarations, was to establish a communist society by means of a proletarian revolution and the dictatorship of the proletariat. Consequently, even if it sought power by solely constitutional methods, recourse to a dictatorship was incompatible with the Convention because it would involve the suppression of a number of rights and freedoms which the Convention guaranteed.

In a sequel to this case, a company incorporated under Swiss law, Retimag S.A., complained of the confiscation without compensation of two of its properties in Germany.[3] The German court which ordered the confiscation had held that the company was unquestionably a legal front which had the dual purpose of safeguarding real property belonging to the dissolved Communist Party and of continuing communist subversive activities. Article 17 was invoked by the German Government but the application was rejected for non-exhaustion of domestic remedies.

The *Kühnen* case[4] concerned a German journalist, who was accused of trying to reinstitute the National Socialist Party, which was allegedly a neo-Nazi party. He sought to rely on Article 10. The Commission said that Article 17 covers essentially those rights which will facilitate the attempt to derive from them a right to engage personally in activities aimed at the destruction of any of the rights and freedoms set forth in the Convention. In particular, the Commission has found that the freedom of expression enshrined in Article 10 of the Convention may not be invoked in a sense contrary to Article 17.[5]

---

[2] Ibid.

[3] App. 712/60, *Retimag SA v. Federal Republic of Germany*, 16 December 1961, (1961) 4 *Yearbook* 384.

[4] App. 12194/86, *Kühnen v. Federal Republic of Germany*, 12 May 1988, (1988) 56 DR 205.

[5] See also Apps. 8348/78 and 8406/78, *Glimmerveen and Hagenbeek v. Netherlands*, 11 October 1979, (1980) 18 DR 187.

THE COURT'S CASE LAW

From the earliest decisions in which Article 17 has been raised, the Court has adopted a much more restrictive view of its application. In the *Lawless* case,[6] the Irish Government maintained that the activities of the IRA, in which Lawless was engaged, fell within the terms of Article 17, and that he was therefore not entitled to rely on Articles 5, 6, 7, or any other Article of the Convention. The Commission expressed the view that Article 17 was not applicable. It stated that the general purpose of Article 17 was to prevent totalitarian groups from exploiting the principles enunciated by the Convention. But to achieve that purpose, it was not necessary to deprive the persons concerned of all the rights and freedoms guaranteed in the Convention. Article 17 covered essentially those rights which, if invoked, would enable them to engage in the activities referred to in Article 17. The Court, in somewhat different language, followed in substance the view of the Commission.[7] Thus Article 17 applies only to rights, such as those in Articles 9, 10, and 11, which entitle a person to engage in activities; it prevents him from relying on those Articles to engage in subversive activities. A person engaging in subversive activities does not, therefore, forfeit the right to a fair trial under Article 6; but he cannot claim the freedom to organize political meetings, for instance, if his purpose in using that freedom is to undermine all civil liberties. It is always a question of the purpose for which the rights are used; the principle is that 'no person may be able to take advantage of the provisions of the Convention to perform acts aimed at destroying the aforesaid rights and freedoms.'[8] Hence, Article 17 cannot be used to deprive an individual of his political freedom simply on the ground that he has supported a totalitarian government in the past.[9]

It follows also that even persons engaging in terrorist activities for subversive ends cannot be deprived of their protection under the Convention. In the result, those who pursue anarchy, for example, by organizing political meetings on a peaceful basis may in a sense be at a disadvantage compared with those who resort to violence. The former may lose, through the application of Article 17, the political freedoms guaranteed by Articles 9, 10, and 11; the latter, since they do not seek to exercise political activities, lose nothing. If, however, the scale of violence is such as to create a national emergency, the rights guaranteed under Articles 5 and 6 may also be suspended in application of Article 15.

The Court gave considerable attention to Article 17 in its judgment in the

---

[6] *Lawless* v. *Ireland*, Judgments of 14 November 1960, 7 April 1961, and 1 July 1961, Series A, Nos. 1–3; (1979–80) 1 EHRR 1, 13 and 15.

[7] Ibid.

[8] Para. 6 of judgment of 1 July 1961.

[9] See *De Becker*, Report of the Commission, 8 January 1960, Series B, No. 2, at 137–8.

Lehideux and Isorni case.[10] The applicants had been convicted for 'public defence of war crimes or the crimes of collaboration' in relation to the publication of a one page advertisement in the French newspaper, *Le Monde*, which spoke favourably about Philippe Pétain. A criminal complaint had been filed by the National Association of Former Members of the Resistance, which had initiated the prosecution. The applicants complained of a violation of Article 10 of the Convention on freedom of expression, and the French Government responded by asking the Court to dismiss the application under Article 17. The Commission had concluded that there was nothing in the advertisement in *Le Monde* which constituted racial hatred or other statements calculated to destroy or restrict the rights and freedoms guaranteed by the Convention. Furthermore, it did not consider that the expression of ideas constituted an 'activity' within the meaning of Article 17.

The Court first gave consideration to the complaint under Article 10, and ultimately found that there was a breach of Article 10 because the applicants' criminal conviction was disproportionate and, so, unnecessary in a democratic society. Having reached this conclusion, the Court decided that it was not appropriate to apply Article 17.[11]

A number of concurring and dissenting opinions are attached to the judgment. Judge Jambrek in a concurring opinion says:

In order that Article 17 may be applied, the aim of the offending actions must be to spread violence or hatred, to resort to illegal or undemocratic methods, to encourage the use of violence, to undermine the nation's democratic and pluralist political system, or to pursue objectives that are racist or likely to destroy the rights and freedoms of others. . . . Therefore, the requirements of Article 17 are strictly scrutinised, and rightly so.[12]

This appears to reflect the underlying approach adopted by the Court. The matter could be resolved by applying Article 10 and the repression of this type of publication through the use of criminal sanctions went beyond the requirements of a democratic society. The defenders of Marshall Pétain could not be said to be undermining democracy in the way envisaged by Article 17. It was therefore inappropriate to permit the French Government to plead that provision to excuse their actions.

This approach seems to be confirmed by the way in which the *ÖZDEP* case[13] was argued. The case involved a court order dissolving a political party in Turkey. The Turkish Constitutional Court had concluded that the Freedom and Democracy Party's (ÖZDEP) activities were subject to the restrictions in Article

---

[10] *Lehideux and Isorni* v. *France* (App. 24662/94), Judgment of 23 September 1998; (2000) 30 EHRR 665.

[11] Para. 58 of the judgment.

[12] Para. 2 of concurring opinion.

[13] *ÖZDEP* v. *Turkey* (App. 23995/94), Judgment of 8 December 1999; (2001) 31 EHRR 675.

11(2) and 17 of the Convention. The application to the Strasbourg organs did not raise issues under Article 17, but considered the matter solely under Article 11.[14]

LIMITATION ON USE OF RESTRICTIONS ON RIGHTS

Article 18 provides:

The restrictions permitted under this Convention to the said rights and freedoms shall not be applied for any purpose other than those for which they have been prescribed.

This Article shows that there can be no inherent or implied limitations on the rights guaranteed. Each limitation must be express and have an explicit purpose. The Article does not have an independent character and will only be relevant in conjunction with an article which contains limitations, though there does not need to be a violation of that other provision before Article 18 bites.

It is not clear why Article 18 was included in the Convention. There is no equivalent provision in the Universal Declaration of Human Rights nor in the United Nations Covenant on Civil and Political Rights, though Article 30 of the American Convention provides:

The restrictions that, pursuant to this Convention, may be placed on the enjoyment or exercise of the rights or freedoms recognized herein may not be applied except in accordance with the laws enacted for reasons of general interest and in accordance with the purpose for which such restrictions have been established.

There is not much guidance in the preparatory work. Article 18 may seem to add little to the Convention except to make explicit what is either implicit in other provisions or else may be thought to be well established under the general principles recognized by international law.[15] But it is useful as putting beyond doubt the scope of the restrictions permitted, and as making clear the requirement of good faith in the application of these restrictions.

Article 18 limits the area of discretion of the national authorities. In effect, it excludes *détournement de pouvoir*[16] or abuse of power, notions familiar in many systems of domestic law. The principle is that where the real purpose of the authorities in imposing a restriction is outside the purposes specified, one of the specified purposes cannot be used as a pretext for imposing that restriction.

---

[14] Thus rendering it, in the view of the Court, unnecessary to consider the applicant's complaints under Article 9, 10, and 14.

[15] See A. Kiss, *L'abus de droit en droit international* (Paris, 1953).

[16] See App. 753/60, *X v. Austria*, 5 August 1960, (1960) 3 *Yearbook* 310; *Lawless v. Ireland*, Judgments of 14 November 1960, 7 April 1961, and 1 July 1961, Series A, Nos. 1–3; (1979–80) 1 EHRR 1, 13 and 15.

The restriction may be one which is legitimate in itself, and lawfully imposed in accordance with the proper procedure. But it will still be prohibited if imposed for an improper purpose. For example, where the right of a convicted prisoner to respect for family life is subject to a restriction on the grounds set out in Article 8(2), such a restriction may be imposed only for the purposes there specified, and not, for example, as a punishment.

One difficulty in using Article 18 is its dependence on showing a particular motivation. In the *Handyside* case[17] the applicant sought to argue that the purpose of the seizure of *The Little Red Schoolbook* was not for the protection of morals, but 'to muzzle a small-scale publisher whose political leanings met with the disapproval of a fragment of the public opinion.'[18] The Commission concluded that there was no evidence to sustain this allegation, and the Court considered the matter solely on the limitations in Article 10(2) and did not consider the issue under Article 18. The Court has incorporated its consideration of motivation into its consideration of whether the limitations are necessary in a democratic society.

The provision is cited with some regularity by applicants, but the Court hardly ever finds the need to consider its terms. Other provisions of the Convention are usually sufficient for the application to be determined without recourse to this provision.[19]

---

[17] *Handyside* v. *United Kingdom*, Judgment of 7 December 1976, Series A, No. 24; (1979–80) 1 EHRR 737.

[18] Ibid., para. 52 of the judgment.

[19] See e.g. *Quinn* v. *France* (App. 18580/91), Judgment of 22 March 1995; (1996) 21 EHRR 529; *Lukanov* v. *Bulgaria* (App. 21915/93), Judgment of 20 March 1997; (1997) 24 EHRR 121; *Kurt* v. *Turkey* (App. 24276/94), Judgment of 25 May 1998; (1999) 27 EHRR 373; and *Beyeler* v. *Italy* (App. 33202/96), Judgment of 5 January 2000.

21

DEROGATIONS IN EMERGENCY SITUATIONS

INTRODUCTION

Article 15 provides:

1. In time of war or other public emergency threatening the life of the nation any High Contracting Party may take measures derogating from its obligations under this Convention to the extent strictly required by the exigencies of the situation, provided that such measures are not inconsistent with its other obligations under international law.
2. No derogation from Article 2, except in respect of deaths resulting from lawful acts of war, or from Articles 3, 4 (paragraph 1) and 7 shall be made under this provision.
3. Any High Contracting Party availing itself of this right of derogation shall keep the Secretary-General of the Council of Europe fully informed of the measures which it has taken and the reasons therefor. It shall also inform the Secretary-General of the Council of Europe when such measures have ceased to operate and the provisions of the Convention are again being fully executed.

Article 15 incorporates, in effect, the principle of necessity common to all legal systems. Most States have provisions for emergency legislation, empowering them to take measures in a state of emergency which would not otherwise be lawful.[1]

However, under Article 15, such measures are subject to the control of the organs of the Convention. If a State avails itself in a case, of its right of derogation, it is for the Court to consider, first, whether a public emergency threatening the life of the nation could be said to exist at the material time; and secondly, whether the measures taken were in fact strictly required by the exigencies of the situation. Thirdly, such measures must be consistent with other obligations under international law. Finally, there must be timely notification to the Secretary-General of the Council of Europe both of the introduction of

---

[1] See generally Pinheiro Farinha, 'L'article 15 de la Convention' in F. Matscher and H. Petzold (eds.), *Protecting Human Rights: The European Dimension. Essays in honour of Gérard Wiarda* (Köln, 1990), 521.

derogating measures and of the reasons for them, and of the lifting of those measures.

Issues relating to Article 15 have normally been examined on the merits and cannot usually be disposed of at the stage of admissibility. In inter-State cases, this is indeed inevitable, since such a case cannot be rejected as being manifestly ill-founded.[2] In the case brought by Ireland against the United Kingdom, the respondent Government invoked, at the stage of admissibility, the notification of derogation which it had made in respect of Northern Ireland. The Irish Government accepted that a public emergency within the meaning of Article 15 existed in Northern Ireland, but denied that the measures taken by the United Kingdom Government were strictly required by the exigencies of the situation. The Commission held that this question could not be determined at the stage of admissibility.[3]

Indeed, even on an individual application, it would be difficult to justify a decision holding that all the conditions of Article 15 were plainly fulfilled at the stage of admissibility; normally such an application should be examined at the merits phase if Article 15 is invoked.[4]

There would seem to be nothing objectionable in a State making use of an Article 15 derogation to avoid granting rights under the Convention when it has been held to be in violation of the Convention. In the *Brogan* case[5] the United Kingdom was found to be in breach of Article 5(3) of the Convention in the period allowed for questioning before a suspect was brought before a judicial officer under the prevention of terrorism legislation. Prior to the judgment of the Court, it had considered that the legislation met the requirements of Article 5(3). In response to the judgment, instead of amending its legislation to ensure compliance with the period for bringing suspects before a judicial officer, the United Kingdom entered a derogation under Article 15. Obviously, that derogation could not apply retrospectively, and would be subject to assessment in the usual way by the Convention organs for compliance with the requirements of Article 15.[6]

Any doubt about the validity of the derogation filed following the judgment in the *Brogan* case was resolved in the *Brannigan and McBride* case[7] where the Court said:

---

[2] See ch. 24.

[3] Apps. 5310/71 and 5151/72, *Ireland* v. *United Kingdom*, 1 October 1972, (1972) 41 CD 3, at 88.

[4] But see App. 493/59, *X* v. *Ireland*, 27 July 1961, (1961) 4 *Yearbook* 302, at 310–16.

[5] *Brogan and others* v. *United Kingdom*, Judgment of 29 November 1988, Series A, No. 145-B; (1989) 11 EHRR 117.

[6] This is the view taken in J. Merrills, *Human Rights in Europe* (Manchester, 2001), at 211, though P. van Dijk and G. van Hoof, *Theory and Practice of the European Convention on Human Rights* (Deventer, 1990), at 557–8 take the view that the UK derogation of 23 December 1988 was unlawful.

[7] *Brannigan and McBride* v. *United Kingdom*, Judgment of 26 May 1993, Series A, No. 253-B; (1994) 17 EHRR 539.

The power of extended detention with such judicial control and the derogation of 23 December 1988 being clearly linked to the persistence of the emergency situation, there is no indication that the derogation was other than a genuine response.[8]

NON-DEROGABLE RIGHTS

Certain rights under the Convention are not susceptible to derogation in any circumstances.

Article 2 on the right to life is non-derogable, save to the extent that derogations are permitted 'in respect of deaths resulting from lawful acts of war'.[9] Article 2 itself does not include intentional deprivation of life in the execution of a sentence of a court following a conviction for a crime for which this penalty is imposed;[10] nor does it include deprivation of life in defence of any person from unlawful violence,[11] in order to effect a lawful arrest or to prevent the escape of a person lawfully detained,[12] and in action lawfully taken for the purpose of quelling a riot or insurrection.[13] Where Protocol 6 has been ratified, the prohibition of derogations in respect of the rights guaranteed by that Protocol contained in Article 3 of Protocol 6 applies. However, Article 2 of Protocol 6 permits States to make provision in their law for the death penalty in respect of acts committed in time of war or imminent threat of war.[14]

No derogations may be made in respect of the prohibition of slavery and servitude in Article 4(1); nor in respect of the requirement that there be no punishment without law under Article 7; nor in respect of the right not to be tried or punished twice under Article 4 of Protocol 7.

SUBSTANTIVE REQUIREMENTS

Permissible derogations under Article 15 must meet both the substantive requirements of Article 15(1) and the procedural requirements in Article 15(3). The substantive requirements require three conditions to be satisfied:

[8] Para. 51 of the judgment.
[9] Art. 15(2).
[10] But see comments on Protocol 6 below.
[11] Art. 2(2)(a).
[12] Art. 2(2)(b).
[13] Art. 2(2)(c)
[14] Where this happens, the State must notify the Secretary-General of the Council of Europe of the relevant provisions of the law governing the death penalty: Art. 2 of Protocol 6.

- There must be a public emergency threatening the life of the nation.
- The measures taken in response to it must be strictly required by the exigencies of the situation.
- The measures taken must be in compliance with the State's other obligations under international law.

The procedural requirements require that there is some formal or public act of derogation, and that notice of the derogation, measures adopted in consequence of it, and of the ending of the derogation, is communicated to the Secretary-General of the Council of Europe.[15]

The use of derogations under Article 15 arose for the first time in the *Cyprus* cases;[16] two applications were brought by Greece against the United Kingdom when Cyprus was still under British rule. The Commission considered that it was 'competent to pronounce on the existence of a public danger which, under Article 15, would grant to the Contracting Party concerned the right to derogate from the obligations laid down in the Convention.' The Commission also considered that it was 'competent to decide whether measures taken by a Party under Article 15 of the Convention had been taken to the extent strictly required by the exigencies of the situation.' It added that 'the Government should be able to exercise a certain measure of discretion in assessing the extent strictly required by the exigencies of the situation.'[17]

Subsequently a political solution to the Cyprus problem was reached, and the Committee of Ministers decided that no further action was called for.

The notion of a government's 'measure of discretion'[18] was to have an influential career in this context. Its scope in relation to derogations is considered below. For the moment it is sufficient to observe that it qualifies, but does not exclude, the control by the Court of the application of Article 15.

The existence of this control was confirmed by the Court in the *Lawless* case.[19] The Irish Government had contended that, provided measures taken under Article 15 were not contrary to Article 18, they were outside the control of the Convention bodies. The Court said, however, 'It is for the Court to determine whether the conditions laid down in Article 15 for the exercise of the exceptional right of derogation have been fulfilled'.[20] It accordingly considered, first, whether there could be said to be a public emergency threatening the life of the nation; second, whether the measures taken in derogation from

---

[15] See Art. 15(3).

[16] App. 176/57, *Greece* v. *United Kingdom* (1958–9) 2 Yearbook 174 and 182; App. 299/57, *Greece* v. *United Kingdom*, (1958–9) 2 *Yearbook* 178 and 186.

[17] App. 176/57, *Greece* v. *United Kingdom*, (1958–9) 2 Yearbook 174, at 176

[18] In French *marge d'appreciation;* the term 'margin of appreciation' is now used in preference to 'measures of discretion'.

[19] *Lawless* v. *Ireland*, Judgments of 14 November 1960, 7 April 1961, and 1 July 1961, Series A, Nos. 1–3; (1979–80) 1 EHRR 1, 13, and 15.

[20] Para. 22 of the judgment of 1 July 1961.

obligations under the Convention were 'strictly required by the exigencies of the situation'; and third, whether the measures were inconsistent with other obligations under international law.

The Commission adopted the position that issues arising under Article 15 will not be examined unless they are raised by the respondent State. The *McVeigh* case[21] concerned the United Kingdom anti-terrorist legislation as it had been applied to the three applicants who had arrived in Liverpool on a ferry from Ireland. They were held for forty-five hours without charge, questioned, searched, finger-printed and photographed. They made complaints under Articles 5, 8, and 10. At the material time, various derogations were in effect in respect of the United Kingdom, but the United Kingdom Government did not seek to invoke them in respect of the situation in Great Britain, as distinct from Northern Ireland.

THERE MUST BE A PUBLIC EMERGENCY THREATENING THE LIFE OF THE NATION

What constitutes a public emergency? In the *Lawless* case, the Court defined it as 'an exceptional situation of crisis or emergency which affects the whole population and constitutes a threat to the organized life of the community of which the State is composed.'[22] The danger must be exceptional in that the normal measures permitted by the Convention are plainly inadequate to deal with the situation. The Court found that the existence of a public emergency was 'reasonably deduced' by the Irish Government. The Court had regard, in particular to three factors: the existence of a secret army (the Irish Republican Army—IRA); the fact that this army was also operating outside the territory of the State; and the steady and alarming increase in terrorist activities in the period before the emergency was declared.[23]

In the *Greek* case, the Commission had to consider the validity of a derogation by a revolutionary government. The respondent Government, which had seized power in Greece by a *coup d'état* on 21 April 1967 and had suspended parts of the Constitution, invoked Article 15 of the Convention. The Commission considered that the Convention applied in the same way to a revolutionary as to a constitutional government.[24]

As regards the definition of a 'public emergency threatening the life of the nation', the Commission followed the definition given by the Court in the

---

[21] Apps. 8022/77, 8025/77, and 8027/77, *McVeigh, O'Neil and Evans* v. *United Kingdom*, Report of the Commission, 18 March 1981, (1982) 25 DR 15.

[22] Para. 28 of the judgment of 1 July 1961.

[23] Ibid.

[24] *The Greek Case*, (1969) II *Yearbook*, at 32.

Lawless case.[25] Methodologically, too, the Commission followed the Court, but only in part. It sought to answer the question whether there was such a public emergency in Greece by examining the elements indicated by the respondent Government as constituting in its view such an emergency.[26] These elements were examined by the Commission under three heads: the danger of a Communist take-over; the crisis of constitutional government; and the breakdown of public order in Greece.[27]

The Commission considered that in the present case the burden lay upon the respondent Government to show that the conditions justifying measures of derogation under Article 15 had been and continued to be met.[28] It concluded that the Government had not satisfied it that there was on 21 April 1967 a public emergency threatening the life of the Greek nation.[29]

However, in one respect the Commission did not follow the Court's view of Article 15. The Commission, while referring to the Government's 'margin of appreciation', did not merely consider whether the Greek Government had sufficient reason to believe that a public emergency existed; it considered whether such an emergency existed in fact. This difference of approach is of great importance since it makes more stringent the requirements of Article 15.

In *Ireland* v. *United Kingdom*[30] both the Commission and the Court had little difficulty in determining that there was a public emergency threatening the life of the nation because of the terrorist threat from the activities of the IRA. This issue was not contested by Ireland. No argument was made on the basis that—certainly at the time—the major threat related only to a part of the United Kingdom.

A rather different situation was presented in the *Sakik* case.[31] The Turkish Government sought, in responding to the applications alleging violations of Article 5 arising from the length of detention in police custody, to rely on derogations filed in respect of Article 5. But those declarations did not apply to the country as a whole, and did not apply to Ankara, where the facts alleged to have resulted in the violation of Article 5 had occurred. The Court said:

[T]he Court would be working against the object and purpose of [Article 15] if, when assessing the territorial scope of the derogation concerned, it were to extend its effects to a part of the Turkish territory not explicitly named in the notice of derogation.

---

[25] At 71–2.
[26] At 44.
[27] At 45.
[28] At 72.
[29] At 76.
[30] *Ireland* v. *United Kingdom*, Judgment of 18 January 1978, Series A, No. 25; (1979–80) 2 EHRR 25.
[31] *Sakik and others* v. *Turkey* (Apps. 23878/94—23883/94), Judgment of 26 November 1997; (1998) 27 EHRR 662.

It follows that the derogation in question is inapplicable *ratione loci* to the facts of this case.[32]

The current position adopted by the Court in reviewing whether there is a public emergency threatening the life of the nation is neatly summarized in the *Aksoy* case.

The Court recalls that it falls to each Contracting State, with its responsibility for 'the life of [its] nation', to determine whether that life is threatened by a 'public emergency' and, if so, how far it is necessary to go in attempting to overcome the emergency. By reason of their direct and continuous contact with the pressing needs of the moment, the national authorities are in principle better placed than the international judge to decide both on the presence of such an emergency and on the nature and scope of the derogations necessary to avert it. Accordingly, in this matter a wide margin of appreciation should be left to the national authorities.[33]

The Court seems certain to find itself called upon to consider whether the United Kingdom derogation[34] in respect of Article 5(1) permitting detention without trial of those suspected of involvement in terrorist activities is based upon a public emergency threatening the life of the nation. The public emergency is said to flow from the terrorist attacks in New York, Washington DC, and Pennsylvania of 11 September 2001 in New York. However, no other party to the European Convention has felt it necessary to derogate from Convention rights in relation to those events, and there have been no terrorist attacks in the United Kingdom attributable to those alleged to be responsible for the attacks of 11 September 2001 in the United States. United Kingdom support for the so-called 'war on terrorism' has, however, had a high visibility, which clearly renders the United Kingdom a *potential* target for such terrorist activity.

To date, apart from the *Greek* case which involved a derogation whose underlying purpose was to support a non-democratic government, the Court has accepted the existence of a State's assessment of the existence of a public emergency threatening the life of the nation. Some dissenting judgments of the Court have suggested that the Court defers too readily to the judgment of States in this context.[35]

THE MEASURES TAKEN MUST BE STRICTLY REQUIRED

If it is established that this first condition of Article 15 is satisfied, it must next be asked whether the measures which are the subject of the application were

[32] Para. 39 of the judgment.
[33] *Aksoy* v. *Turkey (App. 21987/93)*, Judgment of 18 December 1996; (1997) 23 EHRR 553, para. 68 of the judgment.
[34] See the Human Rights Act 1998 (Designated Derogation) Order 2001, SI 2001, No. 3644.
[35] See e.g. the dissenting opinion of Judge Walsh in *Brannigan and McBride* v. *United Kingdom*, Judgment of 26 May 1993, Series A, No. 258-B; (1994) 17 EHRR 539.

'strictly required by the exigencies of the situation'. In the *Aksoy* case, the Court said:

It is for the Court to rule whether, *inter alia*, the States have gone beyond the 'extent strictly required by the exigencies' of the crisis. The domestic margin of appreciation is thus accompanied by a European supervision. In exercising this supervision, the Court must give appropriate weight to such relevant factors as the nature of the rights affected by the derogation and the circumstances leading to, and the duration of, the emergency situation.[36]

In the *Greek* case, as the Commission was not satisfied that there was a public emergency, the measures could not in any event be justified under Article 15. It was not therefore necessary to consider whether the measures taken were strictly required by the exigencies of the situation. Nevertheless, the Commission decided to examine that question also, on the hypothesis that there was a public emergency in Greece threatening the life of the nation.[37] The Commission found that, even on that hypothesis, the measures taken could not be justified under Article 15, because they went beyond what the situation required.[38]

In the *Lawless* case, the Court held, following the opinion of the Commission, that detention without trial was justified under Article 15. In considering whether such a measure was strictly required by the exigencies of the situation, the Court had particular regard, not only to the dangers of the situation, but also to the existence of a number of safeguards designed to prevent abuses in the operation of the system of administrative detention.[39] Examination of the safeguards provided where there is a derogation has taken on great significance in cases where the Court is called upon to review the compatibility of derogations with the requirements of Article 15.

In *Ireland* v. *United Kingdom*[40] the Court made an independent examination of the circumstances, but in doing so placed considerable emphasis on the margin of appreciation to be accorded to the State. The Court found that the system of extrajudicial deprivation of liberty was justified by the circumstances as perceived by the United Kingdom between August 1971 and March 1975.

The determination of whether measures taken are strictly required by the exigencies of the situation requires consideration of three elements. First, are the derogations necessary to cope with the threat to the life of the nation?

[36] *Aksoy* v. *Turkey (App. 21987/93)*, Judgment of 18 December 1996; (1997) 23 EHRR 553, para. 68 of the judgment, referring to *Brannigan and McBride* v. *United Kingdom*, Judgment of 26 May 1993, Series A, No. 258-B; (1994) 17 EHRR 539, para. 43 of the judgment.
[37] *The Greek Case*, (1969) *II Yearbook*, at 104.
[38] At 135–6 and 148–9.
[39] *Lawless* v. *Ireland*, Judgments of 14 November 1960, 7 April 1961, and 1 July 1961, Series A, Nos. 1–3; (1979–80) 1 EHRR 1, 13 and 15, paras. 31–8 of the judgment of 1 July 1961.
[40] *Ireland* v. *United Kingdom*, Judgment of 18 January 1978, Series A, No. 25; (1979–80) 2 EHRR 25.

Secondly, are the measures taken no greater than those required to deal with the emergency? This is a test of proportionality. Finally, how long have the derogating measures been applied? There is no case law in which duration of the measures has been a crucial issue, but it is certainly arguable that measures, which at their inception were clearly required, could cease to be so if they proved either to be ineffectual or if it could no longer be established that they were strictly required by the situation. The Court said in *Ireland* v. *United Kingdom* that 'The interpretation of Article 15 must leave a place for progressive adaptation.'[41]

It is possible to detect in the *Brannigan and McBride* case [42] a greater willingness by the Court to question the effectiveness of the safeguards which the State puts in place to compensate for suspension of the rights required by the Convention provision in respect of which the derogation is filed. This tougher stand on the safeguards required to ensure that the derogations do not go beyond what is strictly required by the exigencies of the situation is supported by the Court's approach in the *Aksoy* case, where the Court declined to accept that the situation required suspects to be held for fourteen days without judicial intervention, noting that the Turkish Government had not detailed any reasons why judicial intervention was impracticable.[43]

THE MEASURES MUST COMPLY WITH OTHER OBLIGATIONS UNDER INTERNATIONAL LAW

Measures which may be taken by a State under Article 15(1) must not be 'inconsistent with its other obligations under international law'. Thus, they must not conflict with its other treaty obligations, or obligations under customary international law. Any such measures are not permitted under Article 15. Hence, a State could not avail itself of Article 15 to release itself from its obligations, for example, under other human rights instruments. This would in any event be precluded by Article 53 of the Convention,[44] which provides:

Nothing in this Convention shall be construed as limiting or derogating from any of the human rights and fundamental freedoms which may be ensured under the laws of any High Contracting Party or under any other agreement to which it is a Party.

The requirement of consistency with international obligations has played little part in the case law of the Court on Article 15 so far. In the *Brannigan and*

---

[41] p. 83 of the judgment.
[42] *Brannigan and McBride* v. *United Kingdom*, Judgment of 26 May 1993, Series A, No. 258-B; (1994) 17 EHRR 539
[43] *Aksoy* v. *Turkey (App. 21987/93)*, Judgment of 18 December 1996; (1997) 23 EHRR 553, paras. 78 and 84 of the judgment.
[44] Formerly Art. 60.

McBride case[45] it was argued that Article 4 of the United Nations International Covenant on Civil and Political Rights required the emergency to be 'officially proclaimed'. Without expressing a view on the precise content of this requirement, the Court observed that the statement of the Home Secretary in Parliament on 22 December 1988 was formal in character and made public the Government's reliance on Article 15, and was 'well in keeping with the notion of an official proclamation'.[46]

PROCEDURAL REQUIREMENTS

Two issues require consideration in addressing the procedural requirements of Article 15. First, is it an inherent requirement that there is some official proclamation of the public emergency threatening the life of the nation? Secondly, what are the requirements of Article 15(3), and what is the consequence of any failure to comply with those requirements?

OFFICIAL PROCLAMATION

There is no express requirement in Article 15 that there is an official proclamation of the public emergency in the national legal order. But it seems that some form of public proclamation of the public emergency is an implicit feature of Article 15.[47] Though there is no direct authority on this issue, the implications of the comments of the Court in the *Brannigan and McBride* case referred to above are to this effect. At the very least, a State which had not made any formal announcements within the national legal order might find itself facing greater difficulties in proving the existence of a public emergency before the Court.

THE NOTIFICATION REQUIREMENTS

Article 15(3) requires notification both of the introduction of derogations and of the lifting of them. The precise nature of the obligation in this paragraph was considered by the Court in the *Lawless* case where it was argued that notification to the Secretary-General in July 1957 did not meet the requirements of the paragraph for three reasons: first, it did not indicate expressly that it was a

---

[45] *Brannigan and McBride* v. *United Kingdom*, Judgment of 26 May 1993, Series A, No. 253-B; (1994) 17 EHRR 539.

[46] Para. 73 of the judgment.

[47] Having regard, in particular, to the requirement under Art. 4 of the International Covenant on Civil and Political Rights.

derogation under Article 15; secondly, it did not refer to the existence of a public emergency threatening the life of the nation; and, thirdly, the matter had not been made public in Ireland until October and so could not be relied upon in respect of acts occurring between July and October. The Court did not consider that any of these factors tainted the notification; it was couched in terms sufficient to enable the Secretary-General to understand the Irish Government's position. Furthermore the paragraph required the matter to be notified to the Secretary-General and did not impose any obligation to publish the derogation within the State.[48] Nor did it regard a delay of twelve days between national adoption and notification outside the scope of a requirement of notification 'without delay'.[49]

In the Greek case, there was a four-month delay between the implementation of derogating measures and notification. Even though the derogation was held to be invalid because the Commission was not satisfied that there was a public emergency threatening the life of the nation, the Commission noted that late notification would not justify action taken before the actual notification.[50]

Three remarks should be added on the scope of derogations ratione temporis. First, in considering whether the measures were permissible under Article 15, regard must be had to the situation before the emergency is declared. This was of course done by the Court in the Lawless case and by the Commission in the Greek case, but arguably not in the Brannigan and McBride case. Secondly, notification under Article 15(3) may have a very limited retroactive effect. No time-limit is laid down for notifications, but the Court appeared to consider in the Lawless case that communication without delay is an element in the sufficiency of information required by that provision.[51] In the Greek case the Commission considered that the initial notice of derogation was given within a reasonable time, but that there was undue delay in communicating the reasons for the measures of derogation.[52] Thirdly, it is evident that if the measures in question remain in force after the circumstances which justify them have disappeared, they represent a breach of the Convention.[53] In the Greek case, accordingly, the Commission examined the evolution of the situation from the date of the coup to the time of compiling its Report.[54]

The paragraph contains no sanction, though, in practice, it may well be that a State would find great difficulty in proving its case if it failed to notify the

---

[48] Lawless v. Ireland, Judgments of 1 July 1961, Series A, No. 1; (1979–80) 1 EHRR 15, p. 62 of the judgment.

[49] Ibid.

[50] The Greek Case, (1969) II Yearbook, at 41–3.

[51] Lawless v. Ireland, Judgments of 14 November 1960, 7 April 1961, and 1 July 1961, Series A, Nos. 1–3; (1979–80) 1 EHRR 1, 13, and 15, paras. 42–7 of the judgment of 1 July 1961.

[52] The Greek Case, (1969) II Yearbook, at 42–3.

[53] App. 214/56, De Becker, Report of the Commission, Series B, No. 2, at 133.

[54] The Greek Case, (1969) II Yearbook, at 92–103.

Secretary-General of the measures taken. After all, the essence of Article 15 is that the State reviews its ability to sustain the protection of the rights guaranteed by the Convention and concludes that certain of them must be limited in order to deal with an extraordinary situation.

22

RESERVATIONS

INTRODUCTION

International law recognizes that a State, in accepting a treaty, may in certain circumstances attach a reservation, that is, make its acceptance subject to some new term which limits or varies the application of the treaty to that State.[1]

Article 57[2] of the Convention provides:

1. Any State may, when signing this Convention or when depositing its instrument of ratification, make a reservation in respect of any particular provision of the Convention to the extent that any law then in force in its territory is not in conformity with the provision. Reservations of a general character shall not be permitted under this Article.
2. Any reservation made under this Article shall contain a brief statement of the law concerned.

Reservations must relate to a particular provision of the Convention and to a particular law in force at the time; in addition, according to paragraph (2), they must contain a brief statement of the law concerned. A fair number of reservations has been made to the Convention and Protocols, but these are mainly very limited in scope.[3] Any far-reaching reservation would in any event be illegal as being incompatible with the object and purpose of the Treaty.[4]

Although there is no legal obligation in this respect, and no express provision for withdrawal of a reservation, it would be in accordance with the spirit of the Convention, and with its object and purpose, to envisage that laws which necessitated reservations would progressively be amended or repealed to ensure that the Contracting States complied without reservation with all the Convention's provisions. This has certainly happened on some occasions. When ratifying the Convention, Norway found it necessary to make a reservation in respect of Article 9, since the Norwegian Constitution of 1814 provided for a ban on Jesuits. In 1956 this provision was abrogated and the reservation withdrawn.

---

[1] See Art. 19 ff. of the Vienna Convention on the Law of Treaties.
[2] Formerly Art. 64 of the Convention.
[3] See **http://conventions.coe.int**
[4] Art. 19 of the Vienna Convention on the Law of Treaties. See also *Reservations to the Convention on Genocide*, [1951] ICJ Rep. 15.

Similarly in Switzerland, a reservation to the same article was considered necessary pending revision of the denominational articles of the Federal Constitution. When the revision was made, the reservation was withdrawn.

RESERVATIONS MADE

Article 57 (formerly 64) of the Convention appears to permit only reservations in respect of those articles of the Convention which lay down substantive obligations, but the practice of States shows that they do attempt to qualify declarations relating to the procedural provisions of the Convention, that is, those provisions dealing with the competence of the Commission and the Court.

SUBSTANTIVE PROVISIONS

Some examples of reservations will give an idea of their scope and range. Malta has made a reservation in respect of Article 2, Portugal in respect of Article 4, and Germany, Malta, Portugal, Sweden, Turkey, and the United Kingdom in respect of Article 2 of Protocol 1 on the right to education. There are several reservations in respect of Articles 5 and 6.

An important reservation relates to the Austrian State Treaty of 1955, the Treaty for the Restoration of an Independent and Democratic Austria, which constitutes Austria's peace treaty with the Western Powers and the Soviet Union. The Austrian reservation, made when Austria ratified the Convention and First Protocol in 1958, provides that Article 1 of the First Protocol, which relates to property rights, should not affect Part IV of the Treaty, 'Claims arising out of the War' and Part V, 'Property, Rights and Interests'. A claim for compensation concerned, not the State Treaty itself, but a law of 1958 not mentioned in the reservation, passed in execution of Part IV of the Treaty. The Commission considered that, in making its reservation, Austria must necessarily have intended to exclude from the scope of the First Protocol everything forming the subject matter of Parts IV and V of the State Treaty; and that the reservation must be interpreted as intended to cover all legislative and administrative measures directly related to this subject matter.[5]

In the *Helle* case,[6] Finland made a reservation which was upheld excluding the right to an oral hearing from certain specified proceedings. The Court

---

[5] App. 3923/69, *X* v. *Austria*, 14 December 1970, (1971) 37 CD 10; App. 4002/69, *X* v. *Austria*, 29 March 1971, (1971) 14 *Yearbook* 178.

[6] *Helle* v. *Finland* (App. 20722/92), Judgment of 19 December 1997; (1998) 26 EHRR 159.

upheld the reservation in its application to matters which would be supervised by the court named in the reservation.[7]

PROCEDURAL PROVISIONS

Since recognition of the Court and acceptance of the right of individual petition are now mandatory requirements of the European Convention, the matters raised in this section are of largely historical interest. However, an understanding of the position adopted by some States may be helpful in reading certain significant cases in which the issue arose. It is very doubtful whether reservations may be made to declarations under former Article 25, accepting the competence of the Commission to receive applications from individuals, or under former Article 46, recognizing the compulsory jurisdiction of the Court. Former Article 46(1), providing for declarations recognizing the Court's jurisdiction 'in all matters', seems to exclude the possibility of a partial recognition, although the second paragraph provides that a declaration may be made on condition of reciprocity or for a limited period. Further, what is now Article 57 seems to envisage only reservations of a substantive character, relating to a specific law in force at the time of signature or ratification; and a reservation is not permissible where a treaty provides for only specified reservations which do not include the reservation in question.[8]

The Turkish Government, however, filed two declarations under former Articles 25(1) and 46 to which conditions are attached that the Commission and Court would almost certainly consider to be attempted reservations. They appear to be intended to exclude the Commission's competence in complaints concerning its conduct in the northern part of Cyprus, while others seek to exclude the right to complain about the activities of Turkish military personnel. The third, fourth, and fifth qualifications seek to limit the interpretation which may be placed on Articles 8 to 11 of the Convention. The Commission held all these 'qualifications' to be invalid in the *Chrysostomos* case.[9]

These declarations have now been considered by the Court in the *Loizidou* case.[10] The Court ruled that a territorial limitation is not permissible, but that, notwithstanding the purported territorial restrictions, the declarations contain valid acceptances of the competence of the Commission and the Court.

The Commission has accepted that declarations under former Article 25 may be subject to the proviso that they have no retroactive effect.

---

[7] Para. 47 of the judgment.
[8] Art. 19 of the Vienna Convention on the Law of Treaties.
[9] Apps. 15299–15311/89, *Chrysostomos* v. *Turkey*, Decision of 4 March 1991, (1991) 12 HRLJ 113.
[10] *Loizidou* v. *Turkey*, Judgment of 23 March 1995, Series A, No. 310; (1995) 20 EHRR 99, paras. 65–98 of the Judgment.

INTERPRETATION OF RESERVATIONS

Applications which must be excluded because of a reservation made by the respondent Government are outside the Court's competence *ratione materiae*. A reservation must be interpreted in the language in which it is made, not in its translation into one of the languages, English or French, of the authentic texts of the Convention.[11]

The Commission gave rather extensive interpretations of those reservations which it had to consider, but its approach has now been overtaken by authority from the Court, which is much more robust.

The Commission had held that a reservation may serve to exclude, not only measures expressly covered by the reservation, but also other related measures.[12] It may extend to exclude a new law which replaces the law in force at the time of the reservation, provided that the new law does not have the effect of enlarging the scope of the reservation.[13] It may extend to legislative and administrative measures to implement the purpose for which the reservation was made.[14] It may even extend to other provisions of the Convention than those expressly mentioned in the reservation if it is clearly intended to cover the entire operation of domestic law in the field concerned.[15]

Quite apart from this point, it would seem that the Commission has departed from the evident intention of what was then Article 64. That article refers expressly to laws in force at the time of signature or ratification, and clearly envisages that all subsequent legislation will be in conformity with the Convention. The Commission appears to have gone too far in accepting that a later law in the same field might be brought within the scope of a reservation.

However, both the Commission[16] and the Court have taken the view that it is for them to determine the legal validity of reservations. The Court has been rather more rigorous in its examination of these issues than the Commission. The leading authority is the *Belilos* case.[17] Marlène Belilos had been fined 120 Swiss francs for having taken part in an unauthorized demonstration. She raised a complaint under Article 6 of the Convention. This brought into play a declaration made by Switzerland in respect of this Article:

The Swiss Federal Council considers that the guarantee of fair trial in Article 6, para-

---

[11] App. 1047/61, *X v. Austria*, 15 December 1961, (1961) 4 *Yearbook* 356; App. 1452/62, *X v. Austria*, 18 December 1963, (1963) 6 *Yearbook* 268; App. 2432/65, *X v. Austria*, 7 April 1967, (1967) 22 CD 124.

[12] App. 2432/65, *X v. Austria*, 7 April 1967, (1967) 22 CD 124.

[13] Ibid. See also *App. 3923/69, X v. Austria*, 14 December 1970, (1971) 37 CD 10.

[14] App. 2765/66, *X v. Austria*, 15 December 1967, (1967) 10 *Yearbook* 412, at 418.

[15] App. 3923/69, *X v. Austria*, 14 December 1970, (1971) 37 CD 10; App. 4002/69, *X v. Austria*, 29 March 1971, (1971) 14 *Yearbook* 178.

[16] Initially in App. 9116/80, *Telemtasch* v. *Switzerland*, 5 May 1982, (1983) 31 DR 120.

[17] *Belilos* v. *Switzerland*, Judgment of 29 April 1988, Series A, No. 132; (1988) 10 EHRR 466.

graph 1 of the Convention, in the determination of civil rights and obligations or any criminal charge against the person in question is intended solely to ensure ultimate control by the judiciary over the acts or decisions of the public authorities relating to such rights or obligations or the determination of such a charge.

The Court had to consider the effect of this declaration on the claim, which the Government argued amounted in substance to a reservation. The Court accepted this argument, noting that the Convention only made provision for reservations. As a reservation its validity fell to be determined against the requirements of former Article 64. The Court asserted jurisdiction relying on what were then Articles 19,[18] 45,[19] and 49.[20] The Court went on to say that reservations of a general character (which are not permitted by the reservations article of the Convention) were those 'couched in terms that were too vague or broad for it to be possible to determine their exact meaning and scope'.[21] The Court also noted that the validity of a reservation would be dependent upon its being accompanied by a brief statement of the law concerned. Since the Swiss reservation met neither of these conditions it was invalid.

In international law, the position under the Vienna Convention in such circumstances would be that the provision in question would not be valid as between the parties.[22] However, the Court rightly, since this was not litigation between two States, decided that the effect of holding the reservation invalid was that the full force of Article 6 applied in the case, and they went on to consider the merits of the case on that basis.

A more formal Swiss reservation was in issue in the *Weber* case.[23] Franz Weber had been fined for breaching the confidentiality of a judicial investigation. He complained that his rights under Articles 6 and 10 had been violated. In relation to Article 6, the Government sought to rely on a reservation.

The rule contained in Article 6(1) of the Convention that hearing shall be in public shall not apply to proceedings relating to the determination ... of any criminal charge which, in accordance with cantonal legislation, are heard before an administrative

---

[18] Which charges the Court with ensuring the observance of the engagements undertaken by the High Contracting Parties.

[19] Giving the Court jurisdiction to consider all cases concerning the interpretation and application of the Convention referred by a State or the Commission under Art. 48.

[20] Providing that in the event of a dispute as to whether the Court has jurisdiction, the matter is to be settled by a decision of the Court.

[21] *Belilos* v. *Switzerland*, Judgment of 29 April 1988, Series A, No. 132; (1988) 10 EHRR 466, p. 26 of the judgment.

[22] Art. 21(3) of the Vienna Convention provides: When a State objecting to a reservation has not opposed the entry into force of the treaty between itself and the reserving State, the provisions to which the reservation relates do not apply as between the two States to the extent of the reservation. See also J. Frowein, 'Reservations to the European Convention on Human Rights' in F. Matscher and H. Petzold (eds.), *Protecting Human Rights: The European Dimension. Studies in Honour of Gérard J. Wiarda* (Köln, 1990), 193–200, at 197.

[23] *Weber* v. *Switzerland*, Judgment of 22 May 1990, Series A, No. 177; (1990) 12 EHRR 508.

authority. The rule that judgment must be pronounced publicly shall not affect the operation of cantonal legislation on civil or criminal procedure providing that judgment shall not be delivered in public but notified to the parties in writing.

The Court found that this reservation was invalid because it was not accompanied by a brief statement of the law concerned; such an omission was not regarded as a purely formal requirement but a condition of substance. The Court proceeded to test the complaint against Article 6(1).

In a case concerning Austria,[24] a reservation to Article 5 was in issue. The Court noted that the domestic law in issue was all in force on the date when Austria ratified the Convention, and that its wording was sufficiently specific to meet the requirements of former Article 64(1). The reservation contained a reference to the Bundesgesetzblatt[25] by way of providing a brief statement of the laws affected. The Court amplified its earlier comments on the requirements of former Article 64(2):

According to the Court's case-law, the 'brief statement' as required by [Article 64(2)] 'both constitutes an evidential factor and contributes to legal certainty'; its purpose 'is to provide a guarantee—in particular for the other Contracting Parties and the Convention institutions—that a reservation does not go beyond the provisions expressly excluded by the State concerned.' . . . This does not mean that it is necessary under Article 64(2) to provide a description, even a concise one, of the substance of the texts in question.

In this instance, the reference to the Federal Official Gazette—preceded moreover by an indication of the subject-matter of the relevant provisions—makes it possible for everyone to identify the precise laws concerned and to obtain any information regarding them. It also provides a safeguard against any interpretation which would unduly extend the field of application of the reservation.

The reservation was held to meet the requirements of what was then Article 64(2).

A different Austrian reservation was in issue in the *Eisenstecken* case.[26] This reservation was broadly worded and concerned the right to a fair trial in Article 6; it reads:

The provisions of Article 6 of the Convention shall be so applied that there shall be no prejudice to the principles governing public court hearings laid down in Article 90 of the 1929 version of the Federal Constitutional Law.

The applicant complained that there was no public hearing in a dispute concerning real property transactions. The reservation had been considered in a number of earlier cases,[27] and in a remarkably short section of one earlier

---

[24] *Choherr* v. *Austria*, Judgment of 25 August 1993, Series A, No. 266-B; (1994) 17 EHRR 358.
[25] Federal Official Gazette.
[26] *Eisenstecken* v. *Austria* (App. 29477/95), Judgment of 3 October 2000; (2002) 34 EHRR 860.
[27] See paras. 24–6 of the judgment.

judgment apparently accepted as valid.[28] The Court in the *Eisenstecken* case observed that the compatibility of the Austrian reservation with the requirements of what is now Article 57 had not previously been tested. The Court goes on to rule the reservation to be invalid for its failure to contain a brief statement of the law which is said not to conform to Article 6 of the Convention, and that it was not necessary to consider its compatibility with other requirements of Article 57.

In two cases against Lithuania,[29] the validity of a reservation in respect of Article 5(3)[30] was in issue. Lithuania had made a reservation for one year after the Convention entered into force in respect of Lithuania. The question was whether on the expiry of the reservation, the obligation to bring a detained person promptly before a judge arose, or whether the opportunity had been missed by reason of the earlier detention. The Court is particularly accommodating (though there is logic in the Court's position) in finding that the obligation arises immediately on entering detention and cannot usefully be resurrected at some time later if the person is still in detention on the expiry of the Lithuanian reservation. There was no renewed obligation after the expiry of the reservation.[31]

CONCLUDING COMMENT

The extent to which reservations are appropriate to a human rights instrument has been questioned. Frowein says:

It is of crucial importance that the member States of the Convention should be willing to exercise their collective responsibility in the matter of reservations and agree that reservations can only be a means whereby a new member can bring its law into line with the Convention. In fact, many of the reservations could easily be made superfluous by sometimes very minor amendments to the legislation in force. The Convention system has in recent years grown more and more into the role of a system of European integration in the sense of its preamble. Unilateral derogations are incompatible with the very idea of such a system.[32]

---

[28] *Ettl* v. *Austria*, Judgment of 23 April 1987, Series A, No. 117; (1988) 10 EHRR 255, para. 42 of the judgment.
[29] *Ječius* v. *Lithuania* (App. 34578/97), Judgment of 31 July 2000; and *Grauslys* v. *Lithuania* (App. 36743/97), Judgment of 10 October 2000.
[30] The entitlement of detained persons to be brought promptly before a competent judicial authority.
[31] *Ječius* v. *Lithuania* (App. 34578/97), Judgment of 31 July 2000, para. 86 of the judgment.
[32] J. Frowein, 'Reservations to the European Convention on Human Rights' in F. Matscher and H. Petzold (eds.), *Protecting Human Rights: The European Dimension. Studies in Honour of Gérard J. Wiarda* (Köln, 1990), 193–200, at 200.

23

THE RIGHT TO AN EFFECTIVE REMEDY

INTRODUCTION

Article 13 provides:

Everyone whose rights and freedoms as set forth in this Convention are violated shall have an effective remedy before a national authority notwithstanding that the violation has been committed by persons acting in an official capacity.

There are significant differences between Article 13 and the corresponding provisions of other human rights instruments. For example, Article 8 of the Universal Declaration on Human Rights is wider in encompassing rights granted to an individual by the constitution or by law, but potentially narrower in only requiring effective remedies from competent national tribunals.[1]

Until comparatively recently, Article 13 occupied something of a twilight zone in the case law of the Convention organs.[2] This is somewhat surprising since the Convention is built upon an obligation that Contracting Parties guarantee to those within their jurisdiction the rights enumerated in the Convention and its Protocols, since the engagement of the Strasbourg organs is subsidiary to the protection of these rights in the national legal orders, and since that protection must be dependent upon the remedies available in the national legal order. Part of the problem is the ambiguities in the drafting of the Article. One ambiguity was whether Article 13 only applied *after* the Convention organs had determined that there had been a breach of the Convention rights.[3] The proper view is, however, that Article 13 is about guaranteeing a process within the national legal order by which a remedy for a violation can be provided. This led to a further difficulty about the use of Article 13 by the Strasbourg organs. Since

---

[1] Art. 8 of the Universal Declaration reads, 'Everyone has the right to an effective remedy by the competent national tribunals for acts violating the fundamental rights granted him by the constitution or by law.'

[2] See R. White, 'Remedies in a Multi-Level Legal Order: The Strasbourg Court and the UK' in C. Kilpatrick, T. Novitz, and P. Skidmore, (eds.), *The Future of Remedies in Europe* (Oxford, 2000) at 191.

[3] See J. Fawcett, *The Application of the European Convention on Human Rights* (Oxford, 1987), 290–1.

Article 13 only required a remedy in the national legal order where a person's rights and freedoms as set forth in the Convention are violated, was it necessary to prove a violation of one of the Convention rights before Article 13 could be pleaded? The question was answered in the *Klass* case in 1978 which ruled that Article 13 is an independent provision which can be violated even if there is no violation of another Convention right.[4]

Although the absence of a remedy before the national authorities will normally be a matter subsidiary to the principal complaint, it is appropriate that it should be examined separately where it is alleged that, as a general feature of the national law, there is no effective remedy. For example, it may be suggested that if an applicant complains of an invasion of privacy, and if domestic law affords no general remedy in such cases, the complaint should be examined under Article 13 as well as under Article 8.

On the other hand, where the principal complaint is itself the absence of an appropriate remedy under another provision of the Convention, it is unnecessary to consider Article 13. Thus, in the *Vagrancy* cases,[5] where the Court found that the applicants did not have the necessary judicial guarantees under Article 5(4) to challenge the lawfulness of their detention, the Court did not consider that it had to examine separately the issue under Article 13.[6]

It appeared from the early case law that the requirements made of the national legal orders were at a relatively low level. It could almost be reduced to the question of whether there was some mechanism, or mechanisms taken together, which might lead to a remedy for the complaint. There are, however, signs in the recent case law that new life is being breathed into Article 13.[7] The current position is neatly recapitulated in the *Keenan* case:[8]

The Court reiterates that Article 13 of the Convention guarantees the availability at the national level of a remedy to enforce the substance of the Convention rights and freedoms in whatever form they might happen to be secured in the domestic legal order. The effect of Article 13 is thus to require the provision of a domestic remedy to deal with the substance of an 'arguable complaint' under the Convention and to grant appropriate relief, although Contracting States are afforded some discretion as to the manner in which they conform to their Convention obligations under this provision. The scope of the obligation under Article 13 varies depending on the nature of the applicant's complaint under the Convention. Nevertheless, the remedy required by Article 13 must be 'effective' in practice as well as in law. In particular its exercise

---

[4] *Klass and others* v. *Germany*, Judgment of 6 September 1978; Series A, No. 28; (1979–80) 2 EHRR 214, para. 63 of the judgment.

[5] *De Wilde, Ooms and Versyp* v. *Belgium*, Judgment of 18 June 1971, Series A, No. 12; (1979–80) 1 EHRR 373.

[6] Para. 95 of the judgment.

[7] See discussion in ch. 8 above on the Court's comments on the need for an effective remedy where there are violations of Art. 6 by reason of the excessive length of proceedings.

[8] *Keenan* v. *United Kingdom* (App. 27229/95), Judgment of 3 April 2001; (2001) 33 EHRR 913.

must not be unjustifiably hindered by the acts or omission of the authorities of the respondent State.[9]

There are two questions which must always be asked: whether there is an arguable complaint; and whether the remedy in the national legal order is effective.

WHAT IS AN ARGUABLE COMPLAINT?

The Court requires the applicant to show only an arguable case in order to be able to complain of a violation of Article 13. The *Klass* case[10] concerned the availability of secret surveillance in Germany. The applicants complained that the legislation authorizing such surveillance violated Articles 6, 8, and 13. The Court differed from the Commission, which had concluded that it must be shown that a substantive provision had been violated before the Article came into play. The test, said the Court, is rather one of whether the applicant has an arguable case.

In the Court's view, Article 13 requires that where an individual considers himself to have been prejudiced by a measure allegedly in breach of the Convention, he should have a remedy before a national authority in order both to have his claim decided and, if appropriate, to obtain redress, Thus, Article 13 must be interpreted as guaranteeing an 'effective remedy before a national authority' to everyone who *claims* that his rights and freedoms under the Convention have been violated.[11]

The test of having an arguable case was explicitly affirmed in the *Silver* case,[12] where the Court said:

Where an individual has an arguable claim to be the victim of a violation of the rights set forth in the Convention, he should have a remedy before a national authority in order both to have his claim decided and, if appropriate, to obtain redress.[13]

The precise delimitation of the arguability test remains difficult.[14] The Court itself has indicated that providing an abstract definition would not help and decides the issue on a case-by-case basis.[15]

---

[9] Para. 122 of the judgment.

[10] *Klass* v. *Germany*, Judgment of 6 September 1978, Series A, No. 28; (1979–80) 2 EHRR 214.

[11] Para. 64 of the judgment.

[12] *Silver* v. *United Kingdom*, Judgment of 25 March 1983, Series A, No. 61; (1983) 5 EHRR 347.

[13] Para. 113 of the judgment, reaffirmed in *Leander* v. *Sweden*, Judgment of 26 March 1987, Series A, No. 116; (1987) 9 EHRR 433.

[14] F. Hampson, 'The Concept of an "Arguable Claim" under Article 13 of the European Convention on Human Rights' (1990) 39 ICLQ 891.

[15] *Boyle and Rice* v. *United Kingdom*, Judgment of 27 April 1988, Series A, No. 131; (1988) 10 EHRR 425.

In the *Boyle and Rice* case[16] the Court addressed the tricky question of how a case could be viewed as arguable when the Commission had concluded that it was manifestly ill-founded. The answer lies in there being two rather different tests. In deciding that a case is manifestly ill-founded, the Commission is making a judgment on the merits, in that, in effect, the finding means that examination of the merits is not required because the applicant has put forward insufficient evidence to justify doing so. In determining whether a case is arguable, the test is rather one of seeing whether there are the makings of a prima facie case. The Commission suggested before the Court in the *Boyle and Rice* case that to be arguable a case needed only to raise a Convention issue which merits further examination. That is a low threshold.[17] It follows from this that, in all those cases where the Court[18] finds that a complaint is admissible, the arguability threshold is met. The position adopted in the *Boyle and Rice* case was elaborated by the Court in the *Powell and Rayner* case,[19] which concerned complaints under Articles 6, 8, 13, and Article 1 of Protocol 1 in relation to excessive noise from air traffic in the vicinity of Heathrow Airport:

[I]t is difficult to see how a claim that is 'manifestly ill-founded' can nevertheless be 'arguable' and *vice versa*. Furthermore Article 13 and Article 27(2) [now 35(3)] are concerned, within their respective spheres, with the availability of remedies for the enforcement of the same Convention rights and freedoms. The coherence of this dual system of enforcement is at risk of being undermined if Article 13 is interpreted as requiring national law to make available 'an effective remedy' for a grievance classified under Article 27(2) as being so weak as not to warrant examination on its merits at international level. Whatever threshold the Commission has set in its case law for declaring claims 'manifestly ill-founded' under Article 27(2), in principle, it should set the same threshold in regard to the parallel notion of 'arguability' under Article 13.[20]

Now that both admissibility and merits questions are determined by the Court, the risk of inconsistencies of approach will be minimized.

---

[16] Ibid.

[17] See e.g. *Powell and Rayner* v. *United Kingdom*, Judgment of 21 February 1990, Series A, No. 172; (1990) 12 EHRR 355.

[18] Note that, prior to 1 November 1998, admissibility decisions were made by the Commission.

[19] *Powell and Rayner* v. *United Kingdom*, Judgment of 21 February 1990, Series A, No. 172; (1990) 12 EHRR 355.

[20] Para. 33 of the judgment.

THE NATURE OF THE REMEDIES REQUIRED

BACKGROUND

Article 13 offers a measure of respect for national procedural autonomy; this refers to the ability of each Contracting State to determine the form of remedies offered to meet its obligations under the article. Those remedies need not be judicial, but must be effective. Ombudsman procedures and other non-judicial procedures will be included. Once a remedy is identified, it is not necessary to show the certainty of a favourable outcome.[21] National procedural autonomy does not, however, extend to the very existence of a remedy, since Article 13 requires that there is an effective remedy to enforce the substance of the Convention rights in the national legal order.[22]

In the *Klass* case[23] the Court indicated that the requirement of effectiveness had to be read in the context of the complaint. So that an effective remedy in respect of secret surveillance meant a remedy 'that was as effective as could be having regard to the restricted scope for recourse inherent in any system of secret surveillance'. The Court expanded on this in the *Leander* case[24] which concerned secret security checks, making clear that although no single remedy might itself entirely satisfy the requirements of Article 13, the aggregate of remedies under the system might do so.[25] In the *Silver* case[26] the Court said that the remedy before the national authority should concern both the determination of the claim and any redress.

The respondent government will be expected to identify the remedies available to the applicant and to show at least a prima-facie case for their effectiveness. So, where the respondent government cannot put forward an example of the application of the remedy offered to a case similar to the one put forward by the applicant, they are unlikely to satisfy the Court that there is an effective remedy available.[27]

The process need not be judicial, but, if it is not, consideration should be given to its powers and the guarantees it affords. Where the process is judicial,

---

[21] *Pine Valley Developments* v. *Ireland*, Judgment of 22 November 1991, Series A, No. 222; (1992) 14 EHRR 319, para. 66 of the judgment, and *Costello-Roberts* v. *United Kingdom*, Series A, No. 247-C; (1995) 19 EHRR 112, para. 40 of the judgment.

[22] See the discussion of what constitutes a domestic remedy for the purpose of the requirement to exhaust domestic remedies in ch. 24.

[23] *Klass* v. *Germany*, Judgment of 6 September 1978, Series A, No. 28; (1979–80) 2 EHRR 214.

[24] *Leander* v. *Sweden*, Judgment of 26 March 1987, Series A, No. 116; (1987) 9 EHRR 433.

[25] *Chahal* v. *United Kingdom* (App. 22414/93), Judgment of 15 November 1996; (1997) 23 EHRR 413, para. 145 of the judgment.

[26] *Silver* v. *United Kingdom*, Judgment of 25 March 1983, Series A, No. 61; (1983) 5 EHRR 347, para. 113 of the judgment.

[27] See e.g. *Vereinigung Demokratischer Soldaten Österreichs and Gubi* v. *Austria*, Judgment of 19 December 1994; Series A, No. 302; (1995) 20 EHRR 56, para. 93 of the judgment.

there will be a breach of Article 13 if an order of a court is not implemented by the State authorities.[28]

ACCESS TO AN EFFECTIVE REMEDY

The tendency of respondent governments has been simply to point to some procedure available within the national legal order for raising aspects of the matters covered by the applicant's complaint to the Strasbourg organs. The Court is, however, increasingly considering whether those remedies provide an effective means of raising the substance of the complaints of violations of the particular Convention rights in issue.[29] Where irreversible harm might ensue, it will not be sufficient that the remedies are merely as effective as can be; they must provide much more certain guarantees of effectiveness.[30]

This approach is well illustrated in the facts of the *Keenan* case.[31] Mark Keenan had been found hanged in his cell one day after the imposition of punishment of further imprisonment and segregation had been imposed on him. He had a history of mental illness. His mother complained of violations of Article 2, 3, and 13. No violation of Article 2 was found by the Court, but a violation of Article 3, in the form of inhuman and degrading treatment, was found because of a lack of effective monitoring and supervision of his mental state and the imposition of a punishment which threatened his physical and moral resistance having regard to the state of his mental health. In relation to remedies, the Court's enquiry focused on the availability of remedies to Mark Keenan to complain of his ill-treatment in prison before his suicide, and of remedies to his next of kin in respect of his death. The Government argued that, during his detention, Mark Keenan had a number of possible remedies open to him: he could have sought judicial review; he could have made a complaint under the prison complaints procedure; he could have begun actions in tort; and he could have brought an action for misfeasance in the exercise of a public office. Furthermore, his mother could, after his death, have brought proceedings in tort in respect of any injury or exacerbation of his mental illness suffered prior to her son's death. The Government did, however, concede that an inquest was not an effective remedy since it did not furnish the applicant with the possibility of establishing the responsibility of the prison authorities or of obtaining damages.

The Court noted that there was no effective remedy available to Mark Keenan to challenge speedily the imposition of the punishment during which he killed

---

[28] *Iatridis* v. *Greece* (App. 31107/96), Judgment of 25 March 1999; (2000) 30 EHRR 97.
[29] See *Chahal* v. *United Kingdom* (App. 22414/93), Judgment of 15 November 1996; (1997) 23 EHRR 413.
[30] Paras. 150–2 of the judgment
[31] *Keenan* v. *United Kingdom* (App. 27229/95), Judgment of 3 April 2001; (2001) 33 EHRR 913.

himself. Such remedies as had been identified were not effective: it would not have been possible for Mark Keenan to have obtained legal aid and legal representation, and lodged an application for judicial review in a short period of time; similarly prison complaints typically took six weeks to adjudicate. In relation to the remedies available to the next of kin after the death, the Court notes the theoretical availability of the remedy, but did not accept that adequate damages would have been recoverable or that legal aid would have been available to pursue the claim. The Court indicates that in relation to a violation of Article 2 or Article 3, 'compensation for the non-pecuniary damage flowing from the breach should in principle be available as part of the range of possible remedies.'[32] Finally, the Court concluded that no effective remedy was available to the applicant which would have established where responsibility lay for the death of her son. This too was regarded as an essential element of a remedy under Article 13 for a bereaved parent. There was a violation of Article 13.

This case represents a degree of encroachment on national procedural autonomy in the interpretation of Article 13. The Court is increasingly indicating what constitutes effectiveness in the remedies available within the national legal order.

THE RIGHT TO AN EFFECTIVE INVESTIGATION

In a number of cases,[33] the Court has stated that the exercise of remedies available within the national legal order must not be unjustifiably hindered by the acts or omissions of the authorities of the respondent State. In the *Keenan* case, the Court said:

Given the fundamental importance of the right to the protection of life, Article 13 requires, in addition to the payment of compensation where appropriate, a thorough and effective investigation capable of leading to the identification and punishment of those responsible for the deprivation of life, including effective access for the complainant to the investigation procedure.[34]

In the *Kaya* case,[35] the applicant's brother had been killed in disputed circumstances by the security forces. A violation of Article 2 was found by reason of the absence of an effective and independent investigation into the

---

[32]   Para. 129 of the judgment.

[33]   e.g. *Aksoy* v. *Turkey* (App. 21987/93), Judgment of 18 December 1996; (1997) 23 EHRR 553, para. 95 of the judgment; *Aydin* v. *Turkey* (App. 23178/94), Judgment of 25 September 1997; (1998) 25 EHRR 251, para. 103 of the judgment; and *Kaya* v. *Turkey* (App. 22729/93), Judgment of 19 February 1998; (1999) 28 EHRR 1, para. 106 of the judgment.

[34]   *Keenan* v. *United Kingdom* (App. 27229/95), Judgment of 3 April 2001; (2001) 33 EHRR 913, para, 122 of the judgment.

[35]   *Kaya* v. *Turkey* (App. 22729/93), Judgment of 19 February 1998; (1999) 28 EHRR 1.

death, but the complaint that there was also a violation of Article 13 was then considered. The Court said:

In particular, where those relatives have an arguable claim that the victim has been unlawfully killed by agents of the State, the notion of an effective remedy for the purposes of Article 13 entails, in addition to the payment of compensation where appropriate, a thorough and effective investigation capable of leading to the identification and punishment of those responsible and including effective access for the relatives to the investigatory procedure. Seen in these terms the requirements of Article 13 are broader than a Contracting State's procedural obligation under Article 2 to conduct an effective investigation.[36]

A similar approach has been adopted in relation to certain claims falling within Article 3. The *Assenov* case[37] concerned, among other complaints, a complaint of violations of Article 3 during police detention. No violation of Article 3 was found in respect of the alleged ill-treatment, but a violation was found by reason of the absence of an effective official investigation into the applicants' complaints.[38] A separate violation of Article 13 was found in virtually identical terms to those quoted from the judgment in the *Kaya* case.[39]

The entitlement to an effective and independent investigation under Article 13 has also been applied to cases where the allegation is of an unlawful deprivation of liberty. In the *Kurt* case[40] the Court found a violation of Article 5 in circumstances where there was evidence of the applicant's son having being detained but where he had subsequently disappeared, but nevertheless went on to consider separately whether there had been a violation of Article 13. The absence of an effective and independent investigation capable of leading to the identification and punishment of those responsible which included effective access for the relative to the investigatory process constituted a violation of Article 13. Again the Court stressed that the content of Article 13 is wider than the requirement for an investigation under Article 5.[41]

The *PG and JH* case[42] has applied the requirement for an effective investigation in the context of violations of Article 8 arising from the use of covert listening devices by the police. The Court went on to consider whether there was a separate violation of Article 13. In this case the Court based part of its conclusion that there was a violation of Article 13 because of the lack of

---

[36] Para. 107 of the judgment. See also comment in ch. 4 above.

[37] *Assenov and others* v. *Bulgaria* (App. 24760/94), Judgment of 28 October 1998; (1998) 28 EHRR 652.

[38] See also comment in ch. 5 above.

[39] *Assenov and others* v. *Bulgaria* (App. 24760/94), Judgment of 28 October 1998; (1998) 28 EHRR 652, para. 117 of the judgment.

[40] *Kurt* v. *Turkey* (App. 24276/94), Judgment of 25 May 1998; (1999) 27 EHRR 373.

[41] Para. 140 of the judgment.

[42] *PG and JH* v. *United Kingdom* (App. 44787/98), Judgment of 25 September 2001.

independence needed to constitute sufficient protection against the abuse of authority in the operation of the police complaints procedures.[43]

These judgments are to be welcomed, since they reflect the realities of the difficulties that are faced by individuals in building a case against powerful State agencies. Those agencies are best placed to collect the information required to determine whether there has been a violation of the rights guaranteed by the Convention. This development in the ambit of Article 13 is an outstanding example of the Court seeking to ensure that Convention rights are practical and effective and not theoretical and illusory. Indeed, in one case,[44] the Court hinted that in some cases only court proceedings might be sufficient to offer sufficiency of redress, noting the strong guarantees of independence offered by such proceedings.

VIOLATIONS BY PERSONS IN AN OFFICIAL CAPACITY

The last words of Article 13, 'notwithstanding that the violation has been committed by persons acting in an official capacity', show that no defence of State privilege or immunity from suit may be allowed. It has been argued that they also show that the scope of the Convention is not limited to persons exercising public authority.[45]

What is, however, clear is that Article 13 is not concerned with challenges to legislation. Where the source of the grievance is the legislation itself, requiring an effective remedy would be tantamount to allowing judicial review of legislation. The Commission has consistently held that Article 13 has no application in such situations, and the Court has not dissented from that view.[46] To read such a requirement into Article 13 would effectively require the incorporation of the Convention, but where the Convention has been incorporated, there will usually be some process by which the compatibility of legislation can be tested against the requirements of the Convention.[47]

---

[43]   Paras 87–8 of the judgment. See also *Khan* v. *United Kingdom* (App. 35394/97), Judgment of 12 May 2000; (2001) 31 EHRR 1016, paras. 41–7 of the judgment.

[44]   *Z and others* v. *United Kingdom* (App. 29392/95), Judgment of 10 May 2001; (2002) 34 EHRR 97, para. 110 of the judgment.

[45]   See ch. 2.

[46]   e.g. App. 1080/184, L v. *Sweden*, Report of the Commission, 3 October 1988, (1989) 61 DR 62, and see *Leander* v. *Sweden*, Judgment of 26 March 1987, Series A, No. 116; (1987) 9 EHRR 433, para. 77 of the judgment; and *Sigurdur Sigurjonsson* v. *Iceland*, Judgment of 30 June 1993, Series A, No. 264; (1993) 16 EHRR 462, para. 77 of Commission Opinion, and para. 44 of the judgment.

[47]   See, for example, the possibility of obtaining a declaration of incompatibility in the United Kingdom under s. 4 of the Human Rights Act 1998.

CONCLUDING COMMENT

It has taken longer for real substance to be given to Article 13 through the case law of the Strasbourg organs than in relation to virtually any other article of the Convention and its Protocols. In particular, the much more practical approach of the Court in recent years to the determination of whether the remedies allegedly available in the national legal order are, in fact, practically available as a means of dealing with the alleged violations of Convention rights is to be welcomed.

The potential for the development through interpretation of the rights contained in Article 13 remains high. Areas ripe for further interpretation include the determination of compensation where the Court has now said that Article 13 requires compensation to be available within national legal orders; and the extension of the requirement for investigations and remedies that have now been attached to Article 13, particularly in the context of violations of Articles 2, 3, and 5. This is all about measuring the sufficiency of the guarantees required within the national legal order in order to determine whether what is on offer there constitutes an effective remedy, not only in relation to the substance of the complaints made but also in relation to the relief granted in cases where a violation of a substantive provision is found.

24

PROCEEDINGS BEFORE THE COURT

INTRODUCTION

On 1 November 1998 Protocol No. 11 to the European Convention came into effect, replacing the former organs of control—the part-time Commission and Court—with a new, permanent European Court of Human Rights. It has the largest territorial jurisdiction of any permanent court in the World, given that the combined population of the forty-one Contracting States[1] is over 800 million people; in addition, of course, non-nationals and non-residents can bring cases under the Convention concerning matters within a Contracting State's jurisdiction.

The Court's principal role is to pronounce on applications, brought both by individuals and States, under the European Convention on Human Rights. Its judgments are legally binding on States and are declaratory in nature: that is, the Court can announce that the facts of the application disclose a violation of one or more Articles of the Convention, and, under Article 41 of the Convention, it can award monetary compensation to an individual victim of any such violation.

The Court's caseload is constantly increasing. In April 2001 there were 17,766 registered applications pending before it. In the first four months of 2001 alone it registered 4,422 applications; this represented a 35 per cent increase over the preceding year, when there had already been a 24 per cent increase compared with January–April 1999. It is faced with the difficult task of striking a balance between efficiency and speed in dealing with a large number of applications, while administering justice in each individual case and maintaining the quality of its judgments.

---

[1] In April 2002 there were 43 members of the Council of Europe, but the two most recent, Armenia and Azerbaijan, had not yet ratified the Convention. For an updated list of signatures and ratifications, see **conventions.coe.int/treaty/EN/cadreprincipal.htm**

COMPOSITION AND GENERAL PROCEDURE

JUDGES

The Court consists of a number of judges equal to that of the High Contracting Parties to the Convention.[2] The judges are elected by the Parliamentary Assembly from a list of three candidates nominated by each State.[3] They are required to be of high moral character and must either possess the qualifications required for appointment to high judicial office or be 'jurisconsults' of recognized competence.[4] Before electing the judges to the new single Court, the Parliamentary Assembly appointed delegates to interview the candidates, examine their curricula vitae and report back to the Assembly. Broadly, one-third of judges in the new Court were former judges in the old Court, a third were formerly Members of the Commission, and a third were newcomers to Strasbourg.

The judges are normally, but not necessarily, nationals of the State in respect of which they are elected. They are, of course, independent.

The judges are elected for a period of six years.[5] However, to avoid the problems that might arise if all their terms of office expired simultaneously, half of them—chosen by lot by the Secretary-General—were initially appointed only for three years.[6] Prior to the coming into force of Protocol No. 11, the judges elect adopted Rules of Court.[7]

COMMITTEES, SECTIONS, AND CHAMBERS

Under Article 27 of the Convention, the Court may sit in Committees of three judges, Chambers of seven judges, and in a Grand Chamber of seventeen judges.

The Committees are competent only to declare applications inadmissible or strike them off the Court's list of cases,[8] and thus deal only with clearly inadmissible cases in the procedure outlined below.

The Court has divided itself into three Sections of ten judges and one of eleven judges. The composition of the Sections is aimed at being geographically and gender balanced and to reflect the different legal systems among the Contracting Parties.[9] Within these Sections, the seven-judge Chambers

[2] Art. 20, ECHR. For an updated list of judges, see www.echr.coe.int/BilingualDocuments/ListOfJudgesNewCourt.html
[3] Art. 22, ECHR.
[4] Art. 21(1), ECHR, which is based on Art. 2 of the Statute of the International Court of Justice.
[5] Art. 23 ECHR.
[6] Art. 23(1) and (2) ECHR.
[7] Available on-line: www.echr.coe.int/Eng/EDocs/RulesOfCourt.html
[8] Art. 28 ECHR.
[9] In October 2001 the judges elected new Vice-Presidents and Presidents of Sections, and the composition of the Sections was changed, to take effect from 1 November 2001.

examine the admissibility and merits of individual applications which are not prima facie inadmissible and of inter-State cases.[10]

Under Article 30 of the Convention, where a case pending before a Chamber raises a serious question affecting the interpretation of the Convention or Protocols, or where it appears that the Chamber is likely to reach a decision which would be inconsistent with earlier case law, the Chamber can relinquish jurisdiction to the Grand Chamber unless one of the parties to the case objects. This proviso, requiring the consent of the parties to relinquishment, places considerable power in the hands of the applicant or government to interfere with the working of the Court. Its force has been slightly mitigated by Rule 72(2), which states that the Registrar shall notify the parties of the Chamber's intention to relinquish jurisdiction, and sets a time-limit of one month for objections, which must be 'duly reasoned'. An objection which does not meet these criteria will be considered invalid by the Chamber.

The Grand Chamber's other principal role is provided for by Article 43 of the Convention, which allows a party to a case to request that it be referred to the Grand Chamber after the Chamber has given judgment. The request must be submitted within three months of the date of judgment, and a panel of five judges of the Grand Chamber decides whether or not it should be accepted. Article 43(2) states that the panel 'shall accept the request if the case raises a serious question affecting the interpretation or application of the Convention or the protocols thereto, or a serious issue of general importance', but the panel's deliberations are secret and, to date, there has been little guidance as to the type of issues which it considers 'serious'.

The judge who is a national of any State Party concerned automatically sits as a member of the Chamber or Grand Chamber.[11] It is arguable that greater independence would be achieved by excluding the national judge, but the inclusion of the judge of the respondent State has the advantage of ensuring acquaintance with the legal system and the background to the case.

PRESIDENCY

The Court has a President and two Vice-Presidents, and each Section has a President, elected by the plenary Court for three years.[12] The President, at present the Swiss judge Luzius Wildhaber, directs the work and administration of the Court and represents it. He sits in the Grand Chamber, but does not take part in the consideration of cases being heard by Chambers except where he is the national judge.[13]

---

[10] Art. 29 ECHR and Rule 25 and 26 of the Rules of Court.
[11] Art. 27(2) ECHR.
[12] Art. 26 ECHR.
[13] Rule 9 of the Rules of Court.

PUBLIC NATURE OF PROCEEDINGS

The judges deliberate in private and details of their deliberations are secret.[14] Apart from that important exception, however, proceedings before the Court are generally public in character, with hearings held in open court and all documents, with the exception of those deposited within the framework of friendly-settlement negotiations, are accessible to the public.[15] In exceptional cases, however, the Rules of Court—echoing Article 6(1) of the Convention— allow for confidentiality of hearings and documents 'in the interest of morals, public order or national security in a democratic society, where the interests of juveniles or the protection of the private life of the parties so require, or to the extent strictly necessary in the opinion of the Chamber in special circumstances where publicity would prejudice the interests of justice.'[16]

REGISTRY

Article 25 of the Convention states that 'The Court shall have a registry.' It consists of approximately 300 lawyers, translators, and administrative and clerical employees from the Member States, recruited by the Secretary-General of the Council of Europe.[17] The Registrar and Deputy Registrar are elected by the Court.[18] Because of the Court's heavy caseload, the registry has an important role. Its main functions are to conduct correspondence with applicants and governments, to prepare cases for examination, to advise the Court on questions of national law and the law of the Convention, and to assist in the drafting of judgments and decisions. The practice has been for an application to be assigned, as it comes in, to a lawyer in the registry, who will prepare the case for the judge chosen as rapporteur,[19] and attend sessions of the Chamber whenever the case is being examined. In a large measure the standard of the Court's work, and its effectiveness, depend on the quality of its registry.

---

[14] Rule 22 of the Rules of Court.
[15] Rule 33 of the Rules of Court.
[16] Ibid.
[17] Rules 18(3) of the Rules of Court.
[18] Rules 15 and 16 of the Rules of Court.
[19] Discussed in more detail later in this chapter.

PROCEDURE PRIOR TO THE DECISION
ON ADMISSIBILITY

INTRODUCTION OF AN APPLICATION

The Court's procedure is primarily in writing. Most applications originate in a letter to the Registrar setting out the complaint. At this stage the case is given a file number and allocated to a lawyer in the registry from the State against which the complaint is made. Applicants may be represented by lawyers, but they have the option of acting in person until the case is communicated to the respondent government,[20] and the Court's procedure in the early stages is designed to facilitate the position of litigants in person as far as possible. Thus although the Court has only two official languages—English and French[21]—before a decision on admissibility is taken applicants may correspond with the Court in any of the official languages of the Contracting Parties.[22] The registry lawyer assigned to the case will assist and advise applicants as far as possible, given the constraints imposed by the heavy caseload and the need to be seen as impartial.

Upon receipt of an introductory letter the registry lawyer will write to the applicant asking for further information and copies of documents and national judgments relevant to the application, and will send him or her an application form.[23] The form must be completed with details such as the applicant's name, age, occupation and address and that of any representative, the name of the respondent government, the subject matter of the claim, as far as possible the provision of the Convention alleged to have been violated, and a statement of the facts and arguments on which the applicant relies.[24]

Until 1 January 2002, before registering an application which appeared unlikely to succeed because of failure to comply with the conditions of admissibility set out in Article 35 of the Convention,[25] the registry lawyer was under instructions to write to the applicant explaining the shortcomings of the application and warning him or her that the Court would be likely to declare the case inadmissible. If, however, the applicant asked for the case to proceed, it would nonetheless be registered.

Since the beginning of 2002, however, in the interests of efficiency, the Court has decided to do away with the warning letter.[26]

---

[20] Rule 36 of the Rules of Court.
[21] Rule 34(1) of the Rules of Court.
[22] Rule 34(2) of the Rules of Court.
[23] Available on-line: www.echr.coe.int/Eng/General.htm
[24] Rule 47 of the Rules of Court.
[25] See below in this chapter for an account of the conditions of admissibility.
[26] Apparently, some registry lawyers were spending up to 60 per cent of their time engaged in correspondence with applicants over inadmissible cases.

Once a case is ready, a judge will be appointed as rapporteur, and he or she will examine the application and decide whether it should be considered by a Committee or a Chamber.[27]

LEGAL AID

There are no fees or charges for applications to the Court and its expenses are met, under Article 50 of the Convention, by the Council of Europe. The Court may grant an applicant free legal aid at any stage of the proceedings after the respondent government's observations on admissibility have been received, or the time-limit for their submission has expired.[28] Applicants must submit a certified declaration of means, showing that they have insufficient means to meet their costs, and this is sent to the respondent government for comment. Legal aid may be granted to cover lawyers' fees, on a scale fixed by the Registrar, and also other necessary expenses.

INTERIM MEASURES AND THE RIGHT TO COMMUNICATE WITH THE COURT

The Court has no power under the Convention to order interim or interlocutory measures to safeguard the position of the parties pending a final decision. However, in urgent cases—for example, where there is a possibility of immediate expulsion of applicants from the territory of the respondent government which might raise an issue under Article 3—the Commission developed the practice of notifying the respondent government as soon as the application was introduced, requesting the government not to take steps which might prejudice the outcome of the case.[29] This competence, adopted by the Court, is now formally recognized in Rule 39 of the Rules of Court.[30]

In the *Cruz Varas* case[31] the Court ruled that such an indication gave rise to no binding obligation on the part of the State. The effect of a State's failure to abide by a Rule 39 recommendation was recently re-examined by the Court in the *Conka* case.[32] The applicants were Slovakian gypsies who sought and were refused asylum in Belgium. Shortly after the application was introduced on 5

[27] Rule 49 of the Rules of Court.
[28] Rules 91–6 of the Rules of Court.
[29] As in App. 11722/85, *B* v. *France*, 22 January 1987, (1987) 51 DR 165, at 174. See also M. Eissen, 'Les mesures provisoires dans la Convention européenne des Droits de l'Homme', *Revue des droits de l'homme* 2 (1969), 252.
[30] Rule 39(1) provides, 'The Chamber or, where appropriate, its President may, at the request of a party or of any other person concerned, or of its own motion, indicate to the parties any interim measure which it considers should be adopted in the interests of the parties or of the proper conduct of the proceedings before it.'
[31] *Cruz Varas* v. *Sweden*, Judgment of 20 March 1991, Series A, No. 201; (1992) 14 EHRR 1.
[32] *Conka and others* v. *Belgium* (App. 51564/99), admissibility decision of 13 March 2001.

October 1999, the Court decided to apply Rule 39, and the Belgian authorities were duly requested by telephone at 4.30 p.m. that same afternoon not to expel the applicants; the request was confirmed by fax an hour and a half later. Nonetheless, at 5.45 p.m., the applicants were deported to Slovakia, without any explanation on the part of the Belgian authorities as to why they had chosen to disregard the Court's recommendation.

The Court confirmed that it had no power to order legally binding interim measures. The failure to respect the indication it had made under Rule 39 could, however, be taken into account as an aggravating feature of any ill-treatment suffered by the applicants which was imputable to the Belgian Government.

Generally, governments do comply with the Court's recommendations under Rule 39. Moreover, the omission in the Convention to grant the Court such a power has been mitigated to a certain extent by the Court's interpretation of Article 34 of the Convention.

Article 34 provides that 'The Court may receive applications from any person . . . claiming to be the victim of a violation . . . of the rights set forth in the Convention. . . . The High Contracting Parties undertake not to hinder in any way the effective exercise of this right.'

The Court has held that the obligation on States under this provision (formerly Article 25(1) of the Convention) not to interfere with the right of an individual effectively to present and pursue his or her complaint before the Court confers a right of a procedural nature which can be asserted in Convention proceedings.[33] If the Court considers that the State has interfered with this right, it can find a violation of Article 34 and award just satisfaction in respect of it. In the *Assenov* case,[34] for example, the Court found a violation of the right of petition based on the fact that the Bulgarian police had visited the applicant's parents, at a time when the applicant was in custody, and put pressure on them to withdraw the application to Strasbourg.

In addition, freedom to correspond with the Court, even in the case of persons in detention whose correspondence is normally subject to control, is protected by the European Agreement relating to persons participating in proceedings of the European Commission and Court of Human Rights. Under this Agreement, parties to the Convention undertake to respect the right of those involved in most capacities before the Commission or Court to correspond freely with the Commission and Court. Article 3(2) contains special provisions relating to those detained in custody. Article 4 guarantees free movement, subject to certain limitations, in connection with the proceedings. Finally, Article 2 offers immunity from legal process in respect of oral or written statements made before, and documents or other evidence submitted to, the Court.

[33] See e.g. *Assenov and others* v. *Bulgaria* (App. 24760/94), Judgment of 28 October 1998; (1999) 28 EHRR 652, para. 169; *Timurtas* v. *Turkey* (App. 23531/94), Judgment of 13 June 2000; (2001) 33 EHRR 121.
[34] Ibid.

EXAMINATION OF ADMISSIBILITY

COMMITTEE PROCEDURE

The admissibility criteria are set out in Article 35 of the Convention.[35] Given the large number of applications which it receives, the Court has had to devise an admissibility procedure which is economical and efficient, reserving as much time as possible for meritorious cases, but which still ensures that justice is done in each individual case.

After registration, applications under Article 34 are referred to an individual judge who, as rapporteur, prepares a report on the admissibility of the application.[36] The rapporteur may request relevant information on matters connected with the application from the applicant or the government, and sends any information so obtained from the government to the applicant for comments.

Where an application appears to the rapporteur clearly to be inadmissible, he or she will draw up a report containing brief statements of the relevant facts and of the reasons underlying the proposal to declare the application inadmissible, and refer the case to a Committee of three judges.[37] Of the 7,460 final decisions and judgments adopted by the Court in 2000, 84 per cent were inadmissibility decisions passed by Committees.

The Committee's decisions must be taken unanimously.[38] Until 1 January 2002 the applicant was sent a copy of the decision, which included very limited reasoning. A typical decision finding a complaint inadmissible as manifestly ill-founded, for example, would state merely:

The Court has examined the application and notes that the applicant has been informed of the possible obstacles to its admissibility. In the light of all the material in its possession, and in so far as the matters complained of are within its competence, the Court finds that they do not disclose any appearance of a violation of the rights and freedoms set out in the Convention or its Protocols. It follows that the application must be rejected, in accordance with Article 35(4) of the Convention.

The statement that 'the applicant has been informed of the possible obstacles to [the application's] admissibility' referred to the warning letter which the applicant received from the registry lawyer,[39] where the problems with the application would have been explained in more detail.

Under the new procedure adopted by the Court from January 2002, however,

---

[35] Examined in more detail below in this chapter.
[36] Rule 49 of the Rules of Court.
[37] Ibid.
[38] Art. 28 ECHR.
[39] See above.

the applicant is sent neither a warning letter nor a copy of the decision. He or she will receive instead only a letter from the registry stating that the application has been declared inadmissible and a brief outline of the grounds: for example, failure to comply with the six months' rule. The letter states that the registry is not able to give any further information or reasons in connection with the decision.

The Committee's decision is final and there is no possibility of appeal.[40]

Many applicants will no doubt feel aggrieved to have their cases disposed of so summarily by the Court. However, given its vast caseload, it is arguable that the Court is justified in adopting as economic procedure as possible in respect of hopeless applications. Other constitutional and final instances, such as the German Constitutional Court and the United States Supreme Court, rely on a similar practice.

More worrying, perhaps, is the fact that as its policy seems increasingly to utilize the committee procedure in respect of all cases except those where it is not immediately clear that the application is inadmissible, the Court will no longer build up an easily consulted body of decisions clarifying the grounds of inadmissibility. Thus, to take as an example a fairly recently created domestic procedure—the power of the Criminal Cases Review Committee to refer convictions back to the Court of Appeal, for instance—the Court may decide that it does not constitute an 'effective remedy' for the purposes of Article 35, and may therefore declare inadmissible all applications not introduced within six months of the final decision prior to the CCRC's report (usually the judgment in the original Court of Appeal proceedings). However, although the Court may rely on this reasoning in tens of cases, all declared inadmissible through the Committee procedure, there is a risk that no such case will ever be considered by a Chamber, and that the Court's stance in the matter will not therefore become publicly known and accessible to lawyers and other interested parties.

ADMISSIBILITY PROCEDURE IN THE CHAMBER

Applications which are not dealt with in a Committee are considered by a Chamber, once again on the basis of a report prepared by the judge rapporteur. The Chamber can immediately decide to declare a case inadmissible,[41] but this happens rarely, for the reasons just mentioned. Instead, the Chamber will usually decide to communicate the application to the government concerned, and request written observations. Before reaching its decision on admissibility, the Chamber may decide to hold a hearing.[42]

When the Chamber finds a case admissible, a written decision containing summaries of the facts and the parties' arguments, and brief reasons for the

---

[40] Art. 28 ECHR.   [41] Rule 54 of the Rules of Court.   [42] Ibid.

Court's decision, will be prepared and adopted. Chamber admissibility decisions are available from the Court and on-line.[43] Decisions of particular interest and importance are published in the Court's case reports.

The procedure for inter-State cases is broadly similar to that outlined above. However, any inter-State case is automatically communicated at once to the respondent government for its observations on admissibility.[44]

CONDITIONS OF ADMISSIBILITY

Before the coming into force of Protocol No. 11, the Commission was primarily responsible for examining the admissibility of applications. Since 1 November 1989, as has been seen, the new permanent Court has taken over this function, and questions of admissibility are determined by judges sitting as a Committee or Chamber. The admissibility criteria, governed by Articles 34 and 35 of the Convention, have not however been altered by the provisions of Protocol No. 11, and the Court draws heavily on the case law of the Commission in this respect.

The principal criteria for admissibility are considered in the following paragraphs.[45]

CAN THE APPLICANT CLAIM TO BE A VICTIM?

The first question to be considered is that of standing: who may bring an application to the Court? Article 33 ('Inter-State cases') presents no problem in this respect; an application may be brought only by a State which has ratified the Convention. Under Article 34 ('Individual applications'), the Court may receive applications

from any person, non-governmental organisation or group of individuals claiming to be the victim of a violation by one of the High Contracting Parties of the rights set forth in this Convention or the protocols thereto.

The term 'person' (*personne physique* in the French text) appears to include only natural persons but an application may be brought also by any corporate or unincorporated body. Thus applications have been brought by companies, trade unions, churches, political parties, and numerous other types of body. A corporate body has some but not all of the rights of individuals: thus it has the right to a fair trial under Article 6, to protection of its correspondence under Article 8,[46] and is expressly granted property rights under Article 1 of the First Protocol, but it does not have the right to education under Article 2 of Protocol No. 1.

---

[43] hudoc.echr.coe.int/hudoc   [44] Rule 51 of the Rules of Court.
[45] For a more extensive discussion of the grounds of admissibility, see e.g. J. Simor and B. Emmerson, (eds.) *Human Rights Practice* (London, 2000), ch. 20.
[46] App. 14369/88, *Noviflora Sweden AB* v. *Sweden*; (1993) 15 EHRR CD6.

There are, of course, no restrictions on the ground of residence, nationality, or any other status. Only if the individual applicant does not claim to be a victim, as for example where he or she complains generally of certain legislation, or where he or she simply alleges that a fellow-prisoner has been ill-treated, will the application be outside the Court's competence *ratione personae*. The Court has no jurisdiction to review national law or practice *in abstracto*. Similarly, associations have no capacity to bring representative applications,[47] though they may act in a representative capacity for specific individuals.[48]

Where a violation of the right to life is alleged, the Court (and the Commission before it) have accepted applications from relatives of the dead person.[49] In other cases close relatives have standing to bring an application only in relation to the effect of any alleged violation on themselves. So an application by close relatives of a person accused of crime who dies before final disposition of the case can make a claim based on the loss of reputation of the family.[50] In contrast, a complaint under Article 6 relating to the length and fairness of proceedings is personal to the litigant and an application by relatives will not be admitted.[51] Where the applicant dies in the course of the proceedings under the Convention, the Court will have regard to the wishes of the heirs of the deceased in deciding whether to permit the application to proceed.[52]

Cases concerning children will normally be brought by parents or guardians, but the Court will accept applications from minors if the complaint concerns government action affecting the relationship of child and parent or guardian.[53] A person who is neither a custodial parent, guardian, nor legal representative of a child will not have standing to make a complaint.[54] There is no bar to applications by persons under a disability.[55]

In certain cases, in order to give effective protection to human rights, the Court has had to give a wide interpretation to the notion of 'victim'. In the

[47] App. 10581/83, *Norris and National Gay Federation* v. *Ireland*, 16 May 1984, (1984) 44 DR 132.

[48] App. 10983/84, *Confédération des Syndicats médicaux français and Fédération nationale des Infirmiers* v. *France*, 12 May 1986, (1986) 47 DR 225; see also App. 10733/84, *Asociación de Aviadores de la República, Jaime Mata and others* v. *Spain*, 11 March 1985, (1985) 41 DR 211.

[49] App. 2758/66, *X* v. *Belgium*, 21 May 1969, (1969) 30 CD 11 (widow); App. 9360/81, *W* v. *Ireland*, 28 February 1983, (1983) 32 DR 211 (widow and sister); App. 11257/84, *Wolfgram* v. *Federal Republic of Germany*, 6 October 1986, (1986) 49 DR 213 (parents); and App. 8416/78, *X* v. *United Kingdom*, 13 May 1980, (1980) 19 DR 244 (putative father in an abortion case).

[50] App. 10300/83, *Nölkenbockhoff and Bergemann* v. *Federal Republic of Germany*, 12 December 1984, (1985) 40 DR 180.

[51] Ibid.

[52] See e.g. *Aksoy* v. *Turkey* (App. 21987/93), Judgment of 26 November 1996; (1997) 23 EHRR 553, para. 2 of the judgment; *Gladkowski* v. *Poland* (App. 29697/96), Judgment of 14 March 2000.

[53] App. 10929/84, *Nielsen* v. *Denmark*, 10 March 1986, (1986) 46 DR 55; Judgment of 28 November 1988 at Series A, No. 144; (1989) 11 EHRR 175; *A.* v. *United Kingdom* (App. 25599/94), Judgment of 23 September 1998; (1999) 27 EHRR 611

[54] App. 22920/93, *MB* v. *United Kingdom*, 6 April 1994, (1994) 77-A DR 42.

[55] App. 527/62, *X* v. *Austria*, 4 October 1962, (1962) 5 *Yearbook* 238.

Klass case,[56] for example, where the applicants complained about legislation in Germany which allowed the State to intercept telephone calls without informing the person concerned, the Court concluded that the applicants could claim to be victims even though they were unable to establish that they had been the subjects of surveillance, since 'in the mere existence of the legislation itself there is involved, for all those to whom the legislation could be applied, a menace of surveillance', which must have placed a restriction on the applicants' confidence freely to use the telephone system. In that case, it would have been virtually impossible for the applicants to adduce evidence of specific measures taken against them—and indeed this very impossibility formed one of the bases of their complaints. However, where the legislation provides for notification of surveillance to a person concerned, a claim that there has been a violation of Article 8 will generally not succeed unless the applicant has received such notification.[57] Moreover, where the applicant complains of a specific instance of surveillance or telephone-tapping, the Court will require evidence establishing a 'reasonable likelihood' that some such measure was applied to him or her.[58]

In the *Norris* case[59] the Court held that a homosexual man could 'claim to be a victim' of legislation in Ireland which criminalized consensual sex between men, because 'either [he] respects the law and refrains from engaging—even in private and with consenting male partners—in prohibited sexual acts to which he is disposed by reason of his homosexual tendencies, or he commits such acts and thereby becomes liable to criminal prosecution.' This was so even though the applicant himself had never been investigated by the police and there was evidence that the Irish authorities had a policy of not bringing prosecutions under the law.

WAS THE ALLEGED VIOLATION COMMITTED BY A HIGH CONTRACTING PARTY?

It is clear from Articles 33 and 34 that an application may be brought only against a State which has ratified the Convention and only in respect of a breach for which the State is in some way responsible. Otherwise the application will be rejected as being outside the Court's competence *ratione personae*.

The State is directly liable for the acts of the legislature, executive, and judiciary, and also for the acts of other public bodies, for example, public corporations with a certain measure of independence, such as a local Health

---

[56] *Klass* v. *Germany*, Judgment of 6 September 1978, Series A, No. 28; (1979–80) 2 EHRR 214; and see also *Malone* v. *United Kingdom*, Judgment of 2 August 1984, Series A, No. 82; (1985) 7 EHRR 14.

[57] Joined Apps. 10439/83, 10440/83, 10441/83, 10452/83, and 10513/83, *Mersch and others* v. *Luxembourg*, 10 May 1985, (1985) 43 DR 34.

[58] *Halford* v. *United Kingdom* (App. 20605/92), Judgment of 25 June 1997; (1997) 24 EHRR 523.

[59] *Norris* v. *Ireland*, Judgment of 26 October 1988, Series A, No. 142; (1991) 13 EHRR 186.

Authority or British Rail.[60] It cannot be held to account for the acts or omissions of private persons, such as private companies, lawyers or legal professional bodies like the Bar Council. As examined elsewhere in this book, however, many of the substantive Articles of the Convention impose positive obligations on the State. Thus the State can be held responsible under Article 8 for failing to ensure that a privately owned factory does not dangerously pollute the surrounding area[61] or under Article 3 for the lack of adequate protection in its criminal law against violence carried out by a private individual.[62]

An application will be declared inadmissible as incompatible *ratione loci* with the Convention if it relates to an alleged violation of the Convention outside the State's jurisdiction.[63] The Court's interpretation of the meaning of 'jurisdiction' is still developing. At first it appeared that the State's jurisdiction was limited to its territorial boundaries,[64] but in the *Loizidou (Preliminary Objections)* judgment[65] it held that a State was, in principle, liable for breaches of the Convention wherever it had 'effective military control'. In the judgment on the merits,[66] the Court went on to hold Turkey, by virtue of its heavy military presence on the island, responsible for denying the applicant access to her property in Northern Cyprus.

The extension of the Convention, by the terms of Article 1, to all persons within the jurisdiction of the contracting States, is subject to Article 56, the 'colonial' clause. The Convention does not extend to dependent territories unless the State concerned has made a declaration under Article 56(1) and the Court is not competent to receive applications in respect of such territories until a declaration under Article 56(4) has been made. Declarations have been made by the Netherlands, in respect of Surinam, and by the United Kingdom in respect of a number of overseas territories, although there appear to have been few, if any, applications from any of these territories. In the absence of such declarations, a complaint against a State in respect of acts in the dependent territories will be outside the Court's competence *ratione loci*.[67]

Finally, the State can be held responsible under the Convention only in respect of events which have occurred after its acceptance of the jurisdiction of the Court[68] (compatibility *ratione temporis*).

---

[60] App. 7601/76, *Young and James* v. *United Kingdom*, 11 July 1977, (1977) 20 *Yearbook* 520; and App. 7866/76, *Webster* v. *United Kingdom*, 3 March 1978, (1978) 12 DR 168.

[61] *López Ostra* v. *Spain*, Judgment of 9 December 1994, Series A, No. 303-C.

[62] *A.* v. *United Kingdom*, Judgment of 23 September 1998.

[63] Art. 1 ECHR.

[64] *Soering* v. *United Kingdom*, Judgment of 7 July 1989, Series A, No. 161; (1989) 11 EHRR 439, para. 86 of the judgment.

[65] *Loizidou* v. *Turkey (Preliminary Objections (App. 15318/89))*, Judgment of 23 March 1993, Series A, No. 310.

[66] *Loizidou* v. *Turkey (Merits)* (App. 15318/89), Judgment of 18 December 1996; (1997) 23 EHRR 513.

[67] *Yonghong* v. *Portugal* (App. 50887/99), admissibility decision of 25 November 1999.

[68] See ch. 1 above.

DO THE MATTERS COMPLAINED OF FALL WITHIN THE SCOPE OF THE CONVENTION OR PROTOCOLS?

The Court cannot deal with complaints concerning rights not covered by the Convention or Protocols, and a State cannot be brought to task in respect of alleged violations of rights included in protocols which it has not ratified.

Such complaints are normally rejected under Article 35(3) as incompatible *ratione materiae* with the provisions of the Convention.

It is the duty of the Court to examine an application not only in relation to any rights that may have been invoked by the applicant, but also, of its own motion, in relation to any rights which, on the facts and submissions before it, may appear to have been infringed.

HAVE DOMESTIC REMEDIES BEEN EXHAUSTED?

According to Article 35(1): 'The Court may only deal with the matter after all domestic remedies have been exhausted, according to the generally recognized rules of international law, and within a period of six months from the date on which the final decision was taken.'

In the *Akdivar and others* v. *Turkey* judgment[69] the Court explained the rationale for this rule:

[T]he rule of exhaustion of domestic remedies . . . obliges those seeking to bring their case against the State before an international judicial or arbitral organ to use first the remedies provided by the national legal system. Consequently, States are dispensed from answering before an international body for their acts before they have had an opportunity to put matters right through their own legal system. The rule is based on the assumption, reflected in Article 13 of the Convention—with which it has close affinity—that there is an effective remedy available in respect of the alleged breach in the domestic system whether or not the provisions of the Convention are incorporated in national law. In this way, it is an important aspect of the principle that the machinery of protection established by the Convention is subsidiary to the national systems safeguarding human rights.[70]

Under Article 35(1), applicants are under an obligation to use the remedies provided by national law which are sufficient to afford redress in respect of the breaches alleged. The complaint must be made to the appropriate judicial or administrative authorities, and should have been taken to the highest instance available. An applicant will not have complied with the rule if he has been unable to pursue national proceedings because of his own failure to comply with the domestic formal requirements and time-limits.[71] In addition, the

---

[69] *Akdivar and others* v. *Turkey* (App. 21893/93), Judgment of 16 September 1996; (1997) 23 EHRR 143.

[70] Para. 65 of the judgment.

[71] See e.g. *Yahiaoui* v. *France* (App. 30962/96), Judgment of 14 January 2000; (2001) 33 EHRR 393.

applicant must have raised before the national authorities, if it is possible to do so, the particular complaints which he or she wishes to make before the Court. If he raises only some of his complaints, only those will be admissible.

There is, however, no obligation to attempt to use a remedy which is inadequate or ineffective. In addition, according to the 'generally recognized rules of international law' there may be special circumstances which absolve the applicant from the obligation to exhaust the domestic remedies at his disposal. So, for example, in the *Akdivar* case, where the Kurdish applicants complained that their village had been destroyed by Turkish soldiers, and the Government was unable to provide evidence of damages having been awarded in a single similar case, the Court held that there was no need for the applicants to bring proceedings in the national courts before complaining in Strasbourg.

Again, if the national case law shows that a remedy, such as an appeal, has no reasonable chance of success, the applicant is not obliged to try it. The Court will accept Counsel's opinion to this effect as a 'final decision' under Article 35.

The domestic remedies rule applies also to inter-State applications under Article 33, unlike the other grounds of inadmissibility specified in Article 35, which are expressly confined to individual applications under Article 34. The rule, however, has only a limited application in inter-State cases: domestic remedies must have been exhausted in respect of violations of the rights of particular individuals, but not where the scope of the application is to determine the compatibility with the Convention of legislative measures and administrative practices in general.[72] An administrative practice exists if there is repetition of acts and official tolerance, even if only at a subordinate level, and despite occasional reactions from the authorities.[73] There is no requirement in such cases that there should be a victim at all. Thus the rule does not apply if the applicant government can show that the treatment complained of constitutes an administrative practice. It did not apply, for this reason, in the *Irish* case,[74] to the Irish Government's complaints concerning the treatment of persons in custody in Northern Ireland. But it is not sufficient merely to allege the existence of such legislative measures or administrative practices; their existence must be shown by means of substantial evidence. On this ground, the complaints in the same case relating to deaths allegedly caused by the United Kingdom Government's security forces were rejected for non-compliance with the rule.

The applicant must provide, in the application, information enabling it to be

---

[72] App. 788/60, *Pfunders Case, Austria* v. *Italy*, 11 January 1961, (1961) 4 *Yearbook* 116, at 146–50; and see, more recently, *Cyprus* v. *Turkey*, Judgment of 10 May 2001.

[73] *Ireland* v. *United Kingdom*, Judgment of 18 January 1978, Series A, No. 25; (1979–80) 2 EHRR 25.

[74] App. 5310/71, *Ireland* v. *United Kingdom*, 1 October 1972, (1972) 15 *Yearbook* 76; see also Joined Apps. 9940–44/82, *France, Norway, Denmark, Sweden, and The Netherlands* v. *Turkey*, 6 December 1983, (1984) 35 DR 143.

shown that the conditions laid down in Article 35 have been satisfied; if this is not done, the Court must examine the question of its own motion. If the respondent government raises the objection of non-exhaustion, it is for that government to prove the existence, in its municipal legal system, of remedies which have not been exercised.[75] If the existence of such a remedy is established, the applicant must show that it has been exhausted, or that it was unlikely to be effective and adequate in regard to the grievance in question, or that in the special circumstances of the case he or she was absolved from compliance with the rule. The rules concerning the burden of proof are based, as is the substantive rule, on the generally recognized rules of international law referred to in Article 35.[76]

HAS THE APPLICATION BEEN INTRODUCED WITHIN THE SIX MONTHS TIME-LIMIT?

Article 35 prescribes a strict period of limitation: an application is inadmissible if it is not brought within six months from the date on which the final decision was taken.

Time starts running from the day after the applicant became aware of the act or decision of which he or she complains. Where domestic remedies have been completed, this is usually the hearing at which the final domestic judgment is delivered,[77] but where no domestic remedies are available, the six-months period runs from the date of the act alleged to constitute the violation of the Convention. The applicant cannot reopen the period by, for example, subsequently applying for a retrial, as such an application does not constitute an 'effective remedy' for the purposes of Article 35. Where the complaint concerns a continuing situation, time runs from the end of the situation, but as long as the situation continues, the six-months rule cannot bite.[78]

The rule is applied strictly by the Court and cannot be waived by the respondent government.[79] In certain cases it may appear to create injustice—where an application is submitted late through the oversight of the applicant's lawyer, for example—but, like all limitation periods, it is intended to promote legal certainty and finality.

[75] *Akdivar and others* v. *Turkey* (App. 21893/93), Judgment of 16 September 1996; (1997) 23 EHRR 143.
[76] Ibid.
[77] App. 34728/97, *West* v. *United Kingdom*, admissibility decision of 20 October 1997.
[78] *Papamichalopoulos and others* v. *Greece*, Judgment of 24 June 1993, Series A, No. 260-B; (1993) 16 EHRR 440.
[79] *Walker* v. *United Kingdom*, Judgment of 25 January 2000.

THE EUROPEAN CONVENTION ON HUMAN RIGHTS

IS THE APPLICATION SIGNED?

Article 35(1)(a) requires that applicants are identified; anonymous applications cannot be entertained. Applications have rarely been rejected on the ground of anonymity. The most common situation in which an application is declared inadmissible on this ground is the case of representative actions brought by associations, where the identity of the members said to have suffered violations of the Convention is not stated.[80]

HAS THE APPLICATION BEEN BROUGHT BEFORE?

Article 35(1)(b) provides that an application is inadmissible if it 'is substantially the same as a matter which has already been examined by the Court or has already been submitted to another procedure of international investigation or settlement and contains no relevant new information.'

There appears to be no decision of the Court or Commission rejecting an application on the ground that it has already been submitted to another procedure of international investigation or settlement. In one case,[81] although the applicant had already applied to the United Nations Human Rights Commission, his complaint to that body had concerned a different issue than that brought before the Strasbourg organs.

In many cases applicants seek to reopen proceedings after the application has been declared inadmissible, alleging errors in the Court's decision or introducing further details of the same complaints. Since there is no provision for reopening a case, it is necessary to treat the new material as a fresh application. Such an application will be doomed to failure if, for example, the new material does not affect the substance of the previous allegations. In other cases, the new material may remedy the ground on which the previous application was rejected. If, for example, an application is rejected for non-exhaustion of domestic remedies, the applicant may still be able to pursue the domestic remedies and then reintroduce the complaint.

IS THE APPLICATION MANIFESTLY ILL-FOUNDED?

Article 35(3) requires the Court to reject as inadmissible an application which is 'manifestly ill-founded'. This provision requires an initial assessment of the substance of the case and enables to Court to deal effectively with its immense caseload by weeding out at an early stage clearly unmeritorious applications.

---

[80] App. 3798/68, *Church of X v. United Kingdom*, 17 December 1968, (1969) 12 *Yearbook* 306; App. 10983/84, *Confédération des Syndicats médicaux français and Fédération nationale des Infirmiers v. France*, 12 May 1986, (1986) 47 DR 225.

[81] *Pauger v. Austria* (App. 16717/90), Judgment of 28 May 1997; (1998) 25 EHRR 105.

A complaint will be declared manifestly ill-founded if, for example, the applicant has made wholly unsubstantiated allegations or where the allegations, even if substantiated, would not suffice to establish a violation. For example, complaints by prisoners under Article 3 concerning the conditions of their detention are frequently rejected as manifestly ill-founded on the ground that, even if the matters complained of were established, they would not constitute 'inhuman or degrading treatment or punishment'.

IS THERE AN ABUSE OF THE RIGHT OF PETITION?

Abuse of the right of petition, as a ground of rejecting an application, must of course be distinguished from the principle of abuse of rights embodied in Article 17. Article 17 lays down, in effect, that no one may be able to take advantage of the provisions of the Convention to perform acts aimed at destroying the rights guaranteed. It is thus concerned with preventing abuse of the substantive rights. Abuse of the right of petition, on the other hand, may arise where an applicant makes improper use of the procedural rights under Article 34 to bring the complaint before the Court.

For example, the Court is the recipient of multiple applications from a number of individuals who would have been (and frequently are), within the English system, subject to vexatious litigant orders. The Commission habitually declared such applications inadmissible for abuse of process, stating:

> It cannot be the task of the Commission, a body which was set up under the Convention 'to ensure the observance of the engagements undertaken by the High Contracting Parties in the present Convention' to deal with a succession of ill-founded and querulous complaints, creating unnecessary work which is incompatible with its real functions, and which hinders it in carrying them out.[82]

EXAMINATION OF THE MERITS

Once an application has been declared inadmissible, whether by a Committee or a Chamber, that is the end of the matter. There is no possibility of appeal.

If an application is declared admissible, the parties will be informed, and the Court will usually put itself at their disposal to assist in the negotiation of a

---

[82] Joined Apps. 5070/71, 5171/71, and 5186/71, *X* v. *Federal Republic of Germany*, 10 July 1971, (1971) 42 CD 58, at 60. Cited with approval in Joined Apps. 5145/71, 5246/71, 5333/72, 5586/72, 5587/72, and 5532/72, *Ringeisen* v. *Austria*, 2 April 1973, (1973) 43 CD 152, and App. 13284/87, *M* v. *United Kingdom*, 15 October 1987, (1987) 54 DR 214.

friendly settlement.[83] If no settlement can be reached, the President of the Chamber will fix deadlines for the submission of further written observations and the Chamber will decide whether or not to hold a hearing.[84]

THIRD-PARTY INTERVENTION

At this stage, subject to the leave of the President of the Chamber, it is possible for a third party to submit written comments or, occasionally, to intervene at the hearing. Third-party comments are usually submitted by non-governmental organizations whose field of expertise touches on the subject matter of the application. However, it is possible for other governments and interested individuals to intervene. In the cases of *T. and V. v. the United Kingdom*,[85] for example, which concerned the trial and sentencing of two children who had murdered another child, the non-governmental organization Justice was permitted to submit a written brief about the criminal responsibility of children, and the dead child's parents were allowed to submit written and oral comments.[86]

ESTABLISHMENT OF THE FACTS

Article 38(1)(a) of the Convention provides that:

If the Court declares the application admissible, it shall pursue the examination of the case, together with the representatives of the parties, and if need be, undertake an investigation, for the effective conduct of which the States concerned shall furnish all necessary facilities.

In most cases, the facts will have been established by domestic courts and the task of the Court of Human Rights will be limited to examining these facts to assess compliance with the Convention. In some cases, however, particularly where the alleged violation arises wholly or in part from a deficiency in the national adjudicatory system, or where, for example, the applicants are dispensed from exhausting domestic remedies,[87] and the facts are in dispute, the Court will be required to establish them itself.[88]

Under Rule 42 of the Rules of Court, the Chamber may, at the request of a

[83] Art. 38(1)(b) and (2) of the Convention and Rule 62 of the Rules of Court.
[84] Rules 58 and 59 of the Rules of Court.
[85] *T. v. United Kingdom* (App. 24724/94); and *V. v. United Kingdom* (App. 24888/94) Judgments of 16 December 1999; (2000) 30 EHRR 121.
[86] See para. 4 of each judgment.
[87] *Akdivar and others* v. *Turkey* (App. 21893/93), Judgment of 16 September 1996; (1997) 23 EHRR 143, and see also above in this chapter.
[88] For an interesting examination of the Strasbourg organs' approach to evidential issues, see U. Erdal, 'Burden and standard of proof in proceedings under the European Convention', (2001) 26 ELRev HR 65.

party to the case or a third party, or of its own motion, obtain any evidence which it considers capable of providing clarification of the facts of the case. It may request—but not order—the parties to produce documentary evidence and decide to hear as a witness or expert any person whose evidence or statements seem likely to be of assistance.[89]

Where necessary, the Court may appoint a delegation of judges to conduct an inquiry or carry out an investigation on the spot.[90] In the past, the Commission carried out *in situ* fact-finding procedures in a number of cases, particularly cases involving allegations of serious human rights violations against Turkey.

As provided by Article 38 of the Convention, it is incumbent on the State concerned to assist the Court in the conduct of any such investigation. In the *Tanrikulu* case,[91] the Commission sent a delegation to South-East Turkey to investigate the alleged killing of the applicant's husband by security forces. The Commission repeatedly requested the Government to give it a copy of the full investigation file, but this was not supplied.[92] In addition, the Commission requested the two State prosecutors who had investigated the case on the national level to appear before its delegates to give evidence. Neither of them appeared, and the Government provided no satisfactory explanation for their failure to attend.[93] In its judgment, the Court made a separate finding that the Government had fallen short of its obligations under Article 28 of the Convention (now Article 38), commenting as follows:

The Court would observe that it is of the utmost importance for the effective operation of the system of individual petition instituted under former Article 25 of the Convention (now replaced by Article 34) not only that applicants or potential applicants should be able to communicate freely with the Convention organs without being subject to any form of pressure from the authorities, but also that States should furnish all necessary facilities to make possible a proper and effective examination of applications (see former Article 28(1) (a) of the Convention, which concerned the fact-finding responsibility of the Commission, now replaced by Article 38 of the Convention as regards the Court's procedures).

---

[89] For example, in App. 41707/98, *Khoklich v. Ukraine*, the Court decided that it needed a medical opinion to enable it to determine the truth of a complaint that the applicant had been infected with tuberculosis while detained on death row. The costs of the medical examination were borne by the Council of Europe under Rule 42(5).

[90] Rule 42(2) of the Rules of Court.

[91] *Tanrikulu v. Turkey* (App. 23763/94), Judgment of 8 July 1999; (2000) 30 EHRR 950.

[92] Para. 31 of the judgment.

[93] Para. 39 of the judgment.

REMEDIES UNDER ARTICLE 41

Article 41 of the Convention provides that:

If the Court finds that there has been a violation of the Convention or the protocols thereto, and if the internal law of the High Contracting Party concerned allows only partial reparation to be made, the Court shall, if necessary, afford just satisfaction to the injured party.

The Court's case law under Article 41 (formerly Article 50) has been criticized for the lack of clear principles as to when damages should be awarded and how they should be measured.[94] Nonetheless, it is possible to identify a few general rules which the Court applies in determining questions of just satisfaction.

In its *Papamichalopoulos* v. *Greece (Just Satisfaction)* judgment,[95] the Court explained the legal consequences for a State of a finding of violation of the Convention:

[A] judgment in which the Court finds a breach imposes on the respondent State a legal obligation to put an end to the breach and make reparation for its consequences in such a way as to restore as far as possible the situation existing before the breach.

The Contracting States that are parties to a case are in principle free to choose the means whereby they will comply with a judgment in which the Court has found a breach. This discretion as to the manner of execution of a judgment reflects the freedom of choice attaching to the primary obligation of the Contracting States under the Convention to secure the rights and freedoms guaranteed (Article 1). If the nature of the breach allows of *restitutio in integrum*, it is for the respondent State to effect it, the Court having neither the power nor the practical possibility of doing so itself.

If, on the other hand, national law does not allow—or allows only partial— reparation to be made for the consequences of the breach, Article 50 empowers the Court to afford the injured party such satisfaction as appears to it to be appropriate.

Thus, the aim of an award of damages by the Court is to return the applicant to the position in which he or she would have been had there not been a breach of the Convention (*restitutio in integrum*).

The Court will not award just satisfaction if fresh proceedings have brought about a situation as close to *restitutio in integrum* as possible. This is illustrated in the *Windisch* case.[96] Windisch had been convicted by a court in Austria of burglary. The conviction had been secured at a trial at which two witnesses gave evidence anonymously. The Court of Human Rights judged

---

[94] See e.g. the report prepared jointly by the English and Scottish Law Commissions, *Damages under the Human Rights Act 1998*, Law Com. No. 266/Scot Law Com. No. 180, para. 3.4 ff.

[95] Judgment of 31 October 1995, Series A, No. 330-B; (1996) 21 EHRR 439.

[96] *Windisch* v. *Austria (Article 50)*, Judgment of 28 June 1993, Series A, No. 255-D.

this to be a violation of the rights protected by Article 6.[97] The issue of the award of damages was deferred. Following the Court of Human Rights' judgment, Windisch was retried and convicted at a trial in which all the requirements of due process were observed; in particular, the two previously anonymous witnesses gave evidence in public. His appeal against sentence was unsuccessful. The Court of Human Rights in the Article 50 decision held that the retrial redressed the violation found by the Court in its substantive decision of 27 September 1990. It concluded that the national court had taken full account of the term of imprisonment previously served, and, recalling its decision in the *Piersack* case,[98] found that the end result of the retrial 'brought about a situation as close to *restitutio in integrum* as was possible in the nature of things.'[99]

In many cases, however, the nature of the violation will render *restitutio* impossible.[100] In such cases, it may be appropriate for the Court to award just satisfaction.

The Court makes awards of financial just satisfaction under three heads: pecuniary loss, non-pecuniary loss, and costs and expenses.

The Court will award damages only in respect of losses which can be shown to have been caused by the violation in question.[101] In the *Findlay* case,[102] for example, where the Court found a violation of Article 6(1) based on the fact that the court-martial board which had sentenced the applicant had not presented the necessary appearance of independence, it declined to compensate him for losses which flowed from the sentence of imprisonment, because it could not be established that a tribunal meeting the requirements of Article 6(1) would have reached a different decision.

Just satisfaction may be substantial[103] or nominal[104] or even the mere declaration that there has been a violation of the rights protected by the Convention.[105] In determining the amount of compensation, the Court seeks to act equitably, having regard to the severity of the breach and the ready quantifiability of any loss.

---

[97] *Windisch v. Austria*, Judgment of 27 September 1990, Series A, No. 186; (1991) 13 EHRR 281.

[98] *Piersack v. Belgium, (Article 50)*, Judgment of 26 October 1984, Series A, No. 85.

[99] Series A, No. 255-D at para. 14.

[100] See e.g. *Konig v. Germany (Just Satisfaction)*, Judgment of 10 March 1980, Series A, No. 36; (1980) 2 EHRR 469, para. 15, where the Court had found a breach of the reasonable time requirement under Art. 6(1).

[101] *Le Compte, Van Leuven and De Meyere v. Belgium (Article 50)*, Series A, No. 54; (1983) 5 EHRR 183.

[102] *Findlay v. United Kingdom*, Judgment of 25 February 1997.

[103] As in *Neumeister v. Austria (Article 50)*, Judgment of 7 May 1974, Series A, No. 17; (1979–80) 1 EHRR 136.

[104] As in *Engel and others v. Netherlands (Article 50)*, Judgment of 23 November 1976, Series A, No. 22; (1979–80) 1 EHRR 706.

[105] As in *Golder v. United Kingdom*, Judgment of 21 February 1975, Series A, No. 18; (1979–80) 1 EHRR 524.

The most frequent award of just satisfaction beyond the declaration of a violation is the award of costs and expenses incurred in the case, either in the material proceedings[106] or in Strasbourg. Where costs are met from insurance[107] or free legal aid,[108] the amount of those costs cannot be recovered by way of just satisfaction. The Court is not, however, bound by domestic scales or standards.[109] The Court's position on domestic costs is neatly summarized in the *Eckle* case:

According to the settled case-law of the Court, to be entitled to an award of costs and expenses under Article 50, the injured party must have incurred them in order to seek, through the domestic legal order, prevention or redress of a violation, to have the same established by the Commission and later by the Court or to obtain reparation therefore. . . . Furthermore the Court has to be satisfied that the costs and expenses were actually incurred, were necessarily incurred and were also reasonable as to quantum.[110]

JUDGMENT

The Court's judgments must contain, *inter alia*, a summary of the facts, the arguments and the reasons for the Court's decision.[111] The names of the judges making up the majority and the dissenters must be made clear, and any judge who has taken part in the consideration of the case can annex a separate opinion.

Unless the Court decides that a judgment is sufficiently important to merit translation into the other official language, it will be delivered in either English or French. All judgments which the Court decides to publish in the official reports are translated.[112]

The Court's judgments may be delivered in open court or, more usually, communicated to the parties in writing.[113] Within three months of the date of a Chamber judgment, it is open to the parties to request that the case be referred to the Grand Chamber.[114] A judgment of the Grand Chamber is final, and those of the Chambers become final either when (a) the parties declare that they will

---

[106] As in *Fox, Campbell & Hartley* v. *United Kingdom (Article 50)*, Judgment of 27 March 1991, Series A, No. 202; (1992) 14 EHRR 108.

[107] *Öztürk* v. *Germany (Article 50)*, Judgment of 23 October 1984, Series A, No. 85.

[108] *Bozano* v. *France (Article 50)*, Judgment of 2 December 1987, Series A, No. 124-F.

[109] *Eckle* v. *Germany (Article 50)*, Judgment of 21 June 1983, Series A No 65; (1991) 13 EHRR 556.

[110] Para. 25 of judgment.

[111] Rule 74, Rules of Court.

[112] Rule 76, Rules of Court.

[113] Rule 77, Rules of Court.

[114] Art. 43 of the Convention, and see above in this chapter.

not be seeking a referral; (2) the three-month period expires without any request having been made; or (3) the panel of the Grand Chamber refuses a request for referral.[115]

A party to the case may request interpretation of a judgment within a year of its delivery.[116] If a new fact is discovered which might have affected the outcome of a case, a party may request revision of the judgment within six months of becoming aware of the fact.[117]

A finding by the Court in its judgment of a violation of the Convention or Protocols places an obligation on the State in question to make the changes required to the domestic legal order to avoid a repetition of the breach. This is inherent in the obligation in Article 46(1) to abide by the decision of the Court in any case to which the State is a party.

Under Article 46(2) of the Convention, the Court's judgments are transmitted to the Committee of Ministers of the Council of Europe, which supervises their execution.[118]

CONCLUDING COMMENT

To a certain extent, the Court has become a victim of its own success. Protocol No. 11 was adopted to assist the Strasbourg organs to deal effectively with the rapidly increasing caseload, but only a few years after its coming into force, the Court has amended its Committee procedure to deal with inadmissible cases even more summarily, and discussions are taking place as to how the procedure should best be amended again.[119]

---

[115] Art. 44 ECHR.
[116] Rule 79, Rules of Court. To date, the Court has delivered only three interpretation judgments: *Ringeisen* v. *Austria (Interpretation)*, Judgment of 23 June 1973, Series A, No. 16; *Allenet de Ribemont* v. *France (Interpretation)*, Judgment of 7 August 1996; and *Hentrich* v. *France (Interpretation)*, Judgment of 3 July 1997.
[117] Rule 80, Rules of Court; and the Court's four revision judgments: *Pardo* v. *France (Revision)*, Judgments of 10 July 1996 and 29 April 1997; *Gustafsson* v. *Sweden (Revision)*, Judgment of 30 July 1998; *McGinley and Egan* v. *United Kingdom (Revision)*, Judgment of 28 January 2000.
[118] See ch. 25 below.
[119] See ch. 25 below.

25

THE ROLE OF THE COMMITTEE OF MINISTERS

INTRODUCTION[1]

As mentioned in the preceding chapter, the Court's judgments are final[2] and binding on respondent States.[3] The Court has held that a judgment in which it finds a violation imposes on the respondent State a legal obligation to put an end to the breach and make reparation for its consequences in such a way as to restore as far as possible the situation existing before the breach.[4] However, aside from awarding monetary compensation, the Court has declined to assume jurisdiction to order a State to carry out particular measures of reparation or to change its law or practice in any particular way so as to prevent similar violations from recurring in the future.[5]

It is self-evident that, without compliance or enforcement, the best of judgments are useless to the victims of human rights violations. As Ms Leni Fischer, the President of the Council of Europe's Parliamentary Assembly, said at the new Court's inauguration ceremony on 3 November 1998:

What the new European Court of Human Rights needs most is unequivocal respect for and follow-up to its decisions in the Council of Europe member countries. This alone will provide the Court with the authority it needs in order to protect the fundamental rights of our people.[6]

The Committee of Ministers is the organ of the Council of Europe charged

---

[1] Thanks to Elena Malagoni and Frederic Sundberg for their help with this chapter.

[2] Art. 44 of the Convention (formerly Article 52).

[3] Art. 46(1) of the Convention as amended by Protocol No. 11 (formerly Art. 53) provides: 'The High Contracting Parties undertake to abide by the final judgment of the Court in any case to which they are parties.'

[4] *Papamichalopoulos* v. *Greece*, Judgment of 31 October 1995, Series A, No. 330-B; (1996) 21 EHRR 439, para. 34 of the judgment.

[5] See *Ireland* v. *United Kingdom*, Judgment of 18 January 1978, Series A, No. 25; (1979–80) 2 EHRR 25, para. 187 and *Scozzari and Giunta* v. *Italy* (Apps. 39221/98 and 41963/98), Judgment of 13 July 2000, para. 249 of the judgment.

[6] Council of Europe Press Release no. 729/98.

with the task of supervising the execution of these judgments.[7] Since 1 November 1998, when Protocol No. 11 to the Convention came into force, the Committee has been able to concentrate on the supervision of the execution of the Court's judgments,[8] since the other two functions which it formerly carried out under the Convention—the election of members of the European Commission of Human Rights[9] and the examination of the merits of cases not referred to the Court[10]—no longer exist.

COMPOSITION AND PROCEDURE

According to Article 14 of the Statute of the Council of Europe, each of the member States is entitled to one representative on the Committee, and each representative is entitled to one vote. In principle these representatives are the Ministers of Foreign Affairs of each Member State, but the Ministers themselves usually meet only twice a year. At the bimonthly meetings which the Committee devotes to its tasks under the Convention, the Ministers act through their Deputies, namely their Permanent Representatives (ambassadors) in Strasbourg. The Committee is assisted by a surprisingly small secretariat provided by the Secretary-General of the Council of Europe.[11]

On 10 January 2001 the Committee adopted new Rules of Procedure in the exercise of its supervisory function under Article 46(2) of the Convention.[12] The Rules codified existing practice, with one important novelty. In a break with tradition, Rule 5 now provides for public access to the information provided by the State to the Committee of Ministers, although the Committee's deliberations remain confidential.

Rule 1 is concerned with the organization and chairmanship of meetings (the Chair rotates between the member States). Rule 2 provides that a judgment of the Court should be included on the Committee's agenda without delay (in practice, within six weeks of the Court's judgment). According to Rule 3(a), respondent States are under an obligation to inform the Committee about the

---

[7] Art. 46(2) of the Convention provides: 'The final judgment of the Court shall be transmitted to the Committee of Ministers, which shall supervise its execution.'

[8] Art. 54 of the Convention before it was amended; now Art. 46.

[9] Art. 21 of the Convention before it was amended by Protocol No. 11.

[10] Art. 32 of the Convention before it was amended.

[11] In September 2001, only ten members of staff in the Directorate of Human Rights, compared with over 300 agents working in the Registry of the Court.

[12] Rules adopted by the Committee of Ministers for the application of Art. 46(2) of the European Convention on Human Rights (text approved by the Committee of Ministers at the 736th Meeting of the Ministers' Deputies), available from the Council of Europe, Strasbourg; see also the Committee of Minister's internet site: **www.cm.coe.int**

measures taken in consequence of a finding of violation by the Court, whether in respect of the payment of any just satisfaction awarded under Article 41 of the Convention; 'individual measures', such as the striking out of an unjustified criminal conviction from the criminal records, the granting of a residence permit or the reopening of impugned domestic proceedings; or with regard to any 'general measures' taken by the State, for example, changes of practice or legislation to prevent the same violation from recurring. If the respondent State informs the Committee that it is not yet in a position to provide information about measures taken in execution of the judgment, which, because of the shortness of the six-week delay, will frequently occur at the first meeting at which the judgment is placed on the agenda, the case will automatically return to the agenda. The Committee will then re-examine the case at every meeting (that is, every two months), until the required individual measures have been effected, and every six months until the general measures necessary to ensure compliance with the judgment have been taken (Rule 4).

Rule 7 allows the Committee to make interim resolutions (for example, to provide information on the state of progress of the execution or to express concern and/or to make relevant suggestions with respect to the execution), and Rule 8 provides that, 'after having established that the State concerned has taken all the necessary measures to abide by the judgment, the Committee of Ministers shall adopt a resolution concluding that its functions under Article 46, paragraph 2, of the Convention have been exercised.' The Committee's resolutions are available from the Council of Europe and on-line.

The question of the extent to which the individual victim of a violation (the original applicant to the Court) and interested third parties, such as non-governmental organizations, are permitted to become involved in the procedure before the Committee of Ministers has long been controversial. The Rules provide as follows (Rule 6):

a. The Committee of Ministers shall be entitled to consider any communication from the injured party with regard to the payment of the just satisfaction or the taking of individual measures.
b. The Secretariat shall bring such communications to the attention of the Committee of Ministers.

This is the only formal acknowledgement of the standing of the individual victim of a violation before the Committee. It extends only to the applicant's complaints relating to his or her personal situation, despite the fact that in a large number of cases brought before the Court, the applicant's prime concern is one of principle, to achieve changes to existing domestic law or practice. Moreover, there is no formal right of access to the Committee's decision-making process for non-governmental organizations or other third parties which might have an interest in seeing that effective general measures are implemented.

It would appear that in practice, however, the Committee's secretariat will, where necessary, seek and receive information from individual applicants, non-governmental and international organizations, even national newspapers, to assist in determining the nature and extent of reforms needed to ensure compliance with the Court's judgment and the extent to which measures recommended to the State through interim resolutions have been carried out. Any material received in this way by the secretariat will not be used directly as a basis for discussion in the Committee, but will instead be forwarded to the respondent State for information.

The Committee's voting procedures are governed by the Statute of the Council of Europe.[13] A quorum consisting of the representatives of two-thirds of the Member States (that is, representatives from twenty-seven States) is necessary before any meeting can proceed. For the adoption of a resolution or interim resolution a simple majority of all the member States (that is, at least twenty-two votes) and a two-thirds majority of all the States present at the meeting is required.

In contrast, unanimity is necessary for the adoption of a recommendation or an answer to a Parliamentary question. The fact that the State concerned can effectively veto any such text with which it disagrees weakens the effectiveness of these measures.

THE EXECUTION OF JUDGMENTS

JUST SATISFACTION

In every case where the Court finds a violation, it has the power under Article 41 of the Convention to award just satisfaction.[14] If it decides to make an award, it will require the respondent State to pay the applicant within three months of the delivery of the judgment. After the Committee's first examination at its meeting immediately following the delivery of the judgment, a case involving an award of just satisfaction will usually come up for renewed examination after the expiry of the three-month time-limit. If the respondent State is unable to supply proof of payment, the case will return to the agenda at every subsequent meeting until the Committee is satisfied that the money has been paid in full. Since January 1996, following discussions between the Court and the Committee, the Court has included in its awards of just satisfaction an order to States to pay simple interest, calculated on a daily basis, from the expiry of the three

---

[13] Rule 20(d) of the Statute.
[14] See ch. 24 above.

months until payment. The purpose of the award of interest is obviously to encourage States to pay up quickly, and to safeguard the value of the award. In some cases, in order to guard against inflation, the Court has expressed the monetary award in US dollars, pounds sterling, French francs or euros, to be converted into the less stable national currency at the date of payment.[15]

Until the *Loizidou* case,[16] the most difficult case involving just satisfaction that the Committee of Ministers has had to deal with, and which was, indeed, largely responsible for the introduction of default interest, was that of *Stran Greek Refineries and Stratis Andreadis v. Greece*.[17] The background to the case was that the applicant company had entered into a contract with the Greek State (which at the time was governed by the military junta) to build an oil refinery, and had incurred considerable expenditure procuring goods and services for the construction of the refinery. When the democratic Government regained power, they decided that it was not in the national interest for the refinery to be built and they terminated the contract. The company commenced proceedings against the State for compensation for the expenditure it had incurred under the terms of the contract, and a substantial arbitration award was made against the Government, which appealed to the Court of Cassation. However, the State then asked for the hearing to be postponed on the ground that a draft law concerning the point in issue was just about to go through Parliament. The new legislation in fact made it inevitable that the Court of Cassation would find against the applicant. The Court of Human Rights unanimously found a violation of Article 6(1), and awarded pecuniary damages of almost $US30,000,000, together with simple interest at 6 per cent from 27 February 1984 (the date of the arbitration award) to the date of judgment.

Because of the size of the award, the Greek Government refused to pay within the three-month limit and asked the Committee if it could pay by instalments over a period of five years, without interest. This request was rejected by the Committee; the President at the time, the Estonian Foreign Minister, wrote to the Greek Minister of Foreign Affairs, stressing that 'the credibility and effectiveness of the mechanism for the collective enforcement of human rights established under the Convention was based on the respect of the obligations freely entered into by the States and in particular in respect of the supervisory bodies.'[18] In the event, the case was not resolved until 17 January 1997, when, as a result of increasing pressure applied by the Committee, the Government transferred $US30,863,828 to the applicants, corresponding to the just satisfaction

---

[15] See e.g. *Selçuk and Asker* v. *Turkey* (Apps. 23184/94 and 23185/94), Judgment of 24 April 1998; *Assenov and others* v. *Bulgaria* (App. 24760/94), Judgment of 28 October 1998; (1999) 28 EHRR 652.

[16] See below.

[17] Judgment of 9 December 1994, Series A, No. 301-B; (1994) 19 EHRR 293

[18] Resolution DH(97)184.

awarded by the Court, increased in order to provide compensation for the loss of value caused by the delay in payment.[19]

OTHER INDIVIDUAL MEASURES

In addition to the payment of compensation, individual measures may be required to ensure that the injured party is put, as far as possible, in the same situation as he or she enjoyed prior to the violation of the Convention (*restitutio in integrum*). For example, where the Court has found a violation of Article 8 of the Convention caused by the refusal to allow adequate contact between a parent and a child in public care, the State will be required to facilitate more frequent access visits; in a deportation case under Article 3 or 8, the deportation order should be quashed; and so on.

The individual measure most commonly required for *restitutio in integrum* is the reopening of domestic legal proceedings. The need for such a measure arises primarily in respect of criminal proceedings, since problems with civil proceedings can frequently be remedied through financial compensation.[20] But a criminal conviction may need to be quashed, or a retrial ordered, in two types of situation: first, where the Court has found procedural injustice in the original trial giving rise to a violation of Article 6; or, secondly, where it has found that the substantive criminal law of a State is incompatible with one of the provisions of the Convention, for example, where an applicant has been tried and convicted for proselytism, contrary to Article 9,[21] or for exercising his or her right to freedom of expression in some way prohibited by national law.[22]

In its Recommendation No. R (2000) 2, adopted on 19 January 2000, the Committee asked States to provide means of reopening proceedings within their national legal systems following a finding of violation by the Court, particularly where:

(i) the injured party continues to suffer very serious negative consequences because of the outcome of the domestic decision at issue, which are not adequately remedied by the just satisfaction and cannot be rectified except by re-examination or reopening, and

(ii) the judgment of the Court leads to the conclusion that (a) the impugned domestic decision is on the merits contrary to the Convention, or (b) the violation found is based on procedural errors or shortcomings of such gravity that a serious doubt is cast on the outcome of the domestic proceedings complained of.

Most States have now incorporated some mechanism into national law to permit criminal proceedings to be reopened in the circumstances outlined

---

[19] Ibid.   [20] As in the *Stran Greek* case, above.
[21] e.g. *Kokkinakis v. Greece*, Judgment of 25 May 1993, Series A, No. 260-A; (1994) 17 EHRR 397: see ch. 12 above.
[22] See ch. 13 above.

above. For example, in the United Kingdom the Criminal Cases Review Commission can refer a case to the Court of Appeal, either *ex officio* or following an application by the convicted person if it considers that there is a real possibility that the conviction or sentence would not be upheld if the reference is made.[23]

A notable exception to this practice is Italy.[24] In Turkey, the position under domestic law is unclear: it is possible that an individual could try to request a new trial on the grounds that a judgment of the Court constituted a 'new fact or new evidence'. The law may, however, be amended as a result of pressure applied by the Committee of Ministers following the Court's judgment in *Socialist Party and others* v. *Turkey*.[25] The Turkish Socialist Party was dissolved pursuant to an order of the Constitutional Court in July 1992, on the grounds that its chairman, Mr Dogu Perinçek, had made certain statements which could be interpreted as advocating Kurdish secession, contrary to the Constitution. In its judgment of 25 May 1998, the European Court held that the Party's dissolution amounted to a violation of Article 11 of the Convention and awarded damages under Article 50 of the Convention (as it then was). The Committee adopted a resolution on 4 March 1999,[26] stating that it was satisfied that Turkey had paid the just satisfaction ordered by the Court, but continued:

The Committee of Ministers . . . [h]aving, however, been informed that by judgment of 8 July 1998—i.e. after the judgment of the European Court of Human Rights—the Court of Cassation of Turkey confirmed a criminal conviction imposed on Mr Perinçek by the first State Security Court of Ankara on 15 October 1996, according to which the sanction of dissolution of the party also carried with it personal criminal responsibility;

Noting that the Court of Cassation based its judgment on the statements which had been pronounced by Mr Perinçek in 1991;

Noting, furthermore, that by virtue of his conviction, Mr Perinçek has been sentenced to a 14-month prison sentence, which he started to serve on 29 September 1998, and has furthermore *inter alia* been banned from further political activities;

Insists on Turkey's obligation under Article 53 of the Convention to erase, without delay, through action by the competent Turkish authorities, all the consequences resulting from the applicant's criminal conviction on 8 July 1998;

Decides, if need be, to resume consideration of the present case at each of its forthcoming meetings.

[23] Criminal Appeal Act 1995, sections 9–12.

[24] A draft bill was presented before the Senate on 24 March 1998 and, in September 2001, had been examined by the Commission of Justice of the Senate (Commissione Giustizia) since 26 October 1998. If adopted it would enable criminal proceedings to be reopened following a judgment of the European Court of Human Rights which finds a violation of Article 6 (3) (c) and (d), of the Convention (but not Article 6 (1), (2) or (3)(a) or (b)).

[25] *Socialist Party and others* v. *Turkey* (App. 21237/93), Judgment of 25 May 1998; (1999) 27 EHRR 51; see ch. 14 above

[26] Interim Resolution DH(99)245.

Following this interim resolution, on 8 August 1999, Mr Perinçek was released from prison having served two-thirds of his sentence, and on 8 September 1999 the Ankara State Security Court decided to lift the execution of all sanctions imposed on him as a result of his criminal conviction.

GENERAL MEASURES

The aim of general measures is to prevent the recurrence of similar violations of the Convention. There are many examples of States taking action as a result of findings of violations of the Convention, including, in the United Kingdom, amendment of the law on contempt of court,[27] changes to rules on prisoners' correspondence,[28] the abolition of corporal punishment on the Isle of Man[29] and in schools,[30] and the decriminalization of consensual homosexual acts in Northern Ireland.[31] Sometimes the changes made are less salutary. For example, the Court held in the *Abdulaziz, Cabales and Balkandali* case[32] that immigration rules which permitted men to bring their non-national wives to live with them in the United Kingdom, but did not allow women in the same position to gain entry clearance for their husbands, gave rise to a violation of Articles 8 and 14 taken together. The Government's response— accepted, as it had to be, by the Committee of Ministers—was to bring an end to the discrimination by removing the right of entry for husbands and wives alike.

Over half of the general measures taken by respondent States involve changes to legislation. Other general measures include administrative reforms, changes to court practice or the introduction of human rights training of the police, for example.

As mentioned above, the Committee's Rules provide that, until it is satisfied with the measures taken by a State to comply with a judgment of the Court, that case will return to the Committee's agenda every six months at least. On the whole, States are relatively quick to implement the recommendations of the Committee in respect of general measures, sometimes even adopting the necessary measures before the case in question comes before the Committee or even

[27] Following *Sunday Times* v. *United Kingdom*, Judgment of 26 April 1979, Series A, No. 30; (1979–80) 2 EHRR 245.

[28] Following *Silver and others* v. *United Kingdom*, Judgment of 25 March 1983, Series A, No. 61; (1983) 5 EHRR 347.

[29] Following *Tyrer* v. *United Kingdom*, Judgment of 25 April 1978, Series A, No. 26; (1979–80) 2 EHRR 1.

[30] Following *Campbell and Cosans* v. *United Kingdom*, Judgment of 25 February 1982, Series A, No. 48; (1982) 4 EHRR 293.

[31] Following *Dudgeon* v. *United Kingdom*, Judgment of 22 October 1981, Series A, No. 45; (1982) 4 EHRR 149.

[32] Judgment of 28 May 1985, Series A, No. 94; (1985) 7 EHRR 471.

the Court.[33] The newer Central and Eastern European Member States have also shown themselves prompt to carry out the changes required for compliance with the Court's judgments: within eight months of the *Assenov* judgment[34], for example, Bulgaria had adopted a major reform of its criminal procedure.[35] A written question put by four members of the Parliamentary Assembly to the Committee in September 1998,[36] identified only seven cases which had at that time been pending before the Committee for more than three years waiting for general measures to be taken for their adequate execution.

Frequently, delays in implementation relate to technical problems rather than political resistance in the State concerned. The case which has so far taken the longest time to be resolved to the Committee's satisfaction was *Gaskin* v. *the United Kingdom*, where the Court, in its judgment of 7 July 1989,[37] found a violation based on the absence of any procedure to determine when the interests of an individual brought up in public care in having access to his or her medical and other records should outweigh the public interest in the confidentiality of such data. Almost immediately the Government enacted legislation to facilitate access to personal data,[38] but the new provisions did not have retroactive effect and did not, as required by the Court's judgment, provide for a fully independent review of a refusal to disclose information. According to the information provided by the Government to the Committee, the legislative work required to ensure full compliance with the judgment became increasingly complex because of a desire to create a general right of access by the public to documents held by the authorities. It was not until July 2000, following the coming into force of the Data Protection Act 1998, that the Committee adopted its final resolution in the case.[39]

In another long-running case, *Modinos* v. *Cyprus*, the Court in a judgment dated 22 April 1993[40] found a violation of Article 8 of the Convention arising from the criminalization in Cyprus of private homosexual relations. Between 1995 and 1998 various draft laws were put before Parliament with a view to lifting the ban, but at each attempt the legislation was blocked following extensive debate. Finally, an Act was passed by the Cypriot Parliament on 21 May

---

[33] e.g. the Court 'noted with satisfaction' in *Findlay* v. *United Kingdom*, Judgment of 25 February 1997 that the UK had implemented changes to its court-martial procedure following the Commission's finding of a violation of Article 6.

[34] *Assenov and others* v. *Bulgaria* (App. 24760/94), Judgment of 28 October 1998; (1999) 28 EHRR 652.

[35] Law no. 70/1999, adopted 22 July 1999, published in the *Official Gazette* on 6 August 1999.

[36] See 'Execution of certain judgments forwarded to, or certain cases pending before, the Committee of Ministers', Reply from the Committee of Ministers to Written Question No. 378, Council of Europe document no. 8253, 29 October 1998.

[37] Series A, No. 160.

[38] The Access to Personal Files Act 1987 and the Access to Personal Files (Social Services) Regulations 1989.

[39] DH (2000) 106, 24 July 2000.

[40] Series A, No. 259.

1998. However, the terms of the new legislation, similar to that included in the United Kingdom's Sexual Offences Act 1967[41], have, at the time of writing, still not finally been approved by the Committee.

Perhaps more serious is the situation where measures are required to remedy a whole series of cases which highlight an ingrained and persistent problem within the respondent State. An example relates to the actions of the Turkish security forces in South-Eastern Turkey. In a large and increasing number of judgments, the Court has found violations of Articles 2, 3, 5, 6, 8, and 13 of the Convention and Article 1 of Protocol No. 1, in respect of villages destroyed by security forces,[42] torture or serious ill-treatment of Kurds held in police custody,[43] and breaches of the right to life or disappearances.[44] In almost all of these cases the Court in addition found breaches of the Convention relating to the absence of adequate official investigations into the allegations in question, giving rise to the virtual impunity of agents of the State and a lack of effective domestic remedies for their Kurdish victims.

The Committee has been grappling with these problems since 1996. To date, the Turkish Government has informed it of certain general measures taken in response to the above findings of violation. These measures include the translation into Turkish of the relevant judgments of the Court and their publication in legal journals and distribution to members of the security forces. In addition, on 2 December 1999 a law was passed transferring the power to investigate alleged human rights abuses by the security forces from local administrative councils to prefects or subprefects. However, a major reform of basic management and continued training of police, recommended by the Committee by an interim resolution in June 1999,[45] has not, at the time of writing, been implemented.

As for measures taken by the Turkish Government specifically to combat the prevalence of torture, the maximum penalty in respect of State agents found guilty of ill-treating suspects has been increased, although no minimum sentence has been set. On 6 May 1997, legislation came into force reducing the maximum length of time during which a person can be detained before being brought before a magistrate; the maximum period for 'collective crimes', allegedly involving more than one person, was reduced from 15 to 7 days (still

[41] Which gave rise to a finding of violation in *ADT* v. *United Kingdom* (App. 35765/97), Judgment of 31 July 2000; (2001) 31 EHRR 803.

[42] The first cases of this type were *Akdivar and others* v. *Turkey*, Judgment of 16 September 1996; *Menteş and others* v. *Turkey*, Judgment of 28 November 1997; *Selçuk and Asker* v. *Turkey*, Judgment of 24 April 1998.

[43] The first findings of torture against Turkey were in *Aksoy* v. *Turkey*, Judgment of 18 December 1996; *Aydin* v. *Turkey*, Judgment of 25 September 1997; and *Tekin* v. *Turkey*, Judgment of 9 June 1998.

[44] The first cases of this type were *Kaya* v. *Turkey*, Judgment of 19 February 1998 and *Kurt* v. *Turkey*, Judgment of 25 May 1998.

[45] Interim Resolution DH(99)434.

too long), and from 30 to 10 days for crimes allegedly committed within the State of Emergency region (which encompasses most of South-East Turkey). For individual crimes, the time-limits have dropped from 96 to 48 hours. In addition, various safeguards for the detainee have been introduced: for example, a person held in preliminary detention now has the right, at any time after the first four days in custody, to see a lawyer and to apply for *habeas corpus*. Such a person must also be examined by a doctor at the beginning and end of the period of detention.

The above measures are far from adequate to resolve the problems highlighted in the Court's judgments. The Committee continues to press the Turkish authorities and holds a comprehensive debate every six months or so.

Another notorious example of persistent and recurring human rights violations is the Italian length of proceedings cases.[46] Here it appears that some small progress is being made, although to a certain extent it appears that the problems within the Italian legal system are so deep-rooted and pernicious that there is a limit to what the Government can do to put bring about effective reform. In order to remedy the situation the Italian Government informed the Committee in early 1995 that it had instituted a new office of justice of the peace and had hired approximately 5,000 magistrates to perform this function. In addition, a number of procedural simplifications were proposed, and the Committee accepted these measures as execution in a number of cases.[47] In the summer of 1997 it took note of additional measures, including the hiring of another thousand new judges to deal specifically with the backlog of cases.[48] On 25 October 2000 the Committee adopted a further interim resolution[49] which 'note[d] with satisfaction' that:

[R]ecently the highest Italian authorities have manifested, both at the national level and before the organs of the Council of Europe, their solemn commitment to finding eventually an effective solution to the present situation and the progress made in the implementation of the major reform of the Italian judicial system, undertaken in order notably to find long-term remedies, to ensure special expediency in the treatment of the oldest and most deserving cases and to alleviate the burden of the Court.

The reforms implemented included 'the deep structural modernization of the judicial system for better long-term efficiency' (notably through the introduction of Article 6 of the Convention into the Italian Constitution, the streamlining of the jurisdictions of the civil and administrative courts, the increased reliance on a single judge, the creation of the office of justices of the peace and also the subsequent extension of their competence to minor criminal offences,

---

[46] See ch. 8 above.
[47] See e.g. *Zanghi* v. *Italy*, Resolution DH(95)82.
[48] DH(97)336.
[49] Res DH(2000)135.

new simplified dispute settlements mechanisms, the modernization of a number of procedural rules), special actions dealing with the oldest cases pending before the national civil courts or aiming at structural improvements which it was hoped would bring results in the near future (in particular the creation of provisional court chambers composed of honorary judges, entrusted with the solution of civil cases pending since May 1995, a substantial increase in the number of judges and administrative personnel and two important resolutions by the Supreme Council of the Magistrature laying down a number of monitoring mechanisms and issuing special guidelines for judges in order to prevent further unreasonably long proceedings and to speed up those which had already been incriminated by the European Court of Human Rights), and the creation of a domestic remedy in cases of excessive length of procedures.

The Committee concluded that Italy, while making undeniable efforts to solve the problem and having adopted measures of various kinds which allowed the concrete hope of an improvement within a reasonable time, had not, so far, thoroughly complied with its obligations to abide by the Court's judgments and the Committee of Ministers' decisions finding violations of Article 6 of the Convention on account of the excessive length of judicial proceedings. It called upon the State to continue with the reforms, and decided to continue examining the matter at yearly intervals.

SANCTIONS

Rolv Ryssdal, former President of the Court, once remarked, '[the Convention], as an international treaty that encroaches on domestic law, relies for its enforcement on a combination of binding legal obligation and the traditional good faith required of the signatories to an international agreement.'[50]

However, in addition to good faith, a number of pressures and interests combine to encourage States to comply with the legal obligation to take restitutory measures created by a finding of a violation by the Court.

The first of these is the common interest in a stable Europe. The Convention was drafted and adopted in the aftermath of the Second World War, when European unity and the promotion and support of strong democracies throughout the continent were seen as essential to the security of all. This objective for the Convention system again came to the fore after the collapse of

---

[50] Lecture given at Masaryk University, 20 March 1996; and see also Mr Ryssdal's article 'The Enforcement System set up under the European Convention of Human Rights' in *Compliance with Judgments of International Courts: Symposium in Honour of Prof. Henry G. Schermers* (Leiden, 1994).

communism in Central and Eastern Europe in 1989, when it became apparent that Europe could no longer hope to rely on the Cold War fear of mutual annihilation to maintain order and stability. If the Member States of the Council of Europe aspire to strengthen democracy and the rule of law in the Balkans or in Turkey, for example, it is essential that every government is seen to comply willingly with the Court's judgments and the Committee's recommendations. This is the very basis of the collective enforcement of human rights.

In addition, in respect of those States which are not yet part of the European Union but that wish to join, a good record in Strasbourg is seen as an important precondition for membership. The Committee of Ministers' powers are thus reinforced by a certain indirect economic incentive.

There are a number of ways in which the Committee can attempt to influence a government. The first of these is confidential peer pressure: the ministers and their representatives are obliged to keep attending the Committee's meetings and will be reluctant to be seen—or rather, to have their governments seen—as unrepentant violators of human rights. The potency of this type of pressure should not be underestimated. In addition, on a more formal and public level, the Chairman of the Committee can make use of bilateral letters to notify the government concerned of the Committee's views on any particular matter.

In recent years the Committee has made increasing use of interim resolutions as a way of publicizing problems it is encountering in the enforcement of judgments. In addition, the Council of Europe's Parliamentary Assembly appears to be taking a greater interest in the Committee's work under the Convention, and, through the use of Parliamentary questions, may elicit information about the progress of a case and highlight a State's failure adequately to cooperate.

The ultimate sanction available to the Committee is the threat of expulsion from the Council of Europe under Articles 8 and 3 of the Council's Statute.[51] So far, in the history of the Council, the Committee has never made use of its powers to suspend a Member State, although it came close to doing so in 1970, when the military dictatorship which had seized power in Greece in 1967

---

[51] The Statute of the Council of Europe (London, 5 May 1949), provides in Article 3:

> Every member of the Council of Europe must accept the principles of the rule of law and of the enjoyment by all persons within its jurisdiction of human rights and fundamental freedoms, and collaborate sincerely and effectively in the realisation of the aim of the Council as specified in Chapter I.

Article 8 states:

> Any member of the Council of Europe which has seriously violated Article 3 may be suspended from its rights of representation and requested by the Committee of Ministers to withdraw under Article 7. If such member does not comply with this request, the Committee may decide that it has ceased to be a member of the Council as from such date as the Committee may determine.

declared that it considered the finding by the Commission in an inter-State case of a number of serious human rights violations, including torture,[52] to be 'null and void' and that it '[did] not consider itself legally bound by the conclusions of the said report'.[53] In the event, however, Greece withdrew from the Council of Europe without being expelled, and did not join again until the dictatorship had been overthrown.

More recently, the Turkish Government similarly repudiated the Court's judgments in the case of *Loizidou* v. *Turkey*,[54] where the Court found that the denial to a Greek Cypriot of access to her property in Northern Cyprus was a breach of Article 1 of the First Protocol to the Convention (right to peaceful enjoyment of property), imputable to Turkey, and ordered the payment of substantial compensation. On 22 September 1998 the Committee's President of the time, the Greek Minister of Foreign Affairs, told the Parliamentary Assembly:[55]

A few weeks ago the Turkish Ministry of Foreign Affairs convened the ambassadors of the Council of Europe member States posted in Ankara and handed them a memorandum. In this memorandum it is clearly stated that Turkey will not comply with the Court's judgment, on the grounds that the Turks consider that they are not liable for what is going on in the occupied part of Cyprus. If Turkey insists on her refusal beyond the three-month term provided for the execution of the Court's judgment, the Committee of Ministers will certainly assume its responsibility, pro-vided by Article 54 of the Convention of Human Rights, and will—I am sure—use all statutory means at its disposal to obtain the execution of the Court's judgment. If Turkey does not pay the compensation and does not take individual measures to restore Mrs Loizidou's rights, putting an end to their violation, then Turkey is simply being consistent with what it has already declared. In such a case the problem is not with Turkey, the problem remains with the other members of the Committee of Ministers.

At the time of writing,[56] Turkey still refuses to pay the just satisfaction awarded by the Court.[57] The Committee of Ministers has adopted a number of interim resolutions, the most recent of which, dated 26 June 2001,[58] read as follows:

---

[52] *Denmark* v. *Greece; Norway* v. *Greece; Sweden* v. *Greece; Netherlands* v. *Greece*, Decision of the Commission, 25 *Yearbook* 92–116.

[53] Resolution DH (70) 1.

[54] Judgments of 23 March 1995 (preliminary objections) Series A, No. 310, 18 December 1996 (merits) and 28 July 1998 (Article 50).

[55] See the verbatim record of the afternoon debate on 22 September 1998, available from the Council of Europe.

[56] April 2002.

[57] It seems likely that similar problems will arise with the execution of the Court's judgment of 10 May 2001 in the inter-State case, *Cyprus* v. *Turkey*.

[58] No. Res DH(2001)80.

The Committee of Ministers . . .

Recalling its Interim Resolution DH (2000) 105, in which it declared that the refusal of Turkey to execute the judgment of the Court demonstrated a manifest disregard for Turkey's international obligations, both as a High Contracting Party to the Convention and as a member State of the Council of Europe, and strongly insisted that, in view of the gravity of the matter, Turkey comply fully and without any further delay with this judgment;

Very deeply deploring the fact that, to date, Turkey has still not complied with its obligations under this judgment;

Stressing that every member State of the Council of Europe must accept the principles of the rule of law and of the enjoyment by all persons within its jurisdiction of human rights and fundamental freedoms;

Stressing that acceptance of the Convention, including the compulsory jurisdiction of the Court and the binding nature of its judgments, has become a requirement for membership of the Organisation;

Stressing that the Convention is a system for the collective enforcement of the rights protected therein,

Declares the Committee's resolve to ensure, with all means available to the Organisation, Turkey's compliance with its obligations under this judgment,

Calls upon the authorities of the member States to take such action as they deem appropriate to this end.

It is not clear what the Committee intended by the final sentence of this interim resolution. It can be interpreted merely as a request for States to exert further diplomatic pressure on Turkey, or to refuse Turkey's request for membership of the European Union until the problem is resolved. In the alternative, this final sentence could be seen as a veiled threat of expulsion.

The situation in Cyprus has long proved intractable, and negotiations under the auspices of the United Nations have, after many years, reached stalemate. It is, perhaps, unrealistic to hope that the Committee of Ministers will succeed in resolving the situation: it does not even appear to have begun considering what general measures may be required, in addition to the payment of compensation. Nonetheless, it is no exaggeration to say that the manner in which the Committee—and, on a wider level, the Governments of the Member States—deal with Turkey on this issue could make or break the entire Convention system. If Turkey is permitted to disregard with impunity the Court's judgments, it will set a highly undesirable precedent. Nonetheless, Turkey's expulsion would seem to be at odds with the prevailing philosophy within the Council of Europe, that human rights can best be protected by working with a State within the organization.[59] The country's strategic position as a buffer between Europe and the Middle East can also not be forgotten.

---

[59] This principle was instrumental in the acceptance as members of a number of new democracies which clearly fell far short, in many areas, of the Convention standards. Thus, for example, the Parliamentary Assembly's Political Affairs Committee, which made an initial assessment as to whether

It would appear, therefore, that the Committee may be called upon to develop a more flexible range of sanctions. One proposal is the award of punitive damages by the Court in cases of violations so frequently repeated that they amount to a 'practice' of violation of the Convention,[60] or a system of daily fines against States which delay too long in making reparation.[61] The Committee could also perhaps draw on the experience of the International Labour Organisation which, in the face of Myanmar's (Burma's) repeated refusal to take concrete action to comply with the ILO's Convention on Forced Labour, adopted, on 14 June 2000, an unprecedented resolution giving the country five months to rectify the situation. If this failed to occur to the satisfaction of the ILO's Governing Body, a number of measures were to apply, including a recommendation to international organizations, governments, employers' and workers' associations to cease all relations with Myanmar which might, directly or indirectly, have the effect of perpetuating the practice of forced labour.[62]

CONCLUDING COMMENTS

In the first few decades of its existence, the organs of the European Convention system, in contrast to those of other regional and international systems for the protection of human rights,[63] were privileged in that their field of application extended, on the whole, to a relatively homogeneous region of Europe where democracy and the rule of law were well established. However, this region has now expanded to the borders of Asia, to incorporate new Member States which have developed very different cultures and traditions from those prevailing in the West. The Committee is increasingly being called upon to deal with grave and endemic breaches of human rights.

Historically, the Committee has largely relied on good faith and diplomatic pressure to ensure compliance with the Court's judgments. Apart from all-out expulsion from the Council of Europe, which risks being counter-productive to

Russia's request for membership should be granted, reported that, although Russia did not meet the Council of Europe's standards, membership of the organization 'would enable the support and pressure that have so often been identified as essential to progress': *Report by the Political Affairs Committee on Russia's Request for Membership of the Council of Europe*, Muehlemann, Council of Europe document no. 7443, 2 January 1996, and see also the views expressed by members of the Parliamentary Assembly in the course of its debate on Russia's request for membership (25 January 1996, Official Report, Council of Europe document no. AS (1996) CR 7).

[60] See the discussion of the *Bottazzi* v. *Italy* judgment of 28 July 1999 in ch. 8 above.

[61] See the Report of the Parliamentary Assembly's Committee on Legal Affairs and Human Rights, Rapporteur, Mr Erik Jurgens, 12 July 2000, Doc. 8808.

[62] See the ILO's press release: www.ilo.org/public/english/bureau/inf/pr/2000/27.htm

[63] Such as the Inter-American and African systems.

the protection of human rights in the offending State, the sanctions available are limited. It is perhaps a testament to the efficacy of the Convention system as a whole that the Committee is only now, following Turkey's repudiation of the *Loizidou* judgment, being called upon to develop a more flexible range of powers.

In addition, measures should be adopted to facilitate the flow of information to the Committee. It is striking that at present, according to its Rules of Procedure, it is almost entirely dependent on information provided by the respondent State. It might, therefore, assist the Committee if it had at its disposal some sort of independent monitoring procedure or, at the very least, if its tiny secretariat were to be expanded to permit more time to be spent on monitoring. The Committee's work might also be greatly assisted by formal recognition of the benefits of receiving information from those with first-hand experience of the domestic situation, namely individual applicants and concerned non-governmental organizations.

26

RESULTS AND PROSPECTS

INTRODUCTION

The European Convention on Human Rights has attained a leading place in the development of international human rights protection. It has been regarded as a 'chapter in a developing European constitution'.[1] The Convention system has become an integral part of the Council of Europe system; States wishing to become parties to the Statute of the Council of Europe are required to sign the Convention. Following the entry into force of Protocol 11, there is now a pan-European judicial system for the protection of human rights which applies to over 800 million people in forty-three countries.

The most significant recent development has been the expansion of the Council of Europe as the newly emerged democracies of Central and Eastern Europe have established closer ties with Western Europe. The Council of Europe took the view that adapting the existing Convention offered a better solution than the introduction of new arrangements for an enlarged Council of Europe. The late President of the European Court of Human Rights, Rolv Ryssdal, commented:

Thoughts—with an eye to Greater Europe—of replacing the Strasbourg system by new European rules and arrangements in the wider framework of the CSCE have become pointless in view of the not unexpected willingness of central and east European States to join the Council of Europe. The danger that European protection of fundamental rights might become fragmented by the introduction of a special catalogue of such rights into European Community law likewise seems to have been averted. Credit for all this is due not least to the Secretary-General of the Council of Europe, Mrs Lalumière, formerly French Minister of European Affairs, who since the end of the eighties has, like me, argued for the consolidation and further development of the Strasbourg system of legal protection. In so doing, she has recognised, doubtless correctly, that a new European agreement on fundamental rights, if at all achievable, would certainly not be able to match what the European Human Rights Convention can guarantee in the way of legal protection.[2]

[1] F. Jacobs, 'Human Rights in Europe: New Dimensions' (1992) 3 KCLJ 49, at 50. See also R. Ryssdal, *Forty Years of the European Convention on Human Rights*, Address at Vienna on 18 January 1991, Council of Europe document Cour (91) 61, at 12; and Ryssdal, 'On the road to a European Constitutional Court' in *Collected Courses of the Academy of European Law*, ii. bk. 2, (Dordrecht, 1993), 1.

[2] Ryssdal, *European Human Rights Protection in the Year 2000*, address to Potsdam University Law Faculty Conference, 3–5 June 1992, at 18. Council of Europe document Cour (92) 173.

The principal achievement of the Convention has been the establishment of a formal system of legal protection available to individuals covering a range of civil and political rights, which has become the European standard. As arguably the most developed system of legal protection worldwide, it has also contributed to the development of the global definition and understanding of the substantive content of the rights it protects. It has been the model for the American Convention on Human Rights of 1969 and was a key text to which reference was made in the drafting of the African Convention on Human and Peoples Rights. It has also been a reference point for courts in countries such as Australia, Canada, and India.[3]

The key challenge the system faces is coping with an ever-increasing caseload. The changes made by Protocol 11 have not set in place the machinery for dealing in a timely fashion with the number of applications currently being received by the Strasbourg machinery. Furthermore, the relationship between the Council of Europe machinery and the system for protecting fundamental rights operating within the Community legal order has not yet been definitively determined. In addition the Convention has never been static in its substantive coverage, and there remains an agenda for extending the range of rights protected under the system.

RESULTS: SUBSTANTIVE PROVISIONS

The catalogue of human rights in the European Convention is a statement of legal human rights,[4] that is, it consists of a system of rules, decisions, and principles. It confers rights, imposes duties, and establishes institutions to monitor and implement the specified rights and duties. The catalogue of rights in the European Convention is generally of civil and political rights based on liberal democratic ideals, though there are some rights, such as the provisions relating to education and property, which touch on economic, social, and cultural rights.[5]

In November 1950, when the Convention was signed, there was little existing material defining the content of human rights. The key document was the

---

[3] Ryssdal, *Europe: the Roads to Democracy. The Council of Europe and the 'architecture' of Europe,* speech at Colloquy organised by the Secretary-General of the Council of Europe in Strasbourg, 18–19 September 1990, Council of Europe document Cour (90) 223, at 2.

[4] On the distinction between legal, political, and moral human rights, see D. Meuwissen, 'Human Rights and the End of History' in R. Lawson and M. de Blois (eds.) *The Dynamics of the Protection of Human Rights in Europe: Essays in Honour of Henry G. Schermers* (Dordrecht, 1994), at 293.

[5] Under the Council of Europe system, such rights are primarily the province of the European Social Charter; see D. Harris, *The European Social Charter* (Charlottesville, 1984).

Universal Declaration of Human Rights which had been adopted by the General Assembly of the United Nations in December 1948.[6] It would be many years before the United Nations International Covenant on Civil and Political Rights introduced a more detailed statement of civil and political rights coupled with measures of implementation. The Strasbourg system accordingly became a pioneer in the elaboration of the content of the rights declared in the Convention. The contribution to an understanding of the content and extent of the rights protected by the case law of the Court, and to a lesser extent the decisions and reports of the European Commission, should not be underestimated both within the legal systems of the Contracting Parties to the Convention and beyond.

There is hardly an article of Section I of the Convention which has not spawned a case law defining and clarifying the content of the rights protected. There is now a body of case law imposing procedural requirements on States under Article 2 which provide additional guarantees that there will be proper respect for the right to life. Such requirements apply not only to those difficult circumstances where States face increasing threats of terrorist activity, but also to deaths arising in prisons and hospitals. Similar procedural requirements have been imposed on States under Article 3. The definitions of torture and inhuman and degrading treatment under Article 3[7] have shaped State conduct, particularly in the methods for dealing with the threats of terrorist activity, and in procedures for considering the deportation or extradition of individuals.

Other examples of the impact of the Convention case law can be found in the development of standards relating to the imposition of corporal punishment.[8] Various provisions of the Convention have interacted to produce a body of new protections for prisoners, for mental patients, and for transsexuals. The tendencies of the modern State to subject some within its jurisdiction to covert surveillance have been controlled by standards developed under the emerging case law under Article 8.[9] Even in areas where State regulation has a clear role to play, the Court has insisted that such basic rights as freedom of expression are given equal weight with the urge to regulate and restrict.[10] There is hardly an area of State regulation untouched by standards which have emerged from the application of Convention provisions to situations presented by individual applicants. For example, nationalizations and planning regulation must respect the right to property spelled out in the Convention.[11] There is emerging case law giving coherence and substance to the right to an effective remedy in the national legal order under Article 13.[12]

---

[6] General Assembly Resolution 217A of 10 December 1948, UNGAOR, 3rd session.
[7] See ch. 5 above.
[8] See ch. 5 above.
[9] See ch. 11 above.   [10] See. ch. 13 above.
[11] See ch. 15 above.   [12] See ch. 23 above.

Since the Convention is subsidiary to the protection of human rights in national law, the task of the Strasbourg organs involves treading a delicate path between developing and enhancing the standards inherent in the Convention text, and respect for the choices which individual States must make in the face of specific situations. Many of the rights protected are subject to limitations.[13] Setting the boundaries of those limitations has proved to be one of the most contentious aspects of the enforcement of the Convention provisions. Critics of the Court accuse it of accommodating States too readily; others recognize the value of the doctrine of the margin of appreciation as a valuable tool in allowing some differences in the standards adopted in Contracting States reflecting the absence of common values even among the States of Western Europe.[14]

RESULTS: PROCEDURAL PROVISIONS

The great success of the European Convention system has been in securing the acceptance of a machinery for the consideration of complaints from individuals, where they believe that their rights have been violated and where no remedy has been provided by the State. The willingness today of States to sign up to an exclusively judicial system and to a Court with automatic jurisdiction is quite remarkable. It is the more so when it is recalled that acceptance of any form of judicial settlement was initially very hesitant and that until relatively recently reference to the Court was very much the exception. Finally, the maturing of the system has to be set in a context where the Court has at times been bold in its interpretation of the substantive provisions of the Convention.

The role of the individual applicant before the Court has been improved. Initially, the individual was little more than a bystander when cases came before the Court, but individuals are now the main enforcer of Convention rights. However, the success of the Convention has brought with it an increase in the volume of individual applications, which has resulted in excessive delays in the determination of applications.

In virtually all Contracting States, the Convention provisions have been incorporated into national law, although this has not reduced the incidence of applications to the Court. The system may be the victim of its own success, and the number of applications an indication that even half a century after the introduction of the Convention's catalogue of fundamental rights, there remain

---

[13] See generally ch.10 above.
[14] Ryssdal, *The Future of the European Court of Human Rights*, Public lecture given at the Centre of European Law, King's College, London on 22 March 1990, Council of Europe document Cour (90) 296, at 6.

serious threats to their guarantee in very many Contracting States. Indeed, reactions to the horrific events of 11 September 2001 in the United States show quite how fragile some rights which had come to be taken for granted are in times of international crisis.

PROSPECTS: EXTENDING THE RIGHTS PROTECTED

The rights protected in the Convention and its Protocols are traditional civil and political rights. Yet even this restricted range of rights has not found universal acceptance even among the existing Contracting Parties. There are significant gaps in the ratifications to Protocol 1 on rights of property, education, and to free elections, to Protocol 4 on freedom of movement and related rights, to Protocol 6 on the death penalty, and to Protocol 7 on certain rights connected with the criminal process and equality in marriage. Protocol 12 adds a general right to equality of treatment and awaits the necessary ratifications to enter into force.[15]

In the past, there have been calls for a protocol dealing with the rights of persons deprived of their liberty, where such current protection as exists arises from the interaction of a number of provisions of the Convention.[16]

There are many Conventions which have been sponsored by the Council of Europe outside the European Convention and which touch on the protection of human rights.[17] The best known are the European Social Charter of 3 May 1996[18] and the European Convention for the Prevention of Torture and Inhuman or Degrading Treatment or Punishment of 26 November 1987.[19] Other examples include the Convention for the Protection of Individuals with regard to Automatic Processing of Personal Data of 28 January 1981,[20] the European Convention on the Legal Status of Children born out of Wedlock of 15 October 1975,[21] and the European Convention on Social Security of 14 December 1972.[22] Of particular significance are the European Charter for Regional or Minority Languages of 5 November 1992,[23] and the Framework Convention for the Protection of National Minorities of 1 February 1995.[24]

[15] See ch. 19 above.

[16] See speech by Ryssdal at the 7th International Colloquy on the European Convention on Human Rights, 30 May to 2 June 1990, Council of Europe document Cour (90) 152, at 4–6.

[17] For a full list of Council of Europe conventions see **conventions.coe.int/Treaty/EN/ CadreListeTraites.htm**

[18] ETS No. 163, in force since 1 July 1999, revising ETS No. 35.

[19] ETS No. 126, in force since 1 February 1989.   [20] ETS No. 108, in force since 1 October 1985.

[21] ETS No. 85, in force since 11 August 1978.   [22] ETS No. 78, in force since 1 March 1974.

[23] ETS No. 148, in force since 1 March 1998. See S. Wheatley, 'Minority Rights and Political Accommodation in the "New" Europe' (1997) 22 E L Rev HRC/63.

[24] ETS No. 157, in force since 1 February 1998.

Within the Council of Europe, there is certain to be a debate concerning the content of the Convention, which very much reflects the agenda of civil and political rights in 1950. Already, there is evidence of specialist arrangements providing for more detailed treatment of particular areas. The range of rights protected under the developing case law under Article 8 of the Convention suggests that there is a place for more detailed rules on the protection of privacy. There are also important rights, which are not touched upon by the Convention. One example is women's rights to equal pay and equal treatment,[25] though there is extensive coverage of these rights in European Community law.

The development of specifically European standards may at some stage produce conflict with other international agreements. The majority of the Contracting Parties to the European Convention are also party to international conventions on human rights protection having a global character.[26] The conflict has so far been avoided because generally the European standards have been more explicit and better developed than any global counterpart. It is also true that where other international bodies have been called upon to determine the content of rights protected, they have made reference to the deliberations of the European Court of Human Rights on similar issues. The result has been that, to date, the other international regimes have provided a base line of protection which the European Convention system has further developed as the minimum guarantee of protection in each of the Contracting States. These, in turn, have been able in many cases to provide a higher level of protection than the minimum level required by the European Convention throughout the jurisdictions of all the Contracting States.

PROSPECTS: THE RELATIONSHIP WITH THE EUROPEAN UNION

The development of the protection of human rights within the European Community is well documented.[27] Following expressions of concern, in particular, by the German and Italian constitutional courts that Community law did not afford the protections guaranteed by their Constitutions, the Court of Justice took its first tentative steps towards a system of human rights protection

[25] Some of these may be addressed by Protocol 12.
[26] See T. Opsahl, 'Ten years' coexistence Strasbourg—Geneva' in F. Matscher and H. Petzold (eds.), *Protecting Human Rights: The European Dimension. Essays in honour of Gérard Wiarda* (Köln, 1990), 431.
[27] See T. Hartley, *The Foundations of European Community Law* (Oxford, 1998), ch. 5; P. Craig and G. de Búrca, *EU Law. Text, Cases and Materials* (Oxford, 1998), ch. 7; P. Alston (ed.) *The EU and Human Rights* (Oxford, 1999); and K. Lenaerts, 'Fundamental rights in the European Union' (2000) 25 E L Rev 575.

for those affected by decisions of the institutions. In the *Stauder* case[28] the Court recognized incidentally that the general principles of Community law include fundamental human rights which are protected by the Court as such. In the *Internationale Handelsgesellschaft* case,[29] the Court ruled that respect for fundamental human rights forms an integral part of the protection of the general principles of law of the Community law, and that the protection of these rights, 'whilst inspired by the constitutional traditions common to the Member States, must be ensured within the framework of the structure and objectives of the Community.'[30] The *Nold* case[31] was the first in which direct reference was made to international treaties to which the Member States are parties, or in which they have collaborated, as providing guidelines which should be following within the framework of Community law. The necessity to refer to international agreements in which Member States had collaborated rather than referring expressly to the European Convention was necessitated by the fact that at the time France had not yet ratified the European Convention. In the *Rutili* case[32] the Court concluded that a particular provision of Community law was a 'specific manifestation of the more general principle' enshrined in the European Convention. This was a significant statement because strictly the recognition of the provision in the European Convention was not necessary for its decision.

In the *Hauer* case,[33] the Court cited specific reference to constitutional provisions in Germany, Ireland, and Italy, as well as to the European Convention, in concluding that the control of the use of property in issue in the case did not exceed the limitations allowed under any of these regimes.

The approach taken in the case law of the Court of Justice was endorsed by the political institutions in their Joint Declaration of 5 April 1977 which stressed the importance they attached to the protection of fundamental rights as derived from the constitutions of the Member States and from the European Convention, and confirmed the respect of all the institutions for such rights. This was followed by the inclusion in the Preamble to the Single European Act of 17 February 1986 of a reference to the European Convention. The Treaty on European Union, which entered into force on 1 November 1993, incorporated reference to the European Convention in Article F.2, which reads:

The Union shall respect fundamental rights, as guaranteed by the European Convention for the Protection of Human Rights and Fundamental Freedoms signed in Rome on 4 November 1950 and as they result from the constitutional traditions common to the Member States, as general principles of Community law.

[28] Case 29/69, *Stauder* v. *Ulm*, [1969] ECR 419.
[29] Case 11/70, *Internationale Handelsgesellschaft*, [1970] ECR 1125.
[30] Para. 4 of the judgment.
[31] Case 4/73, *Nold* v. *Commission*, [1974] ECR 491.
[32] Case 36/75, *Rutili*, [1975] ECR 1219.
[33] Case 44/79, *Hauer*, [1979]ECR 3727.

This provision takes over the language of the Court itself in its case law.[34] Despite this progress, the context in which human rights questions have arisen in Community law remains rather meagre. It is, however, now the position that the Court will review measures of the institutions for their compatibility with fundamental rights protected by the European Convention.

The Court of Justice has, however, not ignored the question of the extent to which the conduct of Member States may also be subject to review for compatibility with human rights standards when they are acting within the field of Community law. In such cases, the conduct of Member States can be called to account by the Court of Justice where they are directly implementing Community provisions.[35] Where the Member States are implementing Community law, the review may go further. So in the *ERT* case,[36] which concerned a Greek television monopoly, the Court took the view that any derogation by a Member State from the freedom to provide services under the EEC Treaty had to be compatible with the freedom of expression recognized under the European Convention on Human Rights. This formulation suggests that in any regulation by Member States of matters falling within the scope of Community, measures taken by Member States must as a matter of *Community law* comply with the Convention.

Differential interpretation is one risk of having two independent systems of human rights protection based upon the same set of rules and traditions.[37] In the *Hoechst* case,[38] the Court of Justice held that there was no fundamental right to the inviolability of the home in the Community legal order in regard to the business premises of undertakings on the grounds that there was insufficient common practice in the legal orders of the Member States on the protection afforded to business premises against intervention by the public authorities. But in three cases[39] the Court of Human Rights held that Article 8 was wide enough to encompass both the home when used for business purposes and professional premises. Despite this difference of interpretation, the Court of Justice went on

---

[34] The location of this provision in the Treaty on European Union (rather than its insertion into the EC Treaty) coupled with the limitations on the Court of Justice's jurisdiction under Art. L of the Treaty on European Union, avoids the incorporation of the European Convention (at least in relation to matters within the scope of the EC Treaty) by the back door.

[35] See Case C-5/88, *Wachauf*, [1989] ECR 2609, and cf. Case C-2/92, *Bostock*, [1994] ECR I-955.

[36] Case C-260/89, *ERT*, [1991] ECR I-2925. See also Opinion of Advocate General Jacobs in Case C-168/91, *Konstantinidis* v. *Altensteig-Standesamt*, [1993] ECR I-2755.

[37] R. Lawson, 'Confusion and Conflict? Diverging Interpretations of the European Convention on Human Rights in Strasbourg and Luxembourg' in R. Lawson and M. de Blois (eds.) *The Dynamics of the Protection of Human Rights in Europe: Essays in Honour of Henry G. Schermers* (Dordrecht, 1994), at 219.

[38] Joined Cases 46/87 and 227/88, *Hoechst* v. *Commission*, [1989] ECR 2859.

[39] *Chappell* v. *United Kingdom*, Judgment of 30 March 1989, Series A, No. 152; (1990) 12 EHRR 1; *Niemetz* v. *Germany*, Judgment of 16 December 1992, Series A, No. 251-B; and *Funke and others* v. *France*, Judgment of 25 February 1993, Series A, No. 256-A; (1993) 16 EHRR 297.

to rule that there was a general principle of Community law which required that any intervention in the private activities of any natural or legal person must have a legal basis, be justified on grounds laid down by law, and not be arbitrary or disproportionate in its application.

The cumulative effect of the case law of the Court of Justice is that the Court must have regard to national constitutions and to international instruments, especially the European Convention. The Convention is not formally binding on the Community, but its provisions can and must be given effect as general principles of Community law. The result is much the same as if the Community were bound by the Convention. This led to the question of whether the Community should accede to the European Convention, which was proposed by the Union's European Commission. The Council of the European Union responded by asking the Court of Justice, in accordance with the procedure in Article 228 of the EC Treaty,[40] for an Opinion on certain questions in connection with the proposed accession.[41] The Court of Justice ruled that 'as Community law now stands, the Community has no competence to accede to the European Convention.' The only possible basis for competence was Article 235 (now 308) of the EC Treaty.[42] Some Member States had argued that the Community was competent to accede to the European Convention because of the penetration of the protection of fundamental rights through the general principles of law. This is referred to in the Court's reasoning, but accession would, in the Court's view, require the integration of two separate systems for the protection of human rights. Such changes 'would be of constitutional significance and would therefore be such as to go beyond the scope of Article 235' and could only be brought about by way of amendments to the EC Treaty. The Opinion is very clever; it is argued that the response is legally correct in the context of the timing and the question asked. It serves to preserve in full the power of protection of fundamental rights by way of the application of the general principles of law. Few reading the Opinion can be left in any doubt about the complexities of integrating the European Community system and the Strasbourg system, and time has shown that there is no political will to make the relatively straightforward Treaty amendments needed to facilitate accession.

The debate about the rights which attach to citizenship of the European Union has, however, not gone away. This debate is fuelled not only by the inclusion of citizenship in the EC Treaty, but also by express reference to the

[40] Now Art. 300 of the EC Treaty.

[41] Opinion 2/94 on accession by the Community to the European Convention on Human Rights, [1996] ECR I-1759.

[42] This provides:

> If action by the Community should prove necessary to attain, in the course of the operation of the common market, one of the objectives of the Community and this Treaty has not provided the necessary powers, the Council shall, acting unanimously on a proposal from the Commission and after consulting the European Parliament, take the appropriate measures.

European Convention in the Treaty on European Union. That separation might, however, have beneficial results. The protections afforded by the European Convention are available to all those within the jurisdiction of the Contracting Parties regardless of their citizenship. Such rights are a core of rights which do not depend on the link of citizenship between the individual and the State. There are, however, other rights which are dependent on citizenship over and above the minimum guarantees of the European Convention. One obvious example is the right of citizens of the European Union to move freely within the territories of the Member States in order to take up employment under Article 39 (ex 48) of the EC Treaty. But it might be questioned whether it is fair to limit the ability to move to another Member States of a non-national who has lived and worked for many years in one of the Member States. Certainly the denial of the right to move is hardly consistent with viewing the territory of the Member States as a single unit for the purposes of economic activity.

The waters have been further clouded by the solemn proclamation of the Charter of Fundamental Rights of the European Union on 7 December 2000[43] at the Nice Council. This document has no legally binding force and there remain intriguing questions about its impact on the protection of fundamental rights within the European Union. It is divided into six sections[44] and includes rights for citizens of the European Union as well as certain rights which are to be applicable to all within the jurisdiction of the Member States. The rights are said to be based on the rights guaranteed by the European Convention, but in many cases there are intriguing differences of wording.[45] Its scope is considerably wider than the rights protected in the European Convention. A limited welcome can be offered to the EU Charter. As a declaratory document standing behind the legal recognition of fundamental rights, it is probably as good as it could be given that its purpose was not formally decided in advance of the Nice Council and given the manner in which it was constructed.[46]

---

[43] Referred to in this chapter as 'the EU Charter'.

[44] Dignity, freedoms, equality, solidarity, citizens' rights, and justice.

[45] e.g. Art. 9 of the EU Charter provides, 'The right to marry and the right to found a family shall be guaranteed in accordance with the national laws governing the exercise of these rights.' This could be interpreted as decoupling the right to marry and the right to found a family which are coupled in Article 12 of the Convention. Elsewhere there is a more sweeping approach to limitations which may be applied to certain rights.

[46] See G. de Búrca, 'The drafting of the European Union Charter of Fundamental Rights' (2001) 26 E L Rev 126.

PROSPECTS: COPING WITH THE
INCREASING WORKLOAD

Protocol 11 has successfully restructured the control machinery of the Strasbourg institutions, merging the part-time Commission and Court into a new permanent Court.[47] However, it has not delivered a lasting system for dealing with the continuing increase in the Court's caseload. This issue has been taken up in the Report of the Evaluation Group to the Committee of Ministers on the European Court of Human Rights.[48] Table 26.1 shows the growth in the work of the Court in recent years. However, the number of applications emanating from the Contracting States varies considerably, as Table 26.2 shows.[49] Finally, Table 26.3 shows the number of cases disposed of in 1999 and 2000. As at 31 July 2001, there were 18,292 case pending before the Court.[50] The projected number of cases which will be disposed of in 2001 is just over 9,000.

The report of the Evaluation Group suggests a fourfold category of judgments of the Court.[51] Category 1 judgments are leading judgments selected for publication in the reports of judgments and decisions of the Court.[52] Category 2 judgments are judgments dealing with new questions but not considered of sufficient importance to justify publication.[53] Category 3 judgments are judgments essentially applying existing case law.[54] Category 4 judgments are

Table 26.1

	1988	1999	2000	2001[a]
Provisional applications	4,044	20,538	26,398	35,553
Registered applications	1,013	8,402	10,486	13,558

Source: Report of the Evaluation Group to the Committee of Ministers on the European Court of Human Rights (2001), para. 25.

[a] Projected figures.

[47] A. Drzemczewski, 'The European Human Rights Convention: Protocol No 11—Entry into force and first year of application' (2000) 21 HRLJ 1.

[48] EG Court (2001) 1 of 27 September 2001. The Evaluation Group consisted of Justin Harman, Irish Ambassador to the Council of Europe, Luzius Wildhaber, President of the Court of Human Rights, and Hans Krüger, Deputy Secretary-General of the Council of Europe.

[49] Applications per million of population are not given for those countries with populations of less than one million.

[50] Either awaiting consideration of admissibility, or at a later stage of the adjudication process.

[51] Para. 32.

[52] In 1999 there were 58 such judgments, and in 2000 there were 94.

[53] In 1999 there were 4 such judgments, and in 2000 there were 35.

[54] In 1999 there were 28 such judgments, and in 2000 there were 81.

Table 26.2

State	Applications registered		Applications registered per 1 million population	
	1999	2000	1999	2000
Albania	1	3	0.3	0.9
Andorra	1	3		
Austria	227	241	28.0	29.8
Belgium	136	73	13.3	7.2
Bulgaria	196	304	25.1	39.1
Croatia	104	86	24.2	20.0
Cyprus	17	17		
Czech Republic	151	198	14.7	19.3
Denmark	56	56	10.6	10.6
Estonia	29	46	20.7	32.9
Finland	144	109	27.7	21.0
France	870	1032	14.7	17.4
FYRO Macedonia	16	18	8.0	9.0
Georgia	0	7	0.0	1.4
Germany	535	592	6.5	7.2
Greece	144	124	13.6	11.7
Hungary	94	161	9.3	16.0
Iceland	1	4		
Ireland	20	18	5.3	4.7
Italy	833	866	15.3	15.1
Latvia	29	80	12.1	33.3
Liechtenstein	1	3		
Lithuania	76	182	21.1	50.8
Luxembourg	12	15		
Malta	6	3		
Moldova	32	62	7.3	14.1
Netherlands	206	173	13.0	10.9
Norway	20	30	4.4	6.7
Poland	692	776	17.9	20.1
Portugal	112	98	11.2	9.8
Romania	295	640	13.2	28.6
Russia	971	1324	6.7	9.1
San Marino	0	1		
Slovak Republic	163	283	30.2	52.6
Slovenia	86	54	45.3	28.4
Spain	227	284	5.7	7.1
Sweden	175	232	19.7	26.2
Switzerland	156	187	21.4	25.6
Turkey	653	734	9.9	11.2
Ukraine	434	727	8.8	15.0
United Kingdom	431	640	7.2	10.8
Total	8,402	10,486	11.0	14.0

Source: Report of the Evaluation Group to the Committee of Ministers on the European Court of Human Rights (2001), para. 26.

Table 26.3

	1999	1999 percentage	2000	2000 percentage
Declared inadmissible or otherwise struck out of the list	3,519	94.2	6,774	87.8
Concluded by friendly settlement	39	1.0	227	2.9
Subject to a judgment on the merits	177	4.7	695	9.0
Struck out after admissibility decision	2	0.1	15	0.3
Total	3,737	100	7,711	100

Source: Report of the Evaluation Group to the Committee of Ministers on the European Court of Human Rights (2001), para. 28.

judgments in straightforward cases concerning the alleged excessive length of proceedings in national courts and tribunals.[55]

The Evaluation Group summarizes the current concerns in the following terms:

It is abundantly from the foregoing that immediate and urgent action is indispensable if the Court is to remain effective. If no steps are taken, the situation will simply deteriorate, with the Court having no prospect of 'catching-up' with its ever-increasing arrears of work. It will no longer be able to determine all cases within a reasonable time, its public image will suffer and it will gradually lose credibility. Moreover, constant seeking for greater 'productivity' obviously entails the risk that applications will not receive sufficient, or sufficient collective, consideration, to the detriment of the quality of judgments; on this account as well, the credibility and authority of the Court would suffer. Finally, it should be remembered that the problem cannot be seen solely in terms of statistics; the figures quoted say nothing as to the ratio of 'more difficult' to 'less difficult' cases, even though it may be that this will remain constant.[56]

In making proposals for addressing the management of workloads, the Evaluation Group adopted a number of premisses, which informed its recommendations:

- There should be no reduction in the substantive rights protected by the Convention.
- The right of individual petition should be maintained, since it lies at the heart of the Strasbourg machinery.
- The Court must be in a position to dispose of applications in a reasonable

---

[55] In 1999 there were 87 such judgments, and in 2000 there were 485.
[56] Report of the Evaluation Group, para. 39.

time while maintaining the quality and authority of its decisions and judgments.

Five avenues are explored as having a contribution to make to the problems presented by the current caseload of the Court.

NATIONAL MEASURES

The Evaluation Group addressed these issues first because the structure of the Convention is that the role of the Strasbourg machinery is subsidiary to the guaranteeing of Convention rights in the national legal orders.[57] The better the system of protection within the national legal orders, both in securing the rights guaranteed by the Convention, and in the machinery available in the national legal order for remedying violations of those rights, the fewer cases there will be that need determination by the Strasbourg organs. A particular area highlighted by the Evaluation Group is the ensuring by Contracting States of the availability of effective domestic remedies to prevent and redress violations of Convention rights. Emphasis is placed on the machinery for the proper investigation and establishment of the facts. The Evaluation Group also calls for the systematic screening of draft legislation and administrative procedures to ensure that they meet Convention standards.

THE EXECUTION OF JUDGMENTS

The Evaluation Group notes that the Court has had to deal with a large number of repetitive applications which have raised issues identical or very similar to matters already covered in judgments of the Court. This reflects a failure by Contracting States to respond fully and promptly to judgments of the Court. Had they done so, applications complaining of similar violations would not have come before the Court. However, the Evaluation Group expresses hesitation over three proposals put to it to address these difficulties:

- empowering the Committee of Ministers to seek interpretative rulings from the Court where problems arise over the execution of judgments;
- the imposition of financial penalties for non-execution of a judgment;
- the giving in judgments of the Court of more precise indications of the measures which the Contracting State must take in the face of the Court's decision in the case.

The Evaluation Group recommends that steps are taken to identify lookalike cases when transmitting a judgment to the Committee of Ministers, so that the lookalike cases can be put into suspense pending action by the respondent State, which might remove the need for adjudication of those cases.

[57] Paras. 44–7.

Consideration of any judgment involving multiple lookalike cases would be expedited by the Committee of Ministers.

MEASURES IN STRASBOURG WHICH REQUIRE NO AMENDMENTS TO THE CONVENTION

The Evaluation Group[58] begins by rejecting two proposals which had been put to it: that legal representation should be compulsory at all stages in order to improve the quality of applications; and the abandonment of the current practice under which an applicant may use any one of the thirty-seven official languages of the Contracting States up to the time when the admissibility decision is taken.[59] Both were rejected because of the possibility that the effect could be to exclude meritorious applicants for financial reasons unless adequate legal aid and translation services were to be available in every Contracting State.

Among proposals under consideration within the Court are the refusal to register certain applications, including those that are 'obviously far-fetched and those that do not satisfy the formal conditions set out in the Rules of Court'.[60] The details of this proposal could run the risk of excluding meritorious applications which are not presented well at the initial stages. Less controversial are proposals that registered applications would be certified by officials of the Court as being admissible and manifestly well-founded, or prima-facie admissible, or be recommended for communication to the respondent State concerned for its observations. Those certified as admissible and manifestly well-founded would be dealt with on the merits by a summary procedure by a Chamber, unless the respondent State objected. Those certified as prima-facie admissible would be dealt with by a Chamber of judges under a summary procedure in which the decision on admissibility and the judgment on the merits would be combined.[61] Where the official recommended communication to the respondent State, the existing procedure before a Chamber would be followed.

The Evaluation Group also recommends that consideration is given to the establishment of a special unit within the registry to deal with the facilitation of friendly settlements.[62]

---

[58] Paras. 54–67.
[59] After admissibility or in communications and pleadings in respect of a hearing, applicants are currently required to use either English or French.
[60] Para. 58.
[61] Both forms of summary procedure would afford an opportunity to conclude a friendly settlement.
[62] This work is currently undertaken by the Section Registrars.

RESOURCES

Running the Court is not, in the context of typical government expenditure, expensive. The draft budget for 2002 is €29.2 million.[63] This section of the Evaluation Group's report is, as might be expected, full of detailed information about staffing and accommodation needs.[64] It is clear that, without further commitment to enhanced resourcing of the Strasbourg machinery, there can be little hope that applications will be determined in a reasonable time with the care they deserve.

MEASURES IN STRASBOURG REQUIRING AMENDMENTS TO THE CONVENTION

The final group of measures would require amendment of the Convention.[65] The Evaluation Group notes that, whatever other steps are taken, there is a limit to the number of cases which can be determined under a system allowing for a single judge from each Contracting State. However, the favoured solution is not an increase in the number of judges, but a reduction in the caseload coming before the Court coupled with the possibility of additional 'stand-by' judges who might be drafted in to deal with peaks in the Court's caseload or to provide relief where the caseload from a Contracting State placed too great a burden on the national judge. A further proposal is for the term of office to become a single non-renewable term of at least nine years.

Other proposals are also rejected. The idea of regional tribunals is rejected on the grounds of expense as well as the risk of diverging standards and case law.[66] Preliminary rulings and an expansion of the competence to give advisory opinions are also rejected; the Evaluation Group suggests that further detailed study of these ideas is needed and priority should be given to resolving the current workload problems before introducing new jurisdictions. Conferment of powers of decision on officials is rejected as being contrary to the principle of a judicial decision. Finally, proposals to reduce the size of Committees and Chambers are rejected because it is Registry more than judicial time which is currently lacking, and that any decrease in the size of Chambers would make it difficult to achieve the requisite balance between members having regard to geographical origin, gender, and legal system of origin.

The Evaluation Group is in favour of changes which would allow much greater discretion to the Court over the cases which it admits for determination in Strasbourg. This would operate as a second-stage admissibility decision, and

---

[63] Para. 17 of the Report of the Evaluation Group.
[64] Paras. 68–79.
[65] Paras. 80–98.
[66] A parenthetical comment refers to improvement of the role played by national courts and tribunals as 'Convention courts': para. 83.

would not replace the current admissibility criteria. An unfettered discretion is rejected, but the Group concludes:

[T]he Evaluation Group has come to the view that a provision should be inserted into the Convention that would, in essence, empower the Court to decline to examine in detail applications which raise no substantial issue under the Convention. The Group does not see it as its task to formulate such a provision, notably since this would require detailed study by the appropriate Council of Europe bodies in conjunction with the Court, with which outside bodies should be associated.[67]

Three points are made about the elaboration of the proposed new power. First, that the interpretation of any such provision would have to be worked out by the Court over a period of time, having regard, among other things, to 'the situation obtaining in the respondent State and the extent to which effective domestic remedies are available'.[68] Secondly, the proposal should not be seen as a panacea for the workload problems. Finally, this is not a proposal designed to restrict the right of individual petition, and should be coupled with some mechanism by which applications which are not accepted because they raise no substantial issue under the Convention can be referred back for reconsideration within the national legal order.

The final proposal calls for a study of the possibility of attaching a new 'division' to the Court composed of 'assessors' which would ensure that judges 'are left with sufficient time to devote to what have been called "constitutional judgments", i.e. fully reasoned and authoritative judgments in cases which raise substantial or new and complex issues of human rights law.'[69] This is very reminiscent of the process by which a Court of First Instance came to be attached to the Court of Justice of the European Communities.[70] The notion of decisions by assessors appears to be a cheap version of a second court; it is difficult to see how what are, in effect, judicial decisions can be taken by other than designated judicial personnel.

At its 109th session in November 2001, the Committee of Ministers adopted a declaration urging all Contracting States to ensure the existence of effective remedies at national level in respect of the rights guaranteed by the European Convention and warmly welcoming the Report of the Evaluation Group. It instructed the Ministers' deputies to pursue urgent consideration of all the recommendations contained in the report and to report back at the 111th session in November 2002.[71]

---

[67] Para. 93.   [68] Para. 94.

[69] Para. 98

[70] See F. Brown and T. Kennedy, *Brown and Jacobs: The Court of Justice of the European Communities* (London, 2000), ch. 5.

[71] Declaration on the protection of human rights and fundamental freedoms in Europe— guaranteeing the long-term effectiveness of the European Court of Human Rights, adopted by the Committee of Ministers at its 109th Session, Strasbourg, 8 November 2001.

CONCLUSION

A former President of the European Court of Human Rights described the Court as emerging as a 'fully fledged international tribunal' which deals with diverse grievances brought to it by individuals which not only allege violations of the right to liberty or the right to the proper administration of justice, but also touch on 'some aspect of social, political or even economic life in the respondent Convention country.'[72]

Though there are certain to be conventions setting detailed standards in particular areas, there will remain a central role for a more general catalogue of rights, which provides the essential core of fundamental rights which surrounds everyone within the jurisdiction of the Contracting States. That catalogue will be extended, and there will come a time when the substantive provisions of the Convention and its Protocols will need to be consolidated.

Together the Commission and the Court have ensured that the European Convention has become the most sophisticated regional machinery for the protection of human rights. Substance has been given to the rights in Section I of the Convention and the accompanying Protocols. The Contracting Parties have all accepted that individuals within their jurisdiction can raise a complaint before the Strasbourg organs if they believe that the State has not accorded them the protection guaranteed by the Convention. The current President of the Court has noted that 'impervious and imperious sovereignty has yielded to a culture of international accountability of states and indeed individuals.'[73] Those are huge achievements in the half century since the Convention was signed. The signing of the European Convention on 4 November 1950 in the Palazzo Barberini represented a milestone in the protection of human rights in Europe. Fifty years later the system introduced by the Convention is at another milestone, facing the challenge of ensuring the continuing effectiveness and development of the protection of human rights for over 800 million people in forty-three countries of a wider democratic Europe.

[72] Ryssdal, 'The European Court of Human Rights and Gérard Wiarda' in F. Matscher and H. Petzold (eds.), *Protecting Human Rights: The European Dimension. Essays in honour of Gérard Wiarda* (Köln, 1990), 1, at 2.

[73] Luzius Wildhaber, President of the Court of Human Rights speaking at the ceremony to commemorate the fiftieth anniversary of the European Convention, reproduced in *The European Convention on Human Rights at 50, Human Rights Information Bulletin No. 50, Special Issue,* 2000, at 41.

Appendix

TEXT OF THE EUROPEAN CONVENTION AS MODIFIED BY PROTOCOL 11

CONVENTION FOR THE PROTECTION OF HUMAN RIGHTS AND FUNDAMENTAL FREEDOMS

The governments signatory hereto, being members of the Council of Europe,
Considering the Universal Declaration of Human Rights proclaimed by the General Assembly of the United Nations on 10th December 1948;
Considering that this Declaration aims at securing the universal and effective recognition and observance of the Rights therein declared;
Considering that the aim of the Council of Europe is the achievement of greater unity between its members and that one of the methods by which that aim is to be pursued is the maintenance and further realisation of human rights and fundamental freedoms;
Reaffirming their profound belief in those fundamental freedoms which are the foundation of justice and peace in the world and are best maintained on the one hand by an effective political democracy and on the other by a common understanding and observance of the human rights upon which they depend;
Being resolved, as the governments of European countries which are like-minded and have a common heritage of political traditions, ideals, freedom and the rule of law, to take the first steps for the collective enforcement of certain of the rights stated in the Universal Declaration,
Have agreed as follows:

Article 1

Obligation to respect human rights
The High Contracting Parties shall secure to everyone within their jurisdiction the rights and freedoms defined in Section I of this Convention.

SECTION I—RIGHTS AND FREEDOMS

Article 2

Right to life

(1) Everyone's right to life shall be protected by law. No one shall be deprived of his life intentionally save in the execution of a sentence of a court following his conviction of a crime for which this penalty is provided by law.

(2) Deprivation of life shall not be regarded as inflicted in contravention of this Article when it results from the use of force which is no more than absolutely necessary:

(a) in defence of any person from unlawful violence;

(b) in order to effect a lawful arrest or to prevent the escape of a person lawfully detained;

(c) in action lawfully taken for the purpose of quelling a riot or insurrection.

Article 3

Prohibition of torture

No one shall be subjected to torture or to inhuman or degrading treatment or punishment.

Article 4

Prohibition of slavery and forced labour

(1) No one shall be held in slavery or servitude.

(2) No one shall be required to perform forced or compulsory labour.

(3) For the purposes of this Article the term 'forced or compulsory labour' shall not include:

(a) any work required to be done in the ordinary course of detention imposed according to the provisions of Article 5 of this Convention or during conditional release from such detention;

(b) any service of a military character or, in the case of conscientious objectors in countries where they are recognised, service exacted instead of compulsory military service;

(c) any service exacted in case of an emergency or calamity threatening the life or well-being of the community;

(d) any work or service which forms part of normal civic obligations.

Article 5

Right to liberty and security

(1) Everyone has the right to liberty and security of the person. No one shall be deprived of his liberty save in the following cases and in accordance with a procedure prescribed by law:

(a) the lawful detention of person after conviction by a competent court;

(b) the lawful arrest or detention of a person for non-compliance with the lawful order of a court or in order to secure the fulfilment of any obligation prescribed by law;

(c) the lawful arrest or detention of a person effected for the purpose of bringing him before the competent legal authority on reasonable suspicion of having committed an offence or when it is reasonably considered necessary to prevent his committing an offence or fleeing after having done so;

(d) the detention of a minor by lawful order for the purpose of educational supervision or his lawful detention for the purpose of bringing him before the competent legal authority;

(e) the lawful detention of persons for the prevention of the spreading of infectious diseases, of persons of unsound mind, alcoholics or drug addicts or vagrants;

(f) the lawful arrest or detention of a person to prevent his effecting an unauthorised entry into the country or of a person against whom action is being taken with a view to deportation or extradition.

(2) Everyone who is arrested shall be informed promptly, in a language which he understands, of the reasons for his arrest and of any charge against him.

(3) Everyone arrested or detained in accordance with the provisions of paragraph (1)(c) of this article shall be brought promptly before a judge or other officer authorised by law to exercise judicial power and shall be entitled to trial within a reasonable time or to release pending trial. Release may be conditioned by guarantees to appear for trial.

(4) Everyone who is deprived of his liberty by arrest or detention shall be entitled to take proceedings by which the lawfulness of his detention shall be decided speedily by a court and his release ordered if the detention is not lawful.

(5) Everyone who has been the victim of arrest or detention in contravention of the provisions of this article shall have an enforceable right to compensation.

Article 6

Right to a fair trial

(1) In the determination of his civil rights and obligations or of any criminal charge against him, everyone is entitled to a fair and public hearing within a reasonable time by an independent and impartial tribunal established by law. Judgment shall be pronounced publicly but the press and public may be excluded from all or part of the trial in the interests of morals, public order or national security in a democratic society, where the interests of juveniles or the protection of the private life of the parties so require, or to the extent strictly necessary in the opinion of the court in special circumstances where publicity would prejudice the interests of justice.

(2) Everyone charged with a criminal offence shall be presumed innocent until proved guilty according to law.

(3) Everyone charged with a criminal offence has the following minimum rights:

    (a) to be informed promptly, in a language which he understands and in detail, of the nature and cause of the accusation against him;

    (b) to have adequate time and facilities for the preparation of his defence;

    (c) to defend himself in person or through legal assistance of his own choosing or, if he has not sufficient means to pay for legal assistance, to be given it free when the interests of justice so require;

    (d) to examine or have examined witnesses against him and to obtain the attendance and examination of witnesses on his behalf under the same conditions as witnesses against him;

    (e) to have the free assistance of an interpreter if he cannot understand or speak the language used in court.

Article 7

No punishment without law

(1) No one shall be held guilty of any criminal offence on account of any act or omission which did not constitute a criminal offence under national or international law at the time when it was committed. Nor shall a heavier penalty be imposed than the one that was applicable at the time the criminal offence was committed.

(2) This Article shall not prejudice the trial and punishment of any person for any act or omission which, at the time when it was committed, was criminal according to the general principles of law recognised by civilised nations.

Article 8

Right to respect for private and family life

(1) Everyone has the right to respect for his private and family life, his home and his correspondence.

(2) There shall be no interference by a public authority with the exercise of this right except such as is in accordance with the law and is necessary in a democratic society in the interests of national security, public safety or the economic well-being of the country, for the prevention of disorder or crime, for the protection of health or morals, or for the protection of the rights and freedoms of others.

Article 9

Freedom of thought, conscience and religion

(1) Everyone has the right to freedom of thought, conscience and religion; this right includes freedom to change his religion or belief and freedom, either alone or in community with others and in public or private, to manifest his religion or belief, in worship, teaching, practice and observance.

(2) Freedom to manifest one's religion or beliefs shall be subject only to such limitations as are prescribed by law and are necessary in a democratic society in the interests of public safety, for the protection of public order, health or morals, or for the protection of the rights and freedoms of others.

Article 10

Freedom of expression

(1) Everyone has the right to freedom of expression. This right shall include freedom to hold opinions and to receive and impart information and ideas without interference by public authority and regardless of frontiers. This article shall not prevent States from requiring the licensing of broadcasting, television or cinema enterprises.

(2) The exercise of these freedoms, since it carries with it duties and responsibilities, may be subject to such formalities, conditions, restrictions or penalties as are prescribed by law and are necessary in a democratic society, in the interests of national security, territorial integrity or public safety, for the prevention of disorder or crime, for the protection of health or morals, for the protection of the reputation or rights of others, for preventing the disclosure of information received in confidence, or for maintaining the authority and impartiality of the judiciary.

Article 11

Freedom of assembly and association

(1) Everyone has the right to freedom of peaceful assembly and to freedom of association with others, including the right to form and to join trade unions for the protection of his interests.

(2) No restrictions shall be placed on the exercise of these rights other than such as are prescribed by law and are necessary in a democratic society in the interests of national security or public safety, for the prevention of disorder or crime, for the protection of health or morals or for the protection of the rights and freedoms of others. This article shall not prevent the imposition of lawful restrictions on the exercise of these rights by members of the armed forces, of the police or of the administration of the State.

Article 12

Right to marry

Men and women of marriageable age have the right to marry and to found a family, according to the national laws governing the exercise of this right.

Article 13

Right to an effective remedy

Everyone whose rights and freedoms as set forth in this Convention are violated shall have an effective remedy before a national authority notwithstanding that the violation has been committed by persons acting in an official capacity.

Article 14

Prohibition of discrimination

The enjoyment of the rights and freedoms set forth in this Convention shall be secured without discrimination on any ground such as sex, race, colour, language, religion, political or other opinion, national or social origin, association with a national minority, property, birth or other status.

Article 15

Derogation in time of emergency

(1) In time of war or other public emergency threatening the life of the nation any High Contracting Party may take measures derogating from its obligations under this Convention to the extent strictly required by the exigencies of the situation, provided that such measures are not inconsistent with its other obligations under international law.

(2) No derogation from Article 2, except in respect of deaths resulting from

lawful acts of war, or from Articles 3, 4 (paragraph 1) and 7 shall be made under this provision.

(3) Any High Contracting Party availing itself of this right of derogation shall keep the Secretary General of the Council of Europe fully informed of the measures which it has taken and the reasons therefor. It shall also inform the Secretary General of the Council of Europe when such measures have ceased to operate and the provisions of the Convention are again being fully executed.

Article 16

Restrictions on political activity of aliens
Nothing in Articles 10, 11 and 14 shall be regarded as preventing the High Contracting Parties from imposing restrictions on the political activities of aliens.

Article 17

Prohibition of abuse of rights
Nothing in this Convention may be interpreted as implying for any State, group or person any right to engage in any activity or perform any act aimed at the destruction of any of the rights and freedoms set forth herein or at their limitation to a greater extent that is provided for in the Convention.

Article 18

Limitation on use of restrictions on rights
The restrictions permitted under this Convention to the said rights and freedoms shall not be applied for any purpose other than those for which they have been prescribed.

SECTION II—EUROPEAN COURT OF HUMAN RIGHTS

Article 19

Establishment of the Court
To ensure the observance of the engagements undertaken by the High Contracting Parties in the Convention and the protocols thereto, there shall be set up a European Court of Human Rights, hereinafter referred to as 'the Court'. It shall function on a permanent basis.

Article 20

Number of judges
The Court shall consist of a number of judges equal to that of the High Contracting Parties.

Article 21

Criteria for office
(1) The judges shall be of high moral character and must either possess the qualifications required for appointment to high judicial office or be jurisconsults of recognised competence.
(2) The judges shall sit on the Court in their individual capacity.
(3) During their term of office the judges shall not engage in any activity which is incompatible with their independence, impartiality or with the demands of a full-time office; all questions arising from the application of this paragraph shall be decided by the Court.

Article 22

Election of judges
(1) The judges shall be elected by the Parliamentary Assembly with respect to each High Contracting Party by a majority of votes cast from a list of three candidates nominated by the High Contracting Party.
(2) The same procedure shall be followed to complete the Court in the event of the accession of new High Contracting Parties and in filling casual vacancies.

Article 23

Terms of office
(1) The judges shall be elected for a period of six years. They may be re-elected. However, the terms of office of one-half of the judges elected at the first election shall expire at the end of three years.
(2) The judges whose terms of office are to expire at the end of the initial period of three years shall be chosen by lot by the Secretary General of the Council of Europe immediately after their election.
(3) In order to ensure that, as far as possible, the terms of office of one-half of the judges are renewed every three years, the Parliamentary Assembly may decide, before proceeding to any subsequent election, that the term or terms of office of one or more judges to be elected shall be for a period other than six years but not more than nine and not less than three years.
(4) In cases where more than one term of office is involved and where the Parliamentary Assembly applies the preceding paragraph, the allocation of

the terms of office shall be effected by a drawing of lots by the Secretary General of the Council of Europe immediately after the election.

(5) A judge elected to replace a judge whose term of office has not expired shall hold office for the remainder of his predecessor's term.

(6) The terms of office of judges shall expire when they reach the age of 70.

(7) The judges shall hold office until replaced. They shall, however, continue to deal with such cases as they already have under consideration.

Article 24

Dismissal

No judge may be dismissed from his office unless the other judges decide by a majority of two-thirds that he has ceased to fulfil the required conditions.

Article 25

Registry and legal secretaries

The Court shall have a registry, the functions and organisation of which shall be laid down in the rules of the Court. The Court shall be assisted by legal secretaries.

Article 26

Plenary Court

The plenary Court shall:

(a) elect its President and one or two Vice-Presidents for a period of three years; they may be re-elected;

(b) set up Chambers, constituted for a fixed period of time;

(c) elect the Presidents of the Chambers of the Court; they may be re-elected;

(d) adopt the rules of the Court; and

(e) elect the Registrar and one or more Deputy Registrars.

Article 27

Committees, Chambers and Grand Chamber

(1) To consider cases brought before it, the Court shall sit in committees of three judges, in Chambers of seven judges and in a Grand Chamber of seventeen judges. The Court's Chambers shall set up committees for a fixed period of time.

(2) There shall sit as an *ex officio* member of the Chamber and the Grand Chamber the judge elected in respect of the State Party concerned or, if there is none or if he is unable to sit, a person of its choice who shall sit in the capacity of judge.

(3) The Grand Chamber shall also include the President of the Court, the Vice-Presidents, the Presidents of the Chambers and other judges chosen in accordance with the rules of the Court. When a case is referred to the Grand Chamber under Article 43, no judge from the Chamber which rendered the judgment shall sit in the Grand Chamber, with the exception of the President of the Chamber and the judge who sat in respect of the State Party concerned.

Article 28

Declaration of inadmissibility by committees
A committee may, by a unanimous vote, declare inadmissible or strike out of its list of cases an individual application submitted under Article 34 where such a decision can be taken without further examination. The decision shall be final.

Article 29

Decisions by Chambers on admissibility and merits
(1) If no decision is taken under Article 28, a Chamber shall decide on the admissibility and merits of individual applications submitted under Article 34.
(2) A Chamber shall decide on the admissibility and merits of inter-State applications submitted under Article 33.
(3) The decision on admissibility shall be taken separately unless the Court, in exceptional cases, decides otherwise.

Article 30

Relinquishment of jurisdiction to the Grand Chamber
Where a case pending before a Chamber raises a serious question affecting the interpretation of the Convention or the protocols thereto or where the resolution of a question before it might have a result inconsistent with a judgment previously delivered by the Court, the Chamber may, at any time before it has rendered its judgment, relinquish jurisdiction in favour of the Grand Chamber, unless one of the parties to the case objects.

Article 31

Powers of the Grand Chamber
The Grand Chamber shall

(a) determine applications submitted either under Article 33 or Article 34 when a Chamber has relinquished jurisdiction under Article 30 or when the case has been referred to it under Article 43; and
(b) consider requests for advisory opinions submitted under Article 47.

Article 32

Jurisdiction of the Court

(1) The jurisdiction of the Court shall extend to all matters concerning the interpretation and application of the Convention and the protocols thereto which are referred to it as provided in Articles 33, 34 and 47.

(2) In the event of dispute as to whether the Court has jurisdiction, the Court shall decide.

Article 33

Inter-State cases

Any High Contracting Party may refer to the Court any alleged breach of the provisions of the Convention and the protocols thereto by another High Contracting Party.

Article 34

Individual applications

The Court may receive applications from any person, non-governmental organisation or group of individuals claiming to be the victim of a violation by one of the High Contracting Parties of the rights set forth in the Convention and the protocols thereto. The High Contracting Parties undertake not to hinder in any way the effective exercise of this right.

Article 35

Admissibility criteria

(1) The Court may only deal with the matter after all domestic remedies have been exhausted, according to the generally recognised rules of international law, and within a period of six months from the date on which the final decision was taken.

(2) The Court shall not deal with any individual application submitted under Article 34 that
   (a) is anonymous; or
   (b) is substantially the same as a matter that has already been examined by the Court or has already been submitted to another procedure of international investigation or settlement and contains no relevant new information.

(3) The Court shall declare inadmissible any individual application submitted under Article 34 which it considers incompatible with the provisions of the Convention or the protocols thereto, manifestly ill-founded, or an abuse of the right of application.

(4) The Court shall reject any application which it considers inadmissible under this Article. It may do so at any stage of the proceedings.

Article 36

Third-party intervention
(1) In all cases before a Chamber or the Grand Chamber, a High Contracting Party one of whose nationals is an applicant shall have the right to submit written comments and to take part in the hearings.
(2) The President of the Court may, in the interest of the proper administration of justice, invite any High Contracting Party which is not a party to the proceedings or any person concerned who is not the applicant to submit written comments or take part in the hearings.

Article 37

Striking out applications
(1) The Court may at any stage of the proceedings decide to strike an application out of its list of cases where the circumstances lead to the conclusion that
　(a) the applicant does not intend to pursue his application; or
　(b) the matters has been resolved; or
　(c) for any other reason established by the Court, it is no longer justified to continue the examination of the application.

However, the Court shall continue the examination of the application if respect for human rights as defined in the Convention and the protocols thereto so requires.

(2) The Court may decide to restore an application to its list of cases if it considers that the circumstances justify such a course.

Article 38

Examination of the case and friendly settlement proceedings
(1) If the Court declares the application admissible, it shall
　(a) pursue the examination of the case, together with the representatives of the parties, and if need be, undertake an investigation, for the effective conduct of which the States concerned shall furnish all necessary facilities;
　(b) place itself at the disposal of the parties concerned with a view to securing a friendly settlement of the matter on the basis of respect for human rights as defined in the Convention and the protocols thereto.
(2) Proceedings conducted under paragraph 1(b) shall be confidential.

Article 39

Finding of a friendly settlement
If a friendly settlement is effected, the Court shall strike the case out of its list by means of a decision which shall be confined to a brief statement of the facts and the solution reached.

Article 40

Public hearings and access to documents
(1) Hearings shall be public unless the Court in exceptional circumstances decides otherwise.
(2) Documents deposited with the Registrar shall be accessible to the public unless the President of the Court decides otherwise.

Article 41

Just satisfaction
If the Court finds that there has been a violation of the Convention or the protocols thereto, and if the internal law of the High Contracting Party concerned allows only partial reparation to be made, the Court shall, if necessary afford just satisfaction to the injured party.

Article 42

Judgments of Chambers
Judgments of Chambers shall become final in accordance with the provisions of Article 44, paragraph 2.

Article 43

Referral to the Grand Chamber
(1) Within a period of three months from the date of the judgment of the Chamber, any party to the case may, in exceptional cases, request that the case be referred to the Grand Chamber.
(2) A panel of five judges of the grand Chamber shall accept the request if the case raises a serious question affecting the interpretation or application of the Convention or the protocols thereto, or a serious issue of general importance.
(3) If the panel accepts the request, the Grand Chamber shall decide the case by means of a judgment.

Article 44

Final judgments

(1) The judgment of the Grand Chamber shall be final.
(2) The judgment of a Chamber shall become final
   (a) when the parties declare that they will not request that the case be referred to the Grand Chamber; or
   (b) three months after the date of the judgment, if reference of the case to the Grand Chamber has not been requested; or
   (c) when the panel of the Grand Chamber rejects the request to refer under Article 43.
(3) The final judgment shall be published.

Article 45

Reasons for judgments and decisions

(1) Reasons shall be given for judgments as well as for decisions declaring applications admissible or inadmissible.
(2) If a judgment does not represent, in whole or in part, the unanimous opinion of the judges, any judge shall be entitled to deliver a separate opinion.

Article 46

Binding force and execution of judgments

(1) The High Contracting Parties undertake to abide by the final judgment of the Court in any case where they are parties.
(2) The final judgment of the Court shall be transmitted to the Committee of Ministers, which shall supervise its execution.

Article 47

Advisory opinions

(1) The Court may, at the request of the Committee of Ministers, give advisory opinions on legal questions concerning the interpretation of the Convention and the protocols thereto.
(2) Such opinions shall not deal with any question relating to the content or scope of the rights or freedoms defined in Section I of the Convention and the protocols thereto, or with any other question which the Court or the Committee of Ministers might have to consider in consequence of any such proceedings as could be instituted in accordance with the Convention.
(3) Decisions of the Committee of Ministers to request an advisory opinion of the Court shall require a majority vote of the representatives entitled to sit on the Committee.

Article 48

Advisory jurisdiction of the court
The Court shall decide whether a request for an advisory opinion submitted by the Committee of Ministers is within its competence as defined in Article 47.

Article 49

Reasons for advisory opinions
(1) Reasons shall be given for advisory opinions of the Court.
(2) If the advisory opinion does not represent, in whole or in part, the unanimous opinion of the judges, any judge shall be entitled to deliver a separate opinion.
(3) Advisory opinions of the Court shall be communicated to the Committee of Ministers.

Article 50

Expenditure on the Court
The expenditure on the Court shall be borne by the Council of Europe.

Article 51

Privileges and immunities of judges
The judges shall be entitled, during the exercise of their functions, to the privileges and immunities provided for in Article 40 of the Statute of the Council of Europe and in the agreements made thereunder.

SECTION III—MISCELLANEOUS PROVISIONS

Article 52

Inquiries by the Secretary General
On receipt of a request from the Secretary General of the Council of Europe any High Contracting Party shall furnish an explanation of the manner in which its internal law ensures the effective implementation of any of the provisions of the Convention.

Article 53

Safeguard for existing human rights
Nothing in this Convention shall be construed as limiting or derogating from any of the human rights and fundamental freedoms which may be ensured under the laws of any High Contracting Party or under any other agreement to which it is a Party.

Article 54

Powers of the Committee of Ministers
Nothing in this Convention shall prejudice the powers conferred on the Committee of Ministers by the Statute of the Council of Europe.

Article 55

Exclusion of other means of dispute settlement
The High Contracting Parties agree that, except by special agreement, they will not avail themselves of treaties, conventions or declarations in force between them for the purpose of submitting, by way of petition, a dispute arising out of the interpretation or application of this Convention to a means of settlement other than those provided for in this Convention.

Article 56

Territorial application
(1) Any State may at the time of its ratification or at any time thereafter declare by notification addressed to the Secretary General of the Council of Europe that the present Convention shall, subject to paragraph 4 of this Article, extend to all or any of the territories for whose international relations it is responsible.
(2) The Convention shall extend to the territory or territories named in the notification as from the thirtieth day after the receipt of this notification by the Secretary General of the Council of Europe.
(3) The provisions of this Convention shall be applied in such territories with due regard, however, to local requirements.
(4) Any State which has made a declaration in accordance with paragraph 1 of this Article may at any time thereafter declare on behalf of one or more of the territories to which the declaration relates that it accepts the competence of the Court to receive applications from individuals, non-governmental organisations or groups of individuals as provided in Article 34 of the Convention.

Article 57

Reservations
(1) Any State may, when signing this Convention or when depositing its instrument of ratification, make a reservation in respect of any particular provision of the Convention to the extent that any law then in force in its territory is not in conformity with the provision. Reservations of a general character shall not be permitted under this Article.
(2) Any reservation made under this Article shall contain a brief statement of the law concerned.

Article 58

Denunciation

(1) A High Contracting Party may denounce the present Convention only after the expiry of five years from the date on which it became a party to it and after six months' notice contained in a notification addressed to the Secretary General of the Council of Europe, who shall inform the other High Contracting Parties.

(2) Such a denunciation shall not have the effect of releasing the High Contracting Party concerned from its obligations under this Convention in respect of any act which, being capable of constituting a violation of such obligations, may have been performed by it before the date at which the denunciation became effective.

(3) Any High Contracting Party which shall cease to be a member of the Council of Europe shall cease to be a Party to this Convention under the same conditions.

(4) The Convention may be denounced in accordance with the provisions of the preceding paragraphs in respect of any territory to which it has been declared to extend under the terms of Article 56.

Article 59

Signature and ratification

(1) This Convention shall be open to the signature of the members of the Council of Europe. It shall be ratified. Ratifications shall be deposited with the Secretary General of the Council of Europe.

(2) The present Convention shall come into force after the deposit of ten instruments of ratification.

(3) As regard any signatory ratifying subsequently, the Convention shall come into force at the date of the deposit of its instrument of ratification.

(4) The Secretary General of the Council of Europe shall notify all the members of the Council of Europe of the entry into force of the Convention, the names of the High Contracting Parties who have ratified it, and the deposit of all instruments of ratification which may be effected subsequently.

Done at Rome, 4 November 1950.

Protocol to the convention for the Protection of Human Rights and Fundamental Freedoms, as amended by Protocol No. 11

The governments signatory hereto, being members of the Council of Europe
Being resolved to take steps to ensure the collective enforcement of certain rights and freedoms other than those already included in Section I of the Convention for the Protection of Human Rights and Fundamental Freedoms signed at Rome on 4 November 1950 (hereinafter referred to as 'the Convention'),
Have agreed as follows:

Article 1

Protection of property
Every natural or legal person is entitled to the peaceful enjoyment of his possessions. No one shall be deprived of his possessions except in the public interest
and subject to the conditions provided for by law and by the general principles
of international law.
The preceding provisions shall not, however, in any way impair the right of a
State to enforce such laws as it deems necessary to control the use of property in
accordance with the general interest or to secure the payment of taxes or other
contributions or penalties.

Article 2

Right to education
No person shall be denied the right to education. In the exercise of any
functions which it assumes in relation to education and to teaching, the State
shall respect the right of parents to ensure such education and teaching in
conformity with their own religious and philosophical convictions.

Article 3

Right to free elections
The High Contracting Parties undertake to hold free elections at reasonable
intervals by secret ballot, under conditions which will ensure the free expression
of the opinion of the people in the choice of the legislature.

Article 4

Territorial application
Any High Contracting Party may at the time of signature or ratification or
at any time thereafter communicate to the Secretary General of the Council
of Europe a declaration stating the extent to which it undertakes that the
provisions of the present Protocol shall apply to such of the territories for
the international relations of which it is responsible as are named therein.
Any High Contracting Party which has communicated a declaration in virtue
of the preceding paragraph may from time to time communicate a further
declaration modifying the terms of any former declaration or terminating the
application of the provisions of this Protocol in respect of any territory.
A declaration made in accordance with this Article shall be deemed to have
been made in accordance with paragraph 1 of Article 56 of the Convention.

Article 5

Relationship to the Convention
As between the High Contracting Parties the provisions of Articles 1, 2, 3 and 4 of this Protocol shall be regarded as additional articles to the Convention and all the provisions of the Convention shall apply accordingly.

Article 6

Signature and ratification
This Protocol shall be open for signature by the members of the Council of Europe, who are the signatories of the Convention; it shall be ratified at the same time as or after the ratification of the Convention. It shall enter into force after the deposit of ten instruments of ratification. As regards any signatory ratifying subsequently, the Protocol shall enter into force at the date of the deposit of its instrument of ratification.
The instruments of ratification shall be deposited with the Secretary General of the Council of Europe, who will notify all members of the names of those who have ratified.
Done at Paris, 20 March 1952.

[Protocol No. 2 becomes otiose, since the provisions on the Court's competence to give advisory opinions is incorporated in Articles 47 to 49 of the Convention]

[Protocol No. 3 has become otiose; it modified the procedure of the Commission by abolishing the system of sub-commissions]

Protocol No. 4 to the Convention for the Protection of Human Rights and Fundamental Freedoms securing certain rights and freedoms other than those already included in the Convention and in the First Protocol thereto

The governments signatory hereto, being members of the Council of Europe,
Being resolved to take steps to ensure the collective enforcement of certain rights and freedoms other than those already included in Section I of the Convention for the Protection of Human Rights and Fundamental Freedoms signed at Rome on 4th November 1950 (hereinafter referred to as 'the Convention') and in Articles 1 to 3 of the First Protocol to the Convention, signed at Paris on 20th March 1952,
Have agreed as follows:

Article 1

Prohibition of imprisonment for debt
No one shall be deprived of his liberty merely on the ground of inability to fulfil a contractual obligation.

Article 2

Freedom of movement
(1) Everyone lawfully within the territory of a State shall, within that territory, have the right to liberty of movement and freedom to choose his residence.
(2) Everyone shall be free to leave any country, including his own.
(3) No restrictions shall be placed on the exercise of these rights other than such as are in accordance with law and are necessary in a democratic society in the interests of national security or public safety, for the maintenance of the *ordre public*, for the prevention of crime, for the protection of health or morals, or for the protection of the rights and freedoms of others.
(4) The rights set forth in paragraph 1 may also be subject, in particular areas, to restrictions imposed in accordance with law and justified by the public interest in a democratic society.

Article 3

Prohibition of expulsion of nationals
(1) No one shall be expelled, by means either of an individual or of a collective measure, from the territory of the State of which he is a national.
(2) No one shall be deprived of the right to enter the territory of the State of which he is a national.

Article 4

Prohibition of collective expulsion of aliens
Collective expulsion of aliens is prohibited.

Article 5

Territorial application
(1) Any High Contracting Party may, at the time of signature or ratification of this protocol, or at any time thereafter, communicate to the Secretary General of the Council of Europe a declaration stating the extent to which it undertakes that the provisions of this Protocol shall apply to such of the territories for the international relations of which it is responsible as are named therein.
(2) Any High Contracting Party which has communicated a declaration in

virtue of the preceding paragraph may, from time to time, communicate a further declaration modifying the terms of any former declaration or terminating the application of the provisions of this Protocol in respect of any territory.

(3) A declaration made in accordance with this Article shall be deemed to have been made in accordance with paragraph 1 of Article 56 of the Convention.

(4) The territory of any State to which this Protocol applies by virtue of ratification or acceptance by that State, and each territory to which this Protocol is applied by virtue of a declaration by that State under this Article, shall be treated as separate territories for the purpose of the references in Articles 2 and 3 to the territory of a State.

(5) Any State which has made a declaration in accordance with paragraph 1 or 2 of this Article may at any time thereafter declare on behalf of one or more of the territories to which the declaration relates that it accepts the competence of the Court to receive applications from individuals, non-governmental organisations or groups of individuals as provided in Article 34 of the Convention in respect of all or any of Articles 1 to 4 of this Protocol.

Article 6

Relationship to the Convention

As between the High Contracting Parties the provisions of Articles 1 to 5 of this Protocol shall be regarded as additional Articles to the Convention, and the provisions of the Convention shall apply accordingly.

Article 7

Signature and ratification

(1) This Protocol shall be open for signature by the members of the Council of Europe who are signatories of the Convention; it shall be ratified at the same time as or after the ratification of the Convention. It shall enter into force after the deposit of five instruments of ratification. As regards any signatory ratifying subsequently, the Protocol shall enter into force at the date of the deposit of its instrument of ratification.

(2) The instruments of ratification shall be deposited with the Secretary General of the Council of Europe, who will notify all members of the names of those who have ratified.

Done at Strasbourg, 16 September 1963.

[Protocol No. 5 has become otiose; it concerned the procedure for the election of members of the Commission and Court]

Protocol No. 6 to the Convention for the Protection of Human Rights and Fundamental Freedoms concerning the abolition of the death penalty

The member States of the Council of Europe, signatory to this Protocol to the Convention for the Protection of Human Rights and Fundamental Freedoms, signed at Rome on 4 November 1950 (hereinafter referred to as 'the Convention'),

Considering that the evolution that has occurred in several member States of the Council of Europe expresses a general tendency in favour of the abolition of the death penalty;

Have agreed as follows:

Article 1

Abolition of the death penalty

The death penalty shall be abolished. No-one shall be condemned to such penalty or executed.

Article 2

Death penalty in time of war

A State may make provision in its law for the death penalty in respect of acts committed in time of war or of imminent threat of war; such penalty shall be applied only in the instances laid down in the law and in accordance with its provisions. The State shall communicate to the Secretary General of the Council of Europe the relevant provisions of that law.

Article 3

Prohibition of derogations

No derogation from the provisions of this Protocol shall be made under Article 15 of the Convention.

Article 4

Prohibition of reservations

No reservation may be made under Article 57 of the Convention in respect of the provisions of this Protocol.

Article 5

Territorial application

(1) Any State may at the time of signature or when depositing its instrument of ratification, acceptance or approval, specify the territory or territories to which this Protocol shall apply.

(2) Any State may at any later date, by a declaration addressed to the Secretary General of the Council of Europe, extend the application of this Protocol to any other territory specified in the declaration. In respect of such territory the Protocol shall enter into force on the first day of the month following the date of receipt of such declaration by the Secretary General.

(3) Any declaration made under the two preceding paragraphs may, in respect of any territory specified in such declaration, be withdrawn by a notification addressed to the Secretary General. The withdrawal shall become effective on the first day of the month following the date of receipt of such notification by the Secretary General.

Article 6

Relationship to the Convention

As between the States Parties the provisions of Articles 1 to 5 of this Protocol shall be regarded as additional articles to the Convention and all the provisions of the Convention shall apply accordingly.

Article 7

Signature and ratification

The Protocol shall be open for signature by the member States of the Council of Europe, signatories to the Convention. It shall be subject to ratification, acceptance or approval. A member State of the Council of Europe may not ratify, accept or approve this Protocol unless it has, simultaneously or previously, ratified the Convention. Instruments of ratification, acceptance or approval shall be deposited with the Secretary General of the Council of Europe.

Article 8

Entry into force

(1) This Protocol shall enter into force on the first day of the month following the date on which five member States of the Council of Europe have expressed their consent to be bound by the Protocol in accordance with the provisions of Article 7.

(2) In respect of any member State which subsequently expresses its consent to be bound by it, the Protocol shall enter into force on the first day of the month following the date of the deposit of the instrument of ratification, acceptance or approval.

Article 9

Depositary functions

The Secretary General of the Council of Europe shall notify the member States of the Council of:

(a) any signature;
(b) the deposit of any instrument of ratification, acceptance or approval;
(c) any date of entry into force of this Protocol in accordance with Articles 5 and 8;
(d) any other act, notification or communication relating to this Protocol.

Done at Strasbourg, 28 April 1983

Protocol No. 7 to the Convention for the Protection of Human Rights and Fundamental Freedoms, as amended by Protocol No. 11

The member States of the Council of Europe signatory hereto,

Being resolved to ensure the collective enforcement of certain rights and freedoms by means of the Convention for the Protection of Human Rights and Fundamental Freedoms signed at Rome on 4 November 1950 (hereinafter referred to as 'the Convention'),

Have agreed as follows:

Article 1

Procedural safeguards relating to expulsion of aliens

(1) An alien lawfully resident in the territory of a State shall not be expelled therefrom except in pursuance of a decision reached in accordance with law and shall be allowed:
(a) to submit reasons against his expulsion;
(b) to have his case reviewed; and
(c) to be represented for these purposes before the competent authority or a person or persons designated by that authority.
(2) An alien may be expelled before the exercise of his rights under paragraph 1 (a), (b) and (c) of this Article, when such expulsion is necessary in the interests of public order or is grounded on reasons of national security.

Article 2

Right of appeal in criminal matters

(1) Everyone convicted of a criminal offence by a tribunal shall have the right to have his conviction or sentence reviewed by a higher tribunal. The exercise of this right, including the grounds on which it may be exercised, shall be governed by law.

(2) This right may be subject to exceptions in regard to offences of a minor character, as prescribed by law, or in cases in which the person concerned was tried in the first instance by the highest tribunal or was convicted following an appeal against acquittal.

Article 3

Compensation for wrongful conviction

When a person has by a final decision been convicted of a criminal offence and when subsequently his conviction has been reversed, or he has been pardoned, on the ground that a new or newly discovered fact shows conclusively that there has been a miscarriage of justice, the person who has suffered punishment as a result of such conviction shall be compensated according to the law or the practice of the State concerned, unless it is proved that the non-disclosure of the unknown fact in time is wholly or partly attributable to him.

Article 4

Right not to be tried or punished twice

(1) No one shall be liable to be tried or punished again in criminal proceedings under the jurisdiction of the same State for an offence for which he has already been finally acquitted or convicted in accordance with the law and penal procedure of that State.

(2) The provisions of the preceding paragraph shall not prevent the reopening of the case in accordance with the law and penal procedure of the State concerned, if there is evidence of new or newly discovered facts, or if there has been a fundamental defect in the previous proceedings, which could affect the outcome of the case.

(3) No derogation from this Article shall be made under Article 15 of the Convention.

Article 5

Equality between spouses

Spouses shall enjoy equality of rights and relationships of a private law character between them, and in their relations with their children, as to marriage, during marriage and in the event of its dissolution. This Article shall not prevent States from taking such measures as are necessary in the interests of the children.

Article 6

Territorial application

(1) Any State may at the time of signature or when depositing its instrument of ratification, acceptance or approval, specify the territory or territories to which the Protocol shall apply and state the extent to which it undertakes that the provisions of this Protocol shall apply to such territory or territories.

(2) Any State may at any later date, by a declaration addressed to the Secretary General of the Council of Europe, extend the application of this Protocol to any other territory specified in the declaration. In respect of such territory the Protocol shall enter into force on the first day of the month following the expiration of a period of two months after the date of receipt of such notification by the Secretary General.

(3) Any declaration made under the preceding two paragraphs may, in respect of any territory specified in such declaration, be withdrawn or modified by a notification addressed to the Secretary General. The withdrawal or modification shall become effective on the first day of the month following the expiration of a period of two months after the date of receipt of such notification by the Secretary General.

(4) A declaration made in accordance with this Article shall be deemed to have been made in accordance with paragraph 1 of Article 56 of the Convention.

(5) The territory of any State to which this Protocol applies by virtue of ratification, acceptance or approval by that State, and each territory to which this Protocol is applied by virtue of a declaration by that State under this Article, may be treated as separate territories for the purpose of the reference in Article 1 to the territory of a State.

(6) Any State which has made a declaration in accordance with paragraph 1 or 2 of this Article may at any time thereafter declare on behalf of one or more of the territories to which the declaration relates that it accepts the competence of the Court to receive applications from individuals, non-governmental organisations or groups of individuals as provided in Article 34 of the Convention in respect of Articles 1 to 5 of this Protocol.

Article 7

Relationship to the Convention

As between the States Parties, the provisions of Article 1 to 6 of this Protocol shall be regarded as additional Articles to the Convention, and all the provisions of the Convention shall apply accordingly.

Article 8

Signature and ratification

This Protocol shall be open for signature by member States of the Council of Europe which have signed the Convention. It is subject to ratification, acceptance or approval. A member State of the Council of Europe may not ratify, accept or approve this Protocol without previously or simultaneously ratifying the Convention. Instruments of ratification, acceptance or approval shall be deposited with the Secretary General of the Council of Europe.

Article 9

Entry into force

(1) This Protocol shall enter into force on the first day of the month following the expiration of a period of two months after the date on which seven member States of the Council of Europe have expressed their consent to be bound by the Protocol in accordance with the provisions of Article 8.

(2) In respect of any member State which subsequently expresses its consent to be bound by it, the Protocol shall enter into force on the first day of the month following the expiration of a period of two months after the date of the deposit of the instrument of ratification, acceptance or approval.

Article 10

Depositary functions

The Secretary General of the Council of Europe shall notify all the member States of the Council of Europe of:

(a) any signature;

(b) the deposit of any instrument of ratification, acceptance or approval;

(c) any date of entry into force of this protocol in accordance with Articles 6 and 9;

(d) any other act, notification or declaration relating to this Protocol.

Done at Strasbourg, 22 November 1984,

[Protocol No. 8 has become otiose; it concerned procedure of the 'old' Commission and Court.

[Protocol No. 9 has become otiose; it amended certain provisions of the Convention to improve the position of individual applicants]

[Protocol No. 10 has become otiose; it changes the majority required for a decision of the Committee of Ministers under the original Article 32]

Protocol No. 11 to the Convention for the Protection of Human Rights and Fundamental Freedoms, restructuring the control machinery established thereby

The member States of the Council of Europe, signatories to this Protocol to the Convention for the Protection of Human Rights and Fundamental Freedoms, signed at Rome on 4 November 1950 (hereinafter referred to as 'the Convention'),

Considering the urgent need to restructure the control machinery established by the Convention in order to maintain and improve the efficiency of its protection of human rights and fundamental freedoms, mainly in view of the increase in the number of applications and the growing membership of the Council of Europe;

Considering that it is therefore desirable to amend certain provisions of the Convention with a view, in particular, to replacing the existing European Commission and Court of Human Rights with a new permanent Court;

Having regard to Resolution No. 1 adopted at the European Ministerial Conference on Human Rights, held in Vienna on 19 and 20 March 1985;

Having regard to recommendation 1194 (1992), adopted by the Parliamentary Assembly of the Council of Europe on 6 October 1992;

Having regard to the decision taken on reform of the Convention control machinery by the Heads of State and Government of the Council of Europe member States in the Vienna Declaration on 9 October 1993,

Have agreed as follows:

Article 1

[Replaces the text of Sections II to IV of the Convention and of Protocol No. 2; the amendments have been incorporated in the text set out above.]

Article 2

[Amends the text of other provisions of the Convention and Protocols; the amendments have been incorporated in the text set out above.]

Article 3

(1) This Protocol shall be open for signature by member States of the Council of Europe signatories to the Convention, which may express their consent to be bound by
  (a) signature without reservation as to ratification, acceptance or approval; or
  (b) signature subject to ratification, acceptance or approval, followed by ratification, acceptance or approval.

(2) The instruments of ratification, acceptance or approval shall be deposited with the Secretary General of the Council of Europe.

Article 4

This Protocol shall enter into force on the first day of the month following the expiration of a period of one year after the date on which all Parties to the Convention have expressed their consent to be bound by the Protocol in accordance with the provisions of Article 3. The election of new judges may take place, and any further necessary steps may be taken to establish the new Court, in accordance with the provisions of this Protocol from the date on which all Parties to the Convention have expressed their consent to be bound by the Protocol.

Article 5

(1) Without prejudice to the provisions in paragraphs 3 and 4 below, the terms of office of the judges, members of the Commission, Registrar and Deputy registrar shall expire at the date of entry into force of this Protocol.

(2) Applications pending before the Commission which have not been declared admissible at the date of the entry into force of this Protocol shall be examined by the Court in accordance with the provisions of this Protocol.

(3) Applications which have been declared admissible at the date of the entry into force of this Protocol shall continue to be dealt with by members of the Commission within a period of one year thereafter. Any applications the examination of which has not been completed within the aforesaid period shall be transmitted to the Court which shall examine them as admissible cases in accordance with the provisions of this Protocol.

(4) With respect to applications in which the Commission, after the entry into force of this Protocol, has adopted a report in accordance with former Article 31 of the Convention, the report shall be transmitted to the parties, who shall not be at liberty to publish it. In accordance with the provisions applicable prior to the entry into force of this Protocol, a case may be referred to the Court. The panel of the Grand Chamber shall determine whether one of the Chambers or the Grand Chamber shall decide the case. If the case is decided by a Chamber, the decision of the Chamber shall be final. Cases not referred to the Court shall be dealt with by the Committee of Ministers acting in accordance with the provisions of former Article 32 of the Convention.

(5) Cases pending before the Court which have not been decided at the date of entry into force of this Protocol shall be transmitted to the Grand Chamber of the Court, which shall examine them in accordance with the provisions of this Protocol.

(6) Cases pending before the Committee of Ministers which have not been decided under former Article 32 of the Convention at the date of entry into force of this Protocol shall be completed by the Committee of Ministers acting in accordance with that Article.

Article 6

Where a High Contracting Party had made a declaration recognising the competence of the Commission or the jurisdiction of the Court under former Article 25 or 46 of the Convention with respect to matters arising after or based on facts occurring subsequent to any such declaration, this limitation shall remain valid for the jurisdiction of the Court under this Protocol.

Article 7

The Secretary General of the Council of Europe shall notify the member States of the Council of
    (a) any signature;
    (b) the deposit of any instrument of ratification, acceptance or approval;
    (c) the date of entry into force of this Protocol or of any of its provisions in accordance with Article 4; and
    (d) any other act, notification or communication relating to this Protocol.

Done at Strasbourg, 11 May 1994

Protocol No. 12 to the Convention for the Protection of Human Rights and Fundamental Freedoms

The member States of the Council of Europe signatory hereto,

Having regard to the fundamental principle according to which all persons are equal before the law and are entitled to the equal protection of the law;

Being resolved to take further steps to promote the equality of all persons through the collective enforcement of a general prohibition of discrimination by means of the Convention for the Protection of Human Rights and Fundamental Freedoms signed at Rome on 4 November 1950 (hereinafter referred to as 'the Convention');

Reaffirming that the principle of non-discrimination does not prevent States Parties from taking measures in order to promote full and effective equality, provided that there is an objective and reasonable justification for those measures,

Have agreed as follows:

Article 1

General prohibition of discrimination

(1) The enjoyment of any right set forth by law shall be secured without discrimination on any ground such as sex, race, colour, language, religion, political or other opinion, national or social origin, association with a national minority, property, birth or other status.

(2) No one shall be discriminated against by any public authority on any ground such as those mentioned in paragraph 1.

Article 2

Territorial application

(1) Any State may, at the time of signature or when depositing its instrument of ratification, acceptance or approval, specify the territory or territories to which this Protocol shall apply.

(2) Any State may at any later date, by a declaration addressed to the Secretary General of the Council of Europe, extend the application of this Protocol to any other territory specified in the declaration. In respect of such territory the Protocol shall enter into force on the first day of the month following the expiration of a period of three months after the date of receipt by the Secretary General of such declaration.

(3) Any declaration made under the two preceding paragraphs may, in respect of any territory specified in such declaration, be withdrawn or modified by a notification addressed to the Secretary General of the Council of Europe. The withdrawal or modification shall become effective on the first day of the month following the expiration of a period of three months after the date of receipt of such notification by the Secretary General.

(4) A declaration made in accordance with this article shall be deemed to have been made in accordance with paragraph 1 of Article 56 of the Convention.

(5) Any State which has made a declaration in accordance with paragraph 1 or 2 of this article may at any time thereafter declare on behalf of one or more of the territories to which the declaration relates that it accepts the competence of the Court to receive applications from individuals, non-governmental organisations or groups of individuals as provided by Article 34 of the Convention in respect of Article 1 of this Protocol.

Article 3

Relationship to the Convention

As between the States Parties, the provisions of Articles 1 and 2 of this Protocol shall be regarded as additional articles to the Convention, and all the provisions of the Convention shall apply accordingly.

Article 4

Signature and ratification

This Protocol shall be open for signature by member states of the Council of Europe which have signed the Convention. It is subject to ratification, acceptance or approval. A member state of the Council of Europe may not ratify, accept or approve this Protocol without previously or simultaneously ratifying the Convention. Instruments of ratification, acceptance or approval shall be deposited with the Secretary General of the Council of Europe.

Article 5

Entry into force

(1) This Protocol shall enter into force on the first day of the month following the expiration of a period of three months after the date on which ten member states of the Council of Europe have expressed their consent to be bound by the Protocol in accordance with the provisions of Article 4.

(2) In respect of any member state which subsequently expresses its consent to be bound by it, the Protocol shall enter into force on the first day of the month following the expiration of a period of three months after the date of the deposit of the instrument of ratification, acceptance or approval.

Article 6

Depository functions

The Secretary General of the Council of Europe shall notify all the member states of the Council of Europe of:

(a) any signature;

(b) the deposit of any instrument of ratification, acceptance or approval;

(c) any date of entry into force of this Protocol in accordance with Articles 2 and 5;

(d) any other act, notification or communication relating to this Protocol.

In witness whereof the undersigned, being duly authorised thereto, have signed this Protocol.

Done at Rome, 4 November 2000

LIST OF CONTRACTING PARTIES AS AT 1 JANUARY 2002

Albania
Andorra
Armenia[1]
Austria
Azerbaijan[2]
Belgium
Bulgaria
Croatia
Cyprus
Czech Republic
Denmark
Estonia
Finland
France
Georgia
Germany
Greece
Hungary
Iceland
Ireland
Italy
Latvia
Liechtenstein
Lithuania
Luxembourg
Malta
Moldova
Netherlands
Norway
Poland
Portugal
Romania
Russia
San Marino
Slovakia
Slovenia
Spain
Sweden
Switzerland

TFYR Macedonia[3]
Turkey
Ukraine
United Kingdom

[1] Signed but not yet ratified
[2] Signed but not yet ratified

[3] The former Yugoslav Republic of Macedonia

SELECT BIBLIOGRAPHY

BOOKS

Alston, P., *The EU and Human Rights* (Oxford, 1999).

Atiyah, P., *Law and Modern Society* (London, 1983).

Beatson, J., and Cripps, Y., *Freedom of Expression and Freedom of Information* (Oxford, 2000).

Blackburn, R., and Polakiewicz, J. (eds.), *Fundamental Rights in Europe: The ECHR and its Member States, 1950–2000* (Oxford, 2001).

—— and Taylor, J. *Human Rights for the 1990s. Legal, Political and Ethical Issues* (London, 1991).

Brown, L. Neville, and Kennedy, T., *Brown and Jacobs: The Court of Justice of the European Communities* (London, 2000).

Brownlie, I., *Principles of Public International Law* (Oxford, 1991).

Casese, A., Clapham, A., and Weiler, J. (eds.), *Human Rights and the European Community: The Substantive Law* (Nomos, 1991).

—— —— —— *Human Rights and the European Community: Methods of Protection* (Nomos, 1991).

Clapham, A., *Human Rights and the European Community: A Critical Overview* (Nomos, 1991).

—— *Human Rights in the Private Sphere* (Oxford, 1993).

Clark, D., and McCoy, G., *The Most Fundamental Legal Right. Habeas Corpus in the Commonwealth* (Oxford, 2000)

Clayton, R., and Tomlinson, H., *The Law of Human Rights* (Oxford, 2000).

Clements, L., Mole, N., and Simmons, A., *European Human Rights. Taking a Case under the Convention* (London, 1999).

Council of Europe, *Collected Edition of the travaux préparatoires of the European Convention on Human Rights* (The Hague, 1977).

Council of Europe, *Manual of the Council of Europe. Its Structure, Functions and Achievements* (London, 1970).

—— *Fundamental Social Rights: Case Law of the European Social Charter* (Council of Europe, 2000).

Council of Europe and the International Commission on Civil Status, *Transsexualism in Europe* (Strasbourg, 2000).

Craig, P., and de Búrca, G., *EU Law. Text, Cases and Materials* (Oxford, 1998).

Curtin, D., and Heukels, T., *Institutional Dynamics of European Integration. Essays in Honour of Henry G Schermers* (Dordrecht, 1994).

Dashwood, A., Hacon, R., and White, R., *A Guide to the Civil Jurisdiction and Judgments Convention* (Deventer, 1986).

Delmas-Marty, M., *The European Convention for the Protection of Human Rights. International Protection versus National Restrictions* (Dordrecht, 1992).

Dickson, B., *Human Rights and the European Convention* (London, 1997)

Denning, Lord, *What Next in the Law?* (London, 1982).

Drzemczewski, A., *European Human Rights Convention in Domestic Law. A Comparative Study* (Oxford, 1983).

Dworkin, R., *A Bill of Rights for Britain* (London, 1990).

Emmerson, B., and Ashworth, A., *Human Rights and Criminal Justice* (London, 2001)

Evans, C., *Freedom of Religion under the European Convention on Human Rights* (Oxford, 2001).

Evans, M., and Morgan, R., *Preventing Torture. A Study of the European Convention for the prevention of Torture and Inhuman or Degrading Treatment* (Oxford, 1998).

Fawcett, J., *The Application of the European Convention on Human Rights* (Oxford, 1987).

Feldman, D., *Civil Liberties and Human Rights in England and Wales* (Oxford, 1993).

Gardner, J. P. (ed.), *Aspects of Incorporation of the European Convention of Human Rights into Domestic Law* (London, 1993).

Gearty, C. (ed.), *European Civil Liberties and the European Convention on Human Rights. A Comparative Study* (The Hague, 1997).

Gomien, D., Harris, D. and Zwaak, L., *Law and Practice of the European Convention on Human Rights and the European Social Charter* (Council of Europe, 1996).

Griffith, J. A. G., *The Politics of the Judiciary* (London, 1991).

Grosz, S., Beatson, J., and Duffy, P., *Human Rights. The 1998 Act and the European Convention* (London, 2000).

Guradze, G., *Europäische Menchenrechtskonvention* (Berlin, 1968).

Harris, D., *The European Social Charter* (Charlottesville, 1984).

Hodkinson, P., and Rutherford, A., *Capital Punishment. Global Issues and Prospects* (Winchester, 1996).

Hunt, M., *Using Human Rights Law in English Courts* (Oxford, 1997).

Janis, M., Kay, R., and Bradley, A., *European Human Rights Law. Text and Materials* (Oxford, 2000).

Khol, H., *Zwischen Staat und Weltstaat* (Vienna, 1969).

Kilkelly, U., *The Child and the European Convention on Human Rights* (Ashgate, 1999).

Kilpatrick, C., Novitz, N., and Skidmore, P., *The Future of Remedies in Europe* (Oxford, 2000).

Kinley, D., *The European Convention on Human Rights. Compliance without Incorporation* (Aldershot, 1993).

Kiss, A., *L'abus de droit en droit international* (Paris, 1953).

Landy, E., *The Effectiveness of International Supervision: Thirty Years of I.L.O. Experience* (London, New York, 1966).

Law Commission, *Damages under the Human Rights Act 1998*, Law Com. No. 266/Scot Law Com. No. 180.

Lawson, R., and Blois, M. de (eds.) *The Dynamics of the Protection of Human Rights in Europe: Essays in Honour of Henry G Schermers* (Dordrecht, 1994).

Leach, P., *Taking a Case to the European Court of Human Rights* (London, 2001).

Lester, A., and Pannick, D., *Human Rights Law and Practice* (London, 1999).

Loucks, N., *A Working Guide to Prison Rules* (London, 1993).

Macdonald, R., F. Matscher, and H. Petzold, *The European System for the Protection of Human Rights* (Dortrecht, 1993).

McGoldrick, D., *The Human Rights Committee* (Oxford, 1992).

Matscher, F., and Petzold, H. (eds.), *Protecting Human Rights: The European Dimension. Studies in Honour of Gerard J. Wiarda* (Cologne, 1988).

Merrills, J. G., *The Development of International Law by the European Court of Human Rights* (Manchester, 1988).

Merrills, J. G., and Robertson, A.H., *Human Rights in Europe* (Manchester, 2001).
Mikaelsen, L., *European Protection of Human Rights. The Practice and Procedure of the European Commission of Human Rights on the Admissibility of Applications from Individuals and States* (Alphen aan den Rijn, 1980).
Monconduit, F., *La Commission Européenne des Droits de l'homme* (Leyden, 1965).
Mowbray, A., *Cases and Materials on the European Convention on Human Rights* (London, 2001).
Oetheimer, M., *'L'Harmonisation de la Liberté d'Expression en Europe'* (Paris, 2001).
O'Keeffe, D. and Twomey, P. (eds.), *Legal Issues of the Maastricht Treaty* (London, 1994).
Plamenatz, J., *Man and Society* (London: 1963).
Partsch, K., *Die Rechte und Freiheiten der europäischen Menschrechtskonvention* (Berlin, 1966).
Reid, K., *A Practitioner's Guide to the European Convention of Human Rights* (London, 1998)
Robertson, A. H. (ed.), *Human Rights in National and International Law* (Manchester, 1968).
—— (ed.), *Privacy and Human Rights* (Manchester, 1973).
Scarman, L., *English Law—The New Dimension* (London, 1974);
Schermers, H. G., *The Influence of the European Commission of Human Rights* (The Hague 1992).
Sieghart, P., *The International Law of Human Rights* (Oxford, 1983).
Simor, J., and Emmerson, B., (eds.), *Human Rights Practice* (London, 2000)
Van Dijk, P., and van Hoof, G. J. H., *Theory and Practice of the European Convention on Human Rights* (Deventer, 1998).
Waaldijk, K., and Clapham, A., *Homosexuality: A European Community Issue* (Dordrecht, 1993).
Walter, *Die Europäische Menschenrechtsordnung* (Köln, 1970).
Wyatt, D., and Dashwood, A., *European Community Law* (London, 1993).
Zander, M., *A Bill of Rights?* (London, 1985).
Zwart, T., *The Admissibility of Human Rights Petitions* (Dordrecht, 1994).

CHAPTERS IN BOOKS, REPORTS AND ARTICLES

Addo, M., and Grief, N., 'Is there a policy behind the decisions and judgments relating to Article 3 of the European Convention on Human Rights?' (1995) 20 E L Rev 178.
Baker, E., 'Dangerousness, Rights and Criminal Justice.' (1993) 56 MLR 528–547.
Bonner, D., '*Ireland* v. *United Kingdom*' (1978) 27 ICLQ 897.
Buergenthal, T., 'The effect of the European Convention on Human Rights on the Internal Law of Member States', in *The European Convention on Human Rights*, British Institute of International and Comparative Law, Supplementary Publication No. 11, 1965, 57 ff.
Buxton, R., 'The Human Rights Act and Private Law' (2000) 116 LQR 48.
Canor, I., '*Primus inter pares.* Who is the ultimate guardian of fundamental rights in Europe?' (2000) 25 E L Rev 3.
Cassese, A., 'A New Approach to Human Rights: The European Convention for the Prevention of Torture' (1989) 83 AJIL 128.
Cassin, R., *Amicorum Discipulorumque Liber* III (Paris, 1971).
Cholewinski, R., 'Strasbourg's "Hidden Agenda"? The Protection of Second-Generation Migrants from Expulsion under Article 8 of the ECHR' (1994) 3 NQHR 287.

Chrysostomides, C., ' "Competence" and "Incompatibility" in the Jurisprudence of the
    European Commission of Human Rights', in *Zeitschrift für ausländisches öffentliches Recht
    und Völkerrecht* (1973), 449.
Coppel, J., and O'Neill, A., 'The European Court of Justice: Taking rights seriously?' (1992)
    29 CMLRev. 669.
Council of Europe, Working Paper of the Parliamentary Assembly, Doc. 3699, *Report on the
    Rights of the Sick and Dying*, 26 January 1976, Rapporteurs: Mrs Hubinek and Mr Voogd.
—— *Collected Texts* (Strasbourg, 1987).
—— *European Commission of Human Rights. Survey of Activities and Statistics 1994.*
Daintith, T., and Wilkinson, G., 'Bail and the Convention: British reflections on the
    Wemhoff and Neumeister cases' (1970) 18 AJCL 326.
Dashwood, A., 'The Advocate General in the Court of Justice of the European Communities'
    (1982) 2 *Legal Studies* 202–16.
Doswald-Beck, L., 'The Meaning of the "Right to respect for Private Life" under the
    European Convention on Human Rights' (1983) 4 HRLJ 283.
Drzemczewski, A., 'The domestic Status of the European Convention on Human Rights.
    New Dimensions' [1977/1] LIEI 1–85.
—— 'A Non-Decision of the Committee of Ministers under Article 32(1) of the
    European Convention on Human Rights: The East African Asian Cases' (1978) 41 MLR
    337–42.
—— 'A major overhaul of the European Human Rights Convention control mechanism:
    Protocol No. 11' in *Collected Courses of the Academy of European Law, vi* (Florence, 1997), at
    121.
—— 'The European Human Rights Convention: Protocol No 11 – Entry into force and first
    year of application (2000) 21 HRLJ 1.
Duffy, P., 'English Law and the European Convention on Human Rights' (1980) 29 ICLQ
    585–618.
—— 'Article 3 of the European Convention on Human Rights' (1983) 32 ICLQ 316.
EC Commission, *The Protection of Fundamental Rights in the European Community*, EC
    Bulletin, Supplement 5/76.
—— *Memorandum on the Accession by the European Communities to the European
    Convention on Human Rights and Fundamental Freedoms*, EC Bulletin, Supplement 2/79.
Eissen, M., 'The European Convention on Human Rights and the Duties of the Individual'
    (1962) 32 *Acta Scandinavica Juris Gentium* 230.
—— 'The Independence of Malta and the European Convention on Human Rights'
    (1965–6) 41 BYBIL 401.
—— 'L'autonomie de l'article 14 de la Convention européenne des droits de l'homme dans
    la jurisprudence de la Commission', in *Mélanges Modinos* (Paris, 1968), at 122.
—— 'Malawi and the European Convention on Human Rights' (1968–9) 43 BYBIL 190.
—— 'Les mesures provisoires dans la Convention européenne des Droits de l'Homme',
    Revue des droits de l'homme 2 (1969), 252.
—— 'La Convention européenne des Droits de l'Homme et les obligations de l'individu:
    une mise à jour', in Rene Cassin, *Amicorum Discipulorumque Liber* III (Paris, 1971).
Erdal, U., 'Burden and standard of proof in proceedings under the European Convention'
    (2001) 26 E L Rev HR65.
Evans, A. and Morgan, R., 'The European Convention for the Prevention of Torture:
    Operational Practice' (1992) 41 ICLQ 590.

Feldman, D., 'The developing scope of Article 8 of the European Convention on Human Rights' [1997] EHRLR 265.

Finlay, A., 'The Human Rights Act: The Lord Chancellor's Department's Preparations for Implementation' [1999] EHRLR 512.

Golsong, H., 'Die europäishe Konvention zum Schutze der Menschenrechte und Grundfreiheiten', *Jaarbuch des öffentlichen Rechts*, Book 10, 1961, pp. 123–57.

—— 'Le droit à la liberté de la personne tel qu'il est garanti par l'article 5 de la Convention européene des Droits de l'Homme' in *Droit pénal européene* (Brussels, 1970), 25.

—— 'On the reform of the supervisory system of the European Convention on Human Rights' (1992) 13 HRLJ 265–9.

Hampson, F., 'The concept of an "arguable claim" under Article 13 of the European Convention on Human Rights' (1990) 39 ICLQ 891.

Harman, J., 'Complementary Mechanisms within the Council of Europe. Perspectives of the Committee of Ministers' (2000) 21 HRLJ 296.

Hovius, T., 'The Limitations Clauses of the European Convention on Human Rights and Freedoms and Section 1 of the Canadian Charter of Rights and Freedoms: A Comparative Analysis' (1986) 6 YEL 1–54.

Hunt, M., 'The "horizontal effect" of the Human Rights Act' [1998] PL 423.

Jacobs, F., 'Varieties of Approach to Treaty Interpretation with Special Reference to the Draft Convention on the Law of Treaties before the Vienna Diplomatic Conference' (1969) 18 ICLQ 318.

Jacobs, F., 'Human Rights in Europe: New Dimensions' (1992) 3 KCLJ 49.

Jurgens, F., *Report on the Execution of Judgments of the European Court of Human Rights* (2000) HRLJ 275.

King, T., 'Ensuring human rights review of inter-governmental acts in Europe' (2000) 25 ELRev 79.

Krogsgaard, T., 'Fundamental Rights in the European Community after Maastricht' [1993] LIEI 99–113.

Krüger, H. C., 'Friendly settlements under the European Convention on Human Rights' in *40 Jaar EVRM 1950–1990*, NJCM Bulletin, Special Nummer 1990, at 127–58.

Lenaerts, K., 'Fundamental Rights to be Included in a Community Catalogue' (1991) 16 E L Rev 367–90.

—— 'Fundamental rights in the European Union' (2000) 25 E L Rev 575.

Leuprecht, P., 'The Protection of Human Rights by Political Bodies – The Example of the Committee of Ministers of the Council of Europe' in M. Nowak, D. Steurer and H. Tretter (eds.), *Progress in the Spirit of Human Rights* (Strasbourg, 1988), at 95–107.

Levasseur, G., 'La Convention et la procédure pénale française' [1970] *Revue des Droits de l'Homme* 595.

Liddy, J., 'The concept of family life under the ECHR' [1998] EHRLR 15.

Loucaides, L., 'Personality and Privacy under the European Convention on Human Rights' (1990) 61 BYIL 175.

McBride, 'The Right to Property' (1996) 21 E L Rev HRC/40.

MacDonald, R., 'The margin of appreciation in the jurisprudence of the European Court of Human Rights' in A. Giuffré (ed), *Le Droit International à l'heure de sa Codification: études en l'honneur de Roberto Ago* (Milan, 1987), at 187–208.

McGlynn, C., 'Families and the European Union Charter of Fundamental Rights: progressive change or entrenching the status quo?' (2001) 26 E L Rev 582.

Marston, G., 'The United Kingdom's Part in the Preparation of the European Convention on Human Rights' (1993) 42 ICLQ 796.

Melander, J. 'Report on "Responses from the Organs of the European Convention including the Committee of Ministers"' and Zanghi, 'Written Communication on "Responsibilties Resulting for the Committee of Ministers and the Secretary General of the Council of Europe for the Implementation of the European Convention on Human Rights"' in Council of Europe, *Proceedings of the Sixth Colloquy about the European Convention on Human Rights, 13–16 November 1985* (Dordrecht, 1988), at 842–904.

Mendelson, M., 'The European Court of Justice and Human Rights' (1981) 1 *Yearbook of European Law* 121.

Merieux, M., 'The German Competition Law and Article 10 ECHR' (1995) 20 E L Rev 388.

Moon, G., 'The Draft Discrimination Protocol to the European Convention on Human Rights: A Progress Report' [2000] EHRLR 49

Moran, L., '*Laskey* v. *The United Kingdom:* Learning the Limits of Privacy' (1998) 61 MLR 77.

Morgan, R., 'European Convention on Human Rights, Article 32: What is Wrong? [1976] *Human Rights Review* 157–76.

Murdoch, J., 'Safeguarding the liberty of the person: recent Strasbourg jurisprudence' (1993) 42 ICLQ 494.

—— 'The work of the Council of Europe's Torture Committee' (1994) 5 *European J of Int'l L* 220.

—— 'The European Convention for the Prevention of Torture and Inhuman or Degrading Treatment or Punishment: Activities in 2000' (2001) 26 E L Rev HR395.

O'Boyle, M., 'Torture and Emergency Powers under the European Convention on Human Rights' (1977) 71 AJIL 674.

Opsahl, T., 'The Right to Life' in R. Macdonald, F. Matscher, and H. Petzold (eds.), *The European System for the Protection of Human Rights* (Dordrecht, 1993), at 207.

Partsch, K., 'Discrimination' in R. Macdonald, F. Matscher, and H. Petzold (eds.) *The European System for the Protection of Human Rights* (Dordrecht, 1993), at 571.

Phillipson, G., 'The Human Rights Act, "Horizontal Effect" and the Common Law: a Bang or a Whimper' (1999) 62 MLR 824.

Richardson, G., 'Discretionary Life Sentences and the European Convention on Human Rights' [1991] PL 34–40.

Robertson, A. H., 'The European Convention for the Protection of Human Rights.' (1950) 27 BYBIL 145–63.

Rowe, N., and Schlette, V., 'The Protection of Human Rights in Europe after the Eleventh Protocol to the ECHR' (1998) 23 E L Rev HR/1.

Ryssdal, R., *The Future of the European Court of Human Rights*, Public lecture given at the Centre of European Law, King's College, London on 22 March 1990, Council of Europe document Cour (90) 296.

—— Address at the 7th International Colloquy on the European Convention on Human Rights, 30 May to 2 June 1990, Council of Europe document Cour (90) 152.

—— *Europe: the Roads to Democracy. The Council of Europe and the 'Architecture' of Europe*, speech at Colloquy organized by the Secretary General of the Council of Europe in Strasbourg, 18–19 September 1990, Council of Europe document Cour (90) 223.

—— Speech to the Informal Ministerial Conference on Human Rights and Celebration of the 40th Anniversary of the European Convention on Human Rights, Rome, 5 November 1990, p. 2, Council of Europe document Cour (90) 289.

—— Speech at the ceremony for the 40th anniversary of the European Convention on Human Rights at Trieste, 18 December 1990, Council of Europe document Cour (90) 318.

—— *Forty Years of the European Convention on Human Rights*, Address at Vienna on 18 January 1991, Council of Europe document Cour (91) 61

—— Address to the Conference of European National Sections on Human Rights Problems in an Enlarged Europe, 23–5 April 1992, Council of Europe, Document Cour (92) 126.

—— Address to Conference of Presidents and Attorney generals of the Supreme Courts of the European Communities, 19–22 May 1992, Council of Europe document Cour (92) 135.

—— *European Human Rights Protection in the Year 2000*, address to Potsdam University Law Faculty Conference, 3–5 June 1992. Council of Europe document Cour (92) 173.

—— 'On the road to a European Constitutional Court' in *Collected Courses of the Academy of European Law, ii, book 2* (Dordrecht, 1993), 1.

—— Speech delivered on 27 January 1994 on the occasion of the first session of the year, p. 2, Council of Europe document Cour (94) 34.

Schermers, H. G., 'European Commission of Human Rights: The Norwegian Dentist Case on Compulsory Labour' [1964] *Nederlands Tijdschrift voor International Recht* 366.

—— 'The European Communities bound by Fundamental Human Rights' (1990) 27 C M L Rev 249.

—— 'The European Court of Human Rights after the Merger' (1993) 18 E L Rev 493–505.

—— 'The Eleventh Protocol to the European Convention on Human Rights' (1994) 19 E L Rev 367.

—— 'Adaptation of the Eleventh Protocol to the European Convention on Human Rights' (1995) 20 E L Rev 559.

—— 'Election of Judges to the European Court of Human Rights' (1998) 23 E L Rev 568.

—— 'European Remedies in the Field of Human Rights' in C. Kilpatrick, N. Novitz, and P. Skidmore, *The Future of Remedies in Europe* (Oxford, 2000) at 205.

Schwelb, E., 'The Protection of Property of Nationals under the First Protocol to the European Convention on Human Rights' (1964) 12 AJCL 518.

Smith, I., 'The Right to Life and the Right to Kill in Law Enforcement', *New Law Journal*, 11 March 1994, 354.

Steyn, Lord, 'The New Legal Landscape' [2000] EHRLR 549.

Tomuschat, C., 'Quo Vadis Argentoratum? The Success Story of the European Convention on Human Rights—and a Few Dark Stains' (1992) 13 HRLJ 401–6.

Türk, O., 'Protection of Minorities in Europe' in *Collected Courses of the Academy of European Law*, iii., book 2 (Dordrecht, 1994), 143.

Van den Wyngaert, C., 'Applying the European Convention on Human Rights to Extradition: Opening Pandora's box?' (1990) 39 ICLQ 757.

Wade, W., 'Horizons of Horizontality' (2000) 116 LQR 217.

Warbrick, C., 'State Responsibility for Damage Sustained in Another State: Article 3' (1989) 9 YEL 387.

—— 'The Structure of Article 8', [1998] EHRLR 32.

White, R., 'Remedies in a Multi-Level Legal Order: The Strasbourg Court and the UK' in C. Kilpatrick, T. Novitz, and P. Skidmore, *The Future of Remedies in Europe* (Oxford, 2000) at 191.

Williams, G., 'Civil liberties and the protection of statute' (1981) 34 CLP 25–41.

WEBSITES

Commissioner of Human Rights	**www.commissioner.coe.int**
Council of Europe	**www.coe.int**
Council of Europe treaties (includes information on current state of ratifications of Council of Europe treaties)	**http://conventions.coe.int**
European Court of Human Rights	**www.echr.coe.int**
Human Rights Documentation (European Court documentation website)	**www.hudoc.echr.coe.int/hudoc/**
The Aire (Advice on Individual Rights in Europe) Centre	**www.airecentre.org**

INDEX

abortion, 53–5
abuses
  limitation on use of restrictions on rights, 365–6
  of power, 365–6
  prohibition of abuse of rights, 361–5
  of right of petition, 413
acquittals, finality of, 195–6
admissibility of complaint, 6–7, 8–9, 388–9,
    403–13
adoption, 230–1, 232–3
adversarial process, 156
advertising, 287–8
advisory opinions of the European Court of
    Human Rights, 9–10
African Convention on Human and Peoples
    Rights, 438
AIDS/HIV, 128–9
alcoholics, detention of, 128
aliens
  political activity of, 216
  see also deportation and extradition;
    immigration
anonymity
  applicants, 412
  witnesses, 186–7
Anton Piller orders, 254
appeals, 169, 196–7
applications and applicants, 6
  abuse of right of petition, 413
  admissibility of, 6–7, 8–9, 388–9, 403–13
  applicant as victim, 405–7
  establishment of facts, 414–15
  examination of merits, 413–16
  failure of, 8
  introduction and registration, 400–1
  manifestly ill-founded, 412–13
  previous submission, 412
  referral to European Court of Human Rights
    new system, 8
    old system, 7
  signature, 412
  time limits, 411
  see also remedies
armed forces
  children and minors in, 96–7
  conscientious objection, 270–2
  disciplinary regimes, 104–5, 112–13, 141
  homosexuality in, 65, 242
  impartiality of military court, 163

  military service, 96–7
  religion in, 267
arrest, 102, 108, 116
  inhuman and degrading treatment and, 73–5
  notification of reasons for, 130–2
  right to compensation, 137
art, 285
assembly, freedom of, 290–1
assisted suicide, 55–6
association, freedom of, 291–9
  freedom not to join an association, 295–7
  political parties, 292–4
  restrictions on particular groups of workers,
    297–8
  trade unions, 294–5
asylum, 82, 84–5, 104, 107
Austria
status of European Convention on Human Rights
    in, 15
autonomous meaning of terms, 31–2

belief
  conscientious objection, 270–2
  expression by prisoners, 268–9
  manifestation of, 266–8
  meaning of, 265
Bernhardt, Judge, 41
blasphemy, 285–6
Bratza, Nicholas, 190–1
broadcasting see media
Buddhism, 268–9
burden of proof, 174, 177–81

capital punishment (death penalty), 24, 47–8,
    83
care proceedings, 229–31
Charter of Fundamental Rights of the European
    Union, 446
Charter of the United Nations, 3
children and minors, 222–3, 406
  access to records, 261
  adoption, 230–1, 232–3
  care proceedings, 229–31
  compulsory education, 122
  corporal punishment, 86–7, 239, 327
  custody and access, 214–15, 228–9, 230–1
  detention, 120, 122–3
  illegitimate, 65, 226, 231, 301
  military service, 96–7